ROADSIDE USE OF NATIVE PLANTS

ROADSIDE USE OF NATIVE PLANTS

Edited by
Bonnie L. Harper-Lore
Maggie Wilson

WATER AND ECOSYSTEMS TEAM
OFFICE OF NATURAL ENVIRONMENT
FEDERAL HIGHWAY ADMINISTRATION
WASHINGTON, D.C.

ISLAND PRESS
Washington, D.C. • Covelo, California

The first printing of this facsimile Island Press edition is published in August 2000

Island Press is a trademark of The Center for Resource Economics.

This project, publication number FHWA-EP-99-014, was originally published by the U.S. Department of Transportation, Federal Highway Administration, and is a work of the U.S. government.

Library of Congress Cataloging-in-Publication Data

Roadside use of native plants / edited by Bonnie Harper-Lore and Maggie Wilson ;
Water and Ecosystem Team, Office of Natural Environment, Federal Highway Administration.
 p. cm.
 Originally published: Washington, D.C. : Federal Highway Administration, 1999.
 Includes bibliographical references.
 ISBN 1-55963-837-0 (alk. paper)
 1. Roadside plants—United States. 2. Natural landscaping—United States. 3. Native plants for cultivation—United States. I. Harper-Lore, Bonnie. II. Wilson, Maggie, 1948- III. United States. Office of Natural Environment. Water and Ecosystem Team.

TE178 .R63 2000
713'.0973—dc21

 00-057547

CONTENTS

FOREWORD

By John T. Kartesz

Born and raised in rural farm country in western Pennsylvania, it was only fitting that I would become acquainted with wildlands and wild plants early in my childhood. Perhaps it was there, along the long meandering country roads where my family faithfully collected black raspberries and hickory nuts, that the influence of the native flora made an indelible impression on my life. Although the specific details of some of my recollections have blurred over the decades, I can still vividly recall how the buttercups, trilliums, columbines, Dutchman's breeches, and squirrel corn dotted the hillsides in the spring, and how they were replaced routinely by the asters, bonesets, and goldenrods in the fall.

In my pursuit to better understand plant diversity across the continent, I have traveled long hours along roadways in every state and virtually every Canadian province. In doing so, I have gained a deep and rich appreciation of the significance of the floras native to each of these areas. Indeed, for many aspiring botanists, their first impressions of nature are often seen through the windows of their family cars, as they travel. From the majestic beauty of the Blue Ridge Parkway flora in the Great Smoky Mountains, to the spectacularly showy roadside desert flora of southern Nevada and Arizona, to the lush and intriguing Californian flora along scenic Route 1, to the vividly colorful native roadside plants of the Parks Highway in Alaska, our North American highways represent some of the most magnificent displays of wild plants in the world.

What is personally gratifying about the roadside floras, at least in those areas mentioned above, is that they are dominated nearly exclusively by native species. Unfortunately, this is not the situation for many of our highways in other locations. Historically, many of our rights-of-way have been deluged with exotic species, mostly by accident, some deliberate, and some by well-intentioned but poorly informed individuals in their attempts to "beautify" roadside landscapes. Regrettably, today, a full 17% of our North American flora, and up to 33% of some of our individual state floras (i.e. Massachusetts), are composed of plants that are exotic or introduced from foreign lands. Nowhere is this more evident than along our highways. Even along some of the most remote roads within our national parks, evidence of introductions abounds.

Over the decades, the management of roadside vegetation has changed dramatically, in part for the better, by adopting policies that are sound and in concert with nature. The various themes and principles that the Federal Highway Administration and contributors have presented in this informative work provide an enlightened understanding of the problems, along with possible solutions. It is essential that the general public along with local and regional managers become aware of the types of problems associated with roadside floras. By becoming more aware of the ideas articulated here, we may realize that more carefully designed plans and scientifically applied strategies can help avoid some of the problems of the past. Therefore, this work is both timely and necessary to stimulate meaningful thought and provocative discussion on how best to manage our roadside floras.

Using Native Plants On Roadsides - Preface

There has always been a need to use and preserve native plants on roadsides. The reasons are many. In the early days of roadside development (landscaping or erosion control in your state), you will find that the notion of planting, preserving, or encouraging native plants was often written as policy. Policy has changed with prevailing objectives of the times. During the 1930s we believed that our roadsides should be maintained as if they were *our nation's front yards*. And for years we laboriously sought that objective. We did so with the best information and tools of the time. The labor-intensive mowing and planting we did during that era was made easier by the 1950s development of agricultural herbicides that had application to our maintenance needs. In the 1960s we were encouraged to include the needs of the highway users by adding *beautification* as a major objective of state highway agencies, especially after the interstate highway building years. When the energy crunch of the 1970s diminished the use of equipment on roadside work, we learned that an *ecological approach* might be the answer. The idea of working with nature and allowing nature to exist, if not encroach into the right-of-way, was contrary to the front yard and beautification objectives. By the 1990s we had learned that these ideas were not mutually exclusive and could coexist on our roadsides. Our nation's "front yards" could reflect the natural beauty and biodiversity of a region. That natural beauty could actually be considered beautification, in terms of a new aesthetic! The new aesthetic was built on an understanding of our natural heritage and good planning.

That new aesthetic, working with nature, amounted to an ecological approach that was affordable. All we had to do was sell the idea to the highway users, by informing them of all the benefits: environmentally sensitive, local character, ecologically diverse, erosion control, wildlife habitat, with reduced use of water, chemicals, mowing, and fertilizer. And if the new approach allowed a natural beauty to be the highway user's view, so much the better. And so the new aesthetic is actually an old aesthetic, reflecting the beauty that attracted our ancestors to different regions of the country. The need for roads followed. And with that need came our responsibility to take care of the roads and roadsides. I suggest that we have found a way, by working with nature, that suits our needs as well of those of future generations. May we drive into the 21st century knowing that we are not only taking care of roadsides but their future as well.

The common sense of the roadside ecological approach has led to the writing of this handbook. Because this old idea is new to many roadside decision-makers, including maintenance, erosion control, landscape, and environmental units, the Federal Highway Administration researched some of the basics needed for this approach, including: what are native, endangered, or noxious plants in each state, where the native plants fit into natural regions, what references and resources are available with an appendix that provides terms, guidelines, and relative Federal policy, even a sample specification outlining the use of native species in contracts. The book begins with a primer, a collection of insights from a cross section of experts from academia, other agencies, and state departments of transportation themselves. The primer answers basic questions about the use and preservation of native plants. It ends with a roadside land ethic, or explanation of roadside decision-makers' important interaction with the environment. We are proud to be able to share the authors' views of the roadside and the opportunities they see in the use and protection of the natural heritage found there.

Acknowledgments

The help of so many people has made this handbook possible:

The Federal Highway Administration (FHWA) thanks the seventeen respected authors who agreed with the goal enough to contribute their views relevant to the use of native plants as problem solvers. Asked to communicate their knowledge to roadside decision-makers, their views are valuable to the science and practice of roadside vegetation management. The seventeen included: John Kartesz, Larry Morse, Peggy Olwell, Evelyn Howell, Darrel Morrison, William Niering, Kirk Henderson, Wayne Pauly, Ira Bickford, Bill Johnson, Reed Noss, Wayne McCully, John Randall, Sarah Reichard, Randy Westbrooks, Baird Callicot and Gary Lore.

We also thank Maria Urice of the National Wildflower Research Center who identified plants native in each State. We thank her and her organization for compiling the initial plant lists. The FHWA thanks Eishenhower student Don Jacobovitz, who contributed pieces of his graduate work to the making of this book.

Bonnie L. Harper-Lore

Editor, Bonnie L. Harper-Lore.

Part One

essays

"The earth's vegetation is part of a web of life in which there are intimate and essential relationships between plants and the earth, between plants and other plants, between plants and animals. Sometimes we have no choice but to disturb these relationships, but we should do so thoughtfully, with full awareness that what we do may have consequences remote in time and place."
Rachel Carson, Silent Spring, 1962.

And the decisions we make, can no longer be the same ones we have always made, especially on the sides of the road that cover and cross millions of acres. One size does not fit all. One standard seed mix will not succeed in every site. One book of standard specifications for seed mixes no longer matches the reality of the objectives of any given planting, in any given state.

Since highway construction began, the engineering objective was to establish a green growing slope stabilizer. Because of NEPA and the Clean Water Act, the environmental objective changed to a quick green growing slope stabilizer. Because of beautification concerns, the esthetic objective was to establish a visually-pleasing, quick, green-growing slope stabilizer. Because of vegetation management issues, the maintenance objective is becoming, establish a noninvasive, visually-pleasing, quick, green-growing slope stabilizer. Because of diminishing resources, a holistic objective must be to establish an affordable, noninvasive, visually-pleasing, quick, green-growing slope stabilizer. This growing list of roadside objectives makes the seed mix solution complex, and one standard specification cannot meet all the objectives.

Just as one size does not fit all, one seed mix will not succeed in every part of a State or every part of the country. Texas has defined 26 natural regions in that State alone. One seed mix to suit all construction sites across any State was always simplistic, albeit convenient. Soils, moisture regimes, topography, adjacent vegetation, existing seed bank, are always variables - no combination of which is the same from site to site. Therefore the notion of one seed mix could never be reliable, unless introduced plant species with wide ranges of tolerance were used. This has been the case across the country. Species like reed canary grass, sweet clover, perennial rye, smooth brome, and crownvetch have consequently become weed problems themselves, in some instances because plants with wide tolerances of soils, climates, etc. tend to be competitive and capable of not only surviving, but moving beyond where we plant them. They are no longer the best practice under any conditions. They are beginning to show up outside the Right-of-Way fence. They are beginning to show up on State noxious weed lists! They are costing us too much environmentally. They are costing us too much in the realm of public opinion, as well.

Therefore we must take the time to be site specific with our analysis and our designed solution in each roadside project. The investment in time will pay off in the long run, both economically and environmentally. Our roadside decisions will be noticed.

Look out the nearest window - and consider the face of the land. What you see is a human creation. The tree or shrub or patch of grass is there, in other words, either because men put it there or because they allowed it to remain.
Roderick Nash, The American Environment, 1976.

The contents of this book are aimed at making those site specific decisions. The primer gives a holistic background for those decisions. It also addresses some basic techniques and misconceptions about using native plants. The State by State section pulls together native, endangered, and noxious plant lists to aid design and management choices. Resources for more information are included. The appendix adds definitions, bibliography, and policy citations to clarify any debates about the purpose and direction of the use of native plants on roadsides.

This ecological approach involves a lot of common sense. This book attempts to provide technical information to supplement that common sense for more successful projects. The Federal Highway Administration has made a commitment to using this approach and hopes that you find this handbook useful.

Defining What is Native

What Is A Native Plant?:

Larry E. Morse, Jil M. Swearingen, and John M. Randall - The Nature Conservancy

The native plant species in any particular area of interest are those which arrived, established, and survived there without direct or indirect human assistance. It is obvious that plants (or animals) accidentally or deliberately imported by people from faraway places are not native, but it is more difficult to determine whether plants in a general region or state are native to a particular site.

There are many definitions for native plants that differ in minor ways. We here adopt and discuss the definition recently developed for the Native Plant Conservation Initiative: A native plant species is one **"that occurs naturally in a particular region, state, ecosystem, and habitat without direct or indirect human actions"** (Federal Native Plant Conservation Committee, 1994). Most native plants have been in the same area for centuries or longer. However, natural spread and dispersal of species (without human intervention) continues to occur, occasionally leading to an expansion of a species' natural geographical range.

The distinction between native and non-native species is important because native species have generally adapted and evolved with the competing species, predators, and diseases of an area over many thousands of years. Native species are therefore generally in reasonable ecological balance with their associates and competitors, and have pests, predators, or diseases that limit their abundance. Many non-natives, on the other hand, lack these checks, and can quickly spread and dominate areas they invade, changing habitats and pushing out many native plants and animals there. Technological advances in transportation over the past few centuries have allowed humans to deliberately and accidentally move plant and animal species to new parts of the world at rates unprecedented in the history of our planet. This unnaturally high rate of exotics introductions places a burden on native plants and animals that are often unable to compete with these unrestrained interlopers. Nothing in our native plants' evolutionary heritage has prepared them to compete with large numbers of new species that arrive free of the predators and pests that kept their numbers in check in their original ranges. Plants that are not native at a site are variously called non-native, exotic, alien, adventive, or non-indigenous species. Well-established non-natives are sometimes said to be naturalized, but that does not make them native, no matter how long ago they were introduced. In the Americas, most exotic plants were spread through travel, trade, and commerce in the past few centuries, after European colonization and the major land-use changes that soon followed.

Several concepts are fundamental to this definition of a native plant:

1. *Naturally occurring.* The plants found growing in a particular area, either currently or in the historical past, are said to occur there. When there is no evidence that human activities brought them there, these plants are considered to occur naturally at that site. Put differently, they are part of the natural landscape of that area, either because they evolved there or because they arrived through natural means, such as dispersal by birds, other animals, the wind, or water.

2. *Area of interest.* A species may be classified as native to a particular nation, state, region, ecosystem or habitat. Obviously a species native to the U.S. may not be native to all 50 states and a species native to a given state, say California, may not be native to all regions, ecosystems or habitats in the state.

a. *Native to nation.* If a plant species is know to be native to at least one site in a nation it is said to be "native to that nation". Plants native only to other continents cannot be considered native in the U.S.

b. *Native to state.* If a plant is known to be native in at least one site in a particular state, it is considered "native to that state." However, it may or may not be native to a different site in the same state. Since numerous botanical references address the question of which plant species are considered to be native in which states, the state level is often a good starting point for determining whether a species is locally native. Many botanical manuals and horticultural references give generalized native ranges for thousands of commonly encountered plant species.

c. *Native to region.* The ecological region which the site represents should also be considered. For example, the state of Maryland has several distinct natural regions, such as the Coastal Plain, Piedmont, Allegheny Mountains, and Appalachian Plateau. If a species is not native to a region of the state, then it is not native to any site in that portion of the state. Tamarack (Larix laricina), for instance, is native in Maryland only in the Appalachian Plateau, and therefore would not be considered native at any Maryland site near the Atlantic Ocean or Chesapeake Bay. Similarly, bald cypress (Taxodium distichum) is native in Maryland only on the Coastal Plain, and would not be considered native at the Plateau sites where tamarack is found, nor in any of the other ecological regions of Maryland. Nevertheless, both species are considered native to Maryland.

d. *Native to ecosystem and habitat.* Many species are confined to particular ecosystems and habitats within a given state or ecological region, and would not be considered native in substantially different ecosystems or habitats, even within the same state and region. For example, tamarack in Maryland and nearby areas is known naturally only in swamp ecosystems; therefore, tamarack would not be expected to occur naturally on dry ridgetops in Maryland, even in the Appalachian Plateau. Ecosystems include interacting habitats, providing additional ecological resolution in considering whether a species is native at a particular site of interest. For example, a species may be known to be native only in tidal marshes (e.g., Spartina alterniflora). This statement gives two clues: it should be expected in the marsh habitat, but only in marshes that are part of tidal ecosystems. However, a different habitat in a tidal ecosystem, such as a densely shaded cypress swamp, would not be a place where this grass would be considered native, even if nearby to the tidal marsh.

3. *Direct and indirect human actions.* Human actions that move plants (or animals) to new places can be direct or indirect. Most obvious are deliberate introductions of plants to new areas, for example in gardening, forestry, or agriculture. Accidental, or unintentional, introductions of weeds to new places also occur regularly. Once introduced to a new area, plants can spread and disperse further; these newly established populations are attributable to the earlier human-caused introduction, however, and are thus the indirect result of human actions. No matter how long a plant persists in an area, or how far it has subsequently spread, it does not become native to the area if its history there is traceable to a human introduction.

The above definition addresses the question of whether a particular plant species is native to a particular site, but not whether a given individual plant is native there. When plants from elsewhere are brought into an area where the same species already occurs naturally, the introduced plants are not considered native to that site. This distinction is important because we know that local populations are often genetically distinctive and adapted to conditions that prevail where they occur.

In determining whether a species can be considered native at a particular site, evidence of apparent natural, native occurrence should be balanced against evidence of introduction. While most cases are easily resolved, there are borderline cases. Expert assistance from botanists or plant conservationists should be sought in questionable cases before making irreversible management decisions, whether eradicating a species which is suspected to be non-native or planting a species at a site where it is thought to have once been native but does not presently grow. Careful study and consideration whether a plant species is native or non-native may prevent the unintended introduction of a species which is not truly native to a site or the elimination of a disjunct, local population of a species that might be an unusual and perhaps evolutionarily important natural stand.

Further background on the topic of native and exotic species, and the policy and management issues involved, can be found in a variety of sources, of which the following are representative:

Randall, J.M. 1997. Defining weeds of natural areas. Pages 18-25 In J. Luken and J. Theiret (eds.) Assessment and management of plant invasions. Springer, New York.

Randall, J.M., and J. Marinelli (eds.) 1996. Invasive plants: weeds of the global garden. Handbook #149, Brooklyn Botanic Garden, New York.

Schwartz, M. 1997. Defining native plants. J. Luken and J. Theiret (eds.) Assessment and management of plant invasions. Springer, New York.

Preserving Roadside Habitats: An Opportunity For Managers —
A Challenge

Peggy Olwell, National Park Service

Lately, a common refrain we hear is how every place we go in this country looks just the same. I was beginning to believe that when I came back to the eastern United States, after being gone for more than 15 years, to see the native vegetation along the Washington, DC beltway covered by kudzu, porcelain berry and tree of heaven. I am saddened to see the monotonous carpet of vines because I know the beauty of the native wildflowers, trees and shrubs in this part of the US.

I have driven in other states across America as well and seen the beauty of each of those state's in the wildflowers along the roadsides, the bluebonnets, winecups, and indian paintbrushes of Texas, the prairie wildflowers of Iowa and Illinois, the poppies of California, and who can forget the majestic saguaro cactus of Arizona. The diversity is endless and the view is spectacular! How can we conserve and protect the diversity along the roadways, while at the same time allowing the safe passage of the millions of travelers along the four million miles of roadways that cross America?

We need to preserve the native vegetation along our roadsides for many reasons and endangered species are just one of those reasons. As chairperson of the Federal Native Plant Committee and Endangered Species Coordinator for the Bureau of Land Management I see the opportunities for endangered species protection and conservation along the roadways of America. Instead of destroying habitat for endangered species, highway managers can play an important role in the recovery effort of endangered species.

With more and more of our native landscape being displaced by invasive non-native plants or lost to shopping malls, offfice buildings, suburbs and other developments, it is vital that we save whatever parcels or fragments of native vegetation we have. And the fragments of native vegetation within the 12 million acres of highway corridors in this country are valuable parcels of habitat for many rare, native plants and animals. However, we need to know what the native vegetation is along the roadsides. Our highway corridors need to be surveyed. Endangered species could be lost within these areas if the maintenance and mowing crews are not aware of the presence of endangered species.

Roadside corridors play an important role in the continued existence of many endangered species, in particular a southeastern sunflower, Helianthus schweinitzii. This almost ten foot tall sunflower is known from only 35 populations in North Carolina and South Carolina, and most of the known locations are on road rights-of-way. Road crews need to know where these populations are as herbiciding or mowing at the wrong time of the year could destroy even more populations of the endangered sunflower.

Another endangered species, the smooth coneflower, Echinacea laevigata, once occurred in over 65 populations in eight states across the southeast. It has been reduced to 24 populations in only 4 states with several of them occurring along roadsides. Again here is an opportunity for the highway maintenance crews to play a much needed role in the recovery of endangered species.

Road rights-of way can also play a role in the recovery of endangered animals if native vegetation is allowed to grow in these areas. The right-of-way provides a limited amount of habitat depending on the size of the right-of-way, but probably, more importantly, it provides a corridor or conduit between large areas of habitat. This is especially important for the larger mammals that need larger habitat areas within which to roam and obtain food.

These few examples show the need for road managers to know and understand the native vegetation that can be present along highways, as well as the role the vegetation plays in the continued existence of many endangered species - both plants and animals. I would like to acknowledge the program the Oregon Department of Transportation, established in 1994, to work with several partners throughout their state to locate the endangered species and to identify and mark those localities that occurred along roadsides so crews could avoid them when mowing or applying herbicides. A training program was also developed using slides, videos, and other educational information in sessions conducted in five districts throughout the state of Oregon.

I challenge all of you maintenance managers to work cooperatively with your State Heritage Program in your home state to develop a program similar to Oregon's. In addition to conserving endangered species, these types of programs are a good investment for your state. Just think of the positive public relations that would come from protecting endangered species along your state's highways, as well as the cost- savings in materials, maintenance, and labor.

Explaining Plant Communities

Why Different Plants Exist in Different Places

Evelyn A. Howell, University of Wisconsin-Madison

Native plants evolved within communities -- groups of plants and animals living together at the same place at the same time. Communities provide the context within which plants interact with their environment, and supply the resources needed for survival and reproduction. For many, the aesthetic appreciation of native plants lies not only in a celebration of the beauty of their individual forms, colors, and textures, but also in an understanding of the complex interrelationships among species in their natural settings.

The structure and composition of plant communities varies across the landscape, largely in response to changes in the physical environment. North America is remarkable in its natural diversity. Patterns of precipitation, temperature, and day length combine with varied land forms and soil types to divide the continent into distinct regions. Native plants tend to group themselves according to these environmental differences, forming units that are easy to recognize and distinguish.

The cactus-shrublands of the southwest, the marshes of the Everglades, the alpine meadows of the western mountains, and the hemlock forests of the northern midwest all have a distinct appearance. They are dominated by different life forms – succulents, shrubs, sedges, grasses, or evergreen trees. The architectural framework created by the growth patterns of the plants provides different spatial experiences; for example, the exhilaration of the open, wind-swept meadows with the ground carpeted by low-growing flowers and grasses; or the calm of the dark and shady high-ceilinged rooms formed by the hemlocks, with nothing on the ground except a carpet of needles and one or two clumps of ferns and wildflowers where the canopy lets in shafts of light and rain.

Botanists use these community attributes – life forms and structure – together with geographic location and the dominant species present to classify vegetation on a regional basis. The Natural Regions Maps, included in this guide, show the distribution patterns of the major plant associations in the United States.

On a more local level, individual communities become more difficult to distinguish. The species groupings often form a continuum, with no obvious boundaries between community types. Landscapes with large variations in microclimate – different slope aspects, soil types, elevations, often have a mosaic of communities present, blending into a seamless whole. In the Driftless Area of the midwest, for example, it is often difficult to tell on a large tract of land with continuous forest cover where a maple forest ends and an oak forest begins.

No two communities are ever exactly the same, and change is constant. Species enter and leave. Some are able to both establish a presence in the community and reproduce to maintain a population over time; others are less permanent residents. As the microclimate changes, either through the actions of the plants themselves – shade increases in an area as trees mature – or through climatic fluctuations, a drought cycle – or the actions of wind and fire, the vegetation shifts and communities change.

Although communities are variable and dynamic in both space and time, the interactions between species lead to patterns of community structure that are characteristic of particular community types. For example, North American forests have vertical layers – canopy, midstory, understory – that are composed of different life forms – trees, shrubs, herbs. Midwestern prairies have species that are active in the spring and fall – cool season species – and others that are active in mid-summer – warm season species. In the northeast, many communities have some species that bloom in spring, some in summer, and some in fall. These other structures are thought to be a result of "resource partitioning", an evolutionary strategy that allows species that are potential competitors for a resource (space, light, pollinators) to co-exist by specializing on different aspects of the resource.

Other mutual survival strategies that shape the structure of communities have developed in reaction to different kinds of species interactions – for example predator/prey relationships. The fact that grasses have their growing points at the base of the leaf, is thought to be due in large part to a reaction to grazing.

These complex interrelationships are the origins of the diversity of our native species.

Designing Roadsides With Native Plant Communities ─────────

How to Work with a Disturbed Site and Reflect Local Character

Darrel G. Morrison, School of Environmental Design, University of Georgia

The roadside environment is one of the most-frequently experienced landscapes in this country. The view from the road is often the only exposure to the local landscape experienced by travelers. The right-of-way, then, provides an opportunity to heighten the public's understanding and appreciation of the unique local or regional landscape. While our sense of place is influenced by many factors (e.g., the presence or absence of rock outcroppings, the color of the soil), the native plant communities of a region provide some of the strongest cues to the unique identity of a place. It follows, then, that a worthwhile objective in the design and management of roadsides would be to incorporate within the roadside landscape groupings of plants which are representative of native plant communities.

There are, of course, many constraints in taking this approach to roadside landscapes. To begin with, the environmental conditions within the roadway corridor may be quite different after construction then they were earlier. For example, where there may have been a uniform slope across the right-of-way before construction, there may now be a complex of slopes and swales with a variety of soil types, moisture conditions, and solar aspects after construction. Furthermore, visibility and safety concerns may dictate that certain zones not be designated for native forest community plantings, but forest edge, savanna, or a native grassland community.

In planning a roadside landscape based on native plant communities of a region, a first step is to analyze and characterize the different zones in terms of environmental conditions; e.g., soil type, moisture characteristics, solar orientation, existing vegetation, and adjacent land use/cover. These zones should be plotted, and then another drawing showing zones with limitations on vegetation size or growth form can be overlain. Using these as a guide, a mass/space diagram can be created, in which the "mass" areas may be designated as target forest/forest edge plant communities, and "spaces" may be designated as relatively low growing plant communities such as prairie, sedge meadow, or other predominantly-herbaceous groupings. Specific plant species to be incorporated into the different designated communities may be determined from a survey of ecological literature for the region, and from field observation of the plant community types designated for the right of-way. It is difficult, if not impossible, to re-create a native community in its entirety, but we often can incorporate key species of a plant community within appropriate zones. These include the dominant species (usually the largest members of the community, influencing everything beneath them) the prevalent species (those which typically occur most abundantly in the community), and the "visual essence" species (those which have some unique trait which give them visual importance in the community).

Because of the nature of roadsides as disturbed environments, it may not be possible to introduce all the desired species of a particular forest community at the initiation of a community-based roadside design, but the initial planting and subsequent management can facilitate their establishment over time, either by natural invasion or by later introduction when conditions are right for their establishment. Grassland/meadow communities in most cases will need to be mowed annually and/or periodically burned, to suppress unwanted woody invaders. And as in any native community planting, vigilant monitoring of invasive exotic species is a necessity, along with strategies for their suppression or removal.

Using a native community approach in the design of roadsides is not a laissez-faire approach, but the potential rewards in terms of perpetuating and restoring native plant communities and a real "sense of place" to the highway environment, are great.

Incorporating Grasses into Clear Zones

Clear Zones As Grasslands

Bonnie L. Harper-Lore, Federal Highway Administration

The clear zone is "the roadside border area, starting at the edge of the traveled way, that is available for corrective action by errant vehicles" (1991 AASHTO Guide for Transportation Landscape and Environmental Design). The designed width of the accident recovery area is determined by the speed limit. No objects, including trees of more than 4" diameter, are allowed within this zone.

As a logical result, the clear zone (not the entire right-of-way) of a roadside is generally maintained as grassland that can be mowed to prevent encroachment by potentially hazardous trees and shrubs. It has become common practice to keep these zones of roadsides mowed continually. The consequences include: high maintenance costs, mower/vehicle accidents, monocultures of grassy vegetation, and a "front lawn" expectation from the traveling public. In the urban environment, that expectation relates well to adjacent designed and manicured landscapes.

In the rural environment, beyond the city limits, that expectation does not relate to the adjacent landscape. I submit that,since clear zones are not scientifically proven, common sense would tell us that planting large trees and shrubs near the traveled way is asking for trouble. However, rural recovery areas can be safe as well as: interesting, diverse and require less maintenance attention if they are planted in native grasses and forbs. Incidental consequences include: regionally recognizable vegetation, a seasonally dynamic landscape, habitat for small mammals, songbirds and insects, deep-rooted erosion control, water quality improvement, and preservation of our natural heritage. If highway users understand this unmowed grassland and its environmental ramifications, they are likely to be supportive. That has been the experience of States like Iowa, Wisconsin, Illinois, Minnesota, Utah, Oregon and Florida. Using native wildflowers and grasses in clear zones makes common sense!

All States have some native grassland community (some called prairie or meadow) within their State. Those grasslands include both native grasses and wildflowers (forbs). Using what is native to your State makes ecological sense. But natural regions change within a State due to climate and geology. The State of Texas has 26 natural regions. You understand why one grass seed mix might not be successful in all 26 regions. The likelihood of finding one grass seed mix for landscaping, erosion control, mitigation, or revegetation purposes is low.This native grassland can be achieved without planting in many regions. By allowing existing seed in the roadside seed bank and adjacent seed sources to grow, a native landscape can be encouraged. However, segments of roadside must be analyzed before using a hands-off approach to vegetation management. Many roadsides and adjacent lands have been highly disturbed and have no native seed in the soil. To allow these areas to grow up will only result in stands of nonnative invasive species, many of which are on noxious weed lists. Care must be taken in this approach. On the other hand, *if* native grass and forb seed does exist and would flourish without mowing, you have discovered the cheapest way to revegetate your roadside with native plants. The only caution is to watch for noxious weed invasion during the early stages, and to control those weeds quickly or they will persist and compromise the natural vegetation.

Preventing Wildflowers From Becoming Weedy ──────────

Wildflowers are Not a Bunch of Weeds

Bonnie L. Harper-Lore, Federal Highway Administration

Weeds are more than plants out of place. Weeds have many definitions. I chose to use one that evolves from State Noxious Weed lists, for which DOTs are responsible. Weeds are invasive plants that compromise agriculture, human health, and/or the environment. States have noxious weed laws to identify and control these problem plants. Because weed problems are escalating across the country and because road corridors often help move weeds across State borders, roadside managers are now beginning to watch for encroaching weeds from adjacent States.

Wildflowers, (per the STURAA requirement), are flowering native herbaceous plants including grasses. They rarely are invasive and rarely make a weed list. On the contrary they are often hanging on to remnant habitats that are being invaded by nonnative plants, or weeds. For example, my native little bluestem lawn border will not move into your Kentucky bluegrass lawn. If it seeded in, it would never take over due to your weekly mowing. However, your nonnative bluegrass is likely to seed into the native area and constrain the native wildflowers.

Native wildflowers do not include naturalized wildflowers like queen-anne's lace, which was noted as a European introduction and pest plant to farmers as early as 1919. The plant is not a problem because it is nonnative, but rather that we moved it from its natural conditions, and removed its natural competition. Other naturalized wildflowers, found on noxious weed lists, include: ox-eye daisey, chicory, batchelor buttons, and dame's rocket. Because they are introduced plants that are invasive and now on weed lists, we will consider them weeds for vegetation management purposes. The problems of naturalized species, including the lowly dandelion, far outweigh the benefits of planting more of them as wildflowers.

The "wild" in wildflowers has led to many misconceptions. Native wildflowers are plants that have evolved over time to fit the soils, moisture, and sunlight of any given area. They are adapted and self-reliant in any given region. They have evolved with the local climate and tolerate high, humid temperatures in the Southeast, as well as 30 below more than one year for obvious results. Most of their growth occurs beneath the surface during that first year. Patience wears thin when projects are seeking immediate colorful products. A tip, to please the public, is to include some annual/biennial wildflowers (native when possible).

Finally, a weedy look often occurs when native grasses are not included in the wildflower mix. At low seeding rates, native grasses visually compliment and physically give structure to the wildflower planting. This is the way native wildflowers naturally occur. Planting a monoculture of one flower species, or a mix of flowers can only result in a weedy look, unless a lot of gardening maintenance occurs. We do not have time or funds to garden on roadsides.

The concern about erosion during establishment can be tempered with the use of native grasses as part of the cover crop and/or seed mix. Some of the native wild ryes (Elymus sp.) are annual or short-lived and therefore perform like a nonnative rye in terms of erosion control, but dwindle in importance as the other species establish.

Remember that site preparation, using appropriate seed species, diverse species and native grasses will help avoid the weedy look when using native wildflowers. Always be on guard to control your State's and adjacent State's noxious weeds which can compromise the integrity, the public relations, and the success of your wildflower project.

Specifying A Native Planting Plan

Specifications from Experience

Bonnie L. Harper-Lore, Federal Highway Administration

Learn as much as you can from your region's woodlands, grasslands, and wetlands. The vegetation of your State has sorted itself over the landscape in successful associations that match the environmental conditions including climate, geology, and hydrology. The best way to learn, in addition to the references listed, is to hike through examples of plant communities protected as preserves by the Natural Heritage Program and The Nature Conservancy. With a visual image and the knowledge of species composition of these remnants, you can better make decisions about the projects that run through similar community types.

To achieve a semblance of a grassland or other community on roadside rights-of-way, begin with a designs described by Morrison. Write a detailed Specification and supervise the installation. Here are some tips to consider:

TIMING is everything in native plant seedings. Because of climate differences, good timing differs across the country. Beware of synchronizing your planting calendar with that of local cool-season crops. Many native grasses and forbs are warm-season species and need to be planted later. Obviously construction contracts are not always flexible enough to accommodate perfect timing. Planting a temporary noninvasive erosion control would be ideal, but most contracts cannot do this. On top of that constraint, some regions are learning that success comes with fall rather than spring plantings of native seed. There is strong evidence that native grass and forb seeds will lie dormant in the soil until climate conditions are appropriate for germination. Bottom line, many seasoned native grass contractors have successfully widened the window of planting opportunity.....proving once more that we have a lot to learn. Landscape contracts let separately from general contracts would improve establishment and save money over time. Ultimately it is the timing of the natural weather patterns that will make or break the planting. Low precipitation, flooding or drought episodes are unforeseeable.

SITE PREPARATION is key to successful establishment. Analyze existing vegetation, adjacent vegetation and soils to define weed problems that could compromise your project. Control as much as possible. Disturb existing soils minimally. Derive a plan for weed follow up.

SEEDING RATES are often too high for the project, wasting precious seed, and budget. Of course the per/acre or hectare rate will vary with equipment used. Higher rates are needed when broadcasting or hydroseeding. Drill seeding is a more efficient delivery system, but tractor-drawn drills cannot be used on steep slopes.

To define a successful seeding rate, it is wise to know the species well. A pound of switch grass contains a lot more seed than a pound of Indian grass. Consequently it is an easy species to accidently overplant. Understanding pure live seed is important to get what you pay for.

Rates for native wildflower seed is usually low at 2-5 pounds/acre. This rate is low for a number of reasons: l) lack of availability, 2) high cost per pound, and 3) natural wildflowers exist as accents in grasslands. Rates for associated native grass seed is higher at 7-10 pounds/acre. This rate is higher because l) native grass seed is more readily available, 2) it is less expensive, and 3) native grasses are the main component of a grassland.

PLANTING METHODS vary across the country. Although hydroseeding is preferred by some, accounts exist of expensive native seed being caught up in the slurry and never reaching the soil. Specialized seeding drills that handle a variety of seed shapes, sizes and pubescence have been successful. They can plant on new construction sites or interseed on established slopes. Specialized broadcasting equipment is better applied to prepared soils. Broadcasting leaves no unnatural rows behind. Some success has occurred with the use of fertilizer spreaders. This kind of broadcasting cannot be calibrated. Planting seed as seedlings is done when equipment cannot be used on steep slopes or when a high visibility planting needs enhancement. Learn what works in your region. Be creative and plan ahead.

FOLLOW-UP is critical to the success of these plantings. Contrary to the idea of no maintenance plantings, some follow-up is necessary. For example, if normal precipitation does not follow, supplemental waterings might be necessary until the seeding is established. Then, if you have matched the species to the site conditions, the plants are on their own. Ideally, there is no need for irrigation systems in native plantings. Remember to build maintenance into the contract when possible.

Also important in new plantings is the need of weed control . Whenever the soil is disturbed or bare-grounded, nature will fill in the spaces with pioneer plants. Many opportunistic pioneers are considered weeds that threaten the planting. Spot spray noxious weeds where necessary. Pioneer weeds should be mowed off to avoid their shading out or out-competing the planted seed. Remember to mow high enough so that desirable seedlings are not affected. As for long term maintenance, prescribed burns where appropriate, annual mowings, and/or spot sprayings will be necessary.

These mowings will give the project a cared for look allowing you some time before public expectations are met. When seeding perennial plants, establishment will take a number of years. Often signing such a planting, can help explain the patience needed. A local newspaper feature can be helpful for public awareness.

SPECIFICATION TIPS are useful since we still operate in a low-bid world for the most part. We must specify all the details of these not-so-common plantings. Many winning contractors have no experience with native plantings. Common mistakes include: l) not ordering these uncommon seeds and plants early, 2) not demanding local origin seed or seedlings, 3) using a conventional grass drill and planting too deeply, 4) making up time on a project and skipping steps in weed control, 5) working with untrained inspectors. NOTE: Specification writing tips are included in the Appendix.

Working With Succession

An Ecological Approach in Preserving Biodiversity

William A. Niering, Connecticut College, New London

The highway rights-of-ways across America represent a vast potential ecological resource in terms of supporting a diversity of natural and semi-natural plant communities. These rights-of-way can contribute significantly in promoting and preserving biodiversity which is now a current environmental issue of international concern. This brief paper will address the potential that exists nationwide along the rights-of-way of our Nation. Here is an untapped landscape resource which, if managed creatively, can support a rich array of plant and animal species and at the same time restore elements of the natural landscape that have been and are being continuously destroyed by development. For example, in the Midwest grassland region, most of the original prairie has been converted to agricultural land supporting agricultural crops. Thus restoring elements of the prairie grassland along highway rights-of-way provides a way to recreate elements of native prairie with their diversity of grasses and colorful forbs. Elsewhere, in the West, the State of Texas has been a leader in promoting colorful floristic roadsides thanks in part to Ladybird Johnson. In even drier regions-the deserts of the Southwest, the Great Basin and Mojave Desert, the sparse native desert vegetation is the logical plant cover to promote along these arid roadsides. Here no mowing is needed and plants are adapted to the extreme xeric conditions.

Elsewhere in forested regions of the nation, there also exists unlimited potential to promote both natural grasslands and shrublands in lieu of a continuum of frequently mowed landscapes along roadside rights-of-way. The extent of regularly mowed areas varies with States - some have extensive areas, others have reduced such activity to a minimum. In terms of roadside management needs, the presence of a regularly mowed strip immediately adjacent to the highways is usually deemed necessary and justified based on visibility and fire hazard conditions. However, beyond this belt, possibly 25-50 feet or less in width, there are opportunities to favor natural meadows with a mixture of native and introduced grasses and showy broad-leaved flowering plants such as goldenrod, asters, and blazing star. Such meadows will develop with the mere cessation of regular mowing. In addition, shrublands can also be favored either by native plantings or by allowing thickets to develop naturally. Trees are associated with such thickets and deemed undesirable. They can be removed with selected herbicides, and the resulting shrubland will remain remarkably stable, as has been documented by numerous studies in the Northeast (Niering & Goodwin 1974, Dreyer & Niering 1986, Niering et al 1986, Canham et al 1993). This idea of shrub stability somewhat counters traditional succession theory; however the ability of many kinds of shrub thickets to arrest tree establishment is an example of the inhibition model of Connell & Slatyer

(1977) in which certain shrubby plant communities can arrest forest development. Thus shrub communities represent a low maintenance vegetation type with high wildlife values. As to meadow maintenance, mowing once a year is adequate to suppress woody development. By integrating natural plant communities into the management of the nation's roadside rights-of-way, maintenance costs and air pollution will be reduced. Adoption of these innovative vegetation management strategies will be the wave of the future for the environmentally enlighted since they favor energy conservation and the preservation of biodiversity (Niering & Goodwin 1975, Taylor et al. 1987).

Literature Cited

Canham, C.D., A.R. Berkowitz, J.B. McAninch, M.J. McDonnell and R.S. Ostfeld. 1993. Vegetation dynamics along utility rights-of-way: factors affecting the ability of shrub and herbaceous communities to resist invasion by trees. Final Technical Report, Central Hudson Gas and Electric Corp. and Empire State Electric Energy Research Corporation. Institute of Ecosystem Studies, Millbrook, N.Y.

Connell, J.H. and R.O. Slatyer. 1977. Mechanisms of succession in natural communities and their role in community stability and organization. American Naturalist III:I I 19-1177.

Dreyer, G.D. and W.A. Niering. 1986. Evolution of two herbicide techniques in electric transmission rights-of-way: development of relatively stable shrublands. Environmental Management 10:113-118.

Niering, W.A. and R.H. Goodwin. 1974. Creation of relatively stable shrublands with herbicides: arresting "succession" on rights-of-way and pasturelands. Ecology 55: 784-795.

Niering, W.A. and R.H. Goodwin. (eds.) 1975. Energy Conservation on the Home Grounds, The Role of Naturalistic Landscaping. Connecticut College Arboretum Bulletin No. 21.

Niering, W.A., G.D. Dreyer, F.E. Egler and J.P. Anderson Jr. 1986. Stability of a Viburnum lentago - shrub community after 30 years. Bulletin of the Torrey Botanical Club 113:23-27.

Taylor S.L., G.D. Dreyer and W.A. Niering. 1987. Native Shrubs for Landscaping. Connecticut College Arboretum Bulletin. No. 30.

Integrating All The Management Tools ─────────────

Integrated Roadside Vegetation Management (IRVM)

Kirk Henderson, University of Northern Iowa, Cedar Falls

Integrate: to form or blend into a whole. - Webster

All roadside programs are integrated. Some roadside programs are more integrated than others. This has nothing to do with busing school children. This form of integration applies to the diversity of practices used to manage roadside vegetation. According to Webster's definition, a State or County roadside program consisting of blanket spraying, wall-to-wall mowing and monoculture seeding is technically an integrated program. It blends three practices to form a whole. These three practices, however do not rank very high on the sustainability chart. The program they form is more hole than whole. Fortunately many States and Counties have discovered a whole lot more can be done in highway rights-of-way (ROW).

Highway departments are discovering there are more plants with which to work, more tools to use, more interests to serve, more resources to protect, more principles to apply and more people to involve. As States attempt to realize the benefits of such multi-faceted management regions, they begin the process of developing truly integrated roadside vegetation management programs.

A primary goal of IRVM is reducing herbicide use in the ROW. People care about ground water protection. And IRVM gives policy-makers a real way of addressing these concerns. Saving money and beautifying the ROW are two more important goals of IRVM. With locally-adapted, naturally-beautiful native plants as the cornerstone of the program, IRVM is able to help achieve all three of these worthwhile goals.

Preventing weeds is key to reducing herbicide use. Since weeds are opportunistic plants that readily colonize disturbed areas, disturbance prevention is an important IRVM tool. Prevention means including the help of adjacent landowners in order to minimize erosion and chemicals from farming and residential development. In the process, landowners will better understand the relationship between their actions and the weeds that show up in the ROW.

Herbicide use is reduced by spraying smarter. That means improved chemicals applied at the proper time with trained applicators who know the difference between weeds and wildflowers. Before going after a particular weed, IRVM roadside managers consider alternatives to chemical weed control. These management practices include: l) evaluating each site to determine if weeds really present a problem, 2) spot-mowing to prevent annual weed seed production, 3) removing a disturbance and allowing nearby desirable species to reclaim the area, 4) prescribed burning of prairie communities to promote healthy vegetation, and 5) using biological controls as alternatives.

Besides controlling weeds, today's comprehensive roadside program must integrate a wide range of interests. Lots of people care what goes on in 'their' right-of-way. While many people are concerned only with controlling weeds and spending less money, others want to protect soil and water, beautify the surroundings, protect rare plants, or provide for wildlife. Diverse interests demand a flexible approach. The definition of IRVM developed for the National Roadside Vegetation Management Association states: "IRVM is a decision-making and quality management process for maintaining roadside vegetation that integrates the following: l) needs of local communities and highway users, 2) knowledge of plant ecology (and natural processes), 3) design, construction and maintenance considerations, 4) government statutes and regulations, and 5) technology - with cultural, biological, mechanical and chemical pest control methods to economically manage roadsides for safety plus environmental and visual quality."

People make the program. Through local participation each City, County, and State develops its own IRVM program tailored to fit local needs. The best programs are developed with ongoing input from all levels of the State highway agency integrating administrative, technical and maintenance personnel. Partnerships beyond the highway department enlist support from a variety of specialists including people from other government agencies, private companies and volunteer organizations. Contributions such as these lead to good roadside management.

With roadsides occupying millions of acres, road departments are land managers on a large scale. A resource as large as our nation's rights-of-way must be managed for the most positive impact on the environment and the economy. A holistic approach like IRVM responsibly addresses the full range of roadside interests and gives the public the best program for their money. There is great fun to be had along the side of the road. People are driving by all the time. And they notice everything we do. Doing it right can be very rewarding!

Implementing Prescribed Burns

Burn Management - as a Roadside Tool

Wayne R. Pauly, Dane County Parks, Wisconsin

There is no substitute for fire in managing some natural plant communities. Here in Wisconsin, grassland fires favor prairie plants and discourage unwanted weeds, while woodland fires favor oaks and discourage most other trees and brush including buckthorn and honeysuckle. Fire stimulates blooming, seed production, and the general health of prairie remnants. However fire does little to discourage "weeds" in most ordinary roadside mixes.

Fire management requires as little as a few hundred dollars in equipment including drip torches, 5 gallon water back packs, flappers, rakes, and safety clothing. Of course several hundred gallons of water with a high pressure pump and hose are also handy to have.

Roadside prescribed burns are fairly easy. The road is one fire break and the others can be a mowed strip, a plowed field, harvested hay, or lawns. Some lessons, though, are learned the hard way. For example, corn stubble burns quite well, old fence posts smolder while newer ones usually don't, and a crack in a wooden telephone pole acts like a chimney conducting the fire to the top.

Common sense and planning, along with lawn mowers and rakes, solve many problems. However, the quickest and safest way to learn fire behavior is the prescribed burn classes sponsored by local conservation organizations or state natural resource staff. Form partnerships with private and governmental conservation organizations and have their fire bosses work with your crews. Solicit help from local volunteer fire departments who want to learn about prescribed burns, since most of their available formal training involves structural fires, or attacking wildfires.

Many highway departments have staff who've had personal experience burning, especially in rural areas where farmers burn out fence rows, roadsides, and drainage areas to keep down weeds and 'clean up' areas. With training, road crews can easily handle the hazards of prescribed burning just as they handle the every day risks of roadside work.

The most frequently overlooked factor affecting a grass fire is relative humidity. On an early morning with a 95% humidity grass won't burn, but a few hours later a rising temperature might reduce it to 60% allowing a nice slow fire. Finally, by late afternoon on a warm, sunny, spring day a 25% humidity would encourage a hot, lively grass fire. Below 15% fire conditions are usually too hot to handle. A frequently used rule of thumb is that a temperature rise of 20 degrees will reduce relative humidity by one-half.

Fire is a powerful tool for improving some native plant communities, but as with all powerful tools, it can cause problems. You should seek training and respect fire as a necessary but untamed force of nature.

Controlling The Spread Of Nonnative Invasive Plants ——————

The Need for State Noxious Weed Law

Ira Bickford, Utah Department of Transportation

I am sometimes asked why should Road Departments care about weed control. Road Departments are here to build and maintain roads. We all know how important roads are to our lives. They provide the means for the rapid transport of goods and services. If someone is injured, they can be transported to a hospital in minutes. If you need a truckload of hay from a feedlot, it can be loaded and moved across the State in just hours. Want to go on vacation to another State? You can drive to most in a few days. So what does this have to do with weeds?

The very vehicles that provide the means for goods and people to move long distances in short periods of time, also provide the means for weed seeds to be transported just as fast. Weed seeds are caught in the frames of vehicles and moved quickly to new places. Many food stuffs are contaminated with weed seeds which are moved from one place to another. Weeds spread from agricultural products or by tourists often show up first on a State or County roadside.

Department of Transportation spray crews are often the first line of defense against a new infestation. Weeds found on roadsides, when there are only a few plants, can be easily controlled. One case in point is a weed brought in with grain by a railroad. When first discovered, it only covered a few acres. It was decided not to spray the weed, but only keep an eye on it. The next time someone took notice, the weed had covered nearly 300,000 acres. There are thousands of miles of roads in America with millions of cars and trucks. Weeds are being transported into new areas of public and private land where they quickly crowd out native vegetation. The impact from weeds is millions of lost acres and millions of dollars in costs. Good weed control by State and County Road Departments cannot only stop new infestations, but can act as physical barriers to stop the spread of infestations.

If we have a serious problem, why are we not doing more? Simply said, most people do not know how bad the problem is. The public's first exposure to noxious weed law comes with enforcement. Land owners or public agencies are given notice to comply - not what one would call a positive experience. A County agent cites you for non compliance with a law you did not know existed. Most State weed laws are fairly weak with minimal enforcement.

State noxious weed laws could be strengthened by forming an organization like that of Utah. Every County has a weed supervisor to control weeds at the County level. They are the legal eyes for the State Department of Agriculture. They can hold taxes, set fines, and declare areas a public nuisance. This group has formed the Weed Supervisors' Association. The Association holds an annual meeting, usually a workshop. Many DOT personnel attend that workshop. Next, Regional

Boards are made up of several County supervisors, DOT supervisors, land managers from the Forest Service and Bureau of Land Management, and farmers. University experts join members of the Regional Boards in the Utah Weed Control Association. This private/public sector network strengthens the control of weeds statewide.

Weed laws do much more than make weeds illegal. These laws give us a way to make landowners and others aware of the size of the problem. In Utah they encouraged a network of partnerships to control a true environmental problem. We can pay now or we will pay later!

Gaining Public Support

Ways to Increase Public Awareness

Bill Johnson, North Carolina Department of Transportation

How might you gain public support for your roadside enhancement programs? Here are some recommendations that have helped in our roadside program here in North Carolina:

1. Start in a focused manner. Pick a special event or a special program to focus on. Our Wildflower Program started in 1985 with just 12 acres and was followed by the Olympic Festival in 1987 in the Research Triangle area. The Wildflower Program, which we could focus on intensely and the Olympic Festival successes with all kinds of plant materials, jump started our roadside enhancement program.

2. Whatever you do, be successful. Look at every detail of the plantings you are undertaking. Remember, color is king and large solid splashes will make you successful.

3. Pinpoint who are the likely support groups for your roadside enhancement program, your State Council of Garden Clubs, local garden clubs, Keep America Beautiful chapters, your state Keep America Beautiful organization, your Commerce Department, travel and tourism organizations, local civic groups, key legislators, local appearance groups, Scenic America chapters, etc. Involve as many groups as you can in your program as you start it up. Here in North Carolina one of our most successful sponsorships is an awards luncheon sponsored by the Garden Club of North Carolina. This is a statewide contest for DOT employees who have planted the best wildflower areas or who have maintained the best program each year.

4. Crank up your department's public relations' machine. Develop news releases during the blooming periods. Identify flowers and where they are located statewide. Develop a wildflower handbook to identify your roadside plants. Other ideas may include promotional items such as front license tags, t-shirts, seed packets that may be provided for monetary donations to your program. Enlist public support in every way possible.

5. Develop slide presentations and videos that can be used at speaking engagements for local garden clubs and civic groups. Go out to the grass roots level to garner support for your program.

6. Develop a packet of information in your central office and be prepared for a flood of phone calls and letters that you will have to respond to about your great work. In summary, involve the public and local support groups early in your program. Start out on a scale that you can manage at a very high level of intensity. One success breeds many more successes in a roadside enhancement program. The resources will be provided to you if you start and develop a successful and popular program.

Restoring Grassland Ecosystems ⸻

An Opportunity to Save the Pieces

Reed F. Noss, Conservation Biology Institute

As a rule, ecologists and conservationists detest roads. Roads fragment wild habitats; create noise, air, and water pollution; increase landslides and erosion, filling rivers with silt; serve as invasion routes for exotic weeds, pests, and diseases; create barriers to the movement of animals; kill millions of animals that are struck by vehicles; and provide access to wildlife poachers. Generally speaking, the fewer roads, the better.

But most roads are here to stay. Is there anything we can do to make them less troublesome? Can roads ever provide benefits to the environment? I am almost surprised to hear myself answering "yes." In an increasing number of regions, roadsides provide some of the only semi-natural habitat left. Everything else has been committed to the plow or turned to asphalt and concrete. In Australia, for example, roadside remnants of forest provide breeding habitat and movement corridors for many species of wildlife that have been extirpated from the intensively used Wheatbelt landscape. Similarly, in much of the American Corn Belt, roadsides, railroad rights-of-way, old cemetery edges, and other marginal habitats that escaped the plow provide the best places to find native prairie plants. Birders know that some uncommon birds, such as loggerhead shrikes, are usually encountered along roads.

In North America, some of the most highly imperiled native habitats are prairies and other grasslands. Actively restoring these grasslands is one of the few things people can do to compensate, in small part, for the destruction that has occurred over the last couple centuries. Roadsides offer excellent opportunities for restoring some components of the prairie ecosystem. In Iowa, for example, 600,000 acres of roadside habitat provide more area than all the state, county, and city parks combined. Because Iowa was a prairie state and has lost some 98% of its native habitat, managing roadsides for native prairie makes abundant sense. These plants are well adapted to roadside conditions, require little maintenance (for example, periodic burning usually suffices), and beautify the landscape. By planting them, we help maintain the gene pools of prairie plants and some of the small animals associated with them. Together, the Iowa Department of Transportation and the Roadside Management Program at the University of Northern Iowa are doing great things to restore roadside prairies. But alas, a roadside prairie is not a complete ecosystem. Such plantings will not help us bring back the buffalo and other animals that need large areas of grassland.

Another way that the effects of roads can be mitigated is to provide corridors for animals that need to cross under (or, in some cases, over) them. "Toad tunnels," for example, have been used for decades in Europe and, recently, in parts of the U.S. to allow frogs, toads, and salamanders to cross roads (during their breeding migrations) without getting squashed. Wider crossings (underpasses) have been used successfully to allow deer and other large mammals to cross highways in many regions. In South Florida, underpasses constructed on Interstate 75 to mitigate fragmentation of Florida panther habitat and prevent roadkills have allowed panthers and dozens of other kinds of animals to cross safely. In these cases, roadside fences help funnel animals into the crossings. In situations where no underpasses are constructed, wide roadside clearings help animals and drivers see and avoid each other. As is the case in Australia, wide swaths of natural habitat adjacent and parallel to roads may help animals and plants disperse across human-dominated landscapes.

I do not believe that roadside enhancement projects will ever completely compensate for the ecological damage done by a road. When the choice is no road, a road with its edges restored to native vegetation, or a road with non-native vegetation, the best choice is no road. But for roads already in existence, the best option is to mitigate the damage by restoring the roadsides. Indeed, the advantages of restoring roadsides to native habitat are accompanied by few, if any, disadvantages. As natural habitats become fewer, smaller, and more isolated everywhere, native roadsides provide a vestige of what once was, living space and movement routes for many native creatures, and a reminder of our responsibility to hang on to whatever we can in an increasingly impoverished world.

Utilizing The Ecotype Concept

An Insight into Native Plant Establishment

Wayne G. McCully, Texas Transportation Institute, Texas A&M University

An Executive Memorandum issued by the President in 1994 calls for planting native grasses and forbs (broad-leaf herbaceous plants) on federally-funded projects. State highway agencies (SHAs) have reported a wide range of success in establishing native plants and feel their use is practicable. Failure to secure a stand may be due to a number of causes such as seeding plants which are not adapted (at home) or planting at the wrong season. More likely, lack of performance may signify that the seeded materials were placed in an unfavorable environment.

All cultivated plant varieties began as wild plants. Range scientists and agronomists have shown that individual species having a large geographic distribution vary considerably in plant height, growth habits, earliness of maturity, leaf characters, reproductive habits, and other characters. These characters are not distributed at random throughout the range of the species. Instead, plants showing these variations are grouped into local ecological units associated with habitat differences. These local ecological plant groups are known as ecotypes or biotypes. Ecotypes are plants in the early stages of varietal development, but lack the refinement in plant characters which come with breeding to fix the desired characters.

Ecotypes were first recognized in the early 1920's by scientists studying taxonomy, morphology, ecology, and physiology. Ecotypes assembled in a common garden demonstrated that:

- Northern ecotypes of sideoats grama flower earlier than more southern ecotypes, resulting in shorter plants.

- Ecotypes of little bluestem growing on either sandy or clay soils do not grow well on soils of the opposite texture.

- Within a single species tall plants grow in lowlands and dwarf plants grow on uplands. Plants with coarse leaves are found in hot, sunny situations while those with broad, thin leaves grow in shade.

In a practical sense, ecotypes are considered best adapted to conditions within 100-200 miles from the center of origin or point of collection. The usual considerations include soil type, day length, elevation, exposure, and climatic factors. All of these factors seem to be associated with a common genetic base. State experiment stations, U.S. Soil Conservation Science and the National Park Service have been involved in plant selection for isolating ecotypes or utilizing ecotypes for operational plantings. A complete program will involve research at the state level, by federal agencies, and endorsed by the seed industry.

Choosing Non-Invasive Plant Species

When is it safe to use non-native plants?

John M. Randall, The Nature Conservancy, and Sarah Reichard, Center for Urban Horticulture, University of Washington

Working to protect our natural areas, parks and preserves by halting the use of invasive non-native plants does not mean you need to avoid using all non-native plants. Invasive plants are those that spread by seed or vegetative growth into natural areas where they often dominate and degrade the native vegetation. Non-native plants that will not spread from plantings into natural or semi-natural vegetation, on the other hand, are safe to use in roadside and ornamental plantings. Special care should be taken for plantings adjacent to or near nature preserves, parks, riversides and other areas with natural vegetation. In urban areas with no natural vegetation somewhat less caution is needed but even here, invasive plants whose seeds may be carried great distances by birds or the wind should not be used.

Lists of invasive non-native species are available for several areas of the U.S. and should be consulted before plant materials are selected. Before planting, consult lists from surrounding areas and areas with similar climate areas too, because the best way we now have of predicting whether a species is likely to become invasive in the future is by determining whether it is invasive somewhere else. For example, if you work in California, check lists for Florida and the Pacific Northwest and carefully consider whether species on these lists could survive without cultivation in their area.

Unfortunately, lists of non-invasive plant species are harder to come by, although several groups around the nation are now working to compile lists for their regions. Some rules of thumb may be used to distinguish those species least likely to be invasive. Sterile cultivars and hybrids are among the safest materials to use. For example, *Syringa xpersica*. Unfortunately, some cultivars of known invasive species that were thought to be sterile proved to be fully or partially fertile on careful examination. For example, 20 cultivars of purple loosestrife, including 'Morden Pink' and others widely advertised as sterile, produce fertile seeds, pollen or both.

Dioecious species for which only males are available are likewise safe to use. *Ginko biloba* is a well-known example.

Species, cultivars, and hybrids that have been widely used and never reported as spreading or invasive in natural or semi-natural vegetation are likely to be safe to use. For example, Xylosma (*Xylosma congestum*), an evergreen or deciduous shrub, commonly used for ornamental and hedge plantings in California and other western states is not known to spread. Lilacs (Syringa spp.) have also been widely planted throughout much of the U.S., particularly in cooler climates and do not become invasive.

Non-invasive groundcovers include: Cotoneaster adpressus, Hypericum calycinum, and Lamium maculatum.

You can also help protect natural areas by reporting any 'new' species you find spreading into native vegetation - whether they are from plantings, accidental introductions or unknown sources. Reports may be made to nearby natural area managers, state Native Plant Societies, or Exotic Pest Plant Councils. If the species has not been reported growing in the state or region outside cultivation it should also be recorded in a note to a regional botanical journal. Early detection of new invaders provides natural area managers with the best chance of eliminating or containing invaders that may have the potential to do great damage.

Additional Information

Some of the best known invasive non-native species used for roadside and other horticultural plantings are listed in:

Randall, J.M. and J. Marinelli (eds.) 1996. Invasive plants: weeds of the global garden. Handbook #149, Brooklyn Botanic Garden, New York.

Other lists of known invasive non-native species which should be avoided (these lists also include many species which that were accidentally introduced and are rarely if ever cultivated):

California - Exotic Pest Plants of Greatest Ecological Concern in California (1996) - For copies, contact Sally Davis, 32912 Calle del Tesoro, San Juan Capistrano, CA 92675 or via e-mail: sallydavis@aol.com.

Florida - Florida Exotic Pest Plant Council's List of Florida's most Invasive Species. For copies, contact: Amy Ferriter, South Florida Water Management District, P.O. Box 24680, West Palm Beach, FL 33416 or via e-mail: amy.ferriter@sfwmd.gov.

Illinois - Exotics of Illinois Forests. by John Schwegman 1994. Erigenia 13:6567.

Maryland - Invasive Exotic Plants that Threaten Native Species and Natural Habitats in Maryland. For copies contact: Maryland Department of Natural Resources, Maryland Natural Heritage Program, Tawes State Office Building, E-1, 580 Taylor Avenue, Annapolis, Maryland 21401.

Oregon & Washington - Non-native Pest Plants of Greatest Concern in Oregon and Washington as of August 1997. For copies contact: Dr. Sarah Reichard, University of Washington, Center for Urban Horticulture, Box 354115, Seattle, WA 98195.

Rhode Island - Plants Invasive in Rhode Island. by Lisa L. Gould and Irene H. Stuckey. 1992. Rhode Island Wild Plant Society Newsletter 6(2):1-6.

Tennessee - Exotic Pest Plants in Tennessee: Threats to our Native Ecosystems. For copies, contact Brian Bowen or Andrea Shea, Department of Environment and Conservation, Division of Natural

Heritage, 8th Floor, L&C Tower, 401 Church Street, Nashville, TN 37243-0447 or via e-mail: blbowen@juno.com; abshea@juno.com.

Virginia - Invasive Alien Plants of Virginia. For copies contact: Virginia Native Plant Society, P.O. Box 844, Annandale, VA 22003 OR Department of Conservation and Recreation, Division of Natural Heritage, 1500 East Main Street, Suite 312, Richmond, VA 23219.

Pulling Together

New Approaches for Weed Prevention and Management in the United States

Randy Westbrooks, Arrival and Plant Health Inspection Service

Weed Prevention - An Important Tool in Traditional Weed Management: Throughout history, weed management in crops has been an all consuming chore for most of the human population. In areas of the world where hand cultivation is still the primary means of weed control, early detection and removal are still regarded as critical aspects of crop production. This was also the norm in the United States until herbicides introduced after WWII reduced the time and labor involved in weed management.

New Strategies for Weed Prevention: Today, with increasing concerns about environmental protection, and ever increasing restrictions on the wide spread use of pesticides, prevention is once again being considered as an important tool in dealing with weeds. Prevention strategies to protect the United States and other countries from introduced invasive plants include production of weed free commodities in exporting countries; preclearance of risk commodities at foreign ports of export; port of entry inspections; and finally, early detection, containment, and eradication of incipient infestations before they become established and begin to spread.

Role of Federal Agencies in Weed Prevention and Management: In 1994, 17 federal agencies headquartered in Washington, D.C., formed the Federal Interagency Committee for the Management of Noxious and Exotic Weeds (FICMNEW) to address the invasive plant issue on a national scale. In 1997, FICMNEW developed and published a National Strategy for Invasive Plant Management. Major goals of the national strategy include weed prevention, weed control, and restoration of degraded lands. Research, education and partnerships are cross cutting elements that are critical to achieving each goal of the strategy.

Strategies for Early Detection and Rapid Response to New Weed Infestations: The establishment of volunteer plant detection and reporting networks and state weed teams in each state, as recommended under the national strategy, would facilitate early detection and rapid response to new infestations of weeds before they become wide spread in the United States.

Highways and Byways - Major Corridors for the Spread of Weeds: Roadways serve as major corridors for spread of serious weeds such as yellow starthistle (Centaurea solstitialis) in the West and cogongrass (Imperata cylindrica) in the Gulf Coast Region. In order to minimize the spread of such weeds along roadsides, weeds should be controlled early in the season to prevent reproduction of seeds and other propagules that hitch hike on traveling vehicles such as trucks and cars. In addition, mowing machines and other highway maintenance equipment should be thoroughly cleaned prior to leaving a known infested area to prevent weeds from being transported to new areas.

Weed prevention is much easier and cheaper than control of widespread infestations!

Reassessing Beautification

More than an Aesthetic Goal

Bonnie L. Harper-Lore, Federal Highway Administration

"For once the battle is lost, once our natural splendor is destroyed, it can never be recaptured. And once man can no longer walk with beauty or wonder at nature, his spirit will wither, and his sustenance be wasted."
President Lyndon B. Johnson, 1965

"To me, in sum, beautification means our total concern for the physical and human quality we pass on to our children and the future."
Mrs. Lyndon Johnson, 1993.

The 1965 Beautification Act was never just about beautification. Lyndon B. Johnson as President wanted to further the cause of conservation. Unfortunately for conservation, the aesthetics of natural beauty became more important than the ecological value. Ecology was not yet a household word. The beautification/landscape requirement became one quickly. Mrs. Johnson's friend, Senator Lloyd Bentson later championed the native wildflower requirement in the 1987 STURAA. To this day, Mrs. Johnson speaks of the value of native plants and that each region should value its natural beauty. She knows full well, the many benefits of the use of native plants. She admits that wildflowers was not the right word for the restoration of native vegetation - our natural heritage, but the word became a rallying word over night. That word conjured up an expectation that many roadside managers could not possibly create in the poor soiled, droughty, wind-blown environment of the typical right-of-way.

Initially many State roadside programs tried by planting Texas wildflower species even when their conditions were very different. Failures followed. But in a culture, where failures are not discussed, those learning experiences were not shared with other States. So each was left to plant, fail, and learn the same hard lesson. Mrs. Johnson once said that "Wherever I go in America, I like it when the land speaks its own language in its own regional accent." In other words, she thought the natural beauty of Texas should look like Texas , and that of Vermont like Vermont.

Beyond natural beauty, the benefits of using natives include:

I. *Erosion control* - Because many of the grasses and forbs have deep and/or fibrous root systems, they add to the strength of the slope and prevent unwanted erosion. The associated problem with their use for erosion control has been their long establishment time, so many species being perennial. However, it has been learned that some cool season, quick-to-establish native grasses do exist and act much like the annual ryes used previously.

2. *Vegetation management* - Often a reduction in mowing and spraying are possible with the use and preservation of existing native plants. The Texas Department of Transportation and many others save millions of dollars annually in reduced maintenance.

3 *Biodiversity* - A diversity of grasses, forbs, shrubs and vines can be maintained in contrast to the conventional mowed grass monocultures. This diversity is ultimately important to global ecology. Locally the biodiversity presents a dynamic landscape through the seasons for the traveling public.

4. *Wildlife habitat* - That biodiversity of planted or preserved native vegetation provides food and shelter for small mammals and song birds, whose habitat is diminishing elsewhere. No study shows an increase in accidents resulting from our increasing roadside inhabitants.

5. *Wetland mitigation* - Using native plants in wetland creation or restoration is more likely to be successful. Our mitigation record needs strengthening. The use of regionally adapted plantings will enhance our chances of success - for functioning, diverse, wetland habitats.

6. *Endangered species* - By protecting native plant remnants, we often inadvertently protect undiscovered endangered species. By planting native plants instead of aggressive introductions, we can protect endangered species from being displaced by exotics. We have a responsibility to do so.

7. *Water quality* - Studies do show that the run-off from sod or common turfs is far greater than from deep rooted native grasses. The native grasses capture much of precipitation before it hits the ground. The deep roots absorb the run off better. Therefore, normal rainfall has less opportunity to pick up fertilizers, agricultural run-off, etc. and end up in your State's waters.

8. *Hardy vegetation* - By taking advantage of your region's native vegetation, you consequently are working with plants that are adapted to your area's climate, soils, etc. Replacements in landscape plantings should be rare. When plants are matched carefully, survival should be assured, eliminating future costs.

And in the end, if the result happens to look pretty, the goal of beautification has also been achieved. I submit this is a new aesthetic, a different kind of "pretty" than the front yard look of the 1930's. But it is a look that reflects your State's natural heritage, regional differences, and natural beauty that highway users travel to see and all take pride in. The use of native plants and this new aesthetic reflect careful decision-making that considers the future of the environment first.

Introducing A Roadside Land Ethic

It's Common Sense

J. Baird Callicot, University of Northern Texas, and Gary K. Lore

"A thing is right if it tends to preserve the beauty, integrity, and stability of the biotic community; it is wrong when it tends otherwise." Aldo Leopold - *"The Land Ethic" A Sand County Almanac.*

When Aldo Leopold formulated his now famous land ethic half a century ago, few people realized the utility, beauty, and intrinsic value of roadsides. Economics controlled the use and management of roadsides with little attention to the roadside environment. The time has come for us to recognize that the land ethic applies to our roadsides no less than to our wilderness areas.

Sitting on the mower or on the Department of Transportation budget committee, operating as a design engineer, a snow plow driver or landscape architect, we make decisions that affect our roadsides virtually every day. We usually base these decisions on cost, ease of operation, and safety to the highway user - all highly practical and common sense concerns. Yet, we rarely carefully consider how the consequences of our decisions impact the roadside environment.

Economics can not — and ought not — be the sole determinate of how we treat our roadsides. We must carefully measure not only the present value of any management practice, but also its future economic and environmental costs. All too often we tend to over-value the present and under value the future, or ignore it altogether. We should seek not economic expediency, but rather the right thing to do by taking a common sense look at the long-term economic and environmental consequences. We should recognize the function, beauty, and intrinsic value of our roadsides and thus our responsibility to properly maintain and care for them. Only by carefully planning our roadside activities with an understanding of roadside ecology can we make the right decisions.

Roadsides provide a buffer between the roadway and the commercial, industrial, agricultural, and other economic activities on the adjoining private lands, protecting both the private land owner and the highway user from one another. Maintaining that protection is our responsibility. Understanding the ecology of the roadside plant community leads to providing that protection. For example, we know that non-native invasive plant species - weeds - follow our roadways, taking advantage of our roadside maintenance practices. Very often, such weeds not only clearly threaten the adjacent land owners economic activities, but also fail to protect the highway user's interests.

Preventing the spread of non-native invasive plant species to our neighbor's property is our responsibility. Year after year roadside crews mow weeds - usually with flail mowers - after their seeds have matured.

While minimally complying with the local weed district's directives, the mowing assures the spread of the weeds. Similarly, many jurisdictions, more out of habit than proven need, mow native grasses and forbs before their seeds mature. The flail mowers expose the soil for the weed seed, giving them a competitive advantage, cultivating even more weeds to mow or spray in the future. That makes very little sense. We must avoid and prevent activities that give weeds an opportunity to spread.

Our roadsides contain important remnants of our nation's biological heritage. Though by definition roadsides are not wilderness or wildlife areas, in many parts of our country, they remain the only safe harbor for many native plants and songbirds. It makes little sense to unwittingly destroy their habitat.

Roadsides also provide increasingly important places of beauty, respite and interest to the highway user, as Aldo Leopold pointed out in A Sand County Almanac, "every highway is bordered by an idle strip as long as it is; keep cow, plow, and mower out of these idle spots and the full native flora . . . could be part of the normal environment of every citizen".

Natural beauty is not limited to mountains, coastal vistas, pine forests, geological sites, or lakes and rivers. Many highway users discern more aesthetic satisfaction and simple pleasure in viewing an autumnal roadside of prairie flowers and grasses than we have yet been able to measure, or value. Interesting roadsides also help keep highway users alert and attentive, providing for greater safety. Protecting that beauty and interest makes better sense than needlessly destroying it.

We should also carefully consider our efforts to change or "improve the roadsides". Roadsides naturally change, from season to season and from year to year. Yet, arbitrary and artificial changes to roadsides are usually more detrimental, violent, and disruptive than natural changes. Instead of improving roadsides, we disturb and destroy their intrinsic natural beauty.

While we can mimic nature when landscaping construction areas, we have yet to master the inner workings of nature. Nature is not only much too complex for us to reproduce, it is unique and irreplaceable. Unlike growing manicured turf grass, replicating natural areas is more costly than simply protecting them.

This is not to say that "nature knows best," but rather that it is extremely arrogant to say that highway engineers, managers or mower operators know best. For example, chemical mowing - once touted as being far less disruptive to the roadsides and more economical than the mowers it replaced - results in the virtually unrestrained spread of some noxious and problem weeds. Basing decisions on poor or incomplete science and ignoring clear evidence insults our common sense.

However, the most profound reasons to protect the beauty, stability and integrity of the roadside plant community are, quite simply, because we can and because it makes sense. In some cases, roadside weeds may do as good a job of preventing soil erosion or other tasks as natives, but we should prefer native plants because they are native. It's the right thing to do, irrespective of the practical or prudent thing to do. We should preserve, protect, and encourage the planting of native plants as a matter of biotic right - and because we love them for what they are in themselves.

Yet, as Leopold also reminded us, "A land ethic of course cannot prevent the alteration, management and use of these 'resources', but it does affirm their right to continued existence, and, at least in spots, their continued existence in a natural state." This means that we must realize that turning our roadsides into highly eroded, barren or weed-infested waste lands, or dump sites for leftover construction materials not only makes very little sense, but also is simply wrong.

Since Leopold, our understanding of roadside management has developed immeasurably, both as a science and as an art. Recognizing our roadsides as valuable treasures and incorporating Leopold's land ethic in our roadside management decisions goes a long way towards following a roadside land ethic that makes sense. Protecting the utility, beauty, and intrinsic value of our roadside biota remains our responsibility. It's the only management decision that makes sense.

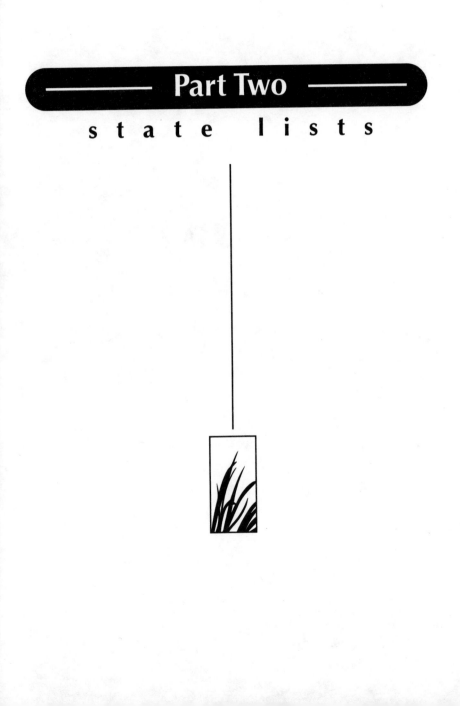

Part Two

s t a t e   l i s t s

State Plant Listings

HOW TO USE PLANT LISTS

Native Plant lists:

The following native plant lists are intended as a beginning reference, and not as a shopping list for your next project. Every State has various natural regions due to climate and geological variation over time. The vegetation of these regions has evolved uniquely to each region. What grows in the southwest part of your State might be impossible to grow in the northeast, and so on. What grows at one elevation will be different from another. What grows on the north slope will look different from the south slope. And what grows on dry sand will be different from wet sand. Using a plant hardiness zone map will not help you make native plant species decisions. Using a natural vegetation map will help you match plant species to the environment to which they are adapted. The Natural Heritage Program, Native Plant Society, and /or The Nature Conservancy in your State can be of further help. Some universities specialize in native plants.

The native trees, shrubs, grasses, forbs, and vines on your State's list are common to your State, but not every region within the State. Not all are commercially available, but should be considered for propagation. Please use resources to further fine tune your list, in terms of desirable roadside characteristics: locally common, early successional, low-growing, seasonal, deep or fibrous-rooted, perennial, drought-resistant, noninvasive, available, affordable and aesthetically pleasing. In other words, to be successful you need to know as much about each species' life history and your objectives as possible. This knowledge will help you match the most appropriate plants to each project.

Endangered Species lists:

There is some precedent to not only protecting but planting endangered plant species to highway rights-of-way. This planting should be done only after careful study. Some States have set up a process and permit system for such reintroductions. This reintroduction is a complex issue, ecologically and politically. Be sure to contact your natural resource department or natural heritage program for guidance. On most sites, these listed species will require extra protection and a specific maintenance plan. Keep your vegetation inventory current and know where these plants exist. Only Federally listed species noted.

Noxious Weeds lists:

Not all States have noxious weed lists. Those that do typically have defined the lists by including those plants that interfere with agriculture (Canada thistle), or cause human health problems (poison ivy). Some

States have added a third reason for inclusion, and that is environmental impact (Purple Loosestrife). Check this list to be sure that you are not inadvertantly planting an invasive species that you are legally responsible to control. Western States are also checking with adjacent States to avoid planting their problem plants. Because weeds do not know political boundaries, and because by their very nature weeds continue to adapt and expand, watching State borders in terms of planting and vegetation management is wise.

Note: Color versions of the state maps showing potential natural vegetation zones are gathered in a section following page 316.

POTENTIAL NATURAL VEGETATION ZONES IN
ALABAMA

Source: A.W. Kuchler's Potential Natural Vegetation Map, 1964, Revised 1985.
Presented in U.S.G.S. National Atlas of the U.S. Series,
U.S. Geological Survey, Reston, VA.

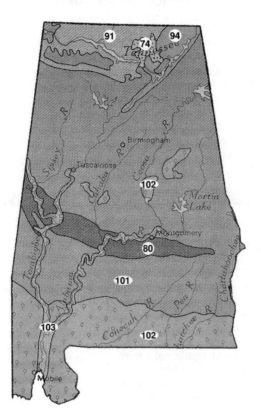

 74 Cedar glades
(Quercus-Juniperus-Sporobolus)

 80 Blackbelt
(Liquidambar-Quercus-Juniperus)

91 Oak-hickory forest
(Quercus-Carya)

94 Mixed mesophytic forest
(Acer-Aesculus-Fagus-Liriodendro

101 Oak-hickory-pine forest
(Quercus-Carya-Pinus)

 102 Southern mixed forest
(Fagus-Liquidambar-Magnolia-Pinus-Quercus)

103 Southern floodplain forest
(Quercus-Nyassa-Taxodium)

(Dominant plant species present in each vegetation type are listed in Appendix 8)

74 Cedar Glades (Quercus-Juniperus-Sporobolus)
80 Blackbelt (Liquidambar-Quercus-Juniperus)
91 Oak-Hickory Forest (Quercus-Carya)
94 Mixed Mesophytic Forest (Acer-Aesculus-Fagus-Liriodendron Quercus-Tilia)
101 Oak-Hickory-Pine Forest (Quercus-Carya-Pinus)
102 Southern Mixed Forest (Fagus-Liquidambar-Magnolia-Pinus-Quercus)
103 Southern Floodplain Forest (Quercus Nyssa-Taxodium)

Botanical Experts

Al Schotz, Community Ecologist/Botanist
Alabama Natural Heritage Program
Huntingdon College, Massey Hall
1500 E. Fairview Avenue
Montgomery, AL 36106
aschotz@zebra.net

Recommended Flora

Radford, A.E.; H.E. Ahles; C.R. Bell. 1968. Manual of the Vascular Flora of the Carolinas. University of North Carolina Press: Chapel Hill, NC. 1183 pgs.

NATIVE PLANTS FOR LANDSCAPE USE IN ALABAMA

Cacti

Opuntia humifusa (prickly pear)

Ferns

Adiantum capillus-veneris (southern maidenhair fern)
Adiantum pedatum (northern maidenhair fern)
Asplenium platyneuron (ebony spleenwort)
Asplenium trichomanes (maidenhair spleenwort)
Athyrium filix-femina (lady fern)
Botrychium virginianum (rattlesnake fern)
Cystopteris bulbifera (bladder fern)
Dennstaedtia punctilobula (hay-scented fern)
Dryopteris marginalis (marginal wood fern)
Onoclea sensibilis (sensitive fern, bead fern)
Osmunda cinnamomea (cinnamon fern)
Osmunda claytoniana (interrupted fern)
Osmunda regalis (royal fern)
Phegopteris hexagonoptera (broad beech fern)
Polystichum acrostichoides (Christmas fern)
Thelypteris kunthii (southern shield fern, wood fern, river fern)
Thelypteris novaboracensis (New York fern, tapering fern)
Woodwardia areolata (netted chain fern)
Woodwardia virginica (Virginia chain fern)

Forbs (annuals/biennials)

Aphanostephus skirrhobasis (lazy daisy)

Campanulastrum americanum (American bellflower, tall bellflower)
Dracopsis amplexicaulis (clasping leaf coneflower)
Gaillardia pulchella (Indian blanket, firewheel)
Glandularia canadensis (rose vervain, sweet William)
Helianthus annuus (common sunflower)
Ipomopsis rubra (standing cypress)
Lobelia spicata (pale lobelia)
Monarda citriodora (horsemint, lemon beebalm, lemon mint)
Oenothera biennis (common evening primrose)
Rudbeckia hirta (black-eyed Susan)
Sabatia brevifolia (narrow-leaved sabatia)
Senecio glabellus (butterweed)

Forbs (perennials)

Acorus calamus (sweet flag, calamus)
Actaea pachypoda (white baneberry)
Ageratina altissima var. altissima (white snakeroot)
Allium canadense (wild garlic)
Allium cernuum (nodding onion)
Amsonia ciliata (blue funnel lily, blue star)
Amsonia tabernaemontana (blue star)
Anemone caroliniana (Carolina anemone, southern thimbleweed)
Antennaria spp. (pussytoes, everlasting)
Apocynum androsaemifolium (spreading dogbane)
Aquilegia canadensis (columbine)
Arisaema triphyllum (Jack-in-the-pulpit, Indian turnip)
Aruncus dioicus (goat's beard)
Asarum canadense (wild ginger)
Asclepias amplexicaulis (milkweed)
Asclepias humistrata (milkweed)
Asclepias tuberosa (butterfly weed)
Asclepias variegata (milkweed)
Asclepias verticillata (whorled milkweed)
Aster dumosus (bushy aster)
Aster pilosus (frost aster)
Aster oolentangiensis (sky blue aster)
Astragalus canadensis (milk vetch, Canada milk vetch)
Baptisia alba (white false indigo)
Callirhoe papaver (poppy mallow)
Calylophus berlandieri (square-bud primrose, sundrops)
Camassia scilloides (wild hyacinth)
Canna flaccida (golden canna)
Caulophyllum thalictroides (blue cohosh)
Chelone lyonii (turtlehead)
Chrysopsis mariana (Maryland golden aster)
Claytonia caroliniana (broad-leaved spring beauty)
Claytonia virginica (narrow-leaved spring beauty)
Collinsonia canadensis (stoneroot, citronella horsebalm)
Coreopsis auriculata (early coreopsis)
Coreopsis grandiflora (coreopsis)
Coreopsis lanceolata (lance-leaved coreopsis)
Coreopsis pubescens (coreopsis)

Coreopsis tripteris (tall coreopsis)
Delphinium carolinianum (blue larkspur)
Delphinium tricorne (dwarf larkspur)
Dicentra cucullaria (dutchman's breeches)
Dodecatheon meadia (shooting star)
Echinacea purpurea (purple coneflower)
Eryngium yuccifolium (rattlesnake master, button snake-root)
Erythronium americanum (eastern trout lily, yellow trout lily)
Eupatorium coelestinum (mist flower)
Eupatorium fistulosum (Joe-pye weed)
Eupatorium perfoliatum (boneset)
Eupatorium purpureum (Joe-pye weed)
Euphorbia corollata (flowering spurge)
Fragaria virginiana (wild strawberry)
Galium triflorum (sweet-scented bedstraw)
Gentiana saponaria (closed gentian, soapwort gentian)
Geranium maculatum (wild geranium, cranesbill)
Hedyotis nigricans (bluets)
Helenium autumnale (common sneezeweed)
Helianthus debilis (sunflower)
Helianthus microcephalus (sunflower)
Helianthus simulans (narrow-leaved sunflower, swamp sunflower)
Helianthus strumosus (woodland sunflower)
Heliopsis helianthoides (ox-eye sunflower, false sunflower)
Heuchera americana var. hirsuticaulis (alumroot)
Hibiscus laevis (halberd-leaved marsh mallow)
Hibiscus moscheutos (swamp rose mallow, marshmallow hibiscus)
Houstonia caerulea (bluets)
Houstonia longifolia var. longifolia (long-leaved bluets, pale bluets)
Houstonia procumbens (innocence)
Hydrastis canadensis (golden seal)
Hymenocallis caroliniana (spider lily, rain lily)
Hypoxis hirsuta (yellow star grass)
Iris cristata (dwarf crested iris)
Iris hexagona (flag iris)
Iris verna (dwarf flag iris)
Iris virginica (southern blue flag)
Iris virginica var. shrevei (blue flag)
Kosteletzkya virginica (seashore mallow)
Lespedeza capitata (roundheaded bush clover)
Liatris aspera (rough blazing star, gayfeather)
Liatris cylindracea (dwarf blazing star, gayfeather)
Liatris elegans (gayfeather)
Liatris spicata (marsh blazing star, gayfeather)
Liatris squarrosa (blazing star)
Lilium canadense (wild yellow lily, Canada lily)
Lilium catesbaei (pine lily)
Lilium michauxii (Carolina lily)
Lobelia cardinalis (cardinal flower)
Lobelia siphilitica (great blue lobelia)
Lupinus perennis (wild lupine)
Lysimachia ciliata (fringed loosestrife)

Maianthemum racemosum ssp. racemosum (false Solomon's seal, false spikenard)
Manfreda virginica (rattlesnake master, false aloe)
Mertensia virginica (bluebells)
Mitchella repens (partridge berry)
Monarda didyma (beebalm, oswego tea)
Monarda fistulosa (wild bergamot, horsemint, beebalm)
Monarda punctata (beebalm)
Nuphar lutea (yellow pond lily, cow lily, spatter dock)
Oenothera fruticosa (sundrops)
Orontium aquaticum (golden club)
Osmorhiza claytoni (sweet cicely, sweet jarvil)
Peltandra virginica (arrow arum)
Penstemon australis (beardtongue)
Penstemon digitalis (beardtongue)
Penstemon smallii (small's beardtongue)
Penstemon tenuiflorus (beardtongue)
Phlox carolina (Carolina phlox)
Phlox divaricata (blue woodland phlox, sweet william)
Phlox divaricata ssp. laphamii (blue phlox, sweet william)
Phlox pilosa (prairie phlox, downy phlox)
Physostegia virginiana (obedient plant, false dragonhead)
Podophyllum peltatum (May apple)
Polemonium reptans (Jacob's ladder, Greek valerian)
Polygonatum biflorum (Solomon's seal)
Potentilla simplex (common cinquefoil)
Pycnanthemum tenuifolium (slender mountain mint)
Ranunculus hispidus (early buttercup, tufted buttercup)
Ratibida pinnata (gray-headed coneflower, yellow coneflower)
Rhexia virginica (meadow beauty)
Rudbeckia fulgida (black-eyed Susan, orange coneflower)
Rudbeckia laciniata (cut-leaf coneflower)
Ruellia humilis (wild petunia)
Salvia lyrata (cancer weed, lyre-leaf sage)
Sanguinaria candensis (bloodroot)
Senecio aureus (golden ragwort)
Silene stellata (starry campion)
Silene virginica (fire pink)
Sisyrinchium angustifolium (narrow-leaved blue-eyed grass)
Sisyrinchium atlanticum (eastern blue-eyed grass)
Solidago caesia (blue-stemmed goldenrod, wreath goldenrod)
Solidago nemoralis (gray goldenrod, old-field goldenrod)
Solidago odora (sweet goldenrod)
Solidago rugosa (rough-leaved goldenrod)
Solidago sempervirens (seaside goldenrod)
Solidago ulmifolia (elm-leaved goldenrod)
Spigelia marilandica (Indian pink)
Stylophorum diphyllum (celandine poppy)
Tephrosia virginiana (goat's rue)
Thalictrum dioicum (early meadow rue)
Thalictrum thalictroides (rue anemone)
Thermopsis villosa (bush pea)

Tradescantia hirsuticaulis (hairy spiderwort)
Tradescantia ohiensis (Ohio spiderwort)
Trillium cernuum (nodding trillium)
Trillium erectum (wakerobin, purple trillium)
Uvularia sessilifolia (wildoats, merrybells)
Vernonia noveboracensis (New York ironweed)
Veronicastrum virginicum (Culver's root)
Viola affinis (Florida violet)
Viola canadensis (Canada violet)
Viola conspersa (American dog violet)
Viola pedata (bird-foot violet)
Viola sororia (common blue violet, meadow violet)
Yucca aloifolia (Spanish dagger)
Zephyranthes atamasca (atamasco lily, Easter lily)
Zizia aptera (heart-leaved golden alexanders)
Zizia aurea (golden alexanders))

Grasses/Grass-like plants

Agrostis scabra (ticklegrass, fly-away grass)
Andropogon gerardii (big bluestem)
Andropogon glomeratus (bushy bluestem)
Andropogon ternarius (splitbeard bluestem)
Andropogon virginicus (broom sedge)
Arundinaria gigantea (giant cane)
Bouteloua curtipendula (sideoats grama)
Carex pensylvanica (Pennsylvania sedge)
Carex plantaginea (plantain-leaved sedge)
Carex stipata (awl-fruited sedge)
Chasmanthium latifolium (inland sea oats, wild oats, river oats, broad-leaf uniola)
Danthonia spicata (poverty grass)
Distichlis spicata (seashore saltgrass)
Elymus hystrix var. hystrix (bottlebrush grass)
Eragrostis spectabilis (purple lovegrass, tumblegrass)
Juncus effusus var. solutus (soft rush)
Leersia oryzoides (rice cut grass)
Muhlenbergia capillaris (gulf muhly, hair grass)
Panicum virgatum (switchgrass)
Saccharum giganteum (sugarcane plume grass)
Schizachyrium scoparium (little bluestem)
Scirpus atrovirens (dark green bulrush)
Scirpus cyperinus (wool grass)
Scirpus tabernaemontani (great bulrush)
Sorghastrum nutans (Indian grass)
Spartina patens (marsh hay cordgrass, salt meadow cordgrass)
Tripsacum dactyloides (eastern gama grass)
Typha latifolia (cattail)

Shrubs (deciduous)

Aesculus sylvatica (buckeye)
Alnus serrulata (smooth alder)
Amelanchier arborea (downy serviceberry, shadbush, Juneberry)
Amorpha fruticosa (false indigo, Indigo bush)

Baccharis halimifolia (sea myrtle, groundsel bush)
Callicarpa americana (American beautyberry, French mulberry)
Calycanthus floridus (Carolina allspice, sweet shrub)
Castanea pumila (chinquapin)
Ceanothus americanus (New Jersey tea, red root)
Cephalanthus occidentalis (buttonbush)
Clethra alnifolia (summer sweet)
Cornus alternifolia (pogoda dogwood, alternate-leaved dogwood)
Corylus americana (American hazelnut or filbert)
Diervilla sessilifolia (southern bush honeysuckle)
Dirca palustris (leatherwood, ropebark)
Erythrina herbacea (coral bean)
Euonymus americana (strawberry bush, brook euonymus, hearts-a-bustin')
Euonymus atropurpurea (wahoo, burning bush)
Forestiera acuminata (swamp privet)
Fothergilla major (witch alder)
Frangula caroliniana (Carolina buckthorn)
Hibiscus coccineus (wild red mallow)
Hydrangea arborescens (wild hydrangea)
Hydrangea quercifolia (oakleaf hydrangea)
Hypericum hypericoides ssp. hypericoides (St. Andrew's cross)
Hypericum prolificum (shrubby St. John's wort)
Ilex verticillata (winterberry, black alder)
Itea virginica (Virginia willow, sweetspire, tassel-white)
Lindera benzoin (spicebush)
Lycium carolinianum (Christmas berry, matrimony vine)
Lyonia ligustrina (male-berry, male-blueberry)
Physocarpus opulifolius (ninebark)
Rhododendron atlanticum (dwarf, or coastal azalea)
Rhododendron canescens (wild, piedmont, or sweet azalea)
Rhododendron calendulaceum (flame azalea)
Rhododendron viscosum (swamp azalea)
Rhododendron arborescens (smooth azalea)
Rhus hirta (staghorn sumac)
Rhus copallinum (dwarf or winged sumac)
Rhus glabra (smooth sumac)
Ribes cynosbati (prickly gooseberry, dogberry)
Rosa carolina (Carolina rose)
Rosa setigera (Illinois or prairie rose)
Sambucus canadensis (elderberry, common elder)
Sideroxylon lanuginosum ssp. lanuginosum (chittamwood, gum elastic tree)
Spiraea tomentosa (steeplebush, hardhack)
Staphylea trifolia (bladdernut)
Stewartia malacodendron (silky camellia)
Styrax americanus (American silverbells)
Symphoricarpos orbiculatus (coralberry, Indian currant)
Vaccinium arboreum (sparkleberry, farkleberry)
Vaccinium corymbosom (highbush blueberry)
Viburnum acerifolium (maple leaf viburnum)
Viburnum dentatum (southern arrowwood)
Viburnum nudum (possumhaw viburnum)
Viburnum nudum var. cassinoides (wild raisin)

Viburnum prunifolium (black haw, nanny berry)
Viburnum rufidulum (southern or rusty black haw)

Shrubs (evergreen)

Epigaea repens (trailing arbutus)
Gordonia lasianthus (loblolly bay, gordonia)
Ilex glabra (inkberry, bitter gallberry)
Ilex vomitoria (yaupon)
Illicium floridanum (Florida anise tree)
Juniperus communis (common juniper)
Kalmia latifolia (mountain laurel)
Leucothoe axillaris (coast leucothoe)
Myrica cerifera (wax myrtle, southern bayberry, candleberry)
Rhododendron carolinianum (Carolina rhododendron)
Rhododendron catawbiense (purple rhododendron, red laurel)
Sabal minor (dwarf palmetto)
Serenoa repens (saw palmetto)

Trees (deciduous)

Acer barbatum (Florida maple, southern sugar maple)
Acer leucoderme (chalk maple)
Acer negundo (box elder)
Acer rubrum (red maple)
Acer saccharum (sugar maple)
Aesculus flava (sweet buckeye, yellow buckeye)
Aesculus glabra (Ohio buckeye, horse chestnut)
Aesculus pavia var. pavia (red buckeye)
Betula lenta (cherry birch)
Betula nigra (river birch)
Carpinus caroliniana (blue beech, hornbeam, muscle wood)
Carya alba (mockernut hickory)
Carya cordiformis (bitternut, swamp hickory)
Carya illinoinensis (pecan)
Carya ovata (shagbark hickory)
Celtis laevigata (sugarberry, hackberry)
Celtis occidentalis (hackberry, sugarberry)
Cercis canadensis (redbud)
Chionanthus virginicus (fringe tree, old man's beard)
Cladrastis kentukea (yellowwood)
Cornus florida (flowering dogwood)
Cotinus obovatus (smoke tree)
Crataegus mollis (downy hawthorn)
Crataegus crus-galli (cockspur hawthorn)
Cyrilla racemiflora (leatherwood, yiti)
Diospyros virginiana (persimmon)
Fagus grandifolia var. caroliniana (beech)
Fraxinus americana (white ash)
Fraxinus pensylvanica (green ash)
Gleditsia triacanthos (honey locust)
Gymnocladus dioica (Kentucky coffee tree)
Halesia diptera (American snowdrop tree, two-winged silverbell)
Halesia tetraptera (Carolina silverbell)

Hamamelis virginiana (witch hazel)
Ilex decidua (possum-haw, deciduous holly)
Juglans cinerea (butternut, white walnut)
Juglans nigra (black walnut)
Liquidambar styraciflua (sweet gum)
Liriodendron tulipifera (tulip tree)
Magnolia acuminata (cucumber tree)
Magnolia pyramidata (pyramid magnolia)
Magnolia tripetala (umbrella tree)
Magnolia virginiana (sweetbay, swampbay)
Malus angustifolia (southern crabapple, wild crabapple)
Nyssa sylvatica (black gum, tupelo)
Ostrya virginiana (ironwood, hop hornbeam)
Oxydendrum arboreum (sourwood)
Platanus occidentalis (sycamore, plane-tree)
Populus deltoides (eastern cottonwood)
Prunus americana (wild plum)
Prunus angustifolia (chickasaw plum)
Prunus mexicana (Mexican plum)
Prunus serotina (black cherry)
Ptelea trifoliata (wafer ash, common hop tree)
Quercus alba (white oak)
Quercus bicolor (swamp white oak)
Quercus coccinea (scarlet oak)
Quercus falcata (southern red oak, Spanish oak)
Quercus laurifolia (laurel oak)
Quercus lyrata (overcup oak)
Quercus macrocarpa (bur oak)
Quercus marilandica (blackjack oak)
Quercus muhlenbergii (chinkapin oak, chestnut oak)
Quercus phellos (willow oak)
Quercus prinus (rock chestnut oak)
Quercus rubra (red oak)
Quercus shumardii (shumard oak)
Quercus stellata (post oak)
Quercus velutina (black oak)
Salix nigra (black willow)
Sassafras albidum (sassafras)
Taxodium distichum (bald cypress)
Ulmus americana (American elm)
Ulmus rubra (red elm, slippery elm)

Trees (evergreen)

Chamaecyparis thyoides (white cedar)
Ilex opaca (American holly, Christmas holly)
Juniperus virginiana (eastern red cedar)
Magnolia grandiflora (southern magnolia)
Magnolia macrophylla (umbrella tree)
Persea borbonia (red bay)
Pinus echinata (shortleaf pine)

Pinus elliotii (slash, pitch, or yellow slash pine)
Pinus glabra (spruce pine)
Pinus palustris (longleaf pine)
Pinus taeda (loblolly pine)
Pinus virginiana (Virginia pine)
Prunus caroliniana (cherry laurel)
Quercus virginiana (live oak, coastal live oak, southern live oak)
Tsuga canadensis (eastern hemlock)

Vines (deciduous)

Bignonia capreolata (cross vine)
Campsis radicans (trumpet creeper, trumpet vine)
Celastrus scandens (American bittersweet)
Clematis crispa (leather flower)
Clematis virginiana (virgin's bower)
Lonicera sempervirens (coral honeysuckle)
Parthenocissus quinquefolia (Virginia creeper)
Passiflora incarnata (passion flower, maypop)
Vitis riparia (riverbank grape)
Vitis rotundifolia (muscadine grape)

Vines (evergreen)

Gelsemium sempervirens (yellow jessamine, Carolina jessamine)

FEDERALLY LISTED ENDANGERED SPECIES

Listed Species under Fish and Wildlife Service jurisdiction

Alabama canebrake pitcher-plant (Sarracenia rubra ssp. Alabamensis)
Alabama leather-flower (Clematis socialis)
Alabama streak-sorus fern (Thelypteris pilosa var. Alabamensis)
American hart's-tongue fern (Asplenium scolopendrium var. Americanum)
Gentian pinkroot (Spigelia gentianoides)
Green pitcher-plant (Sarracenia oreophila)
Harperella (Ptilimnium nodosum (fluviatile)
Kral's water plantain (Sagittaria secundifuolia)
Leafy prairie-clover (Dalea (Petalostemum foliosa)
Little amphianthus (Amphianthus pusillus)
Lyrate bladderpod (Lesquerella lyrata)
Mohr's Barbara's buttons (Marshallia mohrii)
Morefield's leather-flower (Clematis morefieldii)
Pondberry (Lindera melissifolia)
Price's potato-bean (Apios priceana)
Relict trillium (Trillium reliquum)
Rock cress (Arabis perstellata)
Tennessee yellow-eyed grass (Xyris tennesseensis)

ALABAMA NOXIOUS SPECIES

Because the noxious weed lists have continually changed since we gathered them in 1994, we are not including them at this time. Not all States have noxious weed lists. Those that do, do not use the same standards of importance and are not comparable. States typically have included plants that interfere with agriculture (Canada thistle), or cause human health problems (poison ivy). Some States are now including a category of plants that invade and degrade the environment (purple loosestrife). Check with your State's Agriculture Department or Weed Scientist listed below. The noxious weed list can be used two ways on roadsides: l) check to not inadvertently plant these invasive plants, and 2) note the plants you are legally responsible to control. Many States now check adjacent State lists to avoid planting their neighbors' problem plants. Because weeds do not respect political boundaries, and because by their very nature weeds continue to adapt and expand, monitoring and controlling invasives at State borders is a wise part of vegetation management.

(Seed Law only)

Plant Protection Division
Department of Agriculture
P.O. Box 3336
Montgomery, AL 36109

John W. Everest
Agronomy and Soils
107 Extension Hall
Auburn University, AL 36849
(334) 844-5493

ALABAMA RESOURCES

Alabama Natural Heritage Program
Huntingdon College, Massey Hall
1500 E. Fairview Avenue
Montgomery, AL 36106
(334) 834-4519
(334) 834-5439 (fax)

The Nature Conservancy Field Office
2821-C Second Avenue South
Birmingham, AL 35233

Alabama Wildflower Society
240 Ivy Lane
Auburn, AL 36830

Department of Agriculture
Birhard Beard Bldg.
P.O. Box 3336
Montgomery, AL 36193
(334) 242-2650

Alabama Forestry Commission
513 Madison Avenue
Montgomery, AL 36130
(334) 240-9300

Alabama Cooperative Extension
Service
109 Duncan Hall
Auburn University, AL 36849
(334) 844-5544

Birmingham Botanical Garden
Kaul Wildflower Garden
2512 Lane Park Road
Birmingham, AL 35223

University of Alabama Arboretum
Department of Biology
Box 870344
Tuscaloosa, AL 35487

POTENTIAL NATURAL VEGETATION ZONES IN

ALASKA

Source: A.W. Kuchler's Potential Natural Vegetation Map, 1964, Revised 1985.
Presented in U.S.G.S. National Atlas of the U.S. Series,
U.S. Geological Survey, Reston, VA.

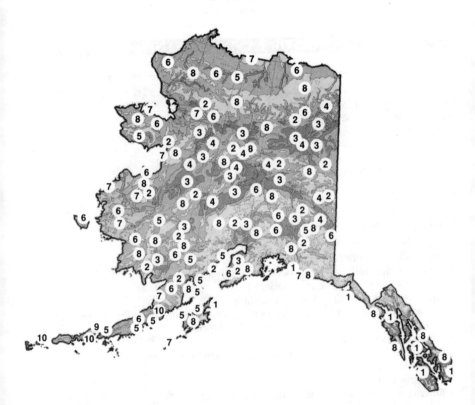

AK1	Hemlock-spruce forest (Tsuga-Picea)	**AK6**	Cottonsedge tundra (Eriophorum)
AK2	Spruce-birch forest (Picea-Betula)	**AK7**	Watersedge tundra (Carex)
AK3	Black spruce forest (Picea)	**AK8**	Dryas meadows and barren (Dryas-Carex-Betula)
AK4	Muskeg (Eriophorum-Sphagnum-Betula)	**AK9**	Aleutian meadows (Calamagrostis-Anemone)
AK5	Alder thickets (Alnus)	**AK10**	Aleutian heath and barren (Empetrum-Vaccinium)

(Dominant plant species present in each vegetation type are listed in Appendix 8)

AK 1 *Hemlock-spruce forest (Tsuga-Picea)*
AK 2 *Spruce-birch forest (Picea-Betula)*
AK 3 *Black spruce forest (Picea)*
AK 4 *Muskeg (Eriophorum-Sphagnum-Betula)*
AK 5 *Alder thickets (Alnus)*
AK 6 *Cottonsedge tundra (Eriophorum)*
AK 7 *Watersedge tundra (Carex)*
AK 8 *Dryas meadows and barren (Dryas-Carex-Betula)*
AK 9 *Aleutian meadows (Calamagrostis-Anemone)*
AK10 *Aleutian heath and barren (Empetrum-Vaccinium)*

NATIVE PLANTS FOR LANDSCAPE USE IN ALASKA

Ferns

Athyrium filix-femina (lady fern)
Botrychium lunaria (Moonwort)
Botrychium virginianum (rattlesnake fern)
Cystopteris fragilis (fragile fern)
Dryopteris dilatata (wood fern)
dryopteris fragrans (fragrant fern)
Gymnocarpium dryopteris (oak fern)
Matteuccia struthiopteris (ostrich fern)
Woodsia ilvenis (rusty woodsia)

Forbs (perennials)

Achillea borealis (northern yarrow)
Achillea sibirica (Siberian yarrow)
Aconitum delphiniifolium (northern monkshood)
Actaea rubra (red or western baneberry)
Anaphalis margaritacea (pearly everlasting)
Anemone multifida (early thimbleweed, cut-leaf anemone, Pacific anemone)
Anemone narcissiflora (narcissis-flowered anemone)
Anemone parviflora (windflower)
Anemone richardsonii (yellow anemone, Richardson's anemone)
Angelica lucida (wild celery)
Antennaria spp. (pussytoes)
Aquilegia formosa (scarlet or crimson columbine)
Arabis lyrata (lyre-leaf rockcress)
Armeria maritima (sea pink, thrift)
Arnica alpina (alpine arnica)
Arnica frigida (fridgid arnica)
Arnica lessingii (Lessing's arnica)
Artemesia arctica (Arctic wormwood)
Artemesia borealis (Northern wormwood)
Artemesia frigida (prairie sagebrush, frigid wormwood)
Artemesia Tilesii (common wormwood)
Aruncus dioicus var. vulgaris (sylvan goat's beard)
Aster sibiricus (Sibirian or arctic aster)
Astragalus alpinus (alpine milk vetch)

Boykinia richardsonii (Alaska boykinia, bear flower)
Caltha palustris ssp. palustris (marsh marigold, cowslip)
Campanula rotundifolia (harebell)
Cerastium Beeringianum (Bering Sea chickweed)
Clintonia uniflora (bride's bonnet, queen cup, bead lily)
Cnidium cnidifolium (Cnidium cnidifolium)
Cornus canadensis (bunchberry, dwarf dogwood)
Corydalis pauciflora (coydalis)
Cypripedium passerinum (Northern white, sparrow's egg, or Franklin's lady
   slipper)
Delphinium glaucum (larkspur)
Dodecatheon frigidum (northern shooting star)
Dodecatheon jeffreyi (Jeffrey's shooting star)
Draba nivalis (draba)
Drosera rotundifolia (round leaf sundew)
Dryas integrifolia (Entire Leaf Avens)
Dryas octopetala (mountain dryas, white mountain avens)
Epilobium angustifolium (fireweed, willow herb)
Epilobium latifolium (dwarf fireweed)
Erigeron acris (blue fleabane)
Erigeron compositus (alpine daisy)
Erigeron peregrinus (coastal fleabane)
Fragaria chiloensis (coast strawberry)
Galium boreale (Northern bedstraw)
Galium triflorum (sweet-scented bedstraw)
Gentiana glauca (glaucous gentian)
Geranium erianthum (northern cranesbill)
Geum Rossii (Ross' Avens)
Hedysarum alpinum (Eskimo potato)
Hedysarum Mackenzii (wild sweet pea)
Honckenya peploides
Iris setosa (wild iris, blue flag)Linnaea borealis (twinflower)
Linum lewisii (wild blue flax)
Luetkea pectinata (Alaska spiraea, partridge foot)
Lupinus arcticus (arctic lupine)
Lupinus nootkatensis (Nootka lupine)
Maianthemum dilatatum (false lily-of-the-valley)
Maianthemum stellatum (starry Solomon's seal)
Melandrium apetalum (bladder campeon)
Menyanthes trifoliata (buckbean, bog bean)
Mertensia paniculata (bluebells, lungwort, languid lady, chiming bells)
Mimulus guttatus (golden monkey flower)
Mimulus lewisii (Lewis monkey flower, great purple monkey flower)
Minuartia arctica (arctic sandwort)
Minuartia obtusiloba (cushion sandwort)
Minuartia rubella
Myosotis alpestris (Alpine forget-me-not)
Nuphar polysepalum (yellow pond lily)
Osmorhiza berteroi (mountain sweet cicely)
Oxyria digyna (mountain sorrel)
Oxytropis campestris (Northern oxytrope)
Oxytropis deflexa (small-flowered oxytrope)
Oxytropis maydelliana (Maydell's oxytrope)

Oxytropis viscida (sticky oxytrope)
Papaver alaskanum (Alaska poppy)
Papaver Macounii (Macoun's poppy)
Pedicularis groenlandica (elephant heads)
Penstemon gormanii (Yukon beardtongue, Gorman penstemon)
Plantago maritima
Plantanthera obtusata (small Northern bog orchid)
Polemonium acutiflorum (tall Jacob's ladder)
Polemonium pulcherrimum (alpine Jacob's ladder, skunk leaf)
Polygonum alaskanum (wild rhubarb)
Polygonum bistorta
Potentilla arguta (white cinquefoil, prairie cinquefoil, tall cinquefoil)
Potentilla Egeddi (silverweed)
Potentilla nivea (villous cinquefoil)
Potentilla palustris (marsh cinquefoil, marsh fivefinger)
Pulsatilla patens ssp. multifida (pasque flower, wild crocus)
Pyrola asarifolia (pink pyrola, wintergreen)
Pyrola grandiflora (large-flowered wintergreen)
Pyrola secunda (sidebells pyrola)
Ranuculus Gmelini (creeping crowfoot)
Ranuculus hyperboreus (dwarf creeping buttercup)
Ranuculus lapponicus (lapland buttercup)
Rumex arcticus (Arctic dock)
Sanguisorba stipulata (Sitka burnet)
Saxifraga bronchialis (yellow spotted saxifrage, matted saxifrage)
Saxifraga cespitosa (tufted saxifrage)
Saxifraga oppositifolia (purple mountain saxifrage)
Sedum rosea (rosewort, roseroot)
Senecio pseudoarnica (seabeach senecio)
Sibbaldia procumbens (sibbaldia procumbens)
Silene acaulis (moss campion)
Solidago multiradiata (northern goldenrod, mountain goldenrod)
Spiranthes Romanzofiana (hooded ladies' tresses)
Stellarian longipes (long stalk starwort, stellaria)
Streptopus roseus (rosy twisted stalk)
Tellima grandiflora (fringe cup)
Thalictrum sparsiflorum (few-flowered meadow rue)
Tiarella trifoliata var. unifoliata (sugar scoop, western foam flower)
Trientalis europaea (star flower)
Tofieldia coccinea (false asphodel)
Tolmiea menziesii (piggyback plant, youth-on-age, thousand mothers)
Valeriana capitata (Capitate Valerian)
Viola canadensis (Canada violet)
Viola glabella (smooth yellow violet)
Viola lansdorfii (Alaska violet)

Grasses/Grass-like plants

Agropyron boreale
Agropyron macrourum
Agropyron pauciflorum
Agropyron Violaceum
Agrostis alaskana

Agrostis borealis
Agrostis exerata
Agrostis scabre.
Beckmannia syzigachne
Bromus Pumpellianus
Bromus sitchensis
Calamagrostis canadensis
Calamagrostis inexpanse
Calamagrostis lapponica
Calamagrostis purpurascens
Carex aquatilis
Carex Bigelowii
Carex dioica
Carex Lyngbyaei
Carex maritima
Carex macloviana
Carex mertensii
Carex microchaeta
Carex rostata
Carex saxitilis
Carex scirpoidea
Deschampsia caespilosa
Deschampsia beringensis
Dupontia Fischeri
Elymus arenarius
Elymus innovatus
Eriophorum angustifolium
Eriophorum russeolum
Eriophorum Scheuchzeri
Festuca altaica
Festuca brachyphylla
Festuca rubra
Glyceria pauciflora
Hierochloe alpina
Hierochloe odorata
Hordeum brachyantherum
Juncus alpinus
Juncus arcticus
Juncus biglumis
Juncus casteneus
Juncus ensifolius
Juncus triglumis
Luzula arcuata
Luzula multiflora
Luzula parviflora
Poa alpigena
Poa arctica
Poa eminens
Poa lanata
Poa paucispicula
Poa stenantha
Puccinellia borealis

Puccinellia Langeana
Puccinellia nutkaensis
Scirpus microcarpus
Scirpus validus
Triglochin maritimum
Triglochin palustris
Trisetum spicatum

Shrubs (deciduous)

Alnus crispa (mountain alder)
Alnus incana (river alder)
Amelanchier alnifolia (Saskatoon, western serviceberry, Juneberry)
Arctostaphylos alpina (alpine bearberry)
Arctostaphylos rubra
Arctostaphylos uva-ursi (bearberry, kinnikinnik)
Artemisia frigida (prairie sagewort, fringed sagebrush)
Betula nana (dwarf arctic birch, bog birch)
Cornus stolonifera (red-twig dogwood, red-osier dogwood)
Elaeagnus commutata (silverberry, wild olive, wolf willow)
Empetrum nigrum (crowberry, mossberry)
Ledum palustre
Myrica gale (sweet gale)
Potentilla fruticosa (bush cinquefoil)
Ribes laxiflorum (trailing black currant)
Ribes triste (Northern red currant)
Rosa acicularis (prickley rose)
Rosa nutkana (Nootka rose)
Rubus arcticus (nagoonberry, dewberry)
Rubus chamaemonrus (cloudberry)
Rubus idaeus (red raspberry)
Rubus spectabilis (salmon berry)
Salix alexensis
Salix arbusculoides
Salix arctica (arctic willow)
Salix bebbiana (Bebb willow, long-beaked willow)
Salix lanata
Salix lasiandre
Salix planifolia
Salix reticulata
Sambucus racemosa (elder)
Shepherdia canadensis (buffaloberry)
Spiraea stevenii (Alaska spiraea, Beauverd's spiraea)
Vaccinium parvifolium (red huckleberryj)
Vaccinium uliginosum (alpine blueberry, bog blueberry)
Viburnum edule (moosewood viburnum, highbush cranberry)

Shrubs (evergreen)

Juniperus communis (common juniper)
Juniperus horizontalis (creeping juniper, creeping savin)
Kalmia polifolia (swamp laurel, bog laurel)
Ledum groenlandicum (Labrador tea, muskeg tea)

Phyllodoce empetriformis (pink mountain heather)
Rhododendron lapponicum (Lapland rosebay)
Vaccinium vitis-idaea (lingonberry)

Trees (deciduous)

Betula occidentalis (mountain birch, water birch)
Betula papyrifera (paper birch)
Larix larcina (tamarack)
Populus balsamifera (balsam poplar)
Populus tremuloides (quaking aspen)
Populus trichocarpa (black cottonwood)

Trees (evergreen)

Abies lasiocarpa (alpine fir)
Chamaecyparis nootkatensis (Alaska cedar, yellow cedar, Nootka cedar)
Picea glauca (white spruce)
Picea sitchensis (Sitka spruce)
Picea mariana (black spruce)
Pinus contorta (Lodgepole or scrub pine)
Taxus brevifolia (western yew, Pacific yew)
Thuja plicata (western red cedar)
Tsuga heterophylla (western hemlock)
Tsuga mertensiana (mountain hemlock)

FEDERALLY LISTED ENDANGERED SPECIES

Aleutian shield-fern (Aleutian holly-fern) (Polystichum aleuticum)

ALABAMA NOXIOUS SPECIES

Because the noxious weed lists have continually changed since we gathered them in 1994, we are not including them at this time. Not all States have noxious weed lists. Those that do, do not use the same standards of importance and are not comparable. States typically have included plants that interfere with agriculture (Canada thistle), or cause human health problems (poison ivy). Some States are now including a category of plants that invade and degrade the environment (purple loosestrife). Check with your State's Agriculture Department or Weed Scientist listed below. The noxious weed list can be used two ways on roadsides: l) check to not inadvertently plant these invasive plants, and 2) note the plants you are legally responsible to control. Many States now check adjacent State lists to avoid planting their neighbors' problem plants. Because weeds do not respect political boundaries, and because by their very nature weeds continue to adapt and expand, monitoring and controlling invasives at State borders is a wise part of vegetation management.

(Seed Law)

Department of Natural Resources
Division of Agriculture
P.O. Box 949
Palmer, AK 99645

Wayne Vandre, U. of A.
Alaska Cooperative Extension
2221 E. Nothern Lights Blvd. #118
Anchorage, AK 99508
(907) 279-6575

ALASKA RESOURCES

Alaska Natural Heritage Program
707 A Street, Ste. 208
Anchorage, AK 99501
(907) 257-2702
(907) 258-9139 (fax)

The Nature Conservancy Field Office
421 West First Avenue, Ste. 200
Anchorage, AK 99501

Alaska Native Plant Society
P.O. Box 141613
Anchorage, AK 99514

Department of Environmental
Conservation
410 Willoughby Avenue
Juneau, AK 99801
(907) 465-5000

Stoney J. Wright
Plant Materials Center
Dept. Of Natural Resources
HC 02, Box 7440
Palmer, AK 99645
(907) 745-4469

Georgeson Botanical Garden
University of Alaska
309 O'Neil Resources Building
West Tanana Drive
Fairbanks, AK 99775

POTENTIAL NATURAL VEGETATION ZONES IN
ARIZONA

Source: A.W. Kuchler's Potential Natural Vegetation Map, 1964, Revised 1985.
Presented in U.S.G.S. National Atlas of the U.S. Series,
U.S. Geological Survey, Reston, VA.

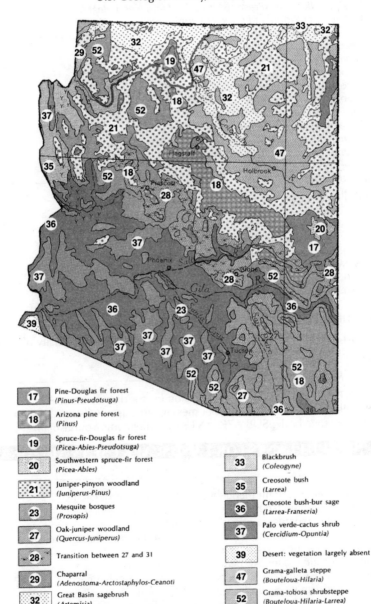

17	Pine-Douglas fir forest *(Pinus-Pseudotsuga)*
18	Arizona pine forest *(Pinus)*
19	Spruce-fir-Douglas fir forest *(Picea-Abies-Pseudotsuga)*
20	Southwestern spruce-fir forest *(Picea-Abies)*
21	Juniper-pinyon woodland *(Juniperus-Pinus)*
23	Mesquite bosques *(Prosopis)*
27	Oak-juniper woodland *(Quercus-Juniperus)*
28	Transition between 27 and 31
29	Chaparral *(Adenostoma-Arctostaphylos-Ceanoti*
32	Great Basin sagebrush *(Artemisia)*

33	Blackbrush *(Coleogyne)*
35	Creosote bush *(Larrea)*
36	Creosote bush-bur sage *(Larrea-Franseria)*
37	Palo verde-cactus shrub *(Cercidium-Opuntia)*
39	Desert: vegetation largely absent
47	Grama-galleta steppe *(Bouteloua-Hilaria)*
52	Grama-tobosa shrubsteppe *(Bouteloua-Hilaria-Larrea)*

(Dominant plant species present in each vegetation type are listed in Appendix 8)

17 Pine-Douglas Fir Forest (Pinus-Pseudotsuga)
18 Arizona Pine Forest (Pinus)
19 Spruce Fir-Douglas Fir Forest (Picea-Abies-Pseudotsuga)
20 Southwestern Spruce Fir Forest (Picea-Abies)
21 Juniper-Pinyon Woodland (Juniperus-Pinus)
23 Mesquite Bosques (Prosopis) Broadleaf and Needleleaf forests
27 Oak-Juniper Woodland (Quercus-Juniperus)
28 Transition Between 27 (Woodland) and 31 (Mountain Mahogany-Oak Scrub)
29 Chaparral (Adenostoma-Arctostaphylos-Ceanothus)
32 Great Basin Sagebrush (Artemisia)
33 Blackbrush (Coleogyne)
35 Creosote Bush (Larrea)
36 Creosote Bush-Bur Sage (Larrea-Franseria)
37 Palo Verde-Cactus Shrub (Cercidium-Opuntia)
39 Desert: Vegetation Largely Absent
47 Grama-Galleta Steppe (Bouteloua-Hilaria)
52 Grama-Tobosa Shrubsteppe (Bouteloua-Hilaria-Larrea)

Botanical Experts

Tricia Roller, Botanist
Angela Brooks, Section Coordinator
U.S. Fish and Wildlife Service
Arizona Ecological Services State Office
2321 W. Royal Palm Rd., Suite 103
Phoenix, AZ 85021
(602) 640-2720
(602) 640-2730 (fax)

Recommended Flora

Kearney, T.H.; R.H. Peebles. 1964. Arizona Flora, 2nd Ed. University of Calfironia Press, Berlekey, CA. 1085 pgs. + illus., maps.

Internet Resource

"AZPLANTS" is an unmoderated discussion list for discussion of Arizona native plants. To subscribe, send an internet message to listserv@listserv.arizona.edu with the message body: SUB AZPLANTS <yourfirstname yourlastname>

NATIVE PLANTS FOR LANDSCAPE USE IN ARIZONA

Cacti

Echinocereus engelmannii (hedgehog cactus, strawberry cactus)
Echinocereus fendleri (strawberry cactus, Fendler hedgehog)
Echinocereus pecinatus (rainbow hedgehog)
Ferocactus wislizeni (fishhook barrel cactus, southwestern barrel cactus)
Opuntia basilaris (beavertail cactus)
Opuntia chlorotica (pancake pear, silver-dollar cactus)
Opuntia erinacea (grizzly, hedgehog, or Mohave prickly pear)
Opuntia imbricata (tree cholla, walkingstick cholla)

Opuntia macrorhiza (common prickly pear)
Opuntia phaeacantha (purple-fruited prickly pear)

Ferns

Adiantum capillus-veneris (southern maidenhair fern)
Asplenium trichomanes (maidenhair spleenwort)
Athyrium filix-femina (lady fern)
Cystopteris bulbifera (bladder fern)
Cystopteris fragilis (fragile fern)
Gymnocarpium dryopteris (oak fern)
Woodwardia fimbriata (chain fern)

Forbs (annuals/biennials)

Baileya multiradiata (desert marigold)
Castilleja exserta ssp. exserta (red owl's clover)
Centaurea americana (basket flower)
Cleome serrulata (Rocky Mountain beeplant)
Collomia grandiflora (collomia)
Dyssodia aurea (dyssodia, dogweed, fetid marigold)
Dyssodia papposa (dyssodia, dogweed, fetid marigold)
Dyssodia tenuiloba (dyssodia, dogweed, fetid marigold)
Eriogonum inflatum (desert trumpet)
Erodium texanum (fillaree, stork's bill)
Erysimum capitatum (western wallflower, prairie rocket)
Eschscholzia californica ssp. mexicana (Mexican gold poppy)
Gaillardia arizonica (Arizona blanket flower)
Gaillardia pulchella (Indian blanket, firewheel)
Helianthus annuus (common sunflower)
Helianthus petiolaris (plains sunflower)
Hymenoxys cooperi (Cooper's goldflower)
Ipomopsis aggregata (sky rocket, scarlet gilia)
Ipomopsis longiflora (white-flowered gilia)
Ipomopsis thurberi (Thurber's gilia)
Kallstroemia grandiflora (desert poppy, Mexican poppy)
Lasthenia californica (goldfields)
Layia glandulosa (tidy tips)
Lepidium montanum (mountain peppergrass)
Lesquerella gordonii (Gordon's bladderpod)
Linum neomexicanum (flax)
Lupinus concinnus (annual lupine, bajada lupine)
Machaeranthera bigelovii var. bigelovii (plains aster, tansy aster)
Machaeranthera tanacetifolia (tahoka daisy, tansy aster)
Mimulus guttatus (golden monkey flower)
Oenothera albicaulis (pale evening primrose)
Oenothera deltoides (fragrant primrose, desert evening primrose)
Oenothera elata ssp. hookeri (giant evening primrose)
Oenothera primiveris (bottle evening primrose, yellow desert primrose)
Pectis angustifolia (limoncillo, fetid marigold)
Phacelia congesta (blue curls)
Phacelia tanacetifolia (lacy phacelia)
Platystemon californicus (creamcups)

Salvia columbariae (chia)
Townsendia exscapa (Easter daisy)

Forbs (perennials)

Abronia fragrans (sweet sand verbena)
Agave deserti (century plant)
Agave palmeri (Palmer agave, blue century plant)
Agave parryi (century plant, Parry agave)
Allium cernuum (nodding onion)
Allium macropetalum (desert onion)
Anaphalis margaritacea (pearly everlasting)
Anemone cylindrica (thimbleweed, candle anemone)
Antennaria spp. (pussytoes, everlasting)
Apocynum androsaemifolium (spreading dogbane)
Aquilegia chrysantha (yellow columbine)
Aquilegia coerulea (Rocky Mountain or blue columbine)
Arnica cordifolia (heartleaf arnica)
Artemisia ludoviciana (white sage, prairie sage, artemisia)
Asclepias asperula (antelope horns)
Asclepias speciosa (showy milkweed)
Asclepias tuberosa (butterfly weed)
Aster ascendens (purple aster, Pacific aster)
Bahia absinthifolia (bahia, yerba raton)
Balsamorrhiza sagittata (balsamroot)
Berlandiera lyrata (green eyes, chocolate flower)
Calochortus kennedyi (desert mariposa, flame mariposa)
Calochortus nuttallii (sego lily, mariposa lily)
Caltha leptosepala (white marsh marigold, elkslip)
Campanula rotundifolia (harebell)
Castilleja angustifolia var. dubia (desert paintbrush)
Castilleja integra (Indian paintbrush)
Castilleja linariifolia (Indian paintbrush)
Castilleja miniata var. miniata (Indian paintbrush)
Castilleja sessiliflora (downy painted cup)
Claytonia lanceolata (spring beauty)
Commelina dianthifolia (dayflower)
Dasylirion wheeleri (sotol, desert pampas grass, desert spoon)
Delphinium barbeyi (subalpine larkspur)
Delphinium carolinianum ssp. virescens (prairie larkspur)
Delphinium parishii (desert larkspur, paleface delphinium)
Delphinium scaposum (barestem larkspur)
Dichelostemma congestum (wild hyacinth)
Epilobium angustifolium (fireweed, willow herb)
Epilobium canum var. latifolia (hummingbird trumpet)
Erigeron compositus (alpine daisy)
Erigeron modestus (prairie fleabane)
Erigeron speciosus (showy fleabane)
Eriogonum racemosum (red root buckwheat)
Eriogonum wrightii (Wright buckwheat)
Eupatorium greggii (palmleaf thoroughwort)
Gaillardia pinnatifida (yellow gaillardia, blanket flower)
Galium triflorum (sweet-scented bedstraw)

Gentiana parryi (Parry gentian)
Glandularia bipinnatifida var. bipinnatifida (prairie verbena, Dakota vervain)
Glandularia gooddingii (pink verbena, southwestern vervain)
Gutierrezia sarothrae (broom snakeweed, matchbrush)
Hedyotis nigricans (bluets)
Hedysarum boreale (sweet vetch, sweet broom)
Heliomeris multiflora (showy goldeneye)
Heterotheca villosa var. villosa (golden aster)
Heuchera rubescens var. versicolor (coral bells, alumroot)
Heuchera sanguinea (New Mexican coral bells)
Heuchera parvifolia (saxifrage, alum root)
Iris missouriensis (Rocky Mountain iris, western blue flag)
Lesquerella fendleri (bladderpod)
Lewisia rediviva (bitter root)
Lilium philadelphicum (wood lily)
Linnaea borealis (twinflower)
Linum lewisii (wild blue flax)
Lithospermum incisum (fringed or narrow-leaved puccoon)
Lobelia cardinalis (cardinal flower)
Lupinus argenteus (silvery lupine)
Lupinus palmeri (Palmer's lupine)
Maianthemum racemosum ssp. racemosum (false Solomon's seal,
    false spikenard)
Maianthemum stellatum (starry Solomon's seal)
Melampodium leucanthum (Blackfoot daisy, rock daisy)
Mimulus cardinalis (crimson monkey flower)
Mimulus primuloides (primrose monkey flower)
Mirabilis multiflora (wild four o'clock)
Monardella odoratissima (coyote mint, mountain pennyroyal)
Nolina bigelovii var. parryi (Parry's nolina, Bigelow nolina)
Nolina microcarpa (sacahuista, bear grass)
Nolina texana (sacahuista, basket grass, Texas beargrass)
Oenothera brachycarpa (evening primrose)
Oenothera cespitosa (gumbo evening primrose, gumbo lily)
Oenothera flava (shortfin evening primrose)
Pedicularis groenlandica (elephant heads)
Penstemon angustifolius (whorled penstemon)
Penstemon eatonii (firecracker penstemon)
Penstemon fendleri (fendler penstemon, purple foxglove)
Penstemon jamesii (James' penstemon)
Penstemon strictus (Rocky Mountain penstemon)
Penstemon palmeri (Palmer's penstemon, scented penstemon)
Penstemon parryi (Parry penstemon)
Penstemon pseudospectabilis (desert beardtongue)
Penstemon rostriflorus (Bridge's penstemon, mountain scarlet penstemon)
Penstemon thurberi (sand penstemon)
Pentaphylloides floribunda (potentilla, shrubby cinquefoil)
Petrophyton caespitosum (dwarf spiraea, petrophytum, tufted rockmat)
Phacelia sericea (silky phacelia)
Phlox nana (Santa Fe phlox, white-eyed phlox, canyon phlox)
Polemonium foliosissimum (Jacob's ladder)
Polemonium viscosum (sky pilot)

Potentilla arguta (white cinquefoil, prairie cinquefoil, tall cinquefoil)
Potentilla thurberi (red cinquefoil)
Psilostrophe tagetina (woolly paper-flower)
Ranunculus cardiophyllus (buttercup)
Ranunculus macranthus (large buttercup)
Ratibida columnifera (prairie or long-headed coneflower, Mexican hat)
Rudbeckia laciniata (cut-leaf coneflower)
Ruellia nudiflora (wild petunia, violet ruellia)
Salvia arizonica (Arizona sage)
Saxifraga cespitosa (tufted saxifrage)
Senna lindheimeriana (Lindheimer senna, velvetleaf senna)
Sidalcea neomexicana (checker mallow, prairie mallow)
Silene laciniata (southern Indian pink, catchfly, Mexican campion)
Solidago canadensis (meadow goldenrod)
Solidago missouriensis (Missouri goldenrod, prairie goldenrod)
Sphaeralcea ambigua (desert mallow)
Sphaeralcea coccinea (scarlet globe mallow)
Sphaeralcea parvifolia (globe mallow)
Stachys coccinea (Texas betony)
Talinum aurantiacum (flame flower)
Tetraneuris acaulis var. acaulis (stemless goldflower, stemless rubber weed, butte marigold)
Thalictrum dasycarpum (tall or purple meadow rue)
Thlaspi montanum var. fendleri (wild candytuft, penny cress)
Verbena hastata (blue verbena, blue vervain)
Viguiera dentata (goldeneye)
Viguiera parishii (shrubby goldeneye)
Viola canadensis (Canada violet)
Viola pedatifida (prairie violet)
Xylorhiza tortifolia var. tortifolia (Mojave aster)
Yucca baccata (blue, banana, or fleshy-fruited yucca)
Yucca brevifolia (Joshua tree)
Yucca elata (soaptree yucca, palmella)
Yucca glauca (yucca, soapweed)
Yucca schottii (hoary yucca, mountain yucca)
Zinnia grandiflora (Rocky Mountain, yellow, or plains zinnia)

Grasses/Grass-like plants

Agrostis exarata (spikebent, spike red top)
Agrostis scabra (ticklegrass, fly-away grass)
Andropogon gerardii (big bluestem)
Andropogon hallii (sand bluestem)
Aristida purpurea (purple three awn)
Aristida purpurea var. longiseta (red three awn)
Bouteloua curtipendula (sideoats grama)
Bouteloua eriopoda (black grama)
Bouteloua gracilis (blue grama)
Bouteloua hirsuta (hairy grama)
Bromus carinatus (California brome)
Calamagrostis canadensis (bluejoint grass)
Carex aquatilis (water sedge)
Carex nebrascensis (Nebraska sedge)

Carex utriculata (beaked sedge)
Chloris crinita (two-flowered trichloris)
Danthonia californica (California oatgrass)
Danthonia intermedia (timber oatgrass)
Deschampsia cespitosa (tufted hairgrass)
Digitaria californica (cottontop)
Distichlis spicata (seashore saltgrass)
Eleocharis palustris (creeping spikesedge, spike rush)
Elymus canadensis (Canada wild rye)
Elymus glaucus (blue wild rye)
Eragrostis intermedia (plains lovegrass)
Eragrostis spectabilis (purple lovegrass, tumblegrass)
Festuca ovina (sheep fescue)
Glyceria grandis (American or tall mannagrass, reed meadowgrass)
Hierochloe odorata (sweet grass)
Hilaria belangeri (curly mesquite)
Hilaria mutica (tobosa grass)
Koeleria macrantha (June grass)
Leersia oryzoides (rice cut grass)
Leptochloa dubia (green sprangletop)
Leymus cinereus (Great Basin wild rye)
Muhlenbergia montana (mountain muhly)
Muhlenbergia porteri (bush muhly)
Muhlenbergia rigida (purple muhly)
Muhlenbergia wrightii (spike muhly)
Panicum obtusum (vine mesquite)
Panicum virgatum (switchgrass)
Pascopyrum smithii (western wheatgrass)
Phleum alpinum (alpine timothy)
Schizachyrium scoparium (little bluestem)
Scirpus acutus (hardstem bulrush)
Scirpus maritimus (alkali, prairie, or bayonet grass)
Scirpus tabernaemontani (great bulrush)
Sorghastrum nutans (Indian grass)
Sporobolus airoides (alkali sacaton)
Sporobolus compositus var. compositus (tall dropseed)
Sporobolus cryptandrus (sand dropseed)
Sporobolus flexuosus (mesa dropseed)
Trisetum spicatum (spike trisetum)
Typha latifolia (cattail)

Shrubs (deciduous)

Acacia angustissima (fern acacia, whiteball acacia)
Amelanchier utahensis (Utah serviceberry)
Amorpha fruticosa (false indigo, Indigo bush)
Anisacanthus thurberi (Chuparosa, desert honeysuckle)
Arctostaphylos patula (greenleaf manzanita)
Arctostaphylos pringlei (pink-bracted manzanita)
Artemisia frigida (prairie sagewort, fringed sage)
Artemisia nova (black sagebrush)
Artemisia tridentata (big sagebrush, Great Basin sagebrush)
Atriplex canescens (four-wing saltbush, wingscale)

Atriplex confertifolia (spiny saltbush, shadscale saltbush, hop sage)
Atriplex lentiformis (saltbush, coastal quail bush)
Bouvardia ternifolia (smooth bouvardia)
Calliandra eriophylla (fairy duster, mesquitilla)
Ceanothus fendleri (Fendler ceanothus, buckbrush)
Ceanothus greggii var. vestitus (desert ceanothus)
Celtis pallida (desert hackberry, granjeno)
Cercocarpus ledifolius (curl-leaf mountain mahogany)
Cercocarpus montanus (mountain mahogany, silverleaf mountain mahogany)
Chamaebatiaria millefolium (fernbush, desert sweet, tansy bush)
Chrysothamnus nauseosus (rabbit brush, chamisa)
Crossosoma bigelovii (crossosoma)
Dalea formosa (feather plume, feather dalea)
Dalea scoparia (broom dalea, broom pea)
Encelia farinosa (brittle bush)
Ephedra nevadensis (Mormon tea)
Ephedra trifurca (ephedra, joint fir)
Ephedra viridis (Mormon tea)
Ericameria laricifolia (larchleaf goldenweed, turpentine bush)
Eriogonum fasciculatum (California buckwheat)
Erythrina flabelliformis (western coral bean, Indian bean, chilicote)
Fallugia paradoxa (Apache plume)
Fendlera rupicola (false mock orange, cliff fendler bush)
Forestiera pubescens (desert olive, elbow-bush, forestiera)
Fouquieria splendens (ocotillo, candlewood)
Frangula californica ssp. californica (coffeeberry)
Fraxinus greggii (littleleaf ash, Gregg ash, escobilla)
Fremontodendron californicum (northern flannelbush, northern fremontia)
Garrya wrightii (Wright's catclaw, Wright's silk tassel)
Grayia spinosa (spiny hopsage)
Hibiscus coulteri (desert rose mallow, Coulter hibiscus)
Hibiscus denudatus (rock hibiscus)
Holodiscus dumosus (bush rock-spires, cream bush, ocean spray)
Juniperus californica (California juniper)
Juniperus monosperma (one-seed juniper)
Krascheninnikovia lanata (winterfat)
Larrea tridentata (creosote bush)
Lonicera involucrata (black twinberry, bear berry honeysuckle)
Lycium andersonii (Anderson wolfberry)
Mahonia haematocarpa (red barberry)
Mahonia fremontii (Fremont barberry, holly grape)
Mahonia trifoliolata (agarito, trifoliate barberry)
Parkinsonia microphylla (foothills palo verde, littleleaf palo verde)
Parthenium incanum (mariola)
Poliomintha incana (mintbush)
Prosopis glandulosa (honey mesquite)
Prunus virginiana (chokecherry)
Psilostrophe cooperi (paperflower, yellow paper daisy)
Purshia stansburiana (cliff rose)
Purshia tridentata (antelope brush)
Quercus turbinella (shrub live oak)
Rhus choriophylla (evergreen sumac)

Rhus glabra (smooth sumac)
Rhus microphylla (desert sumac, littleleaf sumac, correosa)
Rhus ovata (sugar bush, sugar sumac)
Rhus trilobata (squawbush, basketbush, skunkbush)
Ribes aureum (golden currant)
Ribes cereum (wax currant, western red currant, squaw currant)
Robinia neomexicana (New Mexico locust, mescal bean)
Rosa stellata (desert rose)
Rosa woodsii var. ultramontana (Arizona wild rose)
Rubus idaeus ssp. strigosus (red raspberry)
Rubus parviflorus (western thimbleberry)
Salix scouleriana (western pussy willow, Scouler's willow)
Salvia dorrii (grayball sage)
Sambucus cerulea (blue elderberry)
Sambucus mexicana (Mexican elderberry)
Sambucus racemosa var. melanocarpa (black elderberry)
Sarcobatus vermiculatus (greasewood)
Senna wislizenii (shrubby senna, canyon senna)
Shepherdia argentea (silver buffaloberry)

Shrubs (evergreen)

Sideroxylon lanuginosum ssp. lanuginosum (chittamwood, gum elastic tree)
Sorbus dumosa (mountain ash)
Symphoricarpos oreophilus (mountain snowberry)
Tecoma stans (yellow bells, trumpet flower)
Vauquelinia californica (Arizona rosewood)

Trees (deciduous)

Acacia farnesiana (huisache, sweet acacia)
Acer negundo (box elder)
Acer glabrum (Rocky Mountain maple)
Acer grandidentatum (bigtooth maple)
Betula occidentalis (mountain birch, water birch)
Celtis laevigata var. reticulata (netleaf hackberry)
Cercis canadensis var. texensis (California redbud)
Chilopsis linearis (desert willow, trumpet flower)
Fraxinus velutina (arizona ash, velvet ash, desert ash)
Fraxinus cuspidata (flowering ash)
Juglans major (Arizona walnut)
Parkinsonia florida (blue palo verde)
Platanus wrightii (Arizona sycamore, Alamo)
Populus fremontii (western cottonwood)
Populus tremuloides (quaking aspen)
Prosopis pubescens (tornillo, screwbean mesquite)
Quercus gambelii (Gambel's oak, Rocky Mountain white oak)
Quercus grisea (gray oak, Mexican blue oak)

Trees (evergreen)

Abies concolor (western white fir)
Abies lasiocarpa (subalpine fir)
Acacia constricta (whitethorn, mescat acacia)
Arbutus arizonica (Arizona madrone)

Cupressus arizonica (Arizona cypress)
Juniperus deppeana (alligator or western juniper)
Juniperus osteosperma (Utah juniper)
Juniperus scopulorum (Rocky Mountain juniper)
Olneya tesota (ironwood, tesota)
Picea engelmannii (Engelmann spruce)
Picea pungens (blue spruce, Colorado spruce)
Pinus cembroides (Mexican pinyon)
Pinus edulis (pinyon pine, Colorado pinyon)
Pinus flexilis (limber pine)
Pinus longaeva (bristlecone pine)
Pinus ponderosa (ponderosa pine)
Pinus strobiformis (southwestern white pine)
Pseudotsuga menziesii (Douglas fir)
Quercus arizonica (Arizona white oak)
Quercus chrysolepis (canyon live oak)
Quercus emoryi

Vines (deciduous)

Clematis ligusticifolia (clematis)
Maurandella antirrhiniflora (snapdragon vine)
Vitis arizonica (Arizona grape, canyon grape)

FEDERALLY LISTED ENDANGERED SPECIES

Arizona agaze (Agave arizonica)
Arizona cliffrose (Purshia subintegra)
Arizona hedgehog cactus (Echinocereus triglochidiatus var. arizonicaus)
Brady pincushion cactus (Pediocactus bradyi)
Cochise pincushion cactus (Coryphantha (Escobaria) robbinsorum)
Jones cycladenia (Cycladenia humilis var. Jonesii)
Kearney's blue-star (Amsonia kearneyana)
Navajo sedge (Carex specuicola)
Nichol's Turk's head cactus (Echinocactus horizonthalonius var. Nicholii)
Peebles Navajo cactus (Pediocactus peeblesianus var. Peeblesianus)
Pima pineapple cactus (Coryphantha scheeri var. Robustispina)
San Francisco Peaks groundsel (Senecio franciscanus)
Sentry milk-vetch (Astrgalus cremnophylax var. Ccremnophylax)
Siler pincushion cactus (Pediocactus sileri)
Welsh's milkweed (Asclepias welshii)

ARIZONA NOXIOUS SPECIES

Because the noxious weed lists have continually changed since we gathered them in 1994, we are not including them at this time. Not all States have noxious weed lists. Those that do, do not use the same standards of importance and are not comparable. States typically have included plants that interfere with agriculture (Canada thistle), or cause human health problems (poison ivy). Some States are now including a category of plants that invade and degrade the environment (purple loosestrife). Check with your State's Agriculture Department or Weed Scientist listed below. The noxious weed list can be used two ways on roadsides: l) check to not inadvertently plant these invasive plants, and 2) note the plants you are legally responsible to control. Many States now check adjacent State lists to avoid planting their neighbors' problem plants. Because weeds do not respect political boundaries, and because by their very nature weeds continue to adapt and expand, monitoring and controlling invasives at State borders is a wise part of vegetation management.

(Weed and Seed Law)

Everett Hall, Plant Services
Arizona Department of Agriculture
1688 West Adams Street
Phoenix, AZ 85007

William McCloskey
Unversity of Arizona, Plant Science
Yuma, AZ 85364
(520) 621-7613

ARIZONA RESOURCES

Arizona Heritage Data Mgt. System
Arizona Game & Fish Department
WM-H
2221 W, Greenway Road
Phoenix, AZ 85023
(602) 789-3612
(602) 789-3928 (fax)

The Nature Conservancy Field Office
300 E. University Boulevard, Ste. 230
Tucson, AZ 85705
(520) 622-3861

Arizona Native Plant Society
P.O. Box 41206
Tucson, AZ 85717

Department of Agriculture
1688 W. Adams
Phoenix, AZ 85997
(602) 542-4373

State Extension Service
Range Management -
Dr. George Ruyle
School of Renewable
Natural Resources
University of Arizona
Tucson, AZ 85721
(602) 621-1384

Arizona-Sonora Desert Museum
2021 N. Kinney Road
Tucson, AZ 85743

Boyce-Thompson Southwestern
Arboretum
37615 E. U.S. Hwy. 60
Superior, AZ 85273

POTENTIAL NATURAL VEGETATION ZONES IN
═══ ARKANSAS ═══

Source: A.W. Kuchler's Potential Natural Vegetation Map, 1964, Revised 1985.
Presented in U.S.G.S. National Atlas of the U.S. Series,
U.S. Geological Survey, Reston, VA.

74 Cedar glades *(Quercus-Juniperus-Sporobolus)*	
75 Cross timbers *(Quercus-Andropogon)*	**101** Oak-hickory-pine forest *(Quercus-Carya-Pinus)*
91 Oak-hickory forest *(Quercus-Carya)*	**103** Southern floodplain forest *(Quercus-Nyassa-Taxodium)*

(Dominant plant species present in each vegetation type are listed in Appendix 8)

74 *Cedar Glades (Quercus-Juniperus-Sporobolus)*
75 *Cross Timbers (Quercus-Andropogon)*
91 *Oak-Hickory Forest (Quercus-Carya)*
101 *Oak-Hickory-Pine Forest (Quercus-Carya-Pinus)*
103 *Southern Floodplain Forest (Quercus-Nyssa-Taxodium)*

Botanical Experts

John Logan, Botanist
Arkansas Natural Heritage Commission
1400 Tower Building
323 Center St.
Little Rock, AR 72201
(501) 324-9615
(501) 324-9618 (fax)
internet: johnl@dah.state.ar.us

Recommended Flora

Smith, E.B. 1988. An Atlas and Annotated List of the Vascular Plants of Arkansas, 2nd Ed. Univ. of Arkansas, Fayetteville, AR. 72701

NATIVE PLANTS FOR LANDSCAPE USE IN ARKANSAS

Cacti

Opuntia humifusa (prickly pear)
Opuntia macrorhiza (common prickly pear)

Ferns

Adiantum capillus-veneris (southern maidenhair fern)
Adiantum pedatum (northern maidenhair fern)
Asplenium platyneuron (ebony spleenwort)
Asplenium trichomanes (maidenhair spleenwort)
Athyrium filix-femina (lady fern)
Botrychium virginianum (rattlesnake fern)
Cystopteris bulbifera (bladder fern)
Cystopteris fragilis (fragile fern)
Dryopteris carthusiana (shield fern, toothed wood fern, spinulose shield fern)
Dryopteris marginalis (marginal wood fern)
Marsilea macropoda (water clover)
Onoclea sensibilis (sensitive fern, bead fern)
Osmunda cinnamomea (cinnamon fern)
Osmunda regalis (royal fern)
Phegopteris hexagonoptera (broad beech fern)
Polystichum acrostichoides (Christmas fern)
Thelypteris novaboracensis (New York fern, tapering fern)
Woodwardia virginica (Virginia chain fern)

Forbs (annuals/biennials)

Aphanostephus skirrhobasis (lazy daisy)

Campanulastrum americanum (American bellflower, tall bellflower)
Castilleja indivisa (Indian paintbrush)
Centaurea americana (basket flower)
Dracopsis amplexicaulis (clasping leaf coneflower)
Eryngium leavenworthii (Leavenworth eryngo)
Euphorbia marginata (snow-on-the-mountain)
Eustoma russellianum (prairie or catchfly gentian, Texas bluebell)
Gaillardia pulchella (Indian blanket, firewheel)
Helianthus annuus (common sunflower)
Helianthus petiolaris (plains sunflower)
Lesquerella gracilis (bladderpod)
Lindheimera texana (Texas star, Lindheimer daisy)
Monarda citriodora (horsemint, lemon beebalm, lemon mint)
Nemophila phacelioides (baby blue eyes)
Palafoxia callosa (small palafoxia)
Sabatia campestris (prairie rose gentian, prairie sabatia, meadow pink)
Sedum nuttallianum (yellow stonecrop)
Senecio glabellus (butterweed)

Forbs (perennials)

Acorus calamus (sweet flag, calamus)
Actaea pachypoda (white baneberry)
Ageratina altissima var. altissima (white snakeroot)
Allium canadense (wild garlic)
Allium cernuum (nodding onion)
Allium stellatum (wild pink onion)
Amsonia ciliata (blue funnel lily, blue star)
Amsonia tabernaemontana (blue star)
Anemone caroliniana (Carolina anemone, southern thimbleweed)
Anemone virginiana (thimbleweed, tall anemone)
Antennaria spp. (pussytoes, everlasting)
Apocynum androsaemifolium (spreading dogbane)
Aquilegia canadensis (columbine)
Arisaema triphyllum (Jack-in-the-pulpit, Indian turnip)
Artemisia ludoviciana (white sage, prairie sage, artemisia)
Aruncus dioicus (goat's beard)
Asarum canadense (wild ginger)
Asclepias incarnata (swamp milkweed)
Asclepias tuberosa (butterfly weed)
Asclepias verticillata (whorled milkweed)
Aster dumosus (bushy aster)
Aster ericoides (heath aster, white wreath aster)
Aster laevis (smooth aster)
Aster novae-angliae (New England aster)
Aster oblongifolius (aromatic aster)
Aster oolentangiensis (sky blue aster)
Aster pilosus (frost aster)
Aster sericeus (silky aster)
Astragalus canadensis (milk vetch, Canada milk vetch)
Baptisia alba (white false indigo)
Baptisia alba var. macrophylla (cream false indigo, plains wild indigo)
Callirhoe digitata (finger poppy mallow)

Callirhoe involucrata (purple poppy mallow, winecup)
Callirhoe papaver (poppy mallow)
Camassia scilloides (wild hyacinth)
Caulophyllum thalictroides (blue cohosh)
Cimicifuga racemosa (bugbane, black cohosh)
Claytonia caroliniana (broad-leaved spring beauty)
Claytonia virginica (narrow-leaved spring beauty)
Cooperia drummondii (rain lily, prairie lily)
Coreopsis grandiflora (coreopsis)
Coreopsis lanceolata (lance-leaved coreopsis)
Coreopsis palmata (stiff coreopsis)
Coreopsis tripteris (tall coreopsis)
Dalea candida (white prairie clover)
Dalea purpurea (purple prairie clover)
Delphinium carolinianum (blue larkspur)
Delphinium carolinianum ssp. virescens (prairie larkspur)
Delphinium tricorne (dwarf larkspur)
Desmodium canadense (Canada tick-trefoil, Canada tickclover)
Desmodium illinoense (Illinois tick-trefoil, Illinois tickclover)
Dicentra cucullaria (dutchman's breeches)
Dodecatheon meadia (shooting star)
Engelmannia pinnatifida (Engelmann daisy)
Eryngium yuccifolium (rattlesnake master, button snake-root)
Erysimum capitatum (western wallflower, prairie rocket)
Erythronium americanum (eastern trout lily, yellow trout lily)
Eupatorium coelestinum (mist flower)
Eupatorium fistulosum (Joe-pye weed)
Eupatorium maculatum (spotted Joe-pye weed)
Eupatorium perfoliatum (boneset)
Eupatorium purpureum (Joe-pye weed)
Euphorbia corollata (flowering spurge)
Fragaria virginiana (wild strawberry)
Galium triflorum (sweet-scented bedstraw)
Gentiana alba (cream gentian, yellow gentian)
Gentiana andrewsii (bottle gentian)
Gentiana saponaria (closed gentian, soapwort gentian)
Geranium maculatum (wild geranium, cranesbill)
Glandularia bipinnatifida var. bipinnatifida (prairie verbena, Dakota vervain)
Glandularia canadensis (rose vervain, sweet William)
Glycyrrhiza lepidota (wild licorice)
Helianthus pauciflorus ssp. pauciflorus (stiff sunflower)
Helianthus strumosus (woodland sunflower)
Helianthus simulans (narrow-leaved sunflower, swamp sunflower)
Heliopsis helianthoides (ox-eye sunflower, false sunflower)
Hepatica nobilis var. acuta (sharp-lobed hepatica)
Heterotheca villosa var. villosa (golden aster)
Heuchera americana var. hirsuticaulis (alumroot)
Hieracium longipilum (hairy hawkweed)
Houstonia caerulea (bluets)
Hydrastis canadensis (golden seal)
Hydrophyllum virginianum (Virginia waterleaf)
Hymenocallis caroliniana (spider lily, rain lily)

Hymenopappus artemisiifolius (old plainsman, woolly white)
Hypoxis hirsuta (yellow star grass)
Ipomopsis rubra (standing cypress)
Iris cristata (dwarf crested iris)
Iris virginica v. shrevei (blue flag)
Lespedeza capitata (roundheaded bush clover)
Liatris aspera (rough blazing star, gayfeather)
Liatris cylindracea (dwarf blazing star, gayfeather)
Liatris elegans (gayfeather)
Liatris mucronata (narrow-leaf gayfeather)
Liatris pycnostachya (prairie blazing star, gayfeather)
Liatris punctata (dotted blazing star, gayfeather)
Liatris spicata (marsh blazing star, gayfeather)
Liatris squarrosa (blazing star)
Lilium michiganense (Turk's cap lily, Michigan lily)
Linum virginianum (woodland flax)
Lithospermum canescens (hoary puccoon)
Lithospermum caroliniense (hairy puccoon, hispid gromwell)
Lithospermum incisum (fringed puccoon, narrow-leaved puccoon)
Lobelia cardinalis (cardinal flower)
Lobelia siphilitica (great blue lobelia)
Lobelia spicata (pale lobelia)
Lysimachia ciliata (fringed loosestrife)
Maianthemum stellatum (starry Solomon's seal)
Manfreda virginica (rattlesnake master, false aloe)
Mertensia virginica (bluebells)
Mimosa quadrivalvis var. angustata (catclaw sensitive briar)
Mitchella repens (partridge berry)
Monarda fistulosa (wild bergamot, horsemint, beebalm)
Nuphar lutea (yellow pond lily, cow lily, spatter dock)
Oenothera biennis (common evening primrose)
Oenothera fruticosa (sundrops)
Oenothera macrocarpa (Missouri evening primrose)
Oenothera speciosa (showy white evening primrose)
Osmorhiza claytoni (sweet cicely, sweet jarvil)
Peltandra virginica (arrow arum)
Penstemon digitalis (beardtongue)
Phlox carolina (Carolina phlox)
Phlox divaricata ssp. laphamii (blue phlox, sweet william)
Phlox paniculata (summer phlox, perennial phlox)
Phlox pilosa (prairie phlox, downy phlox)
Physostegia digitalis (obedient plant)
Physostegia intermedia (obedient plant)
Physostegia virginiana (obedient plant, false dragonhead)
Podophyllum peltatum (May apple)
Polemonium reptans (Jacob's ladder, Greek valerian)
Polygonatum biflorum (Solomon's seal)
Potentilla arguta (white cinquefoil, prairie cinquefoil, tall cinquefoil)
Potentilla simplex (common cinquefoil)
Pycnanthemum tenuifolium (slender mountain mint)
Pycnanthemum virginianum (mountain mint)
Ranunculus hispidus (early buttercup, tufted buttercup)

Ratibida columnifera (prairie coneflower, long-headed coneflower, Mexican hat)
Ratibida pinnata (gray-headed coneflower, yellow coneflower)
Rhexia virginica (meadow beauty)
Rudbeckia fulgida (black-eyed Susan, orange coneflower)
Rudbeckia grandiflora (large coneflower)
Rudbeckia hirta (black-eyed Susan)
Rudbeckia laciniata (cut-leaf coneflower)
Rudbeckia subtomentosa (sweet black-eyed Susan)
Ruellia humilis (wild petunia)
Salvia azurea var. grandiflora (blue sage)
Salvia lyrata (cancer weed, lyre-leaf sage)
Sanguinaria candensis (bloodroot)
Sedum ternatum (wild stonecrop)
Senecio aureus (golden ragwort)
Senecio plattensis (prairie ragwort, prairie groundsel)
Silene stellata (starry campion)
Silene virginica (fire pink)
Silphium integrifolium (rosinweed)
Silphium laciniatum (compass plant)
Silphium perfoliatum (cup plant)
Silphium terebinthinaceum (prairie dock)
Sisyrinchium mucronatum (eastern blue-eyed grass)
Sisyrinchium campestre (white-eyed grass, prairie blue-eyed grass)
Sisyrinchium angustifolium (narrow-leaved blue-eyed grass)
Solidago caesia (blue-stemmed goldenrod, wreath goldenrod)
Solidago canadensis (meadow goldenrod)
Solidago juncea (early goldenrod, plume goldenrod)
Solidago missouriensis (Missouri goldenrod, prairie goldenrod)
Solidago nemoralis (gray goldenrod, old-field goldenrod)
Solidago odora (sweet goldenrod)
Solidago rigida (stiff goldenrod)
Solidago rugosa (rough-leaved goldenrod)
Solidago speciosa (showy goldenrod)
Solidago ulmifolia (elm-leaved goldenrod)
Spigelia marilandica (Indian pink)
Stylophorum diphyllum (celandine poppy)
Tephrosia virginiana (goat's rue)
Thalictrum dasycarpum (tall or purple meadow rue)
Thalictrum dioicum (early meadow rue)
Thalictrum thalictroides (rue anemone)
Thelesperma filifolium var. filifolium (thelesperma, greenthread)
Tradescantia hirsuticaulis (hairy spiderwort)
Tradescantia ohiensis (Ohio spiderwort)
Uvularia grandiflora (bellwort, merrybells)
Uvularia sessilifolia (wildoats, merrybells)
Verbena hastata (blue verbena, blue vervain)
Verbena stricta (hoary vervain)
Vernonia baldwinii (ironweed, western ironweed)
Vernonia fasciculata (ironweed)
Veronicastrum virginicum (Culver's root)
Viola canadensis (Canada violet)
Viola missouriensis (Missouri violet)

Viola pedata (bird-foot violet)
Viola pedatifida (prairie violet)
Viola pubescens (downy or smooth yellow violet)
Viola soraria (common blue violet, meadow violet)
Yucca arkansana (Arkansas yucca, softleaf yucca)
Zizia aptera (heart-leaved golden alexanders)
Zizia aurea (golden alexanders)

Grasses/Grass-like plants

Agrostis scabra (ticklegrass, fly-away grass)
Andropogon gerardii (big bluestem)
Andropogon glomeratus (bushy bluestem)
Andropogon ternarius (splitbeard bluestem)
Andropogon virginicus (broom sedge)
Aristida purpurea (purple three awn)
Arundinaria gigantea (giant cane)
Bouteloua curtipendula (sideoats grama)
Bouteloua hirsuta (hairy grama)
Buchloe dactyloides (buffalograss)
Carex pensylvanica (Pennsylvania sedge)
Carex stipata (awl-fruited sedge)
Carex stricta (tussock sedge)
Chasmanthium latifolium (inland sea oats, wild oats, river oats, broad-leaf uniola)
Danthonia spicata (poverty grass)
Elymus canadensis (Canada wild rye)
Elymus glaucus (blue wild rye)
Elymus hystrix var. hystrix (bottlebrush grass)
Eragrostis intermedia (plains lovegrass)
Eragrostis spectabilis (purple lovegrass, tumblegrass)
Juncus effusus var. solutus (soft rush)
Juncus interior (inland rush)
Koeleria macrantha (June grass)
Leersia oryzoides (rice cut grass)
Melica nitens (three-flower melic grass)
Muhlenbergia capillaris (gulf muhly, hair grass)
Panicum virgatum (switchgrass)
Pascopyrum smithii (western wheatgrass)
Saccharum giganteum (sugarcane plume grass)
Schizachyrium scoparium (little bluestem)
Scirpus atrovirens (dark green bulrush)
Scirpus cyperinus (wool grass)
Scirpus tabernaemontani (great bulrush)
Sorghastrum nutans (Indian grass)
Spartina pectinata (prairie cordgrass, freshwater cordgrass)
Sporobolus cryptandrus (sand dropseed)
Sporobolus heterolepis (northern prairie dropseed)
Tripsacum dactyloides (eastern gama grass)
Typha angustifolia (narrow-leaved cattail)
Typha latifolia (cattail)

Shrubs (deciduous)

Acacia angustissima (fern acacia, whiteball acacia)
Alnus serrulata (smooth alder)
Amelanchier arborea (downy serviceberry, shadbush, Juneberry)
Amorpha canescens (leadplant)
Amorpha fruticosa (false indigo, Indigo bush)
Aronia melanocarpa (black chokeberry)
Baccharis halimifolia (sea myrtle, groundsel bush)
Callicarpa americana (American beautyberry, French mulberry)
Castanea pumila (chinquapin)
Ceanothus americanus (New Jersey tea, red root)
Cephalanthus occidentalis (buttonbush)
Cornus alternifolia (pogoda dogwood, alternate-leaved dogwood)
Cornus amomum ssp. obliqua (swamp dogwood, silky dogwood)
Cornus drummondii (rough-leaf dogwood)
Cornus racemosa (gray dogwood)
Corylus americana (American hazelnut or filbert)
Dirca palustris (leatherwood, ropebark)
Erythrina herbacea (coral bean)
Euonymus americana (strawberry bush, brook euonymus, hearts-a-bustin')
Euonymus atropurpurea (wahoo, burning bush)
Forestiera acuminata (swamp privet)
Fothergilla major (witch alder)
Frangula caroliniana (Carolina buckthorn)
Hamamelis vernalis (vernal witch hazel)
Hydrangea arborescens (wild hydrangea)
Hypericum hypericoides ssp. hypericoides (St. Andrew's cross)
Hypericum prolificum (shrubby St. John's wort)
Ilex verticillata (winterberry, black alder)
Itea virginica (Virginia willow, sweetspire, tassel-white)
Lindera benzoin (spicebush)
Lonicera dioica (limber or wild honeysuckle)
Lyonia ligustrina (male-berry, male-blueberry)
Physocarpus opulifolius (ninebark)
Prunus gracilis (Oklahoma plum)
Prunus virginiana (chokecherry)
Rhododendron canescens (wild, piedmont, or sweet azalea)
Rhododendron prinophyllum (roseshell azalea, early azalea)
Rhododendron viscosum (swamp azalea)
Rhus aromatica (fragrant sumac)
Rhus copallinum (dwarf or winged sumac)
Rhus glabra (smooth sumac)
Ribes cynosbati (prickly gooseberry, dogberry)
Ribes odoratum (buffalo currant, golden currant)
Rosa arkansana (prairie rose)
Rosa carolina (Carolina rose)
Rosa setigera (Illinois or prairie rose)
Rubus occidentalis (black raspberry, thimbleberry)
Sambucus canadensis (elderberry, common elder)
Spiraea tomentosa (steeplebush, hardhack)
Staphylea trifolia (bladdernut)
Styrax americanus (American silverbells)

Vaccinium arboreum (sparkleberry, farkleberry)
Viburnum acerifolium (maple leaf viburnum)
Viburnum dentatum (southern arrowwood)
Viburnum nudum (possumhaw viburnum)
Viburnum prunifolium (black haw, nanny berry)
Viburnum rufidulum (southern or rusty black haw)

Shrubs (evergreen)

Ilex vomitoria (yaupon)
Myrica cerifera (wax myrtle, southern bayberry, candleberry)
Sabal minor (dwarf palmetto)

Trees (deciduous)

Acer barbatum (Florida maple, southern sugar maple)
Acer leucoderme (chalk maple)
Acer negundo (box elder)
Acer rubrum (red maple)
Acer saccharinum (silver maple)
Acer saccharum (sugar maple)
Aesculus glabra (Ohio buckeye, horse chestnut)
Aesculus pavia var. pavia (red buckeye)
Betula nigra (river birch)
Carpinus caroliniana (blue beech, hornbeam, musclewood)
Carya alba (mockernut hickory)
Carya cordiformis (bitternut, swamp hickory)
Carya illinoinensis (pecan)
Carya ovata (shagbark hickory)
Carya texana (black hickory)
Catalpa speciosa (northern catalpa)
Celtis laevigata (sugarberry, hackberry)
Celtis occidentalis (hackberry, sugarberry)
Cercis canadensis (redbud)
Chionanthus virginicus (fringe tree, old man's beard)
Cladrastis kentukea (yellowwood)
Cornus florida (flowering dogwood)
Cotinus obovatus (smoke tree)
Crataegus crus-galli (cockspur hawthorn)
Crataegus marshallii (parsley hawthorn)
Crataegus mollis (downy hawthorn)
Crataegus phaenopyrum (Washington hawthorn)
Diospyros virginiana (persimmon)
Fagus grandifolia var. caroliniana (beech)
Fraxinus americana (white ash)
Fraxinus pensylvanica (green ash)
Gleditsia triacanthos (honey locust)
Gymnocladus dioica (Kentucky coffee tree)
Hamamelis virginiana (witch hazel)
Ilex decidua (possum-haw, deciduous holly)
Juglans cinerea (butternut, white walnut)
Juglans nigra (black walnut)
Liquidambar styraciflua (sweet gum)
Liriodendron tulipifera (tulip tree)

Magnolia acuminata (cucumber tree)
Magnolia virginiana (sweetbay, swampbay)
Malus angustifolia (southern crabapple, wild crabapple)
Malus ioensis var. ioensis (prairie crabapple)
Nyssa sylvatica (black gum, tupelo)
Ostrya virginiana (ironwood, hophornbeam)
Platanus occidentalis (sycamore, plane-tree)
Populus deltoides (eastern cottonwood)
Prunus americana (wild plum)
Prunus angustifolia (chickasaw plum)
Prunus mexicana (Mexican plum)
Prunus serotina (black cherry)
Ptelea trifoliata (wafer ash, common hoptree)
Quercus alba (white oak)
Quercus coccinea (scarlet oak)
Quercus falcata (southern red oak, Spanish oak)
Quercus lyrata (overcup oak)
Quercus macrocarpa (bur oak)
Quercus marilandica (blackjack oak)
Quercus muhlenbergii (chinkapin oak, chestnut oak)
Quercus palustris (pin oak)
Quercus phellos (willow oak)
Quercus rubra (red oak)
Quercus shumardii (shumard oak)
Quercus stellata (post oak)
Quercus velutina (black oak)
Salix nigra (black willow)
Sapindus saponaria var. drummondii (soapberry)
Sassafras albidum (sassafras)
Tilia americana (American linden, basswood)
Ulmus americana (American elm)
Ulmus crassifolia (cedar elm)
Ulmus rubra (red elm, slippery elm)

Trees (evergreen)

Ilex opaca (American holly, Christmas holly)
Juniperus ashei (rock or post cedar, Ashe or Mexican juniper)
Juniperus virginiana (eastern red cedar)
Pinus echinata (shortleaf pine)
Pinus taeda (loblolly pine)
Taxodium distichum (bald cypress)

Vines (deciduous)

Bignonia capreolata (cross vine)
Celastrus scandens (American bittersweet)
Clematis crispa (leatherflower)
Clematis pitcheri (leather flower, purple clematis)
Clematis virginiana (virgin's bower)
Lonicera sempervirens (coral honeysuckle)
Parthenocissus quinquefolia (Virginia creeper)
Passiflora incarnata (passion flower, maypop)
Vitis riparia (riverbank grape)

Vitis rotundifolia (muscadine grape)
Wisteria frutescens (wisteria)

Vine (evergreen)
Gelsemium sempervirens (yellow jessamine, Carolina jessamine)

FEDERALLY LISTED ENDANGERED SPECIES
Eastern prairie fringed orchid (Platanthera leucophaea)
Geocarpon minimum (no common name)
Harperella (Ptilimnium nodosum (=fluviatile)
Pondberry (Lindera melissifolia)
Running buffalo clover (Trifolium stonloniferum)

ARKANSAS NOXIOUS SPECIES
Because the noxious weed lists have continually changed since we gathered them in 1994, we are not including them at this time. Not all States have noxious weed lists. Those that do, do not use the same standards of importance and are not comparable. States typically have included plants that interfere with agriculture (Canada thistle), or cause human health problems (poison ivy). Some States are now including a category of plants that invade and degrade the environment (purple loosestrife). Check with your State's Agriculture Department or Weed Scientist listed below. The noxious weed list can be used two ways on roadsides: l) check to not inadvertently plant these invasive plants, and 2) note the plants you are legally responsible to control. Many States now check adjacent State lists to avoid planting their neighbors' problem plants. Because weeds do not respect political boundaries, and because by their very nature weeds continue to adapt and expand, monitoring and controlling invasives at State borders is a wise part of vegetation management.

(Seed Law only)

State Plant Board
Plant Industry Division
P.O. Box 1069
Little Rock, AR 72203

John Boyd
University of Arkansas, Box 391
2301 South University
Little Rock, AR 72203

ARKANSAS RESOURCES

Arkansas Natural Heritage
Commission
1400 Tower Building
323 Center Street
Little Rock, AR 72201
(501) 324-9150
(501) 324-9618 (fax)

The Nature Conservancy Field Office
601 N. University Avenue
Little Rock, AR72205
(501) 663-6699

Arkansas Native Plant Society
Department of Forest Resources
University of Arkansas at Monticello
Monticello, AR 71655

State Plant Board
1 Natural Resources Drive
P.O. Box 1069
Little Rock, AR 72203
(501) 225-1598

State Extension Services - Forestry
University of Arkansas
P.O. Box 3468
Monticello, AR 71665
(501) 460-1049

Arkansas Arboretum
Pinnacle Mountain State Park
11901 Pinnacle Valley Road
Roland, AR 72135

POTENTIAL NATURAL VEGETATION ZONES IN
CALIFORNIA

Source: A.W. Kuchler's Potential Natural Vegetation Map, 1964, Revised 1985.
Presented in U.S.G.S. National Atlas of the U.S. Series,
U.S. Geological Survey, Reston, VA.

2	Cedar-hemlock-Douglas fir forest (*Thuja-Tsuga-Pseudotsuga*)
5	Mixed conifer forest (*Abies-Pinus-Pseudotsuga*)
6	Redwood forest (*Sequoia-Pseudotsuga*)
7	Red fir forest (*Abies*)
8	Lodgepole pine-subalpine forest (*Pinus-Tsuga*)
9	Pine-cypress forest (*Pinus-Cupressus*)
10	Western ponderosa forest (*Pinus*)
22	Oregon oakwoods (*Quercus*)
25	California mixed evergreen forest (*Quercus-Arbutus-Pseudotsuga*)
26	California oakwoods (*Quercus*)
29	Chaparral (*Adenostoma-Arctostaphylos-Ceanoti*)
30	Coastal sagebrush (*Salvia-Eriogonum*)
32	Great Basin sagebrush (*Artemisia*)
34	Saltbush-greasewood (*Atriplex-Sarcobatus*)
35	Creosote bush (*Larrea*)
36	Creosote bush-bur sage (*Larrea-Franseria*)
37	Palo verde-cactus shrub (*Cercidium-Opuntia*)
40	Fescue-oatgrass (*Festuca-Danthonia*)
41	California steppe (*Stipa*)
42	Tule marshes (*Scirpus-Typha*)
45	Alpine meadows and barren (*Agrostis, Carex, Festuca, Poa*)
49	Sagebrush steppe (*Artemisia-Agropyron*)

VEGETATION REFERENCES

(Dominant plant species present in each vegetation type are listed in Appendix 8)

2   *Cedar-Hemlock-Douglas Fir Forest (Thuja-Tsuga-Pseudotsuga)*
5   *Mixed Conifer Corest (Abies-Pinus-Pseudotsuga)*
6   *Redwood Forest (Sequoia-Pseudotsuga)*
7   *Red Fir Forest (Abies)*
8   *Lodgepole Pine-Subalpine Forest (Pinus-Tsuga)*
9   *Pine-Cypress Forest (Pinus-Cupressus)*
10 *Western Ponderosa forest (Pinus)*
22 *Oregon Oakwoods (Quercus)*
25 *California Mixed Evergreen Forest (Quercus-Arbutus-Pseudotsuga)*
26 *California Oakwoods (Quercus)*
29 *Chaparral (Adenostoma-Arctostaphylos-Ceanothus)*
30 *Coastal Sagebrush (Salvia-Eriogonum)*
32 *Great Basin Sagebrush (Artemisia)*
34 *Saltbrush-Geasewood (Artiplex-Sarcobatus)*
35 *Creosote Bush (Larrea)*
36 *Creosote Bush-Bur Sage (Larrea-Franseria)*
37 *Palo Verde-Cactus Shrub (Cercidium-Opuntia)*
40 *Fescue-Oatgrass (Festuca-Danthonia)*
41 *California Steppe (Stipa)*
42 *Tule Marshes (Scirpus-Typha)*
45 *Alpine Meadows and Barren (Agrostis, Carex, Festuca, Poa)*
49 *Sagebrush Steppe (Artemisia-Agropyron)*

Botanical Experts

Roxanne Bittman, Botanist
Natural Heritage Division
California Department of Fish and Game
1200 S St.
Sacramento, CA 95814
(916) 323-8970
(916) 324-0475 (fax)
internet: rlb@gishost.dfg.ca.gov

Recommended Flora

Hickman, James C. 1993. The Jepson Manual of Higher Plants of California, Revision and Update of 1925 Original Edition. University of California Press, Berkeley and Los Angeles, CA. 1400 pgs. ISBN: 0520082559.

NATIVE PLANTS FOR LANDSCAPE USE IN CALIFORNIA

Cacti

Echinocereus engelmannii (hedgehog cactus, strawberry cactus)
Opuntia basilaris (beavertail cactus)
Opuntia chlorotica (pancake pear, silver-dollar cactus)
Opuntia erinacea (grizzly, hedgehog, or Mohave prickly pear)

Ferns

Adiantum capillus-veneris (southern maidenhair fern)
Aspidotis densa (rock brake, cliff brake, Indian's dream)

Asplenium trichomanes (saidenhair spleenwort)
Athyrium filix-femina (lady fern)
Blechnum spicant (deer fern)
Cheilanthes gracillima (lace fern)
Cystopteris fragilis (fragile fern)
Dryopteris arguta (coast wood fern)
Pellaea mucronata (bird's-foot fern)
Polypodium glycyrrhiza (licorice fern)
Polypodium scouleri (rock polypody)
Polystichum imbricans (dwarf western sword fern)
Polystichum munitum (western sword fern)
Woodwardia fimbriata (chain fern)

Forbs (annuals/biennials)

Castilleja exserta ssp. exserta (red owl's clover)
Clarkia concinna (red ribbons)
Clarkia unguiculata (mountain garland)
Collinsia heterophylla (Chinese houses)
Collinsia parviflora var. grandiflora (blue lips)
Layia glandulosa (tidy tips)
Mimulus guttatus (golden monkey flower)
Nemophila breviflora (Great Basin nemophila)

Forbs (perennials)

Achlys triphylla (vanilla leaf)
Aconitum columbianum (western monkshood)
Agave deserti (century plant)
Allium validum (swamp onion)
Anaphalis margaritacea (pearly everlasting)
Antennaria spp. (pussytoes, everlasting)
Apocynum androsaemifolium (spreading dogbane)
Aquilegia formosa (scarlet columbine)
Armeria maritima (sea pink, thrift)
Arnica cordifolia (heartleaf arnica)
Artemisia douglasiana (Douglas mugwort)
Artemisia ludoviciana (white sage, prairie sage, artemisia)
Asarum caudatum (wild ginger)
Asclepias asperula (antelope horns)
Asclepias speciosa (showy milkweed)
Aster ascendens (purple aster, Pacific aster)
Aster foliaceus (leafy aster)
Astragalus canadensis (milk vetch, Canada milk vetch)
Balsamorrhiza sagittata (balsamroot)
Calochortus kennedyi (desert mariposa, flame mariposa)
Calochortus macrocarpus (bigpod mariposa)
Calochortus venustus (white mariposa lily)
Camissonia cheiranthifolia (beach evening primrose)
Campanula rotundifolia (harebell)
Castilleja linariifolia (Indian paintbrush)
Claytonia lanceolata (spring beauty)
Clintonia uniflora (bride's bonnet, queen cup, bead lily)
Coreopsis gigantea (giant coreopsis, tree coreopsis)

Cornus canadensis (bunchberry)
Delphinium cardinale (scarlet larkspur)
Delphinium glaucum (tower larkspur)
Delphinium nudicaule (red larkspur)
Delphinium parishii (desert larkspur, paleface delphinium)
Dicentra formosa (western bleeding heart)
Dichelostemma congestum (wild hyacinth)
Disporum smithii (fairy bells)
Dodecatheon hendersonii (Henderson's shooting stars)
Dodecatheon jeffreyi (Jeffrey's shooting stars)
Dudleya cymosa (dudleya)
Dudleya pulverulenta (chalk lettuce)
Epilobium angustifolium (fireweed, willow herb)
Epilobium canum (California fuschia)
Epilobium latifolium (dwarf fireweed)
Epilobium obcordatum (rock fringe)
Erigeron compositus (alpine daisy)
Erigeron glaucus (seaside daisy)
Eriogonum umbellatum (sulfur buckwheat)
Eriogonum wrightii (Wright buckwheat)
Eriophyllum confertifolium (golden yarrow)
Eriophyllum lanatum (woolly sunflower, Oregon sunshine)
Erythronium grandiflorum (glacier lily, yellow fawn lily, dogtooth violet)
Erythronium revolutum (bog fawn lily)
Eschscholzia californica (California poppy)
Fragaria chiloensis (coast strawberry)
Galium triflorum (sweet-scented bedstraw)
Geranium viscossisimum (sticky wild geranium)
Geum triflorum (prairie smoke, purple avens)
Glandularia gooddingii (pink verbena, southwestern vervain)
Glycyrrhiza lepidota (wild licorice)
Gutierrezia sarothrae (broom snakeweed, matchbrush)
Helenium autumnale (common sneezeweed)
Helianthus californicus (California sunflower)
Helianthus gracilentus (dwarf sunflower)
Heterotheca villosa var. villosa (golden aster)
Heuchera micrantha (common alumroot)
Heuchera rubescens (mountain alumroot, red alumroot, wild coralbells)
Hypericum concinnum (goldwire)
Iris douglasiana (Douglas iris, western iris)
Iris missouriensis (Rocky Mountain iris, western blue flag)
Keckiella cordifolia (climbing penstemon)
Lewisia cotyledon (broadleaf lewisia)
Lewisia rediviva (bitter root)
Lilium columbianum (Columbia lily, Oregon lily, wild tiger lily)
Lilium humboldtii (Humboldt lily)
Lilium pardalinum (leopard lily, tiger lily)
Linnaea borealis (twinflower)
Linum lewisii (wild blue flax)
Luetkea pectinata (Alaska spiraea, partridge foot)
Lupinus albifrons (silver bush lupine)
Lupinus arboreus (bush lupine)
Lupinus argenteus (silvery lupine)

Lupinus polyphyllus (meadow lupine, bog lupine)
Lupinus variicolor (bluff lupine, varicolored lupine)
Maianthemum dilatatum (false lily-of-the-valley)
Maianthemum racemosum ssp. racemosum (false Solomon's seal, false spikenard)
Maianthemum stellatum (starry Solomon's seal)
Mertensia ciliata (mountain bluebells)
Mimulus cardinalis (crimson monkey flower)
Mimulus lewisii (Lewis monkey flower, great purple monkey flower)
Mimulus primuloides (primrose monkey flower)
Monardella odoratissima (coyote mint, mountain pennyroyal)
Nolina bigelovii var. parryi (Parry's nolina, Bigelow nolina)
Nothochelone nemorosa (woodland penstemon)
Oenothera cespitosa (gumbo evening primrose, gumbo lily)
Oenothera flava (shortfin evening primrose)
Osmorhiza berteroi (mountain sweet cicely)
Oxalis oregana (redwood sorrel)
Paeonia californica (California peony)
Pedicularis groenlandica (elephant heads)
Penstemon azureus (azure penstemon)
Penstemon centranthifolius (scarlet bugler)
Penstemon davidsonii (blue color mat, alpine penstemon)
Penstemon deustus (hot rock penstemon)
Penstemon eatonii (firecracker penstemon)
Penstemon heterophyllus (foothill penstemon)
Penstemon palmeri (Palmer's penstemon, scented penstemon)
Penstemon pseudospectabilis (desert beardtongue)
Penstemon rupicola (penstemon)
Penstemon speciosus (sagebrush penstemon)
Penstemon spectabilis (royal penstemon)
Pentaphylloides floribunda (potentilla, shrubby cinquefoil)
Petrophyton caespitosum (dwarf spiraea, petrophytum, tufted rockmat)
Phacelia bolanderi (flowered grape leaf)
Phlox diffusa (mat phlox)
Phlox speciosa (showy phlox)
Polemonium occidentale (Jacob's ladder)
Polemonium pulcherrimum (alpine Jacob's ladder, skunk leaf)
Ranunculus alismifolius (meadow buttercup)
Sairocarpus multiflorus (multi-flowered snapdragon)
Salvia sonomensis (creeping sage)
Salvia spathacea (hummingbird sage)
Satureja douglasii (yerba buena)
Sedum spathulifolium (common stonecrop, broad-leaved sedum)
Sidalcea malvaeflora (checkerbloom, checker mallow)
Silene californica (California Indian pink)
Silene hookeri (Hooker's pink, ground pink)
Silene laciniata (southern Indian pink, catchfly, Mexican campion)
Sisyrinchium bellum (blue-eyed grass)
Sisyrinchium californicum (golden-eyed grass)
Solidago canadensis (meadow goldenrod)
Solidago multiradiata (northern goldenrod, mountain goldenrod)
Sphaeralcea ambigua (desert mallow)

Sphaeralcea parvifolia (globe mallow)
Tellima grandiflora (fringe cup)
Tetraneuris acaulis var. acaulis (stemless goldflower, stemless rubber weed, butte marigold)
Thermopsis macrophylla (false lupine)
Tolmiea menziesii (piggyback plant, youth-on-age, thousand mothers)
Trientalis borealis ssp. latifolia (western starflower)
Trillium ovatum (coast trillium, western wakerobin)
Vancouveria hexandra (inside-out flower)
Verbena hastata (blue verbena, blue vervain)
Viguiera parishii (shrubby goldeneye)
Viola glabella (smooth yellow or stream violet)
Viola macloskeyi (white mountain violet)
Whipplea modesta (whipplevine, modesty, yerba de selva)
Wyethia angustifolia (narrowleaf mule ears)
Xerophyllum tenax (beargrass)
Xylorhiza tortifolia var. tortifolia (Mojave aster)
Yucca baccata (blue yucca, banana yucca, fleshy-fruited yucca)
Yucca brevifolia (Joshua tree)
Yucca whipplei (chaparral yucca, our Lord's candle)

Grasses/Grass-like plants

Agrostis exarata (spikebent, spike red top)
Agrostis scabra (ticklegrass, fly-away grass)
Aristida purpurea (purple three awn)
Bouteloua curtipendula (sideoats grama)
Bouteloua eriopoda (black grama)
Bouteloua gracilis (blue grama)
Bromus carinatus (California brome)
Calamagrostis canadensis (bluejoint grass)
Carex aquatilis (water sedge)
Carex barbarae (Santa Barbara sedge)
Carex heteroneura (sedge)
Carex nebrascensis (Nebraska sedge)
Carex spissa (San Diego sedge)
Carex stipata (awl-fruited sedge)
Carex utriculata (beaked sedge)
Carex vernacula (sedge)
Danthonia californica (California oatgrass)
Danthonia intermedia (timber oatgrass)
Deschampsia cespitosa (tufted hairgrass)
Dichanthelium acuminatum var. acuminatum (panic grass)
Distichlis spicata (seashore saltgrass)
Eleocharis palustris (creeping spikesedge, spike rush)
Elymus glaucus (blue wild rye)
Festuca californica (California fescue)
Festuca idahoensis (Idaho fescue, blue bunchgrass)
Hierochloe occidentalis (vanilla grass, California sweet grass)
Juncus dubius (little bamboo)
Koeleria macrantha (June grass)
Leersia oryzoides (rice cut grass)
Leymus mollis (American dune grass, beach wild rye)

Melica imperfecta (coast range melic)
Muhlenbergia montana (mountain muhly)
Muhlenbergia porteri (bush muhly)
Muhlenbergia rigens (meadow muhly, deergrass)
Nassella cernua (nodding stipa)
Pascopyrum smithii (western wheatgrass)
Phleum alpinum (alpine timothy)
Poa secunda (pine bluegrass)
Pseudoroegneria spicata (bluebunch wheatgrass)
Scirpus acutus (hardstem bulrush)
Scirpus maritimus (alkali bulrush, prairie bulrush, bayonet grass)
Scirpus tabernaemontani (great bulrush)
Sporobolus airoides (alkali sacaton)
Sporobolus cryptandrus (sand dropseed)
Sporobolus flexuosus (mesa dropseed)
Stipa comata (needle-and-thread grass)
Stipa nelsonii (Columbia needlegrass)
Stipa speciosa (desert needlegrass, spear grass)
Trisetum spicatum (spike trisetum)

Shrubs (deciduous)

Aesculus californica (California buckeye)
Alnus incana (speckled alder, mountain alder)
Alnus viridis ssp. sinuata (Sitka alder, mountain alder)
Amelanchier alnifolia (saskatoon, western serviceberry, Juneberry)
Amelanchier utahensis (Utah serviceberry)
Amorpha fruticosa (false indigo, Indigo bush)
Atriplex canescens (four-wing saltbush, wingscale)
Atriplex confertifolia (spiny saltbush, shadscale saltbush, hop sage)
Baccharis pilularis (chaparral broom)
Betula nana (bog birch, dwarf birch)
Calliandra eriophylla (fairy duster, mesquitilla)
Calycanthus occidentalis (California sweet shrub, spice bush)
Ceanothus greggii var. vestitus (desert ceanothus)
Ceanothus integerrimus (deer brush)
Ceanothus sanguineus (redstem ceanothus, wild lilac)
Chamaebatiaria millefolium (fernbush, desert sweet, tansy bush)
Chrysothamnus nauseosus (rabbit brush, chamisa)
Cornus sericea (red-twig dogwood, red-osier dogwood)
Corylus cornuta (beaked hazelnut or filbert)
Crataegus douglasii (black hawthorn)
Crossosoma bigelovii (crossosoma)
Empetrum nigrum (crowberry)
Ephedra nevadensis (Mormon tea)
Ephedra trifurca (ephedra, joint fir)
Ephedra viridis (Mormon tea)
Eriogonum arborescens (Santa Cruz Island buckwheat)
Eriogonum fasciculatum (California buckwheat)
Fallugia paradoxa (Apache plume)
Hibiscus denudatus (rock hibiscus)
Holodiscus discolor (cream bush, ocean spray, mountain spray)
Holodiscus dumosus (bush rock-spires, cream bush, ocean spray)

Justicia californica (chuparosa)
Lonicera involucrata (black twinberry, bear berry honeysuckle)
Lycium andersonii (Anderson wolfberry)
Oemleria cerasiformis (Indian plum, oso berry)
Parkinsonia microphylla (foothills palo verde, littleleaf palo verde)
Philadelphus lewisii (wild mock orange, syringa)
Physocarpus capitatus (western ninebark)
Poliomintha incana (mintbush)
Prosopis glandulosa (honey mesquite)
Prunus andersonii (desert peach)
Prunus virginiana (chokecherry)
Psilostrophe cooperi (paperflower, yellow paper daisy)
Purshia tridentata (antelope brush)
Rhododendron occidentale (western azalea)
Rhus trilobata (squawbush, basketbush, skunkbush)
Ribes aureum (golden currant)
Ribes cereum (wax currant, western red currant, squaw currant)
Ribes laxiflorum (trailing black currant)
Ribes menziesii (chaparral currant)
Ribes sanguineum (pink-flowered currant, red flowering currant)
Rosa californica (California rose)
Rosa nutkana (nootka rose)
Rosa woodsii (western wild rose, woods rose)
Rubus idaeus ssp. strigosus (red raspberry)
Rubus parviflorus (western thimbleberry)
Rubus spectabilis (salmon berry)
Rubus ursinus (western blackberry)
Salix arctica (arctic willow)
Salix scouleriana (western pussy willow, Scouler's willow)
Salvia apiana (shite sage)
Salvia dorrii (grayball sage)
Sambucus cerulea (blue elderberry)
Sambucus racemosa var. melanocarpa (black elderberry)
Sarcobatus vermiculatus (greasewood)
Shepherdia argentea (silver buffaloberry)
Sorbus scopulina (western mountain ash)
Spiraea douglasii (western spiraea, hardhack spiraea)
Spiraea splendens var. splendens (subalpine spiraea)
Styrax officinalis (snowdrop bush)
Symphoricarpos albus (snowberry)
Vaccinium parvifolium (red huckleberry)
Vaccinium uliginosum (alpine blueberry, bog blueberry)

Shrubs (evergreen)

Arctostaphylos columbiana (hairy manzanita)
Arctostaphylos glandulosa (eastwood manzanita)
Arctostaphylos manzanita (manzanita)
Arctostaphylos nevadensis (pinemat manzanita)
Arctostaphylos patula (greenleaf manzanita)
Arctostaphylos pringlei (pink-bracted manzanita)
Arctostaphylos uva-ursi (bearberry, kinnikinnik)
Artemisia californica (California sagebrush)

Artemisia nova (black sagebrush)
Artemisia tridentata (big sagebrush, Great Basin sagebrush)
Atriplex lentiformis (saltbush, coastal quail bush)
Carpenteria californica (bush anemone)
Castanopsis sempervirens (Sierra chinquapin, bush chinquapin)
Ceanothus arboreus (island ceanothus, island mountain lilac)
Ceanothus thyrsiflorus (blue blossom)
Ceanothus velutinus (mountain balm, buckbush)
Cercocarpus ledifolius (curl-leaf mountain mahogany)
Comarostaphylis diversifolia (summer holly)
Dendromecon rigida (tree poppy, bush poppy)
Encelia californica (bush sunflower)
Encelia farinosa (brittle bush)
Ericameria laricifolia (larchleaf goldenweed, turpentine bush)
Frangula californica ssp. californica (coffeeberry)
Fremontodendron californicum (northern flannelbush, northern fremontia)
Garrya elliptica (silk-tassel bush)
Gaultheria shallon (salal)
Grayia spinosa (spiny hopsage)
Heteromeles arbutifolia var. arbutifolia (toyon, Christmas berry, California holly)
Juniperus californica (California juniper)
Juniperus communis (common juniper)
Kalmia polifolia (swamp laurel, bog laurel)
Larrea tridentata (creosote bush)
Lavatera assurgentiflora (tree mallow)
Leucothoe davisiae (western leucothoe)
Mahonia aquifolium (Oregon grape)
Mahonia fremontii (Fremont barberry, holly grape)
Mahonia haematocarpa (red barberry)
Mahonia nervosa var. nervosa (Cascade Oregon grape)
Malacothamnus fasciculatus (bush mallow)
Myrica californica (California wax myrtle)
Paxistima myrsinites (Oregon box, myrtle boxwood, mountain lover)
Phyllodoce empetriformis (pink mountain heather)
Prunus ilicifolia (holly-leaved cherry)
Quercus turbinella (shrub live oak)
Rhamnus crocea (redberry)
Rhododendron macrophyllum (Pacific rhododendron, California rose-bay)
Rhus ovata (sugar bush, sugar sumac)
Ribes speciosum (fuschia flowering gooseberry)
Trichostema lanatum (woolly blue-curls, romero)
Vaccinium ovatum (evergreen huckleberry)

Trees (deciduous)

Acer circinatum (Oregon vine maple)
Acer glabrum (Rocky Mountain maple)
Acer macrophyllum (bigleaf maple, canyon maple)
Acer negundo (box elder)
Alnus rhombifolia (white alder)
Betula occidentalis (mountain birch, water birch)
Celtis laevigata var. reticulata (netleaf hackberry)
Cercis canadensis var. texensis (California redbud)

Chilopsis linearis (desert willow, trumpet flower)
Cornus nuttalii (Pacific dogwood, mountain dogwood)
Fraxinus latifolia (Oregon ash)
Fraxinus velutina (Arizona ash, velvet ash, desert ash)
Juglans californica (California black walnut)
Parkinsonia florida (blue palo verde)
Platanus racemosa (California sycamore)
Populus balsamifera (black cottonwood)
Populus fremontii (western cottonwood)
Populus tremuloides (quaking aspen)
Prosopis pubescens (tornillo, screwbean mesquite)
Quercus douglasii (blue oak)
Quercus garryana (Oregon post oak)
Quercus kelloggii (California black oak)
Salix laevigata (red willow)

Trees (evergreen)

Abies concolor (western white fir)
Abies grandis (grand fir, giant fir)
Abies procera (noble fir)
Arbutus menziesii (Pacific madrone, Oregon laurel, laurelwood)
Calocedrus decurrens (incense cedar)
Chamaecyparis lawsoniana (Lawson falsecypress, Port Orford cedar)
Chamaecyparis nootkatensis (Alaska cedar, yellow cedar, Nootka cedar)
Cupressus macnabiana (McNab cypress)
Juniperus osteosperma (Utah juniper)
Lithocarpus densiflorus (tanbark oak)
Lyonothamnus floribundus (fernleaf Catalina ironwood)
Olneya tesota (ironwood, tesota)
Picea sitchensis (Sitka spruce)
Pinus attenuata (knobcone pine)
Pinus contorta (beach pine)
Pinus contorta var. murrayana (lodgepole pine)
Pinus flexilis (limber pine)
Pinus lambertiana (sugar pine)
Pinus monticola (western white pine)
Pinus ponderosa (ponderosa pine)
Pinus sabiniana (gray or foothill pine)
Pseudotsuga macrocarpa (big-cone spruce)
Pseudotsuga menziesii (Douglas fir)
Quercus agrifolia (coast live oak)
Quercus chrysolepis (canyon live oak)
Quercus wislizeni (Interior live oak)
Sequoia sempervirens (redwood)
Sequoiadendron giganteum (giant sequoia)
Taxus brevifolia (western yew, Pacific yew)
Thuja plicata (western red cedar)
Torreya californica (California nutmeg)
Tsuga heterophylla (western hemlock)
Tsuga mertensiana (mountain hemlock)
Umbellularia californica (California bay laurel, myrtle)

Vines (deciduous)

Aristolochia californica (Dutchman's pipe)
Clematis lasiantha (pipestem clematis)
Clematis ligusticifolia (clematis)
Lathyrus splendens (pride of California, campo pea)
Lonicera ciliosa (orange honeysuckle)
Maurandella antirrhiniflora (snapdragon vine)
Vitis californica (California wild grape)
Vitis girdiana (southern California grape)

FEDERALLY LISTED ENDANGERED SPECIES

Amargosa niterwort (Nitrophila mohavensis)
Antioch Dunes evening-primrose (Oenothera deltoides ssp. howellii)
Ash Meadows gumplant (Grindelia fraxino-pratensis)
Bakersfield cactus (Opuntia treleasei)
Beach layia (Layia carnosa)
Ben Lomond spineflower (Chorizanthe pungens var. hartwegiana)
Ben Lomond wallflower (Erysimum teretifolium)
Big-leaved crownbeard (Verbesina dissita)
Burke's goldfields (Lasthenia burkei)
Butte County meadowfoam (Limnanthes floccosa ssp. californica)
California Orcutt grass (Orcuttia californica)
California jewelflower (Caulanthus californicus)
California seablite (Suaeda californica)
Chorro Creek bob thistle (Cirsium fontinale obispoense), (Lupinus tidestromii)
Contra Costa wallflower (Erysimum)
Clover lupine (capitatum var. angustatum)
Coyote ceanothus (Coyote Valley California-lilac) (Ceanothus ferrisae)
Cushenbury buckwheat (Eriogonum ovalifolium var. Vineum)
Cushenbury milk-vetch (Astrgalus albens)
Cushenbury oxytheca (Oxytheca parishii var. goodmaniana)
Del Mar Manzanita (Arctostaphylos glandulosa ssp. crassifolia)
El Dorado bedstraw (Galium californicum ssp. Sierrae)
Encinitis baccharis (Coyote bush), (Baccharis vanessae)
Eureka Dune grass (Swallenia alexandrae)
Eureka Valley evening-primrose (Oenothera avita ssp. eurekensis)
Fountain thistle (Cirsium fontinale var. fontinale)
Gambel's watercress (Rorippa gambellii)
Hoover's wooly-star (Eriastrum hooveri)
Howell's spineflower (Chorizanthe howellii)
Indian Knob mountain balm (Eriodictyon altisssimum)
Kern mallow (Eremalche kernensis)
Large-flowered fiddleneck (Amsinckia grandiflora)
Layne's butterweed (Senecio layneae)
Loch Lomond coyote-thistle (Eryngium constancei)
Marin dwarf-flax (Hesperolinon congestum)
Marsh sandwort (Arenaria paludicola)
McDonald's rock-cress (Arabis mcdonaldiana)
Menzies' wallflower (Erysimum menziesii)
Metcalf Canyon jewelflower (Streptatnthus albidus ssp. albidus)
Monterey gilia (Gilia tenuiflora ssp. Arenaria)

Monterey spineflower (Chorizanthe pungens var. pungens)
Morro manzanita (Arctostaphylos morroensis)
Orcutt's spineflower (Chorizanthe orcuttiana)
Otay mesa miint (Pogogyne nudiuscula)
Palmate-bracted bird's-beak (Cordylanthus tenuis ssp. capillaris)
Pine Hill ceanothus roderickii)
Pine Hill flannelbush (Fremontodendron californicum ssp. decumbens)
Pismo clarkia (Clarkia speciosa immaculata)
Presidio (Raven's) manzanita (Arctostaphylos hookeri var. ravenii)
Presidio clarkia (Clarkia franciscana)
Robust spineflower (includes Scotts Valley spineflower (Chorizanthe robusta)
Salt marsh bird'sbeak (Cordylanthus maritimus ssp. maritimus)
San Benito evening-primrose (Camissonia benitensis)
San Bernardino Mountains bladderpod (Lesquerella kingii ssp. bernadina)
San Clemente Island Indian paintbrush (Castilleja grisea)
San Clemente Island broom (Lotus dendroideus ssp. traskiae)
San Clemente Island bush-mallow (Malacothamnus clementinus)
San Clemente Island larkspur (Delphinium variegatum ssp. kinkiense)
SanDiego button-celery (Eryngium aristulatum var. parishii)
San Diego mesa mint (Pogogyne abramsii)
San Joaquin wooly-threads (Lembertia congdonii)
San Mateo thornmint (Acanthomintha obovata ssp. duttonii)
San Mateo woolly sunflower (Eriophyllum latilobum)
Santa Ana River wooly-star (Eriasturm densifolium ssp. sanctorum)
Santa Barbara Island liveforever (Dudleya traskiae)
Santa Clara Valley dudleya (Dudleya setchellii)
Santa Cruz cypress (Cupressus abramsiana)
Sebastopol meadowfoam (Limnanthes vinculans)
Slender-horned spineflower (Dodecahema leptoceras)
Slender-petaled mustard (Thelypodium stenopetalum)
Solano grass (Tuctoria mucronata)
Sonoma spineflower (Chorizanthe valida)
Sonoma sunshine (Baker's stickyseed) (Blennosperma bakeri)
Spring-loving centaury (Centaurium namophilum)
Stebbins' morning-glory (Calystegia stebbinsii)
Tiburon mariposa lily (Calochortus tiburonensis)
Tiburon jewelflower (Streptanthus niger)
Tiburon paintbrush (Castilleja affinis ssp. neglecta)
Truckee barberry (Berberis sonnei)
Water howellia (Howellia aquatilis)
Western lily (Lilium occidental)
White-rayed pentachaeta (Pentachaeta bellidiflora)

CALIFORNIA NOXIOUS SPECIES

Because the noxious weed lists have continually changed since we gathered them in 1994, we are not including them at this time. Not all States have noxious weed lists. Those that do, do not use the same standards of importance and are not comparable. States typically have included plants that interfere with agriculture (Canada thistle), or cause human health problems (poison ivy). Some States are now including a category of plants that invade and degrade the environment (purple loosestrife). Check with your State's Agriculture Department or Weed Scientist listed below. The noxious weed list can be used two ways on roadsides: l) check to not inadvertently plant these invasive plants, and 2) note the plants you are legally responsible to control. Many States now check adjacent State lists to avoid planting their neighbors' problem plants. Because weeds do not respect political boundaries, and because by their very nature weeds continue to adapt and expand, monitoring and controlling invasives at State borders is a wise part of vegetation management.

(Weed and Seed Law)

Department of Agriculture
Division of Plant Industry
P.O. Box 942871
Sacramento, CA 94271

Clyde Elmore
Weed Science Program
University of California
Davis, CA 95616
(916) 752-9978

CALIFORNIA RESOURCES

California Natural Heritage Division
Department of Fish & Game
1220 S. Street
Sacramento, CA 95814
(916) 322-2493, (FAX) 324-0475

The Nature Conservancy Regional Office
201 Mission Street, 4th Floor
San Francisco, CA 94105
(415) 777-0487

California Native Plant Society
1722 "J" Street, Ste. 17
Sacramento, CA 95814

California Native Grass Society
Box 566
Dixon, CA 95620

Department of Food and Agriculture
P.O. Box 942871
1220 N Street
Sacramento, CA 94271
(916) 654-0466

CalEPPC
Exotic Pest Plant Council
31872 Joshua Drive #25D
Trabuco Cnhyon, CA 92679

The Living Desert
47900 South Portola Avenue
Palm Desert, CA 92269

Santa Barbara Botanic Garden
1212 Mission Canyon Road
Santa Barbara, CA 93205

John Randall
Department of Vegetable Crops
University of California
Davis, CA 95616
(530) 754-8890

POTENTIAL NATURAL VEGETATION ZONES IN
COLORADO

Source: A.W. Kuchler's Potential Natural Vegetation Map, 1964, Revised 1985.
Presented in U.S.G.S. National Atlas of the U.S. Series,
U.S. Geological Survey, Reston, VA.

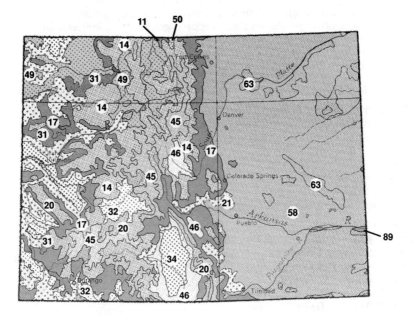

11	Douglas fir forest (*Pseudotsuga*)			
14	Western spruce-fir forest (*Picea-Abies*)		**45**	Alpine meadows and barren (*Agrostis, Carex, Festuca, Poa*)
17	Pine-Douglas fir forest (*Pinus-Pseudotsuga*)		**46**	Fescue-mountain muhly prairie (*Festuca-Muhlenbergia*)
20	Southwestern spruce-fir forest (*Picea-Abies*)		**49**	Sagebrush steppe (*Artemisia-Agropyron*)
21	Juniper-pinyon woodland (*Juniperus-Pinus*)		**50**	Wheatgrass-needlegrass shrubsteppe (*Agropyron-Stipa-Artemisia*)
31	Mountain mahogany-oak scrub (*Cercocarpus-Quercus*)		**58**	Grama-buffalo grass (*Bouteloua-Buchloë*)
32	Great Basin sagebrush (*Artemisia*)		**63**	Sandsage-bluestem prairie (*Artemisia-Andropogon*)
34	Saltbush-greasewood (*Atriplex-Sarcobatus*)		**89**	Northern floodplain forest (*Populus-Salix-Ulmus*)

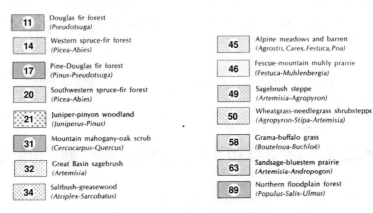

(Dominant plant species present in each vegetation type are listed in Appendix 8)

11 Douglas Fir Forest (Pseudotsuga)
14 Western Spruce-Fir Forest (Picea-Abies)
17 Pine-Douglas Fir Forest (Pinus-Pseudotsuga)
20 Southwestern Spruce Fir Forest (Picea-Abies)
21 Juniper-Pinyon Woodland (Juniperus-Pinus)
31 Mountain Mahogany-Oak Scrub (Cercocarpus-Quercus)
32 Great Basin Sagebrush (Artemisia)
34 Saltbrush-Geasewood (Artiplex-Sarcobatus)
45 Alpine Meadows and Barren (Agrostis, Carex, Festuca, Poa)
46 Fescue-Mountain Muhly Prairie (Festuca-Muhlenbergia)
49 Sagebrush Steppe (Artemisia-Agropyron)
50 Wheatgrass-Needlegrass Shrubsteppe (Agropyron-Stipa-Artemisia)
58 Grama-Buffalo Grass (Bouteloua-Buchloë)
63 Sandsage-Bluestem Prairie (Artemisia-Andropogon)
89 Northern Floodplain Forest (Populus Salix-Ulmus)

Botanical Experts

William A. Weber, Professor Emeritus
University of Colorado Museum Herbarium
Clare Small Gymnasium (Basement)
Campus Box 350
Boulder, CO 80309-0350
(303) 492-6171
(303) 303-492-5105 (fax)
internet: weberw@spot.colorado.edu

Susan Spackman
Colorado Natural Heritage Program
Colorado State University
103 Natural Resources Bldg.
Fort Collins, CO 80523
(970) 491-1309
(970) 970-491-0279/3349 (fax)

Recommended Flora

Weber, W.A.; R.C. Wittmann. 1996a. Colorado Flora, Eastern Slope, 2nd Ed. University Press of Colorado, P.O. Box 849, Niwot, CO 80544. ISBN: 0870813870.

Weber, W.A.; R.C. Wittmann. 1996b. Colorado Flora, Western Slope, 2nd Ed. University Press of Colorado, P.O. Box 849, Niwot, CO 80544. ISBN: 0870813889.

Weber, W.A.; R.C. Wittmann. 1992. Catalog of the Flora of Colorado. University Press of Colorado, P.O. Box 849, Niwot, CO 80544.

NATIVE PLANTS FOR LANDSCAPE USE IN COLORADO

Forbs (annuals/biennials)

Cleome serrulata (Rocky Mountain beeplant)
Erysimum capitatum (western wallflower, prairie rocket)

Helianthus annuus (common sunflower)
Helianthus petiolaris (plains sunflower)
Ipomopsis aggregata (sky rocket, scarlet gilia)
Machaeranthera bigelovii var. bigelovii (plains aster, tansy aster)
Machaeranthera tanacetifolia (tahoka daisy, tansy aster)
Oenothera elata ssp. hookeri (giant evening primrose)

Forbs (perennials)

Abronia fragrans (sweet sand verbena)
Aconitum columbianum (western monkshood)
Anaphalis margaritacea (pearly everlasting)
Apocynum androsaemifolium (spreading dogbane)
Arnica cordifolia (heartleaf arnica)
Artemisia ludoviciana (white sage, prairie sage, artemisia)
Aster ascendens (purple aster, Pacific aster)
Aster ericoides (heath aster, white wreath aster)
Aster foliaceus (leafy aster)
Aster laevis (smooth aster)
Campanula rotundifolia (harebell)
Castilleja integra (Indian paintbrush)
Clematis hirsutissima (clematis, vase flower, leather flower, lion's beard)
Dalea candida (white prairie clover)
Dalea purpurea (purple prairie clover)
Epilobium angustifolium (fireweed, willow herb)
Erigeron compositus (alpine daisy)
Erigeron speciosus (showy fleabane)
Gaillardia aristata (blanket flower, gaillardia, brown-eyed Susan)
Gaura coccinea (scarlet gaura)
Geranium viscossisimum (sticky wild geranium)
Glandularia bipinnatifida var. bipinnatifida (prairie verbena, Dakota vervain)
Hedysarum boreale (sweet vetch, sweet broom)
Heliomeris multiflora (showy goldeneye)
Heterotheca villosa var. villosa (golden aster)
Iris missouriensis (Rocky Mountain iris, western blue flag)
Liatris punctata (dotted blazing star, gayfeather)
Linum lewisii (wild blue flax)
Lupinus argenteus (silvery lupine)
Melampodium leucanthum (Blackfoot daisy, rock daisy)
Mirabilis multiflora (wild four o'clock)
Oenothera cespitosa (gumbo evening primrose, gumbo lily)
Penstemon ambiguus (sand penstemon)
Penstemon angustifolius (whorled penstemon)
Penstemon barbatus (red penstemon, scarlet bugler)
Penstemon glaber v. alpinus (blue penstemon, alpine penstemon)
Penstemon strictus (Rocky Mountain penstemon)
Phacelia sericea (silky phacelia)
Ratibida columnifera (prairie coneflower, long-headed coneflower, Mexican hat)
Ratibida tagetes (
Rudbeckia laciniata (cut-leaf coneflower)
Saxifraga bronchialis (spotted saxifrage, matted saxifrage)
Sidalcea neomexicana (checker mallow, prairie mallow)
Silene acaulis (moss campion)

Silphium integrifolium (rosinweed)
Solidago canadensis (meadow goldenrod)
Solidago missouriensis (Missouri goldenrod, prairie goldenrod)
Solidago rigida (stiff goldenrod)
Sphaeralcea coccinea (scarlet globe mallow))
Sphaeralcea parvifolia (globe mallow)
Stanleya pinnata (desert or prince's plume)
Thalictrum dasycarpum (tall or purple meadow rue)
Yucca baccata (blue yucca, banana yucca, fleshy-fruited yucca)
Yucca glauca (yucca, soapweed)
Zinnia grandiflora (Rocky Mountain zinnia, yellow zinnia, plains zinnia)

Grasses/Grass-like plants

Andropogon gerardii (big bluestem)
Andropogon hallii (sand bluestem)
Aristida purpurea (purple three awn)
Bouteloua curtipendula (sideoats grama)
Bouteloua gracilis (blue grama)
Bouteloua hirsuta (hairy grama)
Buchloe dactyloides (buffalograss)
Calamagrostis canadensis (bluejoint grass)
Calamovilfa longifolia (sandreed grass, prairie sandreed)
Carex nebrascensis (Nebraska sedge)
Carex utriculata (beaked sedge)
Deschampsia cespitosa (tufted hairgrass)
Distichlis spicata (seashore saltgrass)
Eleocharis macrostachya spike rush)
Elymus canadensis (Canada wild rye)
Elymus lanceolatus (thickspike wheatgrass)
Festuca idahoensis (Idaho fescue, blue bunchgrass)
Glyceria grandis (American mannagrass, tall mannagrass, reed meadowgrass)
Koeleria macrantha (June grass)
Leymus cinereus (Great Basin wild rye)
Muhlenbergia montana (mountain muhly)
Muhlenbergia porteri (bush muhly)
Oryzopsis hymenoides (Indian ricegrass)
Panicum obtusum (vine mesquite)
Panicum virgatum (switchgrass)
Pascopyrum smithii (western wheatgrass)
Poa secunda (pine bluegrass)
Pseudoroegneria spicata (bluebunch wheatgrass)
Schizachyrium scoparium (little bluestem)
Scirpus acutus (hardstem bulrush)
Scirpus maritimus (alkali bulrush, prairie bulrush, bayonet grass)
Sorghastrum nutans (Indian grass)
Spartina pectinata (prairie cordgrass, freshwater cordgrass)
Sporobolus airoides (alkali sacaton)
Sporobolus cryptandrus (sand dropseed)
Stipa comata (needle-and-thread grass)
Trisetum spicatum (spike trisetum)
Typha angustifolia (narrow-leaved cattail)
Typha latifolia (cattail)

Shrubs (deciduous)

Amorpha fruticosa (false indigo, indigo bush)
Artemisia frigida (prairie sagewort, fringed sage)
Atriplex canescens (four-wing saltbush, wingscale)
Atriplex confertifolia (spiny saltbush, shadscale saltbush, hop sage)
Chrysothamnus nauseosus (rabbit brush, chamisa)
Cornus sericea (red-twig dogwood, red-osier dogwood)
Fallugia paradoxa (Apache plume)
Holodiscus dumosus (bush rock-spires, cream bush, ocean spray)
Krascheninnikovia lanata (winterfat)
Prunus pumila var. besseyi (sand cherry)
Prunus virginiana (chokecherry)
Purshia tridentata (antelope brush)
Rhus glabra (smooth sumac)
Rhus trilobata (squawbush, basketbush, skunkbush)
Ribes aureum (golden currant)
Ribes cereum (wax currant, western red currant, squaw currant)
Ribes odoratum (buffalo currant, golden currant)
Rosa arkansana (prairie rose)
Rosa woodsii (western wild rose, woods rose)
Rubus idaeus ssp. strigosus (red raspberry)
Rubus parviflorus (western thimbleberry)
Salix bebbiana (Bebb willow, long-beaked willow)
Salix scouleriana (western pussy willow, Scouler's willow)
Shepherdia argentea (silver buffaloberry)
Shepherdia canadensis (buffaloberry)
Symphoricarpos albus (snowberry)
Symphoricarpos oreophilus (mountain snowberry)

Shrubs (evergreen)

Artemisia nova (black sagebrush)
Artemisia tridentata (big sagebrush, Great Basin sagebrush)
Ceanothus fendleri (Fendler ceanothus, buckbrush)
Ceanothus velutinus (mountain balm, buckbush)
Cercocarpus montanus (mountain mahogany, silverleaf mountain mahogany)
Juniperus monosperma (one-seed juniper)
Kalmia polifolia (swamp laurel, bog laurel)

Trees (deciduous)

Acer glabrum (Rocky Mountain maple)
Betula fontinalis (water birch)
Celtis laevigata var. reticulata (netleaf hackberry)
Populus deltoides (eastern cottonwood)
Populus tremuloides (quaking aspen)
Prunus americana (wild plum)
Quercus gambelii (Gambel's oak, Rocky Mountain white oak)
Salix amygdaloides (peachleaf willow)

Trees (evergreen)

Abies concolor (western white fir)
Abies bifolia (fir)

Juniperus osteosperma (Utah juniper)
Juniperus scopulorum (Rocky Mountain juniper)
Picea engelmannii (Engelmann spruce)
Picea pungens (blue spruce, Colorado spruce)
Pinus contorta var. murrayana (lodgepole pine)
Pinus edulis (pinyon pine, Colorado pinyon)
Pinus flexilis (limber pine)
Pinus longaeva (bristlecone pine)
Pinus ponderosa (ponderosa pine)
Pseudotsuga menziesii (Douglas fir)

FEDERALLY LISTED ENDANGERED SPECIES

Clay-loving buckwheat (Eriogonum pelinophiulum)
Dudley Bluffs bladderpod (Lesquerella congesta)
Dudley Bluffs twinpod (Physaria obcordata)
Knowlton cactus (Pediocactus knowltonii)
Mancos milk-vetch (Astrgalus humillimus)
Mesa Verde cactus (Schlerocactus mesae-verdae)
North Park phacelia (Phacelia formosula)
Osterhout milk-vetch (Astragalus osterhoutii)
Penland alpine fen mustard (Eutrema penlandii)
Penland beardtongue (Penstemon penlandii)
Uinta Basin hookless cactus (Sclerocactus glaucus)
Ute ladies'-tresses (Spiranthes diluvialis)

COLORADO NOXIOUS SPECIES

Because the noxious weed lists have continually changed since we gathered them in 1994, we are not including them at this time. Not all States have noxious weed lists. Those that do, do not use the same standards of importance and are not comparable. States typically have included plants that interfere with agriculture (Canada thistle), or cause human health problems (poison ivy). Some States are now including a category of plants that invade and degrade the environment (purple loosestrife). Check with your State's Agriculture Department or Weed Scientist listed below. The noxious weed list can be used two ways on roadsides: l) check to not inadvertently plant these invasive plants, and 2) note the plants you are legally responsible to control. Many States now check adjacent State lists to avoid planting their neighbors' problem plants. Because weeds do not respect political boundaries, and because by their very nature weeds continue to adapt and expand, monitoring and controlling invasives at State borders is a wise part of vegetation management.

(Weed and Seed Law)

Department of Agriculture
Division of Plant Industry
700 Kipling Street # 4000
Lakewood, CO 80215

K.George Beck
Colorado State University
Weed Research, Room 116
Ft. Collins, CO 80523
(303) 491-7568

COLORADO RESOURCES

Colorado Natural Heritage Program
Colorado State University
103 Natural Resources Building
Fort Collins, CO 80523
(970) 491-1309

The Nature Conservancy Field Office
1244 Pine Street
Boulder, CO 80302
(303) 444-2950

Colorado Native Plant Society
P.O. Box 200
Fort Collins, CO 80522

Department of Agriculture
700 Kipling ST., Ste. 4000
Lakewood, CO 80215
(303) 239-4100

State Forest Service
Forestry Bldg., State University
Ft. Collins, CO 80523
(970) 491-6303

State Cooperative Extension
l Administration Bldg.
Colorado State University
Ft. Collins, CO 80523
(970) 491-628l

Denver Botanic Garden
100 S. York Street
Denver, CO 80206
(303) 331-4000

Aspen Center for Environmental Studies
100 Puppy Smith Street
Aspen, CO 81611

POTENTIAL NATURAL VEGETATION ZONES IN
CONNECTICUT

Source: A.W. Kuchler's Potential Natural Vegetation Map, 1964, Revised 1985.
Presented in U.S.G.S. National Atlas of the U.S. Series,
U.S. Geological Survey, Reston, VA.

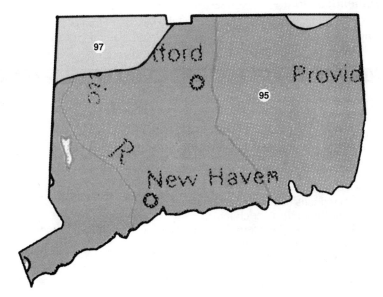

95 | Appalachian oak forest
(Quercus)

97 | Northern hardwoods
(Acer-Betula-Fagus-Tsuga)

(Dominant plant species present in each vegetation type are listed in Appendix 8)

95 *Appalachian Oak Forest (Quercus)*
97 *Northern Hardwoods (Acer-Betula-Fagus-Tsuga)*

Botanical Experts

Kenneth Metzler
Connecticut Geological and Natural History Survey
Department of Environmental Protection
79 Elm St.
Hartford, CT 06106-5127
(860) 424-3585
(860) 424-4058 (fax)

Recommended Flora

Dowhan, J.J. 1979. Preliminary Checklist of the Vascular Flora of Connecticut (Growing Without Cultivation). State Geological and Natural History Survey of Connecticut. Dept. of Investigations #8. Hartford, CT. 176 pgs.

NATIVE PLANTS FOR LANDSCAPE USE IN CONNECTICUT

Ferns

Adiantum pedatum (northern maidenhair fern)
Asplenium platyneuron (ebony spleenwort)
Asplenium trichomanes (maidenhair spleenwort)
Athyrium filix-femina (lady fern)
Dennstaedtia punctilobula (hay-scented fern)
Dryopteris cristata (crested wood fern, buckler fern)
Dryopteris marginalis (marginal wood fern)
Matteuccia struthiopteris (ostrich fern)
Onoclea sensibilis (sensitive fern, bead fern)
Osmunda cinnamomea (cinnamon fern)
Osmunda claytoniana (interrupted fern)
Osmunda regalis (royal fern)
Polystichum acrostichoides (Christmas fern)
Thelypteris novaboracensis (New York fern, tapering fern)
Thelypteris palustris (marsh fern)
Woodsia ilvensis (rusty woodsia)

Forbs (annuals/biennials)

Corydalis sempervirens (pale corydalis)
Gentianopsis crinita (fringed gentian)
Lobelia spicata (pale lobelia)
Oenothera biennis (common evening primrose)

Forbs (perennials)

Acorus calamus (sweet flag, calamus)
Actaea pachypoda (white baneberry)
Ageratina altissima var. altissima (white snakeroot)
Allium canadense (wild garlic)

Allium tricoccum (wild leek)
Anaphalis margaritacea (pearly everlasting)
Anemone cylindrica (thimbleweed, candle anemone)
Anemone virginiana (thimbleweed, tall anemone)
Apocynum androsaemifolium (spreading dogbane)
Aquilegia canadensis (columbine)
Asarum canadense (wild ginger)
Asclepias incarnata (swamp milkweed)
Asclepias tuberosa (butterfly weed)
Asclepias verticillata (whorled milkweed)
Aster divaricatus (white wood aster)
Aster dumosus (bushy aster)
Aster ericoides (heath aster, white wreath aster)
Aster laevis (smooth aster)
Aster novae-angliae (New England aster)
Aster pilosus (frost aster)
Aster puniceus (red-stem aster, swamp aster)
Caltha palustris (marsh marigold, cowslip)
Campanula rotundifolia (harebell)
Cardamine diphylla (two-leaved toothwort)
Caulophyllum thalictroides (blue cohosh)
Chelone glabra (turtlehead)
Claytonia caroliniana (broad-leaved spring beauty)
Claytonia virginica (narrow-leaved spring beauty)
Clintonia borealis (clintonia, blue-bead lily)
Collinsonia canadensis (stoneroot, citronella horsebalm)
Coptis trifolia ssp. groenlandica (goldthread)
Desmodium canadense (Canada tick-trefoil, Canada tickclover)
Dicentra cucullaria (Dutchman's breeches)
Epilobium angustifolium (fireweed, willow herb)
Erythronium americanum (eastern trout lily, yellow trout lily)
Eupatorium fistulosum (Joe-pye weed)
Eupatorium maculatum (spotted Joe-pye weed)
Eupatorium perfoliatum (boneset)
Eupatorium purpureum (Joe-pye weed)
Fragaria virginiana (wild strawberry)
Galium triflorum (sweet-scented bedstraw)
Gentiana clausa (bottle gentian)
Geranium maculatum (wild geranium, cranesbill)
Geum rivale (purple avens, water avens)
Helianthus strumosus (woodland sunflower)
Houstonia longifolia var. longifolia (long-leaved bluets, pale bluets)
Hypoxis hirsuta (yellow star grass)
Iris versicolor (blue flag)
Lespedeza capitata (roundheaded bush clover)
Lilium canadense (wild yellow lily, Canada lily)
Lilium philadelphicum (wood lily)
Linum virginianum (woodland flax)
Lobelia cardinalis (cardinal flower)
Lobelia siphilitica (great blue lobelia)
Lupinus perennis (wild lupine)
Lysimachia ciliata (fringed loosestrife)

Maianthemum canadense (wild lily-of-the-valley, Canada mayflower)
Maianthemum racemosum ssp. racemosum (false Solomon's seal,
    false spikenard)
Maianthemum stellatum (starry Solomon's seal)
Mitchella repens (partridge berry)
Monarda fistulosa (wild bergamot, horsemint, beebalm)
Nuphar lutea (yellow pond lily, cow lily, spatter dock)
Osmorhiza claytoni (sweet cicely, sweet jarvil)
Peltandra virginica (arrow arum)
Penstemon hirsutus (hairy beardtongue)
Pentaphylloides floribunda (potentilla, shrubby cinquefoil)
Phlox pilosa (prairie phlox, downy phlox)
Polygonatum biflorum (Solomon's seal)
Potentilla simplex (common cinquefoil)
Pycnanthemum tenuifolium (slender mountain mint)
Pycnanthemum virginianum (mountain mint)
Pyrola elliptica (shinleaf)
Ranunculus hispidus (early buttercup, tufted buttercup)
Rhexia virginica (meadow beauty)
Rudbeckia laciniata (cut-leaf coneflower)
Sanguinaria candensis (bloodroot)
Senecio aureus (golden ragwort)
Sisyrinchium angustifolium (narrow-leaved blue-eyed grass)
Sisyrinchium atlanticum (eastern blue-eyed grass)
Solidago caesia (blue-stemmed goldenrod, wreath goldenrod)
Solidago canadensis (meadow goldenrod)
Solidago juncea (early goldenrod, plume goldenrod)
Solidago nemoralis (gray goldenrod, old-field goldenrod)
Solidago odora (sweet goldenrod)
Solidago sempervirens (seaside goldenrod)
Solidago speciosa (showy goldenrod)
Solidago ulmifolia (elm-leaved goldenrod)
Tephrosia virginiana (goat's rue)
Thalictrum dasycarpum (tall or purple meadow rue)
Thalictrum dioicum (early meadow rue)
Thalictrum pubescens (tall meadow rue)
Thalictrum thalictroides (rue anemone)
Tiarella cordifolia (foam flower)
Tradescantia ohiensis (Ohio spiderwort)
Tradescantia virginiana (Virginia spiderwort, spider lily)
Trientalis borealis ssp. borealis (starflower)
Trillium cernuum (nodding trillium)
Trillium erectum (wakerobin, purple trillium)
Trillium undulatum (painted trillium)
Uvularia sessilifolia (wildoats, merrybells)
Verbena hastata (blue verbena, blue vervain)
Vernonia noveboracensis (New York ironweed)
Viola conspersa (American dog violet)
Viola pedata (bird-foot violet)
Viola pubescens (downy or smooth yellow violet)
Viola soraria (common blue violet, meadow violet)
Zizia aurea (golden alexanders)

Grasses/Grass-like plants

Agrostis scabra (ticklegrass, fly-away grass)
Andropogon gerardii (big bluestem)
Andropogon virginicus (broom sedge)
Bromus kalmii (prairie brome, wild chess)
Calamagrostis canadensis (bluejoint grass)
Carex pensylvanica (Pennsylvania sedge)
Carex plantaginea (plantain-leaved sedge)
Carex stipata (awl-fruited sedge)
Carex stricta (tussock sedge)
Danthonia spicata (poverty grass)
Deschampsia cespitosa (tufted hairgrass)
Distichlis spicata (seashore saltgrass)
Eleocharis palustris (creeping spikesedge, spike rush)
Elymus canadensis (Canada wild rye)
Elymus hystrix var. hystrix (bottlebrush grass)
Eragrostis spectabilis (purple lovegrass, tumblegrass)
Glyceria grandis (American mannagrass, tall mannagrass, reed meadowgrass)
Hierochloe odorata (sweet grass)
Juncus effusus var. solutus (soft rush)
Leersia oryzoides (rice cut grass)
Panicum virgatum (switchgrass)
Schizachyrium scoparium (little bluestem)
Scirpus atrovirens (dark green bulrush)
Scirpus cyperinus (wool grass)
Scirpus maritimus (alkali bulrush, prairie bulrush, bayonet grass)
Scirpus tabernaemontani (great bulrush)
Sorghastrum nutans (Indian grass)
Spartina patens (marsh hay cordgrass, salt meadow cordgrass)
Spartina pectinata (prairie cordgrass, freshwater cordgrass)
Tripsacum dactyloides (eastern gama grass)
Typha latifolia (cattail)

Shrubs (deciduous)

Alnus incana (speckled alder, mountain alder)
Alnus serrulata (smooth alder)
Amelanchier arborea (downy serviceberry, shadbush, Juneberry)
Aronia melanocarpa (black chokeberry)
Baccharis halimifolia (sea myrtle, groundsel bush)
Ceanothus americanus (New Jersey tea, red root)
Cephalanthus occidentalis (buttonbush)
Clethra alnifolia (summer sweet)
Cornus alternifolia (pogoda dogwood, alternate-leaved dogwood)
Cornus amomum ssp. obliqua (swamp dogwood, silky dogwood)
Cornus racemosa (gray dogwood)
Corylus americana (American hazelnut or filbert)
Corylus cornuta (beaked hazelnut or filbert)
Diervilla lonicera (bush honeysuckle)
Dirca palustris (leatherwood, ropebark)
Ilex verticillata (winterberry, black alder)
Lindera benzoin (spicebush)
Lonicera dioica (limber or wild honeysuckle)

Lyonia ligustrina (male-berry, male-blueberry)
Prunus virginiana (chokecherry)
Rhododendron periclymenoides (pinxterbloom azalea)
Rhododendron viscosum (swamp azalea)
Rhus aromatica (fragrant sumac)
Rhus copallinum (dwarf or winged sumac)
Rhus glabra (smooth sumac)
Rhus hirta (staghorn sumac)
Ribes cynosbati (prickly gooseberry, dogberry)
Rosa blanda (early wild rose, smooth rose)
Rosa carolina (Carolina rose)
Rubus occidentalis (black raspberry, thimbleberry)
Rubus odoratus (thimbleberry)
Salix bebbiana (Bebb willow, long-beaked willow)
Salix discolor (pussy willow)
Sambucus canadensis (elderberry, common elder)
Sambucus racemosa var. pubens (scarlet elderberry, red-berried elder)
Spiraea tomentosa (steeplebush, hardhack)
Vaccinium angustifolium (low-bush blueberry)
Vaccinium corymbosom (highbush blueberry)
Viburnum acerifolium (maple leaf viburnum)
Viburnum lentago (black haw, nannyberry)
Viburnum nudum var. cassinoides (wild raisin)
Viburnum opulus var. americanum (high-bush cranberry, American
cranberrybush viburnum)

Shrubs (evergreen)

Arctostaphylos uva-ursi (bearberry, kinnikinnik)
Epigaea repens (trailing arbutus)
Gaultheria procumbens (wintergreen, checkerberry)
Juniperus communis (common juniper)
Kalmia angustifolia (sheep laurel, lambkill kalmia)
Kalmia latifolia (mountain laurel)
Kalmia polifolia (swamp laurel, bog laurel)
Taxus canadensis (Canada yew)

Trees (deciduous)

Acer pensylvanicum (striped maple)
Acer rubrum (red maple)
Acer saccharinum (silver maple)
Acer saccharum (sugar maple)
Acer spicatum (mountain maple)
Amelanchier canadensis (shadblow serviceberry, Juneberry)
Betula lenta (cherry birch)
Betula papyrifera (paper birch)
Carpinus caroliniana (blue beech, hornbeam, musclewood)
Carya alba (mockernut hickory)
Carya cordiformis (bitternut, swamp hickory)
Carya ovata (shagbark hickory)
Celtis occidentalis (hackberry, sugarberry)
Cornus florida (flowering dogwood)
Crataegus crus-galli (cockspur hawthorn)

Fagus grandifolia var. caroliniana (beech)
Fagus grandifolia var. grandifolia (beech)
Fraxinus americana (white ash)
Fraxinus pensylvanica (green ash)
Hamamelis virginiana (witch hazel)
Larix laricina (tamarack, American larch)
Liriodendron tulipifera (tulip tree)
Nyssa sylvatica (black gum, tupelo)
Ostrya virginiana (ironwood, hophornbeam)
Platanus occidentalis (sycamore, plane-tree)
Populus deltoides (eastern cottonwood)
Populus grandidentata (large-toothed aspen)
Populus tremuloides (quaking aspen)
Prunus americana (wild plum)
Prunus pensylvanica (fire or pin cherry)
Prunus serotina (black cherry)
Quercus alba (white oak)
Quercus bicolor (swamp white oak)
Quercus coccinea (scarlet oak)
Quercus muhlenbergii (chinkapin oak, chestnut oak)
Quercus palustris (pin oak)
Quercus rubra (red oak)
Quercus stellata (post oak)
Quercus velutina (black oak)
Salix nigra (black willow)
Sassafras albidum (sassafras)
Sorbus americana (mountain ash)
Tilia americana (American linden, basswood)
Ulmus americana (American elm)
Ulmus rubra (red elm, slippery elm)

Trees (evergreen)

Chamaecyparis thyoides (white cedar)
Juniperus virginiana (eastern red cedar)
Pinus rigida (pitch pine)
Pinus strobus (eastern white pine)
Tsuga canadensis (eastern hemlock)

Vines (deciduous)

Clematis virginiana (virgin's bower)
Lonicera sempervirens (trumpet honeysuckle)
Parthenocissus quinquefolia (Virginia creeper)
Parthenocissus quinquefolia var. quinquefolia (woodbine)
Vitis riparia (riverbank grape)

FEDERALLY LISTED ENDANGERED SPECIES

Sandplain gerardia (Agalinis acuta)
Small whorled pogonia (Isotria medeoloides)

CONNECTICUT NOXIOUS SPECIES

Because the noxious weed lists have continually changed since we gathered them in 1994, we are not including them at this time. Not all States have noxious weed lists. Those that do, do not use the same standards of importance and are not comparable. States typically have included plants that interfere with agriculture (Canada thistle), or cause human health problems (poison ivy). Some States are now including a category of plants that invade and degrade the environment (purple loosestrife). Check with your State's Agriculture Department or Weed Scientist listed below. The noxious weed list can be used two ways on roadsides: l) check to not inadvertently plant these invasive plants, and 2) note the plants you are legally responsible to control. Many States now check adjacent State lists to avoid planting their neighbors' problem plants. Because weeds do not respect political boundaries, and because by their very nature weeds continue to adapt and expand, monitoring and controlling invasives at State borders is a wise part of vegetation management.

(No Laws)

Agricultural Experiment Station
123 Huntington Street, Box 1106
New Haven, CT 06504

Frank Himmelstein
University of Connecticut
14 Hyde Avenue
Vernon, CT 06066
(860) 875-3331

CONNECTICUT RESOURCES

Connecticut Natural Diversity
Database
Hartford, CT
(203) 424-3540

The Nature Conservancy, Field Office
55 High Street
Middletown, CT 06457
(860) 344-0716

Connecticut Botanical Society
10 Hillside Court
Storrs, CT 06268

William Niering
Connecticut College Arboretum
270 Mohegan Avenue
New London, CT 06320
(203) 439-2143

POTENTIAL NATURAL VEGETATION ZONES IN

DELAWARE

Source: A.W. Kuchler's Potential Natural Vegetation Map, 1964, Revised 1985.
Presented in U.S.G.S. National Atlas of the U.S. Series,
U.S. Geological Survey, Reston, VA.

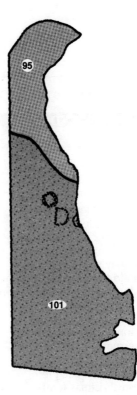

95 Appalachian oak forest
(Quercus)

101 Oak-hickory-pine forest
(Quercus-Carya-Pinus)

(Dominant plant species present in each vegetation type are listed in Appendix 8)

95   Appalachian Oak Forest (Quercus)
101   Oak-Hickory-Pine Forest (Quercus-Carya-Pinus)

Botanical Experts

Bill McAvoy, Botanist
Delaware Natural Heritage Program
Division of Fish and Wildlife
4876 Hay Point Landing
Smyrna, DE 19977
(302) 653-2880
(302) 653-3431 (fax)

Recommended Flora

McAvoy, W.A. Annotated checklist of the flora of Delaware (in preparation).

NATIVE PLANTS FOR LANDSCAPE USE IN DELAWARE

Cactus

Opuntia humifusa (prickly pear)

Ferns

Adiantum pedatum (northern maidenhair fern)
Asplenium platyneuron (ebony spleenwort)
Athyrium filix-femina (lady fern)
Botrychium virginianum (rattlesnake fern)
Dennstaedtia punctilobula (hay-scented fern)
Dryopteris carthusiana (shield fern, toothed wood fern, spinulose shield fern)
Dryopteris cristata (crested wood fern, buckler fern)
Dryopteris marginalis (marginal wood fern)
Onoclea sensibilis (sensitive fern, bead fern)
Osmunda cinnamomea (cinnamon fern)
Osmunda claytoniana (interrupted fern)
Osmunda regalis (royal fern)
Phegopteris hexagonoptera (broad beech fern)
Polystichum acrostichoides (Christmas fern)
Thelypteris novaboracensis (New York fern, tapering fern)
Woodwardia areolata (netted chain fern)
Woodwardia virginica (Virginia chain fern)

Forbs (annuals/biennials)

Oenothera biennis (common evening primrose)
Rudbeckia hirta (black-eyed Susan)

Forbs (perennials)

Acorus calamus (sweet flag, calamus)
Allium canadense (wild garlic)
Anemone virginiana (thimbleweed, tall anemone)

Antennaria spp. (pussytoes, everlasting)
Arisaema triphyllum (Jack-in-the-pulpit, Indian turnip)
Asarum canadense (wild ginger)
Asclepias incarnata (swamp milkweed)
Asclepias tuberosa (butterfly weed)
Aster divaricatus (white wood aster)
Aster novae-angliae (New England aster)
Aster pilosus (frost aster)
Aster puniceus (red-stem aster, swamp aster)
Chelone glabra (turtlehead)
Chrysopsis mariana (Maryland golden aster)
Claytonia virginica (narrow-leaved spring beauty)
Collinsonia canadensis (stoneroot, citronella horsebalm)
Desmodium canadense (Canada tick-trefoil, Canada tickclover)
Dicentra cucullaria (Dutchman's breeches)
Epilobium angustifolium (fireweed, willow herb)
Erythronium americanum (eastern trout lily, yellow trout lily)
Eupatorium coelestinum (mist flower)
Eupatorium fistulosum (Joe-pye weed)
Eupatorium perfoliatum (boneset)
Euphorbia corollata (flowering spurge)
Euthamia graminifolia var. graminifolia (grass-leaved goldenrod)
Fragaria virginiana (wild strawberry)
Geranium maculatum (wild geranium, cranesbill)
Heuchera americana var. hirsuticaulis (alumroot)
Hibiscus moscheutos (swamp rose mallow, marshmallow hibiscus)
Houstonia caerulea (bluets)
Hydrophyllum virginianum (Virginia waterleaf)
Hypoxis hirsuta (yellow star grass)
Lespedeza capitata (roundheaded bush clover)
Lilium superbum (Turk's cap lily)
Linum virginianum (woodland flax)
Lobelia cardinalis (cardinal flower)
Lobelia siphilitica (great blue lobelia)
Lysimachia ciliata (fringed loosestrife)
Maianthemum canadense (wild lily-of-the-valley, Canada mayflower)
Maianthemum racemosum ssp. racemosum (false Solomon's seal,
    false spikenard)
Mitchella repens (partridge berry)
Nuphar lutea (yellow pond lily, cow lily, spatter dock)
Oenothera fruticosa (sundrops)
Orontium aquaticum (golden club)
Osmorhiza claytoni (sweet cicely, sweet jarvil)
Peltandra virginica (arrow arum)
Penstemon digitalis (beardtongue)
Penstemon hirsutus (hairy beardtongue)
Podophyllum peltatum (May apple)
Polemonium reptans (Jacob's ladder, Greek valerian)
Polygonatum biflorum (Solomon's seal)
Potentilla simplex (common cinquefoil)
Rhexia virginica (meadow beauty)
Rudbeckia laciniata (cut-leaf coneflower)

Salvia lyrata (cancer weed, lyre-leaf sage)
Sanguinaria candensis (bloodroot)
Senecio aureus (golden ragwort)
Silene stellata (starry campion)
Sisyrinchium angustifolium (narrow-leaved blue-eyed grass)
Solidago caesia (blue-stemmed goldenrod, wreath goldenrod)
Solidago canadensis (meadow goldenrod)
Solidago juncea (early goldenrod, plume goldenrod)
Solidago odora (sweet goldenrod)
Solidago rugosa (rough-leaved goldenrod)
Solidago sempervirens (seaside goldenrod)
Tephrosia virginiana (goat's rue)
Thalictrum pubescens (tall meadow rue)
Thalictrum thalictroides (rue anemone)
Uvularia sessilifolia (wildoats, merrybells)
Verbena hastata (blue verbena, blue vervain)
Vernonia noveboracensis (New York ironweed)
Viola soraria (common blue violet, meadow violet)

Grasses/Grass-like plants

Andropogon glomeratus (bushy bluestem)
Andropogon ternarius (splitbeard bluestem)
Andropogon virginicus (broom sedge)
Carex pensylvanica (Pennsylvania sedge)
Carex stipata (awl-fruited sedge)
Carex stricta (tussock sedge)
Danthonia spicata (poverty grass)
Distichlis spicata (seashore saltgrass)
Eleocharis palustris (creeping spikesedge, spike rush)
Eragrostis spectabilis (purple lovegrass, tumblegrass)
Juncus effusus (soft rush)
Leersia oryzoides (rice cut grass)
Muhlenbergia capillaris (gulf muhly, hair grass)
Panicum virgatum (switchgrass)
Saccharum giganteum (sugarcane plume grass)
Schizachyrium scoparium (little bluestem)
Scirpus Georgianus (Georgia bulrush)
Scirpus cyperinus (wool grass)
Scirpus tabernaemontani (great bulrush)
Sorghastrum nutans (Indian grass)
Spartina patens (marsh hay cordgrass, salt meadow cordgrass)
Tripsacum dactyloides (eastern gama grass)
Typha angustifolia (narrow-leaved cattail)
Typha latifolia (cattail)

Shrubs (deciduous)

Alnus serrulata (smooth alder)
Amelanchier arborea (downy serviceberry, shadbush, Juneberry)
Baccharis halimifolia (sea myrtle, groundsel bush)
Castanea pumila (chinquapin)
Ceanothus americanus (New Jersey tea, red root)
Cephalanthus occidentalis (buttonbush)

Clethra alnifolia (summer sweet)
Cornus alternifolia (pogoda dogwood, alternate-leaved dogwood)
Cornus sericea (red-twig dogwood, red-osier dogwood)
Corylus americana (American hazelnut or filbert)
Euonymus americana (strawberry bush, brook euonymus, hearts-a-bustin')
Hypericum hypericoides ssp. hypericoides (St. Andrew's cross)
Ilex verticillata (winterberry, black alder)
Itea virginica (Virginia willow, sweetspire, tassel-white)
Lindera benzoin (spicebush)
Lyonia ligustrina (male-berry, male-blueberry)
Rhododendron atlanticum (dwarf, or coastal azalea)
Rhododendron periclymenoides (pinxterbloom azalea)
Rhododendron viscosum (swamp azalea)
Rhus copallinum (dwarf or winged sumac)
Rhus glabra (smooth sumac)
Rhus hirta (staghorn sumac)
Rosa carolina (Carolina rose)
Rubus occidentalis (black raspberry, thimbleberry)
Salix discolor (pussy willow)
Sambucus canadensis (elderberry, common elder)
Spiraea tomentosa (steeplebush, hardhack)
Vaccinium corymbosom (highbush blueberry)
Viburnum acerifolium (maple leaf viburnum)
Viburnum dentatum (southern arrowwood)
Viburnum nudum (possumhaw viburnum)
Viburnum prunifolium (black haw, nanny berry)

Shrubs (evergreen)

Epigaea repens (trailing arbutus)
Ilex glabra (inkberry, bitter gallberry)
Kalmia latifolia (mountain laurel)
Myrica cerifera (wax myrtle, southern bayberry, candleberry)

Trees (deciduous)

Acer negundo (box elder)
Acer rubrum (red maple)
Acer saccharinum (silver maple)
Acer saccharum (sugar maple)
Amelanchier canadensis (shadblow serviceberry, Juneberry)
Betula lenta (cherry birch)
Betula nigra (river birch)
Carpinus caroliniana (blue beech, hornbeam, musclewood)
Carya alba (mockernut hickory)
Carya cordiformis (bitternut, swamp hickory)
Carya ovata (shagbark hickory)
Celtis occidentalis (hackberry, sugarberry)
Chionanthus virginicus (fringe tree, old man's beard)
Cornus florida (flowering dogwood)
Crataegus crus-galli (cockspur hawthorn)
Crataegus phaenopyrum (Washington hawthorn)
Diospyros virginiana (persimmon)
Fagus grandifolia var. grandifolia (beech)

Fraxinus americana (white ash)
Fraxinus pensylvanica (green ash)
Gleditsia triacanthos (honey locust)
Hamamelis virginiana (witch hazel)
Juglans nigra (black walnut)
Liquidambar styraciflua (sweet gum)
Liriodendron tulipifera (tulip tree)
Magnolia virginiana (sweetbay, swampbay)
Nyssa sylvatica (black gum, tupelo)
Platanus occidentalis (sycamore, plane-tree)
Populus grandidentata (large-toothed aspen)
Prunus serotina (black cherry)
Quercus alba (white oak)
Quercus bicolor (swamp white oak)
Quercus coccinea (scarlet oak)
Quercus falcata (southern red oak, Spanish oak)
Quercus lyrata (overcup oak)
Quercus marilandica (blackjack oak)
Quercus nigra (black oak)
Quercus phellos (willow oak)
Quercus rubra (red oak)
Quercus stellata (post oak)
Quercus velutina (black oak)
Salix nigra (black willow)
Sassafras albidum (sassafras)
Ulmus americana (American elm)
Ulmus rubra (red elm, slippery elm)

Trees (evergreen)

Chamaecyparis thyoides (white cedar)
Ilex opaca (American holly, Christmas holly)
Juniperus virginiana (eastern red cedar)
Pinus echinata (shortleaf pine)
Pinus rigida (pitch pine)
Pinus taeda (loblolly pine)
Pinus virginiana (Virginia pine)

Vines (deciduous)

Campsis radicans (trumpet creeper, trumpet vine)
Clematis virginiana (virgin's bower)
Lonicera sempervirens (coral honeysuckle)
Parthenocissus quinquefolia (Virginia creeper)
Vitis rotundifolia (muscadine grape)

FEDERALLY LISTED ENDANGERED SPECIES

Canby's dropwort (Oxypolis canbyi)
Knieskern'ss beaked-rush (Rhynchospora knieskernii)
Small whorled pogonia (Isotria medeoloides)
Swamp pink (Helonias bullata)

DELAWARE NOXIOUS SPECIES

Because the noxious weed lists have continually changed since we gathered them in 1994, we are not including them at this time. Not all States have noxious weed lists. Those that do, do not use the same standards of importance and are not comparable. States typically have included plants that interfere with agriculture (Canada thistle), or cause human health problems (poison ivy). Some States are now including a category of plants that invade and degrade the environment (purple loosestrife). Check with your State's Agriculture Department or Weed Scientist listed below.   The noxious weed list can be used two ways on roadsides: I) check to not inadvertantly plant these invasive plants, and 2) note the plants you are legally responsible to control. Many States now check adjacent State lists to avoid planting their neighbors' problem plants. Because weeds do not respect political boundaries, and because by their very nature weeds continue to adapt and expand, monitoring and controlling invasives at State borders is a wise part of vegetation management.

(Weed Law)

Department of Agriculture
Plant Industry Section
2320 South Dupont Highway
Dover, DE 19901

Mark Van Goessel
University of Delaware
RD 6 Box 48

DELAWARE RESOURCES

Department of Natural Resources
89 Kings Highway,
P.O. Box 1401
Dover, DE 19903

University of Delaware
College of Agricultural Sciences
Newark, DE 19717
(302) 831-2526

The Nature Conservancy - Field Office
260 Chapman Road #201D
Newark, DE 19702
(302) 369-4144

Mount Cuba Center for the Study of
Piedmont Flora
P.O. Box 3570
Greenville, DE 19807

Winterthur
Winterthur, DE 19735
(302) 656-8591

POTENTIAL NATURAL VEGETATION ZONES IN
—DISTRICT OF COLUMBIA—

Source: A.W. Kuchler's Potential Natural Vegetation Map, 1964, Revised 1985.
Presented in U.S.G.S. National Atlas of the U.S. Series,
U.S. Geological Survey, Reston, VA.

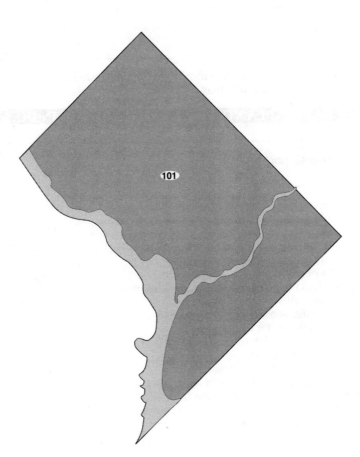

 Oak-hickory-pine forest
(Quercus-Carya-Pinus)

(Dominant plant species present in each vegetation type are listed in Appendix 8)

101   Oak-Hickory-Pine Forest (Quercus-Carya-Pinus)

Botanical Expert

Ginny Crouch, Botanist
D.C. Natural Heritage Program
13025 Riley's Lock Road
Poolesville, MD 20837
(301) 427-1302
(301) 427-1305 (fax)

Recommended Flora

No recommended flora exists specifically for DC. Suggested flora for neighboring states of Maryland and Virginia may be helpful.

NATIVE PLANTS FOR LANDSCAPE USE IN DC

Cactus

Opuntia humifusa (prickly pear)

Ferns

Adiantum pedatum (northern maidenhair fern)
Asplenium platyneuron (ebony spleenwort)
Asplenium trichomanes (maidenhair spleenwort)
Athyrium filix-femina (lady fern)
Botrychium virginianum (rattlesnake fern)
Dennstaedtia punctilobula (hay-scented fern)
Dryopteris cristata (crested wood fern, buckler fern)
Dryopteris marginalis (marginal wood fern)
Onoclea sensibilis (sensitive fern, bead fern)
Osmunda cinnamomea (cinnamon fern)
Osmunda claytoniana (interrupted fern)
Osmunda regalis (royal fern)
Polystichum acrostichoides (Christmas fern)
Woodwardia areolata (netted chain fern)
Woodwardia virginica (Virginia chain fern)

Forbs (annuals/biennials)

Campanulastrum americanum (American bellflower, tall bellflower)
Lobelia spicata (pale lobelia)
Oenothera biennis (common evening primrose)
Rudbeckia hirta (black-eyed Susan)

Forbs (perennials)

Acorus calamus (sweet flag, calamus)
Allium canadense (wild garlic)
Allium cernuum (nodding onion)
Allium tricoccum (wild leek)

Anemone virginiana (thimbleweed, tall anemone)
Antennaria spp. (pussytoes, everlasting)
Aquilegia canadensis (columbine)
Arisaema triphyllum (Jack-in-the-pulpit, Indian turnip)
Asarum canadense (wild ginger)
Asclepias incarnata (swamp milkweed)
Asclepias tuberosa (butterfly weed)
Asclepias verticillata (whorled milkweed)
Aster divaricatus (white wood aster)
Aster dumosus (bushy aster)
Aster laevis (smooth aster)
Aster novae-angliae (New England aster)
Aster oblongifolius (aromatic aster)
Aster pilosus (frost aster)
Aster puniceus (red-stem aster, swamp aster)
Chelone glabra (turtlehead)
Chrysogonum virginianum (green-and-gold)
Cimicifuga racemosa (bugbane, black cohosh)
Claytonia virginica (narrow-leaved spring beauty)
Collinsonia canadensis (stoneroot, citronella horsebalm)
Coreopsis verticillata (whorled coreopsis)
Dicentra cucullaria (dutchman's breeches)
Erythronium americanum (eastern trout lily, yellow trout lily)
Eupatorium coelestinum (mist flower)
Eupatorium fistulosum (Joe-pye weed)
Eupatorium perfoliatum (boneset)
Eupatorium purpureum (Joe-pye weed)
Fragaria virginiana (wild strawberry)
Galium triflorum (sweet-scented bedstraw)
Gentiana clausa (bottle gentian)
Geranium maculatum (wild geranium, cranesbill)
Helenium autumnale (common sneezeweed)
Helianthus strumosus (woodland sunflower)
Heliopsis helianthoides (ox-eye sunflower, false sunflower)
Heuchera americana var. hirsuticaulis (alumroot)
Hibiscus moscheutos (swamp rose mallow, marshmallow hibiscus)
Houstonia longifolia var. longifolia (long-leaved bluets, pale bluets)
Hydrophyllum virginianum (Virginia waterleaf)
Hypericum ascyron (great St. John's wort)
Hypoxis hirsuta (yellow star grass)
Iris virginica (southern blue flag)
Lespedeza capitata (roundheaded bush clover)
Lilium canadense (wild yellow lily, Canada lily)
Linnaea borealis (twinflower)
Linum virginianum (woodland flax)
Lithospermum canescens (hoary puccoon)
Lobelia cardinalis (cardinal flower)
Lobelia siphilitica (great blue lobelia)
Lysimachia ciliata (fringed loosestrife)
Maianthemum racemosum ssp. racemosum (false Solomon's seal, false spikenard)
Mertensia virginica (bluebells)

Mitchella repens (partridge berry)
Monarda fistulosa (wild bergamot, horsemint, beebalm)
Nuphar lutea (yellow pond lily, cow lily, spatter dock)
Oenothera fruticosa (sundrops)
Orontium aquaticum (golden club)
Peltandra virginica (arrow arum)
Penstemon digitalis (beardtongue)
Phlox divaricata (blue woodland phlox, sweet william)
Phlox paniculata (summer phlox, perennial phlox)
Podophyllum peltatum (May apple)
Polygonatum biflorum (Solomon's seal)
Potentilla simplex (common cinquefoil)
Pycnanthemum tenuifolium (slender mountain mint)
Rhexia virginica (meadow beauty)
Rudbeckia fulgida (black-eyed Susan, orange coneflower)
Rudbeckia laciniata (cut-leaf coneflower)
Salvia lyrata (cancer weed, lyre-leaf sage)
Sanguinaria candensis (bloodroot)
Sedum ternatum (wild stonecrop)
Senecio aureus (golden ragwort)
Silene stellata (starry campion)
Sisyrinchium angustifolium (narrow-leaved blue-eyed grass)
Solidago caesia (blue-stemmed goldenrod, wreath goldenrod)
Solidago canadensis (meadow goldenrod)
Solidago juncea (early goldenrod, plume goldenrod)
Solidago nemoralis (gray goldenrod, old-field goldenrod)
Solidago rugosa (rough-leaved goldenrod)
Solidago ulmifolia (elm-leaved goldenrod)
Tephrosia virginiana (goat's rue)
Thalictrum dioicum (early meadow rue)
Tradescantia virginiana (Virginia spiderwort, spider lily)
Uvularia sessilifolia (wildoats, merrybells)
Verbena hastata (blue verbena, blue vervain)
Veronicastrum virginicum (Culver's root)
Viola pedata (bird-foot violet)
Viola pubescens (downy or smooth yellow violet)
Zizia aptera (heart-leaved golden alexanders)

Grasses/Grass-like plants

Andropogon gerardii (big bluestem)
Andropogon ternarius (splitbeard bluestem)
Andropogon virginicus (broom sedge)
Carex pensylvanica (Pennsylvania sedge)
Carex stipata (awl-fruited sedge)
Danthonia spicata (poverty grass)
Eleocharis palustris (creeping spikesedge, spike rush)
Eragrostis spectabilis (purple lovegrass, tumblegrass)
Juncus effusus var. solutus (soft rush)
Leersia oryzoides (rice cut grass)
Panicum virgatum (switchgrass)
Schizachyrium scoparium (little bluestem)
Scirpus cyperinus (wool grass)

Sorghastrum nutans (Indian grass)
Spartina pectinata (prairie cordgrass, freshwater cordgrass)
Sporobolus heterolepis (northern prairie dropseed)
Tripsacum dactyloides (eastern gama grass)
Typha latifolia (cattail)

Shrubs (deciduous)

Alnus serrulata (smooth alder)
Amelanchier arborea (downy serviceberry, shadbush, Juneberry)
Aronia melanocarpa (black chokeberry)
Baccharis halimifolia (sea myrtle, groundsel bush)
Castanea pumila (chinquapin)
Ceanothus americanus (New Jersey tea, red root)
Cephalanthus occidentalis (buttonbush)
Comptonia peregrina (sweet fern)
Cornus alternifolia (pogoda dogwood, alternate-leaved dogwood)
Cornus racemosa (gray dogwood)
Cornus sericea (red-twig dogwood, red-osier dogwood)
Corylus americana (American hazelnut or filbert)
Euonymus americana (strawberry bush, brook euonymus, hearts-a-bustin')
Euonymus atropurpurea (wahoo, burning bush)
Hydrangea arborescens (wild hydrangea)
Hypericum hypericoides ssp. hypericoides (St. Andrew's cross)
Ilex verticillata (winterberry, black alder)
Itea virginica (Virginia willow, sweetspire, tassel-white)
Lindera benzoin (spicebush)
Lyonia ligustrina (male-berry, male-blueberry)
Physocarpus opulifolius (ninebark)
Rhododendron periclymenoides (pinxterbloom azalea)
Rhododendron viscosum (swamp azalea)
Rhus aromatica (fragrant sumac)
Rhus copallinum (dwarf or winged sumac)
Rhus glabra (smooth sumac)
Rhus hirta (staghorn sumac)
Rosa carolina (Carolina rose)
Rubus occidentalis (black raspberry, thimbleberry)
Sambucus canadensis (elderberry, common elder)
Staphylea trifolia (bladdernut)
Vaccinium corymbosom (highbush blueberry)
Viburnum acerifolium (maple leaf viburnum)
Viburnum dentatum (southern arrowwood)
Viburnum nudum (possumhaw viburnum)
Viburnum prunifolium (black haw, nanny berry)

Shrubs (evergreen)

Epigaea repens (trailing arbutus)
Gaultheria procumbens (wintergreen, checkerberry)
Gaylussacia brachycera (box huckleberry)
Kalmia latifolia (mountain laurel)

Trees (deciduous)

Acer negundo (box elder)
Acer rubrum (red maple)
Acer saccharinum (silver maple)
Acer saccharum (sugar maple)
Amelanchier canadensis (shadblow serviceberry, Juneberry)
Betula nigra (river birch)
Carpinus caroliniana (blue beech, hornbeam, musclewood)
Carya cordiformis (bitternut, swamp hickory)
Carya ovata (shagbark hickory)
Celtis laevigata (sugarberry, hackberry)
Celtis occidentalis (hackberry, sugarberry)
Cercis canadensis (redbud)
Chionanthus virginicus (fringe tree, old man's beard)
Crataegus crus-galli (cockspur hawthorn)
Diospyros virginiana (persimmon)
Fagus grandifolia (beech)
Fraxinus americana (white ash)
Fraxinus pensylvanica (green ash)
Hamamelis virginiana (witch hazel)
Juglans nigra (black walnut)
Larix laricina (tamarack, American larch)
Liquidambar styraciflua (sweet gum)
Liriodendron tulipifera (tulip tree)
Magnolia virginiana (sweetbay, swampbay)
Malus angustifolia (southern crabapple, wild crabapple)
Nyssa sylvatica (black gum, tupelo)
Ostrya virginiana (ironwood, hophornbeam)
Platanus occidentalis (sycamore, plane-tree)
Populus deltoides (eastern cottonwood)
Populus grandidentata (large-toothed aspen)
Prunus americana (wild plum)
Prunus angustifolia (chickasaw plum)
Prunus serotina (black cherry)
Ptelea trifoliata (wafer ash, common hoptree)
Quercus alba (white oak)
Quercus bicolor (swamp white oak)
Quercus coccinea (scarlet oak)
Quercus falcata (southern red oak, Spanish oak)
Quercus marilandica (blackjack oak)
Quercus muhlenbergii (chinkapin oak, chestnut oak)
Quercus palustris (pin oak)
Quercus phellos (willow oak)
Quercus rubra (red oak)
Quercus stellata (post oak)
Quercus velutina (black oak)
Salix nigra (black willow)
Sassafras albidum (sassafras)
Tilia americana (American linden, basswood)
Ulmus americana (American elm)
Ulmus rubra (red elm, slippery elm)

Trees (evergreen)

Ilex opaca (American holly, Christmas holly)
Juniperus virginiana (eastern red cedar)
Pinus echinata (shortleaf pine)
Pinus rigida (pitch pine)
Pinus virginiana (Virginia pine)

Vines (deciduous)

Campsis radicans (trumpet creeper, trumpet vine)
Clematis virginiana (virgin's bower)
Lonicera sempervirens (coral honeysuckle)
Parthenocissus quinquefolia (Virginia creeper)
Passiflora incarnata (passion flower, maypop)
Vitis riparia (riverbank grape)

FEDERALLY LISTED ENDANGERED SPECIES
DISTRICT OF COLUMBIA NOXIOUS SPECIES

Because the noxious weed lists have continually changed since we gathered them in 1994, we are not including them at this time. Not all States have noxious weed lists. Those that do, do not use the same standards of importance and are not comparable. States typically have included plants that interfere with agriculture (Canada thistle), or cause human health problems (poison ivy). Some States are now including a category of plants that invade and degrade the environment (purple loosestrife). Check with your State's Agriculture Department or Weed Scientist listed below. The noxious weed list can be used two ways on roadsides: l) check to not inadvertantly plant these invasive plants, and 2) note the plants you are legally responsible to control. Many States now check adjacent State lists to avoid planting their neighbors' problem plants. Because weeds do not respect political boundaries, and because by their very nature weeds continue to adapt and expand, monitoring and controlling invasives at State borders is a wise part of vegetation management.

State Extension Services
University of the District of Columbia
4200 Connecticut Ave. NW, Ste. 3009
Washington DC, 20008
(202) 274-6470

Agriculture and Natural Resources
Dr. Mohamid Kahn
DC Cooperative Extension Service
901 Newton St. NE
Washington, DC 20017
(202) 274-6907

DISTRICT OF COLUMBIA RESOURCES

District of Columbia Natural Heritage Program
13025 Riley's Lock Road
Poolesville, MD 20838
(301) 427-1354

Botanical Society of Washington
Depatment of Biology - NHB/166
Smithsonian Institution
Washington DC 20560

National Arboretum (USDA)
3501 New York Avenue NE
Washington, DC 20002
(202) 475-4815

National Park Service (USDI)
National Capital Parks East
1099 Anacostia Drive SE
Washington, DC 20020
(202) 433-1190

The Nature Conservancy
Maryand/DC Office
Chevy Chase Metro Building
2 Wisconsin Circle, Ste. 300
Chevy Chase, MD 20815
(301) 656-8673

POTENTIAL NATURAL VEGETATION ZONES IN

FLORIDA

Source: A.W. Kuchler's Potential Natural Vegetation Map, 1964, Revised 1985.
Presented in U.S.G.S. National Atlas of the U.S. Series,
U.S. Geological Survey, Reston, VA.

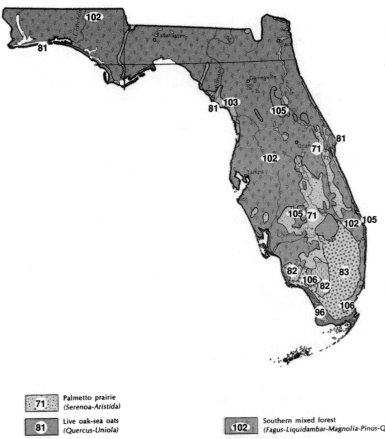

71 Palmetto prairie
(Serenoa-Aristida)

81 Live oak-sea oats
(Quercus-Uniola)

82 Cypress savanna
(Taxodium-Mariscus)

83 Everglades
(Mariscus and Magnolia-Persea)

96 Mangrove
(Avicennia-Rhizophora)

102 Southern mixed forest
(Fagus-Liquidambar-Magnolia-Pinus-Quercus)

103 Southern floodplain forest
(Quercus-Nyassa-Taxodium)

105 Sand pine scrub
(Pinus-Quercus)

106 Sub-tropical pine forest
(Pinus)

VEGETATION REFERENCES

(Dominant plant species present in each vegetation type are listed in Appendix 8)

71   *Palmetto Prairie (Serenoa-Aristida)*
81   *Live Oak-Sea Oats (Quercus-Uniola)*
82   *Cypress Savanna (Taxodium-Mariscus)*
83   *Everglades (Mariscus and Magnolia-Persea)*
96   *Mangrove (Avicennia-Rhizophora)*
102 *Sandhill (Pinus Palustrus-Aristida Stricta)*
103 *Southern Floodplain Forest (Quercus-Nyssa-Taxodium)*
105 *Sand Pine Scrub (Pinus-Quercus)*
106 *Subtropical Pine Forest (Pinus)*

Botanical Experts

Linda G. Chafin, Botanist
Florida Natural Areas Inventory
1018 Thomasville Road, Suite 200-C
Tallahassee, FL 32303
(850) 224-8207

Recommended Flora

Clewell, A.F. 1985. Guide to the Vascular Plants of the Florida Panhandle. University Presses of Florida, Florida State University, Gainesville, FL. 605 pgs. + illus. ISBN 0813007798.

Wunderlin, R.P. 1998. Guide to the Vascular Plants of Florida. University Presses of Florida, Florida State University, Gainesville, FL. 806 pgs. Map. ISBN 081301556-1.

NATIVE PLANTS FOR LANDSCAPE USE IN FLORIDA

Cactus

Opuntia humifusa (prickly pear)

Ferns

Adiantum capillus-veneris (southern maidenhair fern)
Asplenium platyneuron (ebony spleenwort)
Athyrium filix-femina (lady fern)
Botrychium virginianum (rattlesnake fern)
Onoclea sensibilis (sensitive fern, bead fern)
Osmunda cinnamomea (cinnamon fern)
Osmunda regalis (royal fern)
Phegopteris hexagonoptera (broad beech fern)
Polystichum acrostichoides (Christmas fern)
Thelypteris kunthii (southern shield fern, wood fern, river fern)
Woodwardia areolata (netted chain fern)
Woodwardia virginica (Virginia chain fern)

Forbs (annuals/biennials)

Aphanostephus skirrhobasis (lazy daisy)
Glandularia canadensis (rose vervain, sweet William)

Ipomopsis rubra (standing cypress)
Rudbeckia hirta (black-eyed Susan)
Sabatia brevifolia (narrow-leaved sabatia)
Senecio glabellus (butterweed)

Forbs (perennials)

Actaea pachypoda (white baneberry)
Ageratina altissima var. altissima (white snakeroot)
Allium canadense (wild garlic)
Amsonia ciliata (blue funnel lily, blue star)
Amsonia tabernaemontana (blue star)
Arisaema triphyllum (Jack-in-the-pulpit, Indian turnip)
Asarum canadense (wild ginger)
Asclepias incarnata (swamp milkweed)
Asclepias tuberosa (butterfly weed)
Asclepias verticillata (whorled milkweed)
Aster dumosus (bushy aster)
Aster pilosus (frost aster)
Baptisia alba (white false indigo)
Callirhoe papaver (poppy mallow)
Canna flaccida (golden canna)
Chrysopsis mariana (Maryland golden aster)
Collinsonia canadensis (stoneroot, citronella horsebalm)
Coreopsis lanceolata (lance-leaved coreopsis)
Delphinium carolinianum (blue larkspur)
Dodecatheon meadia (shooting star)
Echinacea purpurea (purple coneflower)
Eryngium yuccifolium (rattlesnake master, button snake-root)
Eupatorium coelestinum (mist flower)
Eupatorium fistulosum (Joe-pye weed)
Eupatorium perfoliatum (boneset)
Eupatorium purpureum (Joe-pye weed)
Euphorbia corollata (flowering spurge)
Fragaria virginiana (wild strawberry)
Gentiana saponaria (closed gentian, soapwort gentian)
Hedyotis nigricans (bluets)
Helenium autumnale (common sneezeweed)
Helianthus simulans (narrow-leaved sunflower, swamp sunflower)
Heliopsis helianthoides (ox-eye sunflower, false sunflower)
Hepatica nobilis var. acuta (sharp-lobed hepatica)
Hibiscus moscheutos (swamp rose mallow, marshmallow hibiscus)
Houstonia procumbens (innocence)
Hymenocallis caroliniana (spider lily, rain lily)
Hypoxis hirsuta (yellow star grass)
Iris virginica (southern blue flag)
Kosteletzkya virginica (seashore mallow)
Lespedeza capitata (roundheaded bush clover)
Liatris elegans (gayfeather)
Liatris spicata (marsh blazing star, gayfeather)
Liatris squarrosa (blazing star)
Lilium canadense (wild yellow lily, Canada lily)
Lilium michauxii (Carolina lily)

Lilium michiganense (Turk's cap lily, Michigan lily)
Lithospermum caroliniense (hairy puccoon, hispid gromwell)
Lobelia cardinalis (cardinal flower)
Lupinus perennis (wild lupine)
Lysimachia ciliata (fringed loosestrife)
Manfreda virginica (rattlesnake master, false aloe)
Mitchella repens (partridge berry)
Nuphar lutea (yellow pond lily, cow lily, spatter dock)
Oenothera fruticosa (sundrops)
Orontium aquaticum (golden club)
Pachysandra procumbens (Alleghany spurge)
Peltandra virginica (arrow arum)
Penstemon australis (beardtongue)
Phlox carolina (Carolina phlox)
Phlox pilosa (prairie phlox, downy phlox)
Physostegia virginiana (obedient plant, false dragonhead)
Podophyllum peltatum (May apple)
Polygonatum biflorum (Solomon's seal)
Rhexia virginica (meadow beauty)
Rudbeckia fulgida (black-eyed Susan, orange coneflower)
Rudbeckia laciniata (cut-leaf coneflower)
Salvia lyrata (cancer weed, lyre-leaf sage)
Sanguinaria candensis (bloodroot)
Senecio aureus (golden ragwort)
Silene virginica (fire pink)
Sisyrinchium angustifolium (narrow-leaved blue-eyed grass)
Sisyrinchium atlanticum (eastern blue-eyed grass)
Solidago nemoralis (gray goldenrod, old-field goldenrod)
Solidago odora (sweet goldenrod)
Solidago sempervirens (seaside goldenrod)
Spigelia marilandica (Indian pink)
Stokesia laevis (stokes' aster)
Tephrosia virginiana (goat's rue)
Thalictrum thalictroides (rue anemone)
Tradescantia ohiensis (Ohio spiderwort)
Uvularia sessilifolia (wildoats, merrybells)
Verbena hastata (blue verbena, blue vervain)
Veronicastrum virginicum (Culver's root)
Viola affinis (Florida violet)
Viola soraria (common blue violet, meadow violet)
Yucca aloifolia (Spanish dagger)
Zephyranthes atamasca (atamasco lily, Easter lily)
Zizia aptera (heart-leaved golden alexanders)
Zizia aurea (golden alexanders)

Grasses/Grass-like plants

Agrostis scabra (ticklegrass, fly-away grass)
Andropogon gerardii (big bluestem)
Andropogon glomeratus (bushy bluestem)
Andropogon ternarius (splitbeard bluestem)
Andropogon virginicus (broom sedge)
Arundinaria gigantea (giant cane)

Carex stipata (awl-fruited sedge)
Chasmanthium latifolium (inland sea oats, wild oats, river oats, broad-leaf uniola)
Danthonia spicata (poverty grass)
Distichlis spicata (seashore saltgrass)
Eragrostis spectabilis (purple lovegrass, tumblegrass)
Juncus effusus var. solutus (soft rush)
Leersia oryzoides (rice cut grass)
Leptochloa dubia (green sprangletop)
Muhlenbergia capillaris (gulf muhly, hair grass)
Panicum virgatum (switchgrass)
Schizachyrium scoparium (little bluestem)
Scirpus cyperinus (wool grass)
Scirpus tabernaemontani (great bulrush)
Sorghastrum nutans (Indian grass)
Spartina patens (marsh hay cordgrass, salt meadow cordgrass)
Tripsacum dactyloides (eastern gama grass)

Shrubs (deciduous)

Alnus serrulata (smooth alder)
Amelanchier arborea (downy serviceberry, shadbush, Juneberry)
Amorpha fruticosa (false indigo, Indigo bush)
Baccharis halimifolia (sea myrtle, groundsel bush)
Callicarpa americana (American beautyberry, French mulberry)
Calycanthus floridus (Carolina allspice, sweet shrub)
Ceanothus americanus (New Jersey tea, red root)
Cephalanthus occidentalis (buttonbush)
Clethra alnifolia (summer sweet)
Cornus alternifolia (pogoda dogwood, alternate-leaved dogwood)
Dirca palustris (leatherwood, ropebark)
Erythrina herbacea (coral bean)
Euonymus americana (strawberry bush, brook euonymus, hearts-a-bustin')
Euonymus atropurpurea (wahoo, burning bush)
Eupatorium odoratum (blue mistflower, crucita)
Forestiera acuminata (swamp privet)
Frangula caroliniana (Carolina buckthorn)
Hibiscus coccineus (wild red mallow)
Hydrangea arborescens (wild hydrangea)
Hydrangea quercifolia (oakleaf hydrangea)
Hypericum hypericoides ssp. hypericoides (St. Andrew's cross)
Ilex verticillata (winterberry, black alder)
Itea virginica (Virginia willow, sweetspire, tassel-white)
Lindera benzoin (spicebush)
Lycium carolinianum (Christmas berry, matrimony vine)
Lyonia ligustrina (male-berry, male-blueberry)
Malvaviscus drummondii (Turk's-cap mallow, Texas wax mallow,
    Mexican apple, manzanilla)
Physocarpus opulifolius (ninebark)
Rhododendron canescens (wild, piedmont, or sweet azalea)
Rhus copallinum (dwarf or winged sumac)
Rhus glabra (smooth sumac)
Rosa carolina (Carolina rose)
Rosa setigera (Illinois or prairie rose)

Sambucus canadensis (elderberry, common elder)
Sideroxylon lanuginosum ssp. lanuginosum (chittamwood, gum elastic tree)
Staphylea trifolia (bladdernut)
Stewartia malacodendron (silky camellia)
Styrax americanus (American silverbells)
Vaccinium arboreum (sparkleberry, farkleberry)
Viburnum acerifolium (maple leaf viburnum)
Viburnum dentatum (southern arrowwood)
Viburnum nudum (possumhaw viburnum)
Viburnum nudum var. cassinoides (wild raisin)
Viburnum rufidulum (southern or rusty black haw)

Shrubs (evergreen)

Avicennia germinans (black mangrove)
Coccoloba uvifera (sea grape)
Epigaea repens (trailing arbutus)
Gordonia lasianthus (loblolly bay, gordonia)
Ilex glabra (inkberry, bitter gallberry)
Ilex vomitoria (yaupon)
Illicium floridanum (Florida anise tree)
Kalmia latifolia (mountain laurel)
Leucothoe axillaris (coast leucothoe)
Myrica cerifera (wax myrtle, southern bayberry, candleberry)
Sabal minor (dwarf palmetto)
Serenoa repens (saw palmetto)

Trees (deciduous)

Acer barbatum (Florida maple, southern sugar maple)
Acer leucoderme (chalk maple)
Acer negundo (box elder)
Acer rubrum (red maple)
Acer saccharinum (silver maple)
Aesculus pavia var. pavia (red buckeye)
Betula nigra (river birch)
Carpinus caroliniana (blue beech, hornbeam, musclewood)
Carya alba (mockernut hickory)
Carya cordiformis (bitternut, swamp hickory)
Celtis laevigata (sugarberry, hackberry)
Cercis canadensis (redbud)
Chionanthus virginicus (fringe tree, old man's beard)
Cornus florida (flowering dogwood)
Crataegus crus-galli (cockspur hawthorn)
Crataegus marshallii (parsley hawthorn)
Crataegus phaenopyrum (Washington hawthorn)
Cyrilla racemiflora (leatherwood, yiti)
Diospyros virginiana (persimmon)
Fagus grandifolia var. caroliniana (beech)
Fraxinus americana (white ash)
Fraxinus pensylvanica (green ash)
Gleditsia triacanthos (honey locust)
Halesia diptera (American snowdrop tree, two-winged silverbell)
Halesia tetraptera (Carolina silverbell)

Hamamelis virginiana (witch hazel)
Ilex decidua (possum-haw, deciduous holly)
Juglans nigra (black walnut)
Liquidambar styraciflua (sweet gum)
Liriodendron tulipifera (tulip tree)
Magnolia acuminata (cucumber tree)
Magnolia pyramidata (pyramid magnolia)
Magnolia virginiana (sweetbay, swampbay)
Malus angustifolia (southern crabapple, wild crabapple)
Nyssa sylvatica (black gum, tupelo)
Ostrya virginiana (ironwood, hophornbeam)
Oxydendrum arboreum (sourwood)
Platanus occidentalis (sycamore, plane-tree)
Populus deltoides (eastern cottonwood)
Prunus americana (wild plum)
Prunus angustifolia (chickasaw plum)
Prunus serotina (black cherry)
Ptelea trifoliata (wafer ash, common hoptree)
Quercus alba (white oak)
Quercus falcata (southern red oak, Spanish oak)
Quercus laurifolia (laurel oak)
Quercus lyrata (overcup oak)
Quercus marilandica (blackjack oak)
Quercus muhlenbergii (chinkapin oak, chestnut oak)
Quercus phellos (willow oak)
Quercus shumardii (shumard oak)
Quercus stellata (post oak)
Quercus velutina (black oak)
Salix nigra (black willow)
Sassafras albidum (sassafras)
Taxodium distichum (bald cypress)
Ulmus americana (American elm)
Ulmus rubra (red elm, slippery elm)

Trees (evergreen)

Chamaecyparis thyoides (white cedar)
Clematis crispa (leatherflower)
Ilex opaca (American holly, Christmas holly)
Juniperus virginiana (eastern red cedar)
Magnolia grandiflora (southern magnolia)
Persea borbonia (red bay)
Pinus echinata (shortleaf pine)
Pinus elliotii (slash, pitch, or yellow slash pine)
Pinus glabra (spruce pine)
Pinus palustris (longleaf pine)
Pinus taeda (loblolly pine)
Prunus caroliniana (cherry laurel)
Quercus virginiana (live oak, coastal live oak, southern live oak)
Sabal palmetto (cabbage palm)

Vines (deciduous)

Bignonia capreolata (cross vine)
Campsis radicans (trumpet creeper, trumpet vine)
Gelsemium sempervirens (yellow jessamine, Carolina jessamine)
Lonicera sempervirens (coral honeysuckle)
Parthenocissus quinquefolia (Virginia creeper)
Passiflora incarnata (passion flower, maypop)
Vitis rotundifolia (muscadine grape)

FEDERALLY LISTED ENDANGERED SPECIES

Americqn chaffseed (Schwalbea americana)
Apalachicola rosemary (Conradina glabra)
Avon Park harebells (Crotalaria avonensis)
Beach jacquemontia (Jacquemontia reclinata)
Beautiful pawpaw (Deeringothamnus pulchellus)
Britton's beargrass (Nolina brittoniana)
Brooksville (Robins') bellflower (Campanula robinsiae)
Carter's mustard (Warea carteri)
Chapman rhododendron (Rhododendron chapmanii)
Cooley's meadowrue (Thalictrum cooleyi)
Cooley's water-willow (Justicia cooleyi)
Crenulate lead-plant (Amorpha crenulata)
Deltoid spurge (Chamaesyce deltoidea ssp. deltoidea)
Etonia rossemary (Conradina etonia)
Florida bonamin (Boanamia grandiflora)
Florida golden aster (Chrysopsis floridana)
Florida perforate cladonia (Cladonia perforata)
Florida skullcap (Scutellaria floridana)
Florida torreya (Torreya taxifolia)
Florida ziziphus (Ziziphus celatat)
Four-petal pawpaw (Asimina tetramera)
Fragrant prickly-apple (Cereus eriophorus var. fragrans)
Fringed campion (Silene polypetala)
Garber's spurge (Chamaesyce garberi)
Garrett's mint (Dicerandra christmanii)
Gentian pinkroot (Spigelia gentianoides)
Godfrey's butterwort (Pinguicula ionantha)
Harper's beauty (Harperocallis flava)
Highlands scrub hypericum (Hypericum cumulicola)
Key tree-cactus (Pilosocereus robinii (Cereus r.))
Lakela's mint (Dicerandra immaculata)
Lewton's polygala (Polygala lewtonii)
Longspurred mint (Dicerandra cornutissima)
Miccosukee gooseberry (Ribes echinellum)
Okeechobee gourd (Cucurbita okeechobeensis ssp. okeechobeensis)
Papery whitlow-wort (Paronychia chartacea)
Pigeon wings (Clitoria fragrans)
Pondberry (Lindera melissifolia)
Pygmy fringe-tree (Chionanthus pygmaeus)
rugel's pawpaw (Deeringothamnus rugelii)
Sandlace (Polygonella myriophylla)

Scrub blazingstar (Liatris ohlingerae)
Scrub buckwheat (Eriogonum longifolium var. gnaphalifolium)
Scrub lupine (Lupinus aridorum)
Scrub mint (Dicerandra frutescens)
Scrub plum (Prunus geniculata)
Short-leaved rosemary (Conradina brevifolia)
Small's milkpea (Galactia smallii)
Snakeroot (Eryngium cuneifolium)
Telephus spurge (Euphorbia telephioides)
Tiny polygala (Polygala smallii)
White birds-in-a-nest (Macbridea alba)
Wide-leaf warea (Warea amplexifolia)
Wireweed (Polygonella basiramia)

FLORIDA NOXIOUS SPECIES

Because the noxious weed lists have continually changed since we gathered them in 1994, we are not including them at this time. Not all States have noxious weed lists. Those that do, do not use the same standards of importance and are not comparable. States typically have included plants that interfere with agriculture (Canada thistle), or cause human health problems (poison ivy). Some States are now including a category of plants that invade and degrade the environment (purple loosestrife). Check with your State's Agriculture Department or Weed Scientist listed below. The noxious weed list can be used two ways on roadsides: l) check to not inadvertently plant these invasive plants, and 2) note the plants you are legally responsible to control. Many States now check adjacent State lists to avoid planting their neighbors' problem plants. Because weeds do not respect political boundaries, and because by their very nature weeds continue to adapt and expand, monitoring and controlling invasives at State borders is a wise part of vegetation management.

(Weed and Seed Law)

Department of Agriculture
Division of Plant Industry
P.O. Box 14700
Gainesville, FL 32614

Donn Shilling
Agronomy Department
University of Florida, Box 110300
Gainesville, FL 32611
(352) 391-1823

FLORIDA RESOURCES

Florida Natural Areas Inventory
1018 Thomasville Road, Ste. 200-C
Tallahassee, FL 32303
(850) 224-8207

The Nature Conservancy
222 Westmonte Drive, Ste. 300
Altamonte Springs, FL 32714

Florida Native Plant Society
P.O. Box 6116
Spring Hill, FL 34606

Archbold Biological Station
Old State Road 8
P.O. Box 2057
Lake Placid, FL 33862

POTENTIAL NATURAL VEGETATION ZONES IN
GEORGIA

Source: A.W. Kuchler's Potential Natural Vegetation Map, 1964, Revised 1985.
Presented in U.S.G.S. National Atlas of the U.S. Series,
U.S. Geological Survey, Reston, VA.

81 Live oak-sea oats *(Quercus-Uniola)*		**101** Oak-hickory-pine forest *(Quercus-Carya-Pinus)*
94 Mixed mesophytic forest *(Acer-Aesculus-Fagus-Liriodendron-Quercus-Tilia)*		**102** Southern mixed forest *(Fagus-Liquidambar-Magnolia-Pinus-Quercus)*
95 Appalachian oak forest *(Quercus)*		**103** Southern floodplain forest *(Quercus-Nyassa-Taxodium)*

(Dominant plant species present in each vegetation type are listed in Appendix 8)

81 *Live Oak-Sea Oats (Quercus-Uniola)*
94 *Mixed Mesophytic Forest (Acer-Aesculus-Fagus-Liriodendron-Quercus-Tilia)*
95 *Appalachian Oak Forest (Quercus)*
101 *Oak-Hickory-Pine Forest (Quercus-Carya-Pinus)*
102 *Southern Mixed Forest (Fagus-Liquidambar-Magnolia-Pinus-Quercus)*
103 *Southern Floodplain Forest (Quercus-Nyssa-Taxodium)*

Botanical Experts

James Allison, Botanist
Georgia Department of Natural Resources
Wildlife Resources Division
Georgia Natural Heritage Program
2117 U.S. Highway 278, S.E.
Social Circle, GA 30025
(706) 557-3032
(706) 557-3033 (fax)
internet: jim_allison@mail.dnr.state.ga.us

Recommended Flora

No recommended flora exists specifically for Georgia. Suggested flora for neighboring states may be helpful.

NATIVE PLANTS FOR LANDSCAPE USE IN GEORGIA

Cactus

Opuntia humifusa (prickly pear)

Ferns

Adiantum capillus-veneris (southern maidenhair fern)
Adiantum pedatum (northern maidenhair fern)
Asplenium platyneuron (ebony spleenwort)
Asplenium trichomanes (maidenhair spleenwort)
Athyrium filix-femina (lady fern)
Botrychium virginianum (rattlesnake fern)
Dennstaedtia punctilobula (hay-scented fern)
Dryopteris marginalis (marginal wood fern)
Onoclea sensibilis (sensitive fern, bead fern)
Osmunda cinnamomea (cinnamon fern)
Osmunda claytoniana (interrupted fern)
Osmunda regalis (royal fern)
Phegopteris hexagonoptera (broad beech fern)
Polystichum acrostichoides (Christmas fern)
Thelypteris kunthii (southern shield fern, wood fern, river fern)
Thelypteris novaboracensis (New York fern, tapering fern)
Woodwardia areolata (netted chain fern)
Woodwardia virginica (Virginia chain fern)

Forbs (annuals/biennials)

Campanulastrum americanum (American bellflower, tall bellflower)
Glandularia canadensis (rose vervain, sweet William)
Lobelia spicata (pale lobelia)
Oenothera biennis (common evening primrose)
Rudbeckia hirta (black-eyed Susan)
Sabatia brevifolia (narrow-leaved sabatia)
Senecio glabellus (butterweed)

Forbs (perennials)

Actaea pachypoda (white baneberry)
Ageratina altissima var. altissima (white snakeroot)
Allium canadense (wild garlic)
Allium cernuum (nodding onion)
Allium tricoccum (wild leek)
Amsonia ciliata (blue funnel lily, blue star)
Amsonia tabernaemontana (blue star)
Anemone virginiana (thimbleweed, tall anemone)
Antennaria spp. (pussytoes, everlasting)
Apocynum androsaemifolium (spreading dogbane)
Aquilegia canadensis (columbine)
Arisaema triphyllum (Jack-in-the-pulpit, Indian turnip)
Aruncus dioicus (goat's beard)
Asarum canadense (wild ginger)
Asclepias tuberosa (butterfly weed)
Asclepias verticillata (whorled milkweed)
Aster divaricatus (white wood aster)
Aster dumosus (bushy aster)
Aster pilosus (frost aster)
Aster puniceus (red-stem aster, swamp aster)
Astilbe biternata (false goatsbeard)
Baptisia alba (white false indigo)
Callirhoe papaver (poppy mallow)
Camassia scilloides (wild hyacinth)
Canna flaccida (golden canna)
Caulophyllum thalictroides (blue cohosh)
Chrysogonum virginianum (green-and-gold)
Chrysopsis mariana (Maryland golden aster)
Cimicifuga racemosa (bugbane, black cohosh)
Claytonia caroliniana (broad-leaved spring beauty)
Claytonia virginica (narrow-leaved spring beauty)
Collinsonia canadensis (stoneroot, citronella horsebalm)
Coreopsis auriculata (early coreopsis)
Coreopsis grandiflora (coreopsis)
Coreopsis lanceolata (lance-leaved coreopsis)
Coreopsis tripteris (tall coreopsis)
Dicentra cucullaria (Dutchman's breeches)
Dodecatheon meadia (shooting star)
Eryngium yuccifolium (rattlesnake master, button snake-root)
Erythronium americanum (eastern trout lily, yellow trout lily)
Eupatorium coelestinum (mist flower)
Eupatorium fistulosum (Joe-pye weed)

Eupatorium perfoliatum (boneset)
Eupatorium purpureum (Joe-pye weed)
Euphorbia corollata (flowering spurge)
Fragaria virginiana (wild strawberry)
Galium triflorum (sweet-scented bedstraw)
Gentiana saponaria (closed gentian, soapwort gentian)
Geranium maculatum (wild geranium, cranesbill)
Hedyotis nigricans (bluets)
Helenium autumnale (common sneezeweed)
Helianthus microcephalus (sunflower)
Helianthus simulans (narrow-leaved sunflower, swamp sunflower)
Helianthus strumosus (woodland sunflower)
Heliopsis helianthoides (ox-eye sunflower, false sunflower)
Hepatica nobilis var. acuta (sharp-lobed hepatica)
Heuchera americana var. hirsuticaulis (alumroot)
Hibiscus moscheutos (swamp rose mallow, marshmallow hibiscus)
Houstonia caerulea (bluets)
Houstonia longifolia var. longifolia (long-leaved bluets, pale bluets)
Houstonia procumbens (innocence)
Hymenocallis caroliniana (spider lily, rain lily)
Hypoxis hirsuta (yellow star grass)
Iris cristata (dwarf crested iris)
Iris hexagona (flag iris)
Iris prismatica (slender blue flag, coastal iris)
Iris verna (dwarf flag iris)
Iris virginica (southern blue flag)
Kosteletzkya virginica (seashore mallow)
Lespedeza capitata (roundheaded bush clover)
Liatris aspera (rough blazing star, gayfeather)
Liatris elegans (gayfeather)
Liatris spicata (marsh blazing star, gayfeather)
Liatris squarrosa (blazing star)
Lilium catesbaei (pine lily)
Lilium michauxii (Carolina lily)
Linum virginianum (woodland flax)
Lithospermum caroliniense (hairy puccoon, hispid gromwell)
Lobelia cardinalis (cardinal flower)
Lobelia siphilitica (great blue lobelia)
Lupinus perennis (wild lupine)
Lysimachia ciliata (fringed loosestrife)
Maianthemum canadense (wild lily-of-the-valley, Canada mayflower)
Maianthemum racemosum ssp. racemosum (false Solomon's seal, false
   spikenard)
Manfreda virginica (rattlesnake master, false aloe)
Mitchella repens (partridge berry)
Monarda didyma (beebalm, oswego tea)
Monarda fistulosa (wild bergamot, horsemint, beebalm)
Monarda punctata (beebalm)
Nuphar lutea (yellow pond lily, cow lily, spatter dock)
Oenothera fruticosa (sundrops)
Orontium aquaticum (golden club)
Osmorhiza claytoni (sweet cicely, sweet jarvil)

Peltandra virginica (arrow arum)
Penstemon australis (beardtongue)
Phlox carolina (Carolina phlox)
Phlox divaricata ssp. laphamii (blue phlox, sweet william)
Phlox paniculata (summer phlox, perennial phlox)
Phlox pilosa (prairie phlox, downy phlox)
Phlox stolonifera (creeping phlox)
Physostegia virginiana (obedient plant, false dragonhead)
Podophyllum peltatum (May apple)
Polygonatum biflorum (Solomon's seal)
Potentilla simplex (common cinquefoil)
Pycnanthemum tenuifolium (slender mountain mint)
Ranunculus hispidus (early buttercup, tufted buttercup)
Ratibida pinnata (gray-headed coneflower, yellow coneflower)
Rhexia nashii (meadow beauty)
Rhexia virginica (meadow beauty)
Rudbeckia fulgida (black-eyed Susan, orange coneflower)
Rudbeckia laciniata (cut-leaf coneflower)
Salvia lyrata (cancer weed, lyre-leaf sage)
Sanguinaria candensis (bloodroot)
Sedum ternatum (wild stonecrop)
Senecio aureus (golden ragwort)
Silene stellata (starry campion)
Silene virginica (fire pink)
Sisyrinchium angustifolium (narrow-leaved blue-eyed grass)
Sisyrinchium mucronatum (eastern blue-eyed grass)
Solidago caesia (blue-stemmed goldenrod, wreath goldenrod)
Solidago nemoralis (gray goldenrod, old-field goldenrod)
Solidago odora (sweet goldenrod)
Solidago rigida (stiff goldenrod)
Solidago rugosa (rough-leaved goldenrod)
Solidago sempervirens (seaside goldenrod)
Solidago speciosa (showy goldenrod)
Solidago ulmifolia (elm-leaved goldenrod)
Spigelia marilandica (Indian pink)
Tephrosia virginiana (goat's rue)
Thalictrum dioicum (early meadow rue)
Thalictrum pubescens (tall meadow rue)
Thalictrum thalictroides (rue anemone)
Thermopsis villosa (bush pea)
Tiarella cordifolia (foam flower)
Tradescantia hirsuticaulis (hairy spiderwort)
Tradescantia ohiensis (Ohio spiderwort)
Tradescantia virginiana (Virginia spiderwort, spider lily)
Trillium erectum (wakerobin, purple trillium)
Trillium undulatum (painted trillium)
Uvularia grandiflora (bellwort, merrybells)
Uvularia sessilifolia (wildoats, merrybells)
Vernonia noveboracensis (New York ironweed)
Veronicastrum virginicum (Culver's root)
Viola affinis (Florida violet)
Viola canadensis (Canada violet)

Viola pedata (bird-foot violet)
Viola soraria (common blue violet, meadow violet)
Yucca aloifolia (Spanish dagger)
Zephyranthes atamasca (atamasco lily, Easter lily)
Zizia aptera (heart-leaved golden alexanders)
Zizia aurea (golden alexanders)

Grasses/Grass-like plants

Agrostis scabra (ticklegrass, fly-away grass)
Andropogon gerardii (big bluestem)
Andropogon glomeratus (bushy bluestem)
Andropogon ternarius (splitbeard bluestem)
Andropogon virginicus (broom sedge)
Arundinaria gigantea (giant cane)
Carex pensylvanica (Pennsylvania sedge)
Carex plantaginea (plantain-leaved sedge)
Carex stipata (awl-fruited sedge)
Chasmanthium latifolium (inland sea oats, wild oats, river oats, broad-leaf uniola)
Danthonia spicata (poverty grass)
Distichlis spicata (seashore saltgrass)
Elymus hystrix var. hystrix (bottlebrush grass)
Elymus villosus (wild rye)
Elymus virginicus (wild rye)
Eragrostis intermedia (plains lovegrass)
Eragrostis spectabilis (purple lovegrass, tumblegrass)
Juncus effusus var. solutus (soft rush)
Leersia oryzoides (rice cut grass)
Muhlenbergia capillaris (gulf muhly, hair grass)
Panicum virgatum (switchgrass)
Saccharum giganteum (sugarcane plume grass)
Schizachyrium scoparium (little bluestem)
Scirpus atrovirens (dark green bulrush)
Scirpus cyperinus (wool grass)
Scirpus tabernaemontani (great bulrush)
Sorghastrum nutans (Indian grass)
Spartina patens (marsh hay cordgrass, salt meadow cordgrass)
Tripsacum dactyloides (eastern gama grass)
Typha angustifolia (narrow-leaved cattail)
Typha latifolia (cattail)

Shrubs (deciduous)

Amelanchier arborea (downy serviceberry, shadbush, Juneberry)
Aronia melanocarpa (black chokeberry)
Baccharis halimifolia (sea myrtle, groundsel bush)
Castanea pumila (chinquapin)
Ceanothus americanus (New Jersey tea, red root)
Cephalanthus occidentalis (buttonbush)
Erythrina herbacea (coral bean)
Forestiera acuminata (swamp privet)
Hypericum hypericoides ssp. hypericoides (St. Andrew's cross)
Physocarpus opulifolius (ninebark)
Rhododendron arborescens (smooth azalea)

Rhododendron atlanticum (dwarf, or coastal azalea)
Rhododendron periclymenoides (pinxterbloom azalea)
Rhododendron viscosum (swamp azalea)
Rhus aromatica (fragrant sumac)
Rhus copallinum (dwarf or winged sumac)
Rhus glabra (smooth sumac)
Rubus occidentalis (black raspberry, thimbleberry)
Rubus odoratus (thimbleberry)
Staphylea trifolia (bladdernut)
Styrax americanus (American silverbells)
Vaccinium arboreum (sparkleberry, farkleberry)
Vaccinium corymbosom (highbush blueberry)
Viburnum nudum (possumhaw viburnum)
Viburnum rufidulum (southern or rusty black haw)

Shrubs (evergreen)

Alnus serrulata (smooth alder)
Amorpha fruticosa (false indigo, Indigo bush)
Callicarpa americana (American beautyberry, French mulberry)
Calycanthus floridus (Carolina allspice, sweet shrub)
Clethra alnifolia (summer sweet)
Cornus alternifolia (pogoda dogwood, alternate-leaved dogwood)
Corylus americana (American hazelnut or filbert)
Corylus cornuta (beaked hazelnut or filbert)
Diervilla sessilifolia (southern bush honeysuckle)
Dirca palustris (leatherwood, ropebark)
Epigaea repens (trailing arbutus)
Euonymus americana (strawberry bush, brook euonymus, hearts-a-bustin')
Euonymus atropurpurea (wahoo, burning bush)
Frangula caroliniana (Carolina buckthorn)
Gaultheria procumbens (wintergreen, checkerberry)
Gordonia lasianthus (loblolly bay, gordonia)
Hydrangea arborescens (wild hydrangea)
Hydrangea quercifolia (oakleaf hydrangea)
Hypericum prolificum (shrubby St. John's wort)
Ilex glabra (inkberry, bitter gallberry)
Ilex verticillata (winterberry, black alder)
Ilex vomitoria (yaupon)
Itea virginica (Virginia willow, sweetspire, tassel-white)
Kalmia latifolia (mountain laurel)
Leucothoe axillaris (coast leucothoe)
Lindera benzoin (spicebush)
Lyonia ligustrina (male-berry, male-blueberry)
Myrica cerifera (wax myrtle, southern bayberry, candleberry)
Rhododendron calendulaceum (flame azalea)
Rhododendron canescens (wild, piedmont, or sweet azalea)
Rhododendron catawbiense (purple rhododendron, red laurel)
Rhododendron maximum (rosebay, great laurel)
Rhus hirta (staghorn sumac)
Ribes cynosbati (prickly gooseberry, dogberry)
Rosa carolina (Carolina rose)
Rosa palustris (swamp rose)

Sabal minor (dwarf palmetto)
Sambucus canadensis (elderberry, common elder)
Serenoa repens (saw palmetto)
Sideroxylon lanuginosum ssp. lanuginosum (chittamwood, gum elastic tree)
Viburnum acerifolium (maple leaf viburnum)
Viburnum dentatum (southern arrowwood)
Viburnum nudum var. cassinoides (wild raisin)
Viburnum prunifolium (black haw, nanny berry)

Trees (deciduous)

Acer barbatum (Florida maple, southern sugar maple)
Acer leucoderme (chalk maple)
Acer negundo (box elder)
Acer pensylvanicum (striped maple)
Acer rubrum (red maple)
Acer saccharinum (silver maple)
Acer saccharum (sugar maple)
Aesculus flava (sweet buckeye, yellow buckeye)
Aesculus pavia var. pavia (red buckeye)
Amelanchier canadensis (shadblow serviceberry, Juneberry)
Betula lenta (cherry birch)
Betula nigra (river birch)
Carpinus caroliniana (blue beech, hornbeam, musclewood)
Carya alba (mockernut hickory)
Carya cordiformis (bitternut, swamp hickory)
Carya ovata (shagbark hickory)
Celtis laevigata (sugarberry, hackberry)
Celtis occidentalis (hackberry, sugarberry)
Cercis canadensis (redbud)
Chionanthus virginicus (fringe tree, old man's beard)
Cornus florida (flowering dogwood)
Crataegus crus-galli (cockspur hawthorn)
Crataegus marshallii (parsley hawthorn)
Crataegus punctata (dotted hawthorn, white thorn)
Cyrilla racemiflora (leatherwood, yiti)
Diospyros virginiana (persimmon)
Fagus grandifolia var. caroliniana (beech)
Fraxinus americana (white ash)
Fraxinus pensylvanica (green ash)
Gleditsia triacanthos (honey locust)
Halesia diptera (American snowdrop tree, two-winged silverbell)
Halesia tetraptera (Carolina silverbell)
Hamamelis virginiana (witch hazel)
Ilex decidua (possum-haw, deciduous holly)
Juglans nigra (black walnut)
Liquidambar styraciflua (sweet gum)
Liriodendron tulipifera (tulip tree)
Magnolia acuminata (cucumber tree)
Magnolia pyramidata (pyramid magnolia)
Magnolia tripetala (umbrella tree)
Magnolia virginiana (sweetbay, swampbay)
Malus angustifolia (southern crabapple, wild crabapple)

Nyssa sylvatica (black gum, tupelo)
Ostrya virginiana (ironwood, hophornbeam)
Oxydendrum arboreum (sourwood)
Platanus occidentalis (sycamore, plane-tree)
Populus deltoides (eastern cottonwood)
Prunus americana (wild plum)
Prunus angustifolia (chickasaw plum)
Prunus serotina (black cherry)
Ptelea trifoliata (wafer ash, common hoptree)
Quercus alba (white oak)
Quercus coccinea (scarlet oak)
Quercus falcata (southern red oak, Spanish oak)
Quercus laurifolia (laurel oak)
Quercus lyrata (overcup oak)
Quercus marilandica (blackjack oak)
Quercus muhlenbergii (chinkapin oak, chestnut oak)
Quercus phellos (willow oak)
Quercus prinus (rock chestnut oak)
Quercus rubra (red oak)
Quercus shumardii (shumard oak)
Quercus stellata (post oak)
Quercus velutina (black oak)
Salix nigra (black willow)
Sassafras albidum (sassafras)
Taxodium distichum (bald cypress)
Ulmus americana (American elm)
Ulmus rubra (red elm, slippery elm)

Trees (evergreen)

Ilex opaca (American holly, Christmas holly)
Juniperus virginiana (eastern red cedar)
Magnolia grandiflora (southern magnolia)
Persea borbonia (red bay)
Pinus echinata (shortleaf pine)
Pinus elliotii (slash, pitch, or yellow slash pine)
Pinus glabra (spruce pine)
Pinus palustris (longleaf pine)
Pinus rigida (pitch pine)
Pinus strobus (eastern white pine)
Pinus taeda (loblolly pine)
Pinus virginiana (Virginia pine)
Quercus virginiana (live oak, coastal live oak, southern live oak)
Sabal palmetto (cabbage palm)
Tsuga canadensis (eastern hemlock)

Vine (deciduous)

Bignonia capreolata (cross vine)
Campsis radicans (trumpet creeper, trumpet vine)
Clematis crispa (leatherflower)
Clematis virginiana (virgin's bower)
Lonicera sempervirens (coral honeysuckle)
Parthenocissus quinquefolia (Virginia creeper)

Passiflora incarnata (passion flower, maypop)
Vitis rotundifolia (muscadine grape)

Vine (evergreen)

Gelsemium sempervirens (yellow jessamine, Carolina jessamine)

FEDERALLY LISTED ENDANGERED SPECIES

American chaffseed (Schwalbea americana)
Black-spored quillwort (Isoetes melanospora)
Canby's dropwort (Oxypolis canbyi)
Florida torreya (Torreya taxifolia)
Finged campion (Silene polypetala)
Green pitcher-plant (Sarracenia oreophila)
Hairy rattleweed (Baptisia arachnifera)
Harperella (Ptilimnium nodosum (fluviatile))
Kral's water-plantain (Sagittaria secundifolia)
Large-flowered skullcap (Scutellaria montana)
Little amphianthus (Amphianthus pusillus)
Mat-forming quillwort (Isoetes tegetiformans)
Michaux's sumac (Rhus michauxii)
Mohr's Barbara's buttons (Marshallia mohrii)
Persistent trillium (Trillium persistens)
Pondberry (Lindera melissifolia)
Relict trillium (Trillium reliquum)
Small whorled pogonia (Isotria medeoloides)
Smooth coneflower (Echinacea laevigata)
Swamp pink (Helonias bullata)
Tennessee yellow-eyed grass (Xyris tennesseensis)
Virginia spiraea (Spiraea virginiana)

GEORGIA NOXIOUS SPECIES

Because the noxious weed lists have continually changed since we gathered them in 1994, we are not including them at this time. Not all States have noxious weed lists. Those that do, do not use the same standards of importance and are not comparable. States typically have included plants that interfere with agriculture (Canada thistle), or cause human health problems (poison ivy). Some States are now including a category of plants that invade and degrade the environment (purple loosestrife). Check with your State's Agriculture Department or Weed Scientist listed below. The noxious weed list can be used two ways on roadsides: l) check to not inadvertently plant these invasive plants, and 2) note the plants you are legally responsible to control. Many States now check adjacent State lists to avoid planting their neighbors' problem plants. Because weeds do not respect political boundaries, and because by their very nature weeds continue to adapt and expand, monitoring and controlling invasives at State borders is a wise part of vegetation management.

(Seed Law only)

Department of Agriculture
Capital Square
Atlanta, GA 30334

Timothy Murphy, Exp. Sta.
University of Georgia
P.O. Box 748
Tifton, GA 31793
(912) 386-3901

Georgia Natural Heritage Program
Wildlife Resources Division
Department of Natural Resources
2117 U.S. Highway 278 S.E.
Social Circle, GA 30279
(706) 557-3032

The Nature Conservancy Field Office
1330 W. Peachtree Street, Ste. 410
Atlanta, GA 30309
(404) 873-6946

Georgia Botanical Society
1676 Andover Court
Doraville, GA 30360

Georgia Native Plant Society
P.O. Box 422085
Atlanta, GA 30342

Atlanta Botanical Garden
1345 Piedmont Avenue
Atlanta, GA 30309

Darrel G. Morrison
University of Georgia
609 Caldwell Hall
Athens, GA 30602
(706) 542-8293

POTENTIAL NATURAL VEGETATION ZONES IN
HAWAII

Source: A.W. Kuchler's Potential Natural Vegetation Map, 1964, Revised 1985.
Presented in U.S.G.S. National Atlas of the U.S. Series,
U.S. Geological Survey, Reston, VA.

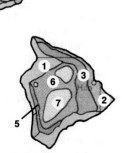

HI 1	Sclerophyllous forest, shrubland, and grassland *(Heteropogon-Opuntia-Prosopis)*	
HI 2	Guava mixed forest *(Aleurites-Hibiscus-Mangifera-Psidium-Schinus)*	**HI 5** Koa forest *(Acacia)*
HI 3	Ohia lehua forest *(Metrosideros-Cibotium)*	**HI 6** Koa-mamani parkland *(Acacia-Deschampsia-Myoporum-Sophora)*
HI 4	Lama-manele forest *(Diospyros-Sapindus)*	**HI 7** Grassland, microphyllous shrubland, and barrer *(Deschampsia-Styphelia-Vaccinium)*

VEGETATION REFERENCES

(Dominant plant species present in each vegetation type are listed in Appendix 8)

HI 1   *Sclerophyllous forest, shrubland, and grassland (Heteropogon-Opuntia-Prosopis)*

HI 2   *Guava mixed forest (Aleurites-Hibiscus-Mangilera-Psidium-Schinus)*

HI 3   *Ohia lehua forest (Metrosideros-Cibotium)*

HI 4   *Lama-manele forest (Diospyros-Sapindus)*

HI 5   *Koa forest (Acacia)*

HI 6   *Koa-mamani parkland (Acacia-Deschampsia-Myoporum-Sophora)*

HI 7   *Grassland, microphyllous shrubland, and barren (Deschampsia-Styphelia-Vaccinium)*

Botanical Experts

Joel Lau - Botanist, Hawaii Specialist
Hawaii Natural Heritage Program
http://aloha.net/~hinhp/

NATIVE PLANTS FOR LANDSCAPE USE IN HAWAII

Abutilon menziesii (ko `oloa `ula)
Acacia koa (koa)
Bacopa monnieri
Canthium odoratum (alahe`e)
Capparis sandwichiana (puapilo)
Chamaesyce spp. (`akoko)
Dodonaea viscosa (`a `ali`i)
Gnaphalium sanwicensium (`ena`ena)
Gossypium tomentosum (ma`o)
Heliotropium anomalum (hinahina kahakai)
Hetropogon contortus (pili)
Hibiscus clayi (koki`o `ula`ula)
Hibiscus kokio (koki`o `ula`ula)
Lipochaeta integrifolia (nehe)
Metrosideros polymorpha (`ohi`a lehua)
Myoporum sandwicense (naio)
Nototrichium sandwicense (kulu`i)
Osteomeles anthyllidifolia (`ulei)
Pittosporum spp. (ho`awa)
Pritchardia spp. (loulu)
Santalum spp. (`iliahi)
Sapindus oahuensis (lonomea)
Sapindus saponaria (manele)
Scaevola sericea (naupaka kahakai)
Sesbania tomentosa (`ohai)
Sida fallax (`ilima)
Sporobolus virginicus (`aki`aki)
Vitex rotundifolia (pohinahina)
Wikstroemia uva-ursi (`akia)

FEDERALLY LISTED ENDANGERED SPECIES

For current list, contact:
Hawaii Natural Heritage Program
1116 Smith Street, Ste. 201
Honolulu, HI 96817
(808) 537-4508

HAWAII NOXIOUS SPECIES

Because the noxious weed lists have continually changed since we gathered them in 1994, we are not including them at this time. Not all States have noxious weed lists. Those that do, do not use the same standards of importance and are not comparable. States typically have included plants that interfere with agriculture (Canada thistle), or cause human health problems (poison ivy). Some States are now including a category of plants that invade and degrade the environment (purple loosestrife). Check with your State's Agriculture Department or Weed Scientist listed below. The noxious weed list can be used two ways on roadsides: l) check to not inadvertantly plant these invasive plants, and 2) note the plants you are legally responsible to control. Many States now check adjacent State lists to avoid planting their neighbors' problem plants. Because weeds do not respect political boundaries, and because by their very nature weeds continue to adapt and expand, monitoring and controlling invasives at State borders is a wise part of vegetation management.

(Weed and Seed Laws)

Department of Agriculture
Plant Industry QBR
701 Ilalo Street
Honolulu, HI 96823

Phillip Motooka, Exp. Sta.
Univeristy of Hawaii at Manoa
Kealakekua, HI 96750
(808) 322-0488

HAWAII RESOURCES

Hawaii Natural Heritage Program
The Nature Conservancy of Hawaii
1116 Smith Street, Ste. 201
Honolulu, HI 96817
(808) 537-4508, (FAX) 545-2019

Hawaiian Botanical Society
% Department of Botany
University of Hawaii
3190 Maile Way
Honolulu, HI 96822

National Tropical Botanical Garden
P.O. Box 340
Lawai, Kauai, HI 96765

Waimea Arboretum
59-864 Kam Highway
Haleiwa, HI 96712

POTENTIAL NATURAL VEGETATION ZONES IN
IDAHO

Source: A.W. Kuchler's Potential Natural Vegetation Map, 1964, Revised 1985.
Presented in U.S.G.S. National Atlas of the U.S. Series,
U.S. Geological Survey, Reston, VA.

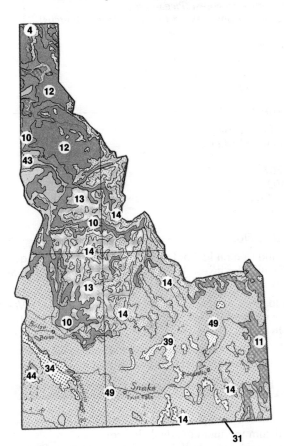

4	Fir-hemlock forest *(Abies-Tsuga)*	**31**	Mountain mahogany-oak scrub *(Cercocarpus-Quercus)*
10	Western ponderosa forest *(Pinus)*	**34**	Saltbush-greasewood *(Atriplex-Sarcobatus)*
11	Douglas fir forest *(Pseudotsuga)*	**39**	Desert: vegetation largely absent
12	Cedar-hemlock-pine forest *(Thuja-Tsuga-Pinus)*	**43**	Fescue-wheatgrass *(Festuca-Agropyron)*
13	Grand fir-Douglas fir forest *(Abies-Pseudotsuga)*	**44**	Wheatgrass-bluegrass *(Agropyron-Poa)*
14	Western spruce-fir forest *(Picea-Abies)*	**49**	Sagebrush steppe *(Artemisia-Agropyron)*

(Dominant plant species present in each vegetation type are listed in Appendix 8)

4   *Fir-Hemlock Forest (Abies-Tsuga)*
10   *Western Ponderosa forest (Pinus)*
11   *Douglas Fir Forest (Pseudotsuga)*
12   *Cedar-Hemlock-Pine Forest (Thuja-Tsuga-Pinus)*
13   *Grand Fir-Douglas Fir Forest (Abies Pseudotsuga)*
14   *Western Spruce-Fir Forest (Picea-Abies)*
31   *Mountain Mahogany-Oak Scrub (Cercocarpus-Quercus)*
34   *Saltbrush-Geasewood (Artiplex-Sarcobatus)*
39   *Desert: Vegetation Largely Absent*
43   *Fescue-Wheatgrass (Festuca-Agropyron)*
44   *Wheatgrass-Bluegrass (Agropyron-Poa)*
49   *Sagebrush Steppe (Artemisia-Agropyron)*

Botanical Experts

Bob Moseley, Plant Ecologist
Idaho Conservation Data Center
P.O. Box 25
Boise, ID 83707
(208) 334-3402
(208) 334-2114 (fax)
internet: bmoseley@idfg.state.id.us

Recommended Flora

For Northern and Central Idaho: Hitchcock, C.L. and A. Cronquist. 1973. Flora of the Pacific Northwest. University of Washington Press, Seattle, WA. 730 pgs. + illus.

For Southern Idaho: Cronquist, A. 1994. Intermountain Flora: Vascular Plants of the Intermountain West, U.S.A: Vol. 5: Asterales. New York Botanical Garden, New York. 496 pgs. + illus. maps. ISBN 0893273759.

Cronquist, A. 1972-97. Intermountain Flora: Vascular Plants of the Intermountain West, U.S.A. New York Botanical Garden, New York.

NATIVE PLANTS FOR LANDSCAPE USE IN IDAHO

Ferns

Adiantum pedatum (northern maidenhair fern)
Aspidotis densa (rock brake, cliff brake, Indian's dream)
Athyrium filix-femina (lady fern)
Botrychium virginianum (rattlesnake fern)
Cheilanthes gracillima (lace fern)
Cystopteris fragilis (fragile fern)
Dryopteris carthusiana (shield fern, toothed wood fern, spinulose shield fern)
Gymnocarpium dryopteris (oak fern)
Polystichum munitum (western sword fern)

Forbs (annuals/biennials)

Cleome serrulata (Rocky Mountain beeplant)
Collinsia parviflora var. grandiflora (blue lips)
Collomia grandiflora (collomia)
Erysimum capitatum (western wallflower, prairie rocket)
Gilia capitata (globe gilia, blue gilia)
Helianthus annuus (common sunflower)
Ipomopsis aggregata (sky rocket, scarlet gilia)
Layia glandulosa (tidy tips)
Lepidium montanum (mountain peppergrass)
Mentzelia laevicaulis (blazing star, evening star, stick leaf)
Mimulus guttatus (golden monkey flower)
Nemophila breviflora (Great Basin nemophila)
Townsendia exscapa (Easter daisy)

Forbs (perennials)

Abronia fragrans (sweet sand verbena)
Aconitum columbianum (western monkshood)
Allium cernuum (nodding onion)
Anaphalis margaritacea (pearly everlasting)
Anemone cylindrica (thimbleweed, candle anemone)
Antennaria spp. (pussytoes, everlasting)
Apocynum androsaemifolium (spreading dogbane)
Aquilegia coerulea (Rocky Mountain or blue columbine)
Aquilegia flavescens (yellow columbine)
Aquilegia formosa (scarlet columbine)
Arnica cordifolia (heartleaf arnica)
Artemisia ludoviciana (white sage, prairie sage, artemisia)
Asarum caudatum (wild ginger)
Asclepias speciosa (showy milkweed)
Aster ascendens (purple aster, Pacific aster)
Aster foliaceus (leafy aster)
Aster laevis (smooth aster)
Aster sibiricus (Sibirian or arctic aster)
Astragalus canadensis (milk vetch, Canada milk vetch)
Balsamorrhiza sagittata (balsamroot)
Calochortus macrocarpus (bigpod mariposa)
Calochortus nuttallii (sego lily, mariposa lily)
Caltha leptosepala (white marsh marigold, elkslip)
Campanula rotundifolia (harebell)
Castilleja angustifolia var. dubia (desert paintbrush)
Castilleja linariifolia (Indian paintbrush)
Castilleja sulphurea (splitleaf Indian paintbrush)
Claytonia lanceolata (spring beauty)
Clematis hirsutissima (clematis, vase flower, leather flower, lion's beard)
Clintonia uniflora (bride's bonnet, queen cup, bead lily)
Cornus canadensis (bunchberry)
Delphinium glaucum (tower larkspur)
Dicentra cucullaria (dutchman's breeches)
Dodecatheon jeffreyi (Jeffrey's shooting stars)
Dryas octopetala (mountain dryas, white mountain avens)
Epilobium angustifolium (fireweed, willow herb)

Epilobium canum var. latifolia (hummingbird trumpet)
Epilobium latifolium (dwarf fireweed)
Epilobium obcordatum (rock fringe)
Erigeron compositus (alpine daisy)
Erigeron speciosus (showy fleabane)
Eriogonum umbellatum (sulfur buckwheat)
Eriophyllum lanatum (woolly sunflower, Oregon sunshine)
Erythronium grandiflorum (glacier lily, yellow fawn lily, dogtooth violet)
Fritillaria lanceolata (checker lily, mission bells, chocolate lily)
Gaillardia aristata (blanket flower, gaillardia, brown-eyed Susan)
Galium triflorum (sweet-scented bedstraw)
Gaura coccinea (scarlet gaura)
Geranium viscossisimum (sticky wild geranium)
Geum triflorum (prairie smoke, purple avens)
Glycyrrhiza lepidota (wild licorice)
Hedysarum boreale (sweet vetch, sweet broom)
Helenium autumnale (common sneezeweed)
Heliomeris multiflora (showy goldeneye)
Heterotheca villosa var. villosa (golden aster)
Heuchera micrantha (common alumroot)
Heuchera parvifolia (saxifrage, alum root)
Heuchera rubescens (mountain alumroot, red alumroot, wild coralbells)
Iris missouriensis (Rocky Mountain iris, western blue flag)
Lewisia rediviva (bitter root)
Lilium columbianum (Columbia lily, Oregon lily, wild tiger lily)
Linnaea borealis (twinflower)
Linum lewisii (wild blue flax)
Luetkea pectinata (Alaska spiraea, partridge foot)
Lupinus argenteus (silvery lupine)
Maianthemum racemosum ssp. racemosum (false Solomon's seal,
    false spikenard)
Maianthemum stellatum (starry Solomon's seal)
Mertensia ciliata (mountain bluebells)
Mimulus lewisii (Lewis monkey flower, great purple monkey flower)
Mimulus primuloides (primrose monkey flower)
Minuartia obtusiloba (cushion sandwort)
Monardella odoratissima (coyote mint, mountain pennyroyal)
Oenothera brachycarpa (evening primrose)
Oenothera cespitosa (gumbo evening primrose, gumbo lily)
Oenothera flava (Shortfin evening primrose)
Pedicularis groenlandica (elephant heads)
Penstemon deustus (hot rock penstemon)
Penstemon fruticosus (shrubby penstemon)
Penstemon speciosus (sagebrush penstemon)
Pentaphylloides floribunda (potentilla, shrubby cinquefoil)
Petrophytum caespitosum (dwarf spiraea, petrophytum, tufted rockmat)
Phacelia sericea (silky phacelia)
Phlox diffusa (mat phlox)
Phlox speciosa (showy phlox)
Polemonium occidentale (Jacob's ladder)
Polemonium pulcherrimum (alpine Jacob's ladder, skunk leaf)
Polemonium viscosum (sky pilot)

Potentilla arguta (white cinquefoil, prairie cinquefoil, tall cinquefoil)
Pyrola elliptica (shinleaf)
Ranunculus alismifolius (meadow buttercup)
Rudbeckia laciniata (cut-leaf coneflower)
Satureja douglasii (yerba buena)
Saxifraga bronchialis (spotted saxifrage, matted saxifrage)
Saxifraga cespitosa (tufted saxifrage)
Saxifraga oppositifolia (purple saxifrage)
Sidalcea neomexicana (checker mallow, prairie mallow)
Silene acaulis (moss campion)
Solidago canadensis (meadow goldenrod)
Solidago missouriensis (Missouri goldenrod, prairie goldenrod)
Solidago multiradiata (northern goldenrod, mountain goldenrod)
Sphaeralcea coccinea (scarlet globe mallow)
Sphaeralcea munroana (Munro's globe mallow, white-leaved globe mallow)
Tellima grandiflora (fringe cup)
Thermopsis rhombifolia var. montana (golden pea, buckbean)
Tiarella trifoliata var. unifoliata (sugar scoop, western foam flower)
Trillium ovatum (coast trillium, western wakerobin)
Verbena hastata (blue verbena, blue vervain)
Verbena stricta (hoary vervain)
Viola glabella (smooth yellow or stream violet)
Viola nuttallii (yellow violet)
Xerophyllum tenax (beargrass)
Zizia aptera (heart-leaved golden alexanders)

Grasses/Grass-like plants

Agrostis exarata (spikebent, spike red top)
Agrostis scabra (ticklegrass, fly-away grass)
Aristida purpurea var. longiseta (red three awn)
Bromus carinatus (California brome)
Calamagrostis canadensis (bluejoint grass)
Carex aquatilis (water sedge)
Carex nebrascensis (Nebraska sedge)
Carex stipata (awl-fruited sedge)
Danthonia californica (California oatgrass)
Danthonia intermedia (timber oatgrass)
Danthonia spicata (poverty grass)
Deschampsia cespitosa (tufted hairgrass)
Dichanthelium acuminatum var. acuminatum (panic grass)
Distichlis spicata (seashore saltgrass)
Eleocharis palustris (creeping spikesedge, spike rush)
Elymus canadensis (Canada wild rye)
Elymus glaucus (blue wild rye)
Elymus lanceolatus (thickspike wheatgrass)
Festuca idahoensis (Idaho fescue, blue bunchgrass)
Festuca ovina (sheep fescue)
Glyceria grandis (American mannagrass, tall mannagrass, reed meadowgrass)
Hierochloe odorata (sweet grass)
Juncus interior (inland rush)
Koeleria macrantha (June grass)
Leersia oryzoides (rice cut grass)

Leymus cinereus (Great Basin wild rye)
Oryzopsis hymenoides (Indian ricegrass)
Pascopyrum smithii (western wheatgrass)
Phleum alpinum (alpine timothy)
Poa alpina (alpine bluegrass)
Poa secunda (pine bluegrass)
Pseudoroegneria spicata (bluebunch wheatgrass)
Scirpus acutus (hardstem bulrush)
Scirpus maritimus (alkali bulrush, prairie bulrush, bayonet grass)
Spartina pectinata (prairie cordgrass, freshwater cordgrass)
Sporobolus airoides (alkali sacaton)
Sporobolus cryptandrus (sand dropseed)
Stipa comata (needle-and-thread grass)
Stipa nelsonii (Columbia needlegrass)
Trisetum spicatum (spike trisetum)
Typha latifolia (cattail)

Shrubs (deciduous)

Alnus incana (speckled alder, mountain alder)
Alnus viridis ssp. sinuata (Sitka alder, mountain alder)
Amelanchier alnifolia (saskatoon, western serviceberry, Juneberry)
Amelanchier utahensis (Utah serviceberry)
Artemisia frigida (prairie sagewort, fringed sage)
Atriplex canescens (four-wing saltbush, wingscale)
Atriplex confertifolia (spiny saltbush, shadscale saltbush, hop sage)
Betula nana (bog birch, dwarf birch)
Ceanothus sanguineus (redstem ceanothus, wild lilac)
Chamaebatiaria millefolium (fernbush, desert sweet, tansy bush)
Chrysothamnus nauseosus (rabbit brush, chamisa)
Cornus sericea (red-twig dogwood, red-osier dogwood)
Corylus cornuta (beaked hazelnut or filbert)
Crataegus douglasii (black hawthorn)
Elaeagnus commutata (silverberry, wild olive, wolf willow)
Holodiscus discolor (cream bush, ocean spray, mountain spray)
Holodiscus dumosus (bush rock-spires, cream bush, ocean spray)
Krascheninnikovia lanata (winterfat)
Lonicera involucrata (black twinberry, bear berry honeysuckle)
Philadelphus lewisii (wild mock orange, syringa)
Physocarpus capitatus (western ninebark)
Physocarpus malvaceus (mallow ninebark)
Prunus virginiana (chokecherry)
Purshia tridentata (antelope brush)
Rhus glabra (smooth sumac)
Rhus trilobata (squawbush, basketbush, skunkbush)
Ribes aureum (golden currant)
Ribes cereum (wax currant, western red currant, squaw currant)
Rosa nutkana (nootka rose)
Rosa woodsii (western wild rose, woods rose)
Rubus idaeus ssp. strigosus (red raspberry)
Rubus parviflorus (western thimbleberry)
Salix bebbiana (Bebb willow, long-beaked willow)
Salix scouleriana (western pussy willow, Scouler's willow)

Sambucus cerulea (blue elderberry)
Sambucus racemosa var. melanocarpa (black elderberry)
Sambucus racemosa var. pubens (scarlet elderberry, red-berried elder)
Sarcobatus vermiculatus (greasewood)
Shepherdia canadensis (buffaloberry)
Sorbus scopulina (western mountain ash)
Spiraea douglasii (western spiraea, hardhack spiraea)
Spiraea splendens var. splendens (subalpine spiraea)
Symphoricarpos oreophilus (mountain snowberry)
Viburnum edule (moosewood viburnum)

Shrubs (evergreen)

Arctostaphylos uva-ursi (bearberry, kinnikinnik)
Artemisia nova (black sagebrush)
Artemisia tridentata (big sagebrush, Great Basin sagebrush)
Ceanothus velutinus (mountain balm, buckbush)
Cercocarpus ledifolius (curl-leaf mountain mahogany)
Juniperus communis (common juniper)
Kalmia microphylla (swamp laurel, bog laurel)
Mahonia aquifolium (Oregon grape)
Mahonia nervosa var. nervosa (Cascade Oregon grape)
Paxistima myrsinites (Oregon box, myrtle boxwood, mountain lover)
Phyllodoce empetriformis (pink mountain heather)

Trees (deciduous)

Acer glabrum (Rocky Mountain maple)
Acer grandidentatum (bigtooth maple)
Acer negundo (box elder)
Alnus rhombifolia (white alder)
Betula occidentalis (mountain birch, water birch)
Betula papyrifera (paper birch)
Celtis laevigata var. reticulata (netleaf hackberry)
Larix occidentalis (western larch, western tamarack)
Populus tremuloides (quaking aspen)
Salix amygdaloides (peachleaf willow)

Trees (evergreen)

Abies grandis (grand fir, giant fir)
Abies lasiocarpa (subalpine fir)
Juniperus osteosperma (Utah juniper)
Juniperus scopulorum (Rocky Mountain juniper)
Picea engelmannii (Engelmann spruce)
Picea pungens (blue spruce, Colorado spruce)
Pinus contorta var. murrayana (lodgepole pine)
Pinus flexilis (limber pine)
Pinus monticola (western white pine)
Pinus ponderosa (ponderosa pine)
Pseudotsuga menziesii (Douglas fir)
Taxus brevifolia (western yew, Pacific yew)
Thuja plicata (western red cedar)
Tsuga heterophylla (western hemlock)
Tsuga mertensiana (mountain hemlock)

Vines (deciduous)

Clematis columbiana (purple virgin's bower)
Clematis ligusticifolia (clematis)
Lonicera ciliosa (orange honeysuckle)

IDAHO NOXIOUS SPECIES

Because the noxious weed lists have continually changed since we gathered them in 1994, we are not including them at this time. Not all States have noxious weed lists. Those that do, do not use the same standards of importance and are not comparable. States typically have included plants that interfere with agriculture (Canada thistle), or cause human health problems (poison ivy). Some States are now including a category of plants that invade and degrade the environment (purple loosestrife). Check with your State's Agriculture Department or Weed Scientist listed below. The noxious weed list can be used two ways on roadsides: l) check to not inadvertantly plant these invasive plants, and 2) note the plants you are legally responsible to control. Many States now check adjacent State lists to avoid planting their neighbors' problem plants. Because weeds do not respect political boundaries, and because by their very nature weeds continue to adapt and expand, monitoring and controlling invasives at State borders is a wise part of vegetation management.

(Weed and Seed Laws)

Department of Agriculture
Plant Industries
120 Klotz, Box 790
Boise, ID 83702

Robert H. Callihan
Plant/Soil Science Dept.
University of Idaho
Moscow, ID 83843
(208) 885-6617

IDAHO RESOURCES

Idaho Conservation Data Center
Department of Fish & Game
600 South Walnut Street, Box 25
Boise, ID 83707
(208) 334-3402

The Nature Conservancy Field Office
P.O. Box 165
Sun Valley, ID 83353
(208) 726-3007

Idaho Native Plant Society
P.O. Box 9451
Boise, ID 83707

Idaho Botanical Garden
2355 N. Penitentiary Road
Boise, ID 83712

POTENTIAL NATURAL VEGETATION ZONES IN
ILLINOIS

Source: A.W. Kuchler's Potential Natural Vegetation Map, 1964, Revised 1985.
Presented in U.S.G.S. National Atlas of the U.S. Series,
U.S. Geological Survey, Reston, VA.

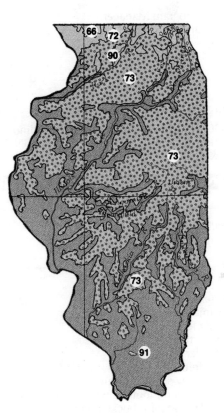

66	Bluestem prairie *(Andropogon-Panicum-Sorghastrum)*
72	Oak savanna *(Quercus-Andropogon)*
73	Mosaic of numbers 66 and 91
90	Maple-basswood forest *(Acer-Tilia)*
91	Oak-hickory forest *(Quercus-Carya)*

(Dominant plant species present in each vegetation type are listed in Appendix 8)

66   *Bluestem Prairie (Andropogon-Panicum-Sorghastrum)*
72   *Oak Savanna (Quercus-Andropogon)*
73   *Mosaic of 66 (Bluestem Prairie) and 91 (Oak-Hickory Forest)*
90   *Maple-Basswood Forest (Acer-Tilia)*
91   *Oak-Hickory Forest (Quercus-Carya)*

Botanical Experts

Bill McClain
Natural Areas Stewardship Program Manager
Illinois Department of Natural Resources
524 South 2nd St.
Springfield, IL 61701
(217) 785-8774
(217) 785-8277 (fax)

Recommended Flora

Mohlenbrock, R.H. 1986. Guide to the Vascular Flora of Illinois. Southern Illinois University Press, Carbondale, IL. 507 pgs., plates, maps. ISBN 0809312727; 0809312735 (paperback).

NATIVE PLANTS FOR LANDSCAPE USE IN ILLINOIS

Cacti

Opuntia humifusa (prickly pear)
Opuntia macrorhiza (common prickly pear)

Ferns

Adiantum pedatum (northern maidenhair fern)
Asplenium platyneuron (ebony spleenwort)
Asplenium trichomanes (maidenhair spleenwort)
Athyrium filix-femina (lady fern)
Botrychium virginianum (rattlesnake fern)
Cystopteris bulbifera (bladder fern)
Cystopteris fragilis (fragile fern)
Dennstaedtia punctilobula (hay-scented fern)
Dryopteris carthusiana (shield fern, toothed wood fern, spinulose shield fern)
Dryopteris cristata (crested wood fern, buckler fern)
Dryopteris marginalis (marginal wood fern)
Matteuccia struthiopteris (ostrich fern)
Onoclea sensibilis (sensitive fern, bead fern)
Osmunda cinnamomea (cinnamon fern)
Osmunda claytoniana (interrupted fern)
Osmunda regalis (royal fern)
Phegopteris hexagonoptera (broad beech fern)
Polystichum acrostichoides (Christmas fern)
Woodsia ilvensis (rusty woodsia)

Forbs (annuals/biennials)

Campanulastrum americanum (American bellflower, tall bellflower)
Erysimum capitatum (western wallflower, prairie rocket)
Glandularia canadensis (rose vervain, sweet William)
Lobelia spicata (pale lobelia)
Oenothera biennis (common evening primrose)
Oenothera rhombipetala (diamond-petal primrose, four-point evening primrose)
Rudbeckia hirta (black-eyed Susan)
Sabatia campestris (prairie rose gentian, prairie sabatia, meadow pink)
Senecio glabellus (butterweed)
Senecio plattensis (prairie ragwort, prairie groundsel)

Forbs (perennials)

Acorus calamus (sweet flag, calamus)
Actaea pachypoda (white baneberry)
Ageratina altissima var. altissima (white snakeroot)
Allium canadense (wild garlic)
Allium cernuum (nodding onion)
Allium stellatum (wild pink onion)
Allium tricoccum (wild leek)
Amsonia tabernaemontana (blue star)
Anemone canadensis (Canada anemone, windflower)
Anemone caroliniana (Carolina anemone, southern thimbleweed)
Anemone cylindrica (thimbleweed, candle anemone)
Anemone virginiana (thimbleweed, tall anemone)
Antennaria spp. (pussytoes, everlasting)
Apocynum androsaemifolium (spreading dogbane)
Aquilegia canadensis (columbine)
Arisaema triphyllum (Jack-in-the-pulpit, Indian turnip)
Artemisia ludoviciana (white sage, prairie sage, artemisia)
Aruncus dioicus (goat's beard)
Asarum canadense (wild ginger)
Asclepias incarnata (swamp milkweed)
Asclepias tuberosa (butterfly weed)
Asclepias verticillata (whorled milkweed)
Aster dumosus (bushy aster)
Aster ericoides (heath aster, white wreath aster)
Aster laevis (smooth aster)
Aster novae-angliae (New England aster)
Aster oblongifolius (aromatic aster)
Aster oolentangiensis (sky blue aster)
Aster pilosus (frost aster)
Aster puniceus (red-stem aster, swamp aster)
Aster sericeus (silky aster)
Astragalus canadensis (milk vetch, Canada milk vetch)
Baptisia alba (white false indigo)
Baptisia alba var. macrophyllla (cream false indigo, plains wild indigo)
Caltha palustris (marsh marigold, cowslip)
Camassia scilloides (wild hyacinth)
Campanula rotundifolia (harebell)
Castilleja sessiliflora (downy painted cup)
Caulophyllum thalictroides (blue cohosh)

Chelone glabra (turtlehead)
Claytonia virginica (narrow-leaved spring beauty)
Collinsonia canadensis (stoneroot, citronella horsebalm)
Coreopsis lanceolata (lance-leaved coreopsis)
Coreopsis palmata (stiff coreopsis)
Coreopsis tripteris (tall coreopsis)
Dalea candida (white prairie clover)
Dalea purpurea (purple prairie clover)
Delphinium carolinianum (blue larkspur)
Delphinium tricorne (dwarf larkspur)
Desmodium canadense (Canada tick-trefoil, Canada tickclover)
Desmodium illinoense (Illinois tick-trefoil, Illinois tickclover)
Dicentra cucullaria (dutchman's breeches)
Dodecatheon meadia (shooting star)
Echinacea purpurea (purple coneflower)
Epilobium angustifolium (fireweed, willow herb)
Eryngium yuccifolium (rattlesnake master, button snake-root)
Erythronium americanum (eastern trout lily, yellow trout lily)
Eupatorium coelestinum (mist flower)
Eupatorium fistulosum (Joe-pye weed)
Eupatorium maculatum (spotted Joe-pye weed)
Eupatorium perfoliatum (boneset)
Eupatorium purpureum (Joe-pye weed)
Euphorbia corollata (flowering spurge)
Euthamia graminifolia var. graminifolia (grass-leaved goldenrod)
Filipendula rubra (queen-of-the-prairie)
Fragaria virginiana (wild strawberry)
Galium triflorum (sweet-scented bedstraw)
Gentiana alba (cream gentian, yellow gentian)
Gentiana andrewsii (bottle gentian)
Gentiana saponaria (closed gentian, soapwort gentian)
Geranium maculatum (wild geranium, cranesbill)
Geum triflorum (prairie smoke, purple avens)
Hedyotis nigricans (bluets)
Helenium autumnale (common sneezeweed)
Helianthus maximiliani (Maximilian sunflower)
Helianthus pauciflorus ssp. pauciflorus (stiff sunflower)
Helianthus strumosus (woodland sunflower)
Heliopsis helianthoides (ox-eye sunflower, false sunflower)
Hepatica nobilis var. acuta (sharp-lobed hepatica)
Heterotheca villosa var. villosa (golden aster)
Heuchera richardsonii (alum root)
Hieracium longipilum (hairy hawkweed)
Houstonia caerulea (bluets)
Houstonia longifolia var. longifolia (long-leaved bluets, pale bluets)
Hydrastis canadensis (golden seal)
Hydrophyllum virginianum (Virginia waterleaf)
Hymenocallis caroliniana (spider lily, rain lily)
Hypericum ascyron (great St. John's wort)
Hypoxis hirsuta (yellow star grass)
Iris cristata (dwarf crested iris)
Iris virginica v. shrevei (blue flag)

Lespedeza capitata (roundheaded bush clover)
Liatris aspera (rough blazing star, gayfeather)
Liatris cylindracea (dwarf blazing star, gayfeather)
Liatris pycnostachya (prairie blazing star, gayfeather)
Liatris spicata (marsh blazing star, gayfeather)
Liatris squarrosa (blazing star)
Lilium michiganense (Turk's cap lily, Michigan lily)
Lilium philadelphicum (wood lily)
Linum virginianum (woodland flax)
Lithospermum canescens (hoary puccoon)
Lithospermum caroliniense (hairy puccoon, hispid gromwell)
Lithospermum incisum (fringed puccoon, narrow-leaved puccoon)
Lobelia cardinalis (cardinal flower)
Lobelia siphilitica (great blue lobelia)
Lupinus perennis (wild lupine)
Lysimachia ciliata (fringed loosestrife)
Maianthemum racemosum ssp. racemosum (false Solomon's seal,
    false spikenard)
Maianthemum stellatum (starry Solomon's seal)
Manfreda virginica (rattlesnake master, false aloe)
Mertensia virginica (bluebells)
Mitchella repens (partridge berry)
Monarda fistulosa (wild bergamot, horsemint, beebalm)
Nuphar lutea (yellow pond lily, cow lily, spatter dock)
Osmorhiza claytoni (sweet cicely, sweet jarvil)
Peltandra virginica (arrow arum)
Penstemon digitalis (beardtongue)
Penstemon grandiflorus (large-flowered penstemon)
Penstemon hirsutus (hairy beardtongue)
Pentaphylloides floribunda (potentilla, shrubby cinquefoil)
Phlox divaricata ssp. laphamii (blue phlox, sweet william)
Phlox paniculata (summer phlox, perennial phlox)
Phlox pilosa (prairie phlox, downy phlox)
Physostegia intermedia (obedient plant)
Physostegia virginiana (obedient plant, false dragonhead)
Podophyllum peltatum (May apple)
Polemonium reptans (Jacob's ladder, Greek valerian)
Polygonatum biflorum (Solomon's seal)
Potentilla arguta (white cinquefoil, prairie cinquefoil, tall cinquefoil)
Potentilla simplex (common cinquefoil)
Pulsatilla patens ssp. multifida (pasque flower, wild crocus)
Pycnanthemum tenuifolium (slender mountain mint)
Pycnanthemum virginianum (mountain mint)
Ranunculus hispidus (early buttercup, tufted buttercup)
Ratibida pinnata (gray-headed coneflower, yellow coneflower)
Rhexia virginica (meadow beauty)
Rudbeckia fulgida (black-eyed Susan, orange coneflower)
Rudbeckia laciniata (cut-leaf coneflower)
Rudbeckia subtomentosa (sweet black-eyed Susan)
Ruellia humilis (wild petunia)
Salvia lyrata (cancer weed, lyre-leaf sage)
Sanguinaria candensis (bloodroot)

Sedum ternatum (wild stonecrop)
Senecio aureus (golden ragwort)
Silene stellata (starry campion)
Silene virginica (fire pink)
Silphium integrifolium (rosinweed)
Silphium laciniatum (compass plant)
Silphium perfoliatum (cup plant)
Silphium terebinthinaceum (prairie dock)
Sisyrinchium angustifolium (narrow-leaved blue-eyed grass)
Sisyrinchium campestre (white-eyed grass, prairie blue-eyed grass)
Solidago caesia (blue-stemmed goldenrod, wreath goldenrod)
Solidago canadensis (meadow goldenrod)
Solidago juncea (early goldenrod, plume goldenrod)
Solidago missouriensis (Missouri goldenrod, prairie goldenrod)
Solidago nemoralis (gray goldenrod, old-field goldenrod)
Solidago rigida (stiff goldenrod)
Solidago rugosa (rough-leaved goldenrod)
Solidago speciosa (showy goldenrod)
Solidago ulmifolia (elm-leaved goldenrod)
Spigelia marilandica (Indian pink)
Tephrosia virginiana (goat's rue)
Thalictrum dasycarpum (tall or purple meadow rue)
Thalictrum dioicum (early meadow rue)
Thalictrum thalictroides (rue anemone)
Tradescantia ohiensis (Ohio spiderwort)
Tradescantia virginiana (Virginia spiderwort, spider lily)
Uvularia grandiflora (bellwort, merrybells)
Uvularia sessilifolia (wildoats, merrybells)
Verbena hastata (blue verbena, blue vervain)
Verbena stricta (hoary vervain)
Vernonia baldwinii (ironweed, western ironweed)
Vernonia fasciculata (ironweed)
Veronicastrum virginicum (Culver's root)
Viola missouriensis (Missouri violet)
Viola pedata (bird-foot violet)
Viola pedatifida (prairie violet)
Viola pubescens (downy or smooth yellow violet)
Viola soraria (common blue violet, meadow violet)
Zizia aptera (heart-leaved golden alexanders)
Zizia aurea (golden alexanders)

Grasses/Grass-like plants

Agrostis scabra (ticklegrass, fly-away grass)
Andropogon gerardii (big bluestem)
Andropogon virginicus (broom sedge)
Arundinaria gigantea (giant cane)
Bouteloua curtipendula (sideoats grama)
Bouteloua hirsuta (hairy grama)
Bromus kalmii (prairie brome, wild chess)
Calamagrostis canadensis (bluejoint grass)
Calamovilfa longifolia (sandreed grass, prairie sandreed)
Carex aquatilis (water sedge)

Carex pensylvanica (Pennsylvania sedge)
Carex stipata (awl-fruited sedge)
Carex stricta (tussock sedge)
Carex utriculata (beaked sedge)
Chasmanthium latifolium (inland sea oats, wild oats, river oats, broad-leaf uniola)
Danthonia spicata (poverty grass)
Eleocharis palustris (creeping spikesedge, spike rush)
Elymus canadensis (Canada wild rye)
Eragrostis spectabilis (purple lovegrass, tumblegrass)
Hierochloe odorata (sweet grass)
Juncus effusus var. solutus (soft rush)
Juncus interior (inland rush)
Koeleria macrantha (June grass)
Leersia oryzoides (rice cut grass)
Melica nitens (three-flower melic grass)
Muhlenbergia capillaris (gulf muhly, hair grass)
Panicum virgatum (switchgrass)
Pascopyrum smithii (western wheatgrass)
Schizachyrium scoparium (little bluestem)
Scirpus acutus (hardstem bulrush)
Scirpus atrovirens (dark green bulrush)
Scirpus cyperinus (wool grass)
Scirpus tabernaemontani (great bulrush)
Sorghastrum nutans (Indian grass)
Spartina pectinata (prairie cordgrass, freshwater cordgrass)
Sporobolus compositus var. compositus (tall dropseed)
Sporobolus cryptandrus (sand dropseed)
Sporobolus heterolepis (northern prairie dropseed)
Stipa spartea (porcupine grass)
Tripsacum dactyloides (eastern gama grass)
Typha latifolia (cattail)

Shrubs (deciduous)

Alnus serrulata (smooth alder)
Amelanchier arborea (downy serviceberry, shadbush, Juneberry)
Amorpha canescens (leadplant)
Amorpha fruticosa (false indigo, Indigo bush)
Aronia melanocarpa (black chokeberry)
Ceanothus americanus (New Jersey tea, red root)
Cephalanthus occidentalis (buttonbush)
Comptonia peregrina (sweet fern)
Cornus alternifolia (pogoda dogwood, alternate-leaved dogwood)
Cornus amomum ssp. obliqua (swamp dogwood, silky dogwood)
Cornus drummondii (rough-leaf dogwood)
Cornus racemosa (gray dogwood)
Cornus sericea (red-twig dogwood, red-osier dogwood)
Corylus americana (American hazelnut or filbert)
Diervilla lonicera (bush honeysuckle)
Dirca palustris (leatherwood, ropebark)
Euonymus americana (strawberry bush, brook euonymus, hearts-a-bustin')
Euonymus atropurpurea (wahoo, burning bush)
Forestiera acuminata (swamp privet)

Frangula caroliniana (Carolina buckthorn)
Hydrangea arborescens (wild hydrangea)
Hypericum hypericoides ssp. hypericoides (St. Andrew's cross)
Hypericum prolificum (shrubby St. John's wort)
Ilex verticillata (winterberry, black alder)
Itea virginica (Virginia willow, sweetspire, tassel-white)
Lindera benzoin (spicebush)
Lonicera dioica (limber or wild honeysuckle)
Physocarpus opulifolius (ninebark)
Prunus virginiana (chokecherry)
Rhododendron prinophyllum (roseshell azalea, early azalea)
Rhus aromatica (fragrant sumac)
Rhus copallinum (dwarf or winged sumac)
Rhus glabra (smooth sumac)
Rhus hirta (staghorn sumac)
Ribes cynosbati (prickly gooseberry, dogberry)
Rosa blanda (early wild rose, smooth rose)
Rosa carolina (Carolina rose)
Rosa setigera (Illinois or prairie rose)
Rubus occidentalis (black raspberry, thimbleberry)
Rubus odoratus (thimbleberry)
Salix bebbiana (Bebb willow, long-beaked willow)
Salix discolor (pussy willow)
Sambucus canadensis (elderberry, common elder)
Sambucus racemosa var. pubens (scarlet elderberry, red-berried elder)
Sideroxylon lanuginosum ssp. lanuginosum (chittamwood, gum elastic tree)
Spiraea alba (meadow sweet)
Spiraea tomentosa (steeplebush, hardhack)
Staphylea trifolia (bladdernut)
Styrax americanus (American silverbells)
Symphoricarpos orbiculatus (coralberry, Indian currant)
Vaccinium angustifolium (low-bush blueberry)
Vaccinium arboreum (sparkleberry, farkleberry)
Viburnum acerifolium (maple leaf viburnum)
Viburnum lentago (black haw, nannyberry)
Viburnum opulus var. americanum (high-bush cranberry, American
cranberrybush viburnum)
Viburnum prunifolium (black haw, nanny berry)
Viburnum rufidulum (southern or rusty black haw)

Shrubs (evergreen)

Arctostaphylos uva-ursi (bearberry, kinnikinnik)
Juniperus communis (common juniper)
Juniperus horizontalis (creeping juniper, creeping savin)
Taxus canadensis (Canada yew)

Trees (deciduous)

Acer negundo (box elder)
Acer rubrum (red maple)
Acer saccharinum (silver maple)
Acer saccharum (sugar maple)
Aesculus glabra (Ohio buckeye, horse chestnut)

Betula nigra (river birch)
Betula papyrifera (paper birch)
Carpinus caroliniana (blue beech, hornbeam, musclewood)
Carya alba (mockernut hickory)
Carya cordiformis (bitternut, swamp hickory)
Carya illinoinensis (pecan)
Carya ovata (shagbark hickory)
Carya texana (black hickory)
Catalpa speciosa (northern catalpa)
Celtis laevigata (sugarberry, hackberry)
Celtis occidentalis (hackberry, sugarberry)
Cercis canadensis (redbud)
Cornus florida (flowering dogwood)
Crataegus crus-galli (cockspur hawthorn)
Crataegus mollis (downy hawthorn)
Crataegus phaenopyrum (Washington hawthorn)
Crataegus punctata (dotted hawthorn, white thorn)
Diospyros virginiana (persimmon)
Fagus grandifolia var. grandifolia (beech)
Fagus grandifolia var. caroliniana (beech)
Fraxinus americana (white ash)
Fraxinus pensylvanica (green ash)
Gleditsia triacanthos (honey locust)
Gymnocladus dioica (Kentucky coffee tree)
Hamamelis virginiana (witch hazel)
Ilex decidua (possum-haw, deciduous holly)
Juglans cinerea (butternut, white walnut)
Juglans nigra (black walnut)
Larix laricina (tamarack, American larch)
Liquidambar styraciflua (sweet gum)
Liriodendron tulipifera (tulip tree)
Magnolia acuminata (cucumber tree)
Malus ioensis var. ioensis (prairie crabapple)
Nyssa sylvatica (black gum, tupelo)
Ostrya virginiana (ironwood, hophornbeam)
Platanus occidentalis (sycamore, plane-tree)
Populus deltoides (eastern cottonwood)
Populus grandidentata (large-toothed aspen)
Populus tremuloides (quaking aspen)
Prunus americana (wild plum)
Prunus angustifolia (chickasaw plum)
Prunus mexicana (Mexican plum)
Prunus pensylvanica (fire or pin cherry)
Prunus serotina (black cherry)
Ptelea trifoliata (wafer ash, common hoptree)
Quercus alba (white oak)
Quercus bicolor (swamp white oak)
Quercus coccinea (scarlet oak)
Quercus falcata (southern red oak, Spanish oak)
Quercus lyrata (overcup oak)
Quercus macrocarpa (bur oak)
Quercus marilandica (blackjack oak)

Quercus muhlenbergii (chinkapin oak, chestnut oak)
Quercus palustris (pin oak)
Quercus rubra (red oak)
Quercus shumardii (shumard oak)
Quercus stellata (post oak)
Quercus velutina (black oak)
Salix amygdaloides (peachleaf willow)
Salix nigra (black willow)
Sassafras albidum (sassafras)
Taxodium distichum (bald cypress)
Tilia americana (American linden, basswood)
Ulmus americana (American elm)
Ulmus rubra (red elm, slippery elm)

Trees (evergreen)

Juniperus virginiana (eastern red cedar)
Pinus echinata (shortleaf pine)
Pinus resinosa (red pine, Norway pine)
Pinus strobus (eastern white pine)
Thuja occidentalis (arbor vitae, northern white cedar)

Vines (deciduous)

Bignonia capreolata (cross vine)
Campsis radicans (trumpet creeper, trumpet vine)
Celastrus scandens (American bittersweet)
Clematis pitcheri (leather flower, purple clematis)
Clematis virginiana (virgin's bower)
Lonicera sempervirens (coral honeysuckle)
Parthenocissus quinquefolia (Virginia creeper)
Parthenocissus quinquefolia var. quinquefolia (woodbine)
Passiflora incarnata (passion flower, maypop)
Vitis riparia (riverbank grape)
Wisteria frutescens (wisteria)

FEDERALLY LISTED ENDANGERED SPECIES

Decurrent false aster (Boltonia decurrens)
Eastern priarie Fringed orchid (Platanthera leucophaea)
Lakeside daisy (Hymenoxys herbacea)
Leafy prarie-clover (Dalea (Petalostemum) foliosa)
Mead's milkweed (Asclepias meadii)
Pitcher's thistle (Cirium pitcheri)
Prairie bush-clover (Lespedeza leptostachya)
Small whorled pogonia (Isotria medeoloides)

ILLINOIS NOXIOUS SPECIES

Because the noxious weed lists have continually changed since we gathered them in 1994, we are not including them at this time. Not all States have noxious weed lists. Those that do, do not use the same standards of importance and are not comparable. States typically have included plants that interfere with agriculture (Canada thistle), or cause human health problems (poison ivy). Some States are now including a category of plants that invade and degrade the environment (purple loosestrife). Check with your State's Agriculture Department or Weed Scientist listed below. The noxious weed list can be used two ways on roadsides: l) check to not inadvertantly plant these invasive plants, and 2) note the plants you are legally responsible to control. Many States now check adjacent State lists to avoid planting their neighbors' problem plants. Because weeds do not respect political boundaries, and because by their very nature weeds continue to adapt and expand, monitoring and controlling invasives at State borders is a wise part of vegetation management.

(Weed Law only)

Department of Agriculture
9511 Harrison Street, Room A169
Des Plaines, IL 60016

Ellery L. Knake, U of I
N-323 Turner Hall
1102 South Goodwin Avenue
Urbana, IL 61801
(217) 333-4424

ILLINOIS RESOURCES

Illinois Natural Heritage Division
Department of Natural Resources
524 South 2nd Street
Springfield, IL 62706
(217) 785-8774

The Nature Conservancy Field Office
8 South Michigan Avenue, Ste. 900
Chicago, IL 60603

Illinois Native Plant Society
Forest Glen Preserve
20301 East 900 N. Road
Westville, IL 61883

Lincoln Memorial Garden
2301 East Lake Drive
Springfield, IL 62707

Liberty Prairie Conservancy
32400 N. Harris Road
Grayslake, IL 60030

Severson Dells Environmental
Education Center
8786 Montague Road
Rockford, IL 61102

Chicago Botanic Garden
1000 Lake Cook Road
Glencoe, IL 60022
(847) 835-5440

Morton Arboretum
4100 Illinois Route 53
Lisle, IL 60532
(630) 968-0074

POTENTIAL NATURAL VEGETATION ZONES IN
INDIANA

Source: A.W. Kuchler's Potential Natural Vegetation Map, 1964, Revised 1985.
Presented in U.S.G.S. National Atlas of the U.S. Series,
U.S. Geological Survey, Reston, VA.

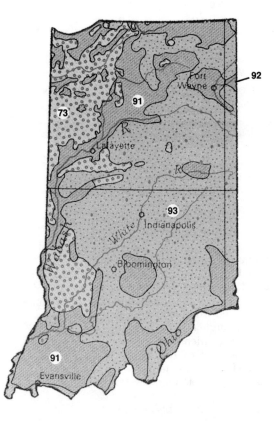

 73 Mosaic of numbers 66 and 91

91 Oak-hickory forest
(Quercus-Carya)

 92 Elm-ash forest
(Ulmus-Fraxinus)

93 Beech-maple forest
(Fagus-Acer)

(Dominant plant species present in each vegetation type are listed in Appendix 8)

73 *Mosaic of 66 (Bluestem Prairie) and 91 (Oak-Hickory Forest)*
91 *Oak-Hickory Forest (Quercus-Carya)*
92 *Elm-Ash Forest (Ulmus-Fraxinus)*
93 *Beech-Maple Forest (Fagus-Acer)*

Botanical Experts

Michael A. Homoya, Botanist
Indiana Department of Natural Resources
Division of Nature Preserves
402 W. Washington St., Rm 267
Indianapolis, IN 46204
(317) 232-4052

Recommended Flora

Deam, C.C. 1940. Flora of Indiana. W.B. Burford, Indianapolis, IN.
1236 pgs. + illus., maps.

NATIVE PLANTS FOR LANDSCAPE USE IN INDIANA

Cactus

Opuntia humifusa (prickly pear)

Ferns

Adiantum pedatum (northern maidenhair fern)
Asplenium platyneuron (ebony spleenwort)
Athyrium filix-femina (lady fern)
Botrychium virginianum (rattlesnake fern)
Cystopteris bulbifera (bladder fern)
Cystopteris protrusa (fragile fern)
Dryopteris carthusiana (shield fern, toothed wood fern, spinulose shield fern)
Dryopteris cristata (crested wood fern, buckler fern)
Dryopteris marginalis (marginal wood fern)
Matteuccia struthiopteris (ostrich fern)
Onoclea sensibilis (sensitive fern, bead fern)
Osmunda cinnamomea (cinnamon fern)
Osmunda claytoniana (interrupted fern)
Osmunda regalis (royal fern)
Phegopteris hexagonoptera (broad beech fern)
Polystichum acrostichoides (Christmas fern)
Thelypteris palustris (marsh fern)
Thelypteris novaboracensis (New York fern, tapering fern)

Forbs (annuals/biennials)

Campanulastrum americanum (American bellflower, tall bellflower)
Gentianopsis crinita (fringed gentian)
Lobelia spicata (pale lobelia)
Oenothera biennis (common evening primrose)
Rudbeckia hirta (black-eyed Susan)

Senecio glabellus (butterweed)
Senecio plattensis (prairie ragwort, prairie groundsel)

Forbs (perennials)

Acorus calamus (sweet flag, calamus)
Actaea pachypoda (white baneberry)
Allium canadense (wild garlic)
Allium cernuum (nodding onion)
Allium tricoccum (wild leek)
Anemone canadensis (Canada anemone, windflower)
Anemone cylindrica (thimbleweed, candle anemone)
Anemone virginiana (thimbleweed, tall anemone)
Apocynum androsaemifolium (spreading dogbane)
Aquilegia canadensis (columbine)
Arisaema triphyllum (Jack-in-the-pulpit, Indian turnip)
Aruncus dioicus (goat's beard)
Asarum canadense (wild ginger)
Asclepias incarnata (swamp milkweed)
Asclepias tuberosa (butterfly weed)
Asclepias verticillata (whorled milkweed)
Aster ericoides (heath aster, white wreath aster)
Aster laevis (smooth aster)
Aster pilosus (frost aster)
Aster puniceus (red-stem aster, swamp aster)
Astragalus canadensis (milk vetch, Canada milk vetch)
Baptisia alba (white false indigo)
Caltha palustris (marsh marigold, cowslip)
Camassia scilloides (wild hyacinth)
Campanula rotundifolia (harebell)
Caulophyllum thalictroides (blue cohosh)
Chelone glabra (turtlehead)
Claytonia virginica (narrow-leaved spring beauty)
Collinsonia canadensis (stoneroot, citronella horsebalm)
Coreopsis lanceolata (lance-leaved coreopsis)
Coreopsis palmata (stiff coreopsis)
Coreopsis tripteris (tall coreopsis)
Dalea candida (white prairie clover)
Dalea purpurea (purple prairie clover)
Delphinium tricorne (dwarf larkspur)
Desmodium canadense (Canada tick-trefoil, Canada tickclover)
Desmodium illinoense (Illinois tick-trefoil, Illinois tickclover)
Dicentra cucullaria (dutchman's breeches)
Dodecatheon meadia (shooting star)
Echinacea purpurea (purple coneflower)
Eryngium yuccifolium (rattlesnake master, button snake-root)
Erythronium americanum (eastern trout lily, yellow trout lily)
Eupatorium coelestinum (mist flower)
Eupatorium fistulosum (Joe-pye weed)
Eupatorium maculatum (spotted Joe-pye weed)
Eupatorium perfoliatum (boneset)
Eupatorium rugosum (white snakeroot)
Eupatorium purpureum (Joe-pye weed)

Euphorbia corollata (flowering spurge)
Fragaria virginiana (wild strawberry)
Galium triflorum (sweet-scented bedstraw)
Gentiana andrewsii (bottle gentian)
Gentiana saponaria (closed gentian, soapwort gentian)
Geranium maculatum (wild geranium, cranesbill)
Helenium autumnale (common sneezeweed)
Helianthus pauciflorus ssp. pauciflorus (stiff sunflower)
Helianthus divericatus (woodland sunflower)
Heliopsis helianthoides (ox-eye sunflower, false sunflower)
Hepatica nobilis var. acuta (sharp-lobed hepatica)
Heuchera americana var. hirsuticaulis (alumroot)
Heuchera richardsonii (alum root)
Hibiscus moscheutos (swamp rose mallow, marshmallow hibiscus)
Hieracium gronovii (hawkweed)
Houstonia caerulea (bluets)
Hydrastis canadensis (golden seal)
Hydrophyllum virginianum (Virginia waterleaf)
Hypoxis hirsuta (yellow star grass)
Iris cristata (dwarf crested iris)
Iris virginica v. shrevei (blue flag)
Lespedeza capitata (roundheaded bush clover)
Liatris aspera (rough blazing star, gayfeather)
Liatris cylindracea (dwarf blazing star, gayfeather)
Liatris spicata (marsh blazing star, gayfeather)
Liatris squarrosa (blazing star)
Lilium michiganense (Turk's cap lily, Michigan lily)
Linum virginianum (woodland flax)
Lithospermum canescens (hoary puccoon)
Lobelia cardinalis (cardinal flower)
Lobelia siphilitica (great blue lobelia)
Lupinus perennis (wild lupine)
Lysimachia ciliata (fringed loosestrife)
Maianthemum canadense (wild lily-of-the-valley, Canada mayflower)
Mertensia virginica (bluebells)
Mitchella repens (partridge berry)
Monarda fistulosa (wild bergamot, horsemint, beebalm)
Nuphar advena (yellow pond lily, cow lily, spatter dock)
Osmorhiza claytonii (sweet cicely, sweet jarvil)
Peltandra virginica (arrow arum)
Penstemon digitalis (beardtongue)
Penstemon hirsutus (hairy beardtongue)
Potentilla fruticosa (potentilla, shrubby cinquefoil)
Phlox divaricata (blue phlox, sweet William)
Phlox paniculata (summer phlox, perennial phlox)
Phlox pilosa (prairie phlox, downy phlox)
Physostegia virginiana (obedient plant, false dragonhead)
Podophyllum peltatum (May apple)
Polemonium reptans (Jacob's ladder, Greek valerian)
Polygonatum biflorum (Solomon's seal)
Potentilla arguta (white cinquefoil, prairie cinquefoil, tall cinquefoil)
Potentilla simplex (common cinquefoil)

Pycnanthemum tenuifolium (slender mountain mint)
Pycnanthemum virginianum (mountain mint)
Ranunculus hispidus (early buttercup, tufted buttercup)
Ratibida pinnata (gray-headed coneflower, yellow coneflower)
Rhexia virginica (meadow beauty)
Rudbeckia laciniata (cut-leaf coneflower)
Rudbeckia subtomentosa (sweet black-eyed Susan)
Ruellia humilis (wild petunia)
Salvia lyrata (cancer weed, lyre-leaf sage)
Sanguinaria candensis (bloodroot)
Sedum ternatum (wild stonecrop)
Senecio aureus (golden ragwort)
Smilacena racemosa (false Solomon's seal, false spikenard)
Smilacena stellata (starry Solomon's seal)
Silene stellata (starry campion)
Silene virginica (fire pink)
Silphium integrifolium (rosinweed)
Silphium laciniatum (compass plant)
Silphium perfoliatum (cup plant)
Silphium terebinthinaceum (prairie dock)
Sisyrinchium albidum (narrow-leaved blue-eyed grass)
Solidago caesia (blue-stemmed goldenrod, wreath goldenrod)
Solidago canadensis (meadow goldenrod)
Solidago juncea (early goldenrod, plume goldenrod)
Solidago nemoralis (gray goldenrod, old-field goldenrod)
Solidago rigida (stiff goldenrod)
Solidago rugosa (rough-leaved goldenrod)
Solidago speciosa (showy goldenrod)
Solidago ulmifolia (elm-leaved goldenrod)
Stylophorum diphyllum (celandine poppy)
Tephrosia virginiana (goat's rue)
Thalictrum dasycarpum (tall or purple meadow rue)
Thalictrum dioicum (early meadow rue)
Thalictrum thalictroides (rue anemone)
Tradescantia ohiensis (Ohio spiderwort)
Tradescantia virginiana (Virginia spiderwort, spider lily)
Uvularia grandiflora (bellwort, merrybells)
Uvularia sessilifolia (wildoats, merrybells)
Verbena hastata (blue verbena, blue vervain)
Verbena stricta (hoary vervain)
Vernonia fasciculata (ironweed)
Veronicastrum virginicum (Culver's root)
Viola pedata (bird-foot violet)
Viola pubescens (yellow violet)
Viola soraria (common blue violet, meadow violet)
Zizia aurea (golden alexander)

Grasses/Grass-like plants

Agrostis parennans (ticklegrass, fly-away grass)
Andropogon gerardii (big bluestem)
Andropogon virginicus (broom sedge)
Bouteloua curtipendula (sideoats grama)

Brachyelytrum erectum (long-awned wood grass)
Bromus kalmii (prairie brome, wild chess)
Calamagrostis canadensis (bluejoint grass)
Carex aquatilis (water sedge)
Carex Jamesii (grass sedge)
Carex pensylvanica (Pennsylvania sedge)
Carex plantaginea (plantain-leaved sedge)
Carex stipata (awl-fruited sedge)
Carex stricta (tussock sedge)
Carex utriculata (beaked sedge)
Chasmanthium latifolium (inland sea oats, wild oats, river oats, broad-leaf uniola)
Danthonia spicata (poverty grass)
Eleocharis palustris (creeping spikesedge, spike rush)
Elymus canadensis (Canada wild rye)
Elymus hystrix var. hystrix (bottlebrush grass)
Eragrostis spectabilis (purple lovegrass, tumblegrass)
Glyceria stricta (American mannagrass, tall mannagrass, reed meadowgrass)
Hierochloe odorata (sweet grass)
Juncus effusus var. solutus (soft rush)
Juncus interior (inland rush)
Koeleria macrantha (June grass)
Leersia oryzoides (rice cut grass)
Panicum virgatum (switchgrass)
Schizachyrium scoparium (little bluestem)
Scirpus acutus (hardstem bulrush)
Scirpus atrovirens (dark green bulrush)
Scirpus cyperinus (wool grass)
Scirpus validus (great bulrush)
Sorghastrum nutans (Indian grass)
Spartina pectinata (prairie cordgrass, freshwater cordgrass)
Sporobolus asper (dropseed)
Stipa spartea (porcupine grass)
Typha latifolia (cattail)

Shrubs (deciduous)

Alnus incana (speckled alder, mountain alder)
Alnus serrulata (smooth alder)
Amelanchier arborea (downy serviceberry, shadbush, Juneberry)
Amorpha canescens (leadplant)
Amorpha fruticosa (false indigo, Indigo bush)
Aronia melanocarpa (black chokeberry)
Ceanothus americanus (New Jersey tea, red root)
Cephalanthus occidentalis (buttonbush)
Comptonia peregrina (sweet fern)
Cornus alternifolia (pogoda dogwood, alternate-leaved dogwood)
Cornus amomum ssp. obliqua (swamp dogwood, silky dogwood)
Cornus drummondii (rough-leaf dogwood)
Cornus racemosa (gray dogwood)
Cornus sericea (red-twig dogwood, red-osier dogwood)
Corylus americana (American hazelnut or filbert)
Diervilla lonicera (bush honeysuckle)
Dirca palustris (leatherwood, ropebark)

Euonymus americana (strawberry bush, brook euonymus, hearts-a-bustin')
Euonymus atropurpurea (wahoo, burning bush)
Rhamnus caroliniana (Carolina buckthorn)
Hydrangea arborescens (wild hydrangea)
Hypericum hypericoides ssp. hypericoides (St. Andrew's cross)
Hypericum prolificum (shrubby St. John's wort)
Ilex verticillata (winterberry, black alder)
Lindera benzoin (spicebush)
Lonicera dioica (limber or wild honeysuckle)
Physocarpus opulifolius (ninebark)
Prunus virginiana (chokecherry)
Rhus copallinum (dwarf or winged sumac)
Rhus glabra (smooth sumac)
Rhus typhina (staghorn sumac)
Ribes cynosbati (prickly gooseberry, dogberry)
Rosa carolina (Carolina rose)
Rosa setigera (Illinois or prairie rose)
Rubus idaeus ssp. strigosus (red raspberry)
Rubus occidentalis (black raspberry, thimbleberry)
Salix bebbiana (Bebb willow, long-beaked willow)
Salix discolor (pussy willow)
Sambucus canadensis (elderberry, common elder)
Spiraea alba (meadow sweet)
Spiraea tomentosa (steeplebush, hardhack)
Staphylea trifolia (bladdernut)
Symphoricarpos orbiculatus (coralberry, Indian currant)
Vaccinium angustifolium (low-bush blueberry)
Viburnum acerifolium (maple leaf viburnum)
Viburnum lentago (black haw, nannyberry)
Viburnum prunifolium (black haw, nanny berry)
Viburnum rufidulum (southern or rusty black haw)

Trees (deciduous)

Acer negundo (box elder)
Acer rubrum (red maple)
Acer saccharinum (silver maple)
Acer saccharum (sugar maple)
Aesculus glabra (Ohio buckeye, horse chestnut)
Betula nigra (river birch)
Carpinus caroliniana (blue beech, hornbeam, musclewood)
Carya alba (mockernut hickory)
Carya cordiformis (bitternut, swamp hickory)
Carya illinoinensis (pecan)
Carya ovata (shagbark hickory)
Celtis laevigata (sugarberry, hackberry)
Celtis occidentalis (hackberry, sugarberry)
Cercis canadensis (redbud)
Cladrastis kentukea (yellowwood)
Cornus florida (flowering dogwood)
Crataegus crus-galli (cockspur hawthorn)
Crataegus mollis (downy hawthorn)
Crataegus phaenopyrum (Washington hawthorn)

Crataegus punctata (dotted hawthorn, white thorn)
Diospyros virginiana (persimmon)
Fagus grandifolia var. caroliniana (beech)
Fagus grandifolia var. grandifolia (beech)
Fraxinus americana (white ash)
Fraxinus pennsylvanica (green ash)
Gleditsia triacanthos (honey locust)
Gymnocladus dioica (Kentucky coffee tree)
Hamamelis virginiana (witch hazel)
Juglans nigra (black walnut)
Liquidambar styraciflua (sweet gum)
Liriodendron tulipifera (tulip tree)
Malus ioensis var. ioensis (prairie crabapple)
Nyssa sylvatica (black gum, tupelo)
Ostrya virginiana (ironwood, hophornbeam)
Platanus occidentalis (sycamore, plane-tree)
Populus deltoides (eastern cottonwood)
Populus grandidentata (large-toothed aspen)
Populus tremuloides (quaking aspen)
Prunus americana (wild plum)
Prunus nigra (Canada plum)
Prunus serotina (black cherry)
Quercus alba (white oak)
Quercus bicolor (swamp white oak)
Quercus coccinea (scarlet oak)
Quercus macrocarpa (bur oak)
Quercus marilandica (blackjack oak)
Quercus muhlenbergii (chinkapin oak, chestnut oak)
Quercus palustris (pin oak)
Quercus rubra (red oak)
Quercus shumardii (shumard oak)
Quercus stellata (post oak)
Quercus velutina (black oak)
Salix amygdaloides (peachleaf willow)
Salix nigra (black willow)
Sassafras albidum (sassafras)
Tilia americana (American linden, basswood)
Ulmus americana (American elm)
Ulmus rubra (red elm, slippery elm)

Trees (evergreen)

Juniperus virginiana (eastern red cedar)
Tsuga canadensis (eastern hemlock)

Vines (deciduous)

Campsis radicans (trumpet creeper, trumpet vine)
Celastrus scandens (American bittersweet)
Clematis virginiana (virgin's bower)
Parthenocissus quinquefolia (Virginia creeper)
Vitis riparia (riverbank grape)
Vitis vulpina (frost grape)
Vitis zestivalis (summer grape)

FEDERALLY LISTED ENDANGERED SPECIES

Mead's milkweed (Asclepias meadii)
Pitcher's thistle (Cirsium pitcheri)
Running buffalo clover (Trifolium stonloniferum)

INDIANA NOXIOUS SPECIES

Because the noxious weed lists have continually changed since we gathered them in 1994, we are not including them at this time. Not all States have noxious weed lists. Those that do, do not use the same standards of importance and are not comparable. States typically have included plants that interfere with agriculture (Canada thistle), or cause human health problems (poison ivy). Some States are now including a category of plants that invade and degrade the environment (purple loosestrife). Check with your State's Agriculture Department or Weed Scientist listed below. The noxious weed list can be used two ways on roadsides: l) check to not inadvertently plant these invasive plants, and 2) note the plants you are legally responsible to control. Many States now check adjacent State lists to avoid planting their neighbors' problem plants. Because weeds do not respect political boundaries, and because by their very nature weeds continue to adapt and expand, monitoring and controlling invasives at State borders is a wise part of vegetation management.

(Weed and Seed laws)

Department of Natural Resources
Division of Entomology & Plant
401 W. Washington Street, Rm. W290
Indianapolis, IN 46204

Thomas N. Jordan
Botany/Plant Pathology
Purdue University
West Lafayette, IN 47907
(317) 494-4629

INDIANA RESOURCES

Indiana Natural Heritage Data Center
Division of Nature Preserves
Department of Natural Resources
402 West Washington Street,
Room W267
Indianapolis, IN 46204
(317) 232-4052

The Nature Conservancy Field Office
1330 West 38th Street
Indianapolis, IN 46208
(317) 923-7547

Association for the Use of
Native Vegetation
871 Shawnee Avenue
Lafayette, IN 47905

Indiana Native Plant and
Wildflower Society
6106 Kingsley Dr.
Indianapolis, IN 46220

Hayes Regional Arboretum
801 Elks Road
Richmond, IN 47374

POTENTIAL NATURAL VEGETATION ZONES IN

IOWA

Source: A.W. Kuchler's Potential Natural Vegetation Map, 1964, Revised 1985.
Presented in U.S.G.S. National Atlas of the U.S. Series,
U.S. Geological Survey, Reston, VA.

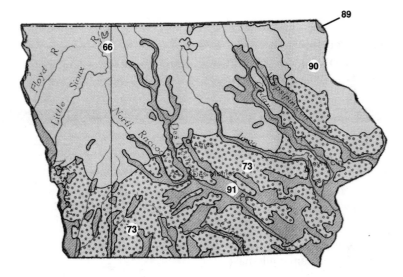

 66 Bluestem prairie
(Andropogon-Panicum-Sorghastrum)

73 Mosaic of numbers 66 and 91

89 Northern floodplain forest
(Populus-Salix-Ulmus)

 90 Maple-basswood forest
(Acer-Tilia)

91 Oak-hickory forest
(Quercus-Carya)

(Dominant plant species present in each vegetation type are listed in Appendix 8

66 *Bluestem Prairie (Andropogon-Panicum-Sorghastrum)*
73 *Mosaic of 66 (Bluestem Prairie) and 91 (Oak-Hickory Forest)*
89 *Northern Floodplain Forest (Populus Salix-Ulmus)*
90 *Maple-Basswood Forest (Acer-Tilia)*
91 *Oak-Hickory Forest (Quercus-Carya)*

Botanical Experts

John Pearson, Plant Ecologist
Iowa Department of Natural Resources
Wallace State Office Building
Des Moines, IA 50319-0034
(515) 281-3891
(515) 281-6794 (fax)

Recommended Flora

Eilers, L.J. and D.M. Roosa. 1994. The Vascular Plants of Iowa: An Annotated Checklist and Natural History. University of Iowa Press, Iowa City, IA. 304 pgs. + illus., maps. ISBN 0877454639; 0877454647 (paperback).

NATIVE PLANTS FOR LANDSCAPE USE IN IOWA

Cacti

Opuntia humifusa (prickly pear)
Opuntia macrorhiza (common prickly pear)

Ferns

Adiantum pedatum (northern maidenhair fern)
Asplenium platyneuron (ebony spleenwort)
Athyrium filix-femina (lady fern)
Botrychium virginianum (rattlesnake fern)
Cystopteris bulbifera (bladder fern)
Cystopteris fragilis (fragile fern)
Dryopteris carthusiana (shield fern, toothed wood fern, spinulose shield fern)
Dryopteris marginalis (marginal wood fern)
Gymnocarpium dryopteris (oak fern)
Matteuccia struthiopteris (ostrich fern)
Onoclea sensibilis (sensitive fern, bead fern)
Osmunda cinnamomea (cinnamon fern)
Osmunda claytoniana (interrupted fern)
Osmunda regalis (royal fern)
Phegopteris hexagonoptera (broad beech fern)
Polystichum acrostichoides (Christmas fern)
Woodsia ilvensis (rusty woodsia)

Forbs (annuals/biennials)

Campanulastrum americanum (American bellflower, tall bellflower)
Gentianopsis crinita (fringed gentian)
Senecio glabellus (butterweed)

Forbs (perennials)

Acorus calamus (sweet flag, calamus)
Actaea pachypoda (white baneberry)
Ageratina altissima var. altissima (white snakeroot)
Allium canadense (wild garlic)
Allium cernuum (nodding onion)
Allium stellatum (wild pink onion)
Allium tricoccum (wild leek)
Anemone canadensis (Canada anemone, windflower)
Anemone caroliniana (Carolina anemone, southern thimbleweed)
Anemone cylindrica (thimbleweed, candle anemone)
Anemone virginiana (thimbleweed, tall anemone)
Antennaria spp. (pussytoes, everlasting)
Apocynum androsaemifolium (spreading dogbane)
Aquilegia canadensis (columbine)
Arisaema triphyllum (Jack-in-the-pulpit, Indian turnip)
Artemisia ludoviciana (white sage, prairie sage, artemisia)
Aruncus dioicus (goat's beard)
Asarum canadense (wild ginger)
Asclepias incarnata (swamp milkweed)
Asclepias speciosa (showy milkweed)
Asclepias tuberosa (butterfly weed)
Asclepias verticillata (whorled milkweed)
Aster ericoides (heath aster, white wreath aster)
Aster laevis (smooth aster)
Aster novae-angliae (New England aster)
Aster oblongifolius (aromatic aster)
Aster oolentangiensis (sky blue aster)
Aster pilosus (frost aster)
Aster puniceus (red-stem aster, swamp aster)
Aster sericeus (silky aster)
Astragalus canadensis (milk vetch, Canada milk vetch)
Baptisia alba (white false indigo)
Baptisia alba var. macrophyllla (cream false indigo, plains wild indigo)
Baptisia australis (blue wild indigo)
Callirhoe involucrata (purple poppy mallow, winecup)
Caltha palustris (marsh marigold, cowslip)
Camassia scilloides (wild hyacinth)
Campanula rotundifolia (harebell)
Castilleja sessiliflora (downy painted cup)
Caulophyllum thalictroides (blue cohosh)
Chelone glabra (turtlehead)
Cimicifuga racemosa (bugbane, black cohosh)
Claytonia virginica (narrow-leaved spring beauty)
Coreopsis palmata (stiff coreopsis)
Coreopsis tripteris (tall coreopsis)
Cornus canadensis (bunchberry)
Corydalis sempervirens (pale corydalis)
Dalea candida (white prairie clover)
Dalea purpurea (purple prairie clover)
Delphinium carolinianum ssp. virescens (prairie larkspur)
Delphinium carolinianum (blue larkspur)

Delphinium tricorne (dwarf larkspur)
Desmodium canadense (Canada tick-trefoil, Canada tickclover)
Desmodium illinoense (Illinois tick-trefoil, Illinois tickclover)
Dicentra cucullaria (Dutchman's breeches)
Dodecatheon meadia (shooting star)
Echinacea angustifolia (narrow-leaved purple coneflower)
Echinacea purpurea (purple coneflower)
Epilobium angustifolium (fireweed, willow herb)
Eryngium yuccifolium (rattlesnake master, button snake-root)
Erythronium americanum (eastern trout lily, yellow trout lily)
Eupatorium maculatum (spotted Joe-pye weed)
Eupatorium perfoliatum (boneset)
Eupatorium purpureum (Joe-pye weed)
Euphorbia corollata (flowering spurge)
Euthamia graminifolia var. graminifolia (grass-leaved goldenrod)
Filipendula rubra (queen-of-the-prairie)
Fragaria virginiana (wild strawberry)
Galium triflorum (sweet-scented bedstraw)
Gaura coccinea (scarlet gaura)
Gentiana alba (cream gentian, yellow gentian)
Gentiana andrewsii (bottle gentian)
Geranium maculatum (wild geranium, cranesbill)
Geum triflorum (prairie smoke, purple avens)
Glycyrrhiza lepidota (wild licorice)
Hedyotis nigricans (bluets)
Helenium autumnale (common sneezeweed)
Helianthus annuus (common sunflower)
Helianthus maximiliani (Maximilian sunflower)
Helianthus pauciflorus ssp. pauciflorus (stiff sunflower)
Helianthus petiolaris (plains sunflower)
Helianthus strumosus (woodland sunflower)
Heliopsis helianthoides (ox-eye sunflower, false sunflower)
Hepatica nobilis var. acuta (sharp-lobed hepatica)
Heterotheca villosa var. villosa (golden aster)
Heuchera richardsonii (alum root)
Hieracium longipilum (hairy hawkweed)
Hydrastis canadensis (golden seal)
Hydrophyllum virginianum (Virginia waterleaf)
Hypericum ascyron (great St. John's wort)
Hypoxis hirsuta (yellow star grass)
Iris versicolor (blue flag)
Iris virginica v. shrevei (blue flag)
Lespedeza capitata (roundheaded bush clover)
Liatris aspera (rough blazing star, gayfeather)
Liatris cylindracea (dwarf blazing star, gayfeather)
Liatris punctata (dotted blazing star, gayfeather)
Liatris pycnostachya (prairie blazing star, gayfeather)
Liatris squarrosa (blazing star)
Lilium michiganense (Turk's cap lily, Michigan lily)
Lilium philadelphicum (wood lily)
Linnaea borealis (twinflower)
Lithospermum canescens (hoary puccoon)

Lithospermum caroliniense (hairy puccoon, hispid gromwell)
Lithospermum incisum (fringed puccoon, narrow-leaved puccoon)
Lobelia cardinalis (cardinal flower)
Lobelia siphilitica (great blue lobelia)
Lobelia spicata (pale lobelia)
Lupinus perennis (wild lupine)
Lysimachia ciliata (fringed loosestrife)
Maianthemum canadense (wild lily-of-the-valley, Canada mayflower)
Maianthemum racemosum ssp. racemosum (false Solomon's seal,
    false spikenard)
Maianthemum stellatum (starry Solomon's seal)
Mertensia virginica (bluebells)
Mitchella repens (partridge berry)
Monarda fistulosa (wild bergamot, horsemint, beebalm)
Nothocalais cuspidata (prairie dandelion)
Nuphar lutea (yellow pond lily, cow lily, spatter dock)
Oenothera rhombipetala (diamond-petal primrose, four-point evening primrose)
Oenothera speciosa (showy white evening primrose)
Osmorhiza claytoni (sweet cicely, sweet jarvil)
Peltandra virginica (arrow arum)
Penstemon albidus (white beardtongue)
Penstemon digitalis (beardtongue)
Penstemon grandiflorus (large-flowered penstemon)
Pentaphylloides floribunda (potentilla, shrubby cinquefoil)
Phlox divaricata ssp. laphamii (blue phlox, sweet william)
Phlox pilosa (prairie phlox, downy phlox)
Physostegia virginiana (obedient plant, false dragonhead)
Podophyllum peltatum (May apple)
Polemonium reptans (Jacob's ladder, Greek valerian)
Polygonatum biflorum (Solomon's seal)
Potentilla arguta (white cinquefoil, prairie cinquefoil, tall cinquefoil)
Potentilla simplex (common cinquefoil)
Pulsatilla patens ssp. multifida (pasque flower, wild crocus)
Pycnanthemum tenuifolium (slender mountain mint)
Pycnanthemum virginianum (mountain mint)
Pyrola elliptica (shinleaf)
Ranunculus hispidus (early buttercup, tufted buttercup)
Ratibida columnifera (prairie coneflower, long-headed coneflower, Mexican hat)
Ratibida pinnata (gray-headed coneflower, yellow coneflower)
Rhexia virginica (meadow beauty)
Rudbeckia hirta (black-eyed Susan)
Rudbeckia laciniata (cut-leaf coneflower)
Rudbeckia subtomentosa (sweet black-eyed Susan)
Ruellia humilis (wild petunia)
Sabatia campestris (prairie rose gentian, prairie sabatia, meadow pink)
Salvia azurea var. grandiflora (blue sage)
Sanguinaria candensis (bloodroot)
Sedum ternatum (wild stonecrop)
Senecio aureus (golden ragwort)
Senecio plattensis (prairie ragwort, prairie groundsel)
Sibbaldiopsis tridentata (three-toothed cinquefoil)
Silene stellata (starry campion)

Silphium integrifolium (rosinweed)
Silphium laciniatum (compass plant)
Silphium perfoliatum (cup plant)
Silphium terebinthinaceum (prairie dock)
Sisyrinchium angustifolium (narrow-leaved blue-eyed grass)
Sisyrinchium campestre (white-eyed grass, prairie blue-eyed grass)
Solidago canadensis (meadow goldenrod)
Solidago missouriensis (Missouri goldenrod, prairie goldenrod)
Solidago nemoralis (gray goldenrod, old-field goldenrod)
Solidago rigida (stiff goldenrod)
Solidago speciosa (showy goldenrod)
Solidago ulmifolia (elm-leaved goldenrod)
Sphaeralcea coccinea (scarlet globe mallow)
Streptopus roseus (rosy twisted stalk)
Tephrosia virginiana (goat's rue)
Thalictrum dasycarpum (tall or purple meadow rue)
Thalictrum dioicum (early meadow rue)
Thalictrum thalictroides (rue anemone)
Tradescantia ohiensis (Ohio spiderwort)
Trillium cernuum (nodding trillium)
Uvularia grandiflora (bellwort, merrybells)
Uvularia sessilifolia (wildoats, merrybells)
Verbena hastata (blue verbena, blue vervain)
Verbena stricta (hoary vervain)
Vernonia baldwinii (ironweed, western ironweed)
Vernonia fasciculata (ironweed)
Veronicastrum virginicum (Culver's root)
Viola canadensis (Canada violet)
Viola missouriensis (Missouri violet)
Viola pedata (bird-foot violet)
Viola pedatifida (prairie violet)
Viola pubescens (downy or smooth yellow violet)
Viola soraria (common blue violet, meadow violet)
Yucca glauca (yucca, soapweed)
Zizia aptera (heart-leaved golden alexanders)
Zizia aurea (golden alexanders)

Grasses/Grass-like plants

Agrostis scabra (ticklegrass, fly-away grass)
Andropogon gerardii (big bluestem)
Andropogon hallii (sand bluestem)
Andropogon virginicus (broom sedge)
Aristida purpurea var. longiseta (red three awn)
Bouteloua curtipendula (sideoats grama)
Bouteloua gracilis (blue grama)
Bouteloua hirsuta (hairy grama)
Bromus kalmii (prairie brome, wild chess)
Buchloe dactyloides (buffalograss)
Calamagrostis canadensis (bluejoint grass)
Calamovilfa longifolia (sandreed grass, prairie sandreed)
Carex aquatilis (water sedge)
Carex pensylvanica (Pennsylvania sedge)

Carex plantaginea (plantain-leaved sedge)
Carex stipata (awl-fruited sedge)
Carex stricta (tussock sedge)
Danthonia spicata (poverty grass)
Distichlis spicata (seashore saltgrass)
Eleocharis palustris (creeping spikesedge, spike rush)
Elymus canadensis (Canada wild rye)
Elymus hystrix var. hystrix (bottlebrush grass)
Eragrostis spectabilis (purple lovegrass, tumblegrass)
Glyceria grandis (American mannagrass, tall mannagrass, reed meadowgrass)
Hierochloe odorata (sweet grass)
Juncus effusus var. solutus (soft rush)
Juncus interior (inland rush)
Koeleria macrantha (June grass)
Leersia oryzoides (rice cut grass)
Melica nitens (three-flower melic grass)
Panicum virgatum (switchgrass)
Pascopyrum smithii (western wheatgrass)
Schizachyrium scoparium (little bluestem)
Scirpus acutus (hardstem bulrush)
Scirpus atrovirens (dark green bulrush)
Scirpus cyperinus (wool grass)
Scirpus maritimus (alkali bulrush, prairie bulrush, bayonet grass)
Scirpus tabernaemontani (great bulrush)
Sorghastrum nutans (Indian grass)
Spartina pectinata (prairie cordgrass, freshwater cordgrass)
Sporobolus compositus var. compositus (tall dropseed)
Sporobolus cryptandrus (sand dropseed)
Sporobolus heterolepis (northern prairie dropseed)
Stipa comata (needle-and-thread grass)
Stipa spartea (porcupine grass)
Tripsacum dactyloides (eastern gama grass)
Typha latifolia (cattail)

Shrubs (deciduous)

Alnus incana (speckled alder, mountain alder)
Amelanchier alnifolia (saskatoon, western serviceberry, Juneberry)
Amelanchier arborea (downy serviceberry, shadbush, Juneberry)
Amorpha canescens (leadplant)
Amorpha fruticosa (false indigo, indigo bush)
Amorpha nana (dwarf wild indigo)
Aronia melanocarpa (black chokeberry)
Ceanothus americanus (New Jersey tea, red root)
Cephalanthus occidentalis (buttonbush)
Cornus alternifolia (pogoda dogwood, alternate-leaved dogwood)
Cornus amomum ssp. obliqua (swamp dogwood, silky dogwood)
Cornus drummondii (rough-leaf dogwood)
Cornus racemosa (gray dogwood)
Cornus sericea (red-twig dogwood, red-osier dogwood)
Corylus americana (American hazelnut or filbert)
Corylus cornuta (beaked hazelnut or filbert)
Diervilla lonicera (bush honeysuckle)

Dirca palustris (leatherwood, ropebark)
Euonymus atropurpurea (wahoo, burning bush)
Hypericum prolificum (shrubby St. John's wort)
Ilex verticillata (winterberry, black alder)
Lonicera dioica (limber or wild honeysuckle)
Physocarpus opulifolius (ninebark)
Prunus pumila var. besseyi (sand cherry)
Prunus virginiana (chokecherry)
Rhus aromatica (fragrant sumac)
Rhus glabra (smooth sumac)
Rhus hirta (staghorn sumac)
Ribes cynosbati (prickly gooseberry, dogberry)
Ribes odoratum (buffalo currant, golden currant)
Rosa arkansana (prairie rose)
Rosa blanda (early wild rose, smooth rose)
Rosa carolina (Carolina rose)
Rosa setigera (Illinois or prairie rose)
Rubus idaeus ssp. strigosus (red raspberry)
Rubus occidentalis (black raspberry, thimbleberry)
Salix bebbiana (Bebb willow, long-beaked willow)
Salix discolor (pussy willow)
Sambucus canadensis (elderberry, common elder)
Sambucus racemosa var. pubens (scarlet elderberry, red-berried elder)
Shepherdia argentea (silver buffaloberry)
Spiraea alba (meadow sweet)
Staphylea trifolia (bladdernut)
Symphoricarpos albus (snowberry)
Symphoricarpos orbiculatus (coralberry, Indian currant)
Vaccinium angustifolium (low-bush blueberry)
Viburnum lentago (black haw, nannyberry)

Shrubs (evergreen)

Juniperus communis (common juniper)
Juniperus horizontalis (creeping juniper, creeping savin)
Taxus canadensis (Canada yew)

Trees (deciduous)

Acer negundo (box elder)
Acer saccharinum (silver maple)
Acer saccharum (sugar maple)
Acer spicatum (mountain maple)
Aesculus glabra (Ohio buckeye, horse chestnut)
Betula nigra (river birch)
Betula papyrifera (paper birch)
Carpinus caroliniana (blue beech, hornbeam, musclewood)
Carya alba (mockernut hickory)
Carya cordiformis (bitternut, swamp hickory)
Carya illinoinensis (pecan)
Carya ovata (shagbark hickory)
Celtis occidentalis (hackberry, sugarberry)
Cercis canadensis (redbud)
Crataegus crus-galli (cockspur hawthorn)

Crataegus mollis (downy hawthorn)
Crataegus punctata (dotted hawthorn, white thorn)
Diospyros virginiana (persimmon)
Fraxinus americana (white ash)
Fraxinus pensylvanica (green ash)
Gleditsia triacanthos (honey locust)
Gymnocladus dioica (Kentucky coffee tree)
Hamamelis virginiana (witch hazel)
Juglans cinerea (butternut, white walnut)
Juglans nigra (black walnut)
Malus ioensis var. ioensis (prairie crabapple)
Ostrya virginiana (ironwood, hophornbeam)
Platanus occidentalis (sycamore, plane-tree)
Populus deltoides (eastern cottonwood)
Populus grandidentata (large-toothed aspen)
Populus tremuloides (quaking aspen)
Prunus americana (wild plum)
Prunus mexicana (Mexican plum)
Prunus nigra (Canada plum)
Prunus pensylvanica (fire or pin cherry)
Prunus serotina (black cherry)
Ptelea trifoliata (wafer ash, common hoptree)
Quercus alba (white oak)
Quercus bicolor (swamp white oak)
Quercus macrocarpa (bur oak)
Quercus marilandica (blackjack oak)
Quercus muhlenbergii (chinkapin oak, chestnut oak)
Quercus palustris (pin oak)
Quercus rubra (red oak)
Quercus stellata (post oak)
Quercus velutina (black oak)
Salix amygdaloides (peachleaf willow)
Salix nigra (black willow)
Tilia americana (American linden, basswood)
Ulmus americana (American elm)
Ulmus rubra (red elm, slippery elm)

Trees (evergreen)

Abies balsamea (balsam fir)
Juniperus virginiana (eastern red cedar)
Pinus strobus (eastern white pine)

Vines (deciduous)

Celastrus scandens (American bittersweet)
Clematis occidentalis var. occidentalis (purple clematis)
Clematis pitcheri (leather flower, purple clematis)
Clematis virginiana (virgin's bower)
Parthenocissus quinquefolia var. quinquefolia (woodbine)
Parthenocissus quinquefolia (Virginia creeper)
Vitis riparia (riverbank grape)

FEDERALLY LISTED ENDANGERED SPECIES

Eastern prairie fringed orchid (Platanthera leucophaea)
Mead's milkweed (Asclepias meadii)
Northern wild monkshood (Aconitum noveboracense)
Prairie bush-clover (Lespedeza leptostachya)
Western prairie fringed orchid (Platanthera praeclara)

IOWA NOXIOUS SPECIES

Because the noxious weed lists have continually changed since we gathered them in 1994, we are not including them at this time. Not all States have noxious weed lists. Those that do, do not use the same standards of importance and are not comparable. States typically have included plants that interfere with agriculture (Canada thistle), or cause human health problems (poison ivy). Some States are now including a category of plants that invade and degrade the environment (purple loosestrife). Check with your State's Agriculture Department or Weed Scientist listed below. The noxious weed list can be used two ways on roadsides: l) check to not inadvertantly plant these invasive plants, and 2) note the plants you are legally responsible to control. Many States now check adjacent State lists to avoid planting their neighbors' problem plants. Because weeds do not respect political boundaries, and because by their very nature weeds continue to adapt and expand, monitoring and controlling invasives at State borders is a wise part of vegetation management.

(Weed Only)

Department of Agriculture
Entomology/Seed Bureau
Wallace Building E. 9th
Des Moines, IA 50319

Robert Hartzler
2104 Agronomy Hall
Iowa State University
Ames, IA 50011
(515) 294-1923

IOWA RESOURCES

Iowa Natural Areas Inventory
Department of Natural Resources
Wallace State Office Building
Des Moines, IA 50319
(515) 281-8524

The Nature Conservancy Field Office
431 East Locust Street, Ste. 200
Des Moines, IA 50309
(515) 244-5044

Des Moines Botanical Center
909 East River Drive
Des Moines, IA 50316

Kirk Henderson
Daryl Smith
Tallgrass Native Vegetation Center
University of Northern Iowa
Cedar Falls, IA 50614
(319) 273-2813

POTENTIAL NATURAL VEGETATION ZONES IN
KANSAS

Source: A.W. Kuchler's Potential Natural Vegetation Map, 1964, Revised 1985.
Presented in U.S.G.S. National Atlas of the U.S. Series,
U.S. Geological Survey, Reston, VA.

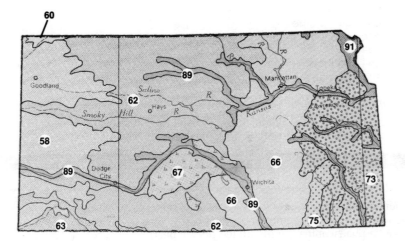

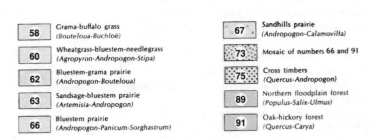

58	Grama-buffalo grass *(Bouteloua-Buchloë)*
60	Wheatgrass-bluestem-needlegrass *(Agropyron-Andropogon-Stipa)*
62	Bluestem-grama prairie *(Andropogon-Bouteloua)*
63	Sandsage-bluestem prairie *(Artemisia-Andropogon)*
66	Bluestem prairie *(Andropogon-Panicum-Sorghastrum)*
67	Sandhills prairie *(Andropogon-Calamovilfa)*
73	Mosaic of numbers 66 and 91
75	Cross timbers *(Quercus-Andropogon)*
89	Northern floodplain forest *(Populus-Salix-Ulmus)*
91	Oak-hickory forest *(Quercus-Carya)*

VEGETATION REFERENCES

(Dominant plant species present in each vegetation type are listed in Appendix 8)

58 *Grama-Buffalo Grass (Bouteloua-Buchloë)*
60 *Wheatgrass-Bluestem-Needlegrass (Agropyron-Andropogon-Stipa)*
62 *Bluestem-Grama Prairie (Andropogon-Bouteloua)*
63 *Sandsage-Bluestem Prairie (Artemisia-Andropogon)*
66 *Bluestem Prairie (Andropogon-Panicum-Sorghastrum)*
67 *Sandhills Prairie (Andropogon-Calamovilfa)*
73 *Mosaic of 66 (Bluestem Prairie) and 91 (Oak-Hickory Forest)*
75 *Cross Timbers (Quercus-Andropogon)*
89 *Northern Floodplain Forest (Populus-Salix-Ulmus)*
91 *Oak-Hickory Forest (Quercus-Carya)*

Botanical Experts

Craig C. Freeman, Associate Curator
R.L. McGregor Herbarium
2045 Constant Avenue
Lawrence, KS 66047-3729
(913) 864-3453
(913) 864-5093 (fax)
internet: c-freeman@ukans.edu

Recommended Flora

Great Plains Flora Association. 1986. Flora of the Great Plains. University Press of Kansas. Lawrence, KS 66045. 1392 pgs. ISBN 0 7006 0295 X.

NATIVE PLANTS FOR LANDSCAPE USE IN KANSAS

Cacti

Opuntia humifosa
Opuntia macrorhiza (common prickly pear)
Opuntia phaeacantha (purple-fruited prickly pear)
Opuntia imbricata (tree cholla, walkingstick cholla)

Ferns

Botrychium virginianum (rattlesnake fern)
Cheilanthes feei (lip fern)
Cystopteris fragilis (fragile fern)
Onoclea sensibilis (sensitive fern)
Phegopteris hexagonoptera (broad beech fern)
Polystichum acrostichoides (Christmas fern)
Thelypteris palustris var. pubescens (marsh fern)

Forbs (annuals/biennials)

Aphanostephus skirrhobasis (lazy daisy)
Campanulastrum americanum (American bellflower, tall bellflower)
Centaurea americana (basket flower)
Cleome serrulata (Rocky Mountain beeplant)
Coreopsis tinctoria (tickseed, goldenwave, plains coreopsis, calliopsis)
Eryngium leavenworthii (Leavenworth eryngo)

Euphorbia marginata (snow-on-the-mountain)
Eustoma russellianum (prairie or catchfly gentian, Texas bluebell)
Gaillardia pulchella (Indian blanket, firewheel)
Glandularia canadensis (rose vervain, sweet William)
Helianthus annuus (common sunflower)
Helianthus petiolaris (plains sunflower)
Ipomopsis longiflora (white-flowered gilia)
Linum rigidum (yellow flax)
Lobelia spicata (pale lobelia)
Machaeranthera tanacetifolia (tahoka daisy, tansy aster)
Monarda citriodora (horsemint, lemon beebalm, lemon mint)
Oenothera albicaulis (pale evening primrose)
Oenothera biennis (common evening primrose)
Oenothera elata ssp. hookeri (giant evening primrose)
Oenothera rhombipetala (diamond-petal primrose, four-point evening primrose)
Pectis angustifolia (limoncillo, fetid marigold)
Rudbeckia hirta (black-eyed Susan)
Sabatia campestris (prairie rose gentian, prairie sabatia, meadow pink)
Sedum nuttallianum (yellow stonecrop)
Senecio glabellus (butterweed)
Senecio plattensis (prairie ragwort, prairie groundsel)
Thelesperma filifolium var. filifolium (thelesperma, greenthread)
Townsendia exscapa (Easter daisy)

Forbs (perennials)

Abronia fragrans (sweet sand verbena)
Ageratina altissima var. altissima (white snakeroot)
Allium canadense (wild garlic)
Allium stellatum (wild pink onion)
Amsonia tabernaemontana (blue star)
Anemone canadensis (Canada anemone, windflower)
Anemone caroliniana (Carolina anemone, southern thimbleweed)
Anemone virginiana (thimbleweed, tall anemone)
Antennaria spp. (pussytoes, everlasting)
Aquilegia canadensis (columbine)
Arisaema triphyllum (Jack-in-the-pulpit, Indian turnip)
Artemisia ludoviciana (white sage, prairie sage, artemisia)
Asclepias asperula (antelope horns)
Asclepias incarnata (swamp milkweed)
Asclepias speciosa (showy milkweed)
Asclepias tuberosa (butterfly weed)
Asclepias verticillata (whorled milkweed)
Aster ericoides (heath aster, white wreath aster)
Aster novae-angliae (New England aster)
Aster oblongifolius (aromatic aster)
Aster oolentangiensis (sky blue aster)
Aster pilosus (frost aster)
Aster sericeus (silky aster)
Astragalus canadensis (milk vetch, Canada milk vetch)
Baptisia alba (white false indigo)
Baptisia alba var. macrophyllla (cream false indigo, plains wild indigo)
Baptisia australis (blue wild indigo)

Berlandiera lyrata (green eyes, chocolate flower)
Boltonia asteroides
Callirhoe digitata (finger poppy mallow)
Callirhoe involucrata (purple poppy mallow, winecup)
Calylophus berlandieri (square-bud primrose, sundrops)
Camassia scilloides (wild hyacinth)
Castilleja sessiliflora (downy painted cup)
Coreopsis grandiflora (coreopsis)
Coreopsis lanceolata (lance-leaved coreopsis)
Coreopsis palmata (stiff coreopsis)
Coreopsis tripteris (tall coreopsis)
Dalea candida (white prairie clover)
Dalea purpurea (purple prairie clover)
Delphinium carolinianum ssp. virescens (prairie larkspur)
Delphinium tricorne (dwarf larkspur)
Desmodium canadense (Canada tick-trefoil, Canada tickclover)
Desmodium illinoense (Illinois tick-trefoil, Illinois tickclover)
Dicentra cucullaria (Dutchman's breeches)
Dodecatheon meadia (shooting star)
Echinacea angustifolia (narrow-leaved purple coneflower)
Echinacea purpurea (purple coneflower)
Engelmannia pinnatifida (Engelmann daisy)
Eryngium yuccifolium (rattlesnake master, button snake-root)
Erythronium americanum (eastern trout lily, yellow trout lily)
Eupatorium coelestinum (mist flower)
Eupatorium maculatum (spotted Joe-pye weed)
Eupatorium perfoliatum (boneset)
Eupatorium purpureum (Joe-pye weed)
Euphorbia corollata (flowering spurge)
Euthamia gymnospermoides (grass-leaved goldenrod)
Fragaria virginiana (wild strawberry)
Gaillardia aristata (blanket flower, gaillardia, brown-eyed Susan)
Galium triflorum (sweet-scented bedstraw)
Gaura coccinea (scarlet gaura)
Gentiana alba (cream gentian, yellow gentian)
Geranium maculatum (wild geranium, cranesbill)
Glandularia bipinnatifida var. bipinnatifida (prairie verbena, Dakota vervain)
Glycyrrhiza lepidota (wild licorice)
Gutierrezia sarothrae (broom snakeweed, matchbrush)
Hedyotis nigricans (bluets)
Helenium autumnale (common sneezeweed)
Helianthus maximiliani (Maximilian sunflower)
Helianthus strumosus (woodland sunflower)
Heliopsis helianthoides (ox-eye sunflower, false sunflower)
Heterotheca villosa var. villosa (golden aster)
Heuchera richardsonii (alum root)
Hieracium longipilum (hairy hawkweed)
Hydrophyllum virginianum (Virginia waterleaf)
Hypoxis hirsuta (yellow star grass)
Ipomoea leptophylla (bush morning glory)
Iris virginica v. shrevei (blue flag)
Lespedeza capitata (roundheaded bush clover)

Lesquerella fendleri (bladderpod)
Liatris aspera (rough blazing star, gayfeather)
Liatris mucronata (narrow-leaf gayfeather)
Liatris punctata (dotted blazing star, gayfeather)
Liatris pycnostachya (prairie blazing star, gayfeather)
Liatris squarrosa (blazing star)
Lilium michiganense (Turk's cap lily, Michigan lily)
Linum lewisii (wild blue flax)
Lithospermum canescens (hoary puccoon)
Lithospermum caroliniense (hairy puccoon, hispid gromwell)
Lithospermum incisum (fringed puccoon, narrow-leaved puccoon)
Lobelia cardinalis (cardinal flower)
Lobelia siphilitica (great blue lobelia)
Lysimachia ciliata (fringed loosestrife)
Maianthemum stellatum (starry Solomon's seal)
Melampodium leucanthum (Blackfoot daisy, rock daisy)
Mimosa quadrivalvis var. angustata (catclaw sensitive briar)
Monarda fistulosa (wild bergamot, horsemint, beebalm)
Nuphar lutea (yellow pond lily, cow lily, spatter dock)
Oenothera brachycarpa (evening primrose)
Oenothera macrocarpa (Missouri evening primrose)
Oenothera speciosa (showy white evening primrose)
Osmorhiza claytoni (sweet cicely, sweet jarvil)
Penstemon albidus (white beardtongue)
Penstemon ambiguus (sand penstemon)
Penstemon cobaea (cobaea penstemon, wild foxglove)
Penstemon digitalis (beardtongue)
Penstemon grandiflorus (large-flowered penstemon)
Phlox divaricata ssp. laphamii (blue phlox, sweet William)
Phlox paniculata (summer phlox, perennial phlox)
Phlox pilosa (prairie phlox, downy phlox)
Physostegia virginiana (obedient plant, false dragonhead)
Podophyllum peltatum (May apple)
Polygonatum biflorum (Solomon's seal)
Potentilla arguta (white cinquefoil, prairie cinquefoil, tall cinquefoil)
Potentilla simplex (common cinquefoil)
Pycnanthemum tenuifolium (slender mountain mint)
Pycnanthemum virginianum (mountain mint)
Ranunculus hispidus (early buttercup, tufted buttercup)
Ratibida columnifera (prairie coneflower, long-headed coneflower, Mexican hat)
Ratibida pinnata (gray-headed coneflower, yellow coneflower)
Rudbeckia grandiflora (large coneflower)
Rudbeckia laciniata (cut-leaf coneflower)
Rudbeckia subtomentosa (sweet black-eyed Susan)
Ruellia humilis (wild petunia)
Salvia azurea var. grandiflora (blue sage)
Silene virginica (fire pink)
Silphium integrifolium (rosinweed)
Silphium laciniatum (compass plant)
Silphium perfoliatum (cup plant)
Sisyrinchium angustifolium (narrow-leaved blue-eyed grass)
Sisyrinchium campestre (white-eyed grass, prairie blue-eyed grass)

Solidago canadensis (meadow goldenrod)
Solidago missouriensis (Missouri goldenrod, prairie goldenrod)
Solidago nemoralis (gray goldenrod, old-field goldenrod)
Solidago rigida (stiff goldenrod)
Solidago speciosa (showy goldenrod)
Solidago ulmifolia (elm-leaved goldenrod)
Tephrosia virginiana (goat's rue)
Tetraneuris acaulis var. acaulis (stemless goldflower, stemless rubber weed, butte marigold)
Tetraneuris scaposa var. scaposa (four-nerve daisy, yellow daisy, Bitterweed)
Thalictrum dasycarpum (tall or purple meadow rue)
Thalictrum thalictroides (rue anemone)
Tradescantia ohiensis (Ohio spiderwort)
Uvularia grandiflora (bellwort, merrybells)
Verbena hastata (blue verbena, blue vervain)
Verbena stricta (hoary vervain)
Vernonia baldwinii (ironweed, western ironweed)
Vernonia fasciculata (ironweed)
Viola missouriensis (Missouri violet)
Viola pedatifida (prairie violet)
Viola pubescens (downy or smooth yellow violet)
Viola sovaria (common blue violet, meadow violet)
Yucca glauca (yucca, soapweed)
Zinnia grandiflora (Rocky Mountain zinnia, yellow zinnia, plains zinnia)
Zizia aurea (golden alexanders)

Grasses/Grass-like plants

Agrostis scabra (ticklegrass, fly-away grass)
Andropogon gerardii (big bluestem)
Andropogon hallii (sand bluestem)
Aristida purpurea (purple three awn)
Bouteloua gracilis (blue grama)
Bouteloua hirsuta (hairy grama)
Buchloe dactyloides (buffalograss)
Calamagrostis canadensis (bluejoint grass)
Calamovilfa longifolia (sandreed grass, prairie sandreed)
Carex aquatilis (water sedge)
Carex emoryi (Emory's sedge)
Carex stricta (tussock sedge)
Chasmanthium latifolium (inland sea oats, wild oats, river oats, broad-leaf uniola)
Danthonia spicata (poverty grass)
Distichlis spicata (seashore saltgrass)
Eleocharis palustris (creeping spikesedge, spike rush)
Elymus canadensis (Canada wild rye)
Elymus hystrix var. hystrix (bottlebrush grass)
Eragrostis intermedia (plains lovegrass)
Eragrostis spectabilis (purple lovegrass, tumblegrass)
Juncus effusus var. solutus (soft rush)
Juncus interior (inland rush)
Krascheninnikovia lanata (winterfat)
Koeleria macrantha (June grass)
Leersia oryzoides (rice cut grass)

Muhlenbergia capillaris (gulf muhly, hair grass)
Oryzopsis hymenoides (Indian ricegrass)
Panicum obtusum (vine mesquite)
Panicum virgatum (switchgrass)
Pascopyrum smithii (western wheatgrass)
Poa arachnifera (Texas bluegrass)
Schizachyrium scoparium (little bluestem)
Scirpus acutus (hardstem bulrush)
Scirpus atrovirens (dark green bulrush)
Scirpus maritimus (alkali bulrush, prairie bulrush, bayonet grass)
Scirpus tabernaemontani (great bulrush)
Sorghastrum nutans (Indian grass)
Spartina pectinata (prairie cordgrass, freshwater cordgrass)
Sporobolus compositus var. compositus (tall dropseed)
Sporobolus cryptandrus (sand dropseed)
Sporobolus heterolepis (northern prairie dropseed)
Stipa comata (needle-and-thread grass)
Stipa spartea (porcupine grass)
Tripsacum dactyloides (eastern gama grass)
Typha latifolia (cattail)

Shrubs (deciduous)

Acacia angustissima (fern acacia, whiteball acacia)
Amelanchier arborea (downy serviceberry, shadbush, Juneberry)
Amorpha canescens (leadplant)
Amorpha fruticosa (false indigo, Indigo bush)
Atriplex canescens (four-wing saltbush, wingscale)
Ceanothus americanus (New Jersey tea, red root)
Cephalanthus occidentalis (buttonbush)
Cercocarpus montanus (mountain mahogany, silverleaf mountain mahogany)
Chrysothamnus nauseosus (rabbit brush, chamisa)
Cornus amomum ssp. obliqua (swamp dogwood, silky dogwood)
Cornus drummondii (rough-leaf dogwood)
Corylus americana (American hazelnut or filbert)
Euonymus atropurpurea (wahoo, burning bush)
Hydrangea arborescens (wild hydrangea)
Hypericum hypericoides ssp. hypericoides (St. Andrew's cross)
Lindera benzoin (spicebush)
Lonicera dioica (limber or wild honeysuckle)
Mimosa borealis (pink mimosa, fragrant mimosa)
Physocarpus opulifolius (ninebark)
Prosopis glandulosa (honey mesquite)
Prunus pumila var. besseyi (sand cherry)
Prunus virginiana (chokecherry)
Rhus aromatica (fragrant sumac)
Rhus glabra (smooth sumac)
Ribes odoratum (buffalo currant, golden currant)
Rosa arkansana (prairie rose)
Rosa blanda (early wild rose, smooth rose)
Rosa setigera (Illinois or prairie rose)
Rosa woodsii (western wild rose, woods rose)
Rubus occidentalis (black raspberry, thimbleberry)

Sambucus canadensis (elderberry, common elder)
Shepherdia argentea (silver buffaloberry)
Sideroxylon lanuginosum ssp. lanuginosum (chittamwood, gum elastic tree)
Staphylea trifolia (bladdernut)
Symphoricarpos orbiculatus (coralberry, Indian currant)
Viburnum prunifolium (black haw, nanny berry)

Trees (deciduous)

Acer negundo (box elder)
Acer saccharinum (silver maple)
Acer saccharum (sugar maple)
Aesculus glabra var. arguta (white buckeye, Texas buckeye)
Betula nigra (river birch)
Carya cordiformis (bitternut, swamp hickory)
Carya illinoinensis (pecan)
Carya ovata (shagbark hickory)
Carya texana (black hickory)
Celtis laevigata (sugarberry, hackberry)
Celtis laevigata var. reticulata (netleaf hackberry)
Celtis occidentalis (hackberry, sugarberry)
Cercis canadensis (redbud)
Crataegus mollis (downy hawthorn)
Fraxinus americana (white ash)
Fraxinus pennsylvanica (green ash)
Gleditsia triacanthos (honey locust)
Gymnocladus dioica (Kentucky coffee tree)
Juglans nigra (black walnut)
Malus ioensis var. ioensis (prairie crabapple)
Ostrya virginiana (ironwood, hophornbeam)
Platanus occidentalis (sycamore, plane-tree)
Populus deltoides (eastern cottonwood)
Prunus americana (wild plum)
Prunus angustifolia (chickasaw plum)
Prunus mexicana (Mexican plum)
Prunus serotina (black cherry)
Ptelea trifoliata (wafer ash, common hoptree)
Quercus alba (white oak)
Quercus macrocarpa (bur oak)
Quercus marilandica (blackjack oak)
Quercus muhlenbergii (chinkapin oak, chestnut oak)
Quercus palustris (pin oak)
Quercus rubra (red oak)
Quercus shumardii (shumard oak)
Quercus stellata (post oak)
Quercus velutina (black oak)
Salix amygdaloides (peachleaf willow)
Salix nigra (black willow)
Sapindus saponaria var. drummondii (soapberry)
Sassafras albidum (sassafras)
Tilia americana (American linden, basswood)
Ulmus americana (American elm)
Ulmus rubra (red elm, slippery elm)

Vines (deciduous)

Celastrus scandens (American bittersweet)
Clematis pitcheri (leather flower, purple clematis)
Clematis virginiana (virgin's bower)
Parthenocissus quinquefolia (Virginia creeper)
Vitis riparia (riverbank grape)

FEDERALLY LISTED ENDANGERED SPECIES

Mead's milkweed (Ascepias meadii)
Western prairie fringed orchid (Platanthera praeclara)

KANSAS NOXIOUS SPECIES

Because the noxious weed lists have continually changed since we gathered them in 1994, we are not including them at this time. Not all States have noxious weed lists. Those that do, do not use the same standards of importance and are not comparable. States typically have included plants that interfere with agriculture (Canada thistle), or cause human health problems (poison ivy). Some States are now including a category of plants that invade and degrade the environment (purple loosestrife). Check with your State's Agriculture Department or Weed Scientist listed below. The noxious weed list can be used two ways on roadsides: l) check to not inadvertently plant these invasive plants, and 2) note the plants you are legally responsible to control. Many States now check adjacent State lists to avoid planting their neighbors' problem plants. Because weeds do not respect political boundaries, and because by their very nature weeds continue to adapt and expand, monitoring and controlling invasives at State borders is a wise part of vegetation management.

(Weed and Seed Laws)

Department of Agriculture
Division of Plant Health
109 SW 9th Street
Topeka, KS 66612

Dallas E. Peterson, Agronomy
Kansas State University
Throckmorton Hall
Manhattan, KS 66506
(913) 532-5776

KANSAS RESOURCES

Kansas Biological Survey
2041 Constant Avenue
Lawrence, KS 66047
(785) 864-3453

The Nature Conservancy Field Office
820 S.E. Quincy, Ste. 301
Topeka, KS 66612
(785) 233-4400

Kansas Wildflower Society
R. L. McGregor Herbarium
2045 Constant Avenue
Lawrence, KS 66047

Save the Tallgrass Prairie, Inc.
4101 West 54th Terrace
Shawnee Missions, KS 66025

Cimarron National Grassland
242 East Highway 56
Elkhart, KS 67950

Tallgrass Prairie National Preserve
Route 1, Box 14
Strong City, KS 66869

POTENTIAL NATURAL VEGETATION ZONES IN
——KENTUCKY——

Source: A.W. Kuchler's Potential Natural Vegetation Map, 1964, Revised 1985.
Presented in U.S.G.S. National Atlas of the U.S. Series,
U.S. Geological Survey, Reston, VA.

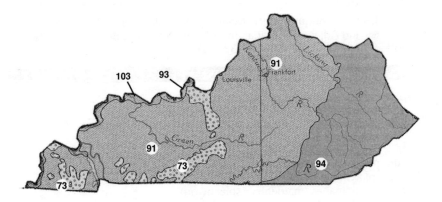

 73 Mosaic of numbers 66 and 91

 91 Oak-hickory forest
(Quercus-Carya)

 93 Beech-maple forest
(Fagus-Acer)

 94 Mixed mesophytic forest
(Acer-Aesculus-Fagus-Liriodendron-Quercus-Tilia)

 103 Southern floodplain forest
(Quercus-Nyassa-Taxodium)

VEGETATION REFERENCES

(Dominant plant species present in each vegetation type are listed in Appendix 8)

73 Mosaic of 66 (Bluestem Prairie) and 91 (Oak-Hickory Forest)
91 Oak-Hickory Forest (Quercus-Carya)
93 Beech-Maple Forest (Fagus-Acer)
94 Mixed Mesophytic Forest (Acer-Aesculus-Fagus-Liriodendron-Quercus-Tilia)
103 Southern Floodplain Forest (Quercus-Nyssa-Taxodium)

Botanical Experts

Deborah White, Senior Botanist
Kentucky State Nature Preserves Commission
801 Schenkel Lane
Frankfort, KY 40601-1403
(502) 573-2886
(502) 573-2355 (fax)

Recommended Flora

Gleason, H.A.; A. Cronquist. 1991. Manual of Vascular Plants of Northeastern United States and Adjacent Canada, 2nd Edition. New York Botanical Garden, New York. 910 pgs. + map. ISBN 0893273651.

NATIVE PLANTS FOR LANDSCAPE USE IN KENTUCKY

Cactus

Opuntia humifusa (prickly pear)

Ferns

Adiantum pedatum (northern maidenhair fern)
Asplenium platyneuron (ebony spleenwort)
Asplenium trichomanes (maidenhair spleenwort)
Athyrium filix-femina (lady fern)
Botrychium virginianum (rattlesnake fern)
Cystopteris bulbifera (bladder fern)
Cystopteris fragilis (fragile fern)
Dennstaedtia punctilobula (hay-scented fern)
Dryopteris carthusiana (shield fern, toothed wood fern, spinulose shield fern)
Dryopteris cristata (crested wood fern, buckler fern)
Dryopteris marginalis (marginal wood fern)
Onoclea sensibilis (sensitive fern, bead fern)
Osmunda cinnamomea (cinnamon fern)
Osmunda claytoniana (interrupted fern)
Osmunda regalis (royal fern)
Phegopteris hexagonoptera (broad beech fern)
Polystichum acrostichoides (Christmas fern)
Thelypteris palustris (marsh fern)
Thelypteris novaboracensis (New York fern, tapering fern)
Woodwardia areolata (netted chain fern)

Forbs (annuals/biennials)

Campanulastrum americanum (American bellflower, tall bellflower)

Glandularia canadensis (rose vervain, sweet William)
Lobelia spicata (pale lobelia)
Monarda citriodora (horsemint, lemon beebalm, lemon mint)
Oenothera biennis (common evening primrose)
Rudbeckia hirta (black-eyed Susan)
Senecio glabellus (butterweed)
Senecio plattensis (prairie ragwort, prairie groundsel)

Forbs (perennials)

Acorus calamus (sweet flag, calamus)
Actaea pachypoda (white baneberry)
Ageratina altissima var. altissima (white snakeroot)
Allium canadense (wild garlic)
Allium cernuum (nodding onion)
Allium tricoccum (wild leek)
Anemone caroliniana (Carolina anemone, southern thimbleweed)
Anemone virginiana (thimbleweed, tall anemone)
Antennaria spp. (pussytoes, everlasting)
Aquilegia canadensis (columbine)
Arisaema triphyllum (Jack-in-the-pulpit, Indian turnip)
Aruncus dioicus (goat's beard)
Asarum canadense (wild ginger)
Asclepias incarnata (swamp milkweed)
Asclepias tuberosa (butterfly weed)
Asclepias verticillata (whorled milkweed)
Aster divaricatus (white wood aster)
Aster dumosus (bushy aster)
Aster ericoides (heath aster, white wreath aster)
Aster laevis (smooth aster)
Aster oblongifolius (aromatic aster)
Aster oolentangiensis (sky blue aster)
Aster pilosus (frost aster)
Aster puniceus (red-stem aster, swamp aster)
Astragalus canadensis (milk vetch, Canada milk vetch)
Baptisia alba (white false indigo)
Baptisia alba var. macrophyllla (cream false indigo, plains wild indigo)
Camassia scilloides (wild hyacinth)
Campanula americana (tall bellflower)
Cardamine diphylla (two-leaved toothwort)
Caulophyllum thalictroides (blue cohosh)
Chelone glabra (turtlehead)
Chrysogonum virginianum (green-and-gold)
Chrysopsis mariana (Maryland golden aster)
Cimicifuga racemosa (bugbane, black cohosh)
Claytonia caroliniana (broad-leaved spring beauty)
Claytonia virginica (narrow-leaved spring beauty)
Collinsonia canadensis (stoneroot, citronella horsebalm)
Coreopsis auriculata (early coreopsis)
Coreopsis grandiflora (coreopsis)
Coreopsis lanceolata (lance-leaved coreopsis)
Coreopsis palmata (stiff coreopsis)
Coreopsis tripteris (tall coreopsis)

Coreopsis verticillata (whorled coreopsis)
Dalea candida (white prairie clover)
Dalea purpurea (purple prairie clover)
Delphinium tricorne (dwarf larkspur)
Desmodium canadense (Canada tick-trefoil, Canada tickclover)
Desmodium illinoense (Illinois tick-trefoil, Illinois tickclover)
Dicentra cucullaria (Dutchman's breeches)
Dodecatheon meadia (shooting star)
Echinacea purpurea (purple coneflower)
Epilobium angustifolium (fireweed, willow herb)
Eryngium yuccifolium (rattlesnake master, button snake-root)
Erythronium americanum (eastern trout lily, yellow trout lily)
Eupatorium coelestinum (mist flower)
Eupatorium fistulosum (Joe-pye weed)
Eupatorium maculatum (spotted Joe-pye weed)
Eupatorium perfoliatum (boneset)
Eupatorium purpureum (Joe-pye weed)
Euphorbia corollata (flowering spurge)
Euthamia graminifolia var. graminifolia (grass-leaved goldenrod)
Fragaria virginiana (wild strawberry)
Galium triflorum (sweet-scented bedstraw)
Gentiana andrewsii (bottle gentian)
Gentiana saponaria (closed gentian, soapwort gentian)
Geranium maculatum (wild geranium, cranesbill)
Glandularia bipinnatifida var. bipinnatifida (prairie verbena, Dakota vervain)
Hedyotis nigricans (bluets)
Helenium autumnale (common sneezeweed)
Helianthus pauciflorus ssp. pauciflorus (stiff sunflower)
Helianthus strumosus (woodland sunflower)
Heliopsis helianthoides (ox-eye sunflower, false sunflower)
Hepatica nobilis var. acuta (sharp-lobed hepatica)
Heterotheca villosa var. villosa (golden aster)
Heuchera americana var. hirsuticaulis (alumroot)
Hibiscus moscheutos (swamp rose mallow, marshmallow hibiscus)
Hieracium longipilum (hairy hawkweed)
Houstonia caerulea (bluets)
Houstonia longifolia var. longifolia (long-leaved bluets, pale bluets)
Hydrastis canadensis (golden seal)
Hymenocallis caroliniana (spider lily, rain lily)
Hypoxis hirsuta (yellow star grass)
Iris cristata (dwarf crested iris)
Iris virginica v. shrevei (blue flag)
Lespedeza capitata (roundheaded bush clover)
Liatris aspera (rough blazing star, gayfeather)
Liatris spicata (marsh blazing star, gayfeather)
Liatris squarrosa (blazing star)
Lilium canadense (wild yellow lily, Canada lily)
Lilium michiganense (Turk's cap lily, Michigan lily)
Linum virginianum (woodland flax)
Lithospermum canescens (hoary puccoon)
Lobelia cardinalis (cardinal flower)
Lobelia siphilitica (great blue lobelia)

Lysimachia ciliata (fringed loosestrife)
Maianthemum racemosum ssp. racemosum (false Solomon's seal,
   false spikenard)
Maianthemum stellatum (starry Solomon's seal)
Manfreda virginica (rattlesnake master, false aloe)
Mertensia virginica (bluebells)
Mitchella repens (partridge berry)
Monarda didyma (beebalm, oswego tea)
Monarda fistulosa (wild bergamot, horsemint, beebalm)
Nuphar lutea (yellow pond lily, cow lily, spatter dock)
Oenothera fruticosa (sundrops)
Osmorhiza claytoni (sweet cicely, sweet jarvil)
Pachysandra procumbens (Alleghany spurge)
Peltandra virginica (arrow arum)
Penstemon hirsutus (hairy beardtongue)
Phlox carolina (Carolina phlox)
Phlox divaricata (blue woodland phlox, sweet William)
Phlox divaricata ssp. laphamii (blue phlox, sweet William)
Phlox paniculata (summer phlox, perennial phlox)
Phlox pilosa (prairie phlox, downy phlox)
Phlox stolonifera (creeping phlox)
Physostegia intermedia (obedient plant)
Physostegia virginiana (obedient plant, false dragonhead)
Podophyllum peltatum (May apple)
Polemonium reptans (Jacob's ladder, Greek valerian)
Polygonatum biflorum (Solomon's seal)
Potentilla simplex (common cinquefoil)
Pycnanthemum tenuifolium (slender mountain mint)
Pycnanthemum virginianum (mountain mint)
Ranunculus hispidus (early buttercup, tufted buttercup)
Ratibida pinnata (gray-headed coneflower, yellow coneflower)
Rhexia virginica (meadow beauty)
Rudbeckia fulgida (black-eyed Susan, orange coneflower)
Rudbeckia grandiflora (large coneflower)
Rudbeckia laciniata (cut-leaf coneflower)
Rudbeckia subtomentosa (sweet black-eyed Susan)
Ruellia humilis (wild petunia)
Salvia azurea var. grandiflora (blue sage)
Sanguinaria candensis (bloodroot)
Sedum ternatum (wild stonecrop)
Senecio aureus (golden ragwort)
Silene stellata (starry campion)
Silene virginica (fire pink)
Silphium integrifolium (rosinweed)
Silphium perfoliatum (cup plant)
Silphium terebinthinaceum (prairie dock)
Sisyrinchium angustifolium (narrow-leaved blue-eyed grass)
Solidago caesia (blue-stemmed goldenrod, wreath goldenrod)
Solidago canadensis (meadow goldenrod)
Solidago juncea (early goldenrod, plume goldenrod)
Solidago missouriensis (Missouri goldenrod, prairie goldenrod)
Solidago nemoralis (gray goldenrod, old-field goldenrod)
Solidago odora (sweet goldenrod)

Solidago rigida (stiff goldenrod)
Solidago rugosa (rough-leaved goldenrod)
Solidago speciosa (showy goldenrod)
Solidago ulmifolia (elm-leaved goldenrod)
Spigelia marilandica (Indian pink)
Stylophorum diphyllum (celandine poppy)
Tephrosia virginiana (goat's rue)
Thalictrum dasycarpum (tall or purple meadow rue)
Thalictrum dioicum (early meadow rue)
Thalictrum pubescens (tall meadow rue)
Thalictrum thalictroides (rue anemone)
Tiarella cordifolia (foam flower)
Tradescantia ohiensis (Ohio spiderwort)
Tradescantia virginiana (Virginia spiderwort, spider lily)
Trientalis borealis ssp. borealis (starflower)
Trillium cernuum (nodding trillium)
Trillium erectum (wakerobin, purple trillium)
Uvularia grandiflora (bellwort, merrybells)
Uvularia sessilifolia (wildoats, merrybells)
Verbena hastata (blue verbena, blue vervain)
Verbena stricta (hoary vervain)
Vernonia baldwinii (ironweed, western ironweed)
Vernonia fasciculata (ironweed)
Veronicastrum virginicum (Culver's root)
Viola canadensis (Canada violet)
Viola conspersa (American dog violet)
Viola missouriensis (Missouri violet)
Viola pedata (bird-foot violet)
Viola pedatifida (prairie violet)
Viola pubescens (downy or smooth yellow violet)
Viola soraria (common blue violet, meadow violet)
Zizia aptera (heart-leaved golden alexanders)
Zizia aurea (golden alexanders)

Grasses/Grass-like plants

Agrostis scabra (ticklegrass, fly-away grass)
Andropogon gerardii (big bluestem)
Andropogon glomeratus (bushy bluestem)
Andropogon ternarius (splitbeard bluestem)
Andropogon virginicus (broom sedge)
Arundinaria gigantea (giant cane)
Bouteloua curtipendula (sideoats grama)
Calamagrostis canadensis (bluejoint grass)
Carex pensylvanica (Pennsylvania sedge)
Carex plantaginea (plantain-leaved sedge)
Carex stipata (awl-fruited sedge)
Carex stricta (tussock sedge)
Carex utriculata (beaked sedge)
Chasmanthium latifolium (inland sea oats, wild oats, river oats, broad-leaf uniola)
Danthonia spicata (poverty grass)
Eleocharis palustris (creeping spikesedge, spike rush)
Elymus hystrix var. hystrix (bottlebrush grass)

Eragrostis spectabilis (purple lovegrass, tumblegrass)
Glyceria grandis (American mannagrass, tall mannagrass, reed meadowgrass)
Juncus effusus var. solutus (soft rush)
Juncus interior (inland rush)
Leersia oryzoides (rice cut grass)
Melica nitens (three-flower melic grass)
Muhlenbergia capillaris (gulf muhly, hair grass)
Panicum virgatum (switchgrass)
Saccharum giganteum (sugarcane plume grass)
Schizachyrium scoparium (little bluestem)
Scirpus acutus (hardstem bulrush)
Scirpus atrovirens (dark green bulrush)
Scirpus cyperinus (wool grass)
Scirpus tabernaemontani (great bulrush)
Sorghastrum nutans (Indian grass)
Spartina pectinata (prairie cordgrass, freshwater cordgrass)
Sporobolus cryptandrus (sand dropseed)
Tripsacum dactyloides (eastern gama grass)
Typha latifolia (cattail)

Shrubs (deciduous)

Alnus serrulata (smooth alder)
Amelanchier arborea (downy serviceberry, shadbush, Juneberry)
Amorpha fruticosa (false indigo, Indigo bush)
Aronia melanocarpa (black chokeberry)
Castanea pumila (chinquapin)
Ceanothus americanus (New Jersey tea, red root)
Cephalanthus occidentalis (buttonbush)
Cornus alternifolia (pogoda dogwood, alternate-leaved dogwood)
Cornus amomum ssp. obliqua (swamp dogwood, silky dogwood)
Cornus drummondii (rough-leaf dogwood)
Cornus racemosa (gray dogwood)
Cornus sericea (red-twig dogwood, red-osier dogwood)
Corylus americana (American hazelnut or filbert)
Dirca palustris (leatherwood, ropebark)
Euonymus americana (strawberry bush, brook euonymus, hearts-a-bustin')
Euonymus atropurpurea (wahoo, burning bush)
Forestiera acuminata (swamp privet)
Frangula caroliniana (Carolina buckthorn)
Hydrangea arborescens (wild hydrangea)
Hypericum hypericoides ssp. hypericoides (St. Andrew's cross)
Hypericum prolificum (shrubby St. John's wort)
Ilex verticillata (winterberry, black alder)
Itea virginica (Virginia willow, sweetspire, tassel-white)
Lindera benzoin (spicebush)
Lonicera dioica (limber or wild honeysuckle)
Lyonia ligustrina (male-berry, male-blueberry)
Physocarpus opulifolius (ninebark)
Prunus virginiana (chokecherry)
Rhododendron arborescens (smooth azalea)
Rhododendron calendulaceum (flame azalea)
Rhododendron viscosum (swamp azalea)

Rhus aromatica (fragrant sumac)
Rhus copallinum (dwarf or winged sumac)
Rhus glabra (smooth sumac)
Rhus hirta (staghorn sumac)
Rosa blanda (early wild rose, smooth rose)
Rosa carolina (Carolina rose)
Rosa setigera (Illinois or prairie rose)
Rubus occidentalis (black raspberry, thimbleberry)
Rubus odoratus (thimbleberry)
Sambucus canadensis (elderberry, common elder)
Spiraea tomentosa (steeplebush, hardhack)
Staphylea trifoliata (bladdernut)
Styrax americanus (American silverbells)
Symphoricarpos orbiculatus (coralberry, Indian currant)
Vaccinium angustifolium (low-bush blueberry)
Vaccinium arboreum (sparkleberry, farkleberry)
Vaccinium corymbosom (highbush blueberry)
Viburnum acerifolium (maple leaf viburnum)
Viburnum dentatum (southern arrowwood)
Viburnum nudum var. cassinoides (wild raisin)
Viburnum prunifolium (black haw, nanny berry)
Viburnum rufidulum (southern or rusty black haw)

Shrubs (evergreen)

Epigaea repens (trailing arbutus)
Gaultheria procumbens (wintergreen, checkerberry)
Gaylussacia brachycera (box huckleberry)
Juniperus communis (common juniper)
Kalmia latifolia (mountain laurel)
Rhododendron catawbiense (purple rhododendron, red laurel)
Rhododendron maximum (rosebay, great laurel)

Trees (deciduous)

Acer barbatum (Florida maple, southern sugar maple)
Acer negundo (box elder)
Acer pensylvanicum (striped maple)
Acer rubrum (red maple)
Acer saccharinum (silver maple)
Acer saccharum (sugar maple)
Aesculus flava (sweet buckeye, yellow buckeye)
Aesculus glabra (Ohio buckeye, horse chestnut)
Betula lenta (cherry birch)
Betula nigra (river birch)
Carpinus caroliniana (blue beech, hornbeam, musclewood)
Carya alba (mockernut hickory)
Carya cordiformis (bitternut, swamp hickory)
Carya illinoinensis (pecan)
Carya ovata (shagbark hickory)
Catalpa speciosa (northern catalpa)
Celtis laevigata (sugarberry, hackberry)
Celtis occidentalis (hackberry, sugarberry)
Cercis canadensis (redbud)

Chionanthus virginicus (fringe tree, old man's beard)
Cladrastis kentukea (yellowwood)
Cornus florida (flowering dogwood)
Crataegus crus-galli (cockspur hawthorn)
Crataegus mollis (downy hawthorn)
Crataegus phaenopyrum (Washington hawthorn)
Crataegus punctata (dotted hawthorn, white thorn)
Diospyros virginiana (persimmon)
Fagus grandifolia var. caroliniana (beech)
Fagus grandifolia var. grandifolia (beech)
Fraxinus americana (white ash)
Fraxinus pensylvanica (green ash)
Gleditsia triacanthos (honey locust)
Gymnocladus dioica (Kentucky coffee tree)
Hamamelis virginiana (witch hazel)
Ilex decidua (possum-haw, deciduous holly)
Juglans nigra (black walnut)
Liquidambar styraciflua (sweet gum)
Liriodendron tulipifera (tulip tree)
Magnolia acuminata (cucumber tree)
Malus angustifolia (southern crabapple, wild crabapple)
Malus ioensis var. ioensis (prairie crabapple)
Nyssa sylvatica (black gum, tupelo)
Ostrya virginiana (ironwood, hophornbeam)
Oxydendrum arboreum (sourwood)
Platanus occidentalis (sycamore, plane-tree)
Populus deltoides (eastern cottonwood)
Prunus americana (wild plum)
Prunus angustifolia (chickasaw plum)
Prunus nigra (Canada plum)
Prunus serotina (black cherry)
Ptelea trifoliata (wafer ash, common hoptree)
Quercus alba (white oak)
Quercus bicolor (swamp white oak)
Quercus coccinea (scarlet oak)
Quercus falcata (southern red oak, Spanish oak)
Quercus lyrata (overcup oak)
Quercus macrocarpa (bur oak)
Quercus marilandica (blackjack oak)
Quercus muhlenbergii (chinkapin oak, chestnut oak)
Quercus palustris (pin oak)
Quercus phellos (willow oak)
Quercus rubra (red oak)
Quercus shumardii (shumard oak)
Quercus stellata (post oak)
Quercus velutina (black oak)
Salix nigra (black willow)
Sassafras albidum (sassafras)
Taxodium distichum (bald cypress)
Tilia americana (American linden, basswood)
Ulmus americana (American elm)
Ulmus rubra (red elm, slippery elm)

Trees (evergreen)

Chamaecyparis thyoides (white cedar)
Ilex opaca (American holly, Christmas holly)
Juniperus virginiana (eastern red cedar)
Pinus echinata (shortleaf pine)
Pinus rigida (pitch pine)
Pinus strobus (eastern white pine)
Pinus virginiana (Virginia pine)
Tsuga canadensis (eastern hemlock)

Vines (deciduous)

Bignonia capreolata (cross vine)
Campsis radicans (trumpet creeper, trumpet vine)
Celastrus scandens (American bittersweet)
Clematis crispa (leatherflower)
Clematis pitcheri (leather flower, purple clematis)
Clematis virginiana (virgin's bower)
Lonicera sempervirens (coral honeysuckle)
Parthenocissus quinquefolia (Virginia creeper)
Passiflora incarnata (passion flower, maypop)
Vitis riparia (riverbank grape)
Vitis rotundifolia (muscadine grape)
Wisteria frutescens (wisteria)

FEDERALLY LISTED ENDANGERED SPECIES

Cumberland rosemary (Conradina verticillata)
Cumberland sandwort (Arenaria cumberlandensis)
Price's potato-bean (Apios priceana)
Rock cress (Arabis perstellata)
Running buffalo clover (Trifolium stoloniferum)
Short's goldenrod (Solidago shortii)
Virginia spiraea (Spiraea virginiana)
White-haried goldenrod (Solidago albopilosa)

KENTUCKY NOXIOUS SPECIES

Because the noxious weed lists have continually changed since we gathered them in 1994, we are not including them at this time. Not all States have noxious weed lists. Those that do, do not use the same standards of importance and are not comparable. States typically have included plants that interfere with agriculture (Canada thistle), or cause human health problems (poison ivy). Some States are now including a category of plants that invade and degrade the environment (purple loosestrife). Check with your State's Agriculture Department or Weed Scientist listed below. The noxious weed list can be used two ways on roadsides: l) check to not inadvertently plant these invasive plants, and 2) note the plants you are legally responsible to control. Many States now check adjacent State lists to avoid planting their neighbors' problem plants. Because weeds do not respect political boundaries, and because by their very nature weeds continue to adapt and expand, monitoring and controlling invasives at State borders is a wise part of vegetation management.

(Weed Law)

Department of Entomology
Division of Pests & Noxious Weeds
S-225 Ag. Sci. Ct. North
Lexington, KY 40546

J.D.Green, Agronomy
University of Kentucky
106B Ag. Science Building
Lexington, KY 40546
(606) 257-4898

KENTUCKY RESOURCES

Kentucky Natural Heritage Program
State Nature Preserves Commission
801 Schenkel Lane
Frankfort, KY 40601
(502) 573-2886

The Nature Conservancy Field Office
642 West Main Street
Lexington, KY 40508

Kentucky-Tennessee Society of
American Foresters
P.O. Box 149
Sawanee, TN 37375

Land Between the Lakes
Tennessee Valley Authority
Golden Pond, KY 42231

Bernheim Arboretum and
Research Forest
State Highway 245,
P.O. Box 130
Clermont, KY 40110

POTENTIAL NATURAL VEGETATION ZONES IN
LOUISIANA

Source: A.W. Kuchler's Potential Natural Vegetation Map, 1964, Revised 1985.
Presented in U.S.G.S. National Atlas of the U.S. Series,
U.S. Geological Survey, Reston, VA.

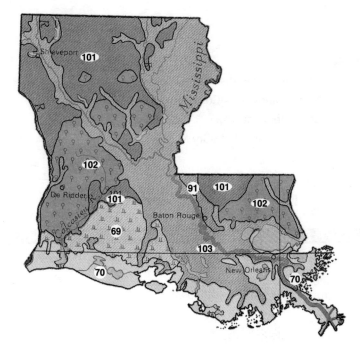

 69 Bluestem-sacahuista prairie
(Andropogon-Spartina)

70 Southern cordgrass prairie
(Spartina)

91 Oak-hickory forest
(Quercus-Carya)

 101 Oak-hickory-pine forest
(Quercus-Carya-Pinus)

102 Southern mixed forest
(Fagus-Liquidambar-Magnolia-Pinus-Quercus)

103 Southern floodplain forest
(Quercus-Nyassa-Taxodium)

(Dominant plant species present in each vegetation type are listed in Appendix 8)

69   *Bluestem-Sacahuista Prairie (Andropogon-Spartina)*
70   *Southern Cordgrass Prairie (Spartina)*
91   *Oak-Hickory Forest (Quercus-Carya)*
101   *Oak-Hickory-Pine Forest (Quercus-Carya-Pinus)*
102   *Southern Mixed Forest (Fagus-Liquidambar-Magnolia-Pinus-Quercus)*
103   *Southern Floodplain Forest (Quercus-Nyssa-Taxodium)*

Botanical Experts

Julia Larke, Botanist
Louisiana Natural Heritage Program
Department of Wildlife and Fisheries
P.O. Box 9800
Baton Rouge, LA 70898-9000
(504) 765-2975
(504) 765-8218 (fax)

Parishes (counties) east of the Mississippi River:

John Marone, Native Landscapes Corp., ph: 504-892-5424

Central and southwestern Louisiana:

Bill Fontenot, Lafayette Natural History Museum and Prairie Basse Nursery,
(318) 896-9187

Recommended Flora

No recommended flora exists specifically for Louisiana. Suggested flora for
neighboring states may be helpful.

NATIVE PLANTS FOR LANDSCAPE USE IN LOUISIANA

Cacti

Opuntia humifusa (prickly pear)
Opuntia macrorhiza (common prickly pear)

Ferns

Asplenium platyneuron (ebony spleenwort)
Athyrium filix-femina (lady fern)
Botrychium virginianum (rattlesnake fern)
Onoclea sensibilis (sensitive fern, bead fern)
Osmunda cinnamomea (cinnamon fern)
Osmunda regalis (royal fern)
Polystichum acrostichoides (Christmas fern)
Thelypteris kunthii (southern shield fern, wood fern, river fern)
Woodwardia areolata (netted chain fern)
Woodwardia virginica (Virginia chain fern)

Forbs (annuals/biennials)

Aphanostephus skirrhobasis (lazy daisy)
Castilleja indivisa (Indian paintbrush)

Dracopsis amplexicaulis (clasping leaf coneflower)
Gaillardia pulchella (Indian blanket, firewheel)
Hymenopappus artemisiifolius (old plainsman, woolly white)
Ipomopsis rubra (standing cypress)
Lobelia spicata (pale lobelia)
Marshallia caespitosa var. caespitosa (Barbara's buttons)
Oenothera biennis (common evening primrose)
Proboscidea louisianica (unicorn plant, proboscis flower, ram's horn)
Rudbeckia hirta (black-eyed Susan)
Sabatia campestris (prairie rose gentian, prairie sabatia, meadow pink)
Senecio glabellus (butterweed)
Senecio plattensis (prairie ragwort, prairie groundsel)

Forbs (perennials)

Acorus calamus (sweet flag, calamus)
Allium canadense (wild garlic)
Amsonia ciliata (blue funnel lily, blue star)
Amsonia tabernaemontana (blue star)
Anemone caroliniana (Carolina anemone, southern thimbleweed)
Antennaria spp. (pussytoes, everlasting)
Apocynum androsaemifolium (spreading dogbane)
Arisaema triphyllum (Jack-in-the-pulpit, Indian turnip)
Artemisia ludoviciana (white sage, prairie sage, artemisia)
Asclepias tuberosa (butterfly weed)
Asclepias verticillata (whorled milkweed)
Aster dumosus (bushy aster)
Aster laevis (smooth aster)
Aster oolentangiensis (sky blue aster)
Aster pilosus (frost aster)
Baptisia alba (white false indigo)
Baptisia alba var. macrophyllla (cream false indigo, plains wild indigo)
Callirhoe papaver (poppy mallow)
Calylophus berlandieri (square-bud primrose, sundrops)
Chrysopsis mariana (Maryland golden aster)
Claytonia virginica (narrow-leaved spring beauty)
Coreopsis auriculata (early coreopsis)
Coreopsis grandiflora (coreopsis)
Coreopsis lanceolata (lance-leaved coreopsis)
Coreopsis tripteris (tall coreopsis)
Dalea candida (white prairie clover)
Dalea purpurea (purple prairie clover)
Delphinium carolinianum (blue larkspur)
Eryngium yuccifolium (rattlesnake master, button snake-root)
Eupatorium coelestinum (mist flower)
Eupatorium fistulosum (Joe-pye weed)
Eupatorium perfoliatum (boneset)
Fragaria virginiana (wild strawberry)
Galium triflorum (sweet-scented bedstraw)
Gentiana saponaria (closed gentian, soapwort gentian)
Hedyotis nigricans (bluets)
Helenium autumnale (common sneezeweed)
Helianthus simulans (narrow-leaved sunflower, swamp sunflower)

Helianthus strumosus (woodland sunflower)
Heliopsis helianthoides (ox-eye sunflower, false sunflower)
Hibiscus moscheutos (swamp rose mallow, marshmallow hibiscus)
Houstonia caerulea (bluets)
Houstonia longifolia var. longifolia (long-leaved bluets, pale bluets)
Houstonia procumbens (innocence)
Hymenocallis caroliniana (spider lily, rain lily)
Hypoxis hirsuta (yellow star grass)
Iris virginica (southern blue flag)
Kosteletzkya virginica (seashore mallow)
Lespedeza capitata (roundheaded bush clover)
Liatris aspera (rough blazing star, gayfeather)
Liatris elegans (gayfeather)
Liatris pycnostachya (prairie blazing star, gayfeather)
Liatris spicata (marsh blazing star, gayfeather)
Liatris squarrosa (blazing star)
Lobelia cardinalis (cardinal flower)
Lobelia siphilitica (great blue lobelia)
Manfreda virginica (rattlesnake master, false aloe)
Mitchella repens (partridge berry)
Monarda fistulosa (wild bergamot, horsemint, beebalm)
Nuphar lutea (yellow pond lily, cow lily, spatter dock)
Oenothera fruticosa (sundrops)
Orontium aquaticum (golden club)
Peltandra virginica (arrow arum)
Penstemon australis (beardtongue)
Penstemon digitalis (beardtongue)
Phlox divaricata ssp. laphamii (blue phlox, sweet William)
Phlox paniculata (summer phlox, perennial phlox)
Phlox pilosa (prairie phlox, downy phlox)
Physostegia digitalis (obedient plant)
Physostegia intermedia (obedient plant)
Podophyllum peltatum (May apple)
Polygonatum biflorum (Solomon's seal)
Potentilla simplex (common cinquefoil)
Pycnanthemum tenuifolium (slender mountain mint)
Ranunculus hispidus (early buttercup, tufted buttercup)
Ratibida pinnata (gray-headed coneflower, yellow coneflower)
Rhexia virginica (meadow beauty)
Rudbeckia grandiflora (large coneflower)
Rudbeckia subtomentosa (sweet black-eyed Susan)
Ruellia humilis (wild petunia)
Salvia lyrata (cancer weed, lyre-leaf sage)
Silphium integrifolium (rosinweed)
Silphium laciniatum (compass plant)
Sisyrinchium angustifolium (narrow-leaved blue-eyed grass)
Sisyrinchium campestre (white-eyed grass, prairie blue-eyed grass)
Solidago caesia (blue-stemmed goldenrod, wreath goldenrod)
Solidago canadensis (meadow goldenrod)
Solidago nemoralis (gray goldenrod, old-field goldenrod)
Solidago odora (sweet goldenrod)
Solidago rigida (stiff goldenrod)

Solidago rugosa (rough-leaved goldenrod)
Solidago sempervirens (seaside goldenrod)
Solidago speciosa (showy goldenrod)
Solidago ulmifolia (elm-leaved goldenrod)
Spigelia marilandica (Indian pink)
Stokesia laevis (stokes' aster)
Thalictrum dasycarpum (tall or purple meadow rue)
Tradescantia ohiensis (Ohio spiderwort)
Vernonia baldwinii (ironweed, western ironweed)
Viola missouriensis (Missouri violet)
Viola pedata (bird-foot violet)
Yucca aloifolia (Spanish dagger)
Zizia aurea (golden alexanders)

Grasses/Grass-like plants

Agrostis scabra (ticklegrass, fly-away grass)
Andropogon gerardii (big bluestem)
Andropogon glomeratus (bushy bluestem)
Andropogon ternarius (splitbeard bluestem)
Andropogon virginicus (broom sedge)
Arundinaria gigantea (giant cane)
Carex caroliniana (sedge)
Carex cherokeensis (sedge)
Carex glaucescans (sedge)
Carex stipata (awl-fruited sedge)
Chasmanthium latifolium (inland sea oats, wild oats, river oats, broad-leaf uniola)
Danthonia spicata (poverty grass)
Elymus canadensis (Canada wild rye)
Eragrostis intermedia (plains lovegrass)
Eragrostis spectabilis (purple lovegrass, tumblegrass)
Juncus effusus var. solutus (soft rush)
Juncus interior (inland rush)
Leersia oryzoides (rice cut grass)
Muhlenbergia capillaris (gulf muhly, hair grass)
Panicum virgatum (switchgrass)
Saccharum giganteum (sugarcane plume grass)
Schizachyrium scoparium (little bluestem)
Scirpus atrovirens (dark green bulrush)
Scirpus cyperinus (wool grass)
Scirpus tabernaemontani (great bulrush)
Sorghastrum nutans (Indian grass)
Spartina patens (marsh hay cordgrass, salt meadow cordgrass)
Sporobolus compositus var. compositus (tall dropseed)
Sporobolus cryptandrus (sand dropseed)
Tripsacum dactyloides (eastern gama grass)
Typha angustifolia (narrow-leaved cattail)
Typha latifolia (cattail)

Shrubs (deciduous)

Alnus serrulata (smooth alder)
Amelanchier arborea (downy serviceberry, shadbush, Juneberry)
Amorpha fruticosa (false indigo, Indigo bush)

Baccharis halimifolia (sea myrtle, groundsel bush)
Callicarpa americana (American beautyberry, French mulberry)
Castanea pumila (chinquapin)
Ceanothus americanus (New Jersey tea, red root)
Cephalanthus occidentalis (buttonbush)
Clethra alnifolia (summer sweet)
Cornus drummondii (rough-leaf dogwood)
Corylus americana (American hazelnut or filbert)
Erythrina herbacea (coral bean)
Euonymus americana (strawberry bush, brook euonymus, hearts-a-bustin')
Forestiera acuminata (swamp privet)
Frangula caroliniana (Carolina buckthorn)
Hydrangea quercifolia (oakleaf hydrangea)
Hypericum prolificum (shrubby St. John's wort)
Ilex verticillata (winterberry, black alder)
Itea virginica (Virginia willow, sweetspire, tassel-white)
Lindera benzoin (spicebush)
Lycium carolinianum (Christmas berry, matrimony vine)
Lyonia ligustrina (male-berry, male-blueberry)
Prunus virginiana (chokecherry)
Rhododendron canescens (wild, piedmont, or sweet azalea)
Rhododendron viscosum (swamp azalea)
Rhus aromatica (fragrant sumac)
Rhus copallinum (dwarf or winged sumac)
Rhus glabra (smooth sumac)
Rosa carolina (Carolina rose)
Rosa setigera (Illinois or prairie rose)
Sambucus canadensis (elderberry, common elder)
Sideroxylon lanuginosum ssp. lanuginosum (chittamwood, gum elastic tree)
Styrax americanus (American silverbells)
Vaccinium arboreum (sparkleberry, farkleberry)
Vaccinium elliottii (Elliott's blueberry)
Vaccinium stamineum (dearberry, squaw-huckleberry)
Vaccinium virgatum
Viburnum acerifolium (maple leaf viburnum)
Viburnum dentatum (southern arrowwood)
Viburnum nudum (possumhaw viburnum)
Viburnum prunifolium (black haw, nanny berry)
Viburnum rufidulum (southern or rusty black haw)

Shrubs (evergreen)

Ilex glabra (inkberry, bitter gallberry)
Ilex vomitoria (yaupon)
Illicium floridanum (Florida anise tree)
Leucothoe axillaris (coast leucothoe)
Myrica cerifera (wax myrtle, southern bayberry, candleberry)
Sabal minor (dwarf palmetto)

Trees (deciduous)

Acacia farnesiana (huisache, sweet acacia)
Acer barbatum (Florida maple, southern sugar maple)
Acer negundo (box elder)

Acer rubrum (red maple)
Acer saccharinum (silver maple)
Aesculus pavia var. pavia (red buckeye)
Betula nigra (river birch)
Carpinus caroliniana (blue beech, hornbeam, musclewood)
Carya alba (mockernut hickory)
Carya cordiformis (bitternut, swamp hickory)
Carya illinoinensis (pecan)
Carya ovata (shagbark hickory)
Carya texana (black hickory)
Celtis laevigata (sugarberry, hackberry)
Cercis canadensis (redbud)
Chionanthus virginicus (fringe tree, old man's beard)
Cornus florida (flowering dogwood)
Crataegus crus-galli (cockspur hawthorn)
Crataegus marshallii (parsley hawthorn)
Cyrilla racemiflora (leatherwood, yiti)
Diospyros virginiana (persimmon)
Fagus grandifolia (beech)
Fagus grandifolia var. grandifolia (beech)
Fraxinus americana (white ash)
Fraxinus pensylvanica (green ash)
Gleditsia triacanthos (honey locust)
Halesia diptera (American snowdrop tree, two-winged silverbell)
Hamamelis virginiana (witch hazel)
Ilex decidua (possum-haw, deciduous holly)
Juglans nigra (black walnut)
Liquidambar styraciflua (sweet gum)
Liriodendron tulipifera (tulip tree)
Magnolia acuminata (cucumber tree)
Magnolia virginiana (sweetbay, swampbay)
Malus angustifolia (southern crabapple, wild crabapple)
Malus ioensis var. ioensis (prairie crabapple)
Nyssa sylvatica (black gum, tupelo)
Ostrya virginiana (ironwood, hophornbeam)
Oxydendrum arboreum (sourwood)
Platanus occidentalis (sycamore, plane-tree)
Populus deltoides (eastern cottonwood)
Prunus angustifolia (chickasaw plum)
Prunus mexicana (Mexican plum)
Prunus serotina (black cherry)
Ptelea trifoliata (wafer ash, common hoptree)
Quercus alba (white oak)
Quercus falcata (southern red oak, Spanish oak)
Quercus laurifolia (laurel oak)
Quercus lyrata (overcup oak)
Quercus macrocarpa (bur oak)
Quercus marilandica (blackjack oak)
Quercus phellos (willow oak)
Quercus shumardii (shumard oak)
Quercus stellata (post oak)
Quercus velutina (black oak)

Salix nigra (black willow)
Sapindus saponaria var. drummondii (soapberry)
Sassafras albidum (sassafras)
Taxodium distichum (bald cypress)
Tilia americana (American linden, basswood)
Ulmus americana (American elm)
Ulmus crassifolia (cedar elm)
Ulmus rubra (red elm, slippery elm)

Trees (evergreen)

Ilex opaca (American holly, Christmas holly)
Juniperus virginiana (eastern red cedar)
Magnolia grandiflora (southern magnolia)
Persea borbonia (red bay)
Pinus echinata (shortleaf pine)
Pinus glabra (spruce pine)
Pinus palustris (longleaf pine)
Pinus taeda (loblolly pine)
Prunus caroliniana (cherry laurel)
Quercus virginiana (live oak, coastal live oak, southern live oak)

Vines (deciduous)

Bignonia capreolata (cross vine)
Campsis radicans (trumpet creeper, trumpet vine)
Clematis crispa (leatherflower)
Clematis virginiana (virgin's bower)
Lonicera sempervirens (coral honeysuckle)
Parthenocissus quinquefolia (Virginia creeper)
Passiflora incarnata (passion flower, maypop)
Vitis riparia (riverbank grape)
Vitis rotundifolia (muscadine grape)
Wisteria frutescens (wisteria)

Vine (evergreen)

Gelsemium sempervirens (yellow jessamine, Carolina jessamine)

FEDERALLY LISTED ENDANGERED SPECIES

American chaffseed (Schwalbea americana)
Geocarpon minimum (no common name)
Louisiana qullwort (Isoetes louisianensis)
Pondberry (Lindera melissifolia)

LOUISIANA NOXIOUS SPECIES

Because the noxious weed lists have continually changed since we gathered them in 1994, we are not including them at this time. Not all States have noxious weed lists. Those that do, do not use the same standards of importance and are not comparable. States typically have included plants that interfere with agriculture (Canada thistle), or cause human health problems (poison ivy). Some States are now including a category of plants that invade and degrade the environment (purple loosestrife). Check with your State's Agriculture Department or Weed Scientist listed below. The noxious weed list can be used two ways on roadsides: l) check to not inadvertantly plant these invasive plants, and 2) note the plants you are legally responsible to control. Many States now check adjacent State lists to avoid planting their neighbors' problem plants. Because weeds do not respect political boundaries, and because by their very nature weeds continue to adapt and expand, monitoring and controlling invasives at State borders is a wise part of vegetation management.

(Seed Law only)

Department of Agriculture
Division of Horticulture & Quarantine
P.O. Box 3118
Baton Rouge, LA 70281

Dearl Sanders, 261 Knapp
Cooperative Extension
Louisiana State University
Baton Rouge, LA 70803
(504) 388-6195

LOUISIANA RESOURCES

Louisiana Natural Heritage Program
Department of Wildlife & Fisheries
P.O. Box 98000
Baton Rouge, LA 70898
(504) 765-2821

The Nature Conservancy Field office
P.O. Box 4125
Baton Rouge, LA 70821
(504) 338-1040

Louisiana Native Plant Society
Route l, Box l5l
Saline, LA 71070

Louisiana Project Wildflower
Lafayette Natural History Museum
637 Girard Park Dr.
Lafayette, LA 70504

POTENTIAL NATURAL VEGETATION ZONES IN
MAINE

Source: A.W. Kuchler's Potential Natural Vegetation Map, 1964, Revised 1985.
Presented in U.S.G.S. National Atlas of the U.S. Series,
U.S. Geological Survey, Reston, VA.

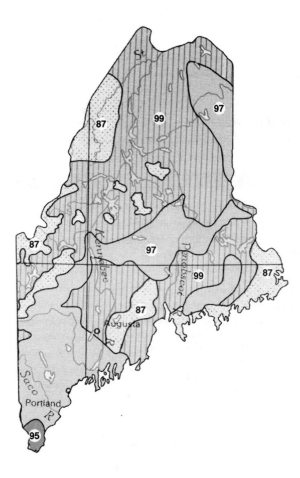

87 Northeastern spruce-fir forest *(Picea-Abies)*	**97** Northern hardwoods *(Acer-Betula-Fagus-Tsuga)*
95 Appalachian oak forest *(Quercus)*	**99** Northern hardwoods-spruce forest *(Acer-Betula-Fagus-Picea-Tsuga)*

(Dominant plant species present in each vegetation type are listed in Appendix 8)

87   Northeastern Spruce-Fir Forest (Picea-Abies)
95   Appalachian Oak Forest (Quercus)
97   Northern Hardwoods (Acer-Betula-Fagus-Tsuga)
99   Northern Hardwoods-Spruce Forests (Acer-Betula-Fagus-Picea-Tsuga)

Botanical Experts

Donald Cameron, Botanist
Maine Natural Areas Program
Department of Conservation
State House Station #93
Augusta, ME 04333
(207) 287-8041
(207) 287-8040 (fax)
internet: don.s.cameron@state.me.us

Recommended Flora

Haines, A. and T.F. Vining. 1998. Flora of Maine. V.F. Thomas Co., Bar Harbor, ME. 837 pp. ISBN 0966487400.

NATIVE PLANTS FOR LANDSCAPE USE IN MAINE

Ferns

Adiantum pedatum (northern maidenhair fern)
Asplenium trichomanes (maidenhair spleenwort)
Athyrium filix-femina (lady fern)
Botrychium virginianum (rattlesnake fern)
Cystopteris bulbifera (bladder fern)
Cystopteris fragilis (fragile fern)
Dennstaedtia punctilobula (hay-scented fern)
Dryopteris carthusiana (shield fern, toothed wood fern, spinulose shield fern)
Dryopteris cristata (crested wood fern, buckler fern)
Dryopteris marginalis (marginal wood fern)
Gymnocarpium dryopteris (oak fern)
Matteuccia struthiopteris (ostrich fern)
Onoclea sensibilis (sensitive fern, bead fern)
Osmunda cinnamomea (cinnamon fern)
Osmunda claytoniana (interrupted fern)
Osmunda regalis (royal fern)
Polystichum acrostichoides (Christmas fern)
Thelypteris novaboracensis (New York fern, tapering fern)
Thelypteris simulata (Massachusetts fern)
Woodsia ilvensis (rusty woodsia)

Forbs (annuals/biennials)

Corydalis sempervirens (pale corydalis)
Lobelia spicata (pale lobelia)
Gentianopsis crinita (fringed gentian)
Oenothera biennis (common evening primrose)

Forbs (perennials)

Acorus calamus (sweet flag, calamus)
Actaea pachypoda (white baneberry)
Actaea rubra (red baneberry)
Ageratina altissima var. altissima (white snakeroot)
Anaphalis margaritacea (pearly everlasting)
Anemone canadensis (Canada anemone, windflower)
Anemone cylindrica (thimbleweed, candle anemone)
Anemone virginiana (thimbleweed, tall anemone)
Antennaria spp. (pussytoes, everlasting)
Apocynum androsaemifolium (spreading dogbane)
Aquilegia canadensis (columbine)
Arisaema triphyllum (Jack-in-the-pulpit, Indian turnip)
Asclepias incarnata (swamp milkweed)
Aster ericoides (heath aster, white wreath aster)
Aster laevis (smooth aster)
Aster novae-angliae (New England aster)
Aster pilosus (frost aster)
Aster puniceus (red-stem aster, swamp aster)
Caltha palustris (marsh marigold, cowslip)
Campanula rotundifolia (harebell)
Cardamine diphylla (two-leaved toothwort)
Caulophyllum thalictroides (blue cohosh)
Chelone glabra (turtlehead)
Claytonia caroliniana (broad-leaved spring beauty)
Clintonia borealis (clintonia, blue-bead lily)
Coptis trifolia ssp. groenlandica (goldthread)
Cornus canadensis (bunchberry)
Desmodium canadense (Canada tick-trefoil, Canada tickclover)
Dicentra cucullaria (Dutchman's breeches)
Epilobium angustifolium (fireweed, willow herb)
Erythronium americanum (eastern trout lily, yellow trout lily)
Eupatorium maculatum (spotted Joe-pye weed)
Eupatorium perfoliatum (boneset)
Euthamia graminifolia var. graminifolia (grass-leaved goldenrod)
Fragaria virginiana (wild strawberry)
Galium triflorum (sweet-scented bedstraw)
Gentiana clausa (bottle gentian)
Gentianopsis crinita (fringed gentian)
Geranium maculatum (wild geranium, cranesbill)
Geum rivale (purple avens, water avens)
Helianthus strumosus (woodland sunflower)
Houstonia caerulea (bluets)
Iris versicolor (blue flag)
Lespedeza capitata (roundheaded bush clover)
Lilium canadense (wild yellow lily, Canada lily)
Lilium philadelphicum (wood lily)
Linnaea borealis (twinflower)
Lobelia cardinalis (cardinal flower)
Lysimachia ciliata (fringed loosestrife)
Maianthemum canadense (wild lily-of-the-valley, Canada mayflower)
Maianthemum racemosum ssp. racemosum (false Solomon's seal,
    false spikenard)

Maianthemum stellatum (starry Solomon's seal)
Mitchella repens (partridge berry)
Monarda fistulosa (wild bergamot, horsemint, beebalm)
Nuphar lutea (yellow pond lily, cow lily, spatter dock)
Osmorhiza claytoni (sweet cicely, sweet jarvil)
Peltandra virginica (arrow arum)
Penstemon digitalis (beardtongue)
Penstemon hirsutus (hairy beardtongue)
Pentaphylloides floribunda (potentilla, shrubby cinquefoil)
Potentilla arguta (white cinquefoil, prairie cinquefoil, tall cinquefoil)
Potentilla simplex (common cinquefoil)
Pycnanthemum tenuifolium (slender mountain mint)
Pycnanthemum virginianum (mountain mint)
Pyrola elliptica (shinleaf)
Ranunculus hispidus (early buttercup, tufted buttercup)
Rhexia virginica (meadow beauty)
Rudbeckia laciniata (cut-leaf coneflower)
Sanguinaria candensis (bloodroot)
Senecio aureus (golden ragwort)
Sibbaldiopsis tridentata (three-toothed cinquefoil)
Sisyrinchium angustifolium (narrow-leaved blue-eyed grass)
Solidago caesia (blue-stemmed goldenrod, wreath goldenrod)
Solidago canadensis (meadow goldenrod)
Solidago juncea (early goldenrod, plume goldenrod)
Solidago nemoralis (gray goldenrod, old-field goldenrod)
Solidago rugosa (rough-leaved goldenrod)
Solidago sempervirens (seaside goldenrod)
Streptopus roseus (rosy twisted stalk)
Thalictrum dioicum (early meadow rue)
Thalictrum pubescens (tall meadow rue)
Tiarella cordifolia (foam flower)
Trientalis borealis ssp. borealis (starflower)
Trillium cernuum (nodding trillium)
Trillium erectum (wakerobin, purple trillium)
Trillium undulatum (painted trillium)
Uvularia sessilifolia (wildoats, merrybells)
Verbena hastata (blue verbena, blue vervain)
Viola conspersa (American dog violet)
Viola pubescens (downy or smooth yellow violet)
Viola sororia (common blue violet, meadow violet)
Zizia aurea (golden alexanders)

Grasses/Grass-like plants

Agrostis scabra (ticklegrass, fly-away grass)
Andropogon gerardii (big bluestem)
Bromus kalmii (prairie brome, wild chess)
Calamagrostis canadensis (bluejoint grass)
Carex aquatilis (water sedge)
Carex lucorum (woodland sedge)
Carex plantaginea (plantain-leaved sedge)
Carex stipata (awl-fruited sedge)
Carex stricta (tussock sedge)

Carex utriculata (beaked sedge)
Danthonia spicata (poverty grass)
Deschampsia cespitosa (tufted hairgrass)
Distichlis spicata (seashore saltgrass)
Eleocharis palustris (creeping spikesedge, spike rush)
Elymus canadensis (Canada wild rye)
Eragrostis spectabilis (purple lovegrass, tumblegrass)
Glyceria grandis (American mannagrass, tall mannagrass, reed meadowgrass)
Hierochloe odorata (sweet grass)
Juncus effusus sp. (soft rush)
Leersia oryzoides (rice cut grass)
Leymus mollis (American dune grass, beach wild rye)
Panicum virgatum (switchgrass)
Schizachyrium scoparium (little bluestem)
Scirpus acutus (hardstem bulrush)
Scirpus atrovirens (dark green bulrush)
Scirpus cyperinus (wool grass)
Scirpus maritimus (alkali bulrush, prairie bulrush, bayonet grass)
Scirpus tabernaemontani (great bulrush)
Spartina patens (marsh hay cordgrass, salt meadow cordgrass)
Spartina pectinata (prairie cordgrass, freshwater cordgrass)
Trisetum spicatum (spike trisetum)
Typha latifolia (cattail)

Shrubs (deciduous)

Alnus incana (speckled alder, mountain alder)
Alnus serrulata (smooth alder)
Amelanchier arborea (downy serviceberry, shadbush, Juneberry)
Aronia melanocarpa (black chokeberry)
Cephalanthus occidentalis (buttonbush)
Cornus alternifolia (pogoda dogwood, alternate-leaved dogwood)
Cornus amomum ssp. obliqua (swamp dogwood, silky dogwood)
Cornus racemosa (gray dogwood)
Corylus americana (American hazelnut or filbert)
Corylus cornuta (beaked hazelnut or filbert)
Diervilla lonicera (bush honeysuckle)
Dirca palustris (leatherwood, ropebark)
Empetrum nigrum (crowberry)
Ilex verticillata (winterberry, black alder)
Lonicera dioica (limber or wild honeysuckle)
Lyonia ligustrina (male-berry, male-blueberry)
Prunus virginiana (chokecherry)
Rhododendron canadense (rhodora)
Rhus copallinum (dwarf or winged sumac)
Rhus glabra (smooth sumac)
Rhus hirta (staghorn sumac)
Ribes cynosbati (prickly gooseberry, dogberry)
Rosa blanda (early wild rose, smooth rose)
Rosa carolina (Carolina rose)
Rubus idaeus (red raspberry)
Rubus occidentalis (black raspberry, thimbleberry)
Rubus odoratus (thimbleberry)

Salix bebbiana (Bebb willow, long-beaked willow)
Salix discolor (pussy willow)
Sambucus canadensis (elderberry, common elder)
Sambucus racemosa var. pubens (scarlet elderberry, red-berried elder)
Spiraea tomentosa (steeplebush, hardhack)
Vaccinium angustifolium (low-bush blueberry)
Vaccinium corymbosom (highbush blueberry)
Viburnum acerifolium (maple leaf viburnum)
Viburnum lentago (black haw, nannyberry)
Viburnum nudum var. cassinoides (wild raisin)
Viburnum opulus var. americanum (high-bush cranberry, American
  cranberrybush viburnum)

Shrubs (evergreen)

Andromeda polifolia var. glaucophylla (bog rosemary)
Arctostaphylos uva-ursi (bearberry, kinnikinnik)
Epigaea repens (trailing arbutus)
Gaultheria hispidula (creeping snowberry)
Gaultheria procumbens (wintergreen, checkerberry)
Ilex glabra (inkberry, bitter gallberry)
Juniperus communis (common juniper)
Juniperus horizontalis (creeping juniper, creeping savin)
Kalmia angustifolia (sheep laurel, lambkill kalmia)
Kalmia polifolia (swamp laurel, bog laurel)
Taxus canadensis (Canada yew)
Vaccinium vitis-idaea (mountain cranberry, lingonberry, cowberry)

Trees (deciduous)

Acer negundo (box elder)
Acer pennsylvanicum (striped maple)
Acer rubrum (red maple)
Acer saccharinum (silver maple)
Acer saccharum (sugar maple)
Acer spicatum (mountain maple)
Amelanchier canadensis (shadblow serviceberry, Juneberry)
Betula lenta (cherry birch)
Betula papyrifera (paper birch)
Carpinus caroliniana (blue beech, hornbeam, musclewood)
Carya ovata (shagbark hickory)
Fagus grandifolia var. grandifolia (beech)
Fraxinus americana (white ash)
Fraxinus pensylvanica (green ash)
Hamamelis virginiana (witch hazel)
Juglans cinerea (butternut, white walnut)
Larix laricina (tamarack, American larch)
Nyssa sylvatica (black gum, tupelo)
Ostrya virginiana (ironwood, hophornbeam)
Platanus occidentalis (sycamore, plane-tree)
Populus deltoides (eastern cottonwood)
Populus grandidentata (large-toothed aspen)
Populus tremuloides (quaking aspen)
Prunus nigra (Canada plum)

Prunus pensylvanica (fire or pin cherry)
Prunus serotina (black cherry)
Quercus alba (white oak)
Quercus macrocarpa (bur oak)
Quercus rubra (red oak)
Quercus velutina (black oak)
Salix nigra (black willow)
Sorbus americana (mountain ash)
Tilia americana (American linden, basswood)
Ulmus americana (American elm)

Trees (evergreen)

Abies balsamea (balsam fir)
Juniperus virginiana (eastern red cedar)
Picea mariana (black spruce)
Picea rubens (red spruce)
Pinus resinosa (red pine, Norway pine)
Pinus rigida (pitch pine)
Pinus strobus (eastern white pine)
Thuja occidentalis (arbor vitae, northern white cedar)
Tsuga canadensis (eastern hemlock)

Vines (deciduous)

Celastrus scandens (American bittersweet)
Clematis virginiana (virgin's bower)
Parthenocissus quinquefolia (Virginia creeper)
Vitis riparia (riverbank grape)

FEDERALLY LISTED ENDANGERED SPECIES

Eastern prairie fringed orchid (Platanthera leucophaea)
Furbish lousewort (Pedicularis furbishiae)
Small whorled pogonia (Isotria medeoloides)

MAINE NOXIOUS SPECIES

Because the noxious weed lists have continually changed since we gathered them in 1994, we are not including them at this time. Not all States have noxious weed lists. Those that do, do not use the same standards of importance and are not comparable. States typically have included plants that interfere with agriculture (Canada thistle), or cause human health problems (poison ivy). Some States are now including a category of plants that invade and degrade the environment (purple loosestrife). Check with your State's Agriculture Department or Weed Scientist listed below. The noxious weed list can be used two ways on roadsides: l) check to not inadvertantly plant these invasive plants, and 2) note the plants you are legally responsible to control. Many States now check adjacent State lists to avoid planting their neighbors' problem plants. Because weeds do not respect political boundaries, and because by their very nature weeds continue to adapt and expand, monitoring and controlling invasives at State borders is a wise part of vegetation management.

(Seed Only)

Department of Agriculture
Division of Plant Industry
18 State House Station
Augusta, ME 04333

Maxwell McCormack
University of Maine
DFRU, PO Box 34
Orono, ME 04473
(207) 581-2903

MAINE RESOURCES

Maine Natural Areas Program
Department of Conservation
State House Station #93
Augusta, ME 04333
(207) 287-8044

The Nature Conservancy Field Office
14 Maine Street, Ste. 401
Brunswick, ME 04011
(207) 729-5181

Josselyn Botanical Society
Deering Hall
University of Maine
Orono, ME 04469

Wild Gardens of Acadia
Sieur de Monts Spring
Bar Harbor, ME 04609

POTENTIAL NATURAL VEGETATION ZONES IN
MARYLAND

Source: A.W. Kuchler's Potential Natural Vegetation Map, 1964, Revised 1985.
Presented in U.S.G.S. National Atlas of the U.S. Series,
U.S. Geological Survey, Reston, VA.

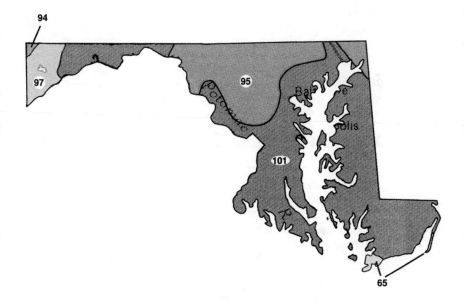

65	Northern cordgrass prairie *(Distichlis-Spartina)*
94	Mixed mesophytic forest *(Acer-Aesculus-Fagus-Liriodendron-Quercu*
95	Appalachian oak forest *(Quercus)*
97	Northern hardwoods *(Acer-Betula-Fagus-Tsuga)*
101	Oak-hickory-pine forest *(Quercus-Carya-Pinus)*

(Dominant plant species present in each vegetation type are listed in Appendix 8)

65 *Northern Cordgrass Prairie (Distichlis-Spartina)*
94 *Mixed Mesophytic Forest (Acer-Aesculus-Fagus-Liriodendron-Quercus-Tilia)*
95 *Appalachian Oak Forest (Quercus)*
97 *Northern Hardwoods (Acer-Betula-Fagus-Tsuga)*
101 *Oak-Hickory-Pine Forest (Quercus-Carya Pinus)*

Botanical Experts

Christopher Frye, State Botanist
Maryland Department of Natural Resources
Tawes State Office Bldg. E-1
580 Taylor Avenue
Annapolis, MD 21401
(410) 260-8565
(410) 260-8595 (fax)
internet: cfrye@dnr.state.md.us

Recommended Flora

Brown, M.L. and R.G. Brown. 1984. Herbaceous Plants of Maryland; Woody Plants of Maryland. Port City Press, Baltimore, MD. 1127 pgs. + illus.

NATIVE PLANTS FOR LANDSCAPE USE IN MARYLAND

Cactus

Opuntia humifusa (prickly pear)

Ferns

Adiantum pedatum (northern maidenhair fern)
Asplenium platyneuron (ebony spleenwort)
Asplenium trichomanes (maidenhair spleenwort)
Athyrium filix-femina (lady fern)
Botrychium virginianum (rattlesnake fern)
Dennstaedtia punctilobula (hay-scented fern)
Dryopteris carthusiana (shield fern, toothed wood fern, spinulose shield fern)
Dryopteris cristata (crested wood fern, buckler fern)
Dryopteris marginalis (marginal wood fern)
Onoclea sensibilis (sensitive fern, bead fern)
Osmunda cinnamomea (cinnamon fern)
Osmunda claytoniana (interrupted fern)
Osmunda regalis (royal fern)
Phegopteris hexagonoptera (broad beech fern)
Polystichum acrostichoides (Christmas fern)
Thelypteris novaboracensis (New York fern, tapering fern)
Thelypteris palustris (marsh fern)
Thelypteris simulata (Massachusetts fern)
Woodwardia areolata (netted chain fern)
Woodwardia virginica (Virginia chain fern)

Forbs (annuals/biennials)

Campanulastrum americanum (American bellflower, tall bellflower)
Lobelia spicata (pale lobelia)
Oenothera biennis (common evening primrose)
Rudbeckia hirta (black-eyed Susan)
Trichostema dichotomum (blue-curls)

Forbs (perennials)

Acorus calamus (sweet flag, calamus)
Ageratina altissima var. altissima (white snakeroot)
Anemone canadensis (Canada anemone, windflower)
Anemone virginiana (thimbleweed, tall anemone)
Apocynum androsaemifolium (spreading dogbane)
Aquilegia canadensis (columbine)
Arisaema triphyllum (Jack-in-the-pulpit, Indian turnip)
Aruncus dioicus (goat's beard)
Asarum canadense (wild ginger)
Asclepias incarnata (swamp milkweed)
Asclepias tuberosa (butterfly weed)
Aster divaricatus (white wood aster)
Aster dumosus (bushy aster)
Aster ericoides (heath aster, white wreath aster)
Aster laevis (smooth aster)
Aster novae-angliae (New England aster)
Aster oblongifolius (aromatic aster)
Aster pilosus (frost aster)
Aster puniceus (red-stem aster, swamp aster)
Caltha palustris (marsh marigold, cowslip)
Cardamine diphylla (two-leaved toothwort)
Caulophyllum thalictroides (blue cohosh)
Chelone glabra (turtlehead)
Chrysogonum virginianum (green-and-gold)
Chrysopsis mariana (Maryland golden aster)
Cimicifuga racemosa (bugbane, black cohosh)
Claytonia virginica (narrow-leaved spring beauty)
Collinsonia canadensis (stoneroot, citronella horsebalm)
Desmodium canadense (Canada tick-trefoil, Canada tickclover)
Dicentra cucullaria (Dutchman's breeches)
Dicentra eximia (wild bleeding heart)
Dodecatheon meadia (shooting star)
Epilobium angustifolium (fireweed, willow herb)
Erythronium americanum (eastern trout lily, yellow trout lily)
Eupatorium fistulosum (Joe-pye weed)
Eupatorium perfoliatum (boneset)
Eupatorium purpureum (Joe-pye weed)
Euphorbia corollata (flowering spurge)
Euthamia graminifolia var. graminifolia (grass-leaved goldenrod)
Fragaria virginiana (wild strawberry)
Galium triflorum (sweet-scented bedstraw)
Gentiana clausa (bottle gentian)
Gentiana saponaria (closed gentian, soapwort gentian)
Geranium maculatum (wild geranium, cranesbill)

Helenium autumnale (common sneezeweed)
Helianthus simulans (narrow-leaved sunflower, swamp sunflower)
Helianthus strumosus (woodland sunflower)
Heliopsis helianthoides (ox-eye sunflower, false sunflower)
Hepatica nobilis var. acuta (sharp-lobed hepatica)
Heuchera americana var. hirsuticaulis (alumroot)
Hibiscus moscheutos (swamp rose mallow, marshmallow hibiscus)
Houstonia caerulea (bluets)
Houstonia longifolia var. longifolia (long-leaved bluets, pale bluets)
Hydrophyllum virginianum (Virginia waterleaf)
Hypoxis hirsuta (yellow star grass)
Iris versicolor (blue flag)
Iris virginica var. shrevei (blue flag)
Kosteletzkya virginica (seashore mallow)
Lespedeza capitata (roundheaded bush clover)
Liatris spicata (marsh blazing star, gayfeather)
Liatris squarrosa (blazing star)
Lilium canadense (wild yellow lily, Canada lily)
Linum virginianum (woodland flax)
Lithospermum canescens (hoary puccoon)
Lobelia cardinalis (cardinal flower)
Lobelia siphilitica (great blue lobelia)
Lysimachia ciliata (fringed loosestrife)
Maianthemum canadense (wild lily-of-the-valley, Canada mayflower)
Maianthemum racemosum ssp. racemosum (false Solomon's seal,
    false spikenard)
Mertensia virginica (bluebells)
Mitchella repens (partridge berry)
Monarda didyma (beebalm, oswego tea)
Monarda fistulosa (wild bergamot, horsemint, beebalm)
Nuphar lutea (yellow pond lily, cow lily, spatter dock)
Oenothera fruticosa (sundrops)
Orontium aquaticum (golden club)
Osmorhiza claytoni (sweet cicely, sweet jarvil)
Peltandra virginica (arrow arum)
Penstemon digitalis (beardtongue)
Penstemon hirsutus (hairy beardtongue)
Phlox divaricata (blue woodland phlox, sweet William)
Phlox stolonifera (creeping phlox)
Podophyllum peltatum (May apple)
Polemonium reptans (Jacob's ladder, Greek valerian)
Polygonatum biflorum (Solomon's seal)
Potentilla arguta (white cinquefoil, prairie cinquefoil, tall cinquefoil)
Potentilla simplex (common cinquefoil)
Pycnanthemum tenuifolium (slender mountain mint)
Pyrola elliptica (shinleaf)
Ranunculus hispidus (early buttercup, tufted buttercup)
Rhexia virginica (meadow beauty)
Rudbeckia fulgida (black-eyed Susan, orange coneflower)
Rudbeckia laciniata (cut-leaf coneflower)
Salvia lyrata (cancer weed, lyre-leaf sage)
Sanguinaria candensis (bloodroot)
Sedum ternatum (wild stonecrop)

Senecio aureus (golden ragwort)
Silene stellata (starry campion)
Silene virginica (fire pink)
Sisyrinchium angustifolium (narrow-leaved blue-eyed grass)
Sisyrinchium atlanticum (eastern blue-eyed grass)
Solidago altissima (tall goldenrod)
Solidago caesia (blue-stemmed goldenrod, wreath goldenrod)
Solidago canadensis (meadow goldenrod)
Solidago juncea (early goldenrod, plume goldenrod)
Solidago nemoralis (gray goldenrod, old-field goldenrod)
Solidago odora (sweet goldenrod)
Solidago rugosa (rough-leaved goldenrod)
Solidago speciosa (showy goldenrod)
Solidago ulmifolia (elm-leaved goldenrod)
Tephrosia virginiana (goat's rue)
Thalictrum dioicum (early meadow rue)
Thalictrum pubescens (tall meadow rue)
Thalictrum thalictroides (rue anemone)
Tiarella cordifolia (foam flower)
Tradescantia ohiensis (Ohio spiderwort)
Tradescantia virginiana (Virginia spiderwort, spider lily)
Trillium erectum (wakerobin, purple trillium)
Uvularia sessilifolia (wildoats, merrybells)
Verbena hastata (blue verbena, blue vervain)
Vernonia noveboracensis (New York ironweed)
Veronicastrum virginicum (Culver's root)
Viola canadensis (Canada violet)
Viola conspersa (American dog violet)
Viola pedata (bird-foot violet)
Viola pubescens (downy or smooth yellow violet)
Viola soraria (common blue violet, meadow violet)
Zizia aptera (heart-leaved golden alexanders)
Zizia aurea (golden alexanders)

Grasses/Grass-like plants

Agrostis scabra (ticklegrass, fly-away grass)
Andropogon gerardii (big bluestem)
Andropogon glomeratus (bushy bluestem)
Andropogon ternarius (splitbeard bluestem)
Andropogon virginicus (broom sedge)
Aristida purpurascens (three-awn grass)
Calamagrostis canadensis (bluejoint grass)
Carex pensylvanica (Pennsylvania sedge)
Carex squarrosa (spreading sedge)
Carex stipata (awl-fruited sedge)
Carex stricta (tussock sedge)
Chasmanthium latifolium (inland sea oats, wild oats, river oats, broad-leaf uniola)
Danthonia spicata (poverty grass)
Distichlis spicata (seashore saltgrass)
Eleocharis palustris (creeping spikesedge, spike rush)
Elymus canadensis (Canada wild rye)
Elymus hystrix var. hystrix (bottlebrush grass)

Eragrostis spectabilis (purple lovegrass, tumblegrass)
Juncus effusus var. solutus (soft rush)
Leersia oryzoides (rice cut grass)
Panicum virgatum (switchgrass)
Saccharum giganteum (sugarcane plume grass)
Schizachyrium scoparium (little bluestem)
Scirpus acutus (hardstem bulrush)
Scirpus atrovirens (dark green bulrush)
Scirpus cyperinus (wool grass)
Scirpus robustus (stout bulrush)
Sorghastrum nutans (Indian grass)
Spartina patens (marsh hay cordgrass, salt meadow cordgrass)
Spartina pectinata (prairie cordgrass, freshwater cordgrass)
Tripsacum dactyloides (eastern gama grass)
Typha angustifolia (narrow-leaved cattail)
Typha latifolia (cattail)

Shrubs (deciduous)

Alnus serrulata (smooth alder)
Amelanchier arborea (downy serviceberry, shadbush, Juneberry)
Amelanchier laevis (smooth serviceberry)
Amelanchier intermedia (intermediate serviceberry)
Aronia melanocarpa (black chokeberry)
Baccharis halimifolia (sea myrtle, groundsel bush)
Castanea pumila (chinquapin)
Ceanothus americanus (New Jersey tea, red root)
Cephalanthus occidentalis (buttonbush)
Clethra alnifolia (summer sweet)
Comptonia peregrina (sweet fern)
Cornus amomum ssp. obliqua (swamp dogwood, silky dogwood)
Cornus racemosa (gray dogwood)
Corylus americana (American hazelnut or filbert)
Diervilla lonicera (bush honeysuckle)
Euonymus americana (strawberry bush, brook euonymus, hearts-a-bustin')
Gaylussacia frondosa (dangleberry)
Hydrangea arborescens (wild hydrangea)
Hypericum hypericoides ssp. hypericoides (St. Andrew's cross)
Hypericum prolificum (shrubby St. John's wort)
Ilex verticillata (winterberry, black alder)
Itea virginica (Virginia willow, sweetspire, tassel-white)
Lindera benzoin (spicebush)
Lonicera dioica (limber or wild honeysuckle)
Lyonia ligustrina (male-berry, male-blueberry)
Physocarpus opulifolius (ninebark)
Prunus virginiana (chokecherry)
Rhododendron periclymenoides (pinxterbloom azalea)
Rhododendron prinophyllum (roseshell azalea, early azalea)
Rhododendron viscosum (swamp azalea)
Rhus aromatica (fragrant sumac)
Rhus copallinum (dwarf or winged sumac)
Rhus glabra (smooth sumac)
Rhus hirta (staghorn sumac)

Rosa carolina (Carolina rose)
Rubus idaeus ssp. strigosus (red raspberry)
Rubus occidentalis (black raspberry, thimbleberry)
Rubus odoratus (thimbleberry)
Sambucus canadensis (elderberry, common elder)
Sambucus racemosa var. pubens (scarlet elderberry, red-berried elder)
Spiraea alba (meadow sweet)
Spiraea tomentosa (steeplebush, hardhack)
Staphylea trifolia (bladdernut)
Symphoricarpos orbiculatus (coralberry, Indian currant)
Vaccinium angustifolium (low-bush blueberry)
Vaccinium corymbosom (highbush blueberry)
Viburnum acerifolium (maple leaf viburnum)
Viburnum dentatum (southern arrowwood)
Viburnum nudum (possumhaw viburnum)
Viburnum nudum var. cassinoides (wild raisin)
Viburnum prunifolium (black haw, nanny berry)

Shrubs (evergreen)

Epigaea repens (trailing arbutus)
Gaultheria procumbens (wintergreen, checkerberry)
Ilex glabra (inkberry, bitter gallberry)
Kalmia latifolia (mountain laurel)
Myrica cerifera (wax myrtle, southern bayberry, candleberry)
Myrica pensylvanica (bayberry)
Rhododendron maximum (rosebay, great laurel)

Trees (deciduous)

Acer negundo (box elder)
Acer pensylvanicum (striped maple)
Acer rubrum (red maple)
Acer saccharinum (silver maple)
Acer saccharum (sugar maple)
Amelanchier canadensis (shadblow serviceberry, Juneberry)
Betula lenta (cherry birch)
Betula nigra (river birch)
Carpinus caroliniana (blue beech, hornbeam, musclewood)
Carya alba (mockernut hickory)
Carya cordiformis (bitternut, swamp hickory)
Carya ovata (shagbark hickory)
Celtis laevigata (sugarberry, hackberry)
Celtis occidentalis (hackberry, sugarberry)
Cercis canadensis (redbud)
Chionanthus virginicus (fringe tree, old man's beard)
Cornus florida (flowering dogwood)
Crataegus crus-galli (cockspur hawthorn)
Crataegus phaenopyrum (Washington hawthorn)
Crataegus punctata (dotted hawthorn, white thorn)
Diospyros virginiana (persimmon)
Fagus grandifolia var. caroliniana (beech)
Fagus grandifolia var. grandifolia (beech)
Fraxinus americana (white ash)

Fraxinus pensylvanica (green ash)
Gleditsia triacanthos (honey locust)
Hamamelis virginiana (witch hazel)
Juglans cinerea (butternut, white walnut)
Juglans nigra (black walnut)
Liquidambar styraciflua (sweet gum)
Liriodendron tulipifera (tulip tree)
Magnolia acuminata (cucumber tree)
Magnolia virginiana (sweetbay, swampbay)
Malus angustifolia (southern crabapple, wild crabapple)
Nyssa sylvatica (black gum, tupelo)
Ostrya virginiana (ironwood, hophornbeam)
Platanus occidentalis (sycamore, plane-tree)
Populus deltoides (eastern cottonwood)
Populus grandidentata (large-toothed aspen)
Populus tremuloides (quaking aspen)
Prunus americana (wild plum)
Prunus nigra (Canada plum)
Prunus pensylvanica (fire or pin cherry)
Prunus serotina (black cherry)
Ptelea trifoliata (wafer ash, common hoptree)
Quercus alba (white oak)
Quercus bicolor (swamp white oak)
Quercus coccinea (scarlet oak)
Quercus falcata (southern red oak, Spanish oak)
Quercus lyrata (overcup oak)
Quercus marilandica (blackjack oak)
Quercus michauxii (swamp chestnut oak)
Quercus muhlenbergii (chinkapin oak, chestnut oak)
Quercus palustris (pin oak)
Quercus phellos (willow oak)
Quercus rubra (red oak)
Quercus stellata (post oak)
Quercus velutina (black oak)
Salix nigra (black willow)
Sassafras albidum (sassafras)
Sorbus americana (mountain ash)
Taxodium distichum (bald cypress)
Tilia americana (American linden, basswood)
Ulmus americana (American elm)
Ulmus rubra (red elm, slippery elm)

Trees (evergreen)

Ilex opaca (American holly, Christmas holly)
Juniperus virginiana (eastern red cedar)
Pinus echinata (shortleaf pine)
Pinus rigida (pitch pine)
Pinus taeda (loblolly pine)
Pinus virginiana (Virginia pine)
Tsuga canadensis (eastern hemlock)

Vines (deciduous)

Bignonia capreolata (cross vine)
Campsis radicans (trumpet creeper, trumpet vine)
Celastrus scandens (American bittersweet)
Clematis occidentalis var. occidentalis (purple clematis)Lonicera sempervirens
  (coral honeysuckle)
Parthenocissus quinquefolia (Virginia creeper)
Passiflora incarnata (passion flower, maypop)
Vitis riparia (riverbank grape)
Vitis rotundifolia (muscadine grape)

FEDERALLY LISTED ENDANGERED SPECIES

Canby's dropwort (Osypolis canbyi)
Harperella (Ptilimnium nodosum (fluviatile))
Northeastern (Barbed bristle) bulrush (Scirpus ancistrochaetus)
Sanplain gerardia (Agalinis acuta)
Sensitive joint-vetch (Aeschynomene virginica)
Swamp pink (Helonias bullata)

MARYLAND NOXIOUS SPECIES

Because the noxious weed lists have continually changed since we gathered them in 1994, we are not including them at this time. Not all States have noxious weed lists. Those that do, do not use the same standards of importance and are not comparable. States typically have included plants that interfere with agriculture (Canada thistle), or cause human health problems (poison ivy). Some States are now including a category of plants that invade and degrade the environment (purple loosestrife). Check with your State's Agriculture Department or Weed Scientist listed below. The noxious weed list can be used two ways on roadsides: l) check to not inadvertently plant these invasive plants, and 2) note the plants you are legally responsible to control. Many States now check adjacent State lists to avoid planting their neighbors' problem plants. Because weeds do not respect political boundaries, and because by their very nature weeds continue to adapt and expand, monitoring and controlling invasives at State borders is a wise part of vegetation management.

(Weed Law only)

Department of Agriculture
Division of Plant Industries
Wayne A. Cawley, Jr. Building
50 Harry S. Truman Parkway
Annapolis, MD 21401

Donald Scott Glenn
University of Maryland
1114 H.J. Patterson Hall
College Park, MD 20742
(301) 405-1329

MARYLAND RESOURCES

Maryland Natural Heritage Program
Department of Natural Resources
Tawes State Office Building, E-l
Annapolis, MD 21401
(410) 260-8400

The Nature Conservancy
Maryland/DC Office
Chevy Chase Metro Building
2 Wisconsin Circle, Ste. 300
Chevy Chase, MD 20815
(301) 656-8673

Maryland Native Plant Society
14720 Claude Lane
Silver Spring, MD 20904

National Arboretum
3501 New York Avenue NE
Washington, DC 20002
(202) 475-4815

POTENTIAL NATURAL VEGETATION ZONES IN
——— MASSACHUSETTS ———

Source: A.W. Kuchler's Potential Natural Vegetation Map, 1964, Revised 1985.
Presented in U.S.G.S. National Atlas of the U.S. Series,
U.S. Geological Survey, Reston, VA.

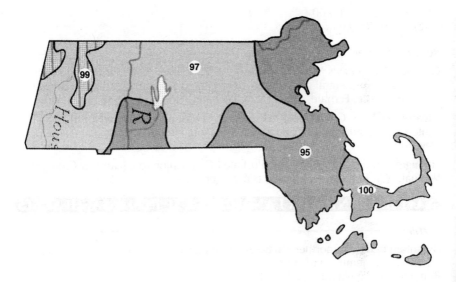

 Appalachian oak forest
(Quercus)

97 Northern hardwoods
(Acer-Betula-Fagus-Tsuga)

 Northern hardwoods-spruce forest
(Acer-Betula-Fagus-Picea-Tsuga)

100 Northeastern oak-pine forest
(Quercus-Pinus)

VEGETATION REFERENCES

(Dominant plant species present in each vegetation type are listed in Appendix 8)

95   *Appalachian Oak Forest (Quercus)*
97   *Northern Hardwoods (Acer-Betula-Fagus-Tsuga)*
99   *Northern Hardwoods-Spruce Forests (Acer-Betula-Fagus-Picea-Tsuga)*
100 *Northeastern Oak-Pine Forest (Quercus-Pinus)*

Botanical Experts

Paul Somers, State Botanist
Massachusetts Natural Heritage and Endangered Species Program
Division of Fisheries and Wildlife
Route 135
Westboro, MA 01581
(508) 792-7270 ext. 200
(508) 792-7275 (fax)

Recommended Flora

Gray, A. 1950. Gray's Manual of Botany: A Handbook of the Flowering Plants and Ferns of the Central and Northeastern United States and Adjacent Canada. 8th Edition (M.L. Fernald, Editor). Van Nostrand, New York, 1632 pgs. + Illus.

Gleason, H.A.; A. Cronquist. 1991. Manual of Vascular Plants of Northeastern United States and Adjacent Canada, 2nd Edition. New York Botanical Garden, New York.

Holmgren, N. H. (Ed.) 1998. The Illustrated Companion to Gleason & Cronquist Manual. N.Y. Bot. Garden, Bronx, NY. 937 pp.

NATIVE PLANTS FOR LANDSCAPE USE IN MASSACHUSETTS

Ferns

Adiantum pedatum (northern maidenhair fern)
Athyrium filix-femina (lady fern)
Botrychium virginianum (rattlesnake fern)
Cystopteris bulbifera (bladder fern)
Dennstaedtia punctilobula (hay-scented fern)
Dryopteris intermedia
Dryopteris marginalis (marginal wood fern)
Gymnocarpium dryopteris (oak fern)
Matteuccia struthiopteris (ostrich fern)
Onoclea sensibilis (sensitive fern, bead fern)
Osmunda cinnamomea (cinnamon fern)
Osmunda claytoniana (interrupted fern)
Osmunda regalis (royal fern)
Phegopteris hexagonoptera (broad beech fern)
Polystichum acrostichoides (Christmas fern)
Thelypteris noveboracensis (New York fern, tapering fern)
Thelypteris palustris (Massachusetts fern)
Woodwardia areolata (netted chain fern)
Woodwardia virginica (Virginia chain fern)

Forbs (annuals/biennials)

Corydalis sempervirens (pale corydalis)
Gentianopsis crinita (fringed gentian)
Lobelia spicata (pale lobelia)
Oenothera biennis (common evening primrose)

Forbs (perennials)

Acorus calamus (sweet flag, calamus)
Actaea pachypoda (white baneberry)
Ageratina altissima var. altissima (white snakeroot)
Allium canadense (wild garlic)
Allium tricoccum (wild leek)
Anaphalis margaritacea (pearly everlasting)
Anemone canadensis (Canada anemone, windflower)
Anemone cylindrica (thimbleweed, candle anemone)
Anemone virginiana (thimbleweed, tall anemone)
Antennaria spp. (pussytoes, everlasting)
Apocynum androsaemifolium (spreading dogbane)
Aquilegia canadensis (columbine)
Arisaema triphyllum (Jack-in-the-pulpit, Indian turnip)
Asarum canadense (wild ginger)
Asclepias amplexicaulis (milkweed)
Asclepias incarnata (swamp milkweed)
Asclepias syriaca (common milkweed)
Asclepias tuberosa (butterfly weed)
Aster divaricatus (white wood aster)
Aster dumosus (bushy aster)
Aster ericoides (heath aster, white wreath aster)
Aster laevis (smooth aster)
Aster novae-angliae (New England aster)
Aster pilosus (frost aster)
Aster puniceus (red-stem aster, swamp aster)
Baptisia tinctoria (wild indigo)
Caltha palustris (marsh marigold, cowslip)
Campanula rotundifolia (harebell)
Cardamine diphylla (two-leaved toothwort)
Caulophyllum thalictroides (blue cohosh)
Chelone glabra (turtlehead)
Claytonia caroliniana (broad-leaved spring beauty)
Clintonia borealis (clintonia, blue-bead lily)
Coptis trifolia ssp. groenlandica (goldthread)
Cornus canadensis (bunchberry)
Desmodium canadense (Canada tick-trefoil, Canada tickclover)
Dicentra cucullaria (Dutchman's breeches)
Epilobium angustifolium (fireweed, willow herb)
Erythronium americanum (eastern trout lily, yellow trout lily)
Eupatorium fistulosum (Joe-pye weed)
Eupatorium maculatum (spotted Joe-pye weed)
Eupatorium perfoliatum (boneset)
Euthamia graminifolia var. graminifolia (grass-leaved goldenrod)
Euthamia tanuifolia
Fragaria virginiana (wild strawberry)

Galium triflorum (sweet-scented bedstraw)
Gentiana clausa (bottle gentian)
Geranium maculatum (wild geranium, cranesbill)
Geum rivale (purple avens, water avens)
Helianthus divaricatus (woodland sunflower)
Helianthus strumosus (woodland sunflower)
Houstonia caerulea (bluets)
Hypoxis hirsuta (yellow star grass)
Iris versicolor (blue flag)
Lespedeza capitata (roundheaded bush clover)
Lilium canadense (wild yellow lily, Canada lily)
Lilium philadelphicum (wood lily)
Lobelia cardinalis (cardinal flower)
Lobelia siphilitica (great blue lobelia)
Lysimachia ciliata (fringed loosestrife)
Maianthemum canadense (wild lily-of-the-valley, Canada mayflower)
Maianthemum racemosum ssp. racemosum (false Solomon's seal,
    false spikenard)
Maianthemum stellatum (starry Solomon's seal)
Mitchella repens (partridge berry)
Monarda fistulosa (wild bergamot, horsemint, beebalm)
Nuphar lutea (yellow pond lily, cow lily, spatter dock)
Osmorhiza longistaalis (sweet cicely, sweet jarvil)
Peltandra virginica (arrow arum)
Pentaphylloides floribunda (potentilla, shrubby cinquefoil)
Potentilla arguta (white cinquefoil, prairie cinquefoil, tall cinquefoil)
Potentilla simplex (common cinquefoil)
Pycnanthemum tenuifolium (slender mountain mint)
Pycnanthemum virginianum (mountain mint)
Pyrola elliptica (shinleaf)
Rhexia virginica (meadow beauty)
Rudbeckia laciniata (cut-leaf coneflower)
Sanguinaria candensis (bloodroot)
Senecio aureus (golden ragwort)
Sibbaldiopsis tridentata (three-toothed cinquefoil)
Sisyrinchium angustifolium (narrow-leaved blue-eyed grass)
Sisyrinchium atlanticum (eastern blue-eyed grass)
Solidago caesia (blue-stemmed goldenrod, wreath goldenrod)
Solidago canadensis (meadow goldenrod)
Solidago juncea (early goldenrod, plume goldenrod)
Solidago nemoralis (gray goldenrod, old-field goldenrod)
Solidago rugosa (rough-leaved goldenrod)
Solidago ulmifolia (elm-leaved goldenrod)
Streptopus roseus (rosy twisted stalk)
Thalictrum dioicum (early meadow rue)
Thalictrum pubescens (tall meadow rue)
Tiarella cordifolia (foam flower)
Trientalis borealis ssp. borealis (starflower)
Trillium cernuum (nodding trillium)
Trillium erectum (wakerobin, purple trillium)
Trillium undulatum (painted trillium)
Uvularia sessilifolia (wildoats, merrybells)

Verbena hastata (blue verbena, blue vervain)
Viola conspersa (American dog violet)
Viola cucullata (blue marsh violet)
Viola pedata (bird-foot violet)
Viola pubescens (downy or smooth yellow violet)
Viola lanceolata
Viola primulifolia (primrose-leaved violet)
Viola sagittata
Viola sororia (common blue violet, meadow violet)
Zizia aurea (golden alexanders)

Grasses/Grass-like plants

Agrostis scabra (ticklegrass, fly-away grass)
Andropogon gerardii (big bluestem)
Bromus pubescens (woodland or Canada brome)
Calamagrostis canadensis (bluejoint grass)
Carex crinita (awned sedge)
Carex echinata
Carex intumescens (bladder sedge)
Carex lurida (sallow sedge)
Carex pensylvanica (Pennsylvania sedge)
Carex plantaginea (plantain-leaved sedge)
Carex scoparia
Carex stipata (awl-fruited sedge)
Carex stricta (tussock sedge)
Carex utriculata (beaked sedge)
Danthonia spicata (poverty grass)
Deschampsia cespitosa (tufted hairgrass)
Eleocharis palustris (creeping spikesedge, spike rush)
Elymus canadensis (Canada wild rye)
Elymus hystrix var. hystrix (bottlebrush grass)
Eragrostis spectabilis (purple lovegrass, tumblegrass)
Hierochloe odorata (sweet grass)
Juncus effusus var. solutus (soft rush)
Leersia oryzoides (rice cut grass)
Muhlenbergia schreberi (nimble Will)
Panicum virgatum (switchgrass)
Schizachyrium scoparium (little bluestem)
Scirpus acutus (hardstem bulrush)
Scirpus atrovirens (dark green bulrush)
Scirpus cyperinus (wool grass)
Scirpus tabernaemontani (great bulrush)
Sorghastrum nutans (Indian grass)
Spartina pectinata (prairie cordgrass, freshwater cordgrass)
Typha latifolia (cattail)

Shrubs (deciduous)

Alnus incana (speckled alder, mountain alder)
Alnus serrulata (smooth alder)
Amelanchier arborea (downy serviceberry, shadbush, Juneberry)
Aronia melanocarpa (black chokeberry)
Ceanothus americanus (New Jersey tea, red root)

Cephalanthus occidentalis (buttonbush)
Clethra alnifolia (summer sweet)
Cornus alternifolia (pogoda dogwood, alternate-leaved dogwood)
Cornus amomum ssp. obliqua (swamp dogwood, silky dogwood)
Cornus racemosa (gray dogwood)
Corylus americana (American hazelnut or filbert)
Corylus cornuta (beaked hazelnut or filbert)
Diervilla lonicera (bush honeysuckle)
Ilex verticillata (winterberry, black alder)
Lindera benzoin (spicebush)
Lonicera dioica (limber or wild honeysuckle)
Lyonia ligustrina (male-berry, male-blueberry)
Prunus virginiana (chokecherry)
Rhododendron canadense (rhodora)
Rhododendron viscosum (swamp azalea)
Rhus copallinum (dwarf or winged sumac)
Rhus glabra (smooth sumac)
Rhus hirta (staghorn sumac)
Ribes cynosbati (prickly gooseberry, dogberry)
Rosa blanda (early wild rose, smooth rose)
Rosa carolina (Carolina rose)
Rubus idaeus ssp. strigosus (red raspberry)
Rubus occidentalis (black raspberry, thimbleberry)
Rubus odoratus (thimbleberry)
Salix bebbiana (Bebb willow, long-beaked willow)
Salix discolor (pussy willow)
Sambucus canadensis (elderberry, common elder)
Sambucus racemosa var. pubens (scarlet elderberry, red-berried elder)
Spiraea tomentosa (steeplebush, hardhack)
Vaccinium angustifolium (low-bush blueberry)
Vaccinium corymbosum (highbush blueberry)
Viburnum acerifolium (maple leaf viburnum)
Viburnum lentago (black haw, nannyberry)
Viburnum nudum var. cassinoides (wild raisin)

Shrubs (evergreen)

Arctostaphylos uva-ursi (bearberry, kinnikinnik)
Epigaea repens (trailing arbutus)
Gaultheria hispidula (creeping snowberry)
Gaultheria procumbens (wintergreen, checkerberry)
Juniperus communis (common juniper)
Kalmia angustifolia (sheep laurel, lambkill kalmia)
Kalmia latifolia (mountain laurel)
Taxus canadensis (Canada yew)

Trees (deciduous)

Acer negundo (box elder)
Acer pensylvanicum (striped maple)
Acer rubrum (red maple)
Acer saccharinum (silver maple)
Acer saccharum (sugar maple)
Acer spicatum (mountain maple)

Amelanchier canadensis (shadblow serviceberry, Juneberry)
Betula lenta (cherry birch)
Betula papyrifera (paper birch)
Carpinus caroliniana (blue beech, hornbeam, musclewood)
Carya cordiformis (bitternut, swamp hickory)
Carya ovata (shagbark hickory)
Cornus florida (flowering dogwood)
Fagus grandifolia var. grandifolia (beech)
Fraxinus americana (white ash)
Fraxinus pensylvanica (green ash)
Hamamelis virginiana (witch hazel)
Larix laricina (tamarack, American larch)
Nyssa sylvatica (black gum, tupelo)
Ostrya virginiana (ironwood, hophornbeam)
Platanus occidentalis (sycamore, plane-tree)
Populus grandidentata (large-toothed aspen)
Populus tremuloides (quaking aspen)
Prunus nigra (Canada plum)
Prunus pensylvanica (fire or pin cherry)
Prunus serotina (black cherry)
Quercus alba (white oak)
Quercus bicolor (swamp white oak)
Quercus coccinea (scarlet oak)
Quercus rubra (red oak)
Quercus velutina (black oak)
Salix nigra (black willow)
Sassafras albidum (sassafras)
Sorbus americana (mountain ash)
Tilia americana (American linden, basswood)
Ulmus americana (American elm)
Ulmus rubra (red elm, slippery elm)

Trees (evergreen)

Abies balsamea (balsam fir)
Chamaecyparis thyoides (white cedar)
Juniperus virginiana (eastern red cedar)
Pinus rigida (pitch pine)
Pinus strobus (eastern white pine)

Vines (deciduous)

Clematis occidentalis var. occidentalis (purple clematis)
Clematis virginiana (virgin's bower)
Parthenocissus quinquefolia (Virginia creeper, woodbine)
Vitis aestivalis (summer grape)
Vitis labrusca (fox grape)
Vitis riparia (riverbank grape)

FEDERALLY LISTED ENDANGERED SPECIES

Northeastern (Barbed bristle) bulrush (Scirpus ancistrochaetus)
Sandplain gerardia (Agalinis acuta)
Small whorled pogonia (Isotria medeoloides)

MASSACHUSETTS NOXIOUS SPECIES

Because the noxious weed lists have continually changed since we gathered them in 1994, we are not including them at this time. Not all States have noxious weed lists. Those that do, do not use the same standards of importance and are not comparable. States typically have included plants that interfere with agriculture (Canada thistle), or cause human health problems (poison ivy). Some States are now including a category of plants that invade and degrade the environment (purple loosestrife). Check with your State's Agriculture Department or Weed Scientist listed below. The noxious weed list can be used two ways on roadsides: l) check to not inadvertently plant these invasive plants, and 2) note the plants you are legally responsible to control. Many States now check adjacent State lists to avoid planting their neighbors' problem plants. Because weeds do not respect political boundaries, and because by their very nature weeds continue to adapt and expand, monitoring and controlling invasives at State borders is a wise part of vegetation management.

(Weed Law Only)

Department of Agriculture
Pest Control Bureau
100 Cambridge Street
Boston, MA 02202

Prasanta Bhowmik, U of M
Plant & Soil Sciences
Stockbridge Hall
Amherst, MA 01003
(413)545-5223

MASSACHUSETTS RESOURCES

Massachusetts Natural Heritage
& Endangered Species Program
Route 135
Westboro, MA 01581
(617) 727-9141

The Nature Conservancy Field Office
79 Milk Street, Ste. 300
Boston, MA 02109
(617) 423-2545

New England Wildflower Society
Garden in the Woods
180 Hemenway Road
Framingham, MA 0170l
(508) 877-7630

The Conway School of
Landscape Design
46 Delabarre Avenue
Conway, MA 01341-01701

Arnold Arboretum
125 Arborway
Jamaica Plain, MA 02130

POTENTIAL NATURAL VEGETATION ZONES IN
MICHIGAN

Source: A.W. Kuchler's Potential Natural Vegetation Map, 1964, Revised 1985.
Presented in U.S.G.S. National Atlas of the U.S. Series,
U.S. Geological Survey, Reston, VA.

73 Mosaic of numbers 66 and 91	**92** Elm-ash forest *(Ulmus-Fraxinus)*
85 Conifer bog *(Picea-Larix-Thuja)*	**93** Beech-maple forest *(Fagus-Acer)*
86 Great Lakes pine forest *(Pinus)*	**97** Northern hardwoods *(Acer-Betula-Fagus-Tsuga)*
91 Oak-hickory forest *(Quercus-Carya)*	**98** Northern hardwoods-fir forest *(Acer-Betula-Abies-Tsuga*

(Dominant plant species present in each vegetation type are listed in Appendix 8)

73 *Mosaic of 66 (Bluestem Prairie) and 91 (Oak-Hickory Forest)*
85 *Conifer Bog (Picea-Larix-Thuja)*
86 *Great Lakes Pine Forest (Pinus)*
91 *Oak-Hickory Forest (Quercus-Carya)*
92 *Elm-Ash Forest (Ulmus-Fraxinus)*
93 *Beech-Maple Forest (Fagus-Acer)*
97 *Northern Hardwoods (Acer-Betula-Fagus-Tsuga)*
98 *Northern Hardwoods-Fir Forests (Acer-Betula-Abies-Tsuga)*

Botanical Experts

Michael R. Penskar, Program Botanist
Michigan Natural Features Inventory
Mason Building
P.O. Box 30444
Lansing, MI 48909-7944
(517) 335-4582
(517) 373-6705 (fax)
internet: penskar@state.mi.us

Recommended Flora

Herman, K.D.; L.A. Masters; M.R. Penskar; A.A. Reznicek; G.S. Wilhelm; W.W. Brodowicz. 1996. Floristic Quality Assessment with Wetland Categories and Computer Applications Programs for the State of Michigan. Michigan Dept. of Natural Resources, Wildlife Division, Natural Heritage Program. Lansing, MI. 21 pp. + append.

Voss, E. G. 1996. Michigan Flora. Part III. Dicots (Pyrolaceae-Compositae). Bull. Cranbrook Inst. Sci. 61 & University of Michigan Herbarium. xix + 622 pp.

Voss, E. G. 1985. Michigan Flora. Part II. Dicots (Saururaceae-Cornaceae). Bull. Cranbrook Inst. Sci. 59 and University of Michigan Herbarium. xix + 724 pp.

Voss, E. G. 1972. Michigan Flora. Part I. Gymnosperms and Monocots. Bull. Cranbrook Inst. Sci. 55 and University of Michigan Herbarium. xv + 488 pp.

NATIVE PLANTS FOR LANDSCAPE USE IN MICHIGAN

Cactus

Opuntia humifusa (prickly pear)

Ferns

Adiantum pedatum (northern maidenhair fern)
Asplenium platyneuron (ebony spleenwort)
Asplenium trichomanes (maidenhair spleenwort)
Athyrium filix-femina (lady fern)
Botrychium virginianum (rattlesnake fern)
Cystopteris bulbifera (bulbet fern)
Cystopteris fragilis (fragile fern)
Dryopteris carthusiana (shield fern, toothed wood fern, spinulose shield fern)
Dryopteris cristata (crested wood fern, buckler fern)

Gymnocarpium dryopteris (oak fern)
Onoclea sensibilis (sensitive fern, bead fern)
Osmunda cinnamomea (cinnamon fern)
Osmunda claytoniana (interrupted fern)
Osmunda regalis (royal fern)
Phegopteris hexagonoptera (broad beech fern)
Polystichum acrostichoides (Christmas fern)
Thelypteris novaboracensis (New York fern, tapering fern)
Woodsia ilvensis (rusty woodsia)
Woodwardia virginica (Virginia chain fern)

Forbs (annuals/biennials)

Corydalis sempervirens (pale corydalis)
Gentianopsis crinita (fringed gentian)
Lobelia spicata (pale lobelia)
Oenothera biennis (common evening primrose)
Rudbeckia hirta (black-eyed Susan)
Senecio plattensis (prairie ragwort, prairie groundsel)

Forbs (perennials)

Acorus calamus (sweet flag, calamus)
Actaea pachypoda (white baneberry)
Allium canadense (wild garlic)
Allium tricoccum (wild leek)
Anaphalis margaritacea (pearly everlasting)
Anemone canadensis (Canada anemone, windflower)
Anemone cylindrica (thimbleweed, candle anemone)
Anemone multifida (early thimbleweed, cut-leaf anemone, Pacific anemone)
Anemone virginiana (thimbleweed, tall anemone)
Antennaria spp. (pussytoes, everlasting)
Apocynum androsaemifolium (spreading dogbane)
Aquilegia canadensis (columbine)
Arisaema triphyllum (Jack-in-the-pulpit, Indian turnip)
Arnica cordifolia (heartleaf arnica)
Asarum canadense (wild ginger)
Asclepias incarnata (swamp milkweed)
Asclepias tuberosa (butterfly weed)
Asclepias verticillata (whorled milkweed)
Aster dumosus (bushy aster)
Aster ericoides (heath aster, white wreath aster)
Aster laevis (smooth aster)
Aster novae-angliae (New England aster)
Aster oolentangiensis (sky blue aster)
Aster pilosus (frost aster)
Aster puniceus (red-stem aster, swamp aster)
Caltha palustris (marsh-marigold, cowslip)
Campanula rotundifolia (harebell)
Cardamine diphylla (two-leaved toothwort)
Caulophyllum thalictroides (blue cohosh)
Chelone glabra (turtlehead)
Cimicifuga racemosa (bugbane, black cohosh)
Claytonia caroliniana (broad-leaved spring beauty)

Claytonia virginica (narrow-leaved spring beauty)
Clintonia borealis (clintonia, blue-bead lily)
Coptis trifolia ssp. groenlandica (goldthread)
Coreopsis lanceolata (lance-leaved coreopsis)
Cornus canadensis (bunchberry)
Desmodium canadense (Canada tick-trefoil, Canada tickclover)
Desmodium illinoense (Illinois tick-trefoil, Illinois tickclover)
Dicentra cucullaria (dutchman's breeches)
Epilobium angustifolium (fireweed, willow herb)
Erythronium americanum (eastern trout lily, yellow trout lily)
Eupatorium maculatum (spotted Joe-pye weed)
Eupatorium perfoliatum (boneset)
Euphorbia corollata (flowering spurge)
Euthamia graminifolia var. graminifolia (grass-leaved goldenrod)
Fragaria virginiana (wild strawberry)
Galium triflorum (sweet-scented bedstraw)
Gentiana andrewsii (bottle gentian)
Geranium maculatum (wild geranium, cranesbill)
Geum rivale (purple avens, water avens)
Helenium autumnale (common sneezeweed)
Helianthus pauciflorus ssp. pauciflorus (stiff sunflower)
Helianthus strumosus (woodland sunflower)
Heliopsis helianthoides (ox-eye sunflower, false sunflower)
Hepatica acutaloba (sharp-lobed hepatica)
Heuchera americana var. hirsuticaulis (alumroot)
Heuchera richardsonii (alum root)
Hieracium longipilum (hairy hawkweed)
Houstonia longifolia var. longifolia (long-leaved bluets, pale bluets)
Hydrophyllum virginianum (Virginia waterleaf)
Hypericum ascyron (great St. John's wort)
Hypoxis hirsuta (yellow star grass)
Iris versicolor (blue flag)
Lespedeza capitata (roundheaded bush clover)
Liatris aspera (rough blazing star, gayfeather)
Liatris cylindracea (dwarf blazing star, gayfeather)
Liatris spicata (marsh blazing star, gayfeather)
Lilium michiganense (Turk's cap lily, Michigan lily)
Lilium philadelphicum (wood lily)
Linnaea borealis (twinflower)
Lithospermum canescens (hoary puccoon)
Lobelia siphilitica (great blue lobelia)
Lupinus perennis (wild lupine)
Lysimachia ciliata (fringed loosestrife)
Maianthemum canadense (wild lily-of-the-valley, Canada mayflower)
Mitchella repens (partridge berry)
Monarda fistulosa (wild bergamot, horsemint, beebalm)
Nuphar lutea (yellow pond-lily, cow-lily, spatter dock)
Osmorhiza claytonii (sweet cicely, sweet jarvil)
Peltandra virginica (arrow arum)
Penstemon digitalis (beardtongue)
Penstemon grandiflorus (large-flowered penstemon)
Pentaphylloides floribunda (potentilla, shrubby cinquefoil)

Phlox divaricata (blue woodland phlox, sweet William)
Phlox pilosa (prairie phlox, downy phlox)
Physostegia virginiana (obedient plant, false dragonhead)
Podophyllum peltatum (May apple)
Potentilla arguta (white cinquefoil, prairie cinquefoil, tall cinquefoil)
Potentilla simplex (common cinquefoil)
Potentilla tridentata (three-toothed cinquefoil)
Pycnanthemum tenuifolium (slender mountain mint)
Pycnanthemum virginianum (mountain mint)
Pyrola elliptica (shinleaf)
Ranunculus hispidus (early buttercup, tufted buttercup)
Ratibida pinnata (gray-headed coneflower, yellow coneflower)
Rhexia virginica (meadow beauty)
Rudbeckia laciniata (cut-leaf coneflower)
Sanguinaria candensis (bloodroot)
Senecio aureus (golden ragwort)
Sisyrinchium angustifolium (narrow-leaved blue-eyed grass)
Smilacina racemosum ssp. racemosum (false Solomon's seal, false spikenard)
Smilacina stellatum (starry Solomon's seal)
Solidago caesia (blue-stemmed goldenrod, wreath goldenrod)
Solidago canadensis (meadow goldenrod)
Solidago juncea (early goldenrod, plume goldenrod)
Solidago nemoralis (gray goldenrod, old-field goldenrod)
Solidago rigida (stiff goldenrod)
Solidago rugosa (rough-leaved goldenrod)
Solidago speciosa (showy goldenrod)
Solidago ulmifolia (elm-leaved goldenrod)
Streptopus roseus (rosy twisted stalk)
Stylophorum diphyllum (celandine poppy)
Tephrosia virginiana (goat's rue)
Thalictrum dasycarpum (tall or purple meadow rue)
Thalictrum dioicum (early meadow rue)
Thalictrum thalictroides (rue anemone)
Tiarella cordifolia (foam flower)
Tradescantia ohiensis (Ohio spiderwort)
Trientalis borealis ssp. borealis (starflower)
Trillium cernuum (nodding trillium)
Trillium erectum (wakerobin, purple trillium)
Uvularia grandiflora (bellwort, merrybells)
Uvularia sessilifolia (wildoats, merrybells)
Verbena hastata (blue verbena, blue vervain)
Veronicastrum virginicum (Culver's root)
Viola canadensis (Canada violet)
Viola conspersa (American dog violet)
Viola pedata (bird-foot violet)
Viola pubescens (downy or smooth yellow violet)
Viola soraria (common blue violet, meadow violet)
Zizia aurea (golden alexanders)

Grasses/Grass-like plants

Agrostis scabra (ticklegrass, fly-away grass)
Andropogon gerardii (big bluestem)

Bromus kalmii (prairie brome, wild chess)
Calamagrostis canadensis (bluejoint grass)
Calamovilfa longifolia (sandreed grass, prairie sandreed)
Carex aquatilis (water sedge)
Carex pensylvanica (Pennsylvania sedge)
Carex plantaginea (plantain-leaved sedge)
Carex stipata (awl-fruited sedge)
Carex stricta (tussock sedge)
Carex utriculata (beaked sedge)
Danthonia spicata (poverty grass)
Deschampsia cespitosa (tufted hairgrass)
Eleocharis palustris (creeping spikesedge, spike-rush)
Elymus canadensis (Canada wild rye)
Elymus hystrix var. hystrix (bottlebrush grass)
Eragrostis spectabilis (purple lovegrass, tumblegrass)
Glyceria grandis (American mannagrass, tall mannagrass, reed meadowgrass)
Hierochloe odorata (sweet grass)
Juncus effusus var. solutus (soft rush)
Juncus interior (inland rush)
Koeleria macrantha (June grass)
Leersia oryzoides (rice cut grass)
Panicum virgatum (switchgrass)
Schizachyrium scoparium (little bluestem)
Scirpus acutus (hardstem bulrush)
Scirpus atrovirens (dark green bulrush)
Scirpus cyperinus (wool grass)
Sorghastrum nutans (Indian grass)
Spartina pectinata (prairie cordgrass, freshwater cordgrass)
Sporobolus neglectus (tall dropseed)
Sporobolus cryptandrus (sand dropseed)
Stipa spartea (porcupine grass)
Typha latifolia (cattail)

Shrubs (deciduous)

Amelanchier arborea (downy serviceberry, shadbush, Juneberry)
Amorpha canescens (leadplant)
Aronia prunifolia (black chokeberry)
Ceanothus americanus (New Jersey tea, red root)
Ceanothus sanguineus (redstem ceanothus, wild lilac)
Cephalanthus occidentalis (buttonbush)
Comptonia peregrina (sweet fern)
Cornus alternifolia (pogoda dogwood, alternate-leaved dogwood)
Cornus amomum ssp. obliqua (swamp dogwood, silky dogwood)
Cornus racemosa (gray dogwood)
Cornus stolonifera (red-twig dogwood, red-osier dogwood)
Corylus americana (American hazelnut or filbert)
Corylus cornuta (beaked hazelnut or filbert)
Crataegus douglasii (black hawthorn)
Diervilla lonicera (bush honeysuckle)
Euonymus atropurpurea (wahoo, burning bush)
Hypericum prolificum (shrubby St. John's wort)
Ilex verticillata (winterberry, black alder)

Lindera benzoin (spicebush)
Lonicera dioica (limber or wild honeysuckle)
Physocarpus opulifolius (ninebark)
Prunus virginiana (chokecherry)
Rhus aromatica (fragrant sumac)
Rhus copallina (dwarf or winged sumac)
Rhus glabra (smooth sumac)
Rhus typhina (staghorn sumac)
Ribes cynosbati (prickly gooseberry, dogberry)
Rosa blanda (early wild rose, smooth rose)
Rosa carolina (Carolina rose)
Rubus strigosus (red raspberry)
Rubus occidentalis (black raspberry, thimbleberry)
Rubus odoratus (thimbleberry)
Salix bebbiana (Bebb willow, long-beaked willow)
Salix discolor (pussy willow)
Sambucus canadensis (elderberry, common elder)
Sambucus pubens (scarlet elderberry, red-berried elder)
Shepherdia canadensis (buffaloberry)
Spiraea alba (meadow sweet)
Spiraea tomentosa (steeplebush, hardhack)
Staphylea trifolia (bladdernut)
Vaccinium angustifolium (low-bush blueberry)
Vaccinium corymbosum (highbush blueberry)
Viburnum acerifolium (maple leaf viburnum)
Viburnum lentago (black haw, nannyberry)
Viburnum cassinoides (wild raisin)
Viburnum opulus var. americanum (high-bush cranberry, American
    cranberrybush viburnum)

Shrubs (evergreen)

Andromeda polifolia var. glaucophylla (bog rosemary)
Arctostaphylos uva-ursi (bearberry, kinnikinnik)
Gaultheria hispidula (creeping snowberry)
Gaultheria procumbens (wintergreen, checkerberry)
Juniperus communis (common juniper)
Juniperus horizontalis (creeping juniper, creeping savin)
Kalmia polifolia (swamp laurel, bog laurel)
Ledum groenlandicum (Labrador tea, muskeg tea)
Taxus canadensis (Canada yew)

Trees (deciduous)

Acer negundo (box elder)
Acer pensylvanicum (striped maple)
Acer rubrum (red maple)
Acer saccharinum (silver maple)
Acer saccharum (sugar maple)
Acer spicatum (mountain maple)
Betula papyrifera (paper birch)
Carpinus caroliniana (blue beech, hornbeam, musclewood)
Carya cordiformis (bitternut, swamp hickory)
Carya ovata (shagbark hickory)

Celtis occidentalis (hackberry, sugarberry)
Cercis canadensis (redbud)
Cornus florida (flowering dogwood)
Crataegus crus-galli (cockspur hawthorn)
Crataegus mollis (downy hawthorn)
Crataegus punctata (dotted hawthorn, white thorn)
Fagus grandifolia (beech)
Fraxinus americana (white ash)
Fraxinus pennsylvanica (green ash)
Hamamelis virginiana (witch hazel)
Juglans cinerea (butternut, white walnut)
Juglans nigra (black walnut)
Larix laricina (tamarack, Eastern larch)
Liriodendron tulipifera (tuliptree)
Nyssa sylvatica (black gum, tupelo)
Ostrya virginiana (ironwood, hophornbeam)
Platanus occidentalis (sycamore, plane-tree)
Populus deltoides (eastern cottonwood)
Populus grandidentata (large-toothed aspen)
Populus tremuloides (quaking aspen)
Prunus americana (wild plum)
Prunus nigra (Canada plum)
Prunus pensylvanica (fire or pin cherry)
Prunus serotina (black cherry)
Ptelea trifoliata (wafer ash, common hoptree)
Quercus alba (white oak)
Quercus bicolor (swamp white oak)
Quercus macrocarpa (bur oak)
Quercus muhlenbergii (chinkapin oak, chestnut oak)
Quercus palustris (pin oak)
Quercus rubra (red oak)
Quercus velutina (black oak)
Salix amygdaloides (peachleaf willow)
Salix nigra (black willow)
Sassafras albidum (sassafras)
Sorbus americana (mountain ash)
Tilia americana (American linden, basswood)
Ulmus americana (American elm)
Ulmus rubra (red elm, slippery elm)

Trees (evergreen)

Abies balsamea (balsam fir)
Juniperus virginiana (Eastern red cedar)
Picea glauca (white spruce)
Pinus resinosa (red pine, Norway pine)
Pinus strobus (eastern white pine)
Thuja occidentalis (arbor vitae, northern white cedar)
Tsuga canadensis (Eastern hemlock)

Vines (deciduous)

Celastrus scandens (American bittersweet)

Clematis occidentalis var. occidentalis (purple clematis)
Clematis virginiana (virgin's bower)
Lonicera sempervirens (coral honeysuckle)
Parthenocissus quinquefolia (Virginia creeper)
Parthenocissus inserta (woodbine)
Vitis riparia (riverbank grape)

FEDERALLY LISTED ENDANGERED SPECIES

American hart's tongue fern (Asplenium scolopendrium var. americanum)
Dwarf lake iris (Iris lacustris)
Eastern prairie fringed orchid (Platanthera leucophaea)
Houghton's goldenrod (Solidago houghtonii)
Michigan monkey-flower (Mimulus glabratus var. michiganensis)
Pitcher's thistle (Cirsium pitcheri)
Small whorled pogonia (Isotria medeoloides)

MICHIGAN NOXIOUS SPECIES

Because the noxious weed lists have continually changed since we gathered
them in 1994, we are not including them at this time. Not all States have
noxious weed lists. Those that do, do not use the same standards of importance
and are not comparable. States typically have included plants that interfere with
agriculture (Canada thistle), or cause human health problems (poison ivy). Some
States are now including a category of plants that invade and degrade the
environment (purple loosestrife). Check with your State's Agriculture Department
or Weed Scientist listed below.   The noxious weed list can be used two ways on
roadsides: l) check to not inadvertantly plant these invasive plants, and 2) note
the plants you are legally responsible to control. Many States now check
adjacent State lists to avoid planting their neighbors' problem plants. Because
weeds do not respect political boundaries, and because by their very nature
weeds continue to adapt and expand, monitoring and controlling invasives at
State borders is a wise part of vegetation management.

(Seed Law only)

Department of Agriculture
Division of Pesticide and Plant
Pest Management,
P.O. Box 30017
Lansing, MI 48909

Karen Ann Renner
Michigan State University
466 Plant/SOIl Science Building
East Lansing, MI 48824
(517) 353-9429

MICHIGAN RESOURCES

Michigan Natural Features Inventory
Mason Building
Box 30444
Lansing, MI 48909
(517) 373-1552

The Nature Conservancy Field Office
2840 East Grand River, Ste. 5
East Lansing, MI 48823
(517) 332-1741

Michigan Botanical Club
Matthaei Botanical Gardens
1800 Dixboro Road
Ann Arbor, MI 48105

Wildflower Association of Michigan
6011 West Joseph Street, Ste. 403
P.O. Box 80527
Lansing, MI 48908

Fernwood Botanic Garden
13988 Range Line Road
Niles, MI 49120

POTENTIAL NATURAL VEGETATION ZONES IN
— MINNESOTA —

Source: A.W. Kuchler's Potential Natural Vegetation Map, 1964, Revised 1985.
Presented in U.S.G.S. National Atlas of the U.S. Series,
U.S. Geological Survey, Reston, VA.

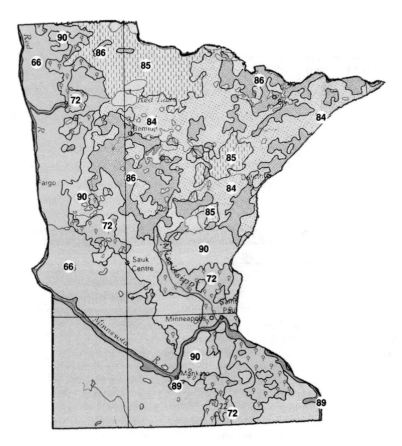

66	Bluestem prairie *(Andropogon-Panicum-Sorghastrum)*	
72	Oak savanna *(Quercus-Andropogon)*	
84	Great Lakes spruce-fir forest *(Picea-Abies)*	
85	Conifer bog *(Picea-Larix-Thuja)*	
86	Great Lakes pine forest *(Pinus)*	
89	Northern floodplain forest *(Populus-Salix-Ulmus)*	
90	Maple-basswood forest *(Acer-Tilia)*	

VEGETATION REFERENCES

(Dominant plant species present in each vegetation type are listed in Appendix 8)

66 *Bluestem Prairie (Andropogon-Panicum-Sorghastrum)*
72 *Oak Savanna (Quercus-Andropogon)*
84 *Great Lakes Spruce-Fir Forest (Picea-Abies)*
85 *Conifer Bog (Picea-Larix-Thuja)*
86 *Great Lakes Pine Forest (Pinus)*
89 *Northern Floodplain Forest (Populus-Salix-Ulmus)*
90 *Maple-Basswood Forest (Acer-Tilia)*

Botanical Experts

Welby Smith, Botanist
Natural Heritage and Nongame Research Program
Division of Fish and Wildlife
500 Lafayette Road Box 7
St. Paul, MN 55155
(612) 297-3733
(612) 297-4961(fax)
internet: welby.smith@dnr.state.mn.us

Recommended Flora

Ownbey, G.B. and T. Morley. 1991. Vascular Plants of Minnesota: A Checklist and Atlas. University of Minnesota Press. Minneapolis, MN. 307 pgs. maps. ISBN 0816619158.

NATIVE PLANTS FOR LANDSCAPE USE IN MINNESOTA

Cactus

Opuntia macrorhiza (common prickly pear)

Ferns

Adiantum pedatum (northern maidenhair fern)
Asplenium platyneuron (ebony spleenwort)
Asplenium trichomanes (maidenhair spleenwort)
Athyrium filix-femina (lady fern)
Botrychium virginianum (rattlesnake fern)
Cystopteris bulbifera (bladder fern)
Cystopteris fragilis (fragile fern)
Dryopteris carthusiana (shield fern, toothed wood fern, spinulose shield fern)
Dryopteris cristata (crested wood fern, buckler fern)
Dryopteris marginalis (marginal wood fern)
Gymnocarpium dryopteris (oak fern)
Matteuccia struthiopteris (ostrich fern)
Onoclea sensibilis (sensitive fern, bead fern)
Osmunda cinnamomea (cinnamon fern)
Osmunda claytoniana (interrupted fern)
Osmunda regalis (royal fern)
Phegopteris hexagonoptera (broad beech fern)
Polystichum acrostichoides (Christmas fern)
Woodsia ilvensis (rusty woodsia)

Forbs (annuals/biennials)

Campanulastrum americanum (American bellflower, tall bellflower)
Corydalis sempervirens (pale corydalis)
Euphorbia marginata (snow-on-the-mountain)
Gentianopsis crinita (fringed gentian)
Helianthus annuus (common sunflower)
Helianthus petiolaris (plains sunflower)
Linum rigidum (yellow flax)
Lobelia spicata (pale lobelia)
Oenothera biennis (common evening primrose)
Oenothera rhombipetala (diamond-petal primrose, four-point evening primrose)
Rudbeckia hirta (black-eyed Susan)
Senecio plattensis (prairie ragwort, prairie groundsel)

Forbs (perennials)

Acorus calamus (sweet flag, calamus)
Actaea pachypoda (white baneberry)
Ageratina altissima var. altissima (white snakeroot)
Allium canadense (wild garlic)
Allium cernuum (nodding onion)
Allium stellatum (wild pink onion)
Allium tricoccum (wild leek)
Anaphalis margaritacea (pearly everlasting)
Anemone canadensis (Canada anemone, windflower)
Anemone caroliniana (Carolina anemone, southern thimbleweed)
Anemone cylindrica (thimbleweed, candle anemone)
Anemone multifida (early thimbleweed, cut-leaf anemone, Pacific anemone)
Anemone virginiana (thimbleweed, tall anemone)
Antennaria spp. (pussytoes, everlasting)
Apocynum androsaemifolium (spreading dogbane)
Aquilegia canadensis (columbine)
Arisaema triphyllum (Jack-in-the-pulpit, Indian turnip)
Asarum canadense (wild ginger)
Asclepias incarnata (swamp milkweed)
Asclepias speciosa (showy milkweed)
Asclepias tuberosa (butterfly weed)
Asclepias verticillata (whorled milkweed)
Aster ericoides (heath aster, white wreath aster)
Aster laevis (smooth aster)
Aster novae-angliae (New England aster)
Aster oblongifolius (aromatic aster)
Aster oolentangiensis (sky blue aster)
Aster pilosus (frost aster)
Aster puniceus (red-stem aster, swamp aster)
Aster sericeus (silky aster)
Astragalus canadensis (milk vetch, Canada milk vetch)
Baptisia alba (white false indigo)
Baptisia alba var. macrophyllla (cream false indigo, plains wild indigo)
Caltha palustris (marsh marigold, cowslip)
Campanula rotundifolia (harebell)
Castilleja sessiliflora (downy painted cup)
Caulophyllum thalictroides (blue cohosh)

Chelone glabra (turtlehead)
Claytonia caroliniana (broad-leaved spring beauty)
Claytonia virginica (narrow-leaved spring beauty)
Clintonia borealis (clintonia, blue-bead lily)
Coptis trifolia ssp. groenlandica (goldthread)
Coreopsis palmata (stiff coreopsis)
Cornus canadensis (bunchberry)
Dalea candida (white prairie clover)
Dalea purpurea (purple prairie clover)
Desmodium canadense (Canada tick-trefoil, Canada tickclover)
Desmodium illinoense (Illinois tick-trefoil, Illinois tickclover)
Dicentra cucullaria (dutchman's breeches)
Dodecatheon meadia (shooting star)
Echinacea angustifolia (narrow-leaved purple coneflower)
Epilobium angustifolium (fireweed, willow herb)
Eryngium yuccifolium (rattlesnake master, button snake-root)
Erythronium americanum (eastern trout lily, yellow trout lily)
Eupatorium maculatum (spotted Joe-pye weed)
Eupatorium perfoliatum (boneset)
Euphorbia corollata (flowering spurge)
Euthamia graminifolia var. graminifolia (grass-leaved goldenrod)
Fragaria virginiana (wild strawberry)
Galium triflorum (sweet-scented bedstraw)
Gentiana alba (cream gentian, yellow gentian)
Gentiana andrewsii (bottle gentian)
Geranium maculatum (wild geranium, cranesbill)
Geum rivale (purple avens, water avens)
Geum triflorum (prairie smoke, purple avens)
Glycyrrhiza lepidota (wild licorice)
Helenium autumnale (common sneezeweed)
Helianthus maximiliani (Maximilian sunflower)
Helianthus pauciflorus ssp. pauciflorus (stiff sunflower)
Helianthus strumosus (woodland sunflower)
Heliopsis helianthoides (ox-eye sunflower, false sunflower)
Hepatica nobilis var. acuta (sharp-lobed hepatica)
Heterotheca villosa var. villosa (golden aster)
Heuchera richardsonii (alum root)
Hieracium longipilum (hairy hawkweed)
Houstonia longifolia var. longifolia (long-leaved bluets, pale bluets)
Hydrastis canadensis (golden seal)
Hydrophyllum virginianum (Virginia waterleaf)
Hypericum ascyron (great St. John's wort)
Iris versicolor (blue flag)
Iris virginica var. shrevei (blue flag)
Lespedeza capitata (roundheaded bush clover)
Liatris aspera (rough blazing star, gayfeather)
Liatris cylindracea (dwarf blazing star, gayfeather)
Liatris punctata (dotted blazing star, gayfeather)
Liatris pycnostachya (prairie blazing star, gayfeather)
Lilium michiganense (Turk's cap lily, Michigan lily)
Lilium philadelphicum (wood lily)
Linnaea borealis (twinflower)

Lithospermum canescens (hoary puccoon)
Lithospermum caroliniense (hairy puccoon, hispid gromwell)
Lithospermum incisum (fringed puccoon, narrow-leaved puccoon)
Lobelia cardinalis (cardinal flower)
Lobelia siphilitica (great blue lobelia)
Lupinus perennis (wild lupine)
Lysimachia ciliata (fringed loosestrife)
Maianthemum canadense (wild lily-of-the-valley, Canada mayflower)
Maianthemum racemosum ssp. racemosum (false Solomon's seal,
    false spikenard)
Maianthemum stellatum (starry Solomon's seal)
Mertensia virginica (bluebells)
Mitchella repens (partridge berry)
Monarda fistulosa (wild bergamot, horsemint, beebalm)
Nothocalais cuspidata (prairie dandelion)
Nuphar lutea (yellow pond lily, cow lily, spatter dock)
Osmorhiza berteroi (mountain sweet cicely)
Osmorhiza claytoni (sweet cicely, sweet jarvil)
Penstemon albidus (white beardtongue)
Penstemon grandiflorus (large-flowered penstemon)
Pentaphylloides floribunda (potentilla, shrubby cinquefoil)
Phlox divaricata ssp. laphamii (blue phlox, sweet William)
Phlox pilosa (prairie phlox, downy phlox)
Physostegia virginiana (obedient plant, false dragonhead)
Podophyllum peltatum (May apple)
Polemonium reptans (Jacob's ladder, Greek valerian)
Polygonatum biflorum (Solomon's seal)
Potentilla arguta (white cinquefoil, prairie cinquefoil, tall cinquefoil)
Potentilla simplex (common cinquefoil)
Pycnanthemum virginianum (mountain mint)
Pyrola elliptica (shinleaf)
Ranunculus hispidus (early buttercup, tufted buttercup)
Ratibida columnifera (prairie coneflower, long-headed coneflower, Mexican hat)
Ratibida pinnata (gray-headed coneflower, yellow coneflower)
Rudbeckia laciniata (cut-leaf coneflower)
Sanguinaria candensis (bloodroot)
Senecio aureus (golden ragwort)
Sibbaldiopsis tridentata (three-toothed cinquefoil)
Silene stellata (starry campion)
Silphium laciniatum (compass plant)
Silphium perfoliatum (cup plant)
Sisyrinchium angustifolium (narrow-leaved blue-eyed grass)
Sisyrinchium campestre (white-eyed grass, prairie blue-eyed grass)
Solidago canadensis (meadow goldenrod)
Solidago juncea (early goldenrod, plume goldenrod)
Solidago missouriensis (Missouri goldenrod, prairie goldenrod)
Solidago nemoralis (gray goldenrod, old-field goldenrod)
Solidago rigida (stiff goldenrod)
Solidago speciosa (showy goldenrod)
Solidago ulmifolia (elm-leaved goldenrod)
Streptopus roseus (rosy twisted stalk)
Tephrosia virginiana (goat's rue)

Thalictrum dasycarpum (tall or purple meadow rue)
Thalictrum dioicum (early meadow rue)
Thalictrum thalictroides (rue anemone)
Tradescantia ohiensis (Ohio spiderwort)
Trientalis borealis ssp. borealis (starflower)
Trillium cernuum (nodding trillium)
Uvularia grandiflora (bellwort, merrybells)
Uvularia sessilifolia (wildoats, merrybells)
Verbena hastata (blue verbena, blue vervain)
Vernonia fasciculata (ironweed)
Veronicastrum virginicum (Culver's root)
Viola canadensis (Canada violet)
Viola conspersa (American dog violet)
Viola missouriensis (Missouri violet)
Viola pedata (bird-foot violet)
Viola pedatifida (prairie violet)
Viola pubescens (downy or smooth yellow violet)
Viola soraria (common blue violet, meadow violet)
Zizia aptera (heart-leaved golden alexanders)
Zizia aurea (golden alexanders)

Grasses/Grass-like plants

Agrostis scabra (ticklegrass, fly-away grass)
Andropogon gerardii (big bluestem)
Aristida purpurea var. longiseta (red three awn)
Bouteloua curtipendula (sideoats grama)
Bouteloua gracilis (blue grama)
Bouteloua hirsuta (hairy grama)
Bromus kalmii (prairie brome, wild chess)
Buchloe dactyloides (buffalograss)
Calamagrostis canadensis (bluejoint grass)
Calamovilfa longifolia (sandreed grass, prairie sandreed)
Carex aquatilis (water sedge)
Carex pensylvanica (Pennsylvania sedge)
Carex plantaginea (plantain-leaved sedge)
Carex stipata (awl-fruited sedge)
Carex stricta (tussock sedge)
Carex utriculata (beaked sedge)
Danthonia spicata (poverty grass)
Deschampsia cespitosa (tufted hairgrass)
Distichlis spicata (seashore saltgrass)
Eleocharis palustris (creeping spikesedge, spike rush)
Elymus canadensis (Canada wild rye)
Elymus hystrix var. hystrix (bottlebrush grass)
Eragrostis spectabilis (purple lovegrass, tumblegrass)
Glyceria grandis (American mannagrass, tall mannagrass, reed meadowgrass)
Hierochloe odorata (sweet grass)
Juncus effusus var. solutus (soft rush)
Juncus interior (inland rush)
Koeleria macrantha (June grass)
Leersia oryzoides (rice cut grass)
Melica nitens (three-flower melic grass)

Oryzopsis hymenoides (Indian ricegrass)
Panicum virgatum (switchgrass)
Pascopyrum smithii (western wheatgrass)
Schizachyrium scoparium (little bluestem)
Scirpus acutus (hardstem bulrush)
Scirpus atrovirens (dark green bulrush)
Scirpus cyperinus (wool grass)
Scirpus maritimus (alkali bulrush, prairie bulrush, bayonet grass)
Scirpus tabernaemontani (great bulrush)
Sorghastrum nutans (Indian grass)
Spartina pectinata (prairie cordgrass, freshwater cordgrass)
Sporobolus compositus var. compositus (tall dropseed)
Sporobolus cryptandrus (sand dropseed)
Sporobolus heterolepis (northern prairie dropseed)
Stipa comata (needle-and-thread grass)
Stipa spartea (porcupine grass)
Trisetum spicatum (spike trisetum)
Typha latifolia (cattail)

Shrubs (deciduous)

Alnus incana (speckled alder, mountain alder)
Amelanchier alnifolia (saskatoon, western serviceberry, Juneberry)
Amelanchier arborea (downy serviceberry, shadbush, Juneberry)
Amorpha canescens (leadplant)
Amorpha fruticosa (false indigo, Indigo bush)
Amorpha nana (dwarf wild indigo)
Aronia melanocarpa (black chokeberry)
Artemisia frigida (prairie sagewort, fringed sage)
Ceanothus americanus (New Jersey tea, red root)
Cephalanthus occidentalis (buttonbush)
Comptonia peregrina (sweet fern)
Cornus alternifolia (pogoda dogwood, alternate-leaved dogwood)
Cornus amomum ssp. obliqua (swamp dogwood, silky dogwood)
Cornus racemosa (gray dogwood)
Cornus sericea (red-twig dogwood, red-osier dogwood)
Corylus americana (American hazelnut or filbert)
Corylus cornuta (beaked hazelnut or filbert)
Crataegus douglasii (black hawthorn)
Diervilla lonicera (bush honeysuckle)
Dirca palustris (leatherwood, ropebark)
Elaeagnus commutata (silverberry, wild olive, wolf willow)
Euonymus atropurpurea (wahoo, burning bush)
Lonicera dioica (limber or wild honeysuckle)
Physocarpus opulifolius (ninebark)
Prunus pumila var. besseyi (sand cherry)
Prunus virginiana (chokecherry)
Rhus glabra (smooth sumac)
Rhus hirta (staghorn sumac)
Ribes cynosbati (prickly gooseberry, dogberry)
Rosa arkansana (prairie rose)
Rosa blanda (early wild rose, smooth rose)
Rubus idaeus ssp. strigosus (red raspberry)

Rubus occidentalis (black raspberry, thimbleberry)
Rubus parviflorus (western thimbleberry)
Salix bebbiana (Bebb willow, long-beaked willow)
Salix discolor (pussy willow)
Sambucus canadensis (elderberry, common elder)
Sambucus racemosa var. pubens (scarlet elderberry, red-berried elder)
Shepherdia argentea (silver buffaloberry)
Shepherdia canadensis (buffaloberry)
Spiraea alba (meadow sweet)
Spiraea tomentosa (steeplebush, hardhack)
Staphylea trifolia (bladdernut)
Symphoricarpos albus (snowberry)
Vaccinium angustifolium (low-bush blueberry)
Vaccinium uliginosum (alpine blueberry, bog blueberry)
Viburnum edule (Moosewood viburnum)
Viburnum opulus var. americanum (high-bush cranberry, American cranberrybush viburnum)

Shrubs (evergreen)

Andromeda polifolia var. glaucophylla (bog rosemary)
Arctostaphylos uva-ursi (bearberry, kinnikinnik)
Gaultheria hispidula (creeping snowberry)
Gaultheria procumbens (wintergreen, checkerberry)
Juniperus communis (common juniper)
Juniperus horizontalis (creeping juniper, creeping savin)
Kalmia polifolia (swamp laurel, bog laurel)
Ledum groenlandicum (Labrador tea, muskeg tea)
Taxus canadensis (Canada yew)
Vaccinium vitis-idaea (mountain cranberry, lingonberry, cowberry)

Trees (deciduous)

Acer negundo (box elder)
Acer rubrum (red maple)
Acer saccharinum (silver maple)
Acer saccharum (sugar maple)
Acer spicatum (mountain maple)
Betula nigra (river birch)
Betula papyrifera (paper birch)
Carpinus caroliniana (blue beech, hornbeam, musclewood)
Carya cordiformis (bitternut, swamp hickory)
Carya ovata (shagbark hickory)
Celtis occidentalis (hackberry, sugarberry)
Crataegus mollis (downy hawthorn)
Crataegus punctata (dotted hawthorn, white thorn)
Fraxinus americana (white ash)
Fraxinus pensylvanica (green ash)
Gymnocladus dioica (Kentucky coffee tree)
Hamamelis virginiana (witch hazel)
Juglans cinerea (butternut, white walnut)
Juglans nigra (black walnut)
Larix laricina (tamarack, American larch)
Malus ioensis var. ioensis (prairie crabapple)

Ostrya virginiana (ironwood, hophornbeam)
Populus deltoides (eastern cottonwood)
Populus grandidentata (large-toothed aspen)
Populus tremuloides (quaking aspen)
Prunus americana (wild plum)
Prunus nigra (Canada plum)
Prunus pensylvanica (fire or pin cherry)
Prunus serotina (black cherry)
Quercus alba (white oak)
Quercus bicolor (swamp white oak)
Quercus macrocarpa (bur oak)
Quercus muhlenbergii (chinkapin oak, chestnut oak)
Quercus rubra (red oak)
Quercus velutina (black oak)
Salix amygdaloides (peachleaf willow)
Salix nigra (black willow)
Sorbus americana (mountain ash)
Tilia americana (American linden, basswood)
Ulmus americana (American elm)
Ulmus rubra (red elm, slippery elm)

Trees (evergreen)

Abies balsamea (balsam fir)
Juniperus virginiana (eastern red cedar)
Picea glauca (white spruce)
Pinus resinosa (red pine, Norway pine)
Pinus strobus (eastern white pine)
Thuja occidentalis (arbor vitae, northern white cedar)
Tsuga canadensis (eastern hemlock)

Vines (deciduous)

Celastrus scandens (American bittersweet)
Clematis occidentalis var. occidentalis (purple clematis)
Clematis virginiana (virgin's bower)
Parthenocissus quinquefolia (Virginia creeper)
Parthenocissus quinquefolia var. quinquefolia (woodbine)
Vitis riparia (riverbank grape)

FEDERALLY LISTED ENDANGERED SPECIES

Leedy's roseroot (Sedum integrifolium ssp. Leedyi)
Minnesota trout lily (Erythronium propullans)
Prairie bush-clover (Lespedeza leptostachya)
Western prairie fringed orchid (Platanthera praeclara)

MINNESOTA NOXIOUS SPECIES

Because the noxious weed lists have continually changed since we gathered them in 1994, we are not including them at this time. Not all States have noxious weed lists. Those that do, do not use the same standards of importance and are not comparable. States typically have included plants that interfere with agriculture (Canada thistle), or cause human health problems (poison ivy). Some States are now including a category of plants that invade and degrade the environment (purple loosestrife). Check with your State's Agriculture Department or Weed Scientist listed below. The noxious weed list can be used two ways on roadsides: l) check to not inadvertently plant these invasive plants, and 2) note the plants you are legally responsible to control. Many States now check adjacent State lists to avoid planting their neighbors' problem plants. Because weeds do not respect political boundaries, and because by their very nature weeds continue to adapt and expand, monitoring and controlling invasives at State borders is a wise part of vegetation management.

(Weed and Seed Laws)

Chuck Dale
Department of Agriculture
Division of Plant Protection
90 West Plato Boulevard
St. Paul, MN 55107

Roger Becker, U. of M.
Agronomy & Plant Genetics
411 Borlaug Hall
St. Paul, MN 55108
(651) 625-5753

MINNESOTA RESOURCES

Minnesota Natural Heritage
& Nongame Research
Department of Natural Resources
500 Lafayette Road, Box 7
St. Paul, MN 55155
(612) 296-3344
(612) 297-4961(fax)

The Nature Conservancy Field Office
1313 Fifth Street S.E., Ste. 320
Minneapolis, MN 55414
(612) 331-0750

Minnesota Native Plant Society
220 Biological Science Center
1446 Gortner Avenue
St. Paul, MN 55108

Prairie Wetlands Learning Center
P.O. Box 23
Fergus Falls, MN 56538

POTENTIAL NATURAL VEGETATION ZONES IN

MISSISSIPPI

Source: A.W. Kuchler's Potential Natural Vegetation Map, 1964, Revised 1985.
Presented in U.S.G.S. National Atlas of the U.S. Series,
U.S. Geological Survey, Reston, VA.

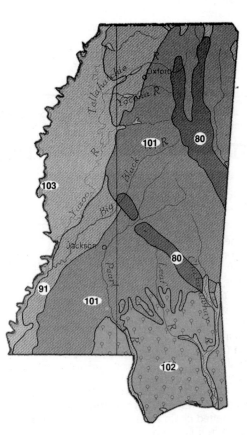

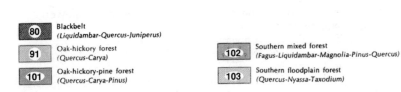

80	Blackbelt *(Liquidambar-Quercus-Juniperus)*	
91	Oak-hickory forest *(Quercus-Carya)*	**102** Southern mixed forest *(Fagus-Liquidambar-Magnolia-Pinus-Quercus)*
101	Oak-hickory-pine forest *(Quercus-Carya-Pinus)*	**103** Southern floodplain forest *(Quercus-Nyassa-Taxodium)*

287

(Dominant plant species present in each vegetation type are listed in Appendix 8)

80   *Blackbelt (Liquidambar-Quercus-Juniperus)*
91   *Oak-Hickory Forest (Quercus-Carya)*
101 *Oak-Hickory-Pine Forest (Quercus-Carya-Pinus)*
102 *Southern Mixed Forest (Fagus-Liquidambar-Magnolia-Pinus-Quercus)*
103 *Southern Floodplain Forest (Quercus-Nyssa-Taxodium)*

Botanical Experts

Ken Gordon, Coordinator/Botanist
Museum of Natural Science
111 North Jefferson St.
Jackson, MS 39202
(601) 354-7303
(601) 354-7227(fax)

Recommended Flora

No recommended flora exists specifically for Mississippi. Suggested flora for neighboring states may be helpful.

NATIVE PLANTS FOR LANDSCAPE USE IN MISSISSIPPI

Cactus

Opuntia humifusa (prickly pear)

Ferns

Adiantum capillus-veneris (southern maidenhair fern)
Adiantum pedatum (northern maidenhair fern)
Asplenium platyneuron (ebony spleenwort)
Asplenium trichomanes (maidenhair spleenwort)
Athyrium filix-femina (lady fern)
Botrychium virginianum (rattlesnake fern)
Onoclea sensibilis (sensitive fern, bead fern)
Osmunda cinnamomea (cinnamon fern)
Osmunda claytoniana (interrupted fern)
Osmunda regalis (royal fern)
Polystichum acrostichoides (Christmas fern)
Thelypteris kunthii (southern shield fern, wood fern, river fern)
Thelypteris novaboracensis (New York fern, tapering fern)
Woodwardia areolata (netted chain fern)
Woodwardia virginica (Virginia chain fern)

Forbs (annuals/biennials)

Campanulastrum americanum (American bellflower, tall bellflower)
Dracopsis amplexicaulis (clasping leaf coneflower)
Glandularia canadensis (rose vervain, sweet William)
Lesquerella gracilis (bladderpod)
Lobelia spicata (pale lobelia)
Oenothera biennis (common evening primrose)
Rudbeckia hirta (black-eyed Susan)

Sabatia campestris (prairie rose gentian, prairie sabatia, meadow pink)
Senecio glabellus (butterweed)
Senecio plattensis (prairie ragwort, prairie groundsel)

Forbs (perennials)

Acorus calamus (sweet flag, calamus)
Actaea pachypoda (white baneberry)
Ageratina altissima var. altissima (white snakeroot)
Allium canadense (wild garlic)
Allium cernuum (nodding onion)
Amsonia tabernaemontana (blue star)
Antennaria spp. (pussytoes, everlasting)
Apocynum androsaemifolium (spreading dogbane)
Aquilegia canadensis (columbine)
Arisaema triphyllum (Jack-in-the-pulpit, Indian turnip)
Asarum canadense (wild ginger)
Asclepias incarnata (swamp milkweed)
Asclepias tuberosa (butterfly weed)
Asclepias verticillata (whorled milkweed)
Aster dumosus (bushy aster)
Aster ericoides (heath aster, white wreath aster)
Aster novae-angliae (New England aster)
Aster pilosus (frost aster)
Aster puniceus (red-stem aster, swamp aster)
Astragalus canadensis (milk vetch, Canada milk vetch)
Baptisia alba (white false indigo)
Callirhoe papaver (poppy mallow)
Camassia scilloides (wild hyacinth)
Canna flaccida (golden canna)
Cardamine diphylla (two-leaved toothwort)
Chrysopsis mariana (Maryland golden aster)
Cimicifuga racemosa (bugbane, black cohosh)
Claytonia virginica (narrow-leaved spring beauty)
Collinsonia canadensis (stoneroot, citronella horsebalm)
Coreopsis auriculata (early coreopsis)
Coreopsis grandiflora (coreopsis)
Coreopsis lanceolata (lance-leaved coreopsis)
Coreopsis tripteris (tall coreopsis)
Dalea purpurea (purple prairie clover)
Delphinium carolinianum (blue larkspur)
Delphinium tricorne (dwarf larkspur)
Desmodium canadense (Canada tick-trefoil, Canada tickclover)
Dicentra cucullaria (dutchman's breeches)
Dodecatheon meadia (shooting star)
Echinacea purpurea (purple coneflower)
Eryngium yuccifolium (rattlesnake master, button snake-root)
Erythronium americanum (eastern trout lily, yellow trout lily)
Eupatorium coelestinum (mist flower)
Eupatorium fistulosum (Joe-pye weed)
Eupatorium perfoliatum (boneset)
Eupatorium purpureum (Joe-pye weed)
Euphorbia corollata (flowering spurge)

Fragaria virginiana (wild strawberry)
Galium triflorum (sweet-scented bedstraw)
Gentiana saponaria (closed gentian, soapwort gentian)
Geranium maculatum (wild geranium, cranesbill)
Glandularia bipinnatifida var. bipinnatifida (prairie verbena, Dakota vervain)
Hedyotis nigricans (bluets)
Helenium autumnale (common sneezeweed)
Helianthus simulans (narrow-leaved sunflower, swamp sunflower)
Helianthus strumosus (woodland sunflower)
Heliopsis helianthoides (ox-eye sunflower, false sunflower)
Heuchera americana var. hirsuticaulis (alumroot)
Houstonia caerulea (bluets)
Houstonia longifolia var. longifolia (long-leaved bluets, pale bluets)
Houstonia procumbens (innocence)
Hydrastis canadensis (golden seal)
Hymenocallis caroliniana (spider lily, rain lily)
Hypoxis hirsuta (yellow star grass)
Iris cristata (dwarf crested iris)
Iris virginica (southern blue flag)
Kosteletzkya virginica (seashore mallow)
Lespedeza capitata (roundheaded bush clover)
Liatris aspera (rough blazing star, gayfeather)
Liatris elegans (gayfeather)
Liatris spicata (marsh blazing star, gayfeather)
Liatris squarrosa (blazing star)
Lilium michauxii (Carolina lily)
Lilium michiganense (Turk's cap lily, Michigan lily)
Lithospermum caroliniense (hairy puccoon, hispid gromwell)
Lobelia cardinalis (cardinal flower)
Lobelia siphilitica (great blue lobelia)
Lupinus perennis (wild lupine)
Maianthemum racemosum ssp. racemosum (false Solomon's seal, false spikenard)
Manfreda virginica (rattlesnake master, false aloe)
Mertensia virginica (bluebells)
Mitchella repens (partridge berry)
Monarda fistulosa (wild bergamot, horsemint, beebalm)
Nuphar lutea (yellow pond lily, cow lily, spatter dock)
Oenothera fruticosa (sundrops)
Orontium aquaticum (golden club)
Pachysandra procumbens (Alleghany spurge)
Peltandra virginica (arrow arum)
Penstemon digitalis (beardtongue)
Phlox carolina (Carolina phlox)
Phlox pilosa (prairie phlox, downy phlox)
Physostegia virginiana (obedient plant, false dragonhead)
Podophyllum peltatum (May apple)
Polemonium reptans (Jacob's ladder, Greek valerian)
Polygonatum biflorum (Solomon's seal)
Potentilla simplex (common cinquefoil)
Pycnanthemum tenuifolium (slender mountain mint)
Ranunculus hispidus (early buttercup, tufted buttercup)

Ratibida pinnata (gray-headed coneflower, yellow coneflower)
Rhexia virginica (meadow beauty)
Rudbeckia fulgida (black-eyed Susan, orange coneflower)
Rudbeckia laciniata (cut-leaf coneflower)
Ruellia humilis (wild petunia)
Salvia lyrata (cancer weed, lyre-leaf sage)
Sanguinaria candensis (bloodroot)
Sedum ternatum (wild stonecrop)
Senecio aureus (golden ragwort)
Silene stellata (starry campion)
Silene virginica (fire pink)
Silphium integrifolium (rosinweed)
Silphium laciniatum (compass plant)
Silphium terebinthinaceum (prairie dock)
Sisyrinchium angustifolium (narrow-leaved blue-eyed grass)
Sisyrinchium mucronatum (eastern blue-eyed grass)
Solidago caesia (blue-stemmed goldenrod, wreath goldenrod)
Solidago canadensis (meadow goldenrod)
Solidago nemoralis (gray goldenrod, old-field goldenrod)
Solidago odora (sweet goldenrod)
Solidago rigida (stiff goldenrod)
Solidago rugosa (rough-leaved goldenrod)
Solidago sempervirens (seaside goldenrod)
Solidago ulmifolia (elm-leaved goldenrod)
Spigelia marilandica (Indian pink)
Stokesia laevis (stokes' aster)
Tephrosia virginiana (goat's rue)
Thalictrum dioicum (early meadow rue)
Thalictrum pubescens (tall meadow rue)
Thalictrum thalictroides (rue anemone)
Tiarella cordifolia (foam flower)
Tradescantia hirsuticaulis (hairy spiderwort)
Tradescantia ohiensis (Ohio spiderwort)
Tradescantia virginiana (Virginia spiderwort, spider lily)
Uvularia grandiflora (bellwort, merrybells)
Uvularia sessilifolia (wildoats, merrybells)
Vernonia fasciculata (ironweed)
Vernonia noveboracensis (New York ironweed)
Veronicastrum virginicum (Culver's root)
Viola affinis (Florida violet)
Viola pedata (bird-foot violet)
Viola pubescens (downy or smooth yellow violet)
Viola sororia (common blue violet, meadow violet)
Yucca aloifolia (Spanish dagger)
Zephyranthes atamasca (atamasco lily, Easter lily)
Zizia aptera (heart-leaved golden alexanders)
Zizia aurea (golden alexanders)

Grasses/Grass-like plants

Agrostis scabra (ticklegrass, fly-away grass)
Andropogon gerardii (big bluestem)
Andropogon glomeratus (bushy bluestem)

Andropogon ternarius (splitbeard bluestem)
Andropogon virginicus (broom sedge)
Arundinaria gigantea (giant cane)
Bouteloua curtipendula (sideoats grama)
Carex stipata (awl-fruited sedge)
Carex stricta (tussock sedge)
Chasmanthium latifolium (inland sea oats, wild oats, river oats, broad-leaf uniola)
Danthonia spicata (poverty grass)
Distichlis spicata (seashore saltgrass)
Elymus canadensis (Canada wild rye)
Eragrostis spectabilis (purple lovegrass, tumblegrass)
Juncus effusus var. solutus (soft rush)
Leersia oryzoides (rice cut grass)
Muhlenbergia capillaris (gulf muhly, hair grass)
Panicum virgatum (switchgrass)
Saccharum giganteum (sugarcane plume grass)
Schizachyrium scoparium (little bluestem)
Scirpus cyperinus (wool grass)
Scirpus tabernaemontani (great bulrush)
Sorghastrum nutans (Indian grass)
Spartina patens (marsh hay cordgrass, salt meadow cordgrass)
Sporobolus compositus var. compositus (tall dropseed)
Tripsacum dactyloides (eastern gama grass)
Typha latifolia (cattail)

Shrubs (deciduous)

Alnus serrulata (smooth alder)
Amelanchier arborea (downy serviceberry, shadbush, Juneberry)
Amorpha fruticosa (false indigo, Indigo bush)
Baccharis halimifolia (sea myrtle, groundsel bush)
Callicarpa americana (American beautyberry, French mulberry)
Calycanthus floridus (Carolina allspice, sweet shrub)
Castanea pumila (chinquapin)
Ceanothus americanus (New Jersey tea, red root)
Cephalanthus occidentalis (buttonbush)
Clethra alnifolia (summer sweet)
Cornus alternifolia (pogoda dogwood, alternate-leaved dogwood)
Cornus drummondii (rough-leaf dogwood)
Corylus americana (American hazelnut or filbert)
Dirca palustris (leatherwood, ropebark)
Erythrina herbacea (coral bean)
Euonymus americana (strawberry bush, brook euonymus, hearts-a-bustin')
Euonymus atropurpurea (wahoo, burning bush)
Forestiera acuminata (swamp privet)
Frangula caroliniana (Carolina buckthorn)
Hibiscus coccineus (wild red mallow)
Hydrangea arborescens (wild hydrangea)
Hydrangea quercifolia (oakleaf hydrangea)
Hypericum hypericoides ssp. hypericoides (St. Andrew's cross)
Hypericum prolificum (shrubby St. John's wort)
Ilex verticillata (winterberry, black alder)
Itea virginica (Virginia willow, sweetspire, tassel-white)

Lindera benzoin (spicebush)
Lycium carolinianum (Christmas berry, matrimony vine)
Lyonia ligustrina (male-berry, male-blueberry)
Rhododendron calendulaceum (flame azalea)
Rhododendron canescens (wild, piedmont, or sweet azalea)
Rhododendron viscosum (swamp azalea)
Rhus copallinum (dwarf or winged sumac)
Rhus glabra (smooth sumac)
Rosa carolina (Carolina rose)
Sambucus canadensis (elderberry, common elder)
Staphylea trifolia (bladdernut)
Stewartia malacodendron (silky camellia)
Styrax americanus (American silverbells)
Vaccinium arboreum (sparkleberry, farkleberry)
Viburnum acerifolium (maple leaf viburnum)
Viburnum dentatum (southern arrowwood)
Viburnum nudum (possumhaw viburnum)
Viburnum nudum var. cassinoides (wild raisin)
Viburnum prunifolium (black haw, nanny berry)
Viburnum rufidulum (southern or rusty black haw)

Shrubs (evergreen)

Epigaea repens (trailing arbutus)
Gordonia lasianthus (loblolly bay, gordonia)
Ilex glabra (inkberry, bitter gallberry)
Ilex vomitoria (yaupon)
Illicium floridanum (Florida anise tree)
Kalmia latifolia (mountain laurel)
Leucothoe axillaris (coast leucothoe)
Myrica cerifera (wax myrtle, southern bayberry, candleberry)
Sabal minor (dwarf palmetto)
Serenoa repens (saw palmetto)

Trees (deciduous)

Acer barbatum (Florida maple, southern sugar maple)
Acer leucoderme (chalk maple)
Acer negundo (box elder)
Acer rubrum (red maple)
Acer saccharinum (silver maple)
Aesculus glabra (Ohio buckeye, horse chestnut)
Aesculus pavia var. pavia (red buckeye)
Betula nigra (river birch)
Carpinus caroliniana (blue beech, hornbeam, musclewood)
Carya alba (mockernut hickory)
Carya cordiformis (bitternut, swamp hickory)
Carya illinoinensis (pecan)
Carya ovata (shagbark hickory)
Celtis laevigata (sugarberry, hackberry)
Cercis canadensis (redbud)
Chionanthus virginicus (fringe tree, old man's beard)
Cladrastis kentukea (yellowwood)
Cornus florida (flowering dogwood)

Crataegus crus-galli (cockspur hawthorn)
Crataegus marshallii (parsley hawthorn)
Crataegus mollis (downy hawthorn)
Cyrilla racemiflora (leatherwood, yiti)
Diospyros virginiana (persimmon)
Fagus grandifolia var. caroliniana (beech)
Fraxinus americana (white ash)
Fraxinus pensylvanica (green ash)
- Gleditsia triacanthos (honey locust)
Gymnocladus dioica (Kentucky coffee tree)
Halesia diptera (American snowdrop tree, two-winged silverbell)
Halesia tetraptera (Carolina silverbell)
Hamamelis virginiana (witch hazel)
Ilex decidua (possum-haw, deciduous holly)
Juglans cinerea (butternut, white walnut)
Juglans nigra (black walnut)
Liquidambar styraciflua (sweet gum)
Liriodendron tulipifera (tulip tree)
Magnolia acuminata (cucumber tree)
Magnolia pyramidata (pyramid magnolia)
Magnolia virginiana (sweetbay, swampbay)
Malus angustifolia (southern crabapple, wild crabapple)
Nyssa sylvatica (black gum, tupelo)
Ostrya virginiana (ironwood, hophornbeam)
Oxydendrum arboreum (sourwood)
Platanus occidentalis (sycamore, plane-tree)
Populus deltoides (eastern cottonwood)
Prunus americana (wild plum)
Prunus angustifolia (chickasaw plum)
Prunus mexicana (Mexican plum)
Prunus serotina (black cherry)
Ptelea trifoliata (wafer ash, common hoptree)
Quercus alba (white oak)
Quercus coccinea (scarlet oak)
Quercus falcata (southern red oak, Spanish oak)
Quercus laurifolia (laurel oak)
Quercus lyrata (overcup oak)
Quercus macrocarpa (bur oak)
Quercus marilandica (blackjack oak)
Quercus muhlenbergii (chinkapin oak, chestnut oak)
Quercus palustris (pin oak)
Quercus phellos (willow oak)
Quercus rubra (red oak)
Quercus shumardii (shumard oak)
Quercus stellata (post oak)
Quercus velutina (black oak)
Salix nigra (black willow)
Sassafras albidum (sassafras)
Taxodium distichum (bald cypress)
Ulmus americana (American elm)
Ulmus crassifolia (cedar elm)
Ulmus rubra (red elm, slippery elm)

Trees (evergreen)

Chamaecyparis thyoides (white cedar)
Ilex opaca (American holly, Christmas holly)
Juniperus virginiana (eastern red cedar)
Magnolia grandiflora (southern magnolia)
Persea borbonia (red bay)
Pinus echinata (shortleaf pine)
Pinus elliotii (slash, pitch, or yellow slash pine)
Pinus glabra (spruce pine)
Pinus palustris (longleaf pine)
Pinus taeda (loblolly pine)
Pinus virginiana (Virginia pine)
Prunus caroliniana (cherry laurel)
Quercus virginiana (live oak, coastal live oak, southern live oak)

Vines (deciduous)

Bignonia capreolata (cross vine)
Campsis radicans (trumpet creeper, trumpet vine)
Celastrus scandens (American bittersweet)
Clematis crispa (leatherflower)
Clematis virginiana (virgin's bower)
Lonicera sempervirens (coral honeysuckle)
Parthenocissus quinquefolia (Virginia creeper)
Passiflora incarnata (passion flower, maypop)
Vitis riparia (riverbank grape)
Vitis rotundifolia (muscadine grape)

Vine (evergreen)

Gelsemium sempervirens (yellow jessamine, Carolina jessamine)

FEDERALLY LISTED ENDANGERED SPECIES

American chaffseed (Schwalbea americana)
Pondberry (Lindera melissifolia)
Price's potato-bean (Apios priceana)

MISSISSIPPI NOXIOUS SPECIES

Because the noxious weed lists have continually changed since we gathered them in 1994, we are not including them at this time. Not all States have noxious weed lists. Those that do, do not use the same standards of importance and are not comparable. States typically have included plants that interfere with agriculture (Canada thistle), or cause human health problems (poison ivy). Some States are now including a category of plants that invade and degrade the environment (purple loosestrife). Check with your State's Agriculture Department or Weed Scientist listed below. The noxious weed list can be used two ways on roadsides: l) check to not inadvertantly plant these invasive plants, and 2) note the plants you are legally responsible to control. Many States now check adjacent State lists to avoid planting their neighbors' problem plants. Because weeds do not respect political boundaries, and because by their very nature weeds continue to adapt and expand, monitoring and controlling invasives at State borders is a wise part of vegetation management.

(Seed Law)

Department of Agriculture
Division of Plant Industry
P.O. Box 5207
Mississippi State, MS 39762

John D. Byrd
Mississippi State University
312 Dorman Hall - Box 9555
Misssissippi State, MS 39762
(601) 325-4537

MISSISSIPPI RESOURCES

Mississippi Natural Heritage Program
Museum of Natural Science
111 North Jefferson Street
Jackson, MS 39201-2897
(601) 354-7303

The Nature Conservancy Field Office
P.O. Box 1028
Jackson, MS 39215
(601) 355-5357

Mississippi Native Plant Society
% Crosby Arboretum
P.O. Box 190
Picayune, MS 39466

Crosby Arboretum
1986 Ridge Road
Picayune, MS 39466
(601) 799-2311

POTENTIAL NATURAL VEGETATION ZONES IN
MISSOURI

Source: A.W. Kuchler's Potential Natural Vegetation Map, 1964, Revised 1985.
Presented in U.S.G.S. National Atlas of the U.S. Series,
U.S. Geological Survey, Reston, VA.

 73 Mosaic of numbers 66 and 91

74 Cedar glades
(Quercus-Juniperus-Sporobolus)

91 Oak-hickory forest
(Quercus-Carya)

 101 Oak-hickory-pine forest
(Quercus-Carya-Pinus)

103 Southern floodplain forest
(Quercus-Nyassa-Taxodium)

(Dominant plant species present in each vegetation type are listed in Appendix 8)

73 Mosaic of 66 (Bluestem Prairie) and 91 (Oak-Hickory Forest)
74 Cedar Glades (Quercus-Juniperus-Sporobolus)
91 Oak-Hickory Forest (Quercus-Carya)
101 Oak-Hickory-Pine Forest (Quercus-Carya-Pinus)
103 Southern Floodplain Forest (Quercus-Nyssa-Taxodium)

Botanical Expert

Tim Smith, Botanist
Missouri Department of Conservation
P.O. Box 180
Jefferson City, MO 65102-0180
(573) 751-4115 ext. 200
(573) 526-5582 (fax)
internet: smitht2@mail.conservation.state.mo.us

Recommended Flora

Steyermark, J.A. 1963. Flora of Missouri. Iowa State University Press, Ames, Iowa.
1728 pgs. + illus. ISBN 0813806550.

NATIVE PLANTS FOR LANDSCAPE USE IN MISSOURI

Cactus

Opuntia humifusa (prickly pear)

Ferns

Adiantum capillus-veneris (southern maidenhair fern)
Adiantum pedatum (northern maidenhair fern)
Asplenium platyneuron (ebony spleenwort)
Asplenium trichomanes (maidenhair spleenwort)
Athyrium filix-femina (lady fern)
Botrychium virginianum (rattlesnake fern)
Cystopteris bulbifera (bladder fern)
Cystopteris fragilis (fragile fern)
Dryopteris carthusiana (shield fern, toothed wood fern, spinulose shield fern)
Dryopteris marginalis (marginal wood fern)
Matteuccia struthiopteris (ostrich fern)
Onoclea sensibilis (sensitive fern, bead fern)
Osmunda cinnamomea (cinnamon fern)
Osmunda claytoniana (interrupted fern)
Osmunda regalis (royal fern)
Phegopteris hexagonoptera (broad beech fern)
Polystichum acrostichoides (Christmas fern)
Thelypteris novaboracensis (New York fern, tapering fern)
Woodwardia areolata (netted chain fern)

Forbs (annuals/biennials)

Campanulastrum americanum (American bellflower, tall bellflower)
Centaurea americana (basket flower)

Coreopsis tinctoria (tickseed, goldenwave, plains coreopsis, calliopsis)
Erysimum capitatum (western wallflower, prairie rocket)
Euphorbia marginata (snow-on-the-mountain)
Glandularia canadensis (rose vervain, sweet William)
Helianthus annuus (common sunflower)
Helianthus petiolaris (plains sunflower)
Lobelia spicata (pale lobelia)
Monarda citriodora (horsemint, lemon beebalm, lemon mint)
Oenothera biennis (common evening primrose)
Palafoxia callosa (small palafoxia)
Rudbeckia hirta (black-eyed Susan)
Sabatia campestris (prairie rose gentian, prairie sabatia, meadow pink)
Sedum nuttallianum (yellow stonecrop)
Senecio glabellus (butterweed)
Senecio plattensis (prairie ragwort, prairie groundsel)

Forbs (perennials)

Acorus calamus (sweet flag, calamus)
Actaea pachypoda (white baneberry)
Allium canadense (wild garlic)
Allium cernuum (nodding onion)
Allium stellatum (wild pink onion)
Allium tricoccum (wild leek)
Amsonia tabernaemontana (blue star)
Anemone canadensis (Canada anemone, windflower)
Anemone caroliniana (Carolina anemone, southern thimbleweed)
Anemone virginiana (thimbleweed, tall anemone)
Antennaria spp. (pussytoes, everlasting)
Apocynum androsaemifolium (spreading dogbane)
Aquilegia canadensis (columbine)
Arisaema triphyllum (Jack-in-the-pulpit, Indian turnip)
Aruncus dioicus (goat's beard)
Asarum canadense (wild ginger)
Asclepias incarnata (swamp milkweed)
Asclepias tuberosa (butterfly weed)
Asclepias verticillata (whorled milkweed)
Aster ericoides (heath aster, white wreath aster)
Aster laevis (smooth aster)
Aster novae-angliae (New England aster)
Aster oblongifolius (aromatic aster)
Aster oolentangiensis (sky blue aster)
Aster pilosus (frost aster)
Aster puniceus (red-stem aster, swamp aster)
Aster sericeus (silky aster)
Astragalus canadensis (milk vetch, Canada milk vetch)
Baptisia alba (white false indigo)
Baptisia alba var. macrophyllla (cream false indigo, plains wild indigo)
Baptisia australis (blue wild indigo)
Callirhoe digitata (finger poppy mallow)
Callirhoe involucrata (purple poppy mallow, winecup)
Camassia scilloides (wild hyacinth)
Campanula rotundifolia (harebell)

Caulophyllum thalictroides (blue cohosh)
Cimicifuga racemosa (bugbane, black cohosh)
Claytonia virginica (narrow-leaved spring beauty)
Collinsonia canadensis (stoneroot, citronella horsebalm)
Coreopsis grandiflora (coreopsis)
Coreopsis lanceolata (lance-leaved coreopsis)
Coreopsis palmata (stiff coreopsis)
Coreopsis tripteris (tall coreopsis)
Dalea candida (white prairie clover)
Dalea purpurea (purple prairie clover)
Delphinium carolinianum (blue larkspur)
Delphinium tricorne (dwarf larkspur)
Desmodium canadense (Canada tick-trefoil, Canada tickclover)
Desmodium illinoense (Illinois tick-trefoil, Illinois tickclover)
Dicentra cucullaria (Dutchman's breeches)
Dodecatheon meadia (shooting star)
Echinacea purpurea (purple coneflower)
Eryngium yuccifolium (rattlesnake master, button snake-root)
Erythronium americanum (eastern trout lily, yellow trout lily)
Eupatorium coelestinum (mist flower)
Eupatorium fistulosum (Joe-pye weed)
Eupatorium perfoliatum (boneset)
Eupatorium purpureum (Joe-pye weed)
Euphorbia corollata (flowering spurge)
Euthamia graminifolia var. graminifolia (grass-leaved goldenrod)
Fragaria virginiana (wild strawberry)
Galium triflorum (sweet-scented bedstraw)
Gentiana alba (cream gentian, yellow gentian)
Gentiana andrewsii (bottle gentian)
Geranium maculatum (wild geranium, cranesbill)
Glycyrrhiza lepidota (wild licorice)
Hedyotis nigricans (bluets)
Helenium autumnale (common sneezeweed)
Helianthus maximiliani (Maximilian sunflower)
Helianthus pauciflorus ssp. pauciflorus (stiff sunflower)
Helianthus simulans (narrow-leaved sunflower, swamp sunflower)
Helianthus strumosus (woodland sunflower)
Heliopsis helianthoides (ox-eye sunflower, false sunflower)
Heterotheca villosa var. villosa (golden aster)
Heuchera richardsonii (alum root)
Hieracium longipilum (hairy hawkweed)
Houstonia longifolia var. longifolia (long-leaved bluets, pale bluets)
Hydrastis canadensis (golden seal)
Hydrophyllum virginianum (Virginia waterleaf)
Hymenocallis caroliniana (spider lily, rain lily)
Hypoxis hirsuta (yellow star grass)
Iris cristata (dwarf crested iris)
Iris virginica var. shrevei (blue flag)
Lespedeza capitata (roundheaded bush clover)
Liatris aspera (rough blazing star, gayfeather)
Liatris cylindracea (dwarf blazing star, gayfeather)
Liatris mucronata (narrow-leaf gayfeather)

Liatris pycnostachya (prairie blazing star, gayfeather)
Liatris squarrosa (blazing star)
Lilium michiganense (Turk's cap lily, Michigan lily)
Lithospermum canescens (hoary puccoon)
Lithospermum caroliniense (hairy puccoon, hispid gromwell)
Lithospermum incisum (fringed puccoon, narrow-leaved puccoon)
Lobelia cardinalis (cardinal flower)
Lobelia siphilitica (great blue lobelia)
Lysimachia ciliata (fringed loosestrife)
Maianthemum racemosum ssp. racemosum (false Solomon's seal,
    false spikenard)
Maianthemum stellatum (starry Solomon's seal)
Manfreda virginica (rattlesnake master, false aloe)
Mertensia virginica (bluebells)
Mimosa quadrivalvis var. angustata (catclaw sensitive briar)
Mitchella repens (partridge berry)
Monarda fistulosa (wild bergamot, horsemint, beebalm)
Nuphar lutea (yellow pond lily, cow lily, spatter dock)
Oenothera fruticosa (sundrops)
Oenothera macrocarpa (Missouri evening primrose)
Oenothera speciosa (showy white evening primrose)
Osmorhiza claytoni (sweet cicely, sweet jarvil)
Peltandra virginica (arrow arum)
Penstemon digitalis (beardtongue)
Phlox carolina (Carolina phlox)
Phlox divaricata ssp. laphamii (blue phlox, sweet william)
Phlox paniculata (summer phlox, perennial phlox)
Phlox pilosa (prairie phlox, downy phlox)
Physostegia intermedia (obedient plant)
Physostegia virginiana (obedient plant, false dragonhead)
Podophyllum peltatum (May apple)
Polemonium reptans (Jacob's ladder, Greek valerian)
Polygonatum biflorum (Solomon's seal)
Potentilla arguta (white cinquefoil, prairie cinquefoil, tall cinquefoil)
Potentilla simplex (common cinquefoil)
Pycnanthemum tenuifolium (slender mountain mint)
Pycnanthemum virginianum (mountain mint)
Pyrola elliptica (shinleaf)
Ranunculus hispidus (early buttercup, tufted buttercup)
Ratibida columnifera (prairie coneflower, long-headed coneflower, Mexican hat)
Ratibida pinnata (gray-headed coneflower, yellow coneflower)
Rhexia virginica (meadow beauty)
Rudbeckia fulgida (black-eyed Susan, orange coneflower)
Rudbeckia grandiflora (large coneflower)
Rudbeckia laciniata (cut-leaf coneflower)
Rudbeckia subtomentosa (sweet black-eyed Susan)
Ruellia humilis (wild petunia)
Salvia azurea var. grandiflora (blue sage)
Salvia lyrata (cancer weed, lyre-leaf sage)
Sanguinaria candensis (bloodroot)
Senecio aureus (golden ragwort)
Silene stellata (starry campion)

Silphium laciniatum (compass plant)
Silphium perfoliatum (cup plant)
Silphium terebinthinaceum (prairie dock)
Sisyrinchium angustifolium (narrow-leaved blue-eyed grass)
Sisyrinchium campestre (white-eyed grass, prairie blue-eyed grass)
Solidago caesia (blue-stemmed goldenrod, wreath goldenrod)
Solidago canadensis (meadow goldenrod)
Solidago juncea (early goldenrod, plume goldenrod)
Solidago missouriensis (Missouri goldenrod, prairie goldenrod)
Solidago nemoralis (gray goldenrod, old-field goldenrod)
Solidago odora (sweet goldenrod)
Solidago rigida (stiff goldenrod)
Solidago rugosa (rough-leaved goldenrod)
Solidago speciosa (showy goldenrod)
Solidago ulmifolia (elm-leaved goldenrod)
Spigelia marilandica (Indian pink)
Tephrosia virginiana (goat's rue)
Thalictrum dasycarpum (tall or purple meadow rue)
Thalictrum dioicum (early meadow rue)
Thalictrum thalictroides (rue anemone)
Tradescantia ohiensis (Ohio spiderwort)
Tradescantia virginiana (Virginia spiderwort, spider lily)
Uvularia grandiflora (bellwort, merrybells)
Uvularia sessilifolia (wildoats, merrybells)
Verbena hastata (blue verbena, blue vervain)
Verbena stricta (hoary vervain)
Vernonia baldwinii (ironweed, western ironweed)
Vernonia fasciculata (ironweed)
Veronicastrum virginicum (Culver's root)
Viola missouriensis (Missouri violet)
Viola pedata (bird-foot violet)
Viola pedatifida (prairie violet)
Viola pubescens (downy or smooth yellow violet)
Viola soraria (common blue violet, meadow violet)
Zizia aptera (heart-leaved golden alexanders)
Zizia aurea (golden alexanders)

Grasses/Grass-like plants

Andropogon gerardii (big bluestem)
Andropogon virginicus (broom sedge)
Bouteloua curtipendula (sideoats grama)
Buchloe dactyloides (buffalograss)
Calamagrostis canadensis (bluejoint grass)
Carex aquatilis (water sedge)
Carex stipata (awl-fruited sedge)
Carex stricta (tussock sedge)
Chasmanthium latifolium (inland sea oats, wild oats, river oats, broad-leaf uniola)
Danthonia spicata (poverty grass)
Distichlis spicata (seashore saltgrass)
Eleocharis palustris (creeping spikesedge, spike rush)
Elymus canadensis (Canada wild rye)
Elymus glaucus (blue wild rye)

Elymus hystrix var. hystrix (bottlebrush grass)
Eragrostis intermedia (plains lovegrass)
Eragrostis spectabilis (purple lovegrass, tumblegrass)
Juncus effusus var. solutus (soft rush)
Juncus interior (inland rush)
Koeleria macrantha (June grass)
Leersia oryzoides (rice cut grass)
Melica nitens (three-flower melic grass)
Muhlenbergia capillaris (gulf muhly, hair grass)
Panicum virgatum (switchgrass)
Pascopyrum smithii (western wheatgrass)
Schizachyrium scoparium (little bluestem)
Scirpus acutus (hardstem bulrush)
Scirpus atrovirens (dark green bulrush)
Scirpus cyperinus (wool grass)
Scirpus maritimus (alkali bulrush, prairie bulrush, bayonet grass)
Scirpus tabernaemontani (great bulrush)
Sorghastrum nutans (Indian grass)
Spartina pectinata (prairie cordgrass, freshwater cordgrass)
Sporobolus compositus var. compositus (tall dropseed)
Sporobolus cryptandrus (sand dropseed)
Sporobolus heterolepis (northern prairie dropseed)
Stipa spartea (porcupine grass)
Tripsacum dactyloides (eastern gama grass)
Typha latifolia (cattail)

Shrubs (deciduous)

Acacia angustissima (fern acacia, whiteball acacia)
Alnus serrulata (smooth alder)
Amelanchier arborea (downy serviceberry, shadbush, Juneberry)
Amorpha canescens (leadplant)
Amorpha fruticosa (false indigo, Indigo bush)
Ceanothus americanus (New Jersey tea, red root)
Cephalanthus occidentalis (buttonbush)
Cornus alternifolia (pogoda dogwood, alternate-leaved dogwood)
Cornus amomum ssp. obliqua (swamp dogwood, silky dogwood)
Cornus drummondii (rough-leaf dogwood)
Cornus racemosa (gray dogwood)
Corylus americana (American hazelnut or filbert)
Dirca palustris (leatherwood, ropebark)
Euonymus atropurpurea (wahoo, burning bush)
Forestiera acuminata (swamp privet)
Frangula caroliniana (Carolina buckthorn)
Hamamelis vernalis (vernal witch hazel)
Hydrangea arborescens (wild hydrangea)
Hypericum hypericoides ssp. hypericoides (St. Andrew's cross)
Hypericum prolificum (shrubby St. John's wort)
Ilex verticillata (winterberry, black alder)
Itea virginica (Virginia willow, sweetspire, tassel-white)
Lindera benzoin (spicebush)
Lonicera dioica (limber or wild honeysuckle)
Physocarpus opulifolius (ninebark)

Prunus virginiana (chokecherry)
Rhododendron prinophyllum (roseshell azalea, early azalea)
Rhus aromatica (fragrant sumac)
Rhus copallinum (dwarf or winged sumac)
Rhus glabra (smooth sumac)
Ribes cynosbati (prickly gooseberry, dogberry)
Ribes odoratum (buffalo currant, golden currant)
Rosa arkansana (prairie rose)
Rosa blanda (early wild rose, smooth rose)
Rosa carolina (Carolina rose)
Rosa setigera (Illinois or prairie rose)
Rubus occidentalis (black raspberry, thimbleberry)
Salix discolor (pussy willow)
Sambucus canadensis (elderberry, common elder)
Sambucus racemosa var. pubens (scarlet elderberry, red-berried elder)
Sideroxylon lanuginosum ssp. lanuginosum (chittamwood, gum elastic tree)
Staphylea trifolia (bladdernut)
Styrax americanus (American silverbells)
Symphoricarpos orbiculatus (coralberry, Indian currant)
Vaccinium arboreum (sparkleberry, farkleberry)
Viburnum prunifolium (black haw, nanny berry)
Viburnum rufidulum (southern or rusty black haw)

Trees (deciduous)

Acer negundo (box elder)
Acer rubrum (red maple)
Acer saccharinum (silver maple)
Acer saccharum (sugar maple)
Aesculus glabra (Ohio buckeye, horse chestnut)
Aesculus pavia var. pavia (red buckeye)
Betula nigra (river birch)
Carpinus caroliniana (blue beech, hornbeam, musclewood)
Carya alba (mockernut hickory)
Carya cordiformis (bitternut, swamp hickory)
Carya illinoinensis (pecan)
Carya ovata (shagbark hickory)
Carya texana (black hickory)
Catalpa speciosa (northern catalpa)
Celtis laevigata (sugarberry, hackberry)
Celtis occidentalis (hackberry, sugarberry)
Cercis canadensis (redbud)
Chionanthus virginicus (fringe tree, old man's beard)
Cladrastis kentukea (yellowwood)
Cornus florida (flowering dogwood)
Cotinus obovatus (smoke tree)
Crataegus crus-galli (cockspur hawthorn)
Crataegus mollis (downy hawthorn)
Crataegus phaenopyrum (Washington hawthorn)
Diospyros virginiana (persimmon)
Fagus grandifolia var. caroliniana (beech)
Fraxinus americana (white ash)
Fraxinus pensylvanica (green ash)

Gleditsia triacanthos (honey locust)
Gymnocladus dioica (Kentucky coffee tree)
Hamamelis virginiana (witch hazel)
Ilex decidua (possum-haw, deciduous holly)
Juglans nigra (black walnut)
Liquidambar styraciflua (sweet gum)
Magnolia acuminata (cucumber tree)
Malus ioensis var. ioensis (prairie crabapple)
Nyssa sylvatica (black gum, tupelo)
Ostrya virginiana (ironwood, hophornbeam)
Platanus occidentalis (sycamore, plane-tree)
Populus deltoides (eastern cottonwood)
Prunus americana (wild plum)
Prunus angustifolia (chickasaw plum)
Prunus mexicana (Mexican plum)
Prunus serotina (black cherry)
Ptelea trifoliata (wafer ash, common hoptree)
Quercus alba (white oak)
Quercus bicolor (swamp white oak)
Quercus coccinea (scarlet oak)
Quercus falcata (southern red oak, Spanish oak)
Quercus lyrata (overcup oak)
Quercus macrocarpa (bur oak)
Quercus marilandica (blackjack oak)
Quercus muhlenbergii (chinkapin oak, chestnut oak)
Quercus palustris (pin oak)
Quercus rubra (red oak)
Quercus shumardii (shumard oak)
Quercus stellata (post oak)
Quercus velutina (black oak)
Salix amygdaloides (peachleaf willow)
Salix nigra (black willow)
Sassafras albidum (sassafras)
Taxodium distichum (bald cypress)
Tilia americana (American linden, basswood)
Ulmus americana (American elm)
Ulmus rubra (red elm, slippery elm)

Trees (evergreen)

Ilex opaca (American holly, Christmas holly)
Juniperus ashei (rock, post cedar, Ashe, or Mexican juniper)
Juniperus virginiana (eastern red cedar)
Pinus echinata (shortleaf pine)

Vines (deciduous)

Bignonia capreolata (cross vine)
Campsis radicans (trumpet creeper, trumpet vine)
Celastrus scandens (American bittersweet)
Clematis pitcheri (leather flower, purple clematis)
Clematis virginiana (virgin's bower)
Parthenocissus quinquefolia (Virginia creeper)
Parthenocissus quinquefolia var. quinquefolia (woodbine)

Passiflora incarnata (passion flower, maypop)
Vitis riparia (riverbank grape)
Wisteria frutescens (wisteria)

FEDERALLY LISTED ENDANGERED SPECIES

Decurrent false aster (Boltonia decurrens)
Geocarpon minimum (no common name)
Mead's milkweed (Asclepias meadii)
Missouri bladderpod (lesquerella filiformis)
Pondberry (Lindera melissifolia)
Running buffalo clover (Trifolium stoloniferum)
Western prairie fringed orchid (Platanthera praeclara)

MISSOURI NOXIOUS SPECIES

Because the noxious weed lists have continually changed since we gathered them in 1994, we are not including them at this time. Not all States have noxious weed lists. Those that do, do not use the same standards of importance and are not comparable. States typically have included plants that interfere with agriculture (Canada thistle), or cause human health problems (poison ivy). Some States are now including a category of plants that invade and degrade the environment (purple loosestrife). Check with your State's Agriculture Department or Weed Scientist listed below. The noxious weed list can be used two ways on roadsides: I) check to not inadvertantly plant these invasive plants, and 2) note the plants you are legally responsible to control. Many States now check adjacent State lists to avoid planting their neighbors' problem plants. Because weeds do not respect political boundaries, and because by their very nature weeds continue to adapt and expand, monitoring and controlling invasives at State borders is a wise part of vegetation management.

(Weed Law)

Department of Agriculture
Division of Plant Industries
1616 Missouri Boulevard
P.O. Box 630
Jefferson City, MO 65102

Fred Fishel, U of M
45 Agriculture Building
Cooperative Extension Box 407
Columbia, MO 65211
(573) 884-6361

MISSOURI RESOURCES

The Nature Conservancy
2800 South Bentwood Boulevard
St. Louis, MO 63144
(314) 968-1105

Missouri Native Plant Society
P.O. Box 20073
St. Louis, MO 63144

The Missouri Department of
Conservation
P.O. Box 180
Jefferson City, MO 65102
(573) 751-4115 (ext.) 200

Shaw Arboretum
Missouri Botanical Garden
P.O. Box 38
Gray Summit, MO 63039

Center for Plant Conservation
Missouri Botanical Garden
P.O. Box 299
St. Louis, MO 63166

Missouri Prairie Foundation
P.O. Box 200
Columbia, MO 65205

POTENTIAL NATURAL VEGETATION ZONES IN
MONTANA

Source: A.W. Kuchler's Potential Natural Vegetation Map, 1964, Revised 1985.
Presented in U.S.G.S. National Atlas of the U.S. Series,
U.S. Geological Survey, Reston, VA.

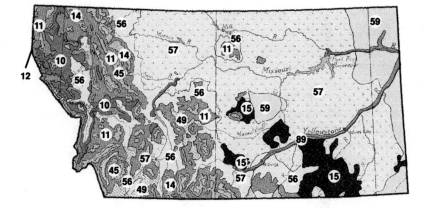

10 Western ponderosa forest
(Pinus)

11 Douglas fir forest
(Pseudotsuga)

12 Cedar-hemlock-pine forest
(Thuja-Tsuga-Pinus)

14 Western spruce-fir forest
(Picea-Abies)

15 Eastern ponderosa forest
(Pinus)

45 Alpine meadows and barren
(Agrostis, Carex, Festuca, Poa)

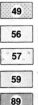

49 Sagebrush steppe
(Artemisia-Agropyron)

56 Foothills prairie
(Agropyron-Festuca-Stipa)

57 Grama-needlegrass-wheatgrass
(Bouteloua-Stipa-Agropyron)

59 Wheatgrass-needlegrass
(Agropyron-Stipa)

89 Northern floodplain forest
(Populus-Salix-Ulmus)

(Dominant plant species present in each vegetation type are listed in Appendix 8)

10   Western Ponderosa forest (Pinus)
11   Douglas Fir Forest (Pseudotsuga)
12   Cedar-Hemlock-Pine Forest (Thuja-Tsuga-Pinus)
14   Western Spruce-Fir Forest (Picea-Abies)
15   Eastern Ponderosa Forest (Pinus)
45   Alpine Meadows and Barren (Agrostis, Carex, Festuca, Poa)
49   Sagebrush Steppe (Artemisia-Agropyron)
56   Foothills Prairie (Agropyron-Festuca-Stipa)
57   Grama-Needlegrass-Wheatgrass (Bouteloua-Stipa-Agropyron)
59   Wheatgrass-Needlegrass (Agropyron-Stipa)
89   Northern Floodplain Forest (Populus-Salix-Ulmus)

Botanical Experts

Bonnie Heidel, Botanist
Montana Natural Heritage Program
1515 East Sixth Avenue P.O. Box 201800
Helena, MT 59620-1800
(406) 444-0536
(406) 444-0581 (fax)
internet: bheidel@nris.msl.mt.gov

Revegetation Botanists:
Phil Johnson
Montana Dept. of Transportation

Jim Olivarez
U.S. Forest Service Region 1 Office

Recommended Flora

Dorn, R.D. 1984. Vascular Plants of Montana. Mountain West Publishing.
Cheyenne, WY. 276 pgs.

NATIVE PLANTS FOR LANDSCAPE USE IN MONTANA

Cactus

Opuntia macrorhiza (common prickly pear)

Ferns

Adiantum pedatum (northern maidenhair fern)
Aspidotis densa (rock brake, cliff brake, Indian's dream)
Athyrium filix-femina (lady fern)
Botrychium virginianum (rattlesnake fern)
Cheilanthes gracillima (lace fern)
Cystopteris fragilis (fragile fern)
Gymnocarpium dryopteris (oak fern)
Polystichum munitum (western sword fern)

Forbs (annuals/biennials)

Achillea millefolium (Western white yarrow)

Cleome serrulata (Rocky Mountain beeplant)
Collomia grandiflora (collomia)
Coreopsis tinctoria (tickseed, goldenwave, plains coreopsis, calliopsis)
Dyssodia papposa (dyssodia, dogweed, fetid marigold)
Euphorbia marginata (snow-on-the-mountain)
Helianthus annuus (common sunflower)
Helianthus petiolaris (plains sunflower)
Ipomopsis aggregata (sky rocket, scarlet gilia)
Lepidium montanum (mountain peppergrass)
Linum rigidum (yellow flax)
Machaeranthera tanacetifolia (tahoka daisy, tansy aster)
Mimulus guttatus (golden monkey flower)
Nemophila breviflora (Great Basin nemophila)
Oenothera albicaulis (pale evening primrose)
Senecio plattensis (prairie ragwort, prairie groundsel)
Townsendia exscapa (Easter daisy)

Forbs (perennials)

Abronia fragrans (sweet sand verbena)
Aconitum columbianum (western monkshood)
Allium cernuum (nodding onion)
Anaphalis margaritacea (pearly everlasting)
Anemone canadensis (Canada anemone, windflower)
Anemone cylindrica (thimbleweed, candle anemone)
Anemone multifida (early thimbleweed, cut-leaf anemone, Pacific anemone)
Antennaria spp. (pussytoes, everlasting)
Apocynum androsaemifolium (spreading dogbane)
Aquilegia coerulea (Rocky Mountain or blue columbine)
Aquilegia flavescens (yellow columbine)
Arnica cordifolia (heartleaf arnica)
Artemisia ludoviciana (white sage, prairie sage, artemisia)
Asarum caudatum (wild ginger)
Asclepias speciosa (showy milkweed)
Asclepias verticillata (whorled milkweed)
Aster ascendens (purple aster, Pacific aster)
Aster foliaceus (leafy aster)
Aster laevis (smooth aster)
Aster modestus
Astragalus americanus (American milk vetch, rattlepod)
Astragalus canadensis (milk vetch, Canada milk vetch)
Balsamorrhiza sagittata (balsamroot)
Calochortus macrocarpus (bigpod mariposa)
Calochortus nuttallii (sego lily, mariposa lily)
Caltha leptosepala (white marsh marigold, elkslip)
Campanula rotundifolia (harebell)
Castilleja angustifolia var. dubia (desert paintbrush)
Castilleja linariifolia (Indian paintbrush)
Castilleja sessiliflora (downy painted cup)
Castilleja sulphurea (splitleaf Indian paintbrush)
Claytonia lanceolata (spring beauty)
Clematis hirsutissima (clematis, vase flower, leather flower, lion's beard)
Clintonia uniflora (bride's bonnet, queen cup, bead lily)
Cornus canadensis (bunchberry)

Dalea candida (white prairie clover)
Dalea purpurea (purple prairie clover)
Delphinium glaucum (tower larkspur)
Dodecatheon jeffreyi (Jeffrey's shooting stars)
Dryas drummondii (yellow dryas)
Dryas octopetala (mountain dryas, white mountain avens)
Echinacea angustifolia (narrow-leaved purple coneflower)
Epilobium angustifolium (fireweed, willow herb)
Epilobium latifolium (dwarf fireweed)
Erigeron compositus (alpine daisy)
Erigeron speciosus (showy fleabane)
Eriogonum umbellatum (sulfur buckwheat)
Eriophyllum lanatum (woolly sunflower, Oregon sunshine)
Erythronium grandiflorum (glacier lily, yellow fawn lily, dogtooth violet)
Fragaria virginiana (wild strawberry)
Gaillardia aristata (blanket flower, gaillardia, brown-eyed Susan)
Galium triflorum (sweet-scented bedstraw)
Gaura coccinea (scarlet gaura)
Geranium viscossisimum (sticky wild geranium)
Geum rivale (purple avens, water avens)
Geum triflorum (prairie smoke, purple avens)
Glycyrrhiza lepidota (wild licorice)
Hedysarum boreale (sweet vetch, sweet broom)
Helenium autumnale (common sneezeweed)
Helianthus maximiliani (Maximilian sunflower)
Helianthus pauciflorus ssp. pauciflorus (stiff sunflower)
Heterotheca villosa var. villosa (golden aster)
Heuchera parvifolia (saxifrage, alum root)
Heuchera richardsonii (alum root)
Ipomoea leptophylla (bush morning glory)
Iris missouriensis (Rocky Mountain iris, western blue flag)
Leptodoctylon pungens
Lewisia rediviva (bitter root)
Liatris punctata (dotted blazing star, gayfeather)
Lilium columbianum (Columbia lily, Oregon lily, wild tiger lily)
Lilium philadelphicum (wood lily)
Linnaea borealis (twinflower)
Linum lewisii (wild blue flax)
Lithospermum incisum (fringed puccoon, narrow-leaved puccoon)
Luetkea pectinata (Alaska spiraea, partridge foot)
Lupinus argenteus (silvery lupine)
Lupinus caudatus (tailcup lupine)
Lupinus polyphyllus (meadow lupine, bog lupine)
Maianthemum racemosum ssp. racemosum (false Solomon's seal,
    false spikenard)
Maianthemum stellatum (starry Solomon's seal)
Mertensia ciliata (mountain bluebells)
Mimulus lewisii (Lewis monkey flower, great purple monkey flower)
Minuartia obtusiloba (cushion sandwort)
Monarda fistulosa (wild bergamot, horsemint, beebalm)
Myosotis asiatica (forget-me-not)
Nothocalais cuspidata (prairie dandelion)

Oenothera cespitosa (gumbo evening primrose, gumbo lily)
Oenothera flava (Shortfin evening primrose)
Osmorhiza berteroi (mountain sweet cicely)
Pedicularis groenlandica (elephant heads)
Penstemon albidus (white beardtongue)
Penstemon cyananthus (Platte River penstemon, Wasatch penstemon)
Penstemon deustus (hot rock penstemon)
Penstemon fruticosus (shrubby penstemon)
Petrophyton caespitosum (dwarf spiraea, petrophytum, tufted rockmat)
Phacelia sericea (silky phacelia)
Phlox diffusa (mat phlox)
Phlox speciosa (showy phlox)
Polemonium occidentale (Jacob's ladder)
Polemonium pulcherrimum (alpine Jacob's ladder, skunk leaf)
Polemonium viscosum (sky pilot)
Potentilla arguta (white cinquefoil, prairie cinquefoil, tall cinquefoil)
Potentilla nivea (villous cinquefoil)
Pyrola elliptica (shinleaf)
Ranunculus alismifolius (meadow buttercup)
Ratibida columnifera (prairie coneflower, long-headed coneflower, Mexican hat)
Rudbeckia laciniata (cut-leaf coneflower)
Saxifraga bronchialis (spotted saxifrage, matted saxifrage)
Saxifraga cespitosa (tufted saxifrage)
Saxifraga oppositifolia (purple saxifrage)
Silene acaulis (moss campion)
Solidago canadensis (meadow goldenrod)
Solidago missouriensis (Missouri goldenrod, prairie goldenrod)
Solidago multiradiata (northern goldenrod, mountain goldenrod)
Solidago nemoralis (gray goldenrod, old-field goldenrod)
Solidago rigida (stiff goldenrod)
Sphaeralcea coccinea (scarlet globe mallow)
Tellima grandiflora (fringe cup)
Tetraneuris acaulis var. acaulis (stemless goldflower, stemless rubber weed, butte marigold)
Thalictrum dasycarpum (tall or purple meadow rue)
Thermopsis rhombifolia var. montana (golden pea, buckbean)
Trillium ovatum (coast trillium, western wakerobin)
Verbena hastata (blue verbena, blue vervain)
Verbena stricta (hoary vervain)
Viola canadensis (Canada violet)
Viola glabella (smooth yellow or stream violet)
Viola macloskeyi (white mountain violet)
Viola nuttallii (yellow violet)
Viola vallicola (yellow violet)
Xerophyllum tenax (beargrass)
Yucca glauca (yucca, soapweed)
Zizia aptera (heart-leaved golden alexanders)

Grasses/Grass-like plants

Agrostis exarata (spikebent, spike red top)
Agrostis scabra (ticklegrass, fly-away grass)
Andropogon gerardii (big bluestem)

Andropogon hallii (sand bluestem)
Andropogaon scoparium (little bluestem)
Aristida purpurea (purple three awn)
Beckmania syzigachne (American sloughgrass)
Bouteloua curtipendula (sideoats grama)
Bouteloua gracilis (blue grama)
Bromus carinatus (California brome)
Bromus cilictus
Bromus marginatus
Buchloe dactyloides (buffalograss)
Calamagrostis canadensis (bluejoint grass)
Calamagrostis stricta
Carex aquatilis (water sedge)
Carex lanuginosa
Carex microptera
Carex nebrascensis
Carex pensylvanica (Pennsylvania sedge)
Carex praegracilis
Carex rossii
Carex stipata (awl-fruited sedge)
Carex utriculata (beaked sedge)
Carex vesicaria
Danthonia californica (California oatgrass)
Danthonia intermedia (timber oatgrass)
Danthonia pareyi
Danthonia spicata (poverty grass)
Deschampsia cespitosa (tufted hairgrass)
Distichlis spicata (seashore saltgrass)
Eleocharis acicularis
Eleocharis palustris (creeping spikesedge, spike rush)
Elymus canadensis (Canada wild rye)
Elymus elynoides (bottlebrush squirreltail)
Elymus trachycaulus (Slender wheatgrass)
Elymus glaucus (blue wild rye)
Elymus lanceolatus (thickspike wheatgrass)
Elymus smithii
Elymus virginicus
Festuca idahoensis (Idaho fescue, blue bunchgrass)
Festuca ovina (sheep fescue)
Festuca scubrella
Glyceria grandis (American mannagrass, tall mannagrass, reed meadowgrass)
Hierochloe odorata (sweet grass)
Juncus balticus (Baltic rush)
Juncus interior (inland rush)
Koeleria macrantha (June grass)
Leersia oryzoides (rice cut grass)
Leymus cinereus (Great Basin wild rye)
Leymus triticoides (creeping (Shoshone) wildrye)
Muhlenbergia montana (mountain muhly)
Oryzopsis hymenoides (Indian ricegrass)
Panicum virgatum (switchgrass)
Pascopyrum smithii (western wheatgrass)

Phleum alpinum (alpine timothy)
Poa alpina (alpine bluegrass)
Poa secunda (pine bluegrass)
Pseudoroegneria spicata (bluebunch wheatgrass)
Puccinellia distans (alkaligrass)
Scirpus americanus
Scirpus acutus (hardstem bulrush)
Scirpus maritimus (alkali bulrush, prairie bulrush, bayonet grass)
Spartina pectinata (prairie cordgrass, freshwater cordgrass)
Sporobolus airoides (alkali sacaton)
Sporobolus compositus var. compositus (tall dropseed)
Sporobolus cryptandrus (sand dropseed)
Stipa comata (needle-and-thread grass)
Stipa spartea (porcupine grass)
Stipa viridula
Typha angustifolia (narrow-leaved cattail)
Typha latifolia (cattail)

Shrubs (deciduous)

Alnus incana (speckled alder, mountain alder)
Amelanchier alnifolia (saskatoon, western serviceberry, Juneberry)
Amelanchier utahensis (Utah serviceberry)
Artemisia cana (siver sagebrush, white sagebrush, hoary sagebrush)
Artemisia frigida (prairie sagewort, fringed sage)
Atriplex confertifolia (spiny saltbush, shadscale saltbush, hop sage)
Atriplex gardneri
Betula glandulosa
Cassiope tetragona
Ceanothus sanguineus (redstem ceanothus, wild lilac)
Chrysothamnus nauseosus (rabbit brush, chamisa)
Cornus stolonifera (red-osier dogwood)
Corylus cornuta (beaked hazelnut or filbert)
Crataegus douglasii (black hawthorn)
Elaeagnus commutata (silverberry, wild olive, wolf willow)
Gaultheria humifusa (wintergreen)
Gaultheria sarothrae
Holodiscus discolor (cream bush, ocean spray, mountain spray)
Kalmia microphylla (laurel)
Ledum glandulosum (labradortea)
Lonicera involucrata (black twinberry, bear berry honeysuckle)
Lonicera utehensis
Pachistima myrsimites
Potentilla fruticosa (potentilla, shrubby cinquefoil, yellow rose)
Prunus virginiana (chokecherry)
Purshia tridentata (antelope brush)
Rhus glabra (smooth sumac)
Rhus trilobata (squawbush, basketbush, skunkbush)
Ribes aureum (golden currant)
Ribes cereum (wax currant, western red currant, squaw currant)
Ribes hudsonianum (wild black currant)
Ribes lacustre (swamp currant)
Rosa acicularis

Rosa arkansana (prairie rose)
Rosa idaeus
Rosa nutkana (nootka rose)
Rosa sayi
Rosa woodsii (western wild rose, woods rose)
Rubus parviflorus (western thimbleberry)
Rubus ursinus (western blackberry)
Salix arctica (arctic willow)
Salix bebbiana (Bebb willow, long-beaked willow)
Salix boothii
Salix discolor (pussy willow)
Salix drummondii
Salix exigua
Salix lutea
Salix scouleriana (western pussy willow, Scouler's willow)
Sambucus cerulea (blue elderberry)
Sarcobatus vermiculatus (greasewood)
Shepherdia argentea (silver buffaloberry)
Shepherdia canadensis (buffaloberry)
Sorbus scopulina (western mountain ash)
Spiraea douglasii (western spiraea, hardhack spiraea)
Symphoricarpos oreophilus (mountain snowberry)
Vaccinium caespitosum (dwarf bilberry)
Vaccinium scoparium
Viburnum edule (moosewood viburnum)
Viburnum lentago (black haw, nannyberry)

Shrubs (evergreen)

Arctostaphylos uva-ursi (bearberry, kinnikinnik)
Artemisia nova (black sagebrush)
Artemisia tridentata (big sagebrush, Great Basin sagebrush)
Ceanothus velutinus (mountain balm, buckbush)
Cercocarpus ledifolius (curl-leaf mountain mahogany)
Grayia spinosa (spiny hopsage)
Juniperus communis (common juniper)
Juniperus horizontalis (creeping juniper, creeping savin)
Mahonia aquifolium (Oregon grape)
Mahonia regpens (
Paxistima myrsinites (Oregon box, myrtle boxwood, mountain lover)
Phyllodoce empetriformis (pink mountain heather)

Trees (deciduous)

Acer glabrum (Rocky Mountain maple)
Acer grandidentatum (bigtooth maple)
Acer negundo (box elder)
Betula occidentalis (mountain birch, water birch)
Betula papyrifera (paper birch)
Fraxinus pensylvanica (green ash)
Larix occidentalis (western larch, western tamarack)
Populus acuminata
Populus angustifolia
Populus deltoides (eastern cottonwood)

Populus tremuloides (quaking aspen)
Populus trichocarpa
Prunus americana (wild plum)
Prunus emarginata
Prunus pennsylvanica (fire or pin cherry)
Salix amygdaloides (peachleaf willow)

Trees (evergreen)

Abies grandis (grand fir, giant fir)
Abies lasiocarpa (subalpine fir)
Juniperus osteosperma (Utah juniper)
Juniperus scopulorum (Rocky Mountain juniper)
Picea engelmannii (Engelmann spruce)
Picea glauca (white spruce)
Pinus albicaulii
Pinus contorta
Pinus flexilis (limber pine)
Pinus monticola (western white pine)
Pinus ponderosa (ponderosa pine)
Pseudotsuga menziesii (Douglas fir)
Taxus brevifolia (western yew, Pacific yew)
Thuja plicata (western red cedar)
Tsuga heterophylla (western hemlock)
Tsuga mertensiana (mountain hemlock)

Vines (deciduous)

Clematis columbiana (purple virgin's bower)
Clematis ligusticifolia (clematis)
Lonicera ciliosa (orange honeysuckle)
Parthenocissus quinquefolia var. quinquefolia (woodbine)
Vitis riparia (riverbank grape)

FEDERALLY LISTED ENDANGERED SPECIES

Ute ladies'-tresses (Spiranthes diluvialis)
Water howellia (Howellia aquatilis)

MONTANA NOXIOUS SPECIES

Because the noxious weed lists have continually changed since we gathered them in 1994, we are not including them at this time. Not all States have noxious weed lists. Those that do, do not use the same standards of importance and are not comparable. States typically have included plants that interfere with agriculture (Canada thistle), or cause human health problems (poison ivy). Some States are now including a category of plants that invade and degrade the environment (purple loosestrife). Check with your State's Agriculture Department or Weed Scientist listed below. The noxious weed list can be used two ways on roadsides: l) check to not inadvertently plant these invasive plants, and 2) note the plants you are legally responsible to control. Many States now check adjacent State lists to avoid planting their neighbors' problem plants. Because weeds do not respect political boundaries, and because by their very nature weeds continue to adapt and expand, monitoring and controlling invasives at State borders is a wise part of vegetation management.

(Weed Law)

Department of Agriculture
Agricultural Sciences Division
P.O. Box 200201
Helena, MT 59620

Roger Sheley
Montana State University
334 Leon Johnson Hall, Box 3120
Bozeman, MT 59715
(406) 994-5686

MONTANA RESOURCES

Montana Natural Heritage Program
State Library Building
1515 East 6th Avenue
Helena, MT 59620
(406) 444-3009

The Nature Conservancy Field Office
32 South Ewing
Helena, MT 59601
(406) 443-0303

Montana Native Plant Society
P.O. Box 992
Bozeman, MT 59771

Montana State University Arboretum
W. College Avenue and
S. 11th Avenue
Bozeman, MT 59717

POTENTIAL NATURAL VEGETATION ZONES IN
ALABAMA

Source: A.W. Kuchler's Potential Natural Vegetation Map, 1964, Revised 1985.
Presented in U.S.G.S. National Atlas of the U.S. Series,
U.S. Geological Survey, Reston, VA.

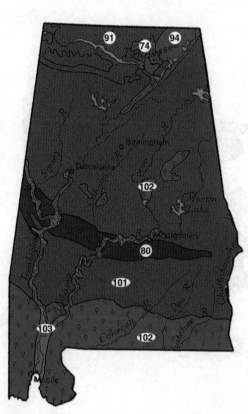

74 Cedar glades
(Quercus-Juniperus-Sporobolus)

80 Blackbelt
(Liquidambar-Quercus-Juniperus)

91 Oak-hickory forest
(Quercus-Carya)

94 Mixed mesophytic forest
(Acer-Aesculus-Fagus-Liriodendro

101 Oak-hickory-pine forest
(Quercus-Carya-Pinus)

102 Southern mixed forest
(Fagus-Liquidambar-Magnolia-Pinus-Quercus)

103 Southern floodplain forest
(Quercus-Nyassa-Taxodium)

POTENTIAL NATURAL VEGETATION ZONES IN
ALASKA

Source: A.W. Kuchler's Potential Natural Vegetation Map, 1964, Revised 1985.
Presented in U.S.G.S. National Atlas of the U.S. Series,
U.S. Geological Survey, Reston, VA.

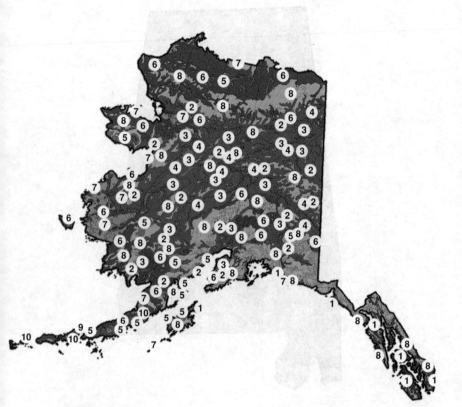

AK1	Hemlock-spruce forest	*(Tsuga-Picea)*
AK2	Spruce-birch forest	*(Picea-Betula)*
AK3	Black spruce forest	*(Picea)*
AK4	Muskeg	*(Eriophorum-Sphagnum-Betula)*
AK5	Alder thickets	*(Alnus)*
AK6	Cottonsedge tundra	*(Eriophorum)*
AK7	Watersedge tundra	*(Carex)*
AK8	Dryas meadows and barren	*(Dryas-Carex-Betula)*
AK9	Aleutian meadows	*(Calamagrostis-Anemone)*
AK10	Aleutian heath and barren	*(Empetrum-Vaccinium)*

POTENTIAL NATURAL VEGETATION ZONES IN

ARIZONA

Source: A.W. Kuchler's Potential Natural Vegetation Map, 1964, Revised 1985.
Presented in U.S.G.S. National Atlas of the U.S. Series,
U.S. Geological Survey, Reston, VA.

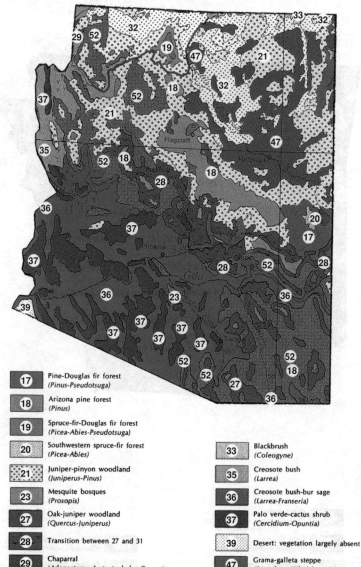

17 Pine-Douglas fir forest
(Pinus-Pseudotsuga)

18 Arizona pine forest
(Pinus)

19 Spruce-fir-Douglas fir forest
(Picea-Abies-Pseudotsuga)

20 Southwestern spruce-fir forest
(Picea-Abies)

21 Juniper-pinyon woodland
(Juniperus-Pinus)

23 Mesquite bosques
(Prosopis)

27 Oak-juniper woodland
(Quercus-Juniperus)

28 Transition between 27 and 31

29 Chaparral
(Adenostoma-Arctostaphylos-Ceanoti

32 Great Basin sagebrush
(Artemisia)

33 Blackbrush
(Coleogyne)

35 Creosote bush
(Larrea)

36 Creosote bush-bur sage
(Larrea-Franseria)

37 Palo verde-cactus shrub
(Cercidium-Opuntia)

39 Desert: vegetation largely absent

47 Grama-galleta steppe
(Bouteloua-Hilaria)

52 Grama-tobosa shrubsteppe
(Bouteloua-Hilaria-Larrea)

POTENTIAL NATURAL VEGETATION ZONES IN
ARKANSAS

Source: A.W. Kuchler's Potential Natural Vegetation Map, 1964, Revised 1985.
Presented in U.S.G.S. National Atlas of the U.S. Series,
U.S. Geological Survey, Reston, VA.

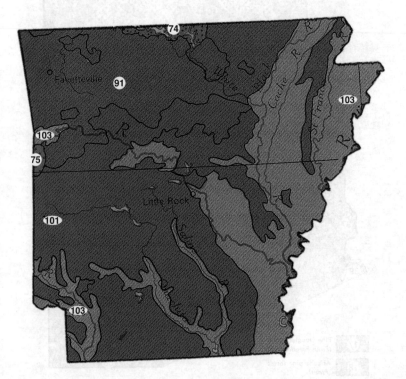

 74 Cedar glades
(Quercus-Juniperus-Sporobolus)

75 Cross timbers
(Quercus-Andropogon)

91 Oak-hickory forest
(Quercus-Carya)

101 Oak-hickory-pine forest
(Quercus-Carya-Pinus)

103 Southern floodplain forest
(Quercus-Nyassa-Taxodium)

POTENTIAL NATURAL VEGETATION ZONES IN

CALIFORNIA

Source: A.W. Kuchler's Potential Natural Vegetation Map, 1964, Revised 1985.
Presented in U.S.G.S. National Atlas of the U.S. Series,
U.S. Geological Survey, Reston, VA.

2	Cedar-hemlock-Douglas fir forest (*Thuja-Tsuga-Pseudotsuga*)
5	Mixed conifer forest (*Abies-Pinus-Pseudotsuga*)
6	Redwood forest (*Sequoia-Pseudotsuga*)
7	Red fir forest (*Abies*)
8	Lodgepole pine-subalpine forest (*Pinus-Tsuga*)
9	Pine-cypress forest (*Pinus-Cupressus*)
10	Western ponderosa forest (*Pinus*)
22	Oregon oakwoods (*Quercus*)
25	California mixed evergreen forest (*Quercus-Arbutus-Pseudotsuga*)
26	California oakwoods (*Quercus*)
29	Chaparral (*Adenostoma-Arctostaphylos-Ceanoti*)
30	Coastal sagebrush (*Salvia-Eriogonum*)
32	Great Basin sagebrush (*Artemisia*)
34	Saltbush-greasewood (*Atriplex-Sarcobatus*)
35	Creosote bush (*Larrea*)
36	Creosote bush-bur sage (*Larrea-Franseria*)
37	Palo verde-cactus shrub (*Cercidium-Opuntia*)
40	Fescue-oatgrass (*Festuca-Danthonia*)
41	California steppe (*Stipa*)
42	Tule marshes (*Scirpus-Typha*)
45	Alpine meadows and barren (*Agrostis, Carex, Festuca, Poa*)
49	Sagebrush steppe (*Artemisia-Agropyron*)

POTENTIAL NATURAL VEGETATION ZONES IN

COLORADO

Source: A.W. Kuchler's Potential Natural Vegetation Map, 1964, Revised 1985.
Presented in U.S.G.S. National Atlas of the U.S. Series,
U.S. Geological Survey, Reston, VA.

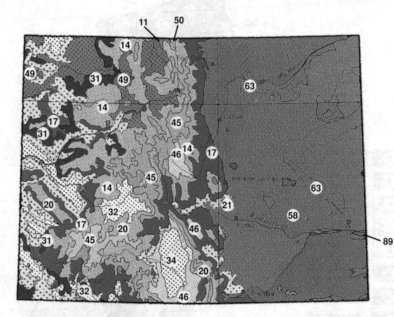

11	Douglas fir forest (*Pseudotsuga*)		
14	Western spruce-fir forest (*Picea-Abies*)	**45**	Alpine meadows and barren (*Agrostis, Carex, Festuca, Poa*)
17	Pine-Douglas fir forest (*Pinus-Pseudotsuga*)	**46**	Fescue-mountain muhly prairie (*Festuca-Muhlenbergia*)
20	Southwestern spruce-fir forest (*Picea-Abies*)	**49**	Sagebrush steppe (*Artemisia-Agropyron*)
21	Juniper-pinyon woodland (*Juniperus-Pinus*)	**50**	Wheatgrass-needlegrass shrubsteppe (*Agropyron-Stipa-Artemisia*)
31	Mountain mahogany-oak scrub (*Cercocarpus-Quercus*)	**58**	Grama-buffalo grass (*Bouteloua-Buchloë*)
32	Great Basin sagebrush (*Artemisia*)	**63**	Sandsage-bluestem prairie (*Artemisia-Andropogon*)
34	Saltbush-greasewood (*Atriplex-Sarcobatus*)	**89**	Northern floodplain forest (*Populus-Salix-Ulmus*)

POTENTIAL NATURAL VEGETATION ZONES IN
—— CONNECTICUT ——

Source: A.W. Kuchler's Potential Natural Vegetation Map, 1964, Revised 1985.
Presented in U.S.G.S. National Atlas of the U.S. Series,
U.S. Geological Survey, Reston, VA.

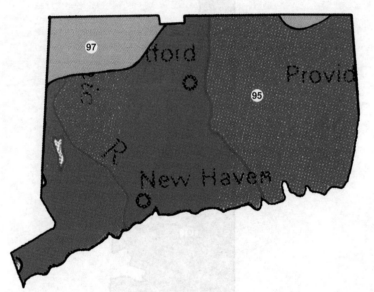

 95   Appalachian oak forest
(Quercus)

97   Northern hardwoods
(Acer-Betula-Fagus-Tsuga)

POTENTIAL NATURAL VEGETATION ZONES IN
DELAWARE

Source: A.W. Kuchler's Potential Natural Vegetation Map, 1964, Revised 1985.
Presented in U.S.G.S. National Atlas of the U.S. Series,
U.S. Geological Survey, Reston, VA.

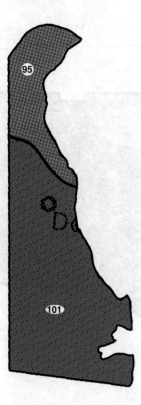

| 95 | Appalachian oak forest *(Quercus)* |
| 101 | Oak-hickory-pine forest *(Quercus-Carya-Pinus)* |

POTENTIAL NATURAL VEGETATION ZONES IN
—DISTRICT OF COLUMBIA—

Source: A.W. Kuchler's Potential Natural Vegetation Map, 1964, Revised 1985.
Presented in U.S.G.S. National Atlas of the U.S. Series,
U.S. Geological Survey, Reston, VA.

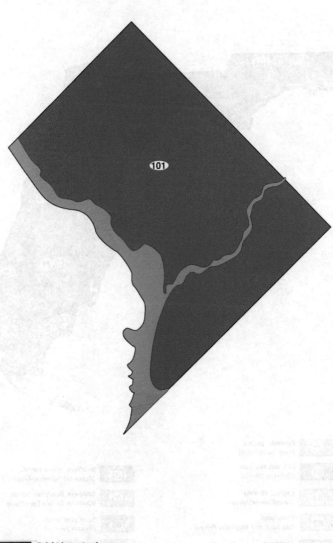

 101   Oak-hickory-pine forest
(Quercus-Carya-Pinus)

POTENTIAL NATURAL VEGETATION ZONES IN
FLORIDA

Source: A.W. Kuchler's Potential Natural Vegetation Map, 1964, Revised 1985.
Presented in U.S.G.S. National Atlas of the U.S. Series,
U.S. Geological Survey, Reston, VA.

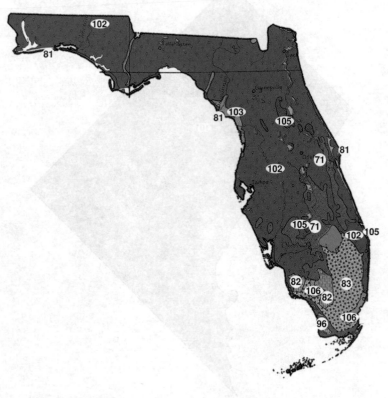

71	Palmetto prairie *(Serenoa-Aristida)*		
81	Live oak-sea oats *(Quercus-Uniola)*	**102**	Southern mixed forest *(Fagus-Liquidambar-Magnolia-Pinus-Quercus)*
82	Cypress savanna *(Taxodium-Mariscus)*	**103**	Southern floodplain forest *(Quercus-Nyassa-Taxodium)*
83	Everglades *(Mariscus and Magnolia-Persea)*	**105**	Sand pine scrub *(Pinus-Quercus)*
96	Mangrove *(Avicennia-Rhizophora)*	**106**	Sub-tropical pine forest *(Pinus)*

POTENTIAL NATURAL VEGETATION ZONES IN
GEORGIA

Source: A.W. Kuchler's Potential Natural Vegetation Map, 1964, Revised 1985.
Presented in U.S.G.S. National Atlas of the U.S. Series,
U.S. Geological Survey, Reston, VA.

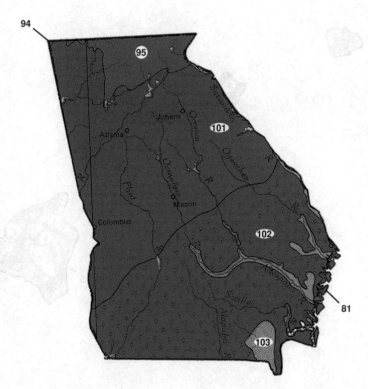

 81 Live oak-sea oats
(Quercus-Uniola)

94 Mixed mesophytic forest
(Acer-Aesculus-Fagus-Liriodendron-Quercus-Tilia)

95 Appalachian oak forest
(Quercus)

101 Oak-hickory-pine forest
(Quercus-Carya-Pinus)

102 Southern mixed forest
(Fagus-Liquidambar-Magnolia-Pinus-Quercus)

103 Southern floodplain forest
(Quercus-Nyassa-Taxodium)

POTENTIAL NATURAL VEGETATION ZONES IN
— HAWAII —

Source: A.W. Kuchler's Potential Natural Vegetation Map, 1964, Revised 1985.
Presented in U.S.G.S. National Atlas of the U.S. Series,
U.S. Geological Survey, Reston, VA.

 HI 1 Sclerophyllous forest, shrubland, and grassland
(Heteropogon-Opuntia-Prosopis)

HI 2 Guava mixed forest
(Aleurites-Hibiscus-Mangifera-Psidium-Schinus)

HI 3 Ohia lehua forest
(Metrosideros-Cibotium)

HI 4 Lama-manele forest
(Diospyros-Sapindus)

HI 5 Koa forest
(Acacia)

HI 6 Koa-mamani parkland
(Acacia-Deschampsia-Myoporum-Sophora)

HI 7 Grassland, microphyllous shrubland, and barrer
(Deschampsia-Styphelia-Vaccinium)

POTENTIAL NATURAL VEGETATION ZONES IN

IDAHO

Source: A.W. Kuchler's Potential Natural Vegetation Map, 1964, Revised 1985.
Presented in U.S.G.S. National Atlas of the U.S. Series,
U.S. Geological Survey, Reston, VA.

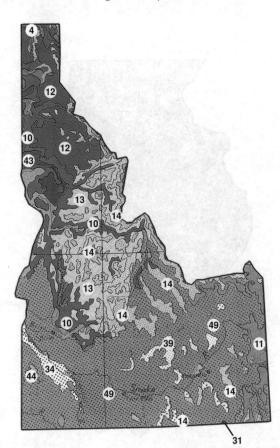

4	Fir-hemlock forest (Abies-Tsuga)	**31**	Mountain mahogany-oak scrub (Cercocarpus-Quercus)
10	Western ponderosa forest (Pinus)	**34**	Saltbush-greasewood (Atriplex-Sarcobatus)
11	Douglas fir forest (Pseudotsuga)	**39**	Desert: vegetation largely absent
12	Cedar-hemlock-pine forest (Thuja-Tsuga-Pinus)	**43**	Fescue-wheatgrass (Festuca-Agropyron)
13	Grand fir-Douglas fir forest (Abies-Pseudotsuga)	**44**	Wheatgrass-bluegrass (Agropyron-Poa)
14	Western spruce-fir forest (Picea-Abies)	**49**	Sagebrush steppe (Artemisia-Agropyron)

POTENTIAL NATURAL VEGETATION ZONES IN
ILLINOIS

Source: A.W. Kuchler's Potential Natural Vegetation Map, 1964, Revised 1985.
Presented in U.S.G.S. National Atlas of the U.S. Series,
U.S. Geological Survey, Reston, VA.

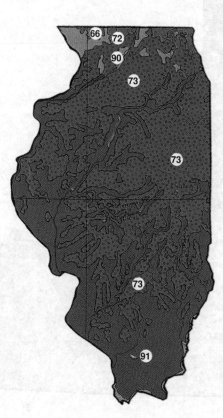

66	**Bluestem prairie** *(Andropogon-Panicum-Sorghastrum)*
72	**Oak savanna** *(Quercus-Andropogon)*
73	**Mosaic of numbers 66 and 91**
90	**Maple-basswood forest** *(Acer-Tilia)*
91	**Oak-hickory forest** *(Quercus-Carya)*

POTENTIAL NATURAL VEGETATION ZONES IN
INDIANA

Source: A.W. Kuchler's Potential Natural Vegetation Map, 1964, Revised 1985.
Presented in U.S.G.S. National Atlas of the U.S. Series,
U.S. Geological Survey, Reston, VA.

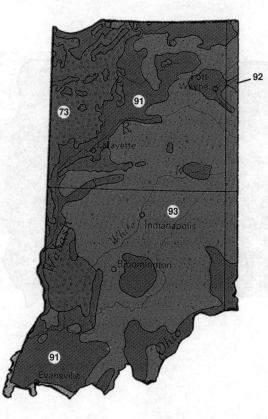

 73   Mosaic of numbers 66 and 91

91   Oak-hickory forest
(Quercus-Carya)

 92   Elm-ash forest
(Ulmus-Fraxinus)

93   Beech-maple forest
(Fagus-Acer)

POTENTIAL NATURAL VEGETATION ZONES IN

IOWA

Source: A.W. Kuchler's Potential Natural Vegetation Map, 1964, Revised 1985.
Presented in U.S.G.S. National Atlas of the U.S. Series,
U.S. Geological Survey, Reston, VA.

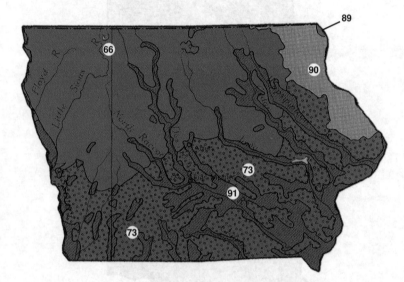

66 Bluestem prairie
(*Andropogon-Panicum-Sorghastrum*)

73 Mosaic of numbers 66 and 91

89 Northern floodplain forest
(*Populus-Salix-Ulmus*)

90 Maple-basswood forest
(*Acer-Tilia*)

91 Oak-hickory forest
(*Quercus-Carya*)

POTENTIAL NATURAL VEGETATION ZONES IN
KANSAS

Source: A.W. Kuchler's Potential Natural Vegetation Map, 1964, Revised 1985.
Presented in U.S.G.S. National Atlas of the U.S. Series,
U.S. Geological Survey, Reston, VA.

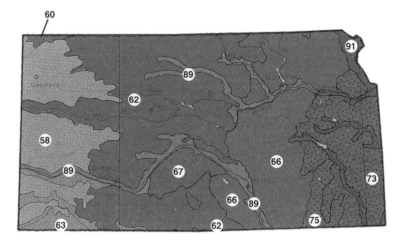

58	Grama-buffalo grass	*(Bouteloua-Buchloë)*
60	Wheatgrass-bluestem-needlegrass	*(Agropyron-Andropogon-Stipa)*
62	Bluestem-grama prairie	*(Andropogon-Bouteloua)*
63	Sandsage-bluestem prairie	*(Artemisia-Andropogon)*
66	Bluestem prairie	*(Andropogon-Panicum-Sorghastrum)*

67	Sandhills prairie	*(Andropogon-Calamovilfa)*
73	Mosaic of numbers 66 and 91	
75	Cross timbers	*(Quercus-Andropogon)*
89	Northern floodplain forest	*(Populus-Salix-Ulmus)*
91	Oak-hickory forest	*(Quercus-Carya)*

POTENTIAL NATURAL VEGETATION ZONES IN
KENTUCKY

Source: A.W. Kuchler's Potential Natural Vegetation Map, 1964, Revised 1985.
Presented in U.S.G.S. National Atlas of the U.S. Series,
U.S. Geological Survey, Reston, VA.

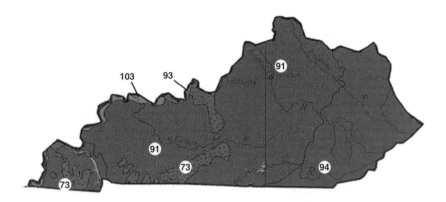

 73 Mosaic of numbers 66 and 91

 91 Oak-hickory forest
(Quercus-Carya)

93 Beech-maple forest
(Fagus-Acer)

94 Mixed mesophytic forest
(Acer-Aesculus-Fagus-Liriodendron-Quercus-Tilia)

103 Southern floodplain forest
(Quercus-Nyassa-Taxodium)

POTENTIAL NATURAL VEGETATION ZONES IN
—— LOUISIANA ——

Source: A.W. Kuchler's Potential Natural Vegetation Map, 1964, Revised 1985.
Presented in U.S.G.S. National Atlas of the U.S. Series,
U.S. Geological Survey, Reston, VA.

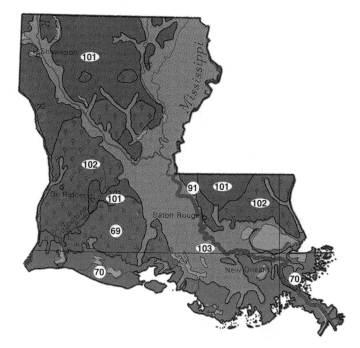

69 Bluestem-sacahuista prairie *(Andropogon-Spartina)*	**101** Oak-hickory-pine forest *(Quercus-Carya-Pinus)*
70 Southern cordgrass prairie *(Spartina)*	**102** Southern mixed forest *(Fagus-Liquidambar-Magnolia-Pinus-Quercus)*
91 Oak-hickory forest *(Quercus-Carya)*	**103** Southern floodplain forest *(Quercus-Nyassa-Taxodium)*

POTENTIAL NATURAL VEGETATION ZONES IN
MAINE

Source: A.W. Kuchler's Potential Natural Vegetation Map, 1964, Revised 1985.
Presented in U.S.G.S. National Atlas of the U.S. Series,
U.S. Geological Survey, Reston, VA.

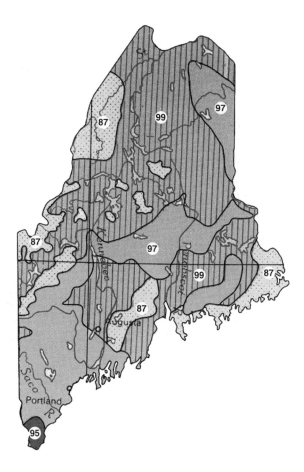

87	Northeastern spruce-fir forest *(Picea-Abies)*	**97**	Northern hardwoods *(Acer-Betula-Fagus-Tsuga)*
95	Appalachian oak forest *(Quercus)*	**99**	Northern hardwoods-spruce forest *(Acer-Betula-Fagus-Picea-Tsuga)*

POTENTIAL NATURAL VEGETATION ZONES IN
MARYLAND

Source: A.W. Kuchler's Potential Natural Vegetation Map, 1964, Revised 1985.
Presented in U.S.G.S. National Atlas of the U.S. Series,
U.S. Geological Survey, Reston, VA.

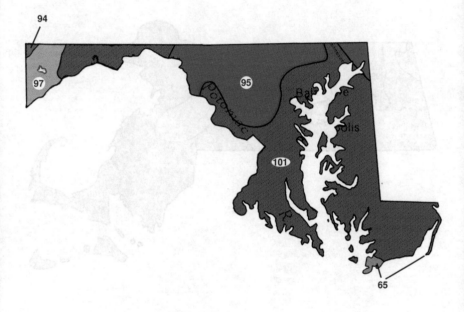

 65 Northern cordgrass prairie
(Distichlis-Spartina)

94 Mixed mesophytic forest
(Acer-Aesculus-Fagus-Liriodendron-Quercu

95 Appalachian oak forest
(Quercus)

97 Northern hardwoods
(Acer-Betula-Fagus-Tsuga)

 101 Oak-hickory-pine forest
(Quercus-Carya-Pinus)

POTENTIAL NATURAL VEGETATION ZONES IN
MASSACHUSETTS

Source: A.W. Kuchler's Potential Natural Vegetation Map, 1964, Revised 1985.
Presented in U.S.G.S. National Atlas of the U.S. Series,
U.S. Geological Survey, Reston, VA.

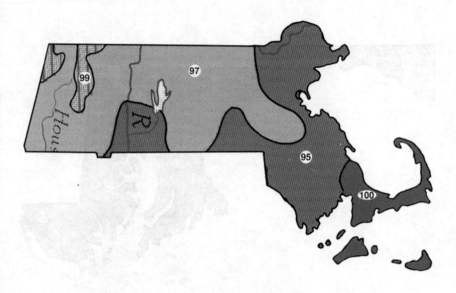

 95 Appalachian oak forest
(Quercus)

97 Northern hardwoods
(Acer-Betula-Fagus-Tsuga)

 99 Northern hardwoods-spruce forest
(Acer-Betula-Fagus-Picea-Tsuga)

100 Northeastern oak-pine forest
(Quercus-Pinus)

POTENTIAL NATURAL VEGETATION ZONES IN

MICHIGAN

Source: A.W. Kuchler's Potential Natural Vegetation Map, 1964, Revised 1985.
Presented in U.S.G.S. National Atlas of the U.S. Series,
U.S. Geological Survey, Reston, VA.

73	Mosaic of numbers 66 and 91
85	Conifer bog *(Picea-Larix-Thuja)*
86	Great Lakes pine forest *(Pinus)*
91	Oak-hickory forest *(Quercus-Carya)*
92	Elm-ash forest *(Ulmus-Fraxinus)*
93	Beech-maple forest *(Fagus-Acer)*
97	Northern hardwoods *(Acer-Betula-Fagus-Tsuga)*
98	Northern hardwoods-fir forest *(Acer-Betula-Abies-Tsuga*

POTENTIAL NATURAL VEGETATION ZONES IN

— MINNESOTA —

Source: A.W. Kuchler's Potential Natural Vegetation Map, 1964, Revised 1985.
Presented in U.S.G.S. National Atlas of the U.S. Series,
U.S. Geological Survey, Reston, VA.

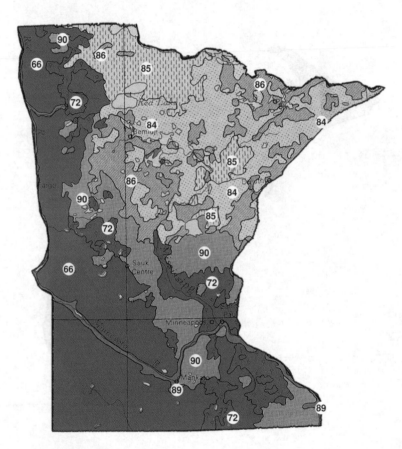

66 Bluestem prairie
(Andropogon-Panicum-Sorghastrum)

72 Oak savanna
(Quercus-Andropogon)

84 Great Lakes spruce-fir forest
(Picea-Abies)

85 Conifer bog
(Picea-Larix-Thuja)

86 Great Lakes pine forest
(Pinus)

89 Northern floodplain forest
(Populus-Salix-Ulmus)

90 Maple-basswood forest
(Acer-Tilia)

POTENTIAL NATURAL VEGETATION ZONES IN

MISSISSIPPI

Source: A.W. Kuchler's Potential Natural Vegetation Map, 1964, Revised 1985.
Presented in U.S.G.S. National Atlas of the U.S. Series,
U.S. Geological Survey, Reston, VA.

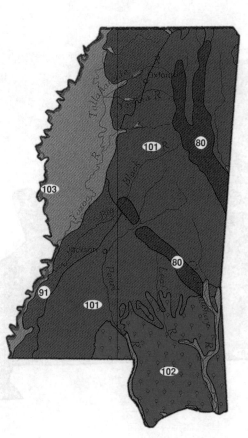

80 Blackbelt
(Liquidambar-Quercus-Juniperus)

91 Oak-hickory forest
(Quercus-Carya)

101 Oak-hickory-pine forest
(Quercus-Carya-Pinus)

102 Southern mixed forest
(Fagus-Liquidambar-Magnolia-Pinus-Quercus)

103 Southern floodplain forest
(Quercus-Nyassa-Taxodium)

POTENTIAL NATURAL VEGETATION ZONES IN

MISSOURI

Source: A.W. Kuchler's Potential Natural Vegetation Map, 1964, Revised 1985.
Presented in U.S.G.S. National Atlas of the U.S. Series,
U.S. Geological Survey, Reston, VA.

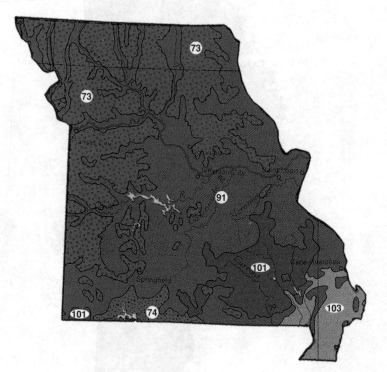

73 Mosaic of numbers 66 and 91

74 Cedar glades
(Quercus-Juniperus-Sporobolus)

91 Oak-hickory forest
(Quercus-Carya)

101 Oak-hickory-pine forest
(Quercus-Carya-Pinus)

103 Southern floodplain forest
(Quercus-Nyassa-Taxodium)

POTENTIAL NATURAL VEGETATION ZONES IN

MONTANA

Source: A.W. Kuchler's Potential Natural Vegetation Map, 1964, Revised 1985.
Presented in U.S.G.S. National Atlas of the U.S. Series,
U.S. Geological Survey, Reston, VA.

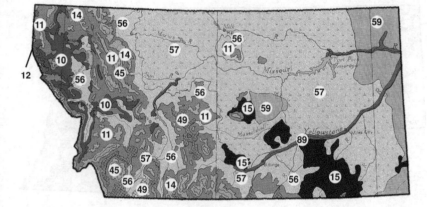

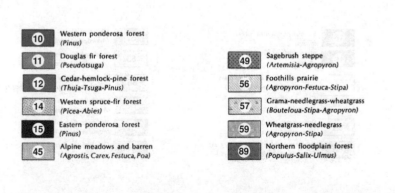

10	Western ponderosa forest *(Pinus)*	
11	Douglas fir forest *(Pseudotsuga)*	
12	Cedar-hemlock-pine forest *(Thuja-Tsuga-Pinus)*	
14	Western spruce-fir forest *(Picea-Abies)*	
15	Eastern ponderosa forest *(Pinus)*	
45	Alpine meadows and barren *(Agrostis, Carex, Festuca, Poa)*	
49	Sagebrush steppe *(Artemisia-Agropyron)*	
56	Foothills prairie *(Agropyron-Festuca-Stipa)*	
57	Grama-needlegrass-wheatgrass *(Bouteloua-Stipa-Agropyron)*	
59	Wheatgrass-needlegrass *(Agropyron-Stipa)*	
89	Northern floodplain forest *(Populus-Salix-Ulmus)*	

POTENTIAL NATURAL VEGETATION ZONES IN
NEBRASKA

Source: A.W. Kuchler's Potential Natural Vegetation Map, 1964, Revised 1985.
Presented in U.S.G.S. National Atlas of the U.S. Series,
U.S. Geological Survey, Reston, VA.

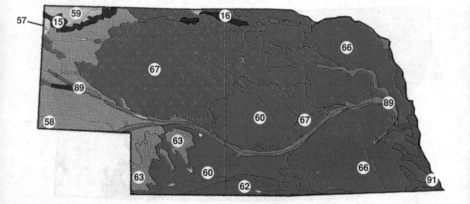

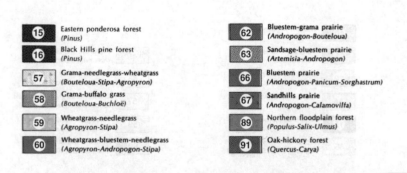

15	Eastern ponderosa forest *(Pinus)*	**62**	Bluestem-grama prairie *(Andropogon-Bouteloua)*
16	Black Hills pine forest *(Pinus)*	**63**	Sandsage-bluestem prairie *(Artemisia-Andropogon)*
57	Grama-needlegrass-wheatgrass *(Bouteloua-Stipa-Agropyron)*	**66**	Bluestem prairie *(Andropogon-Panicum-Sorghastrum)*
58	Grama-buffalo grass *(Bouteloua-Buchloë)*	**67**	Sandhills prairie *(Andropogon-Calamovilfa)*
59	Wheatgrass-needlegrass *(Agropyron-Stipa)*	**89**	Northern floodplain forest *(Populus-Salix-Ulmus)*
60	Wheatgrass-bluestem-needlegrass *(Agropyron-Andropogon-Stipa)*	**91**	Oak-hickory forest *(Quercus-Carya)*

POTENTIAL NATURAL VEGETATION ZONES IN
NEVADA

Source: A.W. Kuchler's Potential Natural Vegetation Map, 1964, Revised 1985.
Presented in U.S.G.S. National Atlas of the U.S. Series,
U.S. Geological Survey, Reston, VA.

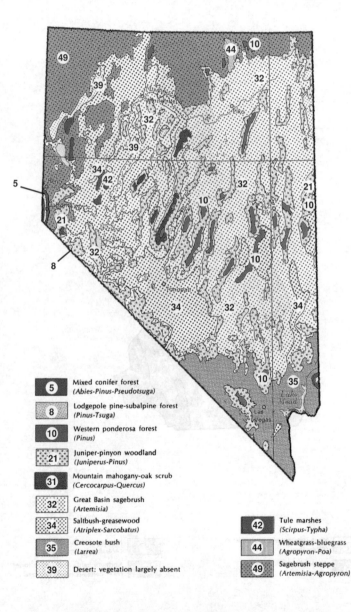

5	Mixed conifer forest (Abies-Pinus-Pseudotsuga)
8	Lodgepole pine-subalpine forest (Pinus-Tsuga)
10	Western ponderosa forest (Pinus)
21	Juniper-pinyon woodland (Juniperus-Pinus)
31	Mountain mahogany-oak scrub (Cercocarpus-Quercus)
32	Great Basin sagebrush (Artemisia)
34	Saltbush-greasewood (Atriplex-Sarcobatus)
35	Creosote bush (Larrea)
39	Desert: vegetation largely absent
42	Tule marshes (Scirpus-Typha)
44	Wheatgrass-bluegrass (Agropyron-Poa)
49	Sagebrush steppe (Artemisia-Agropyron)

POTENTIAL NATURAL VEGETATION ZONES IN
NEW HAMPSHIRE

Source: A.W. Kuchler's Potential Natural Vegetation Map, 1964, Revised 1985.
Presented in U.S.G.S. National Atlas of the U.S. Series,
U.S. Geological Survey, Reston, VA.

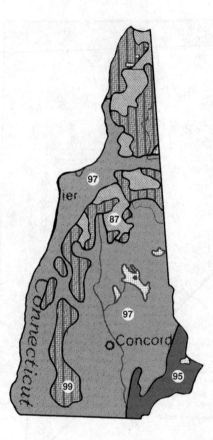

 87 Northeastern spruce-fir forest
(Picea-Abies)

 95 Appalachian oak forest
(Quercus)

97 Northern hardwoods
(Acer-Betula-Fagus-Tsuga)

99 Northern hardwoods-spruce forest
(Acer-Betula-Fagus-Picea-Tsuga)

POTENTIAL NATURAL VEGETATION ZONES IN
NEW JERSEY

Source: A.W. Kuchler's Potential Natural Vegetation Map, 1964, Revised 1985.
Presented in U.S.G.S. National Atlas of the U.S. Series,
U.S. Geological Survey, Reston, VA.

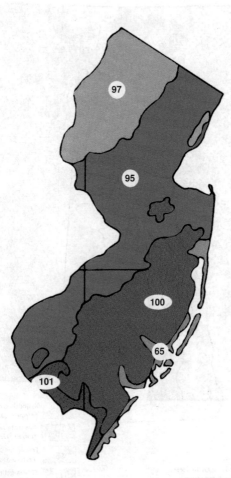

65 Northern cordgrass prairie
(Distichlis-Spartina)

95 Appalachian oak forest
(Quercus)

97 Northern hardwoods
(Acer-Betula-Fagus-Tsuga)

100 Northeastern oak-pine forest
(Quercus-Pinus)

101 Oak-hickory-pine forest
(Quercus-Carya-Pinus)

POTENTIAL NATURAL VEGETATION ZONES IN

NEW MEXICO

Source: A.W. Kuchler's Potential Natural Vegetation Map, 1964, Revised 1985.
Presented in U.S.G.S. National Atlas of the U.S. Series,
U.S. Geological Survey, Reston, VA.

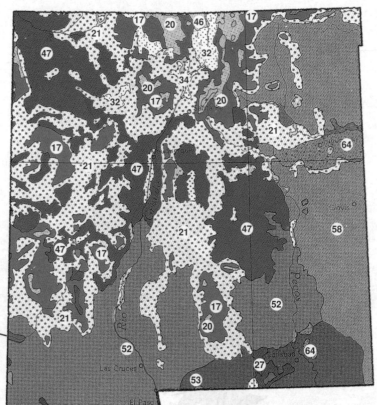

17 Pine-Douglas fir forest
(Pinus-Pseudotsuga)

20 Southwestern spruce-fir forest
(Picea-Abies)

21 Juniper-pinyon woodland
(Juniperus-Pinus)

27 Oak-juniper woodland
(Quercus-Juniperus)

32 Great Basin sagebrush
(Artemisia)

34 Saltbush-greasewood
(Atriplex-Sarcobatus)

36 Creosote bush-bur sage
(Larrea-Franseria)

46 Fescue-mountain muhly prairie
(Festuca-Muhlenbergia)

47 Grama-galleta steppe
(Bouteloua-Hilaria)

52 Grama-tobosa shrubsteppe
(Bouteloua-Hilaria-Larrea)

53 Trans-Pecos shrub savanna
(Flourensia-Larrea)

58 Grama-buffalo grass
(Bouteloua-Buchloë)

64 Shinnery
(Quercus-Andropogon)

POTENTIAL NATURAL VEGETATION ZONES IN
NEW YORK

Source: A.W. Kuchler's Potential Natural Vegetation Map, 1964, Revised 1985.
Presented in U.S.G.S. National Atlas of the U.S. Series,
U.S. Geological Survey, Reston, VA.

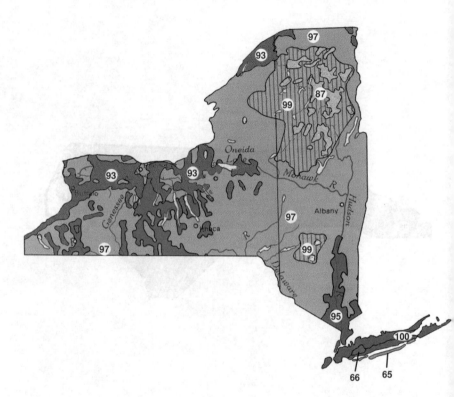

65	Northern cordgrass prairie *(Distichlis-Spartina)*	
66	Bluestem prairie *(Andropogon-Panicum-Sorghastrum)*	
87	Northeastern spruce-fir forest *(Picea-Abies)*	
93	Beech-maple forest *(Fagus-Acer)*	
95	Appalachian oak forest *(Quercus)*	
97	Northern hardwoods *(Acer-Betula-Fagus-Tsuga)*	
99	Northern hardwoods-spruce forest *(Acer-Betula-Fagus-Picea-Tsuga)*	
100	Northeastern oak-pine forest *(Quercus-Pinus)*	

POTENTIAL NATURAL VEGETATION ZONES IN
— NORTH CAROLINA —

Source: A.W. Kuchler's Potential Natural Vegetation Map, 1964, Revised 1985.
Presented in U.S.G.S. National Atlas of the U.S. Series,
U.S. Geological Survey, Reston, VA.

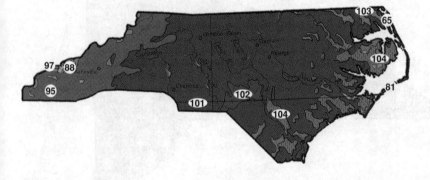

	Northern cordgrass prairie
65	*(Distichlis-Spartina)*
81	Live oak-sea oats *(Quercus-Uniola)*
88	Southeastern spruce-fir forest *(Picea-Abies)*
95	Appalachian oak forest *(Quercus)*
97	Northern hardwoods *(Acer-Betula-Fagus-Tsuga)*

	Oak-hickory-pine forest
101	*(Quercus-Carya-Pinus)*
102	Southern mixed forest *(Fagus-Liquidambar-Magnolia-Pinus-Quercus)*
103	Southern floodplain forest *(Quercus-Nyassa-Taxodium)*
104	Pocosin *(Pinus-Ilex)*

POTENTIAL NATURAL VEGETATION ZONES IN
NORTH DAKOTA

Source: A.W. Kuchler's Potential Natural Vegetation Map, 1964, Revised 1985.
Presented in U.S.G.S. National Atlas of the U.S. Series,
U.S. Geological Survey, Reston, VA.

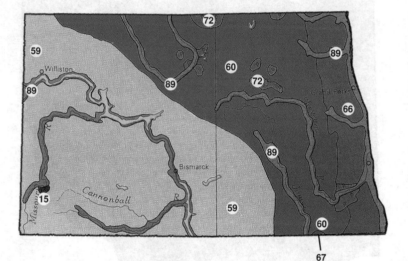

15 Eastern ponderosa forest *(Pinus)*	
59 Wheatgrass-needlegrass *(Agropyron-Stipa)*	**67** Sandhills prairie *(Andropogon-Calamovilfa)*
60 Wheatgrass-bluestem-needlegrass *(Agropyron-Andropogon-Stipa)*	**72** Oak savanna *(Quercus-Andropogon)*
66 Bluestem prairie *(Andropogon-Panicum-Sorghastrum)*	**89** Northern floodplain forest *(Populus-Salix-Ulmus)*

POTENTIAL NATURAL VEGETATION ZONES IN
OHIO

Source: A.W. Kuchler's Potential Natural Vegetation Map, 1964, Revised 1985.
Presented in U.S.G.S. National Atlas of the U.S. Series,
U.S. Geological Survey, Reston, VA.

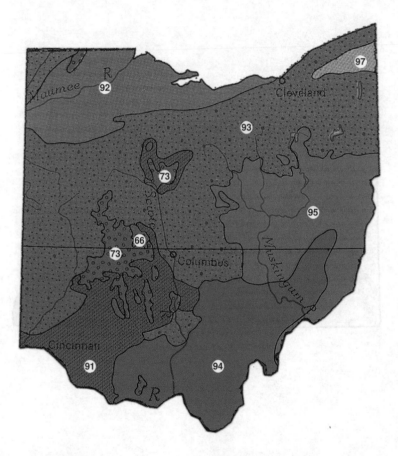

66 Bluestem prairie
(Andropogon-Panicum-Sorghastrum)

73 Mosaic of numbers 66 and 91

91 Oak-hickory forest
(Quercus-Carya)

92 Elm-ash forest
(Ulmus-Fraxinus)

93 Beech-maple forest
(Fagus-Acer)

94 Mixed mesophytic forest
(Acer-Aesculus-Fagus-Liriodendron-Quercus-Tilia)

95 Appalachian oak forest
(Quercus)

97 Northern hardwoods
(Acer-Betula-Fagus-Tsuga)

POTENTIAL NATURAL VEGETATION ZONES IN
OKLAHOMA

Source: A.W. Kuchler's Potential Natural Vegetation Map, 1964, Revised 1985.
Presented in U.S.G.S. National Atlas of the U.S. Series,
U.S. Geological Survey, Reston, VA.

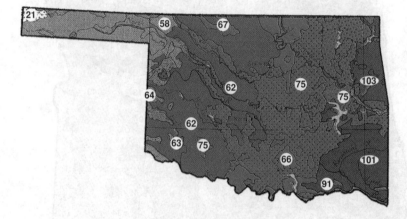

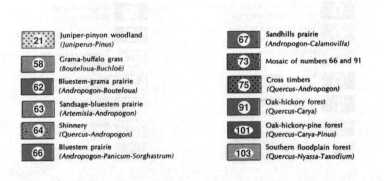

21 Juniper-pinyon woodland *(Juniperus-Pinus)*	**67** Sandhills prairie *(Andropogon-Calamovilfa)*
58 Grama-buffalo grass *(Bouteloua-Buchloë)*	**73** Mosaic of numbers 66 and 91
62 Bluestem-grama prairie *(Andropogon-Bouteloua)*	**75** Cross timbers *(Quercus-Andropogon)*
63 Sandsage-bluestem prairie *(Artemisia-Andropogon)*	**91** Oak-hickory forest *(Quercus-Carya)*
64 Shinnery *(Quercus-Andropogon)*	**101** Oak-hickory-pine forest *(Quercus-Carya-Pinus)*
66 Bluestem prairie *(Andropogon-Panicum-Sorghastrum)*	**103** Southern floodplain forest *(Quercus-Nyassa-Taxodium)*

POTENTIAL NATURAL VEGETATION ZONES IN
OREGON

Source: A.W. Kuchler's Potential Natural Vegetation Map, 1964, Revised 1985.
Presented in U.S.G.S. National Atlas of the U.S. Series,
U.S. Geological Survey, Reston, VA.

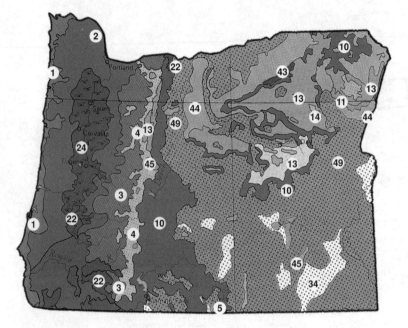

1 Spruce-cedar-hemlock forest (*Picea-Thuja-Tsuga*)	**14** Western spruce-fir forest (*Picea-Abies*)
2 Cedar-hemlock-Douglas fir forest (*Thuja-Tsuga-Pseudotsuga*)	**22** Oregon oakwoods (*Quercus*)
3 Silver fir-Douglas fir forest (*Abies-Pseudotsuga*)	**24** Mosaic of numbers 2 and 22
4 Fir-hemlock forest (*Abies-Tsuga*)	**34** Saltbush-greasewood (*Atriplex-Sarcobatus*)
5 Mixed conifer forest (*Abies-Pinus-Pseudotsuga*)	**43** Fescue-wheatgrass (*Festuca-Agropyron*)
10 Western ponderosa forest (*Pinus*)	**44** Wheatgrass-bluegrass (*Agropyron-Poa*)
11 Douglas fir forest (*Pseudotsuga*)	**45** Alpine meadows and barren (*Agrostis, Carex, Festuca, Poa*)
13 Grand fir-Douglas fir forest (*Abies-Pseudotsuga*)	**49** Sagebrush steppe (*Artemisia-Agropyron*)

POTENTIAL NATURAL VEGETATION ZONES IN
— PENNSYLVANIA —

Source: A.W. Kuchler's Potential Natural Vegetation Map, 1964, Revised 1985.
Presented in U.S.G.S. National Atlas of the U.S. Series,
U.S. Geological Survey, Reston, VA.

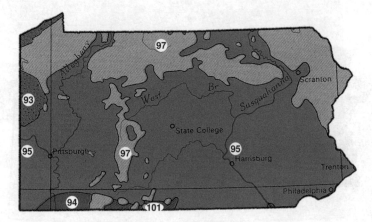

 93   Beech-maple forest
(Fagus-Acer)

94   Mixed mesophytic forest
(Acer-Aesculus-Fagus-Liriodendron-Quercus-Tilia)

95   Appalachian oak forest
(Quercus)

 97   Northern hardwoods
(Acer-Betula-Fagus-Tsuga)

101   Oak-hickory-pine forest
(Quercus-Carya-Pinus)

POTENTIAL NATURAL VEGETATION ZONES IN
PUERTO RICO

Source: Ecological Life Zones of Puerto Rico
J. J. Ewel & J. L. Whitmore 1993
USDA Forest Service

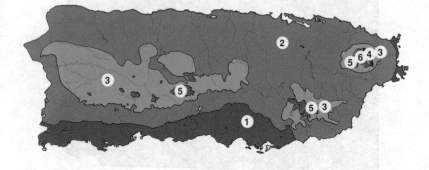

PR1 — Subtropical dry forest *(Bosque seco subtropical)*	PR4 — Subtropical rain forest *(Bosque pluvial subtropical)*
PR2 — Subtropical dry forest *(Bosque seco subtropical)*	PR5 — Lower montane wet forest *(Bosque muy humedo montano*
PR3 — Subtropical wet forest *(Bosque muy humedo subtropic*	PR6 — Lower montane rain forest *(Bosque pluvial montano bajo)*

POTENTIAL NATURAL VEGETATION ZONES IN
RHODE ISLAND

Source: A.W. Kuchler's Potential Natural Vegetation Map, 1964, Revised 1985.
Presented in U.S.G.S. National Atlas of the U.S. Series,
U.S. Geological Survey, Reston, VA.

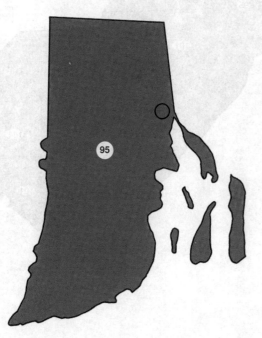

 Appalachian oak forest
(Quercus)

POTENTIAL NATURAL VEGETATION ZONES IN
SOUTH CAROLINA

Source: A.W. Kuchler's Potential Natural Vegetation Map, 1964, Revised 1985.
Presented in U.S.G.S. National Atlas of the U.S. Series,
U.S. Geological Survey, Reston, VA.

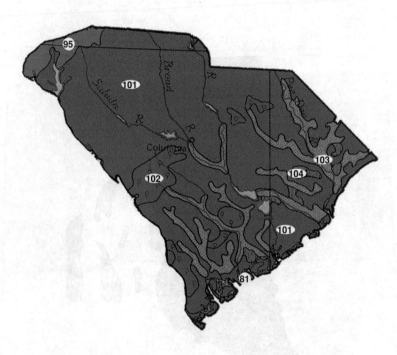

 81 Live oak-sea oats
(Quercus-Uniola)

95 Appalachian oak forest
(Quercus)

101 Oak-hickory-pine forest
(Quercus-Carya-Pinus)

 102 Southern mixed forest
(Fagus-Liquidambar-Magnolia-Pinus-Quercus)

103 Southern floodplain forest
(Quercus-Nyassa-Taxodium)

104 Pocosin
(Pinus-Ilex)

POTENTIAL NATURAL VEGETATION ZONES IN
——— SOUTH DAKOTA ———

Source: A.W. Kuchler's Potential Natural Vegetation Map, 1964, Revised 1985.
Presented in U.S.G.S. National Atlas of the U.S. Series,
U.S. Geological Survey, Reston, VA.

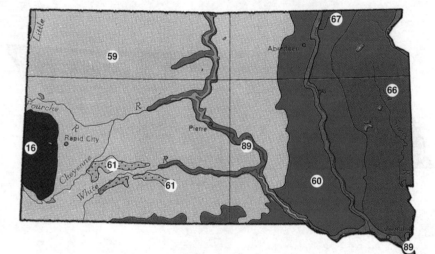

 Black Hills pine forest
(Pinus)

59 Wheatgrass-needlegrass
(Agropyron-Stipa)

60 Wheatgrass-bluestem-needlegrass
(Agropyron-Andropogon-Stipa)

 Wheatgrass-grama-buffalo grass
(Agropyron-Bouteloua-Buchloë)

 Bluestem prairie
(Andropogon-Panicum-Sorghastrum)

67 Sandhills prairie
(Andropogon-Calamovilfa)

89 Northern floodplain forest
(Populus-Salix-Ulmus)

POTENTIAL NATURAL VEGETATION ZONES IN
TENNESSEE

Source: A.W. Kuchler's Potential Natural Vegetation Map, 1964, Revised 1985.
Presented in U.S.G.S. National Atlas of the U.S. Series,
U.S. Geological Survey, Reston, VA.

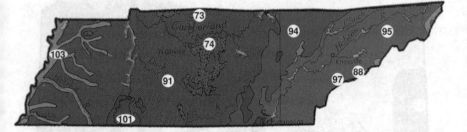

73 Mosaic of numbers 66 and 91	
74 Cedar glades *(Quercus-Juniperus-Sporobolus)*	**95** Appalachian oak forest *(Quercus)*
88 Southeastern spruce-fir forest *(Picea-Abies)*	**97** Northern hardwoods *(Acer-Betula-Fagus-Tsuga)*
91 Oak-hickory forest *(Quercus-Carya)*	**101** Oak-hickory-pine forest *(Quercus-Carya-Pinus)*
94 Mixed mesophytic forest *(Acer-Aesculus-Fagus-Liriodendron-Quercus-Tilia)*	**103** Southern floodplain forest *(Quercus-Nyassa-Taxodium)*

POTENTIAL NATURAL VEGETATION ZONES IN

TEXAS

Source: A.W. Kuchler's Potential Natural Vegetation Map, 1964, Revised 1985.
Presented in U.S.G.S. National Atlas of the U.S. Series,
U.S. Geological Survey, Reston, VA.

27 Oak-juniper woodland
(Quercus-Juniperus)

34 Saltbush-greasewood
(Atriplex-Sarcobatus)

38 Ceniza shrub
(Leucophyllum-Larrea-Prosopis)

48 Grama-tobosa prairie
(Bouteloua-Hilaria)

52 Grama-tobosa shrubsteppe
(Bouteloua-Hilaria-Larrea)

53 Trans-Pecos shrub savanna
(Flourensia-Larrea)

54 Mesquite-acacia-savanna
(Andropogon-Setaria-Prosopis-Acacia

55 Mesquite-live oak savanna
(Andropogon-Prosopis-Quercus)

58 Grama-buffalo grass
(Bouteloua-Buchloë)

62 Bluestem-grama prairie
(Andropogon-Bouteloua)

64 Shinnery
(Quercus-Andropogon)

68 Blackland prairie
(Andropogon-Stipa)

69 Bluestem-sacahuista prairie
(Andropogon-Spartina)

70 Southern cordgrass prairie
(Spartina)

75 Cross timbers
(Quercus-Andropogon)

76 Mesquite-buffalo grass
(Bouteloua-Buchloë-Prosopis)

77 Juniper-oak savanna
(Andropogon-Quercus-Juniperus)

78 Mesquite-oak savanna
(Andropogon-Prosopis-Quercus)

79 Fayette prairie
(Andropogon-Buchloë)

91 Oak-hickory forest
(Quercus-Carya)

101 Oak-hickory-pine forest
(Quercus-Carya-Pinus)

102 Southern mixed forest
(Fagus-Liquidambar-Magnolia-Pinus-Quercus)

103 Southern floodplain forest
(Quercus-Nyassa-Taxodium)

POTENTIAL NATURAL VEGETATION ZONES IN

UTAH

Source: A.W. Kuchler's Potential Natural Vegetation Map, 1964, Revised 1985.
Presented in U.S.G.S. National Atlas of the U.S. Series,
U.S. Geological Survey, Reston, VA.

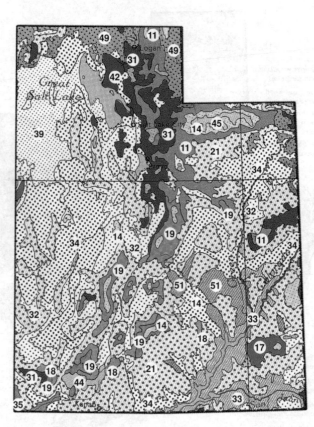

11 Douglas fir forest *(Pseudotsuga)*	**31** Mountain mahogany-oak scrub *(Cercocarpus-Quercus)*	**42** Tule marshes *(Scirpus-Typha)*
14 Western spruce-fir forest *(Picea-Abies)*	**32** Great Basin sagebrush *(Artemisia)*	**44** Wheatgrass-bluegrass *(Agropyron-Poa)*
17 Pine-Douglas fir forest *(Pinus-Pseudotsuga)*	**33** Blackbrush *(Coleogyne)*	**45** Alpine meadows and barren *(Agrostis, Carex, Festuca, Poa)*
18 Arizona pine forest *(Pinus)*	**34** Saltbush-greasewood *(Atriplex-Sarcobatus)*	**49** Sagebrush steppe *(Artemisia-Agropyron)*
19 Spruce-fir-Douglas fir forest *(Picea-Abies-Pseudotsuga)*	**35** Creosote bush *(Larrea)*	**51** Galleta-three awn shrubsteppe *(Hilaria-Aristida)*
21 Juniper-pinyon woodland *(Juniperus-Pinus)*	**39** Desert: vegetation largely absent	

POTENTIAL NATURAL VEGETATION ZONES IN
VERMONT

Source: A.W. Kuchler's Potential Natural Vegetation Map, 1964, Revised 1985.
Presented in U.S.G.S. National Atlas of the U.S. Series,
U.S. Geological Survey, Reston, VA.

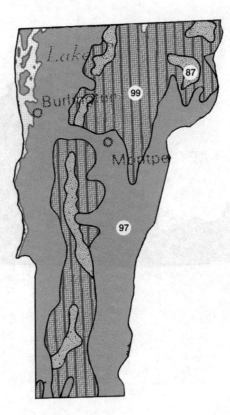

 87 Northeastern spruce-fir forest
(Picea-Abies)

97 Northern hardwoods
(Acer-Betula-Fagus-Tsuga)

99 Northern hardwoods-spruce fores
(Acer-Betula-Fagus-Picea-Tsuga)

POTENTIAL NATURAL VEGETATION ZONES IN
VIRGINIA

Source: A.W. Kuchler's Potential Natural Vegetation Map, 1964, Revised 1985.
Presented in U.S.G.S. National Atlas of the U.S. Series,
U.S. Geological Survey, Reston, VA.

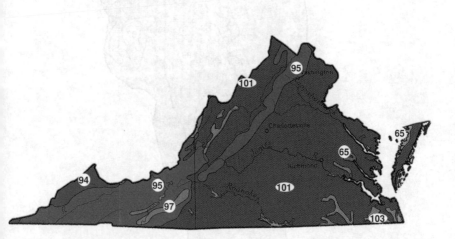

65	Northern cordgrass prairie *(Distichlis-Spartina)*	**97**	Northern hardwoods *(Acer-Betula-Fagus-Tsuga)*
94	Mixed mesophytic forest *(Acer-Aesculus-Fagus-Liriodendron-Quercus-Tilia)*	**101**	Oak-hickory-pine forest *(Quercus-Carya-Pinus)*
95	Appalachian oak forest *(Quercus)*	**103**	Southern floodplain forest *(Quercus-Nyassa-Taxodium)*

POTENTIAL NATURAL VEGETATION ZONES IN
WASHINGTON

Source: A.W. Kuchler's Potential Natural Vegetation Map, 1964, Revised 1985.
Presented in U.S.G.S. National Atlas of the U.S. Series,
U.S. Geological Survey, Reston, VA.

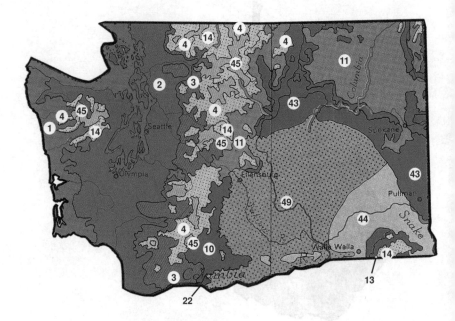

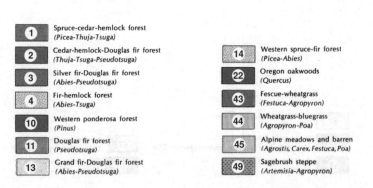

1	Spruce-cedar-hemlock forest (Picea-Thuja-Tsuga)
2	Cedar-hemlock-Douglas fir forest (Thuja-Tsuga-Pseudotsuga)
3	Silver fir-Douglas fir forest (Abies-Pseudotsuga)
4	Fir-hemlock forest (Abies-Tsuga)
10	Western ponderosa forest (Pinus)
11	Douglas fir forest (Pseudotsuga)
13	Grand fir-Douglas fir forest (Abies-Pseudotsuga)
14	Western spruce-fir forest (Picea-Abies)
22	Oregon oakwoods (Quercus)
43	Fescue-wheatgrass (Festuca-Agropyron)
44	Wheatgrass-bluegrass (Agropyron-Poa)
45	Alpine meadows and barren (Agrostis, Carex, Festuca, Poa)
49	Sagebrush steppe (Artemisia-Agropyron)

POTENTIAL NATURAL VEGETATION ZONES IN
—— WEST VIRGINIA ——

Source: A.W. Kuchler's Potential Natural Vegetation Map, 1964, Revised 1985.
Presented in U.S.G.S. National Atlas of the U.S. Series,
U.S. Geological Survey, Reston, VA.

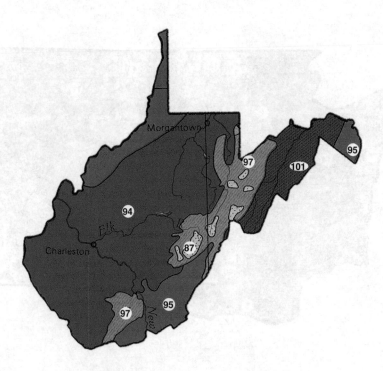

 87 Northeastern spruce-fir forest
(Picea-Abies)

94 Mixed mesophytic forest
(Acer-Aesculus-Fagus-Liriodendron-Quercus-Tilia)

95 Appalachian oak forest
(Quercus)

 97 Northern hardwoods
(Acer-Betula-Fagus-Tsuga)

101 Oak-hickory-pine forest
(Quercus-Carya-Pinus)

POTENTIAL NATURAL VEGETATION ZONES IN
WISCONSIN

Source: A.W. Kuchler's Potential Natural Vegetation Map, 1964, Revised 1985.
Presented in U.S.G.S. National Atlas of the U.S. Series,
U.S. Geological Survey, Reston, VA.

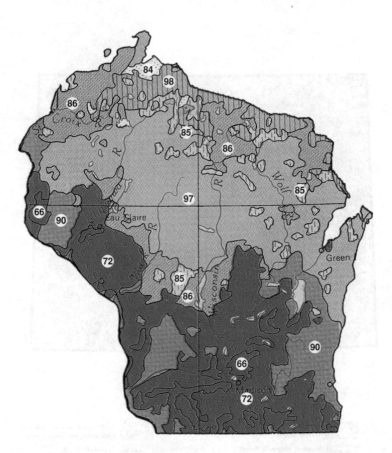

66	Bluestem prairie *(Andropogon-Panicum-Sorghastrum)*	**86**	Great Lakes pine forest *(Pinus)*
72	Oak savanna *(Quercus-Andropogon)*	**90**	Maple-basswood forest *(Acer-Tilia)*
84	Great Lakes spruce-fir forest *(Picea-Abies)*	**97**	Northern hardwoods *(Acer-Betula-Fagus-Tsuga)*
85	Conifer bog *(Picea-Larix-Thuja)*	**98**	Northern hardwoods-fir forest *(Acer-Betula-Abies-Tsuga)*

POTENTIAL NATURAL VEGETATION ZONES IN
WYOMING

Source: A.W. Kuchler's Potential Natural Vegetation Map, 1964, Revised 1985.
Presented in U.S.G.S. National Atlas of the U.S. Series,
U.S. Geological Survey, Reston, VA.

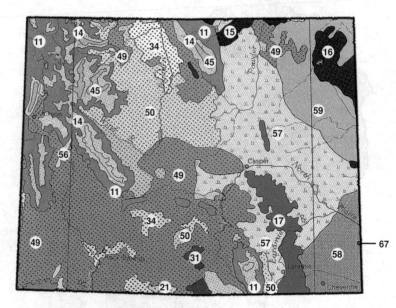

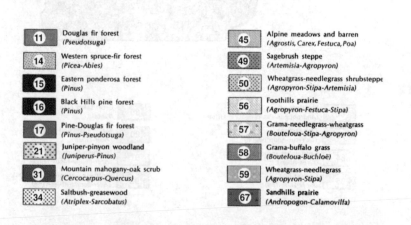

11 Douglas fir forest *(Pseudotsuga)*	**45** Alpine meadows and barren *(Agrostis, Carex, Festuca, Poa)*
14 Western spruce-fir forest *(Picea-Abies)*	**49** Sagebrush steppe *(Artemisia-Agropyron)*
15 Eastern ponderosa forest *(Pinus)*	**50** Wheatgrass-needlegrass shrubsteppe *(Agropyron-Stipa-Artemisia)*
16 Black Hills pine forest *(Pinus)*	**56** Foothills prairie *(Agropyron-Festuca-Stipa)*
17 Pine-Douglas fir forest *(Pinus-Pseudotsuga)*	**57** Grama-needlegrass-wheatgrass *(Bouteloua-Stipa-Agropyron)*
21 Juniper-pinyon woodland *(Juniperus-Pinus)*	**58** Grama-buffalo grass *(Bouteloua-Buchloë)*
31 Mountain mahogany-oak scrub *(Cercocarpus-Quercus)*	**59** Wheatgrass-needlegrass *(Agropyron-Stipa)*
34 Saltbush-greasewood *(Atriplex-Sarcobatus)*	**67** Sandhills prairie *(Andropogon-Calamovilfa)*

POTENTIAL NATURAL VEGETATION ZONES IN
NEBRASKA

Source: A.W. Kuchler's Potential Natural Vegetation Map, 1964, Revised 1985.
Presented in U.S.G.S. National Atlas of the U.S. Series,
U.S. Geological Survey, Reston, VA.

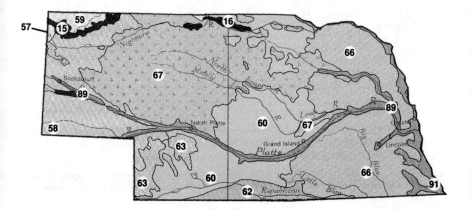

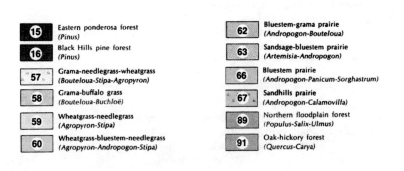

15 Eastern ponderosa forest *(Pinus)*	**62** Bluestem-grama prairie *(Andropogon-Bouteloua)*
16 Black Hills pine forest *(Pinus)*	**63** Sandsage-bluestem prairie *(Artemisia-Andropogon)*
57 Grama-needlegrass-wheatgrass *(Bouteloua-Stipa-Agropyron)*	**66** Bluestem prairie *(Andropogon-Panicum-Sorghastrum)*
58 Grama-buffalo grass *(Bouteloua-Buchloë)*	**67** Sandhills prairie *(Andropogon-Calamovilfa)*
59 Wheatgrass-needlegrass *(Agropyron-Stipa)*	**89** Northern floodplain forest *(Populus-Salix-Ulmus)*
60 Wheatgrass-bluestem-needlegrass *(Agropyron-Andropogon-Stipa)*	**91** Oak-hickory forest *(Quercus-Carya)*

VEGETATION REFERENCES

(Dominant plant species present in each vegetation type are listed in Appendix 8)

15   *Eastern Ponderosa Forest (Pinus)*
16   *Black Hills Pine forest (Pinus)*
57   *Grama-Needlegrass-Wheatgrass (Bouteloua-Stipa-Agropyron)*
58   *Grama-Buffalo Grass (Bouteloua-Buchloë)*
59   *Wheatgrass-Needlegrass (Agropyron-Stipa)*
60   *Wheatgrass-Bluestem-Needlegrass (Agropyron-Andropogon-Stipa)*
62   *Bluestem-Grama Prairie (Andropogon-Bouteloua)*
63   *Sandsage-Bluestem Prairie (Artemisia-Andropogon)*
66   *Bluestem Prairie (Andropogon-Panicum-Sorghastrum)*
67   *Sandhills Prairie (Andropogon-Calamovilfa)*
89   *Northern Floodplain Forest (Populus-Salix-Ulmus)*
91   *Oak-Hickory Forest (Quercus-Carya)*

Botanical Expert

Gerry Steinauer, Botanist/Ecologist
Nebraska Natural Heritage Program
2200 North 33rd St.
Lincoln, NE 68503
(402) 471-5469
(402) 471-5528 (fax)
internet: gstein@ngpsun.ngpc.state.ne.us

Recommended Flora

Great Plains Flora Association. 1986. Flora of the Great Plains. University Press of Kansas. Lawrence, KS 66045. Other authors: R.L. McGregor and T.M. Barkley. 1392 pgs. ISBN 0 7006 0295 X.

NATIVE PLANTS FOR LANDSCAPE USE IN NEBRASKA

Cacti

Opuntia fragilis (little prickly pear)
Opuntia macrorhiza (common prickly pear)
Opuntia polyacantha (plains prickly pear)

Ferns

Athyrium filix-femina (lady fern)
Botrychium virginianum (rattlesnake fern)
Cystopteris fragilis (fragile fern)
Dryopteris cristata (crested wood fern, buckler fern)
Onoclea sensibilis (sensitive fern)
Thalypteris palustris (marsh fern)

Forbs (annuals/biennials)

Cleome serrulata (Rocky Mountain beeplant)
Coreopsis tinctoria (tickseed, goldenwave, plains coreopsis, calliopsis)
Euphorbia marginata (snow-on-the-mountain)
Eustoma grandiflorum(prairie or catchfly gentian, Texas bluebell)
Gaillardia pulchella (Indian blanket, firewheel)

Helianthus annuus (common sunflower)
Helianthus petiolaris (plains sunflower)
Ipomopsis longiflora (white-flowered gilia)
Linum rigidum (yellow flax)
Machaeranthera tanacetifolia (tahoka daisy, tansy aster)
Oenothera albicaulis (pale evening primrose)
Oenothera biennis (common evening primrose)
Oenothera rhombipetala (diamond-petal primrose, four-point evening primrose)
Pectis angustifolia (limoncillo, fetid marigold)
Rudbeckia hirta (black-eyed Susan)
Senecio glabellus (butterweed)
Senecio plattensis (prairie ragwort, prairie groundsel)
Thelesperma filifolium var. filifolium (thelesperma, greenthread)
Townsendia exscapa (Easter daisy)

Forbs (perennials)

Abronia fragrans (sweet sand verbena)
Ageratina altissima var. altissima (white snakeroot)
Allium cernuum (nodding onion)
Allium textile (white wild onion)
Allium tricoccum (wild leek)
Anemone canadensis (Canada anemone, windflower)
Anemone caroliniana (Carolina anemone, southern thimbleweed)
Anemone multifida (early thimbleweed, cut-leaf anemone, Pacific anemone)
Antennaria spp. (pussytoes, everlasting)
Apocynum androsaemifolium (spreading dogbane)
Aquilegia canadensis (columbine)
Arisaema triphyllum (Jack-in-the-pulpit, Indian turnip)
Artemisia ludoviciana (white sage, prairie sage, artemisia)
Asarum canadense (wild ginger)
Asclepias incarnata (swamp milkweed)
Asclepias speciosa (showy milkweed)
Asclepias tuberosa (butterfly weed)
Asclepias verticillata (whorled milkweed)
Aster ericoides (heath aster, white wreath aster)
Aster novae-angliae (New England aster)
Aster oblongifolius (aromatic aster)
Aster oolentangiensis (sky blue aster)
Aster pilosus (frost aster)
Aster puniceus (red-stem aster, swamp aster)
Aster sericeus (silky aster)
Astragalus canadensis (milk vetch, Canada milk vetch)
Baptisia alba (white false indigo)
Baptisia lactea (white wild indigo)
Baptisia bracteata (plains wild indigo)
Callirhoe involucrata (purple poppy mallow, winecup)
Calochortus nuttallii (sego lily, mariposa lily)
Campanula rotundifolia (harebell)
Castilleja sessiliflora (downy painted cup)
Claytonia virginica (narrow-leaved spring beauty)
Dalea candida (white prairie clover)
Dalea purpurea (purple prairie clover)

Desmodium canadense (Canada tick-trefoil, Canada tickclover)
Desmodium illinoense (Illinois tick-trefoil, Illinois tickclover)
Dodecatheon meadia (shooting star)
Echinacea angustifolia (narrow-leaved purple coneflower)
Eupatorium maculatum (spotted Joe-pye weed)
Eupatorium perfoliatum (boneset)
Eupatorium purpureum (Joe-pye weed)
Euphorbia corollata (flowering spurge)
Euthamia graminifolia var. graminifolia (grass-leaved goldenrod)
Fragaria virginiana (wild strawberry)
Galium triflorum (sweet-scented bedstraw)
Gaura coccinea (scarlet gaura)
Gentiana andrewsii (bottle gentian)
Geranium maculatum (wild geranium, cranesbill)
Geranium viscossisimum (sticky wild geranium)
Glandularia bipinnatifida var. bipinnatifida (prairie verbena, Dakota vervain)
Glycyrrhiza lepidota (wild licorice)
Helenium autumnale (common sneezeweed)
Helianthus maximiliani (Maximilian sunflower)
Helianthus pauciflorus ssp. pauciflorus (stiff sunflower)
Heliopsis helianthoides (ox-eye sunflower, false sunflower)
Heuchera richardsonii (alum root)
Hydrophyllum virginianum (Virginia waterleaf)
Hypoxis hirsuta (yellow star grass)
Ipomoea leptophylla (bush morning glory)
Iris missouriensis (Rocky Mountain iris, western blue flag)
Iris virginica var. Shrevei (southern blue flag)
Iris virginica var. shrevei (blue flag)
Lespedeza capitata (roundheaded bush clover)
Liatris aspera (rough blazing star, gayfeather)
Liatris punctata (dotted blazing star, gayfeather)
Liatris pycnostachya (prairie blazing star, gayfeather)
Liatris squarrosa (blazing star)
Lilium michiganense (Turk's cap lily, Michigan lily)
Lilium philadelphicum (wood lily)
Lithospermum canescens (hoary puccoon)
Lithospermum caroliniense (hairy puccoon, hispid gromwell)
Lithospermum incisum (fringed puccoon, narrow-leaved puccoon)
Lobelia siphilitica (great blue lobelia)
Lupinus argenteus (silvery lupine)
Lysimachia ciliata (fringed loosestrife)
Maianthemum stellatum (starry Solomon's seal)
Monarda fistulosa (wild bergamot, horsemint, beebalm)
Nuphar lutea (yellow pond lily, cow lily, spatter dock)
Oenothera cespitosa (gumbo evening primrose, gumbo lily)
Oenothera macrocarpa (Missouri evening primrose)
Osmorhiza claytoni (sweet cicely, sweet jarvil)
Penstemon albidus (white beardtongue)
Penstemon angustifolius (whorled penstemon)
Penstemon cobaea (cobaea penstemon, wild foxglove)
Penstemon grandiflorus (large-flowered penstemon)
Phlox divaricata ssp. laphamii (blue phlox, sweet William)

Phlox pilosa (prairie phlox, downy phlox)
Physostegia virginiana (obedient plant, false dragonhead)
Podophyllum peltatum (May apple)
Polygonatum biflorum (Solomon's seal)
Potentilla arguta (white cinquefoil, prairie cinquefoil, tall cinquefoil)
Pulsatilla patens ssp. multifida (pasque flower, wild crocus)
Pycnanthemum tenuifolium (slender mountain mint)
Pycnanthemum virginianum (mountain mint)
Ranunculus hispidus (early buttercup, tufted buttercup)
Ratibida columnifera (prairie coneflower, long-headed coneflower, Mexican hat)
Ratibida pinnata (gray-headed coneflower, yellow coneflower)
Rudbeckia hirta (black-eyed Susan)
Ruellia humilis (wild petunia)
Salvia azurea var. grandiflora (blue sage)
Sanguinaria candensis (bloodroot)
Silphium integrifolium (rosinweed)
Silphium laciniatum (compass plant)
Silphium perfoliatum (cup plant)
Sisyrinchium angustifolium (narrow-leaved blue-eyed grass)
Sisyrinchium campestre (white-eyed grass, prairie blue-eyed grass)
Solidago canadensis (meadow goldenrod)
Solidago missouriensis (Missouri goldenrod, prairie goldenrod)
Solidago nemoralis (gray goldenrod, old-field goldenrod)
Solidago rigida (stiff goldenrod)
Solidago speciosa (showy goldenrod)
Solidago ulmifolia (elm-leaved goldenrod)
Tetraneuris acaulis var. acaulis (stemless goldflower, stemless rubber weed,
    butte marigold)
Thalictrum dasycarpum (tall or purple meadow rue)
Verbena hastata (blue verbena, blue vervain)
Verbena stricta (hoary vervain)
Vernonia baldwinii (ironweed, western ironweed)
Vernonia fasciculata (ironweed)
Veronicastrum virginicum (Culver's root)
Viola missouriensis (Missouri violet)
Viola pedata (bird-foot violet)
Viola pedatifida (prairie violet)
Viola pubescens (downy or smooth yellow violet)
Viola soraria (common blue violet, meadow violet)
Yucca glauca (yucca, soapweed)
Zizia aurea (golden alexanders)

Grasses/Grass-like plants

Agrostis exarata (spikebent, spike red top)
Agrostis scabra (ticklegrass, fly-away grass)
Andropogon gerardii (big bluestem)
Andropogon hallii (sand bluestem)
Aristida purpurea var. longiseta (red three awn)
Bouteloua curtipendula (sideoats grama)
Bouteloua gracilis (blue grama)
Bouteloua hirsuta (hairy grama)
Buchloe dactyloides (buffalograss)

Calamagrostis canadensis (bluejoint grass)
Calamovilfa longifolia (sandreed grass, prairie sandreed)
Carex filifolia
Carex heliphila
Carex nebrascensis (Nebraska sedge)
Distichlis spicata (seashore saltgrass)
Eleocharis palustris (creeping spikesedge, spike rush)
Elymus canadensis (Canada wild rye)
Elymus hystrix var. hystrix (bottlebrush grass)
Elymus lanceolatus (thickspike wheatgrass)
Elymus villosus (wild rye)
Elymus virginicus (wild rye)
Eragrostis spectabilis (purple lovegrass, tumblegrass)
Glyceria grandis (American mannagrass, tall mannagrass, reed meadowgrass)
Juncus interior (inland rush)
Koeleria macrantha (June grass)
Leersia oryzoides (rice cut grass)
Melica nitens (three-flower melic grass)
Oryzopsis hymenoides (Indian ricegrass)
Panicum virgatum (switchgrass)
Pascopyrum smithii (western wheatgrass)
Pseudoroegneria spicata (bluebunch wheatgrass)
Schizachyrium scoparium (little bluestem)
Scirpus acutus (hardstem bulrush)
Scirpus atrovirens (dark green bulrush)
Scirpus maritimus (alkali bulrush, prairie bulrush, bayonet grass)
Scirpus tabernaemontani (great bulrush)
Sorghastrum nutans (Indian grass)
Spartina pectinata (prairie cordgrass, freshwater cordgrass)
Sporobolus airoides (alkali sacaton)
Sporobolus compositus var. compositus (tall dropseed)
Sporobolus cryptandrus (sand dropseed)
Sporobolus heterolepis (northern prairie dropseed)
Stipa comata (needle-and-thread grass)
Stipa spartea (porcupine grass)
Stipa viridula (green needle grass)
Typha latifolia (cattail)

Shrubs (deciduous)

Amelanchier alnifolia (saskatoon, western serviceberry, Juneberry)
Amelanchier arborea (downy serviceberry, shadbush, Juneberry)
Amorpha canescens (leadplant)
Amorpha fruticosa (false indigo, Indigo bush)
Atriplex canescens (four-wing saltbush, wingscale)
Ceanothus americanus (New Jersey tea, red root)
Chrysothamnus nauseosus (rabbit brush, chamisa)
Cornus amomum ssp. obliqua (swamp dogwood, silky dogwood)
Cornus drummondii (rough-leaf dogwood)
Cornus sericea (red-twig dogwood, red-osier dogwood)
Corylus americana (American hazelnut or filbert)
Corylus cornuta (beaked hazelnut or filbert)
Euonymus atropurpurea (wahoo, burning bush)

Krascheninnikovia lanata (winterfat)
Lonicera dioica (limber or wild honeysuckle)
Prunus pumila var. besseyi (sand cherry)
Prunus virginiana (chokecherry)
Rhus glabra (smooth sumac)
Ribes odoratum (buffalo currant, golden currant)
Rosa arkansana (prairie rose)
Rosa blanda (early wild rose, smooth rose)
Rosa setigera (Illinois or prairie rose)
Rosa woodsii (western wild rose, woods rose)
Rubus idaeus ssp. strigosus (red raspberry)
Rubus occidentalis (black raspberry, thimbleberry)
Salix interior (sand-bar willow)
Sambucus canadensis (elderberry, common elder)
Sarcobatus vermiculatus (greasewood)
Shepherdia argentea (silver buffaloberry)
Symphoricarpos occidentalis (wolfberry)
Symphoricarpos orbiculatus (coralberry, Indian currant)
Viburnum lentago (black haw, nannyberry)

Shrubs (evergreen)

Artemisia tridentata (big sagebrush, Great Basin sagebrush)
Cercocarpus montanus (mountain mahogany, silverleaf mountain mahogany)
Juniperus communis (common juniper)
Juniperus horizontalis (creeping juniper, creeping savin)

Trees (deciduous)

Acer glabrum (Rocky Mountain maple)
Acer saccharinum (silver maple)
Aesculus glabra (Ohio buckeye, horse chestnut)
Betula occidentalis (mountain birch, water birch)
Carya cordiformis (bitternut, swamp hickory)
Carya ovata (shagbark hickory)
Celtis occidentalis (hackberry, sugarberry)
Cercis canadensis (redbud)
Crataegus mollis (downy hawthorn)
Fraxinus americana (white ash)
Fraxinus pensylvanica (green ash)
Gymnocladus dioica (Kentucky coffee tree)
Juglans nigra (black walnut)
Malus ioensis var. ioensis (prairie crabapple)
Ostrya virginiana (ironwood, hophornbeam)
Platanus occidentalis (sycamore, plane-tree)
Populus deltoides (eastern cottonwood)
Populus tremuloides (quaking aspen)
Prunus americana (wild plum)
Prunus mexicana (Mexican plum)
Prunus serotina (black cherry)
Quercus macrocarpa (bur oak)
Quercus marilandica (blackjack oak)
Quercus muhlenbergii (chinkapin oak, chestnut oak)
Quercus rubra (red oak)

Quercus velutina (black oak)
Salix amygdaloides (peachleaf willow)
Tilia americana (American linden, basswood)
Ulmus americana (American elm)
Ulmus rubra (red elm, slippery elm)

Trees (evergreen)

Juniperus scopulorum (Rocky Mountain juniper)
Juniperus virginiana (eastern red cedar)
Pinus ponderosa (ponderosa pine)

Vines (deciduous)

Celastrus scandens (American bittersweet)
Clematis ligusticifolia (clematis)
Clematis pitcheri (leather flower, purple clematis)
Clematis virginiana (virgin's bower)
Parthenocissus quinquefolia (Virginia creeper)
Parthenocissus quinquefolia var. quinquefolia (woodbine)
Vitis riparia (riverbank grape)

FEDERALLY LISTED ENDANGERED SPECIES

Blowout penstemon (Penstemon haydenii)
Western prairie fringed orchid (Platanthera praeclara)

NEBRASKA NOXIOUS SPECIES

Because the noxious weed lists have continually changed since we gathered them in 1994, we are not including them at this time. Not all States have noxious weed lists. Those that do, do not use the same standards of importance and are not comparable. States typically have included plants that interfere with agriculture (Canada thistle), or cause human health problems (poison ivy). Some States are now including a category of plants that invade and degrade the environment (purple loosestrife). Check with your State's Agriculture Department or Weed Scientist listed below. The noxious weed list can be used two ways on roadsides: l) check to not inadvertently plant these invasive plants, and 2) note the plants you are legally responsible to control. Many States now check adjacent State lists to avoid planting their neighbors' problem plants. Because weeds do not respect political boundaries, and because by their very nature weeds continue to adapt and expand, monitoring and controlling invasives at State borders is a wise part of vegetation management.

(Weed and Seed Laws)

Department of Agriculture
P.O. Box 94756
Lincoln, NE 68509

Alexander R. Martin
Agronomy Department
362 Plant Science Building
Lincoln, NE 6858a3
(402) 472-1527

NEBRASKA RESOURCES

Nebraska Natural Heritage Program
Game and Parks Commission
2200 North 33rd Street
Lincoln, NE 68503
(402) 471-5421

The Nature Conservancy, Field Office
1722 St. Mary's Avenue, Ste. 403
Omaha, NE 68102
(402) 342-0282

Wildflower Society of Nebraska
402 Ridgeway Drive
Norfolk, NE 68701

Prairie/Plains Resource Institute
1307 "L" St.
Aurora, NE 68818
(402) 694-5535

Chet Ager Nature Center
Pioneers Park
Lincoln, NE 68502

Institute of Agriculture and
Natural Resources
University of Nebraska-Lincoln
P.O. Box 830915
Lincoln, NE 68583

POTENTIAL NATURAL VEGETATION ZONES IN
NEVADA

Source: A.W. Kuchler's Potential Natural Vegetation Map, 1964, Revised 1985.
Presented in U.S.G.S. National Atlas of the U.S. Series,
U.S. Geological Survey, Reston, VA.

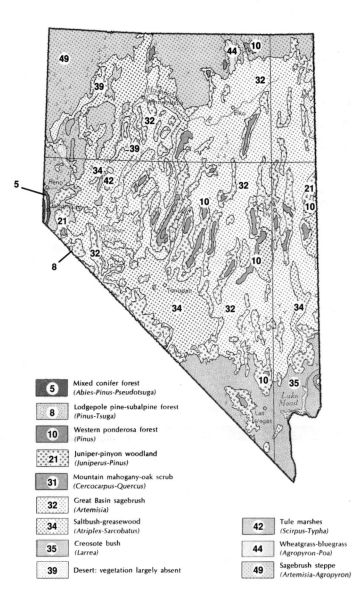

5 Mixed conifer forest
(Abies-Pinus-Pseudotsuga)

8 Lodgepole pine-subalpine forest
(Pinus-Tsuga)

10 Western ponderosa forest
(Pinus)

21 Juniper-pinyon woodland
(Juniperus-Pinus)

31 Mountain mahogany-oak scrub
(Cercocarpus-Quercus)

32 Great Basin sagebrush
(Artemisia)

34 Saltbush-greasewood
(Atriplex-Sarcobatus)

35 Creosote bush
(Larrea)

39 Desert: vegetation largely absent

42 Tule marshes
(Scirpus-Typha)

44 Wheatgrass-bluegrass
(Agropyron-Poa)

49 Sagebrush steppe
(Artemisia-Agropyron)

(Dominant plant species present in each vegetation type are listed in Appendix 8)

5 *Mixed Conifer Forest (Abies-Pinus-Pseudotsuga)*
8 *Lodgepole Pine-Subalpine Forest (Pinus-Tsuga)*
10 *Western Ponderosa Forest (Pinus)*
21 *Juniper-Pinyon Woodland (Juniperus-Pinus)*
31 *Mountain Mahogany-Oak Scrub (Cercocarpus-Quercus)*
32 *Great Basin Sagebrush (Artemisia)*
34 *Saltbrush-Geasewood (Artiplex-Sarcobatus)*
35 *Creosote Bush (Larrea)*
39 *Desert: Vegetation Largely Absent*
42 *Tule Marshes (Scirpus-Typha)*
44 *Wheatgrass-Bluegrass (Agropyron-Poa)*
49 *Sagebrush Steppe (Artemisia-Agropyron)*

Botanical Expert

James D. Morefield, Botanist
Nevada Natural Heritage Program
Department of Conservation and Natural Resources
1550 East College Parkway, Suite 145
Carson City, NV 89706-7921
(775) 687-4245
internet: www.state.nv.us/nvnhp/

Recommended Flora

Cronquist, A. 1977-97. Intermountain Flora: Vascular Plants of the Intermountain West, U.S.A. New York Botanical Garden, New York.

Hickman, James C. 1993. The Jepson Manual of Higher Plants of California, Revision and Update of 1925 Original Edition. University of California Press, Berkeley and Los Angeles, CA. 1400 pgs. ISBN: 0520082559.

Kartesz, J.T. 1987. A Flora of Nevada. Unpublished Doctoral Dissertation. University of Nevada, Reno, NV.

Welsh, S.L. 1993. A Utah Flora. 2nd Edition, Revision. Brigham Young University. Provo, UT. 986 pgs. maps. ISBN 0842523138.

Flora of North America Editorial Committee, eds. 1993 +. Flora of North America North of Mexico. 3 + vols. Oxford University Press, New York and Oxford.

NATIVE PLANTS FOR LANDSCAPE USE IN NEVADA

Cacti

Echinocereus engelmannii (hedgehog cactus, strawberry cactus)
Opuntia acanthocarpa
Opuntia basilaris (beavertail cactus)
Opuntia chlorotica (pancake pear, silver-dollar cactus)
Opuntia echinocarpa
Opuntia erinacea (grizzly, hedgehog, or Mohave prickly pear)
Opuntia phaeacantha (purple-fruited prickly pear)
Opuntia ramosissima

Ferns

Adiantum capillus-veneris (southern maidenhair fern)
Adiantum pedatum (northern maidenhair fern)
Aspidotis densa (rock brake, cliff brake, Indian's dream)
Asplenium trichomanes (maidenhair spleenwort)
Athyrium filix-femina (lady fern)
Cheilanthes gracillima (lace fern)
Cystopteris fragilis (fragile fern)
Woodwardia fimbriata (chain fern)

Forbs (annuals/biennials)

Baileya multiradiata (desert marigold)
Collomia grandiflora (collomia)
Eriogonum inflatum (desert trumpet)
Erysimum capitatum (western wallflower, prairie rocket)
Gaillardia arizonica (Arizona blanket flower)
Helianthus petiolaris (plains sunflower)
Hymenoxys cooperi (Cooper's goldflower)
Ipomopsis aggregata (sky rocket, scarlet gilia)
Lupinus concinnus (annual lupine, bajada lupine)
Mentzelia laevicaulis (blazing star, evening star, stick leaf)
Mimulus guttatus (golden monkey flower)
Nemophila breviflora (Great Basin nemophila)
Oenothera albicaulis (pale evening primrose)
Oenothera deltoides (fragrant primrose, desert evening primrose)
Oenothera elata ssp. hookeri (giant evening primrose)
Salvia columbariae (chia)
Townsendia exscapa (Easter daisy)

Forbs (perennials)

Aconitum columbianum (western monkshood)
Allium validum (swamp onion)
Anemone multifida (early thimbleweed, cut-leaf anemone, Pacific anemone)
Antennaria spp. (pussytoes, everlasting)
Aquilegia chrysantha (yellow columbine)
Aquilegia coerulea (Rocky Mountain or blue columbine)
Aquilegia formosa (scarlet columbine)
Arnica cordifolia (heartleaf arnica)
Artemisia arbuscula (sagebrush)
Artemisia cana (sagebrush)
Artemisia douglasiana (Douglas mugwort)
Artemisia ludoviciana (white sage, prairie sage, artemisia)
Asclepias asperula (antelope horns)
Asclepias incarnata (swamp milkweed)
Asclepias speciosa (showy milkweed)
Aster ascendens (purple aster, Pacific aster)
Aster foliaceus (leafy aster)
Aster laevis (smooth aster)
Balsamorrhiza sagittata (balsamroot)
Calochortus kennedyi (desert mariposa, flame mariposa)
Calochortus macrocarpus (bigpod mariposa)

Calochortus nuttallii (sego lily, mariposa lily)
Caltha leptosepala (white marsh marigold, elkslip)
Castilleja angustifolia var. dubia (desert paintbrush)
Castilleja linariifolia (Indian paintbrush)
Claytonia lanceolata (spring beauty)
Delphinium glaucum (tower larkspur)
Delphinium parishii (desert larkspur, paleface delphinium)
Delphinium scaposum (barestem larkspur)
Dichelostemma congestum (wild hyacinth)
Epilobium angustifolium (fireweed, willow herb)
Epilobium canum var. latifolia (hummingbird trumpet)
Epilobium latifolium (dwarf fireweed)
Epilobium obcordatum (rock fringe)
Erigeron compositus (alpine daisy)
Erigeron speciosus (showy fleabane)
Eriogonum heracleoides (buckwheat)
Eriogonum microthecum (buckwheat)
Eriogonum racemosum (red root buckwheat)
Eriogonum umbellatum (sulfur buckwheat)
Eriogonum wrightii (Wright buckwheat)
Eriophyllum lanatum (woolly sunflower, Oregon sunshine)
Gaillardia pinnatifida (yellow gaillardia, blanket flower)
Gaura coccinea (scarlet gaura)
Geranium caespitosum (wild geranium)
Geranium viscossisimum (sticky wild geranium)
Geum triflorum (prairie smoke, purple avens)
Gutierrezia sarothrae (broom snakeweed, matchbrush)
Hedysarum boreale (sweet vetch, sweet broom)
Heterotheca villosa var. villosa (golden aster)
Heuchera parvifolia (saxifrage, alum root)
Heuchera rubescens (mountain alumroot, red alumroot, wild coralbells)
Ipomopsis congesta (gilia)
Lewisia rediviva (bitter root)
Linum lewisii (wild blue flax)
Lithospermum incisum (fringed puccoon, narrow-leaved puccoon)
Lobelia cardinalis (cardinal flower)
Lupinus argenteus (silvery lupine)
Lupinus caudatus (tailcup lupine)
Lupinus confertus (lupine)
Lupinus palmeri (Palmer's lupine)
Lupinus polyphyllus (meadow lupine, bog lupine)
Maianthemum racemosum ssp. racemosum (false Solomon's seal,
    false spikenard)
Maianthemum stellatum (starry Solomon's seal)
Mertensia ciliata (mountain bluebells)
Mimulus cardinalis (crimson monkey flower)
Mimulus lewisii (Lewis monkey flower, great purple monkey flower)
Mimulus primuloides (primrose monkey flower)
Mirabilis multiflora (wild four o'clock)
Monardella odoratissima (coyote mint, mountain pennyroyal)
Nolina microcarpa (sacahuista, bear grass)
Oenothera brachycarpa (evening primrose)

Oenothera cespitosa (gumbo evening primrose, gumbo lily)
Oenothera flava (shortfin evening primrose)
Pedicularis groenlandica (elephant heads)
Penstemon ambiguus (sand penstemon)
Penstemon davidsonii (blue color mat, alpine penstemon)
Penstemon deustus (hot rock penstemon)
Penstemon eatonii (firecracker penstemon)
Penstemon palmeri (Palmer's penstemon, scented penstemon)
Penstemon speciosus (sagebrush penstemon)
Penstemon thurberi (sand penstemon)
Pentaphylloides floribunda (potentilla, shrubby cinquefoil)
Petrophyton caespitosum (dwarf spiraea, petrophytum, tufted rockmat)
Phacelia sericea (silky phacelia)
Phlox diffusa (mat phlox)
Polemonium foliosissimum (Jacob's ladder)
Polemonium occidentale (Jacob's ladder)
Polemonium pulcherrimum (alpine Jacob's ladder, skunk leaf)
Polemonium viscosum (sky pilot)
Potentilla arguta (white cinquefoil, prairie cinquefoil, tall cinquefoil)
Potentilla gracilis (cinqufoil)
Ranunculus alismifolius (meadow buttercup)
Saxifraga cespitosa (tufted saxifrage)
Sidalcea neomexicana (checker mallow, prairie mallow)
Silene acaulis (moss campion)
Solidago californica (California goldenrod)
Solidago multiradiata (northern goldenrod, mountain goldenrod)
Sphaeralcea ambigua (desert mallow)
Sphaeralcea coccinea (scarlet globe mallow)
Sphaeralcea grossulariifolia (gooseberry leaf globemallow)
Sphaeralcea munroana (Munro's globe mallow, white-leaved globe mallow)
Sphaeralcea parvifolia (globe mallow)
Stanleya pinnata (desert or prince's plume)
Tetraneuris acaulis var. acaulis (stemless goldflower, stemless rubber weed, butte marigold)
Thalictrum fendleri var. polycarpum (meadow rue)
Thermopsis rhombifolia var. montana (golden pea, buckbean)
Verbena stricta (hoary vervain)
Viguiera parishii (shrubby goldeneye)
Viola macloskeyi (white mountain violet)
Viola nuttallii (yellow violet)
Yucca baccata (blue yucca, banana yucca, fleshy-fruited yucca)
Yucca brevifolia (Joshua tree)
Yucca schidigera (yucca)
Zizia aptera (heart-leaved golden alexanders)

Grasses/Grass-like plants

Agrostis scabra (ticklegrass, fly-away grass)
Aristida purpurea (purple three awn)
Aristida purpurea var. longiseta (red three awn)
Bouteloua curtipendula (sideoats grama)
Bouteloua eriopoda (black grama)
Bouteloua gracilis (blue grama)

Bouteloua hirsuta (hairy grama)
Bromus carinatus (California brome)
Calamagrostis canadensis (bluejoint grass)
Carex aquatilis (water sedge)
Carex heteroneura (sedge)
Carex nebrascensis (Nebraska sedge)
Carex utriculata (beaked sedge)
Carex vernacula (sedge)
Danthonia californica (California oatgrass)
Danthonia intermedia (timber oatgrass)
Deschampsia cespitosa (tufted hairgrass)
Eleocharis palustris (creeping spikesedge, spike rush)
Elymus elymoides
Elymus glaucus (blue wild rye)
Elymus lanceolatus (thickspike wheatgrass)
Festuca idahoensis (Idaho fescue, blue bunchgrass)
Glyceria grandis (American mannagrass, tall mannagrass, reed meadowgrass)
Hierochloe odorata (sweet grass)
Koeleria macrantha (June grass)
Leersia oryzoides (rice cut grass)
Leymus cinereus (Great Basin wild rye)
Muhlenbergia porteri (bush muhly)
Muhlenbergia richardsonis (muhly)
Oryzopsis hymenoides (Indian ricegrass)
Panicum virgatum (switchgrass)
Pascopyrum smithii (western wheatgrass)
Phleum alpinum (alpine timothy)
Poa alpina (alpine bluegrass)
Poa secunda (pine bluegrass)
Pseudoroegneria spicata (bluebunch wheatgrass)
Scirpus acutus (hardstem bulrush)
Scirpus maritimus (alkali bulrush, prairie bulrush, bayonet grass)
Sporobolus airoides (alkali sacaton)
Sporobolus cryptandrus (sand dropseed)
Sporobolus flexuosus (mesa dropseed)
Stipa comata (needle-and-thread grass)
Stipa nelsonii (Columbia needlegrass)
Stipa speciosa (desert needlegrass, spear grass)
Trisetum spicatum (spike trisetum)
Typha latifolia (cattail)

Shrubs (deciduous)

Alnus incana (speckled alder, mountain alder)
Ambrosia dumosa
Amelanchier alnifolia (saskatoon, western serviceberry, Juneberry)
Amelanchier utahensis (Utah serviceberry)
Artemisia frigida (prairie sagewort, fringed sage)
Atriplex canescens (four-wing saltbush, wingscale)
Atriplex confertifolia (spiny saltbush, shadscale saltbush, hop sage)
Ceanothus greggii var. vestitus (desert ceanothus)
Chamaebatiaria millefolium (fernbush, desert sweet, tansy bush)
Chrysothamnus nauseosus (rabbit brush, chamisa)

Chrysothamnus parryi (rabbit brush, chamisa)
Cornus sericea (red-twig dogwood, red-osier dogwood)
Ephedra nevadensis (Mormon tea)
Ephedra viridis (Mormon tea)
Eriogonum fasciculatum (California buckwheat)
Fallugia paradoxa (Apache plume)
Hibiscus denudatus (rock hibiscus)
Holodiscus dumosus (bush rock-spires, cream bush, ocean spray)
Krascheninnikovia lanata (winterfat)
Lonicera involucrata (black twinberry, bear berry honeysuckle)
Lycium andersonii (Anderson wolfberry)
Lycium shockleyi (wolfberry)
Parthenium incanum (mariola)
Physocarpus alternans
Physocarpus malvaceus (mallow ninebark)
Prosopsis glandulosa (honey mesquite)
Prunus andersonii (desert peach)
Prunus virginiana (chokecherry)
Purshia tridentata (antelope brush)
Rhus glabra (smooth sumac)
Rhus trilobata (squawbush, basketbush, skunkbush)
Ribes aureum (golden currant)
Ribes cereum (wax currant, western red currant, squaw currant)
Robinia neomexicana (New Mexico locust, mescal bean)
Rosa woodsii (western wild rose, woods rose)
Rubus idaeus ssp. strigosus (red raspberry)
Rubus parviflorus (western thimbleberry)
Salix arctica (arctic willow)
Salix bebbiana (Bebb willow, long-beaked willow)
Salix boothi (willow)
Salix exigua (willow)
Salix geyeriana (willow)
Salix lasiolepis (willow)
Salix lucida (willow)
Salix lutea (willow)
Salix scouleriana (western pussy willow, Scouler's willow)
Salvia dorrii (grayball sage)
Sambucus cerulea (blue elderberry)
Sambucus racemosa var. melanocarpa (black elderberry)
Sarcobatus vermiculatus (greasewood)
Shepherdia argentea (silver buffaloberry)
Shepherdia canadensis (buffaloberry)
Sorbus scopulina (western mountain ash)
Symphoricarpos oreophilus (mountain snowberry)
Vaccinium uliginosum (alpine blueberry, bog blueberry)

Shrubs (evergreen)

Arctostaphylos nevadensis (pinemat manzanita)
Arctostaphylos patula (greenleaf manzanita)
Arctostaphylos uva-ursi (bearberry, kinnikinnik)
Artemisia nova (black sagebrush)
Artemisia tridentata (big sagebrush, Great Basin sagebrush)

Atriplex lentiformis (saltbush, coastal quail bush)
Atriplex torreyi (saltbush)
Ceanothus velutinus (mountain balm, buckbush)
Cercocarpus ledifolius (curl-leaf mountain mahogany)
Cercocarpus montanus (mountain mahogany, silverleaf mountain mahogany)
Encelia farinosa (brittle bush)
Frangula californica ssp. californica (coffeeberry)
Grayia spinosa (spiny hopsage)
Juniperus californica (California juniper)
Juniperus communis (common juniper)
Kalmia polifolia (swamp laurel, bog laurel)
Larrea tridentata (creosote bush)
Mahonia fremontii (Fremont barberry, holly grape)
Mahonia haematocarpa (red barberry)
Purshia stansburiana (cliff rose)
Quercus turbinella (shrub live oak)

Trees (deciduous)

Acer glabrum (Rocky Mountain maple)
Acer grandidentatum (bigtooth maple)
Alnus rhombifolia (white alder)
Betula occidentalis (mountain birch, water birch)
Celtis laevigata var. reticulata (netleaf hackberry)
Cercis canadensis var. texensis (California redbud)
Chilopsis linearis (desert willow, trumpet flower)
Fraxinus velutina (Arizona ash, Velvet ash, desert ash)
Populus balsamifera (black cottonwood)
Populus fremontii (western cottonwood)
Populus tremuloides (quaking aspen)
Prosopis pubescens (tornillo, screwbean mesquite)
Quercus gambelii (Gambel's oak, Rocky Mountain white oak)
Salix amygdaloides (peachleaf willow)
Salix laevigata (red willow)

Trees (evergreen)

Abies concolor (western white fir)
Abies lasiocarpa (subalpine fir)
Calocedrus decurrens (incense cedar)
Cupressus arizonica (Arizona cypress)
Juniperus osteosperma (Utah juniper)
Juniperus scopulorum (Rocky Mountain juniper)
Picea engelmannii (Engelmann spruce)
Pinus flexilis (limber pine)
Pinus lambertiana (sugar pine)
Pinus longaeva (bristlecone pine)
Pinus monophylla (single-leaf pinyon pine)
Pinus monticola (western white pine)
Pinus ponderosa (ponderosa pine)
Pseudotsuga menziesii (Douglas fir)
Quercus chrysolepis (canyon live oak)
Taxus brevifolia (western yew, Pacific yew)
Tsuga mertensiana (mountain hemlock)

Vines (deciduous) ———————————————————————————

Clematis ligusticifolia (clematis)
Vitis arizonica (Arizona grape, canyon grape)

FEDERALLY LISTED ENDANGERED SPECIES

Amargosa niterwort (Nitrophila mohavensis)
Ash Meadows blazing-star (Mentzelia leucophylla)
Ash Meadows gumplant (Grindelia frxino-ratensis)
Ash Meadows ivesia (Ivesia kingii var. eremica)
Ash Meadows milk-vetch (Astragalus phoenix)
Ash Meadows sunray (Enceliopsis nudicaulis var. corrugata)
Spring-loving centaury (Centaurium namophilum)
Steamboad buckwheat (Eriogonum ovalifolium var. williamsiae)

NEVADA NOXIOUS SPECIES

Because the noxious weed lists have continually changed since we gathered them in 1994, we are not including them at this time. Not all States have noxious weed lists. Those that do, do not use the same standards of importance and are not comparable. States typically have included plants that interfere with agriculture (Canada thistle), or cause human health problems (poison ivy). Some States are now including a category of plants that invade and degrade the environment (purple loosestrife). Check with your State's Agriculture Department or Weed Scientist listed below. The noxious weed list can be used two ways on roadsides: l) check to not inadvertantly plant these invasive plants, and 2) note the plants you are legally responsible to control. Many States now check adjacent State lists to avoid planting their neighbors' problem plants. Because weeds do not respect political boundaries, and because by their very nature weeds continue to adapt and expand, monitoring and controlling invasives at State borders is a wise part of vegetation management.

(Weed and Seed Laws)

Department of Agriculture
Division of Plant Industry,
P.O. Box 11100
350 Capitol Hill Avenue
Reno, NV 89510

Robert Wilson, U of N
White Pine County Extension
P.O. Box 210
Ely, NV 89301
(702) 289-4459

NEVADA RESOURCES

Nevada Natural Heritage Program
Department of Conservation
1550 E. College Parkway, Ste. 145
Carson City, NV 89710
(775) 687-4245
(775) 687-1288 (fax)
internet: www.state.nv.us/nvnhp/

The Nature Conservancy Field Office
1771 East Flamingo, Ste. 111B
Las Vegas, NV 89ll9
(702) 737-8744

Northern Nevada Native Plant Society
Box 8965
Reno, NV 89507

POTENTIAL NATURAL VEGETATION ZONES IN
—— NEW HAMPSHIRE ——

Source: A.W. Kuchler's Potential Natural Vegetation Map, 1964, Revised 1985.
Presented in U.S.G.S. National Atlas of the U.S. Series,
U.S. Geological Survey, Reston, VA.

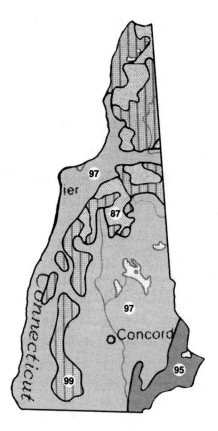

87	Northeastern spruce-fir forest *(Picea-Abies)*
95	Appalachian oak forest *(Quercus)*
97	Northern hardwoods *(Acer-Betula-Fagus-Tsuga)*
99	Northern hardwoods-spruce forest *(Acer-Betula-Fagus-Picea-Tsuga)*

337

VEGETATION REFERENCES

(Dominant plant species present in each vegetation type are listed in Appendix 8)

87 Northeastern Spruce-Fir Forest (Picea-Abies)
95 Appalachian Oak Forest (Quercus)
97 Northern Hardwoods (Acer-Betula-Fagus-Tsuga)
99 Northern Hardwoods-Spruce Forests (Acer-Betula-Fagus-Picea-Tsuga)

Botanical Expert

Dr. Garrett Crow, Professor of Botany
Director, Hodgdon Herbarium
Department of Plant Biology, Nesmith Hall
University of New Hampshire
Duram, NH 03824
(603) 862-3865
(603) 862-4757 (fax)

Recommended Flora

Gleason, H.A.; A. Cronquist. 1991. Manual of Vascular Plants of Northeastern United States and Adjacent Canada, 2nd Edition. New York Botanical Garden, New York. 910 pgs. + map. ISBN 0893273651.

NATIVE PLANTS FOR LANDSCAPE USE IN NEW HAMPSHIRE

Ferns

Athyrium filix-femina (lady fern)
Botrychium virginianum (rattlesnake fern)
Dennstaedtia punctilobula (hay-scented fern)
Dryopteris carthusiana (shield fern, toothed wood fern, spinulose shield fern)
Dryopteris cristata (crested wood fern, buckler fern)
Dryopteris marginalis (marginal wood fern)
Gymnocarpium dryopteris (oak fern)
Matteuccia struthiopteris (ostrich fern)
Onoclea sensibilis (sensitive fern, bead fern)
Osmunda cinnamomea (cinnamon fern)
Osmunda claytoniana (interrupted fern)
Osmunda regalis (royal fern)
Phegopteris hexagonoptera (broad beech fern)
Polystichum acrostichoides (Christmas fern)
Thelypteris novaboracensis (New York fern, tapering fern)
Thelypteris simulata (Massachusetts fern)
Woodwardia virginica (Virginia chain fern)

Forbs (annuals/biennials)

Corydalis sempervirens (pale corydalis)
Lobelia spicata (pale lobelia)
Oenothera biennis (common evening primrose)

Forbs (perennials)

Acorus americanus (sweet flag, calamus)
Actaea pachypoda (white baneberry)

Ageratina altissima var. altissima (white snakeroot)
Allium canadense (wild garlic)
Anaphalis margaritacea (pearly everlasting)
Anemone canadensis (Canada anemone, windflower)
Anemone cylindrica (thimbleweed, candle anemone)
Anemone virginiana (thimbleweed, tall anemone)
Antennaria spp. (pussytoes, everlasting)
Apocynum androsaemifolium (spreading dogbane)
Aquilegia canadensis (columbine)
Arisaema triphyllum (Jack-in-the-pulpit, Indian turnip)
Asclepias incarnata (swamp milkweed)
Aster divaricatus (white wood aster)
Aster dumosus (bushy aster)
Aster ericoides (heath aster, white wreath aster)
Aster foliaceus (leafy aster)
Aster laevis (smooth aster)
Aster novae-angliae (New England aster)
Aster pilosus (frost aster)
Aster puniceus (red-stem aster, swamp aster)
Caltha palustris (marsh marigold, cowslip)
Campanula rotundifolia (harebell)
Chelone glabra (turtlehead)
Clintonia borealis (clintonia, blue-bead lily)
Coptis trifolia ssp. groenlandica (goldthread)
Cornus canadensis (bunchberry)
Desmodium canadense (Canada tick-trefoil, Canada tickclover)
Epilobium angustifolium (fireweed, willow herb)
Erythronium americanum (eastern trout lily, yellow trout lily)
Eupatorium fistulosum (Joe-pye weed)
Eupatorium maculatum (spotted Joe-pye weed)
Eupatorium purpureum (Joe-pye weed)
Euthamia graminifolia var. graminifolia (grass-leaved goldenrod)
Fragaria virginiana (wild strawberry)
Galium triflorum (sweet-scented bedstraw)
Geranium maculatum (wild geranium, cranesbill)
Geum rivale (purple avens, water avens)
Helianthus strumosus (woodland sunflower)
Iris versicolor (blue flag)
Lespedeza capitata (roundheaded bush clover)
Lilium canadense (wild yellow lily, Canada lily)
Lilium philadelphicum (wood lily)
Linnaea borealis (twinflower)
Lobelia cardinalis (cardinal flower)
Lysimachia ciliata (fringed loosestrife)
Maianthemum canadense (wild lily-of-the-valley, Canada mayflower)
Mitchella repens (partridge berry)
Monarda fistulosa (wild bergamot, horsemint, beebalm)
Nuphar variegata (yellow pond lily, cow lily, spatter dock)
Osmorhiza berteroi (mountain sweet cicely)
Osmorhiza claytoni (sweet cicely, sweet jarvil)
Peltandra virginica (arrow arum)
Penstemon digitalis (beardtongue)

Potentilla arguta (white cinquefoil, prairie cinquefoil, tall cinquefoil)
Potentilla simplex (common cinquefoil)
Pycnanthemum tenuifolium (slender mountain mint)
Pyrola elliptica (shinleaf)
Rudbeckia laciniata (cut-leaf coneflower)
Senecio aureus (golden ragwort)
Sisyrinchium angustifolium (narrow-leaved blue-eyed grass)
Sisyrinchium mucronatum (eastern blue-eyed grass)
Smilacina racemosum ssp. racemosum (false Solomon's seal, false spikenard)
Smilacina stellatum (starry Solomon's seal)
Solidago caesia (blue-stemmed goldenrod, wreath goldenrod)
Solidago canadensis (meadow goldenrod)
Solidago juncea (early goldenrod, plume goldenrod)
Solidago nemoralis (gray goldenrod, old-field goldenrod)
Solidago odora (sweet goldenrod)
Solidago rugosa (rough-leaved goldenrod)
Streptopus roseus (rosy twisted stalk)
Thalictrum dioicum (early meadow rue)
Thalictrum pubescens (tall meadow rue)
Tiarella cordifolia (foam flower)
Trientalis borealis ssp. borealis (starflower)
Trillium erectum (wakerobin, purple trillium)
Trillium undulatum (painted trillium)
Uvularia sessilifolia (wildoats, merrybells)
Verbena hastata (blue verbena, blue vervain)
Viola conspersa (American dog violet)
Viola soraria (common blue violet, meadow violet)
Zizia aurea (golden alexanders)

Grasses/Grass-like plants

Agrostis scabra (ticklegrass, fly-away grass)
Andropogon gerardii (big bluestem)
Calamagrostis canadensis (bluejoint grass)
Carex pensylvanica (Pennsylvania sedge)
Carex stipata (awl-fruited sedge)
Carex stricta (tussock sedge)
Carex utriculata (beaked sedge)
Danthonia spicata (poverty grass)
Deschampsia cespitosa (tufted hairgrass)
Distichlis spicata (seashore saltgrass)
Eleocharis smallii (creeping spikesedge, spike rush)
Elymus canadensis (Canada wild rye)
Eragrostis spectabilis (purple lovegrass, tumblegrass)
Glyceria grandis (American mannagrass, tall mannagrass, reed meadowgrass)
Hierochloe odorata (sweet grass)
Juncus effusus var. solutus (soft rush)
Leersia oryzoides (rice cut grass)
Panicum virgatum (switchgrass)
Schizachyrium scoparium (little bluestem)
Scirpus acutus (hardstem bulrush)
Scirpus atrovirens (dark green bulrush)
Scirpus cyperinus (wool grass)

Scirpus maritimus (alkali bulrush, prairie bulrush, bayonet grass)
Scirpus tabernaemontani (great bulrush)
Sorghastrum nutans (Indian grass)
Spartina patens (marsh hay cordgrass, salt meadow cordgrass)
Spartina pectinata (prairie cordgrass, freshwater cordgrass)
Trisetum spicatum (spike trisetum)
Typha latifolia (cattail)

Shrubs (deciduous)

Alnus incana (speckled alder, mountain alder)
Alnus serrulata (smooth alder)
Amelanchier arborea (downy serviceberry, shadbush, Juneberry)
Aronia melanocarpa (black chokeberry)
Ceanothus americanus (New Jersey tea, red root)
Cephalanthus occidentalis (buttonbush)
Clethra alnifolia (summer sweet)
Cornus alternifolia (pogoda dogwood, alternate-leaved dogwood)
Cornus amomum ssp. obliqua (swamp dogwood, silky dogwood)
Cornus racemosa (gray dogwood)
Corylus americana (American hazelnut or filbert)
Corylus cornuta (beaked hazelnut or filbert)
Diervilla lonicera (bush honeysuckle)
Ilex verticillata (winterberry, black alder)
Lindera benzoin (spicebush)
Lonicera dioica (limber or wild honeysuckle)
Lyonia ligustrina (male-berry, male-blueberry)
Prunus virginiana (chokecherry)
Rhododendron canadense (rhodora)
Rhus glabra (smooth sumac)
Rhus hirta (staghorn sumac)
Ribes cynosbati (prickly gooseberry, dogberry)
Rosa blanda (early wild rose, smooth rose)
Rosa carolina (Carolina rose)
Rubus idaeus ssp. strigosus (red raspberry)
Rubus occidentalis (black raspberry, thimbleberry)
Rubus odoratus (thimbleberry)
Salix discolor (pussy willow)
Sambucus canadensis (elderberry, common elder)
Sambucus racemosa var. pubens (scarlet elderberry, red-berried elder)
Spiraea tomentosa (steeplebush, hardhack)
Vaccinium angustifolium (low-bush blueberry)
Vaccinium corymbosom (highbush blueberry)
Viburnum acerifolium (maple leaf viburnum)
Viburnum edule (moosewood viburnum)
Viburnum lentago (black haw, nannyberry)
Viburnum nudum var. cassinoides (wild raisin)
Viburnum opulus var. americanum (high-bush cranberry, American
   cranberrybush viburnum)

Shrubs (evergreen)

Andromeda polifolia var. glaucophylla (bog rosemary)
Arctostaphylos uva-ursi (bearberry, kinnikinnik)

Epigaea repens (trailing arbutus)
Gaultheria hispidula (creeping snowberry)
Gaultheria procumbens (wintergreen, checkerberry)
Juniperus communis (common juniper)
Kalmia angustifolia (sheep laurel, lambkill kalmia)
Kalmia latifolia (mountain laurel)
Kalmia polifolia (swamp laurel, bog laurel)
Ledum groenlandicum (Labrador tea, muskeg tea)
Taxus canadensis (Canada yew)

Trees (deciduous)

Acer negundo (box elder)
Acer pensylvanicum (striped maple)
Acer rubrum (red maple)
Acer saccharinum (silver maple)
Acer saccharum (sugar maple)
Acer spicatum (mountain maple)
Amelanchier canadensis (shadblow serviceberry, Juneberry)
Betula alleghaniensis (yellow birch)
Betula lenta (cherry birch)
Betula papyrifera (paper birch)
Carpinus caroliniana (blue beech, hornbeam, musclewood)
Carya ovata (shagbark hickory)
Fagus grandifolia var. grandifolia (beech)
Fraxinus americana (white ash)
Fraxinus pensylvanica (green ash)
Hamamelis virginiana (witch hazel)
Larix laricina (tamarack, American larch)
Ostrya virginiana (ironwood, hophornbeam)
Populus deltoides (eastern cottonwood)
Populus grandidentata (large-toothed aspen)
Populus tremuloides (quaking aspen)
Prunus nigra (Canada plum)
Prunus pensylvanica (fire or pin cherry)
Prunus serotina (black cherry)
Quercus alba (white oak)
Quercus rubra (red oak)
Quercus velutina (black oak)
Sorbus americana (mountain ash)
Tilia americana (American linden, basswood)
Ulmus americana (American elm)
Ulmus rubra (red elm, slippery elm)

Trees (evergreen)

Abies balsamea (balsam fir)
Juniperus virginiana (eastern red cedar)
Picea glauca (white spruce)
Pinus resinosa (red pine, Norway pine)
Pinus rigida (pitch pine)
Pinus strobus (eastern white pine)
Thuja occidentalis (arbor vitae, northern white cedar)
Tsuga canadensis (eastern hemlock)

Vines (deciduous)

Clematis occidentalis var. occidentalis (purple clematis)
Clematis virginiana (virgin's bower)
Lonicera sempervirens (coral honeysuckle)
Parthenocissus quinquefolia (Virginia creeper)
Parthenocissus quinquefolia var. quinquefolia (woodbine)
Vitis riparia (riverbank grape)

FEDERALLY LISTED ENDANGERED SPECIES

Jesup's milk-vetch (Astragalus robbinsii var. Jesupi)
Northeastern (Barbed bristle) bulrush (Scirpus ancistrochaetus)
Robbins' cinquefoil (Potentilla robbinsiana)
Small whorled pogonia (Isotria medeoloides)

NEW HAMPSHIRE NOXIOUS SPECIES

Because the noxious weed lists have continually changed since we gathered them in 1994, we are not including them at this time. Not all States have noxious weed lists. Those that do, do not use the same standards of importance and are not comparable. States typically have included plants that interfere with agriculture (Canada thistle), or cause human health problems (poison ivy). Some States are now including a category of plants that invade and degrade the environment (purple loosestrife). Check with your State's Agriculture Department or Weed Scientist listed below. The noxious weed list can be used two ways on roadsides: l) check to not inadvertantly plant these invasive plants, and 2) note the plants you are legally responsible to control. Many States now check adjacent State lists to avoid planting their neighbors' problem plants. Because weeds do not respect political boundaries, and because by their very nature weeds continue to adapt and expand, monitoring and controlling invasives at State borders is a wise part of vegetation management.

(Seed Only)

Department of Agriculture
St. Lab Bld. Lab D
6 Hazen Drive
Concord, NH 03301

James Mitchell, U of NH
Nesmith Hall
131 Main Street
Durham, NH 03824
(603) 862-3204

NEW HAMPSHIRE RESOURCES

New Hampshire Natural Heritage
Inventory
Department of Resources &
Economic Development
172 Pembroke Street
Concord, NH 03302
(603) 271-3623

The Nature Conservancy Field Office
2 1/2 Beacon Steet, Ste. 6
Concord, NH 03301
(603) 224-5853

POTENTIAL NATURAL VEGETATION ZONES IN
─── NEW JERSEY ───

Source: A.W. Kuchler's Potential Natural Vegetation Map, 1964, Revised 1985.
Presented in U.S.G.S. National Atlas of the U.S. Series,
U.S. Geological Survey, Reston, VA.

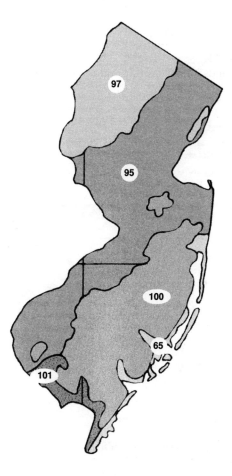

65	Northern cordgrass prairie *(Distichlis-Spartina)*
95	Appalachian oak forest *(Quercus)*
97	Northern hardwoods *(Acer-Betula-Fagus-Tsuga)*
100	Northeastern oak-pine forest *(Quercus-Pinus)*
101	Oak-hickory-pine forest *(Quercus-Carya-Pinus)*

(Dominant plant species present in each vegetation type are listed in Appendix 8)

65 *Northern Cordgrass Prairie (Distichlis-Spartina)*
95 *Appalachian Oak Forest (Quercus)*
97 *Northern Hardwoods (Acer-Betula-Fagus-Tsuga)*
100 *Northeastern Oak-Pine Forest (Quercus-Pinus)*
101 *Oak-Hickory-Pine Forest (Quercus-Carya-Pinus)*

Botanical Expert

David Snyder, Botanist
New Jersey Natural Heritage Program
Department of Environmental Protection
Division of Parks and Forestry
Office of Natural Lands Management
22 South Clinton Avenue, CN 404
Trenton, NJ 08625-0404
(609) 984-1139
(609) 984-1427 (fax)

Recommended Flora

No recommended flora exists specifically for New Jersey. Suggested flora for neighboring states may be helpful.

NATIVE PLANTS FOR LANDSCAPE USE IN NEW JERSEY

Ferns

Adiantum pedatum (northern maidenhair fern)
Asplenium platyneuron (ebony spleenwort)
Asplenium trichomanes (maidenhair spleenwort)
Athyrium filix-femina (lady fern)
Botrychium virginianum (rattlesnake fern)
Dennstaedtia punctilobula (hay-scented fern)
Dryopteris carthusiana (shield fern, toothed wood fern, spinulose shield fern)
Dryopteris cristata (crested wood fern, buckler fern)
Dryopteris marginalis (marginal wood fern)
Matteuccia struthiopteris (ostrich fern)
Onoclea sensibilis (sensitive fern, bead fern)
Osmunda cinnamomea (cinnamon fern)
Osmunda claytoniana (interrupted fern)
Osmunda regalis (royal fern)
Phegopteris hexagonoptera (broad beech fern)
Polystichum acrostichoides (Christmas fern)
Thelypteris novaboracensis (New York fern, tapering fern)
Thelypteris simulata (Massachusetts fern)
Woodwardia areolata (netted chain fern)
Woodwardia virginica (Virginia chain fern)

Forbs (annuals/biennials)

Lobelia spicata (pale lobelia)
Oenothera biennis (common evening primrose)

Forbs (perennials)

Actaea pachypoda (white baneberry)
Ageratina altissima var. altissima (white snakeroot)
Allium canadense (wild garlic)
Allium tricoccum (wild leek)
Anaphalis margaritacea (pearly everlasting)
Anemone virginiana (thimbleweed, tall anemone)
Apocynum androsaemifolium (spreading dogbane)
Aquilegia canadensis (columbine)
Arisaema triphyllum (Jack-in-the-pulpit, Indian turnip)
Asarum canadense (wild ginger)
Asclepias incarnata (swamp milkweed)
Asclepias tuberosa (butterfly weed)
Aster divaricatus (white wood aster)
Aster dumosus (bushy aster)
Aster laevis (smooth aster)
Aster novae-angliae (New England aster)
Aster pilosus (frost aster)
Aster puniceus (red-stem aster, swamp aster)
Caltha palustris (marsh marigold, cowslip)
Caulophyllum thalictroides (blue cohosh)
Chelone glabra (turtlehead)
Chrysopsis mariana (Maryland golden aster)
Cimicifuga racemosa (bugbane, black cohosh)
Claytonia virginica (narrow-leaved spring beauty)
Collinsonia canadensis (stoneroot, citronella horsebalm)
Desmodium canadense (Canada tick-trefoil, Canada tickclover)
Dicentra cucullaria (dutchman's breeches)
Erythronium americanum (eastern trout lily, yellow trout lily)
Eupatorium fistulosum (Joe-pye weed)
Eupatorium perfoliatum (boneset)
Eupatorium purpureum (Joe-pye weed)
Euthamia graminifolia var. graminifolia (grass-leaved goldenrod)
Galium triflorum (sweet-scented bedstraw)
Geranium maculatum (wild geranium, cranesbill)
Helianthus strumosus (woodland sunflower)
Heliopsis helianthoides (ox-eye sunflower, false sunflower)
Heuchera americana var. hirsuticaulis (alumroot)
Hibiscus moscheutos (swamp rose mallow, marshmallow hibiscus)
Hydrophyllum virginianum (Virginia waterleaf)
Hypoxis hirsuta (yellow star grass)
Lespedeza capitata (roundheaded bush clover)
Lobelia cardinalis (cardinal flower)
Lobelia siphilitica (great blue lobelia)
Lysimachia ciliata (fringed loosestrife)
Maianthemum canadense (wild lily-of-the-valley, Canada mayflower)
Maianthemum racemosum ssp. racemosum (false Solomon's seal,
   false spikenard)
Mitchella repens (partridge berry)
Monarda fistulosa (wild bergamot, horsemint, beebalm)
Nuphar lutea (yellow pond lily, cow lily, spatter dock)
Oenothera fruticosa (sundrops)

Peltandra virginica (arrow arum)
Penstemon digitalis (beardtongue)
Podophyllum peltatum (May apple)
Polygonatum biflorum (Solomon's seal)
Potentilla simplex (common cinquefoil)
Pycnanthemum tenuifolium (slender mountain mint)
Pycnanthemum virginianum (mountain mint)
Pyrola elliptica (shinleaf)
Rhexia virginica (meadow beauty)
Rudbeckia laciniata (cut-leaf coneflower)
Sanguinaria candensis (bloodroot)
Senecio aureus (golden ragwort)
Sisyrinchium angustifolium (narrow-leaved blue-eyed grass)
Solidago caesia (blue-stemmed goldenrod, wreath goldenrod)
Solidago canadensis (meadow goldenrod)
Solidago juncea (early goldenrod, plume goldenrod)
Solidago nemoralis (gray goldenrod, old-field goldenrod)
Solidago odora (sweet goldenrod)
Solidago rugosa (rough-leaved goldenrod)
Solidago ulmifolia (elm-leaved goldenrod)
Tephrosia virginiana (goat's rue)
Thalictrum dioicum (early meadow rue)
Thalictrum pubescens (tall meadow rue)
Thalictrum thalictroides (rue anemone)
Tradescantia virginiana (Virginia spiderwort, spider lily)
Trientalis borealis ssp. borealis (starflower)
Uvularia sessilifolia (wildoats, merrybells)
Verbena hastata (blue verbena, blue vervain)
Vernonia noveboracensis (New York ironweed)
Viola conspersa (American dog violet)
Viola soraria (common blue violet, meadow violet)
Zizia aurea (golden alexanders)

Grasses/Grass-like plants

Agrostis scabra (ticklegrass, fly-away grass)
Andropogon gerardii (big bluestem)
Andropogon glomeratus (bushy bluestem)
Andropogon ternarius (splitbeard bluestem)
Andropogon virginicus (broom sedge)
Calamagrostis canadensis (bluejoint grass)
Carex pensylvanica (Pennsylvania sedge)
Carex stipata (awl-fruited sedge)
Carex stricta (tussock sedge)
Danthonia spicata (poverty grass)
Deschampsia cespitosa (tufted hairgrass)
Distichlis spicata (seashore saltgrass)
Eleocharis palustris (creeping spikesedge, spike rush)
Elymus canadensis (Canada wild rye)
Elymus hystrix var. hystrix (bottlebrush grass)
Eragrostis spectabilis (purple lovegrass, tumblegrass)
Juncus effusus var. solutus (soft rush)
Leersia oryzoides (rice cut grass)

Panicum virgatum (switchgrass)
Schizachyrium scoparium (little bluestem)
Scirpus atrovirens (dark green bulrush)
Scirpus cyperinus (wool grass)
Scirpus tabernaemontani (great bulrush)
Sorghastrum nutans (Indian grass)
Spartina patens (marsh hay cordgrass, salt meadow cordgrass)
Spartina pectinata (prairie cordgrass, freshwater cordgrass)
Sporobolus compositus var. compositus (tall dropseed)
Tripsacum dactyloides (eastern gama grass)
Typha angustifolia (narrow-leaved cattail)
Typha latifolia (cattail)

Shrubs (deciduous)

Alnus serrulata (smooth alder)
Amelanchier arborea (downy serviceberry, shadbush, Juneberry)
Aronia melanocarpa (black chokeberry)
Baccharis halimifolia (sea myrtle, groundsel bush)
Cephalanthus occidentalis (buttonbush)
Clethra alnifolia (summer sweet)
Comptonia peregrina (sweet fern)
Cornus alternifolia (pogoda dogwood, alternate-leaved dogwood)
Cornus racemosa (gray dogwood)
Cornus sericea (red-twig dogwood, red-osier dogwood)
Corylus americana (American hazelnut or filbert)
Corylus cornuta (beaked hazelnut or filbert)
Euonymus americana (strawberry bush, brook euonymus, hearts-a-bustin')
Hypericum hypericoides ssp. hypericoides (St. Andrew's cross)
Ilex verticillata (winterberry, black alder)
Lindera benzoin (spicebush)
Lyonia ligustrina (male-berry, male-blueberry)
Physocarpus opulifolius (ninebark)
Prunus virginiana (chokecherry)
Rhododendron periclymenoides (pinxterbloom azalea)
Rhododendron viscosum (swamp azalea)
Rhus copallinum (dwarf or winged sumac)
Rhus glabra (smooth sumac)
Rhus hirta (staghorn sumac)
Rosa carolina (Carolina rose)
Rubus idaeus ssp. strigosus (red raspberry)
Rubus occidentalis (black raspberry, thimbleberry)
Rubus odoratus (thimbleberry)
Salix bebbiana (Bebb willow, long-beaked willow)
Salix discolor (pussy willow)
Sambucus canadensis (elderberry, common elder)
Sambucus racemosa var. pubens (scarlet elderberry, red-berried elder)
Spiraea tomentosa (steeplebush, hardhack)
Staphylea trifolia (bladdernut)
Vaccinium angustifolium (low-bush blueberry)
Vaccinium corymbosom (highbush blueberry)
Viburnum acerifolium (maple leaf viburnum)
Viburnum dentatum (southern arrowwood)

Viburnum lentago (black haw, nannyberry)
Viburnum nudum (possumhaw viburnum)
Viburnum nudum var. cassinoides (wild raisin)
Viburnum prunifolium (black haw, nanny berry)

Shrubs (evergreen)

Epigaea repens (trailing arbutus)
Gaultheria procumbens (wintergreen, checkerberry)
Ilex glabra (inkberry, bitter gallberry)
Kalmia angustifolia (sheep laurel, lambkill kalmia)
Kalmia latifolia (mountain laurel)
Myrica cerifera (wax myrtle, southern bayberry, candleberry)
Rhododendron maximum (rosebay, great laurel)

Trees (deciduous)

Acer negundo (box elder)
Acer pensylvanicum (striped maple)
Acer rubrum (red maple)
Acer saccharinum (silver maple)
Acer saccharum (sugar maple)
Amelanchier canadensis (shadblow serviceberry, Juneberry)
Betula lenta (cherry birch)
Betula nigra (river birch)
Carpinus caroliniana (blue beech, hornbeam, musclewood)
Carya alba (mockernut hickory)
Carya cordiformis (bitternut, swamp hickory)
Carya ovata (shagbark hickory)
Celtis occidentalis (hackberry, sugarberry)
Chamaecyparis thyoides (white cedar)
Cornus florida (flowering dogwood)
Crataegus crus-galli (cockspur hawthorn)
Diospyros virginiana (persimmon)
Fagus grandifolia var. caroliniana (beech)
Fagus grandifolia var. grandifolia (beech)
Fraxinus americana (white ash)
Fraxinus pensylvanica (green ash)
Hamamelis virginiana (witch hazel)
Juglans nigra (black walnut)
Liquidambar styraciflua (sweet gum)
Liriodendron tulipifera (tulip tree)
Magnolia virginiana (sweetbay, swampbay)
Nyssa sylvatica (black gum, tupelo)
Ostrya virginiana (ironwood, hophornbeam)
Platanus occidentalis (sycamore, plane-tree)
Populus grandidentata (large-toothed aspen)
Populus tremuloides (quaking aspen)
Prunus americana (wild plum)
Prunus pensylvanica (fire or pin cherry)
Prunus serotina (black cherry)
Quercus alba (white oak)
Quercus bicolor (swamp white oak)
Quercus coccinea (scarlet oak)

Quercus falcata (southern red oak, Spanish oak)
Quercus marilandica (blackjack oak)
Quercus palustris (pin oak)
Quercus phellos (willow oak)
Quercus rubra (red oak)
Quercus stellata (post oak)
Quercus velutina (black oak)
Salix nigra (black willow)
Sassafras albidum (sassafras)
Tilia americana (American linden, basswood)
Ulmus americana (American elm)
Ulmus rubra (red elm, slippery elm)

Trees (evergreen)

Ilex opaca (American holly, Christmas holly)
Juniperus virginiana (eastern red cedar)
Pinus echinata (shortleaf pine)
Pinus rigida (pitch pine)
Pinus strobus (eastern white pine)
Pinus virginiana (Virginia pine)

Vines (deciduous)

Celastrus scandens (American bittersweet)
Clematis virginiana (virgin's bower)
Parthenocissus quinquefolia (Virginia creeper)
Vitis riparia (riverbank grape)

FEDERALLY LISTED ENDANGERED SPECIES

American chaffseed (Schwalbea americana)
Knieskern's beaked-rush (Rhynchospora knieskernii)
Sensitive joint-vetch (Aeschynomene virginica)
Small whorled pogonia (Isotria medeoloides)
Swamp pink (Helonias bullata)

NEW JERSEY NOXIOUS SPECIES

Because the noxious weed lists have continually changed since we gathered them in 1994, we are not including them at this time. Not all States have noxious weed lists. Those that do, do not use the same standards of importance and are not comparable. States typically have included plants that interfere with agriculture (Canada thistle), or cause human health problems (poison ivy). Some States are now including a category of plants that invade and degrade the environment (purple loosestrife). Check with your State's Agriculture Department or Weed Scientist listed below. The noxious weed list can be used two ways on roadsides: l) check to not inadvertently plant these invasive plants, and 2) note the plants you are legally responsible to control. Many States now check adjacent State lists to avoid planting their neighbors' problem plants. Because weeds do not respect political boundaries, and because by their very nature weeds continue to adapt and expand, monitoring and controlling invasives at State borders is a wise part of vegetation management.

(Seed Law)

Department of Agriculture
Division of Plant Industry
CN330
Trenton, NJ 08625

Bradley Majek
Rutgers University
121 Northville Road
Bridgeton, NJ 08302
(609) 455-3100

NEW JERSEY RESOURCES

New Jersey Natural Heritage Program
 22 South Clinton Avenue, CN404
Trenton, NJ 08625
(609) 984-1339

The Nature Conservancy Field Office
200 Pottersville Road
Chester, NJ 07939
(908) 879-7262

New Jersey Native Plant Society
Frelinghuysen Arboretum
P.O. Box 1295 R
Morristown, NJ 07960

Tourne County Park
53 E. Hanover Avenue
Morristown, NJ 07962

Rutgers University
The State University of New Jersey
New Brunswick, NJ 08903
(908) 932-9271

POTENTIAL NATURAL VEGETATION ZONES IN
NEW MEXICO

Source: A.W. Kuchler's Potential Natural Vegetation Map, 1964, Revised 1985.
Presented in U.S.G.S. National Atlas of the U.S. Series,
U.S. Geological Survey, Reston, VA.

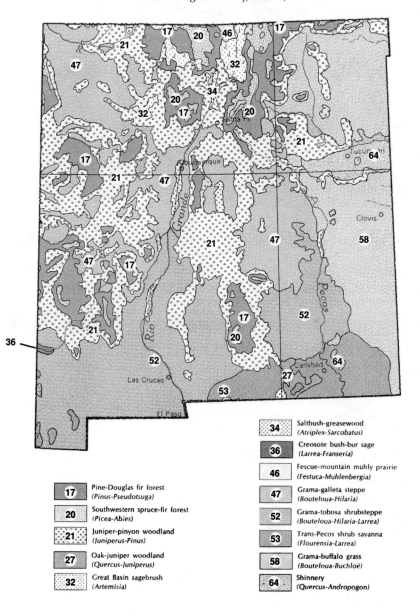

17	Pine-Douglas fir forest *(Pinus-Pseudotsuga)*
20	Southwestern spruce-fir forest *(Picea-Abies)*
21	Juniper-pinyon woodland *(Juniperus-Pinus)*
27	Oak-juniper woodland *(Quercus-Juniperus)*
32	Great Basin sagebrush *(Artemisia)*

34	Saltbush-greasewood *(Atriplex-Sarcobatus)*
36	Creosote bush-bur sage *(Larrea-Franseria)*
46	Fescue-mountain muhly prairie *(Festuca-Muhlenbergia)*
47	Grama-galleta steppe *(Bouteloua-Hilaria)*
52	Grama-tobosa shrubsteppe *(Bouteloua-Hilaria-Larrea)*
53	Trans-Pecos shrub savanna *(Flourensia-Larrea)*
58	Grama-buffalo grass *(Bouteloua-Buchloë)*
64	Shinnery *(Quercus-Andropogon)*

(Dominant plant species present in each vegetation type are listed in Appendix 8)

17 *Pine-Douglas Fir Forest (Pinus-Pseudotsuga)*
20 *Southwestern Spruce Fir Forest (Picea-Abies)*
21 *Juniper-Pinyon Woodland (Juniperus-Pinus)*
27 *Oak-Juniper Woodland (Quercus-Juniperus)*
32 *Great Basin Sagebrush (Artemisia)*
34 *Saltbrush-Geasewood (Artiplex-Sarcobatus)*
36 *Creosote Bush-Bur Sage (Larrea-Franseria)*
46 *Fescue-Mountain Muhly Prairie (Festuca-Muhlenbergia)*
47 *Grama-Galleta Steppe (Bouteloua-Hilaria)*
52 *Grama-Tobosa Shrubsteppe (Bouteloua-Hilaria-Larrea)*
53 *Trans-Pecos Savanna (Flourensia-Larrea)*
58 *Grama-Buffalo Grass (Bouteloua-Buchloë)*
64 *Shinnery (Quercus-Andropogon)*

Botanical Expert

Juanita A. R. Ladyman, Research Botanist
Museum of Southwestern Biology-Herbarium
Casteller Hall
University of New Mexico
Albuquerque, NM 87131
(505) 292-5783
(505) 292-0304 (fax)
internet: ladyman@unm.edu

Recommended Flora

Martin, W.W.; C.R. Hutchins. 1980. A Flora of New Mexico, Vols. 1 and 2. J. Cramer: Gantaer Verlag Kommandiutgesellschaft.

NATIVE PLANTS FOR LANDSCAPE USE IN NEW MEXICO

Cacti

Echinocereus fendleri (strawberry cactus, Fendler hedgehog)
Echinocereus pecinatus (rainbow hedgehog)
Ferocactus wislizeni (fishhook barrel cactus, southwestern barrel cactus)
Opuntia chlorotica (pancake pear, silver-dollar cactus)
Opuntia imbricata (tree cholla, walkingstick cholla)
Opuntia macrorhiza (common prickly pear)
Opuntia plaecantha (purple-fruited prickly pear)

Ferns

Adiantum capillus-veneris (southern maidenhair fern)
Asplenium platyneuron (ebony spleenwort)
Athyrium filix-femina (lady fern)
Cystopteris bulbifera (bladder fern)
Cystopteris fragilis (fragile fern)

Forbs (annuals/biennials)

Baileya multiradiata (desert marigold)

Centaurea americana (basket flower)
Cleome serrulata (Rocky Mountain beeplant)
Coreopsis tinctoria (tickseed, goldenwave, plains coreopsis, calliopsis)
Dimorphocarpa wislizeni (spectacle pod)
Dyssodia spp. (aurea, papposa, tenuiloba (dyssodia, dogweed, fetid marigold)
Erodium texanum (fillaree, stork's bill)
Erysimum capitatum (western wallflower, prairie rocket)
Eschscholzia californica ssp. mexicana (Mexican gold poppy)
Euphorbia marginata (snow-on-the-mountain)
Gaillardia pulchella (Indian blanket, firewheel)
Helianthus annuus (common sunflower)
Helianthus petiolaris (plains sunflower)
Ipomopsis aggregata (sky rocket, scarlet gilia)
Ipomopsis longiflora (white-flowered gilia)
Ipomopsis thurberi (Thurber's gilia)
Kallstroemia grandiflora (desert poppy, Mexican poppy)
Layia glandulosa (tidy tips)
Lepidium montanum (mountain peppergrass)
Lesquerella gordonii (Gordon's bladderpod)
Linum neomexicanum (flax)
Linum rigidum (yellow flax)
Lupinus concinnus (annual lupine, bajada lupine)
Machaeranthera bigelovii var. bigelovii (plains aster, tansy aster)
Machaeranthera tanacetifolia (tahoka daisy, tansy aster)
Mimulus guttatus (golden monkey flower)
Monarda citriodora (horsemint, lemon beebalm, lemon mint)
Oenothera albicaulis (pale evening primrose)
Oenothera elata ssp. hookeri (giant evening primrose)
Oenothera primiveris (bottle evening primrose, yellow desert primrose)
Pectis angustifolia (limoncillo, fetid marigold)
Phacelia congesta (blue curls)
Teucrium laciniatum (dwarf germander, cutleaf germander)
Townsendia exscapa (Easter daisy)

Forbs (perennials)

Abronia fragrans (sweet sand verbena)
Aconitum columbianum (western monkshood)
Agave neomexicana (century plant, New Mexico agave)
Agave palmeri (Palmer agave, blue century plant)
Agave parryi (century plant, Parry agave)
Allium macropetalum (desert onion)
Anaphalis margaritacea (pearly everlasting)
Anemone canadensis (Canada anemone, windflower)
Anemone cylindrica (thimbleweed, candle anemone)
Antennaria spp. (pussytoes, everlasting)
Apocynum androsaemifolium (spreading dogbane)
Aquilegia chrysantha (yellow columbine)
Aquilegia coerulea (Rocky Mountain or blue columbine)
Arnica cordifolia (heartleaf arnica)
Artemisia ludoviciana (white sage, prairie sage, artemisia)
Asclepias asperula (antelope horns)
Asclepias incarnata (swamp milkweed)

Asclepias speciosa (showy milkweed)
Asclepias tuberosa (butterfly weed)
Aster ascendens (purple aster, Pacific aster)
Aster ericoides (heath aster, white wreath aster)
Aster laevis (smooth aster)
Aster novae-angliae (New England aster)
Bahia absinthifolia (bahia, yerba raton)
Balsamorrhiza sagittata (balsamroot)
Berlandiera lyrata (green eyes, chocolate flower)
Callirhoe involucrata (purple poppy mallow, winecup)
Calochortus nuttallii (sego lily, mariposa lily)
Caltha leptosepala (white marsh marigold, elkslip)
Calylophus berlandieri (square-bud primrose, sundrops)
Campanula rotundifolia (harebell)
Castilleja angustifolia var. dubia (desert paintbrush)
Castilleja integra (Indian paintbrush)
Castilleja linariifolia (Indian paintbrush)
Castilleja miniata var. miniata (Indian paintbrush)
Castilleja sessiliflora (downy painted cup)
Claytonia lanceolata (spring beauty)
Commelina dianthifolia (dayflower)
Cooperia drummondii (rain lily, prairie lily)
Coreopsis lanceolata (lance-leaved coreopsis)
Coreopsis tripteris (tall coreopsis)
Dasylirion leiophyllum
Dasylirion wheeleri (Sotol, desert pampas grass, desert spoon)
Delphinium barbeyi (subalpine larkspur)
Delphinium carolinianum ssp. virescens (prairie larkspur)
Delphinium scaposum (barestem larkspur)
Dugaldia hoopesii (orange sneezeweed, owlsclaws)
Echinacea angustifolia (narrow-leaved purple coneflower)
Engelmannia pinnatifida (Engelmann daisy)
Epilobium angustifolium (fireweed, willow herb)
Epilobium canum var. latifolia (hummingbird trumpet)
Erigeron modestus (prairie fleabane)
Erigeron speciosus (showy fleabane)
Eriogonum racemosum (red root buckwheat)
Eriogonum wrightii (Wright buckwheat)
Eupatorium greggii (palmleaf thoroughwort)
Eupatorium maculatum (spotted Joe-pye weed)
Gaillardia pinnatifida (yellow gaillardia, blanket flower)
Galium triflorum (sweet-scented bedstraw)
Gentiana parryi (Parry gentian)
Geum rivale (purple avens, water avens)
Geum triflorum (prairie smoke, purple avens)
Glandularia bipinnatifida var. bipinnatifida (prairie verbena, Dakota vervain)
Hedyotis nigricans (bluets)
Hedysarum boreale (sweet vetch, sweet broom)
Heliomeris multiflora (showy goldeneye)
Heliopsis helianthoides (ox-eye sunflower, false sunflower)
Heuchera rubescens var. versicolor (coral bells, alumroot)
Heuchera parvifolia (saxifrage, alum root)

Heuchera sanguinea (New Mexican coral bells)
Ipomoea leptophylla (bush morning glory)
Iris missouriensis (Rocky Mountain iris, western blue flag)
Lesquerella fendleri (bladderpod)
Lewisia rediviva (bitter root)
Lilium philadelphicum (wood lily)
Linnaea borealis (twinflower)
Linum lewisii (wild blue flax)
Lithospermum incisum (fringed puccoon, narrow-leaved puccoon)
Lobelia cardinalis (cardinal flower)
Lupinus argenteus (silvery lupine)
Lupinus palmeri (Palmer's lupine)
Maianthemum stellatum (starry Solomon's seal)
Melampodium leucanthum (Blackfoot daisy, rock daisy)
Minuartia obtusiloba (cushion sandwort)
Mirabilis multiflora (wild four o'clock)
Monardella odoratissima (coyote mint, mountain pennyroyal)
Nolina microcarpa (sacahuista, bear grass)
Nolina texana (sacahuista, basket grass, Texas beargrass)
Oenothera brachycarpa (evening primrose)
Oenothera cespitosa (gumbo evening primrose, gumbo lily)
Oenothera flava (Shortfin evening primrose)
Pedicularis groenlandica (elephant heads)
Penstemon albidus (white beardtongue)
Penstemon ambiguus (sand penstemon)
Penstemon angustifolius (whorled penstemon)
Penstemon barbatus (red penstemon, scarlet bugler)
Penstemon fendleri (fendler penstemon, purple foxglove)
Penstemon glaber var. alpinus (blue penstemon, alpine penstemon)
Penstemon jamesii (James' penstemon)
Penstemon pseudospectabilis (desert beardtongue)
Penstemon rostriflorus (Bridge's penstemon, Mountain scarlet penstemon)
Penstemon strictus (Rocky Mountain penstemon)
Penstemon thurberi (sand penstemon)
Pentaphylloides floribunda (potentilla, shrubby cinquefoil)
Petrophyton caespitosum (dwarf spiraea, petrophytum, tufted rockmat)
Phacelia sericea (silky phacelia)
Phlox nana (Santa Fe phlox, white-eyed phlox, canyon phlox)
Polemonium foliosissimum (Jacob's ladder)
Polemonium viscosum (sky pilot)
Potentilla arguta (white cinquefoil, prairie cinquefoil, tall cinquefoil)
Potentilla thurberi (red cinquefoil)
Psilostrophe tagetina (woolly paper-flower)
Pulsatilla patens ssp. multifida (pasque flower, wild crocus)
Pyrola elliptica (shinleaf)
Ranunculus cardiophyllus (buttercup)
Ranunculus macranthus (large buttercup)
Ratibida columnifera (prairie coneflower, long-headed coneflower, Mexican hat)
Ruellia nudiflora (wild petunia, violet ruellia)
Salvia arizonica (Arizona sage)
Salvia farinacea (mealy sage)
Saxifraga bronchialis (spotted saxifrage, matted saxifrage)

Saxifraga cespitosa (tufted saxifrage)
Senna lindheimeriana (Lindheimer senna, velvetleaf senna)
Senna roemeriana (two-leaved senna)
Sidalcea neomexicana (checker mallow, prairie mallow)
Silene laciniata (southern Indian pink, catchfly, Mexican campion)
Solidago canadensis (meadow goldenrod)
Solidago missouriensis (Missouri goldenrod, prairie goldenrod)
Solidago multiradiata (northern goldenrod, mountain goldenrod)
Solidago rigida (stiff goldenrod)
Sphaeralcea coccinea (scarlet globe mallow)
Sphaeralcea parvifolia (globe mallow)
Stachys coccinea (Texas betony)
Talinum aurantiacum (flame flower)
Tetraneuris acaulis var. acaulis (stemless goldflower, stemless rubber weed,
    butte marigold)
Tetraneuris scaposa var. scaposa (four-nerve daisy, yellow daisy, bitterweed)
Thalictrum dasycarpum (tall or purple meadow rue)
Thlaspi montanum var. fendleri (wild candytuft, penny cress)
Verbena hastata (blue verbena, blue vervain)
Verbena stricta (hoary vervain)
Viguiera dentata (goldeneye)
Viola canadensis (Canada violet)
Viola missouriensis (Missouri violet)
Viola pedatifida (prairie violet)
Yucca baccata (blue yucca, banana yucca, fleshy-fruited yucca)
Yucca elata (soaptree yucca, palmella)
Yucca glauca (yucca, soapweed)
Yucca schottii (hoary yucca, mountain yucca)
Zinnia grandiflora (Rocky Mountain zinnia, yellow zinnia, plains zinnia)

Grasses/Grass-like plants

Agrostis exarata (spikebent, spike red top)
Agrostis scabra (ticklegrass, fly-away grass)
Andropogon gerardii (big bluestem)
Andropogon hallii (sand bluestem)
Aristida purpurea (purple three awn)
Aristida purpurea var. longiseta (red three awn)
Bouteloua curtipendula (sideoats grama)
Bouteloua eriopoda (black grama)
Bouteloua gracilis (blue grama)
Bouteloua hirsuta (hairy grama)
Bromus carinatus (California brome)
Buchloe dactyloides (buffalograss)
Calamagrostis canadensis (bluejoint grass)
Carex aquatilis (water sedge)
Carex nebrascensis (Nebraska sedge)
Carex utriculata (beaked sedge)
Chloris crinita (two-flowered trichloris)
Danthonia californica (California oatgrass)
Danthonia intermedia (timber oatgrass)
Deschampsia cespitosa (tufted hairgrass)
Digitaria californica (cottontop)

Distichlis spicata (seashore saltgrass)
Eleocharis palustris (creeping spikesedge, spike rush)
Elymus canadensis (Canada wild rye)
Elymus cinereus (Great Basin wild rye)
Elymus glaucus (blue wild rye)
Eragrostis intermedia (plains lovegrass)
Eragrostis spectabilis (purple lovegrass, tumblegrass)
Festuca ovina (sheep fescue)
Glyceria grandis (American mannagrass, tall mannagrass, reed meadowgrass)
Hierochloe odorata (sweet grass)
Hilaria belangeri (curly mesquite)
Hilaria mutica (tobosa grass)
Koeleria macrantha (June grass)
Leersia oryzoides (rice cut grass)
Leptochloa dubia (green sprangletop)
Muhlenbergia montana (mountain muhly)
Muhlenbergia porteri (bush muhly)
Muhlenbergia rigida (purple muhly)
Muhlenbergia wrightii (spike muhly)
Oryzopsis hymenoides (Indian ricegrass)
Panicum obtusum (vine mesquite)
Panicum virgatum (switchgrass)
Pascopyrum smithii (western wheatgrass)
Phleum alpinum (alpine timothy)
Schizachyrium scoparium (little bluestem)
Scirpus acutus (hardstem bulrush)
Scirpus maritimus (alkali bulrush, prairie bulrush, bayonet grass)
Scirpus tabernaemontani (great bulrush)
Sorghastrum nutans (Indian grass)
Spartina pectinata (prairie cordgrass, freshwater cordgrass)
Sporobolus airoides (alkali sacaton)
Sporobolus compositus var. compositus (tall dropseed)
Sporobolus cryptandrus (sand dropseed)
Sporobolus flexuosus (mesa dropseed)
Stipa comata (needle-and-thread grass)
Stipa nelsonii (Columbia needlegrass)
Stipa spartea (porcupine grass)
Trisetum spicatum (spike trisetum)
Typha latifolia (cattail)

Shrubs (deciduous)

Alnus incana (speckled alder, mountain alder)
Amorpha fruticosa (false indigo, Indigo bush)
Atriplex canescens (four-wing saltbush, wingscale)
Atriplex confertifolia (spiny saltbush, shadscale saltbush, hop sage)
Choisya dumosa (Mexican orange, zorrillo)
Dalea scoparia (broom dalea, broom pea)
Forestiera pubescens (desert olive, elbow-bush, forestiera)
Krascheninnikovia lanata (winterfat)
Lonicera involucrata (black twinberry, bear berry honeysuckle)
Rosa woodsii var. ultramontana (Arizona wild rose)
Rubus parviflorus (western thimbleberry)

Salix scouleriana (western pussy willow, Scouler's willow)
Sambucus cerulea (blue elderberry)
Sambucus mexicana (Mexican elderberry)
Shepherdia argentea (silver buffaloberry)
Sideroxylon lanuginosum ssp. lanuginosum (chittamwood, gum elastic tree)
Sorbus dumosa (mountain ash)
Sorbus scopulina (western mountain ash)
Symphoricarpos oreophilus (mountain snowberry)
Tecoma stans (yellow bells, trumpet flower)

Shrubs (evergreen)

Artemisia nova (black sagebrush)
Artemisia tridentata (big sagebrush, Great Basin sagebrush)
Ceanothus fendleri (Fendler ceanothus, buckbrush)
Cercocarpus montanus (mountain mahogany, silverleaf mountain mahogany)
Chrysactinia mexicana (damianita)
Ericameria laricifolia (larchleaf goldenweed, turpentine bush)
Garrya wrightii (Wright's catclaw, Wright's silk tassel)
Juniperus monosperma (one-seed juniper)
Larrea tridentata (creosote bush)
Mahonia fremontii (Fremont barberry, holly grape)
Mahonia haematocarpa (red barberry)
Mahonia trifoliolata (agarito, trifoliate barberry)
Paxistima myrsinites (Oregon box, myrtle boxwood, mountain lover)
Purshia stansburiana (cliff rose)
Quercus turbinella (shrub live oak)
Rhus choriophylla (evergreen sumac)
Viguiera stenoloba (resin bush)

Trees (deciduous)

Acacia farnesiana (huisache, sweet acacia)
Acer glabrum (Rocky Mountain maple)
Acer grandidentatum (bigtooth maple)
Acer negundo (box elder)
Betula occidentalis (mountain birch, water birch)
Celtis laevigata var. reticulata (netleaf hackberry)
Chilopsis linearis (desert willow, trumpet flower)
Fraxinus berlandieriana (Mexican ash)
Fraxinus cuspidata (flowering ash)
Fraxinus velutina (Arizona ash, velvet ash, desert ash)
Juglans major (Arizona walnut)
Juglans microcarpa (Texas walnut, river walnut, little walnut)
Platanus wrightii (Arizona sycamore, Alamo)
Populus fremontii (western cottonwood)
Populus tremuloides (quaking aspen)
Prosopis pubescens (tornillo, screwbean mesquite)
Prunus americana (wild plum)
Quercus gambelii (Gambel's oak, Rocky Mountain white oak)
Quercus grisea (gray oak, Mexican blue oak)
Sapindus saponaria var. drummondii (soapberry)

Trees (evergreen)

Abies concolor (western white fir)
Abies lasiocarpa (subalpine fir)
Acacia constricta (whitethorn, mescat acacia)
Arbutus arizonica (Arizona madrone)
Arbutus xalapensis (Texas madrone)
Juniperus ashei (rock or post cedar, Ashe or Mexican juniper)
Juniperus deppeana (alligator or western juniper)
Juniperus osteosperma (Utah juniper)
Juniperus pinchotii (red-berry juniper)
Juniperus scopulorum (Rocky Mountain juniper)
Picea engelmannii (Engelmann spruce)
Picea pungens (blue spruce, Colorado spruce)
Pinus aristata (bristlecone pine)
Pinus cembroides (Mexican pinyon)
Pinus edulis (pinyon pine, Colorado pinyon)
Pinus flexilis (limber pine)
Pinus ponderosa (ponderosa pine)
Pinus strobiformis (southwestern white pine)
Pseudotsuga menziesii (Douglas fir)
Quercus arizonica (Arizona white oak)
Quercus emoryi

Vines (deciduous)

Clematis ligusticifolia (clematis)
Maurandella antirrhiniflora (snapdragon vine)
Parthenocissus quinquefolia var. quinquefolia (woodbine)
Vitis arizonica (Arizona grape, canyon grape)
Vitis riparia (riverbank grape)

FEDERALLY LISTED ENDANGERED SPECIES

Gypsum wild-buckwheat (eriogonum gypsophilum)
Holy Ghost ipomopsis (Ipomopsis sancti-spiritus)
Knowlton cactus (Pediocactus knowltonii)
Kuenzler hedgehog cuctus (Echinocereus fendleri var. kuenzleri)
Lee pincushion cactus (Croyphantha sneedii var. leei)
Lloyd's Mariposa cactus (Echinomastus)
Lloyd's hedgehog cactus (E. Lloydii)
Mancos milk-vetch (Astragalus hmillimus)
Mesa Verde cactus (Sclerocactus mesae-verdae)
Sacramento Mountains thistle (Cirsium vinaceum)
Sacramento prickly-poppy (Argemone pleiacantha ssp. pinnatisecta)
Sneed pincushion cactus (Coryphantha sneedii var. Sneedii)
Todsen's pennyroyal (Hedeoma todsenii)
Zuni (rhizome) fleabane (Erigeron rhizomatus)

NEW MEXICO NOXIOUS SPECIES

Because the noxious weed lists have continually changed since we gathered them in 1994, we are not including them at this time. Not all States have noxious weed lists. Those that do, do not use the same standards of importance and are not comparable. States typically have included plants that interfere with agriculture (Canada thistle), or cause human health problems (poison ivy). Some States are now including a category of plants that invade and degrade the environment (purple loosestrife). Check with your State's Agriculture Department or Weed Scientist listed below. The noxious weed list can be used two ways on roadsides: l) check to not inadvertently plant these invasive plants, and 2) note the plants you are legally responsible to control. Many States now check adjacent State lists to avoid planting their neighbors' problem plants. Because weeds do not respect political boundaries, and because by their very nature weeds continue to adapt and expand, monitoring and controlling invasives at State borders is a wise part of vegetation management.

(Seed Law)

Department of Agriculture
Ag./Environmental Services
Box 300005, Dpt. 3BA
Las Cruces, NM 88003

Richard Lee, U of NM
Plant Sciences Department
P.O. Box 30003, Dept. 3AE
Las Cruces, NM 88003
(505) 646-2888

NEW MEXICO RESOURCES

New Mexico Natural Heritage Program
University of New Mexico
2500 Yale Boulevard, SE, Ste. 100
Albuquerque, NM 87131
(505) 277-1991)

The Nature Conservancy Field Office
212 East Marcy, Ste. 200
Santa Fe, NM 8750l
(505) 988-3867

Native Plant Society of New Mexico
P.O. Box 5917
Santa Fe, NM 87502

Living Desert Zoo and Gardens
P.O. Box 100
Carlsbad, NM 88221

POTENTIAL NATURAL VEGETATION ZONES IN
NEW YORK

Source: A.W. Kuchler's Potential Natural Vegetation Map, 1964, Revised 1985.
Presented in U.S.G.S. National Atlas of the U.S. Series,
U.S. Geological Survey, Reston, VA.

65	Northern cordgrass prairie	*(Distichlis-Spartina)*
66	Bluestem prairie	*(Andropogon-Panicum-Sorghastrum)*
87	Northeastern spruce-fir forest	*(Picea-Abies)*
93	Beech-maple forest	*(Fagus-Acer)*
95	Appalachian oak forest	*(Quercus)*
97	Northern hardwoods	*(Acer-Betula-Fagus-Tsuga)*
99	Northern hardwoods-spruce forest	*(Acer-Betula-Fagus-Picea-Tsuga)*
100	Northeastern oak-pine forest	*(Quercus-Pinus)*

(Dominant plant species present in each vegetation type are listed in Appendix 8)

65 *Northern Cordgrass Prairie (Distichlis Spartina)*
66 *Bluestem Prairie (Andropogon-Panicum Sorghastrum)*
87 *Northeastern Spruce-Fir Forest (Picea-Abies)*
93 *Beech-Maple Forest (Fagus-Acer)*
95 *Appalachian Oak Forest (Quercus)*
97 *Northern Hardwoods (Acer-Betula-Fagus-Tsuga)*
99 *Northern Hardwoods-Spruce Forests (Acer-Betula-Fagus-Picea-Tsuga)*
100 *Northeastern Oak-Pine Forest (Quercus Pinus)*

Botanical Experts

Dr. Richard S. Mitchell, State Botanist
New York State Museum
3140 CEC
Albany, NY 12230
(518) 486-2027

Donald Cameron
Maine Natural Areas Program
State House Station #93
Augusta, ME 04333-0093
(207) 287-8041

Recommended Flora

Mitchell, R.S. & G. C. Tucker. 1997. Revised Checklist of New York State Plants. Contr. to a Flora of N.Y. State, Checklist IV. New York State Mus. Bull. 790. 400 pp.

NATIVE PLANTS FOR LANDSCAPE USE IN NEW YORK

Cactus

Opuntia humifusa (prickly pear)

Ferns

Adiantum pedatum (northern maidenhair fern)
Asplenium platyneuron (ebony spleenwort)
Asplenium trichomanes (maidenhair spleenwort)
Athyrium filix-femina (lady fern)
Botrychium virginianum (rattlesnake fern)
Cystopteris bulbifera (bladder fern)
Cystopteris fragilis (fragile fern)
Dryopteris carthusiana (shield fern, toothed wood fern, spinulose shield fern)
Dryopteris cristata (crested wood fern, buckler fern)
Dryopteris marginalis (marginal wood fern)
Gymnocarpium dryopteris (oak fern)
Matteuccia struthiopteris (ostrich fern)
Onoclea sensibilis (sensitive fern, bead fern)
Osmunda cinnamomea (cinnamon fern)
Osmunda claytoniana (interrupted fern)
Osmunda regalis (royal fern)
Phegopteris hexagonoptera (broad beech fern)

Polystichum acrostichoides (Christmas fern)
Thelypteris novaboracensis (New York fern, tapering fern)
Thelypteris simulata (Massachusetts fern)
Woodsia ilvensis (rusty woodsia)
Woodwardia areolata (netted chain fern)
Woodwardia virginica (Virginia chain fern)

Forbs (annuals/biennials)

Corydalis sempervirens (pale corydalis)
Gentianopsis crinita (fringed gentian)
Lobelia spicata (pale lobelia)
Oenothera biennis (common evening primrose)

Forbs (perennials)

Acorus calamus (sweet flag, calamus)
Actaea pachypoda (white baneberry)
Allium canadense (wild garlic)
Allium tricoccum (wild leek)
Anaphalis margaritacea (pearly everlasting)
Anemone canadensis (Canada anemone, windflower)
Anemone cylindrica (thimbleweed, candle anemone)
Anemone virginiana (thimbleweed, tall anemone)
Antennaria spp. (pussytoes, everlasting)
Apocynum androsaemifolium (spreading dogbane)
Aquilegia canadensis (columbine)
Arisaema triphyllum (Jack-in-the-pulpit, Indian turnip)
Asarum canadense (wild ginger)
Asclepias incarnata (swamp milkweed)
Asclepias tuberosa (butterfly weed)
Aster divaricatus (white wood aster)
Aster dumosus (bushy aster)
Aster ericoides (heath aster, white wreath aster)
Aster laevis (smooth aster)
Aster novae-angliae (New England aster)
Aster novi-belgii (New York aster)
Aster pilosus (frost aster)
Astragalus canadensis (milk vetch, Canada milk vetch)
Caltha palustris (marsh marigold, cowslip)
Campanula rotundifolia (harebell)
Cardamine diphylla (two-leaved toothwort)
Caulophyllum thalictroides (blue cohosh)
Chelone glabra (turtlehead)
Cimicifuga racemosa (bugbane, black cohosh)
Claytonia caroliniana (broad-leaved spring beauty)
Claytonia virginica (narrow-leaved spring beauty)
Clintonia borealis (clintonia, blue-bead lily)
Collinsonia canadensis (stoneroot, citronella horsebalm)
Coptis trifolia ssp. groenlandica (goldthread)
Cornus canadensis (bunchberry)
Desmodium canadense (Canada tick-trefoil, Canada tickclover)
Dicentra cucullaria (Dutchman's breeches)
Epilobium angustifolium (fireweed, willow herb)

Erythronium americanum (eastern trout lily, yellow trout lily)
Eupatorium fistulosum (Joe-pye weed)
Eupatorium maculatum (spotted Joe-pye weed)
Eupatorium perfoliatum (boneset)
Eupatorium rugosum (white snakeroot)
Eupatorium purpureum (Joe-pye weed)
Euphorbia corollata (flowering spurge)
Euthamia graminifolia var. graminifolia (grass-leaved goldenrod)
Fragaria virginiana (wild strawberry)
Galium triflorum (sweet-scented bedstraw)
Gentiana andrewsii (bottle gentian)
Gentiana clausa (bottle gentian)
Gentiana saponaria (closed gentian, soapwort gentian)
Geranium maculatum (wild geranium, cranesbill)
Geum rivale (purple avens, water avens)
Helenium autumnale (common sneezeweed)
Helianthus divaricatus (narrow-leaved sunflower, swamp sunflower)
Helianthus strumosus (woodland sunflower)
Heliopsis helianthoides (ox-eye sunflower, false sunflower)
Hepatica nobilis var. acuta (sharp-lobed hepatica)
Heuchera american (alumroot)
Houstonia caerulea (bluets)
Houstonia longifolia (long-leaved bluets, pale bluets)
Hydrophyllum virginianum (Virginia waterleaf)
Hypericum ascyron (great St. John's wort)
Hypoxis hirsuta (yellow star grass)
Iris versicolor (blue flag)
Lespedeza capitata (roundheaded bush clover)
Lilium canadense (wild yellow lily, Canada lily)
Lilium philadelphicum (wood lily)
Linnaea borealis (twinflower)
Linum virginianum (woodland flax)
Lobelia cardinalis (cardinal flower)
Lobelia siphilitica (great blue lobelia)
Lupinus perennis (wild lupine)
Lysimachia ciliata (fringed loosestrife)
Maianthemum canadense (wild lily-of-the-valley, Canada mayflower)
Maianthemum racemosum ssp. racemosum (false Solomon's seal,
    false spikenard)
Maianthemum stellatum (starry Solomon's seal)
Mitchella repens (partridge berry)
Monarda didyma (beebalm, oswego tea)
Monarda fistulosa (wild bergamot, horsemint, beebalm)
Nuphar lutea (yellow pond lily, cow lily, spatter dock)
Oenothera fruticosa (sundrops)
Osmorhiza claytoni (sweet cicely, sweet jarvil)
Peltandra virginica (arrow arum)
Penstemon digitalis (beardtongue)
Penstemon hirsutus (hairy beardtongue)
Potentilla fruticosa (potentilla, shrubby cinquefoil)
Phlox paniculata (summer phlox, perennial phlox)
Physostegia virginiana (obedient plant, false dragonhead)

Podophyllum peltatum (May apple)
Polemonium reptans (Jacob's ladder, Greek valerian)
Polygonatum biflorum (Solomon's seal)
Potentilla arguta (white cinquefoil, prairie cinquefoil, tall cinquefoil)
Potentilla simplex (common cinquefoil)
Pycnanthemum tenuifolium (slender mountain mint)
Pycnanthemum virginianum (mountain mint)
Pyrola elliptica (shinleaf)
Ranunculus hispidus (early buttercup, tufted buttercup)
Rhexia virginica (meadow beauty)
Rudbeckia laciniata (cut-leaf coneflower)
Salvia lyrata (cancer weed, lyre-leaf sage)
Sanguinaria candensis (bloodroot)
Senecio aureus (golden ragwort)
Potentilla tridentata (three-toothed cinquefoil)
Silene stellata (starry campion)
Sisyrinchium angustifolium (narrow-leaved blue-eyed grass)
Solidago caesia (blue-stemmed goldenrod, wreath goldenrod)
Solidago canadensis (meadow goldenrod)
Solidago juncea (early goldenrod, plume goldenrod)
Solidago nemoralis (gray goldenrod, old-field goldenrod)
Solidago odora (sweet goldenrod)
Solidago rugosa (rough-leaved goldenrod)
Solidago sempervirens (seaside goldenrod)
Solidago speciosa (showy goldenrod)
Solidago ulmifolia (elm-leaved goldenrod)
Streptopus roseus (rosy twisted stalk)
Tephrosia virginiana (goat's rue)
Thalictrum dioicum (early meadow rue)
Thalictrum pubescens (tall meadow rue)
Thalictrum thalictroides (rue anemone)
Tiarella cordifolia (foam flower)
Trientalis borealis ssp. borealis (starflower)
Trillium cernuum (nodding trillium)
Trillium erectum (wakerobin, purple trillium)
Trillium undulatum (painted trillium)
Uvularia grandiflora (bellwort, merrybells)
Uvularia sessilifolia (wildoats, merrybells)
Verbena hastata (blue verbena, blue vervain)
Vernonia noveboracensis (New York ironweed)
Veronicastrum virginicum (Culver's root)
Viola canadensis (Canada violet)
Viola conspersa (American dog violet)
Viola pedata (bird-foot violet)
Viola pubescens (downy or smooth yellow violet)
Viola soraria (common blue violet, meadow violet)
Zizia aptera (heart-leaved golden alexanders)
Zizia aurea (golden alexanders)

Grasses/Grass-like plants

Agrostis scabra (ticklegrass, fly-away grass)
Andropogon gerardii (big bluestem)

Andropogon glomeratus (bushy bluestem)
Andropogon virginicus (broom sedge)
Bromus kalmii (prairie brome, wild chess)
Calamagrostis canadensis (bluejoint grass)
Carex aquatilis (water sedge)
Carex pensylvanica (Pennsylvania sedge)
Carex plantaginea (plantain-leaved sedge)
Carex stipata (awl-fruited sedge)
Carex stricta (tussock sedge)
Carex rostrata var. utriculata (beaked sedge)
Danthonia spicata (poverty grass)
Deschampsia cespitosa (tufted hairgrass)
Distichlis spicata (seashore saltgrass)
Eleocharis palustris (creeping spikesedge, spike rush)
Elymus canadensis (Canada wild rye)
Elymus hystrix var. hystrix (bottlebrush grass)
Eragrostis spectabilis (purple lovegrass, tumblegrass)
Glyceria grandis (American mannagrass, tall mannagrass, reed meadowgrass)
Juncus effusus var.pylaei (soft rush)
Leersia oryzoides (rice cut grass)
Panicum virgatum (switchgrass)
Schizachyrium scoparium (little bluestem)
Scirpus acutus (hardstem bulrush)
Scirpus atrovirens (dark green bulrush)
Scirpus cyperinus (wool grass)
Scirpus tabernaemontani (great bulrush)
Sorghastrum nutans (Indian grass)
Spartina patens (marsh hay cordgrass, salt meadow cordgrass)
Spartina pectinata (prairie cordgrass, freshwater cordgrass)
Sporobolus asper (dropseed)
Trisetum spicatum (spike trisetum)
Typha latifolia (cattail)

Shrubs (deciduous)

Alnus incana ssp. rugosa (speckled alder, mountain alder)
Alnus serrulata (smooth alder)
Amelanchier arborea (downy serviceberry, shadbush, Juneberry)
Aronia melanocarpa (black chokeberry)
Baccharis halimifolia (sea myrtle, groundsel bush)
Castanea pumila (chinquapin)
Ceanothus americanus (New Jersey tea, red root)
Cephalanthus occidentalis (buttonbush)
Clethra alnifolia (summer sweet)
Cornus alternifolia (pogoda dogwood, alternate-leaved dogwood)
Cornus amomum ssp. obliqua (swamp dogwood, silky dogwood)
Cornus foemina ssp. racemosa (gray dogwood)
Corylus americana (American hazelnut or filbert)
Corylus cornuta (beaked hazelnut or filbert)
Diervilla lonicera (bush honeysuckle)
Dirca palustris (leatherwood, ropebark)
Euonymus americana (strawberry bush, brook euonymus, hearts-a-bustin')
Hydrangea arborescens (wild hydrangea)

Ilex verticillata (winterberry, black alder)
Lindera benzoin (spicebush)
Lonicera dioica (limber or wild honeysuckle)
Lyonia ligustrina (male-berry, male-blueberry)
Physocarpus opulifolius (ninebark)
Prunus virginiana (chokecherry)
Rhododendron periclymenoides (pinksterbloom azalea)
Rhododendron prinophyllum (roseshell azalea, early azalea)
Rhododendron viscosum (swamp azalea)
Rhus aromatica (fragrant sumac)
Rhus copallinum (dwarf or winged sumac)
Rhus glabra (smooth sumac)
Rhus hirta (staghorn sumac)
Ribes cynosbati (prickly gooseberry, dogberry)
Rosa arkansana var. suffulta (prairie rose)
Rosa blanda (early wild rose, smooth rose)
Rosa carolina (Carolina rose)
Rubus idaeus ssp. strigosus (red raspberry)
Rubus occidentalis (black raspberry, thimbleberry)
Rubus odoratus (thimbleberry)
Salix bebbiana (Bebb willow, long-beaked willow)
Salix discolor (pussy willow)
Salix nigra (black willow)
Sambucus canadensis (elderberry, common elder)
Sambucus racemosa var. pubens (scarlet elderberry, red-berried elder)
Spiraea alba (meadow sweet)
Spiraea tomentosa (steeplebush, hardhack)
Staphylea trifolia (bladdernut)
Symphoricarpos albus (snowberry)
Vaccinium angustifolium (low-bush blueberry)
Vaccinium corymbosom (highbush blueberry)
Viburnum acerifolium (maple leaf viburnum)
Viburnum dentatum (southern arrowwood)
Viburnum lentago (black haw, nannyberry)
Viburnum nudum var. cassinoides (wild raisin)
Viburnum opulus var. americanum (high-bush cranberry, American cranberrybush viburnum)
Viburnum prunifolium (black haw, nanny berry)

Shrubs (evergreen)

Andromeda polifolia var. glaucophylla (bog rosemary)
Arctostaphylos uva-ursi (bearberry, kinnikinnik)
Epigaea repens (trailing arbutus)
Gaultheria hispidula (creeping snowberry)
Gaultheria procumbens (wintergreen, checkerberry)
Ilex glabra (inkberry, bitter gallberry)
Juniperus communis (common juniper)
Kalmia angustifolia (sheep laurel, lambkill kalmia)
Kalmia latifolia (mountain laurel)
Kalmia polifolia (swamp laurel, bog laurel)
Rhododendron maximum (rosebay, great laurel)
Taxus canadensis (Canada yew)

Trees (deciduous)

Acer pennsylvanicum (striped maple)
Acer rubrum (red maple)
Acer saccharinum (silver maple)
Acer saccharum (sugar maple)
Acer spicatum (mountain maple)
Amelanchier canadensis (shadblow serviceberry, Juneberry)
Betula lenta (cherry birch)
Betula nigra (river birch)
Betula papyrifera (paper birch)
Carpinus caroliniana (blue beech, hornbeam, musclewood)
Carya alba (mockernut hickory)
Carya cordiformis (bitternut, swamp hickory)
Carya ovata (shagbark hickory)
Celtis occidentalis (hackberry, sugarberry)
Cornus florida (flowering dogwood)
Crataegus crusgalli (cockspur hawthorn)
Crataegus punctata (dotted hawthorn, white thorn)
Diospyros virginiana (persimmon)
Fagus grandifolia var. caroliniana (beech)
Fagus grandifolia (beech)
Fraxinus americana (white ash)
Fraxinus pensylvanica (green ash)
Gymnocladus dioica (Kentucky coffee tree)
Hamamelis virginiana (witch hazel)
Juglans cinerea (butternut, white walnut)
Juglans nigra (black walnut)
Larix laricina (tamarack, American larch)
Liquidambar styraciflua (sweet gum)
Liriodendron tulipifera (tulip tree)
Magnolia acuminata (cucumber tree)
Nyssa sylvatica (black gum, tupelo)
Ostrya virginiana (ironwood, hophornbeam)
Platanus occidentalis (sycamore, plane-tree)
Populus deltoides (eastern cottonwood)
Populus grandidentata (large-toothed aspen)
Populus tremuloides (quaking aspen)
Prunus americana (wild plum)
Prunus nigra (Canada plum)
Prunus pensylvanica (fire or pin cherry)
Prunus serotina (black cherry)
Quercus alba (white oak)
Quercus bicolor (swamp white oak)
Quercus coccinea (scarlet oak)
Quercus macrocarpa (bur oak)
Quercus muhlenbergii (chinkapin oak, chestnut oak)
Quercus palustris (pin oak)
Quercus rubra (red oak)
Quercus stellata (post oak)
Quercus velutina (black oak)
Salix amygdaloides (peachleaf willow)
Salix nigra (black willow)

Sassafras albidum (sassafras)
Sorbus americana (mountain ash)
Tilia americana (American linden, basswood)
Ulmus americana (American elm)
Ulmus rubra (red elm, slippery elm)

Trees (evergreen)

Abies balsamea (balsam fir)
Ilex opaca (American holly, Christmas holly)
Juniperus virginiana (eastern red cedar)
Picea glauca (white spruce)
Pinus resinosa (red pine)
Pinus rigida (pitch pine)
Pinus strobus (eastern white pine)
Thuja occidentalis (arbor vitae, northern white cedar)
Tsuga canadensis (eastern hemlock)

Vines (deciduous)

Celastrus scandens (American bittersweet)
Clematis occidentalis (purple clematis)
Clematis virginiana (virgin's bower)
Lonicera sempervirens (coral honeysuckle)
Parthenocissus quinquefolia (Virginia creeper)
Vitis aestivalis (summer grape)
Vitis labrusca (fox grape)
Vitis riparia (riverbank grape)

FEDERALLY LISTED ENDANGERED SPECIES

American hart's-tongue fern (Asplenium scolopendrium var. americanum)
Houghton's goldenrod (Solidago houghtonii)
Leedy's roseroot (Sedum integrifolium ssp. leedyi)
Northeastern (Barbed bristle) bulrush (Scirpus ancistrochaetus)
Northern wild monkshood (Aconitum noveboracense)
Sandplain gerardia (Agalinis acuta)
Seabeach amaranth (Amaranthus pumilus)

NEW YORK NOXIOUS SPECIES

Because the noxious weed lists have continually changed since we gathered them in 1994, we are not including them at this time. Not all States have noxious weed lists. Those that do, do not use the same standards of importance and are not comparable. States typically have included plants that interfere with agriculture (Canada thistle), or cause human health problems (poison ivy). Some States are now including a category of plants that invade and degrade the environment (purple loosestrife). Check with your State's Agriculture Department or Weed Scientist listed below. The noxious weed list can be used two ways on roadsides: l) check to not inadvertently plant these invasive plants, and 2) note the plants you are legally responsible to control. Many States now check adjacent State lists to avoid planting their neighbors' problem plants. Because weeds do not respect political boundaries, and because by their very nature weeds continue to adapt and expand, monitoring and controlling invasives at State borders is a wise part of vegetation management.

(Seed Law)

Department of Agriculture
Division of Plant Industry
1 Winners Circle
Albany, NY 12235

Bernd Blossey
Natural Resources, 207 Fernow
Cornell University
Ithaca, NY 14853
(607) 255-5314

NEW YORK RESOURCES

New York State Museum
Biological Survey
3140 CEC
Albany, NY 12230

New York Natural Heritage Program
Department of Environmental
Conservation
700 Troy-Schenectady Road
Latham, NY 12110
(518) 783-3932

The Nature Conservancy Regional
Office
91 Broadway
Albany, NY 12204
(518) 463-6133

Torrey Botanical Club
New York Botanical Garden
Bronx, NY 10458

Brooklyn Botanic Garden
1000 Washington Avenue
Brooklyn, NY 11225

Mary Ragler Cary Arboretum
Route 44A
Milbrook, NY 12545

Cooperative Sanctuary Program
Audubon International
46 Rarick Road
Selkirk, NY 12158
(518) 767-9051

POTENTIAL NATURAL VEGETATION ZONES IN
——NORTH CAROLINA——

Source: A.W. Kuchler's Potential Natural Vegetation Map, 1964, Revised 1985.
Presented in U.S.G.S. National Atlas of the U.S. Series,
U.S. Geological Survey, Reston, VA.

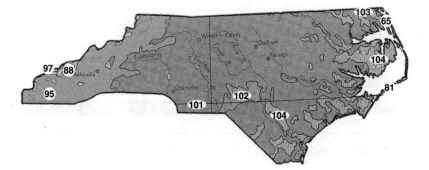

65	Northern cordgrass prairie	*(Distichlis-Spartina)*
81	Live oak-sea oats	*(Quercus-Uniola)*
88	Southeastern spruce-fir forest	*(Picea-Abies)*
95	Appalachian oak forest	*(Quercus)*
97	Northern hardwoods	*(Acer-Betula-Fagus-Tsuga)*
101	Oak-hickory-pine forest	*(Quercus-Carya-Pinus)*
102	Southern mixed forest	*(Fagus-Liquidambar-Magnolia-Pinus-Quercus)*
103	Southern floodplain forest	*(Quercus-Nyassa-Taxodium)*
104	Pocosin	*(Pinus-Ilex)*

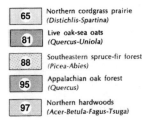

VEGETATION REFERENCES

(Dominant plant species present in each vegetation type are listed in Appendix 8)

65   *Northern Cordgrass Prairie (Distichlis-Spartina)*
81   *Live Oak-Sea Oats (Quercus-Uniola)*
88   *Southeastern Spruce-Fir Forest (Picea-Abies)*
95   *Appalachian Oak Forest (Quercus)*
97   *Northern Hardwoods (Acer-Betula-Fagus-Tsuga)*
101   *Oak-Hickory-Pine Forest (Quercus-Carya-Pinus)*
102   *Southern Mixed Forest (Fagus-Liquidambar-Magnolia-Pinus-Quercus)*
103   *Southern Floodplain Forest (Quercus-Nyssa-Taxodium)*
104   *Pocosin (Pinus-Ilex)*

Botanical Experts

Dr. John Karteasz
University of North Carolina
CD 3280, Coker Hall
Chapel Hill, NC 27599-3280
(919) 962-0578
internet: jkartesz@jkartesz.bio.unc.edu

Recommended Flora

Radford, A.E.; H.E. Ahles; C.R. Bell. 1968. Manual of the
Vascular Flora of the Carolinas. University of North Carolina Press: Chapel Hill,
NC. 1183 pgs.

NATIVE PLANTS FOR LANDSCAPE USE IN NORTH CAROLINA

Cactus

Opuntia humifusa (prickly pear)

Ferns

Adiantum capillus-veneris (southern maidenhair fern)
Adiantum pedatum (northern maidenhair fern)
Asplenium platyneuron (ebony spleenwort)
Asplenium trichomanes (maidenhair spleenwort)
Athyrium filix-femina (lady fern)
Botrychium virginianum (rattlesnake fern)
Cystopteris bulbifera (bladder fern)
Dennstaedtia punctilobula (hay-scented fern)
Dryopteris carthusiana (shield fern, toothed wood fern, spinulose shield fern)
Dryopteris cristata (crested wood fern, buckler fern)
Dryopteris marginalis (marginal wood fern)
Onoclea sensibilis (sensitive fern, bead fern)
Osmunda cinnamomea (cinnamon fern)
Osmunda claytoniana (interrupted fern)
Osmunda regalis (royal fern)
Phegopteris hexagonoptera (broad beech fern)
Polystichum acrostichoides (Christmas fern)
Thelypteris novaboracensis (New York fern, tapering fern)
Woodsia ilvensis (rusty woodsia)

Woodwardia areolata (netted chain fern)
Woodwardia virginica (Virginia chain fern)

Forbs (annuals/biennials)

Campanulastrum americanum (American bellflower, tall bellflower)
Corydalis sempervirens (pale corydalis)
Gaillardia pulchella (Indian blanket, firewheel)
Gentianopsis crinita (fringed gentian)
Glandularia canadensis (rose vervain, sweet William)
Ipomopsis rubra (standing cypress)
Lobelia spicata (pale lobelia)
Oenothera biennis (common evening primrose)
Rudbeckia hirta (black-eyed Susan)
Senecio glabellus (butterweed)

Forbs (perennials)

Acorus calamus (sweet flag, calamus)
Actaea pachypoda (white baneberry)
Ageratina altissima var. altissima (white snakeroot)
Allium canadense (wild garlic)
Allium cernuum (nodding onion)
Allium tricoccum (wild leek)
Amsonia ciliata (blue funnel lily, blue star)
Amsonia tabernaemontana (blue star)
Anemone caroliniana (Carolina anemone, southern thimbleweed)
Anemone virginiana (thimbleweed, tall anemone)
Antennaria spp. (pussytoes, everlasting)
Apocynum androsaemifolium (spreading dogbane)
Aquilegia canadensis (columbine)
Arisaema triphyllum (Jack-in-the-pulpit, Indian turnip)
Aruncus dioicus (goat's beard)
Asarum canadense (wild ginger)
Asclepias amplexicaulis (milkweed)
Asclepias humistrata (milkweed)
Asclepias incarnata (swamp milkweed)
Asclepias tuberosa (butterfly weed)
Asclepias variegata (milkweed)
Asclepias verticillata (whorled milkweed)
Aster divaricatus (white wood aster)
Aster dumosus (bushy aster)
Aster laevis (smooth aster)
Aster novae-angliae (New England aster)
Aster oblongifolius (aromatic aster)
Aster pilosus (frost aster)
Aster puniceus (red-stem aster, swamp aster)
Astilbe biternata (false goatsbeard)
Astragalus canadensis (milk vetch, Canada milk vetch)
Baptisia alba (white false indigo)
Baptisia australis (blue wild indigo)
Caltha palustris (marsh marigold, cowslip)
Camassia scilloides (wild hyacinth)
Cardamine diphylla (two-leaved toothwort)

Caulophyllum thalictroides (blue cohosh)
Chelone lyonii (turtlehead)
Chrysogonum virginianum (green-and-gold)
Chrysopsis mariana (Maryland golden aster)
Cimicifuga racemosa (bugbane, black cohosh)
Claytonia caroliniana (broad-leaved spring beauty)
Claytonia virginica (narrow-leaved spring beauty)
Clintonia borealis (clintonia, blue-bead lily)
Collinsonia canadensis (stoneroot, citronella horsebalm)
Coreopsis auriculata (early coreopsis)
Coreopsis grandiflora (coreopsis)
Coreopsis lanceolata (lance-leaved coreopsis)
Coreopsis pubescens (coreopsis)
Coreopsis tripteris (tall coreopsis)
Coreopsis verticillata (whorled coreopsis)
Delphinium tricorne (dwarf larkspur)
Dicentra cucullaria (dutchman's breeches)
Dicentra eximia (wild bleeding heart)
Dodecatheon meadia (shooting star)
Echinacea purpurea (purple coneflower)
Epilobium angustifolium (fireweed, willow herb)
Eryngium yuccifolium (rattlesnake master, button snake-root)
Erythronium americanum (eastern trout lily, yellow trout lily)
Eupatorium coelestinum (mist flower)
Eupatorium fistulosum (Joe-pye weed)
Eupatorium maculatum (spotted Joe-pye weed)
Eupatorium perfoliatum (boneset)
Eupatorium purpureum (Joe-pye weed)
Euphorbia corollata (flowering spurge)
Filipendula rubra (queen-of-the-prairie)
Fragaria virginiana (wild strawberry)
Galium triflorum (sweet-scented bedstraw)
Gentiana alba (cream gentian, yellow gentian)
Gentiana clausa (bottle gentian)
Gentiana saponaria (closed gentian, soapwort gentian)
Geranium maculatum (wild geranium, cranesbill)
Hedyotis nigricans (bluets)
Helenium autumnale (common sneezeweed)
Helianthus angustifolius (sunflower)
Helianthus debilis (sunflower)
Helianthus microcephalus (sunflower)
Helianthus simulans (narrow-leaved sunflower, swamp sunflower)
Helianthus strumosus (woodland sunflower)
Heliopsis helianthoides (ox-eye sunflower, false sunflower)
Hepatica nobilis var. acuta (sharp-lobed hepatica)
Heuchera americana var. hirsuticaulis (alumroot)
Hibiscus laevis (halberd-leaved marsh mallow)
Hibiscus moscheutos (swamp rose mallow, marshmallow hibiscus)
Houstonia caerulea (bluets)
Houstonia longifolia var. longifolia (long-leaved bluets, pale bluets)
Hydrastis canadensis (golden seal)
Hydrophyllum virginianum (Virginia waterleaf)

Hymenocallis caroliniana (spider lily, rain lily)
Hypoxis hirsuta (yellow star grass)
Iris cristata (dwarf crested iris)
Iris prismatica (slender blue flag, coastal iris)
Iris verna (dwarf flag iris)
Iris virginica (southern blue flag)
Iris virginica var. shrevei (blue flag)
Kosteletzkya virginica (seashore mallow)
Lespedeza capitata (roundheaded bush clover)
Liatris aspera (rough blazing star, gayfeather)
Liatris spicata (marsh blazing star, gayfeather)
Liatris squarrosa (blazing star)
Lilium canadense (wild yellow lily, Canada lily)
Lilium catesbaei (pine lily)
Lilium michauxii (Carolina lily)
Lilium michiganense (Turk's cap lily, Michigan lily)
Lilium philadelphicum (wood lily)
Linum virginianum (woodland flax)
Lithospermum canescens (hoary puccoon)
Lobelia cardinalis (cardinal flower)
Lobelia siphilitica (great blue lobelia)
Lupinus perennis (wild lupine)
Lysimachia ciliata (fringed loosestrife)
Maianthemum canadense (wild lily-of-the-valley, Canada mayflower)
Maianthemum racemosum ssp. racemosum (false Solomon's seal,
    false spikenard)
Manfreda virginica (rattlesnake master, false aloe)
Mertensia virginica (bluebells)
Mitchella repens (partridge berry)
Monarda didyma (beebalm, oswego tea)
Monarda fistulosa (wild bergamot, horsemint, beebalm)
Monarda punctata (beebalm)
Nuphar lutea (yellow pond lily, cow lily, spatter dock)
Oenothera fruticosa (sundrops)
Orontium aquaticum (golden club)
Osmorhiza claytoni (sweet cicely, sweet jarvil)
Pachysandra procumbens (Alleghany spurge)
Peltandra virginica (arrow arum)
Penstemon australis (beardtongue)
Penstemon smallii (small's beardtongue)
Phlox carolina (Carolina phlox)
Phlox divaricata (blue woodland phlox, sweet william)
Phlox divaricata ssp. laphamii (blue phlox, sweet william)
Phlox paniculata (summer phlox, perennial phlox)
Phlox pilosa (prairie phlox, downy phlox)
Phlox stolonifera (creeping phlox)
Physostegia virginiana (obedient plant, false dragonhead)
Podophyllum peltatum (May apple)
Polemonium reptans (Jacob's ladder, Greek valerian)
Polygonatum biflorum (Solomon's seal)
Potentilla simplex (common cinquefoil)
Pycnanthemum tenuifolium (slender mountain mint)

Pycnanthemum virginianum (mountain mint)
Rhexia nashii (meadow beauty)
Rhexia virginica (meadow beauty)
Rudbeckia fulgida (black-eyed Susan, orange coneflower)
Rudbeckia laciniata (cut-leaf coneflower)
Ruellia humilis (wild petunia)
Salvia lyrata (cancer weed, lyre-leaf sage)
Sanguinaria candensis (bloodroot)
Sedum ternatum (wild stonecrop)
Senecio aureus (golden ragwort)
Sibbaldiopsis tridentata (three-toothed cinquefoil)
Silene stellata (starry campion)
Silene virginica (fire pink)
Silphium perfoliatum (cup plant)
Silphium terebinthinaceum (prairie dock)
Sisyrinchium angustifolium (narrow-leaved blue-eyed grass)
Sisyrinchium mucronatum (eastern blue-eyed grass)
Solidago caesia (blue-stemmed goldenrod, wreath goldenrod)
Solidago juncea (early goldenrod, plume goldenrod)
Solidago nemoralis (gray goldenrod, old-field goldenrod)
Solidago odora (sweet goldenrod)
Solidago rigida (stiff goldenrod)
Solidago rugosa (rough-leaved goldenrod)
Solidago sempervirens (seaside goldenrod)
Solidago speciosa (showy goldenrod)
Solidago ulmifolia (elm-leaved goldenrod)
Stokesia laevis (stokes' aster)
Streptopus roseus (rosy twisted stalk)
Tephrosia virginiana (goat's rue)
Thalictrum dioicum (early meadow rue)
Thalictrum pubescens (tall meadow rue)
Thalictrum thalictroides (rue anemone)
Thermopsis villosa (bush pea)
Tiarella cordifolia (foam flower)
Tradescantia hirsuticaulis (hairy spiderwort)
Tradescantia ohiensis (Ohio spiderwort)
Tradescantia virginiana (Virginia spiderwort, spider lily)
Trientalis borealis ssp. borealis (starflower)
Trillium cernuum (nodding trillium)
Trillium erectum (wakerobin, purple trillium)
Trillium undulatum (painted trillium)
Uvularia grandiflora (bellwort, merrybells)
Uvularia sessilifolia (wildoats, merrybells)
Verbena hastata (blue verbena, blue vervain)
Vernonia noveboracensis (New York ironweed)
Veronicastrum virginicum (Culver's root)
Viola affinis (Florida violet)
Viola canadensis (Canada violet)
Viola conspersa (American dog violet)
Viola pedata (bird-foot violet)
Viola soraria (common blue violet, meadow violet)
Yucca aloifolia (Spanish dagger)

Zephyranthes atamasca (atamasco lily, Easter lily)
Zizia aptera (heart-leaved golden alexanders)
Zizia aurea (golden alexanders)

Grasses/Grass-like plants

Agrostis scabra (ticklegrass, fly-away grass)
Andropogon gerardii (big bluestem)
Andropogon glomeratus (bushy bluestem)
Andropogon ternarius (splitbeard bluestem)
Andropogon virginicus (broom sedge)
Arundinaria gigantea (giant cane)
Calamagrostis canadensis (bluejoint grass)
Carex plantaginea (plantain-leaved sedge)
Carex stipata (awl-fruited sedge)
Carex stricta (tussock sedge)
Chasmanthium latifolium (inland sea oats, wild oats, river oats, broad-leaf uniola)
Danthonia spicata (poverty grass)
Deschampsia cespitosa (tufted hairgrass)
Distichlis spicata (seashore saltgrass)
Elymus canadensis (Canada wild rye)
Elymus hystrix var. hystrix (bottlebrush grass)
Elymus villosus (wild rye)
Elymus virginicus (wild rye)
Eragrostis spectabilis (purple lovegrass, tumblegrass)
Juncus effusus var. solutus (soft rush)
Leersia oryzoides (rice cut grass)
Melica nitens (three-flower melic grass)
Muhlenbergia capillaris (gulf muhly, hair grass)
Panicum virgatum (switchgrass)
Saccharum giganteum (sugarcane plume grass)
Schizachyrium scoparium (little bluestem)
Scirpus acutus (hardstem bulrush)
Scirpus atrovirens (dark green bulrush)
Scirpus cyperinus (wool grass)
Scirpus tabernaemontani (great bulrush)
Sorghastrum nutans (Indian grass)
Spartina patens (marsh hay cordgrass, salt meadow cordgrass)
Spartina pectinata (prairie cordgrass, freshwater cordgrass)
Sporobolus cryptandrus (sand dropseed)
Sporobolus heterolepis (northern prairie dropseed)
Tripsacum dactyloides (eastern gama grass)
Trisetum spicatum (spike trisetum)
Typha angustifolia (narrow-leaved cattail)
Typha latifolia (cattail)

Shrubs (deciduous)

Aesculus sylvatica (buckeye)
Alnus serrulata (smooth alder)
Amelanchier arborea (downy serviceberry, shadbush, Juneberry)
Amorpha fruticosa (false indigo, Indigo bush)
Aronia melanocarpa (black chokeberry)
Baccharis halimifolia (sea myrtle, groundsel bush)

Callicarpa americana (American beautyberry, French mulberry)
Calycanthus floridus (Carolina allspice, sweet shrub)
Castanea pumila (chinquapin)
Ceanothus americanus (New Jersey tea, red root)
Cephalanthus occidentalis (buttonbush)
Clethra alnifolia (summer sweet)
Comptonia peregrina (sweet fern)
Cornus alternifolia (pogoda dogwood, alternate-leaved dogwood)
Cornus racemosa (gray dogwood)
Corylus americana (American hazelnut or filbert)
Corylus cornuta (beaked hazelnut or filbert)
Diervilla lonicera (bush honeysuckle)
Diervilla sessilifolia (southern bush honeysuckle)
Dirca palustris (leatherwood, ropebark)
Erythrina herbacea (coral bean)
Euonymus americana (strawberry bush, brook euonymus, hearts-a-bustin')
Euonymus atropurpurea (wahoo, burning bush)
Fothergilla major (witch alder)
Frangula caroliniana (Carolina buckthorn)
Hydrangea arborescens (wild hydrangea)
Hypericum hypericoides ssp. hypericoides (St. Andrew's cross)
Hypericum prolificum (shrubby St. John's wort)
Ilex verticillata (winterberry, black alder)
Itea virginica (Virginia willow, sweetspire, tassel-white)
Lindera benzoin (spicebush)
Lonicera dioica (limber or wild honeysuckle)
Lyonia ligustrina (male-berry, male-blueberry)
Physocarpus opulifolius (ninebark)
Prunus virginiana (chokecherry)
Rhododendron arborescens (smooth azalea)
Rhododendron atlanticum (dwarf, or coastal azalea)
Rhododendron calendulaceum (flame azalea)
Rhododendron canescens (wild, piedmont, or sweet azalea)
Rhododendron periclymenoides (pinxterbloom azalea)
Rhododendron prinophyllum (roseshell azalea, early azalea)
Rhododendron viscosum (swamp azalea)
Rhus aromatica (fragrant sumac)
Rhus copallinum (dwarf or winged sumac)
Rhus glabra (smooth sumac)
Rhus hirta (staghorn sumac)
Ribes cynosbati (prickly gooseberry, dogberry)
Rosa carolina (Carolina rose)
Rosa palustris (swamp rose)
Rosa setigera (Illinois or prairie rose)
Rubus idaeus ssp. strigosus (red raspberry)
Rubus occidentalis (black raspberry, thimbleberry)
Rubus odoratus (thimbleberry)
Sambucus canadensis (elderberry, common elder)
Sambucus racemosa var. pubens (scarlet elderberry, red-berried elder)
Spiraea alba (meadow sweet)
Spiraea tomentosa (steeplebush, hardhack)
Staphylea trifolia (bladdernut)

Stewartia malacodendron (silky camellia)
Styrax americanus (American silverbells)
Symphoricarpos orbiculatus (coralberry, Indian currant)
Vaccinium arboreum (sparkleberry, farkleberry)
Vaccinium corymbosom (highbush blueberry)
Viburnum acerifolium (maple leaf viburnum)
Viburnum dentatum (southern arrowwood)
Viburnum nudum (possumhaw viburnum)
Viburnum nudum var. cassinoides (wild raisin)
Viburnum prunifolium (black haw, nanny berry)
Viburnum rufidulum (southern or rusty black haw)

Shrubs (evergreen)

Epigaea repens (trailing arbutus)
Gaultheria procumbens (wintergreen, checkerberry)
Gordonia lasianthus (loblolly bay, gordonia)
Ilex glabra (inkberry, bitter gallberry)
Ilex vomitoria (yaupon)
Juniperus communis (common juniper)
Kalmia angustifolia (sheep laurel, lambkill kalmia)
Kalmia latifolia (mountain laurel)
Leucothoe axillaris (coast leucothoe)
Myrica cerifera (wax myrtle, southern bayberry, candleberry)
Pieris floribunda (fetter-bush, mountain andromeda)
Rhododendron carolinianum (Carolina rhododendron)
Rhododendron catawbiense (purple rhododendron, red laurel)
Rhododendron maximum (rosebay, great laurel)
Sabal minor (dwarf palmetto)
Taxus canadensis (Canada yew)

Trees (deciduous)

Acer barbatum (Florida maple, southern sugar maple)
Acer leucoderme (chalk maple)
Acer negundo (box elder)
Acer pensylvanicum (striped maple)
Acer rubrum (red maple)
Acer saccharinum (silver maple)
Acer saccharum (sugar maple)
Acer spicatum (mountain maple)
Aesculus flava (sweet buckeye, yellow buckeye)
Aesculus pavia var. pavia (red buckeye)
Amelanchier canadensis (shadblow serviceberry, Juneberry)
Betula lenta (cherry birch)
Betula nigra (river birch)
Carpinus caroliniana (blue beech, hornbeam, musclewood)
Carya alba (mockernut hickory)
Carya cordiformis (bitternut, swamp hickory)
Carya ovata (shagbark hickory)
Celtis laevigata (sugarberry, hackberry)
Celtis occidentalis (hackberry, sugarberry)
Cercis canadensis (redbud)
Chionanthus virginicus (fringe tree, old man's beard)

Cladrastis kentukea (yellowwood)
Cornus florida (flowering dogwood)
Crataegus crus-galli (cockspur hawthorn)
Crataegus marshallii (parsley hawthorn)
Crataegus phaenopyrum (Washington hawthorn)
Crataegus punctata (dotted hawthorn, white thorn)
Cyrilla racemiflora (leatherwood, yiti)
Diospyros virginiana (persimmon)
Fagus grandifolia var. caroliniana (beech)
Fagus grandifolia var. grandifolia (beech)
Fraxinus americana (white ash)
Fraxinus pensylvanica (green ash)
Gleditsia triacanthos (honey locust)
Halesia tetraptera (Carolina silverbell)
Hamamelis virginiana (witch hazel)
Ilex decidua (possum-haw, deciduous holly)
Juglans cinerea (butternut, white walnut)
Juglans nigra (black walnut)
Liquidambar styraciflua (sweet gum)
Liriodendron tulipifera (tulip tree)
Magnolia acuminata (cucumber tree)
Magnolia tripetala (umbrella tree)
Magnolia virginiana (sweetbay, swampbay)
Malus angustifolia (southern crabapple, wild crabapple)
Nyssa sylvatica (black gum, tupelo)
Ostrya virginiana (ironwood, hophornbeam)
Oxydendrum arboreum (sourwood)
Platanus occidentalis (sycamore, plane-tree)
Populus deltoides (eastern cottonwood)
Populus grandidentata (large-toothed aspen)
Prunus americana (wild plum)
Prunus angustifolia (chickasaw plum)
Prunus mexicana (Mexican plum)
Prunus pensylvanica (fire or pin cherry)
Prunus serotina (black cherry)
Ptelea trifoliata (wafer ash, common hoptree)
Quercus alba (white oak)
Quercus bicolor (swamp white oak)
Quercus coccinea (scarlet oak)
Quercus falcata (southern red oak, Spanish oak)
Quercus laurifolia (laurel oak)
Quercus lyrata (overcup oak)
Quercus marilandica (blackjack oak)
Quercus muhlenbergii (chinkapin oak, chestnut oak)
Quercus palustris (pin oak)
Quercus phellos (willow oak)
Quercus prinus (rock chestnut oak)
Quercus rubra (red oak)
Quercus shumardii (shumard oak)
Quercus stellata (post oak)
Quercus velutina (black oak)
Salix nigra (black willow)

Sassafras albidum (sassafras)
Sorbus americana (mountain ash)
Taxodium distichum (bald cypress)
Tilia americana (American linden, basswood)
Ulmus americana (American elm)
Ulmus rubra (red elm, slippery elm)

Trees (evergreen)

Chamaecyparis thyoides (white cedar)
Ilex opaca (American holly, Christmas holly)
Juniperus virginiana (eastern red cedar)
Magnolia grandiflora (southern magnolia)
Persea borbonia (red bay)
Pinus echinata (shortleaf pine)
Pinus palustris (longleaf pine)
Pinus rigida (pitch pine)
Pinus strobus (eastern white pine)
Pinus taeda (loblolly pine)
Pinus virginiana (Virginia pine)
Prunus caroliniana (cherry laurel)
Quercus virginiana (live oak, coastal live oak, southern live oak)
Sabal palmetto (cabbage palm)
Thuja occidentalis (arbor vitae, northern white cedar)
Tsuga canadensis (eastern hemlock)
Tsuga caroliniana (Carolina hemlock)

Vines (deciduous)

Bignonia capreolata (cross vine)
Campsis radicans (trumpet creeper, trumpet vine)
Celastrus scandens (American bittersweet)
Clematis crispa (leatherflower)
Clematis occidentalis var. occidentalis (purple clematis)
Clematis virginiana (virgin's bower)
Lonicera sempervirens (coral honeysuckle)
Parthenocissus quinquefolia (Virginia creeper)
Passiflora incarnata (passion flower, maypop)
Vitis riparia (riverbank grape)
Vitis rotundifolia (muscadine grape)

Vine (evergreen)

Gelsemium sempervirens (yellow jessamine, Carolina jessamine)

FEDERALLY LISTED ENDANGERED SPECIES

American chaffseed (Schwalbea americana)
Blue Ridge goldenrod (Solidago spithamaea)
Bunched arrowhead (Sagittaria fasciculata)
Canby's dropwort (Oxypolis canbyi)
Cooley's meadowrue (Thalictrum cooleyi)
Dwarf-flowered heartleaf (Hexastylis naniflora)
Green ppitcher-plant (Sarracenia oreophila)
Harperella (Ptilimnium nodosum (fluviatile))
Heller's blazingstar (Liatris helleri)
Michaux's sumac (Rhus michauxii)
Mountain golden heather (Hudsonia montana)
Mountain sweet pitcher-plant (Sarracenia rubra ssp. jonesii)
Pondberry (Lindera melissifolia)
Roan Mountain bluet (Hedyotis purpurea var. montana)
Rock gnome lichen (Gymnoderma lineare)
Rough-leaved loosestrife (Lysimachia asperulaefolia)
Schweinitz's sunflower (Helianthus schweinitzii)
Seabeach amaranth (Amaranthus pumilus)
Sensitive joint-vetch (Aeschynomene virginica)
Small whorled pogonia (Isotria medeoloides)
Smalll-anthered bittercress (Cardamine micranthera)
Smooth coneflower (Echinaea laevigata)
Spreading avens (Geum radiatum)
Swamp pink (helonias bullata)
Virginia spiraea (Spiraea virginiana)
White irisette (Sisyrinchium dichotomum)

NORTH CAROLINA NOXIOUS SPECIES

Because the noxious weed lists have continually changed since we gathered them in 1994, we are not including them at this time. Not all States have noxious weed lists. Those that do, do not use the same standards of importance and are not comparable. States typically have included plants that interfere with agriculture (Canada thistle), or cause human health problems (poison ivy). Some States are now including a category of plants that invade and degrade the environment (purple loosestrife). Check with your State's Agriculture Department or Weed Scientist listed below. The noxious weed list can be used two ways on roadsides: l) check to not inadvertantly plant these invasive plants, and 2) note the plants you are legally responsible to control. Many States now check adjacent State lists to avoid planting their neighbors' problem plants. Because weeds do not respect political boundaries, and because by their very nature weeds continue to adapt and expand, monitoring and controlling invasives at State borders is a wise part of vegetation management.

(Weed Law)

Gene Cross
Department of Agriculture
Plant Industry Division
P.O. Box 27647
Raleigh, NC 27611

Stratford Kay
NC State University
]4401-B Williams Hall #7620
Raleigh, NC 27695
(919) 515-5654

North Carolina Heritage Program
NC Department of Environment,
Health & Natural Resources,
Division of Parks & Rec.
P.O. Box 27687
Rleigh, NC 27611
(919) 733-7701

The Nature Conservancy Field Office
4011 University Drive, Ste. 201
Durham, NC 27707
(919) 403-8558

NC Wildflower Preservation Society
900 West Nash Street
Wilson, NC 27893

North Carolina Arboretum
Western Carolina University
Cullowhee, NC 28723

The Daniel Boone Native Gardens
Daniel Boone Park
Off Highway 421
Boone, NC

John Kartesz
Biota of North America Program
North Carolina Botanical Garden
CD3280, Coker Hall
Chapel Hill, NC 27599
(919) 962-0578

POTENTIAL NATURAL VEGETATION ZONES IN
NORTH DAKOTA

Source: A.W. Kuchler's Potential Natural Vegetation Map, 1964, Revised 1985.
Presented in U.S.G.S. National Atlas of the U.S. Series,
U.S. Geological Survey, Reston, VA.

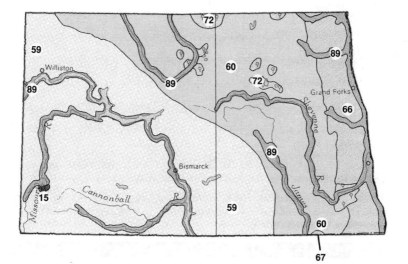

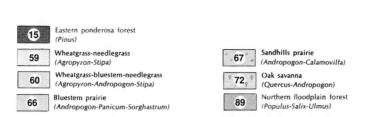

15 Eastern ponderosa forest *(Pinus)*		
59 Wheatgrass-needlegrass *(Agropyron-Stipa)*	**67** Sandhills prairie *(Andropogon-Calamovilfa)*	
60 Wheatgrass-bluestem-needlegrass *(Agropyron-Andropogon-Stipa)*	**72** Oak savanna *(Quercus-Andropogon)*	
66 Bluestem prairie *(Andropogon-Panicum-Sorghastrum)*	**89** Northern floodplain forest *(Populus-Salix-Ulmus)*	

(Dominant plant species present in each vegetation type are listed in Appendix 8)

15   *Eastern Ponderosa Forest (Pinus)*
59   *Wheatgrass-Needlegrass (Agropyron-Stipa)*
60   *Wheatgrass-Bluestem-Needlegrass (Agropyron-Andropogon-Stipa)*
66   *Bluestem Prairie (Andropogon-Panicum-Sorghastrum)*
67   *Sandhills Prairie (Andropogon-Calamovilfa)*
72   *Oak Savanna (Quercus-Andropogon)*
89   *Northern Floodplain Forest (Populus-Salix-Ulmus)*

Botanical Experts

Darla Lenz, Botanist/Plant Ecologist
North Dakota Natural Heritage Program
1835 Bismarck Expressway
Bismarck, ND 58504
(701) 328-5368
(701) 328-5363 (fax)
internet: dlenz@state.nd.us

Susan Rinehart, Botanist
U.S. Forest Service
Medora Ranger District
161 21st St. W
Dickinson, ND 58601
(701) 225-5151

Recommended Flora

Stevens, O.A. 1963. Handbook of North Dakota Plants. North Dakota Institute for Regional Studies. Fargo, ND. 324 pgs. + illus. maps.

Great Plains Flora Association. 1986. Flora of the Great Plains. University Press of Kansas. Lawrence, KS 66045. Other authors: R.L. McGregor and T.M. Barkley. 1392 pgs. ISBN 0 7006 0295 X.

NATIVE PLANTS FOR LANDSCAPE USE IN NORTH DAKOTA

Ferns

Botrychium virginianum (rattlesnake fern)
Cystopteris fragilis (fragile fern)
Matteuccia struthiopteris (ostrich fern)

Forbs (annuals/biennials)

Cleome serrulata (Rocky Mountain beeplant)
Coreopsis tinctoria (tickseed, goldenwave, plains coreopsis, calliopsis)
Euphorbia marginata (snow-on-the-mountain)
Helianthus annuus (common sunflower)
Helianthus petiolaris (plains sunflower)
Linum rigidum (yellow flax)
Lobelia spicata (pale lobelia)
Mimulus guttatus (golden monkey flower)
Oenothera albicaulis (pale evening primrose)

Oenothera biennis (common evening primrose)
Rudbeckia hirta (black-eyed Susan)
Senecio plattensis (prairie ragwort, prairie groundsel)
Townsendia exscapa (Easter daisy)

Forbs (perennials)

Ageratina altissima var. altissima (white snakeroot)
Allium canadense (wild garlic)
Allium stellatum (wild pink onion)
Anemone canadensis (Canada anemone, windflower)
Anemone cylindrica (thimbleweed, candle anemone)
Anemone multifida (early thimbleweed, cut-leaf anemone, Pacific anemone)
Anemone virginiana (thimbleweed, tall anemone)
Antennaria spp. (pussytoes, everlasting)
Apocynum androsaemifolium (spreading dogbane)
Aquilegia canadensis (columbine)
Arisaema triphyllum (Jack-in-the-pulpit, Indian turnip)
Artemisia ludoviciana (white sage, prairie sage, artemisia)
Asclepias incarnata (swamp milkweed)
Asclepias speciosa (showy milkweed)
Asclepias verticillata (whorled milkweed)
Aster ericoides (heath aster, white wreath aster)
Aster laevis (smooth aster)
Aster novae-angliae (New England aster)
Aster oblongifolius (aromatic aster)
Aster puniceus (red-stem aster, swamp aster)
Astragalus canadensis (milk vetch, Canada milk vetch)
Calochortus nuttallii (sego lily, mariposa lily)
Campanula rotundifolia (harebell)
Castilleja sessiliflora (downy painted cup)
Dalea candida (white prairie clover)
Dalea purpurea (purple prairie clover)
Desmodium canadense (Canada tick-trefoil, Canada tickclover)
Echinacea angustifolia (narrow-leaved purple coneflower)
Epilobium angustifolium (fireweed, willow herb)
Erigeron compositus (alpine daisy)
Eupatorium maculatum (spotted Joe-pye weed)
Eupatorium perfoliatum (boneset)
Euthamia graminifolia var. graminifolia (grass-leaved goldenrod)
Fragaria virginiana (wild strawberry)
Gaillardia aristata (blanket flower, gaillardia, brown-eyed Susan)
Galium triflorum (sweet-scented bedstraw)
Gaura coccinea (scarlet gaura)
Gentiana andrewsii (bottle gentian)
Geum triflorum (prairie smoke, purple avens)
Glycyrrhiza lepidota (wild licorice)
Gutierrezia sarothrae (broom snakeweed, matchbrush)
Hedysarum boreale (sweet vetch, sweet broom)
Helenium autumnale (common sneezeweed)
Helianthus maximiliani (Maximilian sunflower)
Helianthus pauciflorus ssp. pauciflorus (stiff sunflower)
Heliopsis helianthoides (ox-eye sunflower, false sunflower)

Heterotheca villosa var. villosa (golden aster)
Heuchera richardsonii (alum root)
Hydrophyllum virginianum (Virginia waterleaf)
Hypoxis hirsuta (yellow star grass)
Liatris aspera (rough blazing star, gayfeather)
Liatris punctata (dotted blazing star, gayfeather)
Lilium philadelphicum (wood lily)
Linum lewisii (wild blue flax)
Lithospermum canescens (hoary puccoon)
Lithospermum incisum (fringed puccoon, narrow-leaved puccoon)
Lobelia siphilitica (great blue lobelia)
Lupinus argenteus (silvery lupine)
Lysimachia ciliata (fringed loosestrife)
Maianthemum stellatum (starry Solomon's seal)
Monarda fistulosa (wild bergamot, horsemint, beebalm)
Nuphar lutea (yellow pond lily, cow lily, spatter dock)
Oenothera cespitosa (gumbo evening primrose, gumbo lily)
Oenothera flava (shortfin evening primrose)
Penstemon albidus (white beardtongue)
Penstemon angustifolius (whorled penstemon)
Penstemon grandiflorus (large-flowered penstemon)
Pentaphylloides floribunda (potentilla, shrubby cinquefoil)
Polygonatum biflorum (Solomon's seal)
Potentilla arguta (white cinquefoil, prairie cinquefoil, tall cinquefoil)
Pulsatilla patens ssp. multifida (pasque flower, wild crocus)
Pycnanthemum virginianum (mountain mint)
Pyrola elliptica (shinleaf)
Ratibida columnifera (prairie coneflower, long-headed coneflower, Mexican hat)
Rudbeckia laciniata (cut-leaf coneflower)
Sibbaldiopsis tridentata (three-toothed cinquefoil)
Silphium perfoliatum (cup plant)
Sisyrinchium angustifolium (narrow-leaved blue-eyed grass)
Solidago canadensis (meadow goldenrod)
Solidago nemoralis (gray goldenrod, old-field goldenrod)
Solidago rigida (stiff goldenrod)
Tetraneuris acaulis var. acaulis (stemless goldflower, stemless rubber weed, butte marigold)
Thalictrum dasycarpum (tall or purple meadow rue)
Verbena hastata (blue verbena, blue vervain)
Verbena stricta (hoary vervain)
Vernonia fasciculata (ironweed)
Viola pedatifida (prairie violet)
Viola soraria (common blue violet, meadow violet)
Yucca glauca (yucca, soapweed)
Zizia aptera (heart-leaved golden alexanders)
Zizia aurea (golden alexanders)

Grasses/Grass-like plants

Agrostis scabra (ticklegrass, fly-away grass)
Andropogon gerardii (big bluestem)
Andropogon hallii (sand bluestem)
Aristida purpurea var. longiseta (red three awn)

Bouteloua curtipendula (sideoats grama)
Bouteloua gracilis (blue grama)
Bouteloua hirsuta (hairy grama)
Bromus carinatus (California brome)
Buchloe dactyloides (buffalograss)
Calamagrostis canadensis (bluejoint grass)
Calamovilfa longifolia (sandreed grass, prairie sandreed)
Carex aquatilis (water sedge)
Carex atherodes
Carex crawei
Carex filifolia
Carex lanuginosa
Carex pensylvanica (Pennsylvania sedge)
Carex sprengelii
Carex stipata (awl-fruited sedge)
Carex stricta (tussock sedge)
Carex utriculata (beaked sedge)
Deschampsia cespitosa (tufted hairgrass)
Distichlis spicata (seashore saltgrass)
Eleocharis palustris (creeping spikesedge, spike rush)
Elymus canadensis (Canada wild rye)
Elymus hystrix var. hystrix (bottlebrush grass)
Elymus lanceolatus (thickspike wheatgrass)
Eragrostis spectabilis (purple lovegrass, tumblegrass)
Festuca ovina (sheep fescue)
Glyceria grandis (American mannagrass, tall mannagrass, reed meadowgrass)
Hierochloe odorata (sweet grass)
Juncus effusus var. solutus (soft rush)
Juncus interior (inland rush)
Koeleria macrantha (June grass)
Leersia oryzoides (rice cut grass)
Nassella viridula (green needle grass)
Oryzopsis hymenoides (Indian ricegrass)
Panicum virgatum (switchgrass)
Pascopyrum smithii (western wheatgrass)
Poa secunda (pine bluegrass)
Pseudoroegneria spicata (bluebunch wheatgrass)
Schizachyrium scoparium (little bluestem)
Scirpus acutus (hardstem bulrush)
Scirpus maritimus (alkali bulrush, prairie bulrush, bayonet grass)
Scirpus tabernaemontani (great bulrush)
Sorghastrum nutans (Indian grass)
Spartina pectinata (prairie cordgrass, freshwater cordgrass)
Sporobolus airoides (alkali sacaton)
Sporobolus compositus var. compositus (tall dropseed)
Sporobolus cryptandrus (sand dropseed)
Sporobolus heterolepis (northern prairie dropseed)
Stipa comata (needle-and-thread grass)
Stipa spartea (porcupine grass)
Typha latifolia (cattail)

Shrubs (deciduous)

Alnus incana (speckled alder, mountain alder)
Amelanchier alnifolia (saskatoon, western serviceberry, Juneberry)
Amorpha canescens (leadplant)
Amorpha fruticosa (false indigo, Indigo bush)
Amorpha nana (dwarf wild indigo)
Artemisia frigida (prairie sagewort, fringed sage)
Atriplex canescens (four-wing saltbush, wingscale)
Atriplex confertifolia (spiny saltbush, shadscale saltbush, hop sage)
Chrysothamnus nauseosus (rabbit brush, chamisa)
Cornus racemosa (gray dogwood)
Cornus sericea (red-twig dogwood, red-osier dogwood)
Corylus americana (American hazelnut or filbert)
Corylus cornuta (beaked hazelnut or filbert)
Elaeagnus commutata (silverberry, wild olive, wolf willow)
Krascheninnikovia lanata (winterfat)
Lonicera dioica (limber or wild honeysuckle)
Prunus pumila var. besseyi (sand cherry)
Prunus virginiana (chokecherry)
Rhus glabra (smooth sumac)
Ribes odoratum (buffalo currant, golden currant)
Rosa blanda (early wild rose, smooth rose)
Rosa woodsii (western wild rose, woods rose)
Rubus idaeus ssp. strigosus (red raspberry)
Rubus occidentalis (black raspberry, thimbleberry)
Salix bebbiana (Bebb willow, long-beaked willow)
Salix discolor (pussy willow)
Sambucus canadensis (elderberry, common elder)
Sarcobatus vermiculatus (greasewood)
Shepherdia argentea (silver buffaloberry)
Shepherdia canadensis (buffaloberry)
Spiraea alba (meadow sweet)
Symphoricarpos albus (snowberry)
Symphoricarpos occidentalis (wolfberry, buckbush)
Viburnum lentago (black haw, nannyberry)
Viburnum opulus var. americanum (high-bush cranberry, American cranberrybush viburnum)

Shrubs (evergreen)

Arctostaphylos uva-ursi (bearberry, kinnikinnik)
Artemisia tridentata (big sagebrush, Great Basin sagebrush)
Juniperus communis (common juniper)
Juniperus horizontalis (creeping juniper, creeping savin)

Trees (deciduous)

Acer negundo (box elder)
Betula occidentalis (mountain birch, water birch)
Betula papyrifera (paper birch)
Celtis occidentalis (hackberry, sugarberry)
Crataegus mollis (downy hawthorn)
Fraxinus pensylvanica (green ash)

Ostrya virginiana (ironwood, hophornbeam)
Populus deltoides (eastern cottonwood)
Populus tremuloides (quaking aspen)
Prunus americana (wild plum)
Prunus pensylvanica (fire or pin cherry)
Quercus macrocarpa (bur oak)
Salix amygdaloides (peachleaf willow)
Tilia americana (American linden, basswood)
Ulmus americana (American elm)
Ulmus rubra (red elm, slippery elm)

Trees (evergreen)

Juniperus scopulorum (Rocky Mountain juniper)

Vines (deciduous)

Celastrus scandens (American bittersweet)
Clematis ligusticifolia (clematis)
Clematis virginiana (virgin's bower)
Parthenocissus quinquefolia var. quinquefolia (woodbine)
Vitis riparia (riverbank grape)

Western prairie fringed orchid (Platanthera praeclara)

NORTH DAKOTA NOXIOUS SPECIES

Because the noxious weed lists have continually changed since we gathered them in 1994, we are not including them at this time. Not all States have noxious weed lists. Those that do, do not use the same standards of importance and are not comparable. States typically have included plants that interfere with agriculture (Canada thistle), or cause human health problems (poison ivy). Some States are now including a category of plants that invade and degrade the environment (purple loosestrife). Check with your State's Agriculture Department or Weed Scientist listed below. The noxious weed list can be used two ways on roadsides: l) check to not inadvertently plant these invasive plants, and 2) note the plants you are legally responsible to control. Many States now check adjacent State lists to avoid planting their neighbors' problem plants. Because weeds do not respect political boundaries, and because by their very nature weeds continue to adapt and expand, monitoring and controlling invasives at State borders is a wise part of vegetation management.

(Weed and Seed Laws)

Department of Agriculture
600 East Boulevard
State Capitol, 6th Floor
Bismarck, ND 58505

Richard K. Zollinger
North Dakota State University
Loftsgard Hall, Box 5051
Fargo, ND 58105
(701) 237-8157

NORTH DAKOTA RESOURCES

Natural Heritage Inventory
ND Parks & Recreation Department
1835 Bismarck Expressway
Bismarck, ND 58504
(701) 328-5357

The Nature Conservancy Field Office
P.O. Box 1156
Bismarck, ND 58502-1156
(701) 222-8464

North Dakota Natural Science Society
8065 51 1/2 St. SE
Montpelier, ND 58472

Gunlogson Nature Preserve
Icelandic State Park
13571 Highway 5 West
Cavalier, ND 58220

POTENTIAL NATURAL VEGETATION ZONES IN

OHIO

Source: A.W. Kuchler's Potential Natural Vegetation Map, 1964, Revised 1985.
Presented in U.S.G.S. National Atlas of the U.S. Series,
U.S. Geological Survey, Reston, VA.

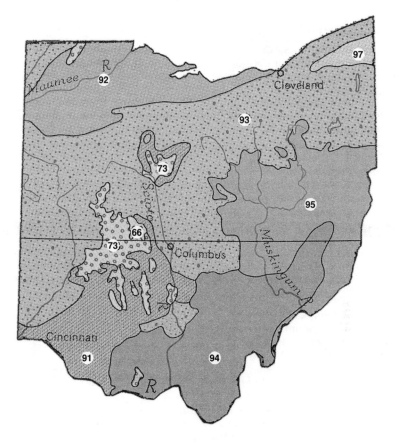

66	Bluestem prairie *(Andropogon-Panicum-Sorghastrum)*	**93**	Beech-maple forest *(Fagus-Acer)*
73	Mosaic of numbers 66 and 91	**94**	Mixed mesophytic forest *(Acer-Aesculus-Fagus-Liriodendron-Quercus-Tilia)*
91	Oak-hickory forest *(Quercus-Carya)*	**95**	Appalachian oak forest *(Quercus)*
92	Elm-ash forest *(Ulmus-Fraxinus)*	**97**	Northern hardwoods *(Acer-Betula-Fagus-Tsuga)*

(Dominant plant species present in each vegetation type are listed in Appendix 8)

66   *Bluestem Prairie (Andropogon-Panicum-Sorghastrum)*
73   *Mosaic of 66 (Bluestem Prairie) and 91 (Oak-Hickory Forest)*
91   *Oak-Hickory Forest (Quercus-Carya)*
92   *Elm-Ash Forest (Ulmus-Fraxinus)*
93   *Beech-Maple Forest (Fagus-Acer)*
94   *Mixed Mesophytic Forest (Acer-Aesculus-Fagus-Liriodendron-Quercus-Tilia)*
95   *Appalachian Oak Forest (Quercus)*
97   *Northern Hardwoods (Acer-Betula-Fagus-Tsuga)*

Botanical Expert

Mr. Allison Cusick, Chief Botanist
Ohio Department of Natural Resources
Divison of Natural Areas and Preserves
Fountain Square
Columbus, Ohio 43224
(614) 265-6471
(614) 267-3096 (fax)
internet: awcusik@aol.com

Recommended Flora

Weishaupt, C.G. 1971. Vascular Plants of Ohio. 3rd ed. Kenday Hunt Publishing
Co., Dubuque, IA.

NATIVE PLANTS FOR LANDSCAPE USE IN OHIO

Ferns

Adiantum pedatum (northern maidenhair fern)
Asplenium platyneuron (ebony spleenwort)
Asplenium trichomanes (maidenhair spleenwort)
Athyrium filix-femina (lady fern)
Botrychium virginianum (rattlesnake fern)
Cystopteris bulbifera (bladder fern)
Cystopteris fragilis (fragile fern)
Dennstaedtia punctilobula (hay-scented fern)
Dryopteris carthusiana (shield fern, toothed wood fern, spinulose shield fern)
Dryopteris marginalis (marginal wood fern)
Onoclea sensibilis (sensitive fern, bead fern)
Osmunda cinnamomea (cinnamon fern)
Osmunda claytoniana (interrupted fern)
Osmunda regalis (royal fern)
Phegopteris hexagonoptera (broad beech fern)
Polystichum acrostichoides (Christmas fern)
Thelypteris novaboracensis (New York fern, tapering fern)

Forbs (annuals/biennials)

Campanulastrum americanum (American bellflower, tall bellflower)
Erysimum capitatum (western wallflower, prairie rocket)
Lobelia spicata (pale lobelia)

Oenothera biennis (common evening primrose)
Rudbeckia hirta (black-eyed Susan)
Senecio plattensis (prairie ragwort, prairie groundsel)

Forbs (perennials)

Actaea pachypoda (white baneberry)
Ageratina altissima var. altissima (white snakeroot)
Allium canadense (wild garlic)
Allium cernuum (nodding onion)
Allium tricoccum (wild leek)
Anaphalis margaritacea (pearly everlasting)
Anemone canadensis (Canada anemone, windflower)
Anemone virginiana (thimbleweed, tall anemone)
Apocynum androsaemifolium (spreading dogbane)
Aquilegia canadensis (columbine)
Arisaema triphyllum (Jack-in-the-pulpit, Indian turnip)
Aruncus dioicus (goat's beard)
Asarum canadense (wild ginger)
Asclepias incarnata (swamp milkweed)
Asclepias tuberosa (butterfly weed)
Asclepias verticillata (whorled milkweed)
Aster divaricatus (white wood aster)
Aster dumosus (bushy aster)
Aster ericoides (heath aster, white wreath aster)
Aster laevis (smooth aster)
Aster novae-angliae (New England aster)
Aster oblongifolius (aromatic aster)
Aster oolentangiensis (sky blue aster)
Aster pilosus (frost aster)
Aster puniceus (red-stem aster, swamp aster)
Astragalus canadensis (milk vetch, canada milk vetch)
Baptisia lactea (white false indigo)
Caltha palustris (marsh marigold, cowslip)
Camassia scilloides (wild hyacinth)
Cardamine diphylla (two-leaved toothwort)
Caulophyllum thalictroides (blue cohosh)
Chelone glabra (turtlehead)
Chrysogonum virginianum (green-and-gold)
Chrysopsis mariana (Maryland golden aster)
Cimicifuga racemosa (bugbane, black cohosh)
Claytonia virginica (narrow-leaved spring beauty)
Collinsonia canadensis (stoneroot, citronella horsebalm)
Coptis trifolia ssp. groenlandica (goldthread)
Coreopsis lanceolata (lance-leaved coreopsis)
Coreopsis tripteris (tall coreopsis)
Dalea purpurea (purple prairie clover)
Delphinium tricorne (dwarf larkspur)
Desmodium canadense (Canada tick-trefoil, Canada tickclover)
Dicentra cucullaria (Dutchman's breeches)
Dodecatheon meadia (shooting star)
Echinacea purpurea (purple coneflower)
Erythronium americanum (eastern trout lily, yellow trout lily)

Eupatorium coelestinum (mist flower)
Eupatorium fistulosum (Joe-pye weed)
Eupatorium maculatum (spotted Joe-pye weed)
Eupatorium perfoliatum (boneset)
Eupatorium purpureum (Joe-pye weed)
Euphorbia corollata (flowering spurge)
Filipendula rubra (queen-of-the-prairie)
Fragaria virginiana (wild strawberry)
Galium triflorum (sweet-scented bedstraw)
Gentiana andrewsii (bottle gentian)
Geranium maculatum (wild geranium, cranesbill)
Helenium autumnale (common sneezeweed)
Helianthus strumosus (woodland sunflower)
Heliopsis helianthoides (ox-eye sunflower, false sunflower)
Hepatica nobilis var. acuta (sharp-lobed hepatica)
Heuchera americana var. hirsuticaulis (alumroot)
Hibiscus moscheutos (swamp rose mallow, marshmallow hibiscus)
Houstonia caerulea (bluets)
Houstonia longifolia var. longifolia (long-leaved bluets, pale bluets)
Hydrastis canadensis (golden seal)
Hydrophyllum virginianum (Virginia waterleaf)
Hypericum ascyron (great St. John's wort)
Iris cristata (dwarf crested iris)
Iris versicolor (blue flag)
Iris virginica var. shrevei (blue flag)
Lespedeza capitata (roundheaded bush clover)
Liatris aspera (rough blazing star, gayfeather)
Liatris spicata (marsh blazing star, gayfeather)
Lilium canadense (wild yellow lily, Canada lily)
Lilium michiganense (Michigan lily)
Linum virginianum (woodland flax)
Lithospermum canescens (hoary puccoon)
Lobelia cardinalis (cardinal flower)
Lobelia siphilitica (great blue lobelia)
Lysimachia ciliata (fringed loosestrife)
Maianthemum canadense (wild lily-of-the-valley, Canada mayflower)
Maianthemum racemosum ssp. racemosum (false Solomon's seal,
    false spikenard)
Maianthemum stellatum (starry Solomon's seal)
Manfreda virginica (rattlesnake master, false aloe)
Mertensia virginica (bluebells)
Mitchella repens (partridge berry)
Monarda didyma (beebalm, oswego tea)
Monarda fistulosa (wild bergamot, horsemint, beebalm)
Nuphar lutea (yellow pond lily, cow lily, spatter dock)
Osmorhiza claytoni (sweet cicely, sweet jarvil)
Peltandra virginica (arrow arum)
Penstemon digitalis (beardtongue)
Penstemon hirsutus (hairy beardtongue)
Pentaphylloides floribunda (potentilla, shrubby cinquefoil)
Phlox divaricata (blue woodland phlox, sweet william)
Phlox paniculata (summer phlox, perennial phlox)

Phlox pilosa (prairie phlox, downy phlox)
Phlox stolonifera (creeping phlox)
Physostegia virginiana (obedient plant, false dragonhead)
Podophyllum peltatum (May apple)
Polemonium reptans (Jacob's ladder, Greek valerian)
Polygonatum biflorum (Solomon's seal)
Potentilla simplex (common cinquefoil)
Pycnanthemum tenuifolium (slender mountain mint)
Pycnanthemum virginianum (mountain mint)
Pyrola elliptica (shinleaf)
Ratibida pinnata (gray-headed coneflower, yellow coneflower)
Rudbeckia fulgida (black-eyed Susan, orange coneflower)
Rudbeckia laciniata (cut-leaf coneflower)
Ruellia humilis (wild petunia)
Salvia lyrata (cancer weed, lyre-leaf sage)
Sanguinaria candensis (bloodroot)
Sedum ternatum (wild stonecrop)
Senecio aureus (golden ragwort)
Silene stellata (starry campion)
Silene virginica (fire pink)
Silphium perfoliatum (cup plant)
Silphium terebinthinaceum (prairie dock)
Sisyrinchium angustifolium (narrow-leaved blue-eyed grass)
Solidago caesia (blue-stemmed goldenrod, wreath goldenrod)
Solidago canadensis (meadow goldenrod)
Solidago juncea (early goldenrod, plume goldenrod)
Solidago nemoralis (gray goldenrod, old-field goldenrod)
Solidago rigida (stiff goldenrod)
Solidago rugosa (rough-leaved goldenrod)
Solidago speciosa (showy goldenrod)
Solidago ulmifolia (elm-leaved goldenrod)
Stylophorum diphyllum (celandine poppy)
Tephrosia virginiana (goat's rue)
Thalictrum dasycarpum (tall or purple meadow rue)
Thalictrum dioicum (early meadow rue)
Thalictrum pubescens (tall meadow rue)
Thalictrum thalictroides (rue anemone)
Tiarella cordifolia (foam flower)
Tradescantia ohiensis (Ohio spiderwort)
Tradescantia virginiana (Virginia spiderwort, spider lily)
Trientalis borealis ssp. borealis (starflower)
Uvularia grandiflora (bellwort, merrybells)
Uvularia sessilifolia (wildoats, merrybells)
Verbena hastata (blue verbena, blue vervain)
Vernonia fasciculata (ironweed)
Vernonia giganteus (tall ironweed)
Veronicastrum virginicum (Culver's root)
Viola canadensis (Canada violet)
Viola conspersa (American dog violet)
Viola pubescens (downy or smooth yellow violet)
Zizia aptera (heart-leaved golden alexanders)
Zizia aurea (golden alexanders)

Grasses/Grass-like plants———————————————————

Agrostis scabra (ticklegrass, fly-away grass)
Andropogon gerardii (big bluestem)
Andropogon virginicus (broom sedge)
Bouteloua curtipendula (sideoats grama)
Bromus kalmii (prairie brome, wild chess)
Calamagrostis canadensis (bluejoint grass)
Carex pensylvanica (Pennsylvania sedge)
Carex plantaginea (plantain-leaved sedge)
Carex stipata (awl-fruited sedge)
Carex stricta (tussock sedge)
Chasmanthium latifolium (inland sea oats, wild oats, river oats, broad-leaf uniola)
Danthonia spicata (poverty grass)
Eleocharis palustris (creeping spikesedge, spike rush)
Elymus canadensis (Canada wild rye)
Elymus hystrix var. hystrix (bottlebrush grass)
Eragrostis spectabilis (purple lovegrass, tumblegrass)
Hierochloe odorata (sweet grass)
Juncus effusus var. solutus (soft rush)
Leersia oryzoides (rice cut grass)
Panicum virgatum (switchgrass)
Scirpus acutus (hardstem bulrush)
Scirpus atrovirens (dark green bulrush)
Scirpus cyperinus (wool grass)
Scirpus tabernaemontani (great bulrush)
Sorghastrum nutans (Indian grass)
Spartina pectinata (prairie cordgrass, freshwater cordgrass)

Shrubs (deciduous) ———————————————————

Alnus incana (speckled alder, mountain alder)
Alnus serrulata (smooth alder)
Amelanchier arborea (downy serviceberry, shadbush, Juneberry)
Aronia melanocarpa (black chokeberry)
Calycanthus floridus (Carolina allspice, sweet shrub)
Ceanothus americanus (New Jersey tea, red root)
Cephalanthus occidentalis (buttonbush)
Comptonia peregrina (sweet fern)
Cornus alternifolia (pogoda dogwood, alternate-leaved dogwood)
Cornus amomum ssp. obliqua (swamp dogwood, silky dogwood)
Cornus drummondii (rough-leaf dogwood)
Cornus racemosa (gray dogwood)
Cornus sericea (red-twig dogwood, red-osier dogwood)
Corylus americana (American hazelnut or filbert)
Diervilla lonicera (bush honeysuckle)
Dirca palustris (leatherwood, ropebark)
Euonymus americana (strawberry bush, brook euonymus, hearts-a-bustin')
Euonymus atropurpurea (wahoo, burning bush)
Frangula caroliniana (Carolina buckthorn)
Hydrangea arborescens (wild hydrangea)
Hypericum hypericoides ssp. hypericoides (St. Andrew's cross)
Hypericum prolificum (shrubby St. John's wort)
Ilex verticillata (winterberry, black alder)

Lindera benzoin (spicebush)
Lonicera dioica (limber or wild honeysuckle)
Physocarpus opulifolius (ninebark)
Prunus virginiana (chokecherry)
Rhododendron periclymenoides (pinxterbloom azalea)
Rhododendron prinophyllum (roseshell azalea, early azalea)
Rhus aromatica (fragrant sumac)
Rhus copallinum (dwarf or winged sumac)
Rhus glabra (smooth sumac)
Rhus hirta (staghorn sumac)
Ribes cynosbati (prickly gooseberry, dogberry)
Rosa carolina (Carolina rose)
Rosa setigera (Illinois or prairie rose)
Rubus idaeus ssp. strigosus (red raspberry)
Rubus occidentalis (black raspberry, thimbleberry)
Rubus odoratus (thimbleberry)
Salix discolor (pussy willow)
Sambucus canadensis (elderberry, common elder)
Sambucus racemosa var. pubens (scarlet elderberry, red-berried elder)
Shepherdia canadensis (buffaloberry)
Spiraea tomentosa (steeplebush, hardhack)
Staphylea trifolia (bladdernut)
Symphoricarpos albus var. albus (snowberry)
Symphoricarpos orbiculatus (coralberry, Indian currant)
Vaccinium angustifolium (low-bush blueberry)
Vaccinium corymbosom (highbush blueberry)
Viburnum acerifolium (maple leaf viburnum)
Viburnum dentatum (southern arrowwood)
Viburnum lentago (black haw, nannyberry)
Viburnum nudum var. cassinoides (wild raisin)
Viburnum opulus var. americanum (high-bush cranberry, American cranberrybush viburnum)
Viburnum prunifolium (black haw, nanny berry)
Viburnum rufidulum (southern or rusty black haw)

Shrubs (evergreen)

Epigaea repens (trailing arbutus)
Gaultheria procumbens (wintergreen, checkerberry)
Juniperus communis (common juniper)
Kalmia latifolia (mountain laurel)
Rhododendron maximum (rosebay, great laurel)
Taxus canadensis (Canada yew)

Trees (deciduous)

Acer negundo (box elder)
Acer rubrum (red maple)
Acer saccharinum (silver maple)
Acer saccharum (sugar maple)
Acer spicatum (mountain maple)
Aesculus flava (sweet buckeye, yellow buckeye)
Aesculus glabra (Ohio buckeye, horse chestnut)
Betula lenta (cherry birch)

Betula nigra (river birch)
Carpinus caroliniana (blue beech, hornbeam, musclewood)
Carya alba (mockernut hickory)
Carya cordiformis (bitternut, swamp hickory)
Carya ovata (shagbark hickory)
Celtis occidentalis (hackberry, sugarberry)
Cercis canadensis (redbud)
Cornus florida (flowering dogwood)
Crataegus crus-galli (cockspur hawthorn)
Crataegus mollis (downy hawthorn)
Crataegus punctata (dotted hawthorn, white thorn)
Diospyros virginiana (persimmon)
Fagus grandifolia var. grandifolia (beech)
Fagus grandifolia var. caroliniana (beech)
Fraxinus americana (white ash)
Fraxinus pensylvanica (green ash)
Gleditsia triacanthos (honey locust)
Gymnocladus dioica (Kentucky coffee tree)
Halesia tetraptera (Carolina silverbell)
Hamamelis virginiana (witch hazel)
Juglans nigra (black walnut)
Liquidambar styraciflua (sweet gum)
Liriodendron tulipifera (tulip tree)
Magnolia acuminata (cucumber tree)
Nyssa sylvatica (black gum, tupelo)
Ostrya virginiana (ironwood, hophornbeam)
Oxydendrum arboreum (sourwood)
Platanus occidentalis (sycamore, plane-tree)
Populus deltoides (eastern cottonwood)
Populus grandidentata (large-toothed aspen)
Populus tremuloides (quaking aspen)
Prunus americana (wild plum)
Prunus mexicana (Mexican plum)
Prunus nigra (Canada plum)
Prunus pensylvanica (fire or pin cherry)
Prunus serotina (black cherry)
Ptelea trifoliata (wafer ash, common hoptree)
Quercus alba (white oak)
Quercus bicolor (swamp white oak)
Quercus coccinea (scarlet oak)
Quercus macrocarpa (bur oak)
Quercus muhlenbergii (chinkapin oak, chestnut oak)
Quercus palustris (pin oak)
Quercus rubra (red oak)
Quercus shumardii (shumard oak)
Quercus stellata (post oak)
Quercus velutina (black oak)
Salix amygdaloides (peachleaf willow)
Salix nigra (black willow)
Sassafras albidum (sassafras)
Tilia americana (American linden, basswood)
Ulmus americana (American elm)
Ulmus rubra (red elm, slippery elm)

Trees (evergreen)

Juniperus virginiana (eastern red cedar)
Pinus echinata (shortleaf pine)
Pinus rigida (pitch pine)
Pinus strobus (eastern white pine)
Pinus virginiana (Virginia pine)
Tsuga canadensis (eastern hemlock)

Vines (deciduous)

Campsis radicans (trumpet creeper, trumpet vine)
Celastrus scandens (American bittersweet)
Clematis occidentalis var. occidentalis (purple clematis)
Clematis virginiana (virgin's bower)
Lonicera sempervirens (coral honeysuckle)
Parthenocissus quinquefolia (Virginia creeper)
Passiflora incarnata (passion flower, maypop)
Vitis riparia (riverbank grape)

FEDERALLY LISTED ENDANGERED SPECIES

Eastern prairie fringed orchid (Platanthera leucophaea)
Lakeside daisy (Hymenoxys herbacea)
Northern wild monkshood (Aconitum noveboracense)
running buffalo clover (Trifolium stoloniferum)
Small whorled pogonia (Isotria medeoloides)
Virginia spireaea (Spiraea virginiana)

OHIO NOXIOUS SPECIES

Because the noxious weed lists have continually changed since we gathered them in 1994, we are not including them at this time. Not all States have noxious weed lists. Those that do, do not use the same standards of importance and are not comparable. States typically have included plants that interfere with agriculture (Canada thistle), or cause human health problems (poison ivy). Some States are now including a category of plants that invade and degrade the environment (purple loosestrife). Check with your State's Agriculture Department or Weed Scientist listed below. The noxious weed list can be used two ways on roadsides: l) check to not inadvertantly plant these invasive plants, and 2) note the plants you are legally responsible to control. Many States now check adjacent State lists to avoid planting their neighbors' problem plants. Because weeds do not respect political boundaries, and because by their very nature weeds continue to adapt and expand, monitoring and controlling invasives at State borders is a wise part of vegetation management.

(Weed and Seed Laws)

Department of Agriculture
Division of Plant Industry
8995 E. Main Street
Reynoldsburg, OH 43068

Mark Loux, 202 Kottman
Ohio State University
2021 Coffey Road
Columbus, OH 43210
(614) 292-9081

OHIO RESOURCES

Natural Heritage Program
Division of Natural Areas & Preserves
Fountain Square, Building F
Columbus, OH 43224
(614) 265-6453

The Nature Conservancy Field Office
6375 Riverside Drive, Ste. 50
Dublin, OH 43017
(614) 717-2770

Ohio Native Plant Society
6 Louise Drive
Chagrin Falls, OH 44022

Aullwood Audubon Center
1000 Aullwood Road
Dayton, OH 45414

Cincinnati Wild Flower Preservation Society
338 Compton Road
Wyoming, OH 45215

Cincinnati Nature Center
4949 Tealtown Road
Milford, OH 45150

POTENTIAL NATURAL VEGETATION ZONES IN
━━━ OKLAHOMA ━━━

Source: A.W. Kuchler's Potential Natural Vegetation Map, 1964, Revised 1985.
Presented in U.S.G.S. National Atlas of the U.S. Series,
U.S. Geological Survey, Reston, VA.

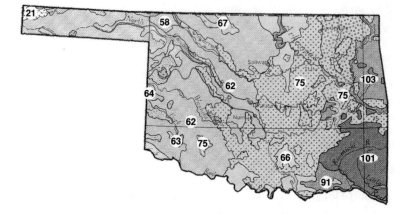

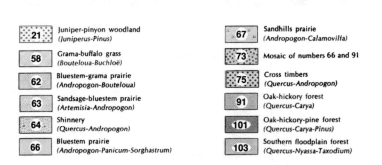

21 Juniper-pinyon woodland *(Juniperus-Pinus)*	**67** Sandhills prairie *(Andropogon-Calamovilfa)*
58 Grama-buffalo grass *(Bouteloua-Buchloë)*	**73** Mosaic of numbers 66 and 91
62 Bluestem-grama prairie *(Andropogon-Bouteloua)*	**75** Cross timbers *(Quercus-Andropogon)*
63 Sandsage-bluestem prairie *(Artemisia-Andropogon)*	**91** Oak-hickory forest *(Quercus-Carya)*
64 Shinnery *(Quercus-Andropogon)*	**101** Oak-hickory-pine forest *(Quercus-Carya-Pinus)*
66 Bluestem prairie *(Andropogon-Panicum-Sorghastrum)*	**103** Southern floodplain forest *(Quercus-Nyassa-Taxodium)*

VEGETATION REFERENCES

(Dominant plant species present in each vegetation type are listed in Appendix A)

21   Juniper-Pinyon Woodland (Juniperus-Pinus)
58   Grama-Buffalo Grass (Bouteloua-Buchloë)
62   Bluestem-Grama Prairie (Andropogon Bouteloua)
63   Sandsage-Bluestem Prairie (Artemisia-Andropogon)
64   Shinnery (Quercus-Andropogon)
66   Bluestem Prairie (Andropogon-Panicum-Sorghastrum)
67   Sandhills Prairie (Andropogon-Calamovilfa)
73   Mosaic of 66 (Bluestem Prairie) and 91 (Oak-Hickory Forest)
75   Cross Timbers (Quercus-Andropogon)
91   Oak-Hickory Forest (Quercus-Carya)
101 Oak-Hickory-Pine Forest (Quercus-Carya-Pinus)
103 Southern Floodplain Forest (Quercus Nyssa-Taxodium)

Botanical Experts

Connie Taylor, State Botanist
Department of Biology
Southeastern Oklahoma State University
Durant, OK 74701
(405) 924-5163

Ron Tryl, State Botanist
Department of Botany
Life Sciences East
Oklahoma State University
Stillwater, OK 74078
(405) 744-9558

Recommended Flora

Taylor, R.J.; C.E.S. Taylor. 1994. An Annotated List of Ferns, Fern Allies, Gymnosperms, and Flowering Plants of Oklahoma. 3rd Edition. Biology Dept. Herbarium, Southeastern Oklahoma State University. Durant, OK. 133 pgs. + illus.

Waterfall, U.T. 1972. Keys to the Flora of Oklahoma, 5th Edition. Published by the author, for sale by the Student Union Bookstore, Oklahoma State University, Stillwater, OK 74078.

NATIVE PLANTS FOR LANDSCAPE USE IN OKLAHOMA

Cacti

Opuntia humifusa (prickly pear)
Opuntia imbricata (tree cholla, walkingstick cholla)
Opuntia macrorhiza (common prickly pear)

Ferns

Adiantum capillus-veneris (southern maidenhair fern)
Adiantum pedatum (northern maidenhair fern)
Asplenium platyneuron (ebony spleenwort)
Asplenium trichomanes (maidenhair spleenwort)

Athyrium filix-femina (lady fern)
Botrychium virginianum (rattlesnake fern)
Cystopteris fragilis (fragile fern)
Dryopteris marginalis (marginal wood fern)
Onoclea sensibilis (sensitive fern, bead fern)
Osmunda cinnamomea (cinnamon fern)
Osmunda regalis (royal fern)
Phegopteris hexagonoptera (broad beech fern)
Polystichum acrostichoides (Christmas fern)

Forbs (annuals/biennials)

Aphanostephus skirrhobasis (lazy daisy)
Castilleja indivisa (Indian paintbrush)
Centaurea americana (basket flower)
Cleome serrulata (Rocky Mountain beeplant)
Coreopsis tinctoria (tickseed, goldenwave, plains coreopsis, calliopsis)
Dracopsis amplexicaulis (clasping leaf coneflower)
Erigeron bellidiastrum (western fleabane)
Eryngium leavenworthii (Leavenworth eryngo)
Eschscholzia californica ssp. mexicana (Mexican gold poppy)
Euphorbia marginata (snow-on-the-mountain)
Eustoma russellianum (prairie or catchfly gentian, Texas bluebell)
Gaillardia pulchella (Indian blanket, firewheel)
Glandularia canadensis (rose vervain, sweet William)
Helianthus petiolaris (plains sunflower)
Ipomopsis longiflora (white-flowered gilia)
Ipomopsis rubra (standing cypress)
Lesquerella gordonii (Gordon's bladderpod)
Lesquerella gracilis (bladderpod)
Linum rigidum (yellow flax)
Lobelia spicata (pale lobelia)
Machaeranthera tanacetifolia (tahoka daisy, tansy aster)
Marshallia caespitosa var. caespitosa (Barbara's buttons)
Monarda citriodora (horsemint, lemon beebalm, lemon mint)
Nemophila phacelioides (baby blue eyes)
Oenothera albicaulis (pale evening primrose)
Oenothera biennis (common evening primrose)
Oenothera rhombipetala (diamond-petal primrose, four-point evening primrose)
Palafoxia callosa (small palafoxia)
Rudbeckia hirta (black-eyed Susan)
Sabatia campestris (prairie rose gentian, prairie sabatia, meadow pink)
Sedum nuttallianum (yellow stonecrop)
Senecio glabellus (butterweed)
Senecio plattensis (prairie ragwort, prairie groundsel)
Teucrium laciniatum (dwarf germander, cutleaf germander)
Thelesperma filifolium var. filifolium (thelesperma, greenthread)
Xanthisma texanum (sleepy daisy)

Forbs (perennials)

Abronia fragrans (sweet sand verbena)
Acorus calamus (sweet flag, calamus)
Ageratina altissima var. altissima (white snakeroot)

Allium canadense (wild garlic)
Allium stellatum (wild pink onion)
Amsonia tabernaemontana (blue star)
Anemone caroliniana (Carolina anemone, southern thimbleweed)
Anemone cylindrica (thimbleweed, candle anemone)
Anemone virginiana (thimbleweed, tall anemone)
Antennaria spp. (pussytoes, everlasting)
Aquilegia canadensis (columbine)
Arisaema triphyllum (Jack-in-the-pulpit, Indian turnip)
Arnoglossum plantagineum
Artemisia ludoviciana (white sage, prairie sage, artemisia)
Aruncus dioicus (goat's beard)
Asclepias asperula (antelope horns)
Asclepias incarnata (swamp milkweed)
Asclepias speciosa (showy milkweed)
Asclepias tuberosa (butterfly weed)
Asclepias verticillata (whorled milkweed)
Aster dumosus (bushy aster)
Aster ericoides (heath aster, white wreath aster)
Aster laevis (smooth aster)
Aster novae-angliae (New England aster)
Aster oblongifolius (aromatic aster)
Aster oolentangiensis (sky blue aster)
Aster pilosus (frost aster)
Astragalus canadensis (milk vetch, Canada milk vetch)
Baptisia alba var. macrophyllla (cream false indigo, plains wild indigo)
Baptisia australis (blue wild indigo)
Callirhoe digitata (finger poppy mallow)
Callirhoe involucrata (purple poppy mallow, winecup)
Callirhoe papaver (poppy mallow)
Calylophus berlandieri (square-bud primrose, sundrops)
Camassia scilloides (wild hyacinth)
Castilleja sessiliflora (downy painted cup)
Claytonia virginica (narrow-leaved spring beauty)
Cooperia drummondii (rain lily, prairie lily)
Coreopsis grandiflora (coreopsis)
Coreopsis lanceolata (lance-leaved coreopsis)
Coreopsis palmata (stiff coreopsis)
Coreopsis tripteris (tall coreopsis)
Dalea purpurea (purple prairie clover)
Delphinium carolinianum (blue larkspur)
Delphinium carolinianum ssp. virescens (prairie larkspur)
Delphinium tricorne (dwarf larkspur)
Desmodium canadense (Canada tick-trefoil, Canada tickclover)
Desmodium illinoense (Illinois tick-trefoil, Illinois tickclover)
Desmodium sessilifolium (tick-trefoil)
Dodecatheon meadia (shooting star)
Echinacea angustifolia (narrow-leaved purple coneflower, black Samson)
Echinacea pallida (pale purple coneflower)
Echinacea purpurea (purple coneflower)
Engelmannia pinnatifida (Engelmann daisy)
Erigeron modestus (prairie fleabane)

Erigeron philadephlius (Philadelphia fleabane)
Erigeron strigosus (white-top fleabane)
Eryngium yuccifolium (rattlesnake master, button snake-root)
Erythronium americanum (eastern trout lily, yellow trout lily)
Eupatorium coelestinum (mist flower)
Eupatorium fistulosum (Joe-pye weed)
Eupatorium perfoliatum (boneset)
Eupatorium purpureum (Joe-pye weed)
Euphorbia corollata (flowering spurge)
Euthamia graminifolia var. graminifolia (grass-leaved goldenrod)
Fragaria virginiana (wild strawberry)
Gaillardia pinnatifida (yellow gaillardia, blanket flower)
Galium triflorum (sweet-scented bedstraw)
Gaura coccinea (scarlet gaura)
Geranium maculatum (wild geranium, cranesbill)
Glandularia bipinnatifida var. bipinnatifida (prairie verbena, Dakota vervain)
Glycyrrhiza lepidota (wild licorice)
Hedyotis nigricans (bluets)
Hedysarum boreale (sweet vetch, sweet broom)
Helenium autumnale (common sneezeweed)
Helianthus maximiliani (Maximilian sunflower)
Helianthus simulans (narrow-leaved sunflower, swamp sunflower)
Heliopsis helianthoides (ox-eye sunflower, false sunflower)
Heterotheca villosa var. villosa (golden aster)
Heuchera americana var. hirsuticaulis (alumroot)
Hieracium longipilum (hairy hawkweed)
Hypoxis hirsuta (yellow star grass)
Ipomoea leptophylla (bush morning glory)
Iris cristata (dwarf crested iris)
Iris virginica (southern blue flag)
Iris virginica var. shrevei (blue flag)
Lespedeza capitata (roundheaded bush clover)
Liatris aspera (rough blazing star, gayfeather)
Liatris elegans (gayfeather)
Liatris mucronata (narrow-leaf gayfeather)
Liatris punctata (dotted blazing star, gayfeather)
Liatris pycnostachya (prairie blazing star, gayfeather)
Liatris squarrosa (blazing star)
Linum lewisii (wild blue flax)
Lithospermum canescens (hoary puccoon)
Lithospermum caroliniense (hairy puccoon, hispid gromwell)
Lithospermum incisum (fringed puccoon, narrow-leaved puccoon)
Lobelia cardinalis (cardinal flower)
Lobelia siphilitica (great blue lobelia)
Ludwigia palustris (marsh purslane)
Ludwigia peploides (water primrose, verdolaga de agua)
Lycopus americanus (bugle-weed, water-horehound)
Lysimachia ciliata (fringed loosestrife)
Manfreda virginica (rattlesnake master, false aloe)
Melampodium leucanthum (Blackfoot daisy, rock daisy)
Mimosa quadrivalvis var. angustata (catclaw sensitive briar)
Mitchella repens (partridge berry)

Monarda fistulosa (wild bergamot, horsemint, beebalm)
Nolina texana (sacahuista, basket grass, Texas beargrass)
Nuphar lutea (yellow pond lily, cow lily, spatter dock)
Oenothera fruticosa (sundrops)
Oenothera macrocarpa (Missouri evening primrose)
Oenothera speciosa (showy white evening primrose)
Peltandra virginica (arrow arum)
Penstemon albidus (white beardtongue)
Penstemon ambiguus (sand penstemon)
Penstemon angustifolius (whorled penstemon)
Penstemon cobaea (cobaea penstemon, wild foxglove)
Penstemon digitalis (beardtongue)
Penstemon fendleri (fendler penstemon, purple foxglove)
Penstemon grandiflorus (large-flowered penstemon)
Penstemon murrayanus (red penstemon, cupleaf beardtongue)
Phlox carolina (Carolina phlox)
Phlox divaricata ssp. laphamii (blue phlox, sweet William)
Phlox pilosa (prairie phlox, downy phlox)
Physostegia intermedia (obedient plant)
Physostegia virginiana (obedient plant, false dragonhead)
Podophyllum peltatum (May apple)
Polygonatum biflorum (Solomon's seal)
Polytaenia nuttallii (prairie parsley)
Potentilla arguta (white cinquefoil, prairie cinquefoil, tall cinquefoil)
Potentilla simplex (common cinquefoil)
Pycnanthemum tenuifolium (slender mountain mint)
Pycnanthemum virginianum (mountain mint)
Ranunculus hispidus (early buttercup, tufted buttercup)
Ratibida columnifera (prairie coneflower, long-headed coneflower, Mexican hat)
Ratibida pinnata (gray-headed coneflower, yellow coneflower)
Rhexia virginica (meadow beauty)
Rudbeckia fulgida (black-eyed Susan, orange coneflower)
Rudbeckia grandiflora (large coneflower)
Rudbeckia subtomentosa (sweet black-eyed Susan)
Ruellia humilis (wild petunia)
Salvia lyrata (cancer weed, lyre-leaf sage)
Sanguinaria candensis (bloodroot)
Silene stellata (starry campion)
Silphium integrifolium (rosinweed)
Silphium laciniatum (compass plant)
Silphium perfoliatum (cup plant)
Sisyrinchium angustifolium (narrow-leaved blue-eyed grass)
Sisyrinchium campestre (white-eyed grass, prairie blue-eyed grass)
Solidago caesia (blue-stemmed goldenrod, wreath goldenrod)
Solidago canadensis (meadow goldenrod)
Solidago missouriensis (Missouri goldenrod, prairie goldenrod)
Solidago nemoralis (gray goldenrod, old-field goldenrod)
Solidago rigida (stiff goldenrod)
Solidago rugosa (rough-leaved goldenrod)
Solidago speciosa (showy goldenrod)
Solidago ulmifolia (elm-leaved goldenrod)
Sphaeralcea coccinea (scarlet globe mallow)
Spigelia marilandica (Indian pink)

Tephrosia virginiana (goat's rue)
Tetraneuris acaulis var. acaulis (stemless goldflower, stemless rubber weed, butte marigold)
Tetraneuris scaposa var. scaposa (four-nerve daisy, yellow daisy, bitterweed)
Thalictrum dasycarpum (tall or purple meadow rue)
Thalictrum thalictroides (rue anemone)
Tradescantia hirsuticaulis (hairy spiderwort)
Tradescantia ohiensis (Ohio spiderwort)
Uvularia grandiflora (bellwort, merrybells)
Uvularia sessilifolia (wildoats, merrybells)
Verbena hastata (blue verbena, blue vervain)
Verbena stricta (hoary vervain)
Vernonia baldwinii (ironweed, western ironweed)
Vernonia fasciculata (ironweed)
Veronicastrum virginicum (Culver's root)
Viola missouriensis (Missouri violet)
Viola pedata (bird-foot violet)
Viola pedatifida (prairie violet)
Viola pubescens (downy or smooth yellow violet)
Viola soraria (common blue violet, meadow violet)
Yucca arkansana (Arkansas yucca, softleaf yucca)
Yucca glauca (yucca, soapweed)
Zinnia grandiflora (Rocky Mountain zinnia, yellow zinnia, plains zinnia)
Zizia aurea (golden alexanders)

Grasses/Grass-like plants

Agrostis scabra (ticklegrass, fly-away grass)
Andropogon gerardii (big bluestem)
Andropogon glomeratus (bushy bluestem)
Andropogon hallii (sand bluestem)
Andropogon ternarius (splitbeard bluestem)
Andropogon virginicus (broom sedge)
Aristida purpurea (purple three awn)
Arundinaria gigantea (giant cane)
Bouteloua curtipendula (sideoats grama)
Bouteloua eriopoda (black grama)
Bouteloua gracilis (blue grama)
Bouteloua hirsuta (hairy grama)
Buchloe dactyloides (buffalograss)
Carex stipata (awl-fruited sedge)
Chasmanthium latifolium (inland sea oats, wild oats, river oats, broad-leaf uniola)
Danthonia spicata (poverty grass)
Digitaria californica (cottontop)
Distichlis spicata (seashore saltgrass)
Eleocharis palustris (creeping spikesedge, spike rush)
Elymus canadensis (Canada wild rye)
Eragrostis intermedia (plains lovegrass)
Eragrostis spectabilis (purple lovegrass, tumblegrass)
Hilaria mutica (tobosa grass)
Juncus effusus var. solutus (soft rush)
Juncus interior (inland rush)
Koeleria macrantha (June grass)

Leersia oryzoides (rice cut grass)
Leptochloa dubia (green sprangletop)
Melica nitens (three-flower melic grass)
Muhlenbergia capillaris (gulf muhly, hair grass)
Muhlenbergia porteri (bush muhly)
Muhlenbergia reverchonii (seep muhly)
Panicum obtusum (vine mesquite)
Panicum virgatum (switchgrass)
Pascopyrum smithii (western wheatgrass)
Poa arachnifera (Texas bluegrass)
Schizachyrium scoparium (little bluestem)
Scirpus acutus (hardstem bulrush)
Scirpus cyperinus (wool grass)
Scirpus maritimus (alkali bulrush, prairie bulrush, bayonet grass)
Sorghastrum nutans (Indian grass)
Spartina pectinata (prairie cordgrass, freshwater cordgrass)
Sporobolus airoides (alkali sacaton)
Sporobolus compositus var. compositus (tall dropseed)
Sporobolus cryptandrus (sand dropseed)
Sporobolus heterolepis (northern prairie dropseed)
Stipa comata (needle-and-thread grass)
Stipa spartea (porcupine grass)
Tripsacum dactyloides (eastern gama grass)
Typha angustifolia (narrow-leaved cattail)

Shrubs (deciduous)

Acacia angustissima (fern acacia, whiteball acacia)
Amelanchier arborea (downy serviceberry, shadbush, Juneberry)
Amorpha canescens (leadplant)
Amorpha fruticosa (false indigo, Indigo bush)
Artemisia frigida (prairie sagewort, fringed sage)
Atriplex canescens (four-wing saltbush, wingscale)
Baccharis halimifolia (sea myrtle, groundsel bush)
Ceanothus americanus (New Jersey tea, red root)
Cephalanthus occidentalis (buttonbush)
Cornus drummondii (rough-leaf dogwood)
Corylus americana (American hazelnut or filbert)
Dalea formosa (feather plume, feather dalea)
Dalea frutescens (black dalea)
Euonymus americana (strawberry bush, brook euonymus, hearts-a-bustin')
Euonymus atropurpurea (wahoo, burning bush)
Forestiera acuminata (swamp privet)
Frangula caroliniana (Carolina buckthorn)
Hamamelis vernalis (vernal witch hazel)
Hypericum hypericoides ssp. hypericoides (St. Andrew's cross)
Hypericum prolificum (shrubby St. John's wort)
Itea virginica (Virginia willow, sweetspire, tassel-white)
Lonicera albiflora (white honeysuckle)
Lonicera dioica (limber or wild honeysuckle)
Lyonia ligustrina (male-berry, male-blueberry)
Mimosa borealis (pink mimosa, fragrant mimosa)
Prunus gracilis (Oklahoma plum)

Prunus virginiana (chokecherry)
Rhododendron canescens (wild, piedmont, or sweet azalea)
Rhododendron oblongifolium (Texas azalea)
Rhus aromatica (fragrant sumac)
Rhus copallinum (dwarf or winged sumac)
Rhus glabra (smooth sumac)
Ribes odoratum (buffalo currant, golden currant)
Rosa arkansana (prairie rose)
Rosa carolina (Carolina rose)
Rosa setigera (Illinois or prairie rose)
Rosa woodsii (western wild rose, woods rose)
Rubus occidentalis (black raspberry, thimbleberry)
Sambucus canadensis (elderberry, common elder)
Sideroxylon lanuginosum ssp. lanuginosum (chittamwood, gum elastic tree)
Staphylea trifolia (bladdernut)
Symphoricarpos orbiculatus (coralberry, Indian currant)
Vaccinium arboreum (sparkleberry, farkleberry)
Vaccinium corymbosom (highbush blueberry)
Viburnum prunifolium (black haw, nanny berry)
Viburnum rufidulum (southern or rusty black haw)

Shrubs (evergreen)

Ilex decidua (possumhaw, deciduous holly)
Ilex vomitoria (yaupon)
Myrica cerifera (wax myrtle, southern bayberry, candleberry)

Trees (deciduous)

Acer negundo (box elder)
Acer rubrum (red maple)
Acer saccharinum (silver maple)
Acer saccharum (sugar maple)
Aesculus glabra (Ohio buckeye, horse chestnut)
Aesculus pavia var. pavia (red buckeye)
Betula nigra (river birch)
Carpinus caroliniana (blue beech, hornbeam, musclewood)
Carya alba (mockernut hickory)
Carya cordiformis (bitternut, swamp hickory)
Carya illinoinensis (pecan)
Carya ovata (shagbark hickory)
Carya texana (black hickory)
Celtis laevigata (sugarberry, hackberry)
Celtis laevigata var. reticulata (netleaf hackberry)
Celtis occidentalis (hackberry, sugarberry)
Cercis canadensis (redbud)
Cornus florida (flowering dogwood)
Cotinus obovatus (smoke tree)
Crataegus crus-galli (cockspur hawthorn)
Crataegus marshallii (parsley hawthorn)
Crataegus mollis (downy hawthorn)
Crataegus viridis (green hawthorn)
Diospyros virginiana (persimmon)
Fraxinus americana (white ash)

Fraxinus pensylvanica (green ash)
Gleditsia triacanthos (honey locust)
Gymnocladus dioica (Kentucky coffee tree)
Halesia tetraptera (Carolina silverbell)
Liquidambar styraciflua (sweet gum)
Malus ioensis var. ioensis (prairie crabapple)
Nyssa sylvatica (black gum, tupelo)
Ostrya virginiana (ironwood, hophornbeam)
Platanus occidentalis (sycamore, plane-tree)
Populus deltoides (eastern cottonwood)
Prunus americana (wild plum)
Prunus angustifolia (chickasaw plum)
Prunus mexicana (Mexican plum)
Prunus serotina (black cherry)
Ptelea trifoliata (wafer ash, common hoptree)
Quercus alba (white oak)
Quercus falcata (southern red oak, Spanish oak)
Quercus macrocarpa (bur oak)
Quercus marilandica (blackjack oak)
Quercus muhlenbergii (chinkapin oak, chestnut oak)
Quercus nigra (water oak)
Quercus palustris (pin oak)
Quercus phellos (willow oak)
Quercus rubra (red oak)
Quercus shumardii (shumard oak)
Quercus stellata (post oak)
Quercus velutina (black oak)
Salix nigra (black willow)
Sapindus saponaria var. drummondii (soapberry)
Sassafras albidum (sassafras)
Tilia americana (American linden, basswood)
Ulmus alata (winged or cork elm, wahoo)
Ulmus americana (American elm)
Ulmus rubra (red elm, slippery elm)

Trees (evergreen)

Pinus echinata (shortleaf pine)
Pinus edulis (pinyon pine, Colorado pinyon)

Vines (deciduous)

Campsis radicans (trumpet creeper, trumpet vine)
Celastrus scandens (American bittersweet)
Clematis crispa (leatherflower)
Clematis pitcheri (leather flower, purple clematis)
Clematis virginiana (virgin's bower)
Lonicera sempervirens (coral honeysuckle)
Parthenocissus quinquefolia (Virginia creeper)
Parthenocissus quinquefolia var. quinquefolia (woodbine)
Passiflora incarnata (passion flower, maypop)
Vitis riparia (riverbank grape)
Vitis rotundifolia (muscadine grape)

FEDERALLY LISTED ENDANGERED SPECIES

Western prairie fringed orchid (Platanthera praeclara)

OKLAHOMA NOXIOUS SPECIES

Because the noxious weed lists have continually changed since we gathered them in 1994, we are not including them at this time. Not all States have noxious weed lists. Those that do, do not use the same standards of importance and are not comparable. States typically have included plants that interfere with agriculture (Canada thistle), or cause human health problems (poison ivy). Some States are now including a category of plants that invade and degrade the environment (purple loosestrife). Check with your State's Agriculture Department or Weed Scientist listed below. The noxious weed list can be used two ways on roadsides: l) check to not inadvertantly plant these invasive plants, and 2) note the plants you are legally responsible to control. Many States now check adjacent State lists to avoid planting their neighbors' problem plants. Because weeds do not respect political boundaries, and because by their very nature weeds continue to adapt and expand, monitoring and controlling invasives at State borders is a wise part of vegetation management.

(Weed and Seed Laws)

Department of Agriculture
Division of Plant Industry
2800 N. Lincoln Boulevard
Oklahoma City, OK 73105

Thomas F. Peeper
Agronomy Dept.
Oklahoma State University
Stillwater, OK 74078
(405) 744-6417

OKLAHOMA RESOURCES

Natural Heritage Inventory
Oklahoma Biological Survey
111 East Chesapeake Street
University of Oklahoma
Norman, OK 73019
(405) 325-1985

The Nature Conservancy Field office
23 West Fourth, Ste. 200
Tulsa, OK 74103
(918) 585-1117

Oklahoma Native Plant Society
2435 S. Peoria Avenue
Tulsa, OK 74114

Redbud Valley Nature Preserve
161 East Avenue
Tulsa, OK 74115

Oxley Nature Center
6700 E. Mohawk Boulevard
Tulsa, OK 74115

POTENTIAL NATURAL VEGETATION ZONES IN
OREGON

Source: A.W. Kuchler's Potential Natural Vegetation Map, 1964, Revised 1985.
Presented in U.S.G.S. National Atlas of the U.S. Series,
U.S. Geological Survey, Reston, VA.

1 Spruce-cedar-hemlock forest (*Picea-Thuja-Tsuga*)	**14** Western spruce-fir forest (*Picea-Abies*)
2 Cedar-hemlock-Douglas fir forest (*Thuja-Tsuga-Pseudotsuga*)	**22** Oregon oakwoods (*Quercus*)
3 Silver fir-Douglas fir forest (*Abies-Pseudotsuga*)	**24** Mosaic of numbers 2 and 22
4 Fir-hemlock forest (*Abies-Tsuga*)	**34** Saltbush-greasewood (*Atriplex-Sarcobatus*)
5 Mixed conifer forest (*Abies-Pinus-Pseudotsuga*)	**43** Fescue-wheatgrass (*Festuca-Agropyron*)
10 Western ponderosa forest (*Pinus*)	**44** Wheatgrass-bluegrass (*Agropyron-Poa*)
11 Douglas fir forest (*Pseudotsuga*)	**45** Alpine meadows and barren (*Agrostis, Carex, Festuca, Poa*)
13 Grand fir-Douglas fir forest (*Abies-Pseudotsuga*)	**49** Sagebrush steppe (*Artemisia-Agropyron*)

417

(Dominant plant species present in each vegetation type are listed in Appendix 8)

1	Spruce-Cedar-Hemlock Forest (Picea-Thuja-Tsuga)
2	Cedar-Hemlock-Douglas Fir Forest (Thuja-Tsuga-Pseudotsuga)
3	Silver Fir-Douglas Fir Forest (Abies-Pseudotsuga)
4	Fir-Hemlock Forest (Abies-Tsuga)
5	Mixed Conifer Forest (Abies-Pinus-Pseudotsuga)
10	Western Ponderosa Forest (Pinus)
11	Douglas Fir Forest (Pseudotsuga)
13	Grand Fir-Douglas Fir Forest (Abies-Pseudotsuga)
14	Western Spruce-Fir Forest (Picea-Abies)
22	Oregon Oakwoods (Quercus)
24	Mosaic of 2 (Cedar-hemlock-Douglas fir forest) and 22 Oregon oakwoods)
34	Saltbrush-Geasewood (Artiplex-Sarcobatus)
43	Fescue-Wheatgrass (Festuca Agropyron)
44	Wheatgrass-Bluegrass (Agropyron-Poa)
45	Alpine Meadows and Barren (Agrostis, Carex, Festuca, Poa)
49	Sagebrush Steppe (Artemisia-Agropyron)

Botanical Expert

Sue Vrilakas, Botanist/Data Manager
Oregon Natural Heritage Program
Oregon Field Office
821 SE 14th Avenue
Portland, OR 97214
(503) 731-3070
(503) 230-9639 (fax)
internet: svrilakas@tnc.org

Recommended Flora

Cronquist, A. et al., 1997. Intermountain Flora: Vascular Plants of the Intermountain West, U.S.A: Vol. 3A: Rosidae (except for Fabales). New York Botanical Garden, New York.

Cronquist, A. et al., 1994. Intermountain Flora: Vascular Plants of the Intermountain West, U.S.A: Vol. 5: Asterales. New York Botanical Garden, New York. 496 pgs. + illus. maps. ISBN 0893273759.

Cronquist, A. et al., 1984. Intermountain Flora: Vascular Plants of the Intermountain West, U.S.A: Vol. 4: Asteridae (except for Asteroceae). New York Botanical Garden, New York. 573 pgs.

Cronquist, A. et al., 1989. Intermountain Flora: Vascular Plants of the Intermountain West, U.S.A. New York Botanical Garden, New York. 279 pgs. + illus. maps. ISBN 0893273473.

Cronquist, A. et al., 1977. Intermountain Flora: Vascular Plants of the Intermountain West, U.S.A: Vol. 6: The Monocotyledons. Columbia University Press, New York. 584 pgs. + illus. maps. ISBN 0231041209.

Cronquist, A. et al., 1972. Intermountain Flora: Vascular Plants of the Intermountain West, U.S.A: Vol. 1: Rosidae (except for Fabales). New York Botanical Garden, New York. 270 pgs.

Hitchcock, C.L. and A. Cronquist. 1974. Flora of the Pacific Northwest. University of Washington Press, Seattle, WA. 730 pgs. + illus.

Hickman, J.C. 1993. The Jepson Manual of Higher Plants of California, Revision and Update of 1925 Original Edition. University of California Press, Berkeley and Los Angeles, CA. 1400 pgs. ISBN: 0520082559.

NATIVE PLANTS FOR LANDSCAPE USE IN OREGON

Ferns

Adiantum pedatum (northern maidenhair fern)
Aspidotis densa (rock brake, cliff brake, Indian's dream)
Asplenium trichomanes (maidenhair spleenwort)
Athyrium filix-femina (lady fern)
Blechnum spicant (deer fern)
Cheilanthes gracillima (lace fern)
Cystopteris fragilis (fragile fern)
Dryopteris arguta (coast wood fern)
Dryopteris carthusiana (shield fern, toothed wood fern, spinulose shield fern)
Gymnocarpium dryopteris (oak fern)
Polypodium glycyrrhiza (licorice fern)
Polypodium scouleri (rock polypody)
Polystichum imbricans (dwarf western sword fern)
Polystichum munitum (western sword fern)
Woodwardia fimbriata (chain fern)

Forbs (annuals/biennials)

Clarkia amoena (farewell-to-spring, herald-of-summer)
Cleome serrulata (Rocky Mountain beeplant)
Collinsia parviflora var. grandiflora (blue lips)
Collomia grandiflora (collomia)
Erysimum capitatum (western wallflower, prairie rocket)
Gilia capitata (globe gilia, blue gilia)
Helianthus annuus (common sunflower)
Ipomopsis aggregata (sky rocket, scarlet gilia)
Lasthenia californica (goldfields)
Layia glandulosa (tidy tips)
Lupinus bicolor (pigmy-leaved lupine, miniature lupine)
Mentzelia laevicaulis (blazing star, evening star, stick leaf)
Mimulus guttatus (monkey flower)
Nemophila breviflora (Great Basin nemophila)
Nemophila menziesii (baby blue eyes)

Forbs (perennials)

Achlys triphylla (vanilla leaf)
Aconitum columbianum (western monkshood)
Allium cernuum (nodding onion)
Allium validum (swamp onion)
Anaphalis margaritacea (pearly everlasting)
Anemone multifida (early thimbleweed, cut-leaf anemone, Pacific anemone)
Antennaria spp. (pussytoes, everlasting)
Apocynum androsaemifolium (spreading dogbane)

Aquilegia flavescens (yellow columbine)
Aquilegia formosa (scarlet columbine)
Armeria maritima (sea pink, thrift)
Arnica cordifolia (heartleaf arnica)
Artemisia douglasiana (Douglas mugwort)
Artemisia ludoviciana (white sage, prairie sage, artemisia)
Aruncus dioicus var. vulgaris (sylvan goat's beard)
Asarum caudatum (wild ginger)
Aster ascendens (purple aster, Pacific aster)
Aster foliaceus (leafy aster)
Aster laevis (smooth aster)
Aster sibiricus (Sibirian or arctic aster)
Astragalus canadensis (milk vetch, Canada milk vetch)
Balsamorrhiza sagittata (balsamroot)
Calochortus macrocarpus (bigpod mariposa)
Caltha leptosepala (white marsh marigold, elkslip)
Caltha palustris ssp. palustris (marsh marigold, cowslip)
Campanula rotundifolia (harebell)
Castilleja angustifolia var. dubia (desert paintbrush)
Castilleja linariifolia (Indian paintbrush)
Castilleja sulphurea (splitleaf Indian paintbrush)
Claytonia lanceolata (spring beauty)
Clematis hirsutissima (clematis, vase flower, leather flower, lion's beard)
Clintonia uniflora (bride's bonnet, queen cup, bead lily)
Cornus canadensis (bunchberry)
Delphinium glareosum (delphinium)
Delphinium glaucum (tower larkspur)
Dicentra cucullaria (Dutchman's breeches)
Dichelostemma congestum (wild hyacinth)
Disporum smithii (fairy bells)
Dodecatheon hendersonii (Henderson's shooting stars)
Dodecatheon jeffreyi (Jeffrey's shooting stars)
Dryas octopetala (mountain dryas, White mountain avens)
Dugaldia hoopesii (orange sneezeweed, owls' claws)
Epilobium angustifolium (fireweed, willow herb)
Epilobium canum (California fuschia)
Epilobium obcordatum (rock fringe)
Erigeron compositus (alpine daisy)
Erigeron glaucus (seaside daisy)
Erigeron speciosus (showy fleabane)
Eriogonum umbellatum (sulfur buckwheat)
Eriophyllum lanatum (woolly sunflower, Oregon sunshine)
Erythronium grandiflorum (glacier lily, yellow fawn lily, dogtooth violet)
Erythronium oregonum (Oregon fawn lily)
Erythronium revolutum (bog fawn lily)
Eschscholzia californica (California poppy)
Fragaria chiloensis (coast strawberry)
Fritillaria lanceolata (checker lily, mission bells, chocolate lily)
Gaillardia aristata (blanket flower, gaillardia, brown-eyed Susan)
Galium triflorum (sweet-scented bedstraw)
Geranium viscossisimum (sticky wild geranium)
Glycyrrhiza lepidota (wild licorice)

Hedysarum boreale (sweet vetch, sweet broom)
Helenium autumnale (common sneezeweed)
Heterotheca villosa var. villosa (golden aster)
Heuchera micrantha (common alumroot)
Iris douglasiana (Douglas iris, western iris)
Iris missouriensis (Rocky Mountain iris, western blue flag)
Iris tenax (Oregon iris)
Lewisia rediviva (bitter root)
Lilium columbianum (Columbia lily, Oregon lily, wild tiger lily)
Linnaea borealis (twinflower)
Linum lewisii (wild blue flax)
Luetkea pectinata (Alaska spiraea, partridge foot)
Lupinus argenteus (silvery lupine)
Lupinus caudatus (tailcup lupine)
Lupinus polyphyllus (meadow lupine, bog lupine)
Lysichiton americanus (skunk cabbage)
Maianthemum dilatatum (false lily-of-the-valley)
Maianthemum racemosum ssp. racemosum (false Solomon's seal,
    false spikenard)
Maianthemum stellatum (starry Solomon's seal)
Mertensia ciliata (mountain bluebells)
Mimulus cardinalis (crimson monkey flower)
Mimulus lewisii (Lewis monkey flower, great purple monkey flower)
Mimulus primuloides (primrose monkey flower)
Minuartia obtusiloba (cushion sandwort)
Monardella odoratissima (coyote mint, mountain pennyroyal)
Myosotis asiatica (forget-me-not)
Nothochelone nemorosa (woodland penstemon)
Oenothera cespitosa (gumbo evening primrose, gumbo lily)
Oenothera flava (shortfin evening primrose)
Osmorhiza berteroi (mountain sweet cicely)
Oxalis oregana (redwood sorrel)
Pedicularis groenlandica (elephant heads)
Penstemon azureus (azure penstemon)
Penstemon fruticosus (shrubby penstemon)
Penstemon rupicola (penstemon)
Penstemon serrulatus (Cascade penstemon, coast penstemon)
Penstemon speciosus (sagebrush penstemon)
Pentaphylloides floribunda (potentilla, shrubby cinquefoil)
Petrophyton caespitosum (dwarf spiraea, petrophytum, tufted rockmat)
Phacelia bolanderi (flowered grape leaf)
Phacelia sericea (silky phacelia)
Phlox diffusa (mat phlox)
Phlox speciosa (showy phlox)
Polemonium occidentale (Jacob's ladder)
Polemonium pulcherrimum (alpine Jacob's ladder, skunk leaf)
Polemonium viscosum (sky pilot)
Potentilla arguta (white cinquefoil, prairie cinquefoil, tall cinquefoil)
Ranunculus alismaefolius (meadow buttercup)
Satureja douglasii (yerba buena)
Saxifraga bronchialis (spotted saxifrage, matted saxifrage)
Saxifraga cespitosa (tufted saxifrage)

Saxifraga oppositifolia (purple saxifrage)
Sedum spathulifolium (common stonecrop, broad-leaved sedum)
Sidalcea neomexicana (checker mallow, prairie mallow)
Silene acaulis (moss campion)
Silene californica (California Indian pink)
Silene hookeri (Hooker's pink, ground pink)
Sisyrinchium bellum (blue-eyed grass)
Sisyrinchium californicum (golden-eyed grass)
Solidago californica (California goldenrod)
Solidago canadensis (meadow goldenrod)
Solidago missouriensis (Missouri goldenrod, prairie goldenrod)
Solidago multiradiata (northern goldenrod, mountain goldenrod)
Sphaeralcea grossulariifolia (gooseberry leaf globemallow)
Sphaeralcea munroana (Munro's globe mallow, white-leaved globe mallow)
Streptopus roseus (rosy twisted stalk)
Tellima grandiflora (fringe cup)
Thalictrum fendleri var. polycarpum (meadow rue)
Thermopsis macrophylla (false lupine)
Thermopsis rhombifolia var. montana (golden pea, buckbean)
Tiarella trifoliata var. unifoliata (sugar scoop, western foam flower)
Tolmiea menziesii (piggyback plant, youth-on-age, thousand mothers)
Trientalis borealis ssp. latifolia (western starflower)
Trillium ovatum (coast trillium, western wakerobin)
Vancouveria hexandra (inside-out flower)
Viola glabella (smooth yellow or stream violet)
Viola macloskeyi (white mountain violet)
Viola nuttallii (yellow violet)
Viola vallicola (yellow violet)
Whipplea modesta (whipplevine, modesty, yerba de selva)
Wyethia angustifolia (narrowleaf mule ears)
Xerophyllum tenax (beargrass)
Zizia aptera (heart-leaved golden alexanders)

Grasses/Grass-like plants

Agrostis exarata (spikebent, spike red top)
Agrostis scabra (ticklegrass, fly-away grass)
Aristida purpurea var. longiseta (red three awn)
Bromus carinatus (California brome)
Calamagrostis canadensis (bluejoint grass)
Carex aquatilis (water sedge)
Carex macrocephala (bighead sedge)
Carex nebrascensis (Nebraska sedge)
Carex stipata (awl-fruited sedge)
Carex utriculata (beaked sedge)
Carex vernacula (sedge)
Danthonia californica (California oatgrass)
Danthonia intermedia (timber oatgrass)
Danthonia spicata (poverty grass)
Deschampsia cespitosa (tufted hairgrass)
Dichanthelium acuminatum var. acuminatum (panic grass)
Distichlis spicata (seashore saltgrass)
Eleocharis palustris (creeping spikesedge, spike rush)

Elymus canadensis (Canada wild rye)
Elymus glaucus (blue wild rye)
Elymus lanceolatus (thickspike wheatgrass)
Festuca californica (California fescue)
Festuca idahoensis (Idaho fescue, blue bunchgrass)
Glyceria grandis (American mannagrass, tall mannagrass, reed meadowgrass)
Hierochloe occidentalis (vanilla grass, California sweet grass)
Hierochloe odorata (sweet grass)
Juncus dubius (little bamboo)
Koeleria macrantha (June grass)
Leersia oryzoides (rice cut grass)
Leymus cinereus (Great Basin wild rye)
Leymus mollis (American dune grass, beach wild rye)
Oryzopsis hymenoides (Indian ricegrass)
Pascopyrum smithii (western wheatgrass)
Phleum alpinum (alpine timothy)
Poa alpina (alpine bluegrass)
Poa secunda (pine bluegrass)
Pseudoroegneria spicata (bluebunch wheatgrass)
Rhynchospora colorata (star-rush whitetop)
Scirpus acutus (hardstem bulrush)
Scirpus maritimus (alkali bulrush, prairie bulrush, bayonet grass)
Scirpus tabernaemontani (great bulrush)
Spartina pectinata (prairie cordgrass, freshwater cordgrass)
Sporobolus airoides (alkali sacaton)
Sporobolus compositus var. compositus (tall dropseed)
Sporobolus cryptandrus (sand dropseed)
Stipa comata (needle-and-thread grass)
Stipa nelsonii (Columbia needlegrass)
Trisetum spicatum (spike trisetum)
Typha latifolia (cattail)

Shrubs (deciduous)

Alnus viridis ssp. sinuata (Sitka alder, mountain alder)
Amelanchier alnifolia (saskatoon, western serviceberry, Juneberry)
Amelanchier utahensis (Utah serviceberry)
Atriplex canescens (four-wing saltbush, wingscale)
Atriplex confertifolia (spiny saltbush, shadscale saltbush, hop sage)
Baccharis pilularis (chaparral broom)
Betula nana (bog birch, dwarf birch)
Ceanothus integerrimus (deer brush)
Ceanothus sanguineus (redstem ceanothus, wild lilac)
Chamaebatiaria millefolium (fernbush, desert sweet, tansy bush)
Chrysothamnus nauseosus (rabbit brush, chamisa)
Cornus sericea (red-twig dogwood, red-osier dogwood)
Corylus cornuta (beaked hazelnut or filbert)
Crataegus douglasii (black hawthorn)
Empetrum nigrum (crowberry)
Ephedra viridis (Mormon tea)
Holodiscus discolor (cream bush, ocean spray, mountain spray)
Holodiscus dumosus (bush rock-spires, cream bush, ocean spray)
Krascheninnikovia lanata (winterfat)

Lonicera involucrata (black twinberry, bear berry honeysuckle)
Oemleria cerasiformis (Indian plum, oso berry)
Philadelphus lewisii (wild mock orange, syringa)
Physocarpus capitatus (western ninebark)
Physocarpus malvaceus (mallow ninebark)
Prunus virginiana (chokecherry)
Purshia tridentata (antelope brush)
Rhododendron occidentale (western azalea)
Rhus glabra (smooth sumac)
Rhus trilobata (squawbush, basketbush, skunkbush)
Ribes aureum (golden currant)
Ribes cereum (wax currant, western red currant, squaw currant)
Ribes laxiflorum (trailing black currant)
Ribes menziesii (chaparral currant)
Ribes sanguineum (pink-flowered currant, red flowering currant)
Rosa californica (California rose)
Rosa nutkana (nootka rose)
Rosa woodsii (western wild rose, woods rose)
Rubus idaeus ssp. strigosus (red raspberry)
Rubus parviflorus (western thimbleberry)
Rubus spectabilis (salmon berry)
Rubus ursinus (western blackberry)
Salix arctica (arctic willow)
Salix bebbiana (Bebb willow, long-beaked willow)
Salix scouleriana (western pussy willow, Scouler's willow)
Salvia dorrii (grayball sage)
Sambucus cerulea (blue elderberry)
Sambucus racemosa var. melanocarpa (black elderberry)
Sarcobatus vermiculatus (greasewood)
Shepherdia argentea (silver buffaloberry)
Shepherdia canadensis (buffaloberry)
Sorbus scopulina (western mountain ash)
Spiraea douglasii (western spiraea, hardhack spiraea)
Spiraea splendens var. splendens (subalpine spiraea)
Symphoricarpos albus (snowberry)
Vaccinium parvifolium (red huckleberry)
Vaccinium uliginosum (alpine blueberry, bog blueberry)
Viburnum edule (moosewood viburnum)

Shrubs (evergreen)

Arctostaphylos columbiana (hairy manzanita)
Arctostaphylos nevadensis (pinemat manzanita)
Arctostaphylos patula (greenleaf manzanita)
Arctostaphylos uva-ursi (bearberry, kinnikinnik)
Artemisia tridentata (big sagebrush, Great Basin sagebrush)
Castanopsis sempervirens (Sierra chinquapin, bush chinquapin)
Ceanothus thyrsiflorus (blue blossom)
Ceanothus velutinus (mountain balm, buckbush)
Cercocarpus ledifolius (curl-leaf mountain mahogany)
Cercocarpus montanus (mountain mahogany, silverleaf mountain mahogany)
Frangula californica ssp. californica (coffeeberry)
Garrya elliptica (silk-tassel bush)

Gaultheria shallon (salal)
Grayia spinosa (spiny hopsage)
Juniperus communis (common juniper)
Kalmia polifolia (swamp laurel, bog laurel)
Ledum glandulosum (Labrador tea, muskeg tea)
Mahonia aquifolium (Oregon grape)
Mahonia nervosa var. nervosa (Cascade Oregon grape)
Myrica californica (California wax myrtle)
Pachystima myrsinites (Oregon box, myrtle boxwood, mountain lover)
Phyllodoce empetriformis (pink mountain heather)
Rhododendron macrophyllum (Pacific rhododendron, California rose-bay)
Vaccinium ovatum (evergreen huckleberry)

Trees (deciduous)

Acer circinatum (Oregon vine maple)
Acer glabrum (Rocky Mountain maple)
Acer macrophyllum (bigleaf maple, canyon maple)
Alnus rhombifolia (white alder)
Betula occidentalis (mountain birch, water birch)
Betula papyrifera (paper birch)
Celtis laevigata var. reticulata (netleaf hackberry)
Cornus nuttallii (Pacific dogwood, mountain dogwood)
Fraxinus latifolia (Oregon ash)
Larix occidentalis (western larch, western tamarack)
Populus balsamifera (black cottonwood)
Populus tremuloides (quaking aspen)
Quercus garryana (Oregon post oak)
Quercus kelloggii (California black oak)

Trees (evergreen)

Abies concolor (western white fir)
Abies grandis (grand fir, giant fir)
Abies lasiocarpa (subalpine fir)
Abies procera (noble fir)
Arbutus menziesii (Pacific madrone, Oregon laurel, Laurelwood)
Calocedrus decurrens (incense cedar)
Chamaecyparis lawsoniana (Lawson falsecypress, Port Orford cedar)
Chamaecyparis nootkatensis (Alaska cedar, yellow cedar, nootka cedar)
Juniperus scopulorum (Rocky Mountain juniper)
Lithocarpus densiflorus (tanbark oak)
Picea breweriana (Brewer's spruce, weeping spruce)
Picea engelmannii (Engelmann spruce)
Picea sitchensis (Sitka spruce)
Pinus attenuata (knobcone pine)
Pinus contorta var. contorta (beach pine)
Pinus contorta var. murrayana (lodgepole pine)
Pinus flexilis (limber pine)
Pinus lambertiana (sugar pine)
Pinus monticola (western white pine)
Pinus ponderosa (ponderosa pine)
Pseudotsuga menziesii (Douglas fir)
Quercus chrysolepis (canyon live oak)

Sequoia sempervirens (redwood)
Taxus brevifolia (western yew, Pacific yew)
Thuja plicata (western red cedar)
Tsuga heterophylla (western hemlock)
Tsuga mertensiana (mountain hemlock)
Umbellularia californica (California bay laurel, myrtle)

Vines (deciduous)

Clematis ligusticifolia (clematis)
Lonicera ciliosa (orange honeysuckle)
Vitis californica (California wild grape)

FEDERALLY LISTED ENDANGERED SPECIES

Applegate's milk-vetch (Astragalus applegatei)
Bradshaw's desert-parsley (lomatium) (Lomatium bradshawii)
MacFarlane's four-o'clock (Mirabilis macfarlanei)
Marsh sandwort (Arenaria paludicola)
Nelson's checker-mallow (Sidalcea nelsoniana)
Water howellia (Howellia aquatilis)
Western lily (Lilium occidental)

OREGON NOXIOUS SPECIES

Because the noxious weed lists have continually changed since we gathered them in 1994, we are not including them at this time. Not all States have noxious weed lists. Those that do, do not use the same standards of importance and are not comparable. States typically have included plants that interfere with agriculture (Canada thistle), or cause human health problems (poison ivy). Some States are now including a category of plants that invade and degrade the environment (purple loosestrife). Check with your State's Agriculture Department or Weed Scientist listed below. The noxious weed list can be used two ways on roadsides: I) check to not inadvertently plant these invasive plants, and 2) note the plants you are legally responsible to control. Many States now check adjacent State lists to avoid planting their neighbors' problem plants. Because weeds do not respect political boundaries, and because by their very nature weeds continue to adapt and expand, monitoring and controlling invasives at State borders is a wise part of vegetation management.

(Weed and Seed Laws)

Department of Agriculture
Division of Plant Industry
635 Capitol Street, NE
Salem, OR 97310

Larry Larson
OSU Agriculture Program
Eastern Oregon State College
LaGrande, OR 997850
(541) 962-3547

Natural Heritage Program
821 SE 14th Avenue
Portland, OR 97
(503) 731-3070

The Nature Conservancy of Oregon
821 SE 14th Avenue
Portland, OR 97214
(503) 230-1221

Native Plant Society of Oregon
2584 N.W. Savier St.
Portland, OR 97210

Natural Areas Association
P.O. Box 1504
Bend, OR 97709

Castle Crest Wildflower Garden
Crater Lake National Park
East Rim Drive
Crater Lake, OR 97604

Oregon State University Herbarium
2082 Cordley Hall
Corvallis, OR 97331-2902
(541) 737-4106

Oregon Dept. of Agriculture
Endangered Plant Species Program
635 Capitol St. NE
Salem OR 97310-0110
(503) 986-4716

Berry Botanic Garden
11505 SW Summerville Avenue
Portland, OR 97219

Leach Botanical Garden
6704 SE 122nd Avenue
Portland, OR 97236

Mount Pisgah Arboretum
Howard Buford Recreational Area
33735 Seavey Loop Road
Eugene, OR 97405

POTENTIAL NATURAL VEGETATION ZONES IN
PENNSYLVANIA

Source: A.W. Kuchler's Potential Natural Vegetation Map, 1964, Revised 1985.
Presented in U.S.G.S. National Atlas of the U.S. Series,
U.S. Geological Survey, Reston, VA.

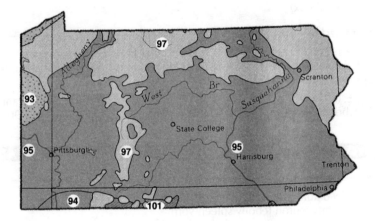

 93 Beech-maple forest
(Fagus-Acer)

 94 Mixed mesophytic forest
(Acer-Aesculus-Fagus-Liriodendron-Quercus-Tilia)

95 Appalachian oak forest
(Quercus)

97 Northern hardwoods
(Acer-Betula-Fagus-Tsuga)

 101 Oak-hickory-pine forest
(Quercus-Carya-Pinus)

VEGETATION REFERENCES

(Dominant plant species present in each vegetation type are listed in Appendix 8)

93   Beech-Maple Forest (Fagus-Acer)
94   Mixed Mesophytic Forest (Acer-Aesculus-Fagus-Liriodendron-Quercus-Tilia)
95   Appalachian Oak Forest (Quercus)
97   Northern Hardwoods (Acer-Betula-Fagus-Tsuga)
101   Oak-Hickory-Pine Forest (Quercus-Carya-Pinus)

Botanical Expert

John Kunsman, Botanist
Pennsylvania Natural Diversity Inventory
PNDI-East
The Nature Conservancy
34 Airport Drive
Middletown, PA 17507
(717) 948-3962
(717) 948-3957 (fax)

Recommended Flora

Rhoads, A.F. and W.M. Klein. 1993. The Vascular Flora of Pennsylvania: Annotated Checklist and Atlas. American Philosophical Society. Philadelphia, PA. 636 pgs. + illus. ISBN 0871692074.

Wherry, E.T.; J.M. Fogg; H.A. Wahl. 1979. Atlas of the Flora of Pennsylvania. Morris Arboretum of the University of Pennsylvania. Philadelphia, PA. 390 pgs. maps.

NATIVE PLANTS FOR LANDSCAPE USE IN PENNSYLVANIA

Ferns

Adiantum pedatum (northern maidenhair fern)
Asplenium platyneuron (ebony spleenwort)
Asplenium trichomanes (maidenhair spleenwort)
Athyrium filix-femina (lady fern)
Botrychium virginianum (rattlesnake fern)
Cystopteris bulbifera (bladder fern)
Cystopteris fragilis (fragile fern)
Dennstaedtia punctilobula (hay-scented fern)
Dryopteris cristata (crested wood fern, buckler fern)
Dryopteris marginalis (marginal wood fern)
Gymnocarpium dryopteris (oak fern)
Onoclea sensibilis (sensitive fern, bead fern)
Osmunda cinnamomea (cinnamon fern)
Osmunda claytoniana (interrupted fern)
Osmunda regalis (royal fern)
Phegopteris hexagonoptera (broad beech fern)
Polystichum acrostichoides (Christmas fern)
Thelypteris novaboracensis (New York fern, tapering fern)
Thelypteris simulata (Massachusetts fern)
Woodsia ilvensis (rusty woodsia)
Woodwardia virginica (Virginia chain fern)

Forbs (annuals/biennials)

Campanulastrum americanum (American bellflower, tall bellflower)
Corydalis sempervirens (pale corydalis)
Gentianopsis crinita (fringed gentian)
Lobelia spicata (pale lobelia)
Oenothera biennis (common evening primrose)
Rudbeckia hirta (black-eyed Susan)

Forbs (perennials)

Acorus calamus (sweet flag, calamus)
Actaea pachypoda (white baneberry)
Ageratina altissima var. altissima (white snakeroot)
Allium canadense (wild garlic)
Allium cernuum (nodding onion)
Allium tricoccum (wild leek)
Anaphalis margaritacea (pearly everlasting)
Anemone canadensis (Canada anemone, windflower)
Anemone virginiana (thimbleweed, tall anemone)
Antennaria spp. (pussytoes, everlasting)
Apocynum androsaemifolium (spreading dogbane)
Aquilegia canadensis (columbine)
Arisaema triphyllum (Jack-in-the-pulpit, Indian turnip)
Aruncus dioicus (goat's beard)
Asarum canadense (wild ginger)
Asclepias incarnata (swamp milkweed)
Asclepias tuberosa (butterfly weed)
Asclepias verticillata (whorled milkweed)
Aster divaricatus (white wood aster)
Aster laevis (smooth aster)
Aster novae-angliae (New England aster)
Aster oblongifolius (aromatic aster)
Aster pilosus (frost aster)
Aster puniceus (red-stem aster, swamp aster)
Baptisia australis (blue wild indigo)
Caltha palustris (marsh marigold, cowslip)
Campanula rotundifolia (harebell)
Cardamine diphylla (two-leaved toothwort)
Caulophyllum thalictroides (blue cohosh)
Chelone glabra (turtlehead)
Cimicifuga racemosa (bugbane, black cohosh)
Claytonia caroliniana (broad-leaved spring beauty)
Claytonia virginica (narrow-leaved spring beauty)
Clintonia borealis (clintonia, blue-bead lily)
Collinsonia canadensis (stoneroot, citronella horsebalm)
Coptis trifolia ssp. groenlandica (goldthread)
Coreopsis tripteris (tall coreopsis)
Cornus canadensis (bunchberry)
Delphinium tricorne (dwarf larkspur)
Desmodium canadense (Canada tick-trefoil, Canada tickclover)
Dicentra cucullaria (Dutchman's breeches)
Dodecatheon meadia (shooting star)
Epilobium angustifolium (fireweed, willow herb)

Erythronium americanum (eastern trout lily, yellow trout lily)
Eupatorium fistulosum (Joe-pye weed)
Eupatorium maculatum (spotted Joe-pye weed)
Eupatorium perfoliatum (boneset)
Eupatorium purpureum (Joe-pye weed)
Euphorbia corollata (flowering spurge)
Euthamia graminifolia var. graminifolia (grass-leaved goldenrod)
Fragaria virginiana (wild strawberry)
Galium triflorum (sweet-scented bedstraw)
Gentiana andrewsii (bottle gentian)
Gentiana clausa (bottle gentian)
Geranium maculatum (wild geranium, cranesbill)
Geum rivale (purple avens, water avens)
Helenium autumnale (common sneezeweed)
Helianthus simulans (narrow-leaved sunflower, swamp sunflower)
Heliopsis helianthoides (ox-eye sunflower, false sunflower)
Hepatica nobilis var. acuta (sharp-lobed hepatica)
Hibiscus moscheutos (swamp rose mallow, marshmallow hibiscus)
Houstonia caerulea (bluets)
Houstonia longifolia var. longifolia (long-leaved bluets, pale bluets)
Hydrophyllum virginianum (Virginia waterleaf)
Hypericum ascyron (great St. John's wort)
Hypoxis hirsuta (yellow star grass)
Iris versicolor (blue flag)
Iris virginica var. shrevei (blue flag)
Lespedeza capitata (roundheaded bush clover)
Liatris spicata (marsh blazing star, gayfeather)
Lilium canadense (wild yellow lily, Canada lily)
Lilium philadelphicum (wood lily)
Linum virginianum (woodland flax)
Lithospermum canescens (hoary puccoon)
Lobelia cardinalis (cardinal flower)
Lobelia siphilitica (great blue lobelia)
Lupinus perennis (wild lupine)
Lysimachia ciliata (fringed loosestrife)
Maianthemum canadense (wild lily-of-the-valley, Canada mayflower)
Maianthemum racemosum ssp. racemosum (false Solomon's seal,
    false spikenard)
Maianthemum stellatum (starry Solomon's seal)
Mertensia virginica (bluebells)
Mitchella repens (partridge berry)
Monarda didyma (beebalm, oswego tea)
Monarda fistulosa (wild bergamot, horsemint, beebalm)
Nuphar lutea (yellow pond lily, cow lily, spatter dock)
Oenothera fruticosa (sundrops)
Osmorhiza claytoni (sweet cicely, sweet jarvil)
Peltandra virginica (arrow arum)
Penstemon digitalis (beardtongue)
Penstemon hirsutus (hairy beardtongue)
Phlox divaricata (blue woodland phlox, sweet William)
Phlox paniculata (summer phlox, perennial phlox)
Phlox stolonifera (creeping phlox)

Physostegia virginiana (obedient plant, false dragonhead)
Podophyllum peltatum (May apple)
Polemonium reptans (Jacob's ladder, Greek valerian)
Polygonatum biflorum (Solomon's seal)
Potentilla arguta (white cinquefoil, prairie cinquefoil, tall cinquefoil)
Potentilla simplex (common cinquefoil)
Pycnanthemum tenuifolium (slender mountain mint)
Pycnanthemum virginianum (mountain mint)
Pyrola elliptica (shinleaf)
Rhexia virginica (meadow beauty)
Rudbeckia fulgida (black-eyed Susan, orange coneflower)
Rudbeckia laciniata (cut-leaf coneflower)
Salvia lyrata (cancer weed, lyre-leaf sage)
Sanguinaria candensis (bloodroot)
Sedum ternatum (wild stonecrop)
Senecio aureus (golden ragwort)
Silene stellata (starry campion)
Silene virginica (fire pink)
Sisyrinchium angustifolium (narrow-leaved blue-eyed grass)
Solidago caesia (blue-stemmed goldenrod, wreath goldenrod)
Solidago canadensis (meadow goldenrod)
Solidago juncea (early goldenrod, plume goldenrod)
Solidago nemoralis (gray goldenrod, old-field goldenrod)
Solidago odora (sweet goldenrod)
Solidago rugosa (rough-leaved goldenrod)
Solidago speciosa (showy goldenrod)
Solidago ulmifolia (elm-leaved goldenrod)
Streptopus roseus (rosy twisted stalk)
Tephrosia virginiana (goat's rue)
Thalictrum dioicum (early meadow rue)
Thalictrum pubescens (tall meadow rue)
Thalictrum thalictroides (rue anemone)
Tiarella cordifolia (foam flower)
Tradescantia ohiensis (Ohio spiderwort)
Tradescantia virginiana (Virginia spiderwort, spider lily)
Trientalis borealis ssp. borealis (starflower)
Trillium cernuum (nodding trillium)
Trillium erectum (wakerobin, purple trillium)
Trillium undulatum (painted trillium)
Uvularia grandiflora (bellwort, merrybells)
Uvularia sessilifolia (wildoats, merrybells)
Verbena hastata (blue verbena, blue vervain)
Vernonia noveboracensis (New York ironweed)
Veronicastrum virginicum (Culver's root)
Viola canadensis (Canada violet)
Viola conspersa (American dog violet)
Viola pedata (bird-foot violet)
Viola pubescens (downy or smooth yellow violet)
Viola soraria (common blue violet, meadow violet)
Zizia aptera (heart-leaved golden alexanders)
Zizia aurea (golden alexanders)

Grasses/Grass-like plants

Agrostis scabra (ticklegrass, fly-away grass)
Andropogon gerardii (big bluestem)
Andropogon virginicus (broom sedge)
Bromus kalmii (prairie brome, wild chess)
Calamagrostis canadensis (bluejoint grass)
Carex aquatilis (water sedge)
Carex pensylvanica (Pennsylvania sedge)
Carex plantaginea (plantain-leaved sedge)
Carex stipata (awl-fruited sedge)
Carex stricta (tussock sedge)
Carex utriculata (beaked sedge)
Danthonia spicata (poverty grass)
Deschampsia cespitosa (tufted hairgrass)
Eleocharis palustris (creeping spikesedge, spike rush)
Elymus canadensis (Canada wild rye)
Elymus hystrix var. hystrix (bottlebrush grass)
Eragrostis spectabilis (purple lovegrass, tumblegrass)
Glyceria grandis (American mannagrass, tall mannagrass, reed meadowgrass)
Juncus effusus var. solutus (soft rush)
Leersia oryzoides (rice cut grass)
Panicum virgatum (switchgrass)
Schizachyrium scoparium (little bluestem)
Scirpus acutus (hardstem bulrush)
Scirpus atrovirens (dark green bulrush)
Scirpus cyperinus (wool grass)
Scirpus tabernaemontani (great bulrush)
Sorghastrum nutans (Indian grass)
Spartina pectinata (prairie cordgrass, freshwater cordgrass)
Sporobolus asper (tall dropseed)
Sporobolus cryptandrus (sand dropseed)
Typha latifolia (cattail)

Shrubs (deciduous)

Alnus incana (speckled alder, mountain alder)
Alnus serrulata (smooth alder)
Amelanchier arborea (downy serviceberry, shadbush, Juneberry)
Aronia melanocarpa (black chokeberry)
Castanea pumila (chinquapin)
Ceanothus americanus (New Jersey tea, red root)
Cephalanthus occidentalis (buttonbush)
Clethra alnifolia (summer sweet)
Comptonia peregrina (sweet fern)
Cornus alternifolia (pogoda dogwood, alternate-leaved dogwood)
Cornus amomum ssp. obliqua (swamp dogwood, silky dogwood)
Cornus racemosa (gray dogwood)
Cornus sericea (red-twig dogwood, red-osier dogwood)
Corylus americana (American hazelnut or filbert)
Corylus cornuta (beaked hazelnut or filbert)
Diervilla lonicera (bush honeysuckle)
Dirca palustris (leatherwood, ropebark)
Euonymus americana (strawberry bush, brook euonymus, hearts-a-bustin')

Euonymus atropurpurea (wahoo, burning bush)
Hydrangea arborescens (wild hydrangea)
Hypericum hypericoides ssp. hypericoides (St. Andrew's cross)
Hypericum prolificum (shrubby St. John's wort)
Ilex verticillata (winterberry, black alder)
Lindera benzoin (spicebush)
Lonicera dioica (limber or wild honeysuckle)
Lyonia ligustrina (male-berry, male-blueberry)
Physocarpus opulifolius (ninebark)
Prunus virginiana (chokecherry)
Rhododendron arborescens (smooth azalea)
Rhododendron canadense (rhodora)
Rhododendron periclymenoides (pinxterbloom azalea)
Rhododendron prinophyllum (roseshell azalea, early azalea)
Rhododendron viscosum (swamp azalea)
Rhus aromatica (fragrant sumac)
Rhus copallinum (dwarf or winged sumac)
Rhus glabra (smooth sumac)
Rhus hirta (staghorn sumac)
Ribes cynosbati (prickly gooseberry, dogberry)
Rosa blanda (early wild rose, smooth rose)
Rosa carolina (Carolina rose)
Rubus idaeus ssp. strigosus (red raspberry)
Rubus occidentalis (black raspberry, thimbleberry)
Rubus odoratus (thimbleberry)
Salix bebbiana (Bebb willow, long-beaked willow)
Salix discolor (pussy willow)
Sambucus canadensis (elderberry, common elder)
Sambucus racemosa var. pubens (scarlet elderberry, red-berried elder)
Spiraea alba (meadow sweet)
Spiraea tomentosa (steeplebush, hardhack)
Staphylea trifolia (bladdernut)
Symphoricarpos albus (snowberry)
Vaccinium angustifolium (low-bush blueberry)
Vaccinium corymbosom (highbush blueberry)
Viburnum acerifolium (maple leaf viburnum)
Viburnum dentatum (southern arrowwood)
Viburnum lentago (black haw, nannyberry)
Viburnum nudum var. cassinoides (wild raisin)
Viburnum prunifolium (black haw, nanny berry)Shrubs (evergreen)
Epigaea repens (trailing arbutus)
Gaultheria procumbens (wintergreen, checkerberry)
Kalmia angustifolia (sheep laurel, lambkill kalmia)
Kalmia latifolia (mountain laurel)
Rhododendron maximum (rosebay, great laurel)
Taxus canadensis (Canada yew)

Trees (deciduous)

Acer negundo (box elder)
Acer pensylvanicum (striped maple)
Acer rubrum (red maple)
Acer saccharinum (silver maple)

Acer saccharum (sugar maple)
Acer spicatum (mountain maple)
Aesculus flava (sweet buckeye, yellow buckeye)
Aesculus glabra (Ohio buckeye, horse chestnut)
Betula lenta (cherry birch)
Betula nigra (river birch)
Betula papyrifera (paper birch)
Carpinus caroliniana (blue beech, hornbeam, musclewood)
Carya alba (mockernut hickory)
Carya cordiformis (bitternut, swamp hickory)
Carya ovata (shagbark hickory)
Celtis occidentalis (hackberry, sugarberry)
Cercis canadensis (redbud)
Cornus florida (flowering dogwood)
Crataegus crus-galli (cockspur hawthorn)
Crataegus mollis (downy hawthorn)
Crataegus punctata (dotted hawthorn, white thorn)
Diospyros virginiana (persimmon)
Fagus grandifolia var. caroliniana (beech)
Fraxinus americana (white ash)
Fraxinus pensylvanica (green ash)
Gleditsia triacanthos (honey locust)
Hamamelis virginiana (witch hazel)
Juglans cinerea (butternut, white walnut)
Juglans nigra (black walnut)
Larix laricina (tamarack, American larch)
Liquidambar styraciflua (sweet gum)
Liriodendron tulipifera (tulip tree)
Magnolia acuminata (cucumber tree)
Nyssa sylvatica (black gum, tupelo)
Ostrya virginiana (ironwood, hophornbeam)
Platanus occidentalis (sycamore, plane-tree)
Populus deltoides (eastern cottonwood)
Populus grandidentata (large-toothed aspen)
Populus tremuloides (quaking aspen)
Prunus americana (wild plum)
Prunus pensylvanica (fire or pin cherry)
Prunus serotina (black cherry)
Quercus alba (white oak)
Quercus bicolor (swamp white oak)
Quercus coccinea (scarlet oak)
Quercus macrocarpa (bur oak)
Quercus marilandica (blackjack oak)
Quercus muhlenbergii (chinkapin oak, chestnut oak)
Quercus palustris (pin oak)
Quercus phellos (willow oak)
Quercus rubra (red oak)
Quercus stellata (post oak)
Quercus velutina (black oak)
Salix amygdaloides (peachleaf willow)
Salix nigra (black willow)
Sassafras albidum (sassafras)

Sorbus americana (mountain ash)
Tilia americana (American linden, basswood)
Ulmus americana (American elm)
Ulmus rubra (red elm, slippery elm)

Trees (evergreen)

Abies balsamea (balsam fir)
Juniperus virginiana (eastern red cedar)
Pinus resinosa (red pine, Norway pine)
Pinus rigida (pitch pine)
Pinus strobus (eastern white pine)
Pinus virginiana (Virginia pine)
Tsuga canadensis (eastern hemlock)

Vines (deciduous)

Celastrus scandens (American bittersweet)
Clematis occidentalis var. occidentalis (purple clematis)
Clematis virginiana (virgin's bower)
Parthenocissus quinquefolia (Virginia creeper)
Vitis riparia (riverbank grape)

FEDERALLY LISTED ENDANGERED SPECIES

Northeastern (Barbed bristle) bulrush (Scirpus ancistrochaetus)
Small whorled pogonia (Isotria medeoloides)
Virginia spiraea (Spiraea virginiana)

PENNSYLVANIA NOXIOUS SPECIES

Because the noxious weed lists have continually changed since we gathered them in 1994, we are not including them at this time. Not all States have noxious weed lists. Those that do, do not use the same standards of importance and are not comparable. States typically have included plants that interfere with agriculture (Canada thistle), or cause human health problems (poison ivy). Some States are now including a category of plants that invade and degrade the environment (purple loosestrife). Check with your State's Agriculture Department or Weed Scientist listed below. The noxious weed list can be used two ways on roadsides: l) check to not inadvertantly plant these invasive plants, and 2) note the plants you are legally responsible to control. Many States now check adjacent State lists to avoid planting their neighbors' problem plants. Because weeds do not respect political boundaries, and because by their very nature weeds continue to adapt and expand, monitoring and controlling invasives at State borders is a wise part of vegetation management.

(Weed Law)

Department of Agriculture
Bureau of Plant Industry
2301 North Cameron Street
Harrisburg, PA 17110

William Curran, Agronomy
Penn State University
116 Agricultural Science Building
University Park, PA 16802
(814) 863-1014

PENNSYLVANIA RESOURCES

Natural Diversity Inventory
Bureau of Forestry
P.O. Box 8552
Harrisburg, PA 17105
(717) 783-0388

The Nature Conservancy Field Office
1100 E. Hector Street, Ste. 470
Conshohocken, PA 19428
(610) 834-1323

Pennsylvania Native Plant Society
1806 Commonwealth Building
316 Fourth Avenue
Pittsburgh, PA 15222

Brandywine Conservancy, Inc.
P.O. Box 141
Chadds Ford, PA 19317

Chesapeake Bay Foundation
214 State St.
Harrisburg, PA 17101

Bowman's Hill Wildflower Preserve
Route 32, River Road
New Hope, PA 18938

Art Gover, Roadside Research Project
Penn State University
University Park, PA 16802
(814) 863-1184

POTENTIAL NATURAL VEGETATION ZONES IN
PUERTO RICO

Source: Ecological Life Zones of Puerto Rico
J. J. Ewel & J. L. Whitmore 1993
USDA Forest Service

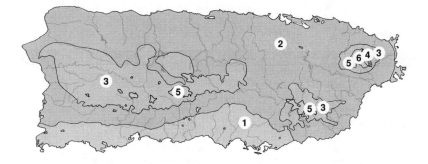

PR1	Subtropical dry forest *(Bosque seco subtropical)*	
PR2	Subtropical dry forest *(Bosque seco subtropical)*	
PR3	Subtropical wet forest *(Bosque muy humedo subtropic:*	
PR4	Subtropical rain forest *(Bosque pluvial subtropical)*	
PR5	Lower montane wet forest *(Bosque muy humedo montano*	
PR6	Lower montane rain forest *(Bosque pluvial montano bajo)*	

PR 1   Subtropical dry forest (Bosque seco subtropical)
PR 2   Subtropical moist forest (Bosque humedo subtropical)
PR 3   Subtropical wet forest (Bosque muy humedo subtropical)
PR 4   Subtropical rain forest (Bosque pluvial subtropical)
PR 5   Lower montane wet forest (Bosque muy humedo montano bajo)
PR 6   Lower montane rain forest (Bosque pluvial montano bajo)

Botanical Experts

Meriam Gonzales
Puerto Rico Heritage Program
Conservation Data Base
787-722-1726

Recommended Flora

Danserau, Pierre and Peter F. Buell. 1966. Studies on the vegetation of Puerto Rico. 1) Description and Integration of the Plant Communities; 2) Analysis and Mapping. University of Puerto Rico, Myagues.

Ecological Life Zones of Puerto Rico and the United States Virgin Islands: J. J. Ewel and J. L. Whitmore, 1973. United State Department of Agriculture. Forest Service. Institute of Tropical Forestry. Rio Piedras, Puerto Rico

NATIVE PLANTS FOR LANDSCAPE USE IN PUERTO RICO

Andira inermis
Buchenavia tetraphylla
Bucida buceras
Bursera simaruba
Byrsonima spicata
Calohyllum calaba
Cecropia schreberiana
Cedrela odorata
Ceiba pentandra
Chrysophyllum
Citharexylum fruticosum
Clusia rosea
Coccoloba uvifera
Conocarpus erecta
Cordia alba
Crescentia cujete
Dacryodes excelsa
Genipa americana
Guaiacum officinale
Guarea guidonia
Guazuma ulmifolia
Hernandia sonora
Hura crepitans
Hyeronima clusioides
Hymenaea courbaril

Inga vera
Juglans jamaicensis
Laguncularia racimosa
Mammea americana
Manilkara bidentata
Melicoccus bijugatus
Montezuma speciosissima
Ochroma pyramidale
Ocotea moschata
Petitia domingensis
Pimenta racimosa
Piptadenia peregrina
Pithecellobium arboreum
Pouteria multiflora
Prunus occidentalis
Rhizophora mangle
Roystonea borinquena
Sabal causiarum
Spondias mombiin
Stahlia monosperma
Tabebuia heterophylla
Tecoma stans
Thespia grandiflora
Zanthoxylum flavum

PUERTO RICO NOXIOUS SPECIES

Because the noxious weed lists have continually changed since we gathered them in 1994, we are not including them at this time. Not all States have noxious weed lists. Those that do, do not use the same standards of importance and are not comparable. States typically have included plants that interfere with agriculture (Canada thistle), or cause human health problems (poison ivy). Some States are now including a category of plants that invade and degrade the environment (purple loosestrife). Check with your State's Agriculture Department or Weed Scientist listed below. The noxious weed list can be used two ways on roadsides: l) check to not inadvertently plant these invasive plants, and 2) note the plants you are legally responsible to control. Many States now check adjacent State lists to avoid planting their neighbors' problem plants. Because weeds do not respect political boundaries, and because by their very nature weeds continue to adapt and expand, monitoring and controlling invasives at State borders is a wise part of vegetation management.

(No Laws)

Department of Agriculture
Plant Quarantine Services
P.O. Box 10163
Santurce, PR 00980

Yamil Oulijano, Ag. Ext.
University of Puerto Rico
Mayaguez, Box 305
Camuy, PR 00627
(787) 898-2270

PUERTO RICO RESOURCES

Frank Axelrod
Biology Department
University of Puerto Rico
787-764-0000

Ariel E. Lugo
USDA Forest Service
International Institute
of Tropical Forestry
Call Box 25,000
Rio Piedras, PR 00928-2500

Pedro Acevedo
Smithsonian
Washington D.C.
202-786-2692

Heritage Program
Department of Natural and
Environmental Resources
P.O. Box 5887
Puerta de Tierra Sta.
San Juan, PR 00906

The Nature Conservancy -
Virgin Islands
148 Norre Gade, 2nd Floor
Charlotte Amali, USCVI 00802
(809) 774-7633

The Puerto Rico Conservation
Foundation
G-11 O'Neill St.
San Juan, PR 00918

POTENTIAL NATURAL VEGETATION ZONES IN
RHODE ISLAND

Source: A.W. Kuchler's Potential Natural Vegetation Map, 1964, Revised 1985.
Presented in U.S.G.S. National Atlas of the U.S. Series,
U.S. Geological Survey, Reston, VA.

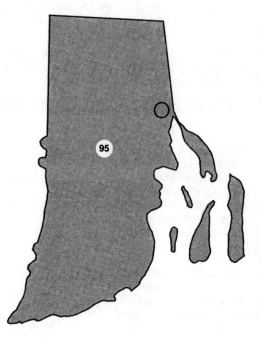

 Appalachian oak forest
(Quercus)

(Dominant plant species present in each vegetation type are listed in Appendix 8)

95 Appalachian Oak Forest (Quercus)

Botanical Expert

Rick Enser, Coordinator/Botanist
Rhode Island Natural Heritage Program
Rhode Island Department of Environmental Management
251 Promenade St.
Providence, RI 02903
(401) 277-2776 ext. 4308
(401) 277-2069 (fax)

Recommended Flora

Gould, L.L., R.W. Enser, R.E. Champlin, and I.S. Stuckey. 1998. Vascular Flora of Rhode Island: A List of Native and Naturalized Plants. Rhode Island Natural History Survey, Kingston, RI. 261 pgs. ISBN 1-887771-01-8.

Gleason, H.A.; A. Cronquist. 1991. Manual of Vascular Plants of Northeastern United States and Adjacent Canada, 2nd Edition. New York Botanical Garden, New York. 910 pgs. + map. ISBN 0893273651.

NATIVE PLANTS FOR LANDSCAPE USE IN RHODE ISLAND

Ferns

Athyrium filix-femina (lady fern)
Dennstaedtia punctilobula (hay-scented fern)
Dryopteris carthusiana (shield fern, toothed wood fern, spinulose shield fern)
Dryopteris cristata (crested wood fern, buckler fern)
Dryopteris marginalis (marginal wood fern)
Onoclea sensibilis (sensitive fern, bead fern)
Osmunda cinnamomea (cinnamon fern)
Osmunda claytoniana (interrupted fern)
Osmunda regalis (royal fern)
Phegopteris hexagonoptera (broad beech fern)
Polystichum acrostichoides (Christmas fern)
Thelypteris novaboracensis (New York fern, tapering fern)
Thelypteris simulata (Massachusetts fern)
Woodwardia areolata (netted chain fern)
Woodwardia virginica (Virginia chain fern)

Forbs (annuals/biennials)

Lobelia spicata (pale lobelia)
Oenothera biennis (common evening primrose)

Forbs (perennials)

Acorus calamus (sweet flag, calamus)
Ageratina altissima var. altissima (white snakeroot)
Allium canadense (wild garlic)
Anaphalis margaritacea (pearly everlasting)

Anemone cylindrica (thimbleweed, candle anemone)
Antennaria spp. (pussytoes, everlasting)
Apocynum androsaemifolium (spreading dogbane)
Aquilegia canadensis (columbine)
Arisaema triphyllum (Jack-in-the-pulpit, Indian turnip)
Asclepias incarnata (swamp milkweed)
Asclepias tuberosa (butterfly weed)
Asclepias verticillata (whorled milkweed)
Aster divaricatus (white wood aster)
Aster dumosus (bushy aster)
Aster ericoides (heath aster, white wreath aster)
Aster laevis (smooth aster)
Aster novae-angliae (New England aster)
Aster pilosus (frost aster)
Aster puniceus (red-stem aster, swamp aster)
Caltha palustris (marsh marigold, cowslip)
Campanula rotundifolia (harebell)
Chelone glabra (turtlehead)
Clintonia borealis (clintonia, blue-bead lily)
Coptis trifolia ssp. groenlandica (goldthread)
Cornus canadensis (bunchberry)
Desmodium canadense (Canada tick-trefoil, Canada tickclover)
Epilobium angustifolium (fireweed, willow herb)
Erythronium americanum (eastern trout lily, yellow trout lily)
Eupatorium fistulosum (Joe-pye weed)
Eupatorium maculatum (spotted Joe-pye weed)
Eupatorium perfoliatum (boneset)
Eupatorium purpureum (Joe-pye weed)
Euthamia graminifolia var. graminifolia (grass-leaved goldenrod)
Fragaria virginiana (wild strawberry)
Galium triflorum (sweet-scented bedstraw)
Geranium maculatum (wild geranium, cranesbill)
Geum rivale (purple avens, water avens)
Helianthus strumosus (woodland sunflower)
Houstonia caerulea (bluets)
Hypoxis hirsuta (yellow star grass)
Iris prismatica (slender blue flag, coastal iris)
Iris versicolor (blue flag)
Lespedeza capitata (roundheaded bush clover)
Lilium canadense (wild yellow lily, Canada lily)
Lilium philadelphicum (wood lily)
Linum virginianum (woodland flax)
Lobelia cardinalis (cardinal flower)
Lupinus perennis (wild lupine)
Lysimachia ciliata (fringed loosestrife)
Maianthemum canadense (wild lily-of-the-valley, Canada mayflower)
Maianthemum racemosum ssp. racemosum (false Solomon's seal,
    false spikenard)
Maianthemum stellatum (starry Solomon's seal)
Mitchella repens (partridge berry)
Monarda fistulosa (wild bergamot, horsemint, beebalm)
Nuphar lutea (yellow pond lily, cow lily, spatter dock)

Osmorhiza claytoni (sweet cicely, sweet jarvil)
Peltandra virginica (arrow arum)
Potentilla simplex (common cinquefoil)
Pycnanthemum tenuifolium (slender mountain mint)
Pycnanthemum virginianum (mountain mint)
Pyrola elliptica (shinleaf)
Rhexia virginica (meadow beauty)
Rudbeckia laciniata (cut-leaf coneflower)
Sibbaldiopsis tridentata (three-toothed cinquefoil)
Silene stellata (starry campion)
Sisyrinchium angustifolium (narrow-leaved blue-eyed grass)
Sisyrinchium mucronatum (eastern blue-eyed grass)
Solidago caesia (blue-stemmed goldenrod, wreath goldenrod)
Solidago juncea (early goldenrod, plume goldenrod)
Solidago nemoralis (gray goldenrod, old-field goldenrod)
Solidago odora (sweet goldenrod)
Solidago rigida (stiff goldenrod)
Solidago rugosa (rough-leaved goldenrod)
Solidago sempervirens (seaside goldenrod)
Solidago speciosa (showy goldenrod)
Solidago ulmifolia (elm-leaved goldenrod)
Thalictrum dasycarpum (tall or purple meadow rue)
Thalictrum dioicum (early meadow rue)
Thalictrum pubescens (tall meadow rue)
Trientalis borealis ssp. borealis (starflower)
Trillium cernuum (nodding trillium)
Uvularia sessilifolia (wildoats, merrybells)
Verbena hastata (blue verbena, blue vervain)
Viola conspersa (American dog violet)
Viola pedata (bird-foot violet)
Viola pubescens (downy or smooth yellow violet)
Viola soraria (common blue violet, meadow violet)

Grasses/Grass-like plants

Agrostis scabra (ticklegrass, fly-away grass)
Andropogon gerardii (big bluestem)
Andropogon glomeratus (bushy bluestem)
Andropogon virginicus (broom sedge)
Calamagrostis canadensis (bluejoint grass)
Carex pensylvanica (Pennsylvania sedge)
Carex stipata (awl-fruited sedge)
Carex stricta (tussock sedge)
Carex utriculata (beaked sedge)
Danthonia spicata (poverty grass)
Deschampsia cespitosa (tufted hairgrass)
Distichlis spicata (seashore saltgrass)
Eleocharis palustris (creeping spikesedge, spike rush)
Elymus hystrix var. hystrix (bottlebrush grass)
Eragrostis spectabilis (purple lovegrass, tumblegrass)
Hierochloe odorata (sweet grass)
Juncus effusus var. solutus (soft rush)
Leersia oryzoides (rice cut grass)

Panicum virgatum (switchgrass)
Schizachyrium scoparium (little bluestem)
Scirpus acutus (hardstem bulrush)
Scirpus atrovirens (dark green bulrush)
Scirpus cyperinus (wool grass)
Scirpus maritimus (alkali bulrush, prairie bulrush, bayonet grass)
Scirpus tabernaemontani (great bulrush)
Sorghastrum nutans (Indian grass)
Spartina patens (marsh hay cordgrass, salt meadow cordgrass)
Spartina pectinata (prairie cordgrass, freshwater cordgrass)
Sporobolus compositus var. compositus (tall dropseed)
Trisetum spicatum (spike trisetum)
Typha angustifolia (narrow-leaved cattail)
Typha latifolia (cattail)

Shrubs (deciduous)

Alnus incana (speckled alder, mountain alder)
Alnus serrulata (smooth alder)
Amelanchier arborea (downy serviceberry, shadbush, Juneberry)
Aronia melanocarpa (black chokeberry)
Baccharis halimifolia (sea myrtle, groundsel bush)
Ceanothus americanus (New Jersey tea, red root)
Cephalanthus occidentalis (buttonbush)
Clethra alnifolia (summer sweet)
Cornus alternifolia (pogoda dogwood, alternate-leaved dogwood)
Cornus amomum ssp. obliqua (swamp dogwood, silky dogwood)
Cornus racemosa (gray dogwood)
Corylus americana (American hazelnut or filbert)
Corylus cornuta (beaked hazelnut or filbert)
Diervilla lonicera (bush honeysuckle)
Ilex verticillata (winterberry, black alder)
Lindera benzoin (spicebush)
Lonicera dioica (limber or wild honeysuckle)
Lyonia ligustrina (male-berry, male-blueberry)
Prunus virginiana (chokecherry)
Rhododendron canadense (rhodora)
Rhododendron viscosum (swamp azalea)
Rhus copallinum (dwarf or winged sumac)
Rhus glabra (smooth sumac)
Rhus hirta (staghorn sumac)
Rosa blanda (early wild rose, smooth rose)
Rosa carolina (Carolina rose)
Rubus idaeus ssp. strigosus (red raspberry)
Rubus occidentalis (black raspberry, thimbleberry)
Salix bebbiana (Bebb willow, long-beaked willow)
Salix discolor (pussy willow)
Sambucus canadensis (elderberry, common elder)
Sambucus racemosa var. pubens (scarlet elderberry, red-berried elder)
Spiraea tomentosa (steeplebush, hardhack)
Vaccinium angustifolium (low-bush blueberry)
Vaccinium corymbosom (highbush blueberry)
Viburnum acerifolium (maple leaf viburnum)

Viburnum dentatum (southern arrowwood)
Viburnum lentago (black haw, nannyberry)
Viburnum nudum (possumhaw viburnum)
Viburnum nudum var. cassinoides (wild raisin)

Shrubs (evergreen)

Arctostaphylos uva-ursi (bearberry, kinnikinnik)
Epigaea repens (trailing arbutus)
Gaultheria hispidula (creeping snowberry)
Gaultheria procumbens (wintergreen, checkerberry)
Ilex glabra (inkberry, bitter gallberry)
Juniperus communis (common juniper)
Kalmia angustifolia (sheep laurel, lambkill kalmia)
Kalmia latifolia (mountain laurel)
Rhododendron maximum (rosebay, great laurel)

Trees (deciduous)

Acer negundo (box elder)
Acer pensylvanicum (striped maple)
Acer rubrum (red maple)
Acer saccharinum (silver maple)
Acer saccharum (sugar maple)
Amelanchier canadensis (shadblow serviceberry, Juneberry)
Betula lenta (cherry birch)
Betula papyrifera (paper birch)
Carpinus caroliniana (blue beech, hornbeam, musclewood)
Carya alba (mockernut hickory)
Carya cordiformis (bitternut, swamp hickory)
Carya ovata (shagbark hickory)
Celtis occidentalis (hackberry, sugarberry)
Cornus florida (flowering dogwood)
Crataegus crus-galli (cockspur hawthorn)
Fagus grandifolia var. grandifolia (beech)
Fraxinus americana (white ash)
Fraxinus pensylvanica (green ash)
Hamamelis virginiana (witch hazel)
Juglans cinerea (butternut, white walnut)
Juglans nigra (black walnut)
Larix laricina (tamarack, American larch)
Liriodendron tulipifera (tulip tree)
Nyssa sylvatica (black gum, tupelo)
Ostrya virginiana (ironwood, hophornbeam)
Platanus occidentalis (sycamore, plane-tree)
Populus deltoides (eastern cottonwood)
Populus grandidentata (large-toothed aspen)
Populus tremuloides (quaking aspen)
Prunus americana (wild plum)
Prunus pensylvanica (fire or pin cherry)
Prunus serotina (black cherry)
Quercus alba (white oak)
Quercus bicolor (swamp white oak)
Quercus coccinea (scarlet oak)

Quercus rubra (red oak)
Quercus stellata (post oak)
Quercus velutina (black oak)
Salix nigra (black willow)
Sassafras albidum (sassafras)
Tilia americana (American linden, basswood)
Ulmus americana (American elm)
Ulmus rubra (red elm, slippery elm)

Trees (evergreen)

Abies balsamea (balsam fir)
Chamaecyparis thyoides (white cedar)
Ilex opaca (American holly, Christmas holly)
Juniperus virginiana (eastern red cedar)
Pinus resinosa (red pine, Norway pine)
Pinus rigida (pitch pine)
Pinus strobus (eastern white pine)
Tsuga canadensis (eastern hemlock)

Vines (deciduous)

Celastrus scandens (American bittersweet)
Clematis virginiana (virgin's bower)
Lonicera sempervirens (coral honeysuckle)
Parthenocissus quinquefolia (Virginia creeper)
Vitis riparia (riverbank grape)

FEDERALLY LISTED ENDANGERED SPECIES

Sandplain gerardia (Agalinis acuta)
Small whorled pogonia (Isotria medeoloides)

RHODE ISLAND NOXIOUS SPECIES

Because the noxious weed lists have continually changed since we gathered them in 1994, we are not including them at this time. Not all States have noxious weed lists. Those that do, do not use the same standards of importance and are not comparable. States typically have included plants that interfere with agriculture (Canada thistle), or cause human health problems (poison ivy). Some States are now including a category of plants that invade and degrade the environment (purple loosestrife). Check with your State's Agriculture Department or Weed Scientist listed below. The noxious weed list can be used two ways on roadsides: l) check to not inadvertantly plant these invasive plants, and 2) note the plants you are legally responsible to control. Many States now check adjacent State lists to avoid planting their neighbors' problem plants. Because weeds do not respect political boundaries, and because by their very nature weeds continue to adapt and expand, monitoring and controlling invasives at State borders is a wise part of vegetation management.

(Seed Law)

Department of Environmental Mgt.
Division of Agriculture
83 Park Street, 6th Floor
Providence, RI 02903

Raymond Taylorson
University of Rhode Island
Department of Plant Sciences
Kingston, RI 02881
(401) 792-2106

RHODE ISLAND RESOURCES

Natural Heritage Program
Department of Environmental
Management
235 Promenade Street
Providence, RI 02908
(401) 222-2776 ext. 4308

Rhode Island Wild Plant Society
P.O. Box 114
Peace Dale, RI 02883-0114
(401) 783-5895

The Nature Conservancy Field Office
45 South Angell Street
Providence, RI 02906
(410) 331-7110

Environment Council of Rhode Island
P.O. Box 8765
Providence, RI 02940

POTENTIAL NATURAL VEGETATION ZONES IN

— SOUTH CAROLINA —

Source: A.W. Kuchler's Potential Natural Vegetation Map, 1964, Revised 1985.
Presented in U.S.G.S. National Atlas of the U.S. Series,
U.S. Geological Survey, Reston, VA.

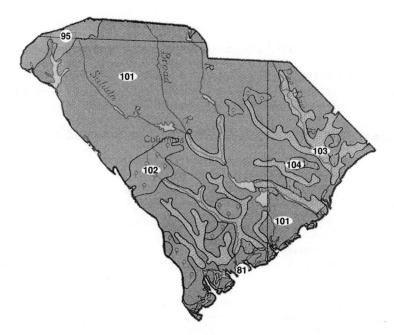

 81 Live oak-sea oats
(Quercus-Uniola)

95 Appalachian oak forest
(Quercus)

101 Oak-hickory-pine forest
(Quercus-Carya-Pinus)

 102 Southern mixed forest
(Fagus-Liquidambar-Magnolia-Pinus-Quercus)

 103 Southern floodplain forest
(Quercus-Nyassa-Taxodium)

104 Pocosin
(Pinus-Ilex)

VEGETATION REFERENCES

(Dominant plant species present in each vegetation type are listed in Appendix 8)

81   *Live Oak-Sea Oats (Quercus-Uniola)*
95   *Appalachian Oak Forest (Quercus)*
101 *Oak-Hickory-Pine Forest (Quercus-Carya-Pinus)*
102 *Southern Mixed Forest (Fagus-Liquidambar-Magnolia-Pinus-Quercus)*
103 *Southern Floodplain Forest (Quercus-Nyssa-Taxodium)*
104 *Pocosin (Pinus-Ilex)*

Botanical Expert

Albert Pittman, Botanist
Heritage Trust Program
P.O. Box 167
Columbia, SC 29202
(803) 734-3920
internet: pittman@water.dnr.state.sc.us

Recommended Flora

Radford, A.E.; H.E. Ahles; C.R. Bell. 1968. Manual of the Vascular Flora of the Carolinas. University of North Carolina Press: Chapel Hill, NC. 1183 pgs.

NATIVE PLANTS FOR LANDSCAPE USE IN SOUTH CAROLINA

Cactus

Opuntia humifusa (prickly pear)

Ferns

Adiantum capillus-veneris (southern maidenhair fern)
Adiantum pedatum (northern maidenhair fern)
Asplenium platyneuron (ebony spleenwort)
Asplenium trichomanes (maidenhair spleenwort)
Athyrium filix-femina (lady fern)
Botrychium virginianum (rattlesnake fern)
Dennstaedtia punctilobula (hay-scented fern)
Dryopteris carthusiana (shield fern, toothed wood fern, spinulose shield fern)
Dryopteris marginalis (marginal wood fern)
Onoclea sensibilis (sensitive fern, bead fern)
Osmunda cinnamomea (cinnamon fern)
Osmunda claytoniana (interrupted fern)
Osmunda regalis (royal fern)
Phegopteris hexagonoptera (broad beech fern)
Polystichum acrostichoides (Christmas fern)
Thelypteris kunthii (southern shield fern, wood fern, river fern)
Thelypteris novaboracensis (New York fern, tapering fern)
Woodwardia areolata (netted chain fern)
Woodwardia virginica (Virginia chain fern)

Forbs (annuals/biennials)

Campanulastrum americanum (American bellflower, tall bellflower)
Corydalis sempervirens (pale corydalis)

Glandularia canadensis (rose vervain, sweet William)
Ipomopsis rubra (standing cypress)
Lobelia spicata (pale lobelia)
Oenothera biennis (common evening primrose)
Rudbeckia hirta (black-eyed Susan)
Sabatia brevifolia (narrow-leaved sabatia)
Senecio glabellus (butterweed)

Forbs (perennials)

Acorus calamus (sweet flag, calamus)
Actaea pachypoda (white baneberry)
Ageratina altissima var. altissima (white snakeroot)
Allium canadense (wild garlic)
Allium cernuum (nodding onion)
Amsonia ciliata (blue funnel lily, blue star)
Amsonia tabernaemontana (blue star)
Anemone caroliniana (Carolina anemone, southern thimbleweed)
Anemone virginiana (thimbleweed, tall anemone)
Antennaria spp. (pussytoes, everlasting)
Aquilegia canadensis (columbine)
Arisaema triphyllum (Jack-in-the-pulpit, Indian turnip)
Asarum canadense (wild ginger)
Asclepias incarnata (swamp milkweed)
Asclepias tuberosa (butterfly weed)
Asclepias verticillata (whorled milkweed)
Aster divaricatus (white wood aster)
Aster dumosus (bushy aster)
Aster laevis (smooth aster)
Aster novae-angliae (New England aster)
Aster pilosus (frost aster)
Aster puniceus (red-stem aster, swamp aster)
Astilbe biternata (false goatsbeard)
Astragalus canadensis (milk vetch, Canada milk vetch)
Baptisia alba (white false indigo)
Camassia scilloides (wild hyacinth)
Canna flaccida (golden canna)
Cardamine diphylla (two-leaved toothwort)
Caulophyllum thalictroides (blue cohosh)
Chelone lyonii (turtlehead)
Chrysogonum virginianum (green-and-gold)
Chrysopsis mariana (Maryland golden aster)
Cimicifuga racemosa (bugbane, black cohosh)
Claytonia virginica (narrow-leaved spring beauty)
Collinsonia canadensis (stoneroot, citronella horsebalm)
Coreopsis auriculata (early coreopsis)
Coreopsis grandiflora (coreopsis)
Coreopsis lanceolata (lance-leaved coreopsis)
Coreopsis tripteris (tall coreopsis)
Coreopsis verticillata (whorled coreopsis)
Delphinium carolinianum (blue larkspur)
Dicentra cucullaria (dutchman's breeches)
Dodecatheon meadia (shooting star)

Eryngium yuccifolium (rattlesnake master, button snake-root)
Erythronium americanum (eastern trout lily, yellow trout lily)
Eupatorium coelestinum (mist flower)
Eupatorium fistulosum (Joe-pye weed)
Eupatorium perfoliatum (boneset)
Eupatorium purpureum (Joe-pye weed)
Euphorbia corollata (flowering spurge)
Fragaria virginiana (wild strawberry)
Galium triflorum (sweet-scented bedstraw)
Gentiana saponaria (closed gentian, soapwort gentian)
Geranium maculatum (wild geranium, cranesbill)
Hedyotis nigricans (bluets)
Helenium autumnale (common sneezeweed)
Helianthus simulans (narrow-leaved sunflower, swamp sunflower)
Helianthus strumosus (woodland sunflower)
Heliopsis helianthoides (ox-eye sunflower, false sunflower)
Hepatica nobilis var. acuta (sharp-lobed hepatica)
Heuchera americana var. hirsuticaulis (alumroot)
Hibiscus moscheutos (swamp rose mallow, marshmallow hibiscus)
Houstonia caerulea (bluets)
Houstonia longifolia var. longifolia (long-leaved bluets, pale bluets)
Houstonia procumbens (innocence)
Hydrophyllum virginianum (Virginia waterleaf)
Hymenocallis caroliniana (spider lily, rain lily)
Hypoxis hirsuta (yellow star grass)
Iris cristata (dwarf crested iris)
Iris prismatica (slender blue flag, coastal iris)
Iris virginica (southern blue flag)
Kosteletzkya virginica (seashore mallow)
Lespedeza capitata (roundheaded bush clover)
Liatris aspera (rough blazing star, gayfeather)
Liatris elegans (gayfeather)
Liatris spicata (marsh blazing star, gayfeather)
Liatris squarrosa (blazing star)
Lilium canadense (wild yellow lily, Canada lily)
Lilium michauxii (Carolina lily)
Linum virginianum (woodland flax)
Lithospermum caroliniense (hairy puccoon, hispid gromwell)
Lobelia cardinalis (cardinal flower)
Lupinus perennis (wild lupine)
Lysimachia ciliata (fringed loosestrife)
Maianthemum racemosum ssp. racemosum (false Solomon's seal,
    false spikenard)
Manfreda virginica (rattlesnake master, false aloe)
Mitchella repens (partridge berry)
Monarda fistulosa (wild bergamot, horsemint, beebalm)
Nuphar lutea (yellow pond lily, cow lily, spatter dock)
Oenothera fruticosa (sundrops)
Orontium aquaticum (golden club)
Osmorhiza claytoni (sweet cicely, sweet jarvil)
Pachysandra procumbens (Alleghany spurge)
Penstemon australis (beardtongue)

Penstemon smallii (small's beardtongue)
Phlox carolina (Carolina phlox)
Phlox pilosa (prairie phlox, downy phlox)
Phlox stolonifera (creeping phlox)
Physostegia virginiana (obedient plant, false dragonhead)
Podophyllum peltatum (May apple)
Polygonatum biflorum (Solomon's seal)
Potentilla simplex (common cinquefoil)
Pycnanthemum tenuifolium (slender mountain mint)
Rhexia virginica (meadow beauty)
Rudbeckia fulgida (black-eyed Susan, orange coneflower)
Rudbeckia laciniata (cut-leaf coneflower)
Salvia lyrata (cancer weed, lyre-leaf sage)
Sanguinaria candensis (bloodroot)
Sedum ternatum (wild stonecrop)
Senecio aureus (golden ragwort)
Silene stellata (starry campion)
Silene virginica (fire pink)
Silphium terebinthinaceum (prairie dock)
Sisyrinchium angustifolium (narrow-leaved blue-eyed grass)
Sisyrinchium atlanticum (eastern blue-eyed grass)
Solidago caesia (blue-stemmed goldenrod, wreath goldenrod)
Solidago juncea (early goldenrod, plume goldenrod)
Solidago nemoralis (gray goldenrod, old-field goldenrod)
Solidago odora (sweet goldenrod)
Solidago rigida (stiff goldenrod)
Solidago rugosa (rough-leaved goldenrod)
Solidago sempervirens (seaside goldenrod)
Solidago speciosa (showy goldenrod)
Solidago ulmifolia (elm-leaved goldenrod)
Spigelia marilandica (Indian pink)
Stokesia laevis (stokes' aster)
Tephrosia virginiana (goat's rue)
Thalictrum pubescens (tall meadow rue)
Thalictrum thalictroides (rue anemone)
Tiarella cordifolia (foam flower)
Tradescantia hirsuticaulis (hairy spiderwort)
Tradescantia ohiensis (Ohio spiderwort)
Tradescantia virginiana (Virginia spiderwort, spider lily)
Trillium cernuum (nodding trillium)
Trillium erectum (wakerobin, purple trillium)
Trillium undulatum (painted trillium)
Uvularia sessilifolia (wildoats, merrybells)
Vernonia noveboracensis (New York ironweed)
Veronicastrum virginicum (Culver's root)
Viola affinis (Florida violet)
Viola canadensis (Canada violet)
Viola pedata (bird-foot violet)
Viola sororia (common blue violet, meadow violet)
Yucca aloifolia (Spanish dagger)
Zephyranthes atamasca (atamasco lily, Easter lily)
Zizia aptera (heart-leaved golden alexanders)
Zizia aurea (golden alexanders)

Grasses/Grass-like plants

Agrostis scabra (ticklegrass, fly-away grass)
Andropogon gerardii (big bluestem)
Andropogon glomeratus (bushy bluestem)
Andropogon ternarius (splitbeard bluestem)
Andropogon virginicus (broom sedge)
Arundinaria gigantea (giant cane)
Carex stipata (awl-fruited sedge)
Chasmanthium latifolium (inland sea oats, wild oats, river oats, broad-leaf uniola)
Danthonia spicata (poverty grass)
Distichlis spicata (seashore saltgrass)
Elymus hystrix var. hystrix (bottlebrush grass)
Eragrostis spectabilis (purple lovegrass, tumblegrass)
Juncus effusus var. solutus (soft rush)
Leersia oryzoides (rice cut grass)
Muhlenbergia capillaris (gulf muhly, hair grass)
Panicum virgatum (switchgrass)
Saccharum giganteum (sugarcane plume grass)
Schizachyrium scoparium (little bluestem)
Scirpus atrovirens (dark green bulrush)
Scirpus cyperinus (wool grass)
Scirpus tabernaemontani (great bulrush)
Sorghastrum nutans (Indian grass)
Spartina patens (marsh hay cordgrass, salt meadow cordgrass)
Tripsacum dactyloides (eastern gama grass)
Typha latifolia (cattail)

Shrubs (deciduous)

Alnus serrulata (smooth alder)
Amelanchier arborea (downy serviceberry, shadbush, Juneberry)
Amorpha fruticosa (false indigo, Indigo bush)
Aronia melanocarpa (black chokeberry)
Baccharis halimifolia (sea myrtle, groundsel bush)
Callicarpa americana (American beautyberry, French mulberry)
Calycanthus floridus (Carolina allspice, sweet shrub)
Castanea pumila (chinquapin)
Ceanothus americanus (New Jersey tea, red root)
Cephalanthus occidentalis (buttonbush)
Clethra alnifolia (summer sweet)
Comptonia peregrina (sweet fern)
Cornus alternifolia (pogoda dogwood, alternate-leaved dogwood)
Cornus racemosa (gray dogwood)
Corylus americana (American hazelnut or filbert)
Corylus cornuta (beaked hazelnut or filbert)
Diervilla sessilifolia (southern bush honeysuckle)
Dirca palustris (leatherwood, ropebark)
Erythrina herbacea (coral bean)
Euonymus americana (strawberry bush, brook euonymus, hearts-a-bustin')
Euonymus atropurpurea (wahoo, burning bush)
Forestiera acuminata (swamp privet)
Fothergilla major (witch alder)
Frangula caroliniana (Carolina buckthorn)

Hydrangea arborescens (wild hydrangea)
Hypericum hypericoides ssp. hypericoides (St. Andrew's cross)
Hypericum prolificum (shrubby St. John's wort)
Ilex verticillata (winterberry, black alder)
Itea virginica (Virginia willow, sweetspire, tassel-white)
Lindera benzoin (spicebush)
Lycium carolinianum (Christmas berry, matrimony vine)
Lyonia ligustrina (male-berry, male-blueberry)
Physocarpus opulifolius (ninebark)
Rhododendron arborescens (smooth azalea)
Rhododendron atlanticum (dwarf, or coastal azalea)
Rhododendron calendulaceum (flame azalea)
Rhododendron canescens (wild, piedmont, or sweet azalea)
Rhododendron periclymenoides (pinxterbloom azalea)
Rhododendron viscosum (swamp azalea)
Rhus aromatica (fragrant sumac)
Rhus copallinum (dwarf or winged sumac)
Rhus glabra (smooth sumac)
Rhus hirta (staghorn sumac)
Rosa carolina (Carolina rose)
Rosa setigera (Illinois or prairie rose)
Rubus occidentalis (black raspberry, thimbleberry)
Rubus odoratus (thimbleberry)
Sambucus canadensis (elderberry, common elder)
Sambucus racemosa var. pubens (scarlet elderberry, red-berried elder)
Spiraea tomentosa (steeplebush, hardhack)
Staphylea trifolia (bladdernut)
Stewartia malacodendron (silky camellia)
Styrax americanus (American silverbells)
Symphoricarpos orbiculatus (coralberry, Indian currant)
Vaccinium arboreum (sparkleberry, farkleberry)
Vaccinium corymbosom (highbush blueberry)
Viburnum acerifolium (maple leaf viburnum)
Viburnum dentatum (southern arrowwood)
Viburnum nudum (possumhaw viburnum)
Viburnum nudum var. cassinoides (wild raisin)
Viburnum prunifolium (black haw, nanny berry)
Viburnum rufidulum (southern or rusty black haw)

Shrubs (evergreen)

Epigaea repens (trailing arbutus)
Gaultheria procumbens (wintergreen, checkerberry)
Gaylussacia brachycera (box huckleberry)
Gordonia lasianthus (loblolly bay, gordonia)
Ilex glabra (inkberry, bitter gallberry)
Ilex vomitoria (yaupon)
Juniperus communis (common juniper)
Kalmia angustifolia (sheep laurel, lambkill kalmia)
Kalmia latifolia (mountain laurel)
Leucothoe axillaris (coast leucothoe)
Myrica cerifera (wax myrtle, southern bayberry, candleberry)
Rhododendron carolinianum (Carolina rhododendron)

Rhododendron catawbiense (purple rhododendron, red laurel)
Rhododendron maximum (rosebay, great laurel)
Serenoa repens (saw palmetto)

Trees (deciduous)

Acer barbatum (Florida maple, southern sugar maple)
Acer leucoderme (chalk maple)
Acer negundo (box elder)
Acer pensylvanicum (striped maple)
Acer rubrum (red maple)
Acer saccharinum (silver maple)
Acer spicatum (mountain maple)
Aesculus flava (sweet buckeye, yellow buckeye)
Aesculus pavia var. pavia (red buckeye)
Amelanchier canadensis (shadblow serviceberry, Juneberry)
Betula lenta (cherry birch)
Betula nigra (river birch)
Carpinus caroliniana (blue beech, hornbeam, musclewood)
Carya alba (mockernut hickory)
Carya cordiformis (bitternut, swamp hickory)
Carya ovata (shagbark hickory)
Celtis laevigata (sugarberry, hackberry)
Celtis occidentalis (hackberry, sugarberry)
Cercis canadensis (redbud)
Chionanthus virginicus (fringe tree, old man's beard)
Cornus florida (flowering dogwood)
Crataegus crus-galli (cockspur hawthorn)
Crataegus marshallii (parsley hawthorn)
Crataegus phaenopyrum (Washington hawthorn)
Crataegus punctata (dotted hawthorn, white thorn)
Cyrilla racemiflora (leatherwood, yiti)
Diospyros virginiana (persimmon)
Fagus grandifolia var. caroliniana (beech)
Fraxinus americana (white ash)
Fraxinus pensylvanica (green ash)
Gleditsia triacanthos (honey locust)
Halesia diptera (American snowdrop tree, two-winged silverbell)
Halesia tetraptera (Carolina silverbell)
Hamamelis virginiana (witch hazel)
Ilex decidua (possum-haw, deciduous holly)
Juglans cinerea (butternut, white walnut)
Juglans nigra (black walnut)
Liquidambar styraciflua (sweet gum)
Liriodendron tulipifera (tulip tree)
Magnolia acuminata (cucumber tree)
Magnolia pyramidata (pyramid magnolia)
Malus angustifolia (southern crabapple, wild crabapple)
Nyssa sylvatica (black gum, tupelo)
Ostrya virginiana (ironwood, hophornbeam)
Oxydendrum arboreum (sourwood)
Platanus occidentalis (sycamore, plane-tree)
Populus deltoides (eastern cottonwood)

Prunus americana (wild plum)
Prunus angustifolia (chickasaw plum)
Prunus mexicana (Mexican plum)
Prunus pensylvanica (fire or pin cherry)
Prunus serotina (black cherry)
Ptelea trifoliata (wafer ash, common hoptree)
Quercus alba (white oak)
Quercus bicolor (swamp white oak)
Quercus coccinea (scarlet oak)
Quercus falcata (southern red oak, Spanish oak)
Quercus laurifolia (laurel oak)
Quercus lyrata (overcup oak)
Quercus marilandica (blackjack oak)
Quercus muhlenbergii (chinkapin oak, chestnut oak)
Quercus phellos (willow oak)
Quercus rubra (red oak)
Quercus shumardii (shumard oak)
Quercus stellata (post oak)
Quercus velutina (black oak)
Salix nigra (black willow)
Sassafras albidum (sassafras)
Sorbus americana (mountain ash)
Taxodium distichum (bald cypress)
Ulmus americana (American elm)
Ulmus rubra (red elm, slippery elm)

Trees (evergreen)

Chamaecyparis thyoides (white cedar)
Ilex opaca (American holly, Christmas holly)
Juniperus virginiana (eastern red cedar)
Magnolia grandiflora (southern magnolia)
Persea borbonia (red bay)
Pinus echinata (shortleaf pine)
Pinus elliotii (slash, pitch, or yellow slash pine)
Pinus glabra (spruce pine)
Pinus palustris (longleaf pine)
Pinus rigida (pitch pine)
Pinus taeda (loblolly pine)
Pinus virginiana (Virginia pine)
Prunus caroliniana (cherry laurel)
Quercus virginiana (live oak, coastal live oak, southern live oak)
Tsuga caroliniana (Carolina hemlock)

Vines (deciduous)

Bignonia capreolata (cross vine)
Campsis radicans (trumpet creeper, trumpet vine)
Celastrus scandens (American bittersweet)
Clematis crispa (leatherflower)
Clematis virginiana (virgin's bower)
Lonicera sempervirens (coral honeysuckle)
Parthenocissus quinquefolia (Virginia creeper)
Passiflora incarnata (passion flower, maypop)

Vitis riparia (riverbank grape)
Vitis rotundifolia (muscadine grape)

Vine (evergreen) —————————————————————
Gelsemium sempervirens (yellow jessamine, Carolina jessamine)

FEDERALLY LISTED ENDANGERED SPECIES

American chaffseed (Schwalbea americana)
Black-spored quillwort (Isoetes melanospora)
Bunched arrowhead (Sagittaria fasciculata)
Canby's dropwort (Oxypolis canbyi)
Dwarf-flowered heartleaf (Hexastylis naniflora)
Harperella (Ptilimnium nodosum (fluviatile))
Little amphianthus (Amphianthus pusillus)
Miccosukee gooseberry (Ribes echinellum)
Michaux's sumac (Rhus michauxii)
Mountain sweet pitcher-plant (Sarracenia rubra ssp. jonesii)
Persistent trillium (Trillium persistens)
Pondberry (Lindera melissifolia)
Relict trillium (Trillium persistens)
Rough-leaved loosestrife (Lysimachia asperulaefolia)
Schweinitz's sunflower (Helianthus schweinitzii)
Seabeach amaranth (Amaranthus pumilus)
Small whorled pogonia (Isotria medeoloides)
Smooth coneflower (Echinacea laevigata)
Swamp pink (Helonias bullata)

SOUTH CAROLINA NOXIOUS SPECIES

Because the noxious weed lists have continually changed since we gathered them in 1994, we are not including them at this time. Not all States have noxious weed lists. Those that do, do not use the same standards of importance and are not comparable. States typically have included plants that interfere with agriculture (Canada thistle), or cause human health problems (poison ivy). Some States are now including a category of plants that invade and degrade the environment (purple loosestrife). Check with your State's Agriculture Department or Weed Scientist listed below. The noxious weed list can be used two ways on roadsides: l) check to not inadvertantly plant these invasive plants, and 2) note the plants you are legally responsible to control. Many States now check adjacent State lists to avoid planting their neighbors' problem plants. Because weeds do not respect political boundaries, and because by their very nature weeds continue to adapt and expand, monitoring and controlling invasives at State borders is a wise part of vegetation management.

(Weed and Seed Laws)

Clemson University
Department of Plant Industry
511 Westinghouse Road
Pendleton, SC 29670

Edward C. Murdock
Clemson University, Agronomy
275 Poole Agricultural Center
Clemson, SC 29634
(864) 656-3517

Heritage Trust
SC Wildlife & Marine Resources
P.O. Box 167
Columbia, SC 29202
(803) 734-3893

The Nature Conservancy Field Office
P.O. Box 5475
Columbia, SC 29250

Wildflower Alliance of South Carolina
P.O. Box 12181
Columbia, SC 29211

Brookgreen Gardens
1931 Brookgreen Drive
Murrells Inlet, SC 29576
(843) 237-4218

Native Plant Society
P.O. Box 12181
Columbia, SC 29211

POTENTIAL NATURAL VEGETATION ZONES IN
── SOUTH DAKOTA ──

Source: A.W. Kuchler's Potential Natural Vegetation Map, 1964, Revised 1985.
Presented in U.S.G.S. National Atlas of the U.S. Series,
U.S. Geological Survey, Reston, VA.

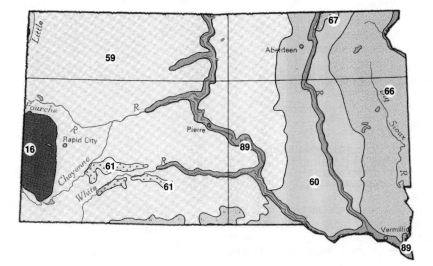

16	Black Hills pine forest *(Pinus)*
59	Wheatgrass-needlegrass *(Agropyron-Stipa)*
60	Wheatgrass-bluestem-needlegrass *(Agropyron-Andropogon-Stipa)*
61	Wheatgrass-grama-buffalo grass *(Agropyron-Bouteloua-Buchloë)*
66	Bluestem prairie *(Andropogon-Panicum-Sorghastrum)*
67	Sandhills prairie *(Andropogon-Calamovilfa)*
89	Northern floodplain forest *(Populus-Salix-Ulmus)*

(Dominant plant species present in each vegetation type are listed in Appendix 8)

16 *Black Hills Pine Forest (Pinus)*
59 *Wheatgrass-Needlegrass (Agropyron-Stipa)*
60 *Wheatgrass-Bluestem-Needlegrass (Agropyron-Andropogon-Stipa)*
61 *Wheatgras-Grama-Buffalo Grass (Andropogon-Bouteloua-Buchloë)*
66 *Bluestem Prairie (Andropogon-Panicum-Sorghastrum)*
67 *Sandhills Prairie (Andropogon-Calamovilfa)*
89 *Northern Floodplain Forest (Populus-Salix-Ulmus)*

Botanical Experts

David Ode, Botanist/Ecologist
South Dakota Game, Fish and Parks Department
523 E. Capitol
Pierre, SD 57501
(605) 773-4227
(605) 773-6245 (fax)
internet: daveo@gfp.state.sd.us

Dr. Gary E. Larson
Biology Department
P.O. Box 2207B
South Dakota State University
Brookings, SD 57007
(605) 688-4552
internet: larsong@ur.sdstate.edu

Dr. Fred Peabody
Biology Department
414 E. Clark Street
University of South Dakota
Vermillion, SD 57069
(605) 677-6176
internet: fpeabody@sunflowr.usd.edu

Recommended Flora

Great Plains Flora Association. 1986. *Flora of the Great Plains*. University Press of Knasas. Lawrence, Kansas

NATIVE PLANTS FOR LANDSCAPE USE IN SOUTH DAKOTA

Forbs (annuals/biennials)

Cleome serrulata (Rocky Mountain beeplant)
Coreopsis tinctoria (tickseed, goldenwave, plains coreopsis, calliopsis)
Euphorbia marginata (snow-on-the-mountain)
Gaillardia pulchella (Indian blanket, firewheel)
Helianthus annuus (common sunflower)
Helianthus petiolaris (plains sunflower)
Linum rigidum (yellow flax)
Oenothera albicaulis (pale evening primrose)
Oenothera biennis (common evening primrose)
Oenothera rhombipetala (diamond-petal primrose, four-point evening primrose)

Rudbeckia hirta (black-eyed Susan)
Senecio plattensis (prairie ragwort, prairie groundsel)
Townsendia exscapa (Easter daisy)

Forbs (perennials)

Aconitum columbianum (western monkshood)
Acorus calamus (sweet flag, calamus)
Ageratina altissima var. altissima (white snakeroot)
Allium canadense (wild garlic)
Allium cernuum (nodding onion)
Allium stellatum (wild pink onion)
Anaphalis margaritacea (pearly everlasting)
Anemone canadensis (Canada anemone, windflower)
Anemone caroliniana (Carolina anemone, southern thimbleweed)
Anemone cylindrica (thimbleweed, candle anemone)
Anemone multifida (early thimbleweed, cut-leaf anemone, Pacific anemone)
Antennaria spp. (pussytoes, everlasting)
Apocynum adndrosaemifolium (spreading dogbane)
Aquilegia canadensis (columbine)
Arisaema triphyllum (Jack-in-the-pulpit, Indian turnip)
Arnica cordifolia (heartleaf arnica)
Artemisia ludoviciana (white sage, prairie sage, artemisia)
Asclepias incarnata (swamp milkweed)
Asclepias speciosa (showy milkweed)
Asclepias verticillata (whorled milkweed)
Aster ericoides (heath aster, white wreath aster)
Aster laevis (smooth aster)
Aster novae-angliae (New England aster)
Aster oblongifolius (aromatic aster)
Aster sericeus (silky aster)
Astragalus americanus (American milk vetch, rattlepod)
Astragalus canadensis (milk vetch, Canada milk vetch)
Calochortus nuttallii (sego lily, mariposa lily)
Campanula rotundifolia (harebell)
Castilleja sessiliflora (downy painted cup)
Coreopsis palmata (stiff coreopsis)
Dalea candida (white prairie clover)
Dalea purpurea (purple prairie clover)
Desmodium canadense (Canada tick-trefoil, Canada tickclover)
Desmodium illinoense (Illinois tick-trefoil, Illinois tickclover)
Echinacea angustifolia (narrow-leaved purple coneflower)
Erigeron compositus (alpine daisy)
Erigeron speciosus (showy fleabane)
Eupatorium maculatum (spotted Joe-pye weed)
Eupatorium perfoliatum (boneset)
Euphorbia corollata (flowering spurge)
Euthamia graminifolia var. graminifolia (grass-leaved goldenrod)
Fragaria virginiana (wild strawberry)
Gaillardia aristata (blanket flower, gaillardia, brown-eyed Susan)
Galium triflorum (sweet-scented bedstraw)
Gaura coccinea (scarlet gaura)
Gentiana andrewsii (bottle gentian)

Geranium viscossisimum (sticky wild geranium)
Geum triflorum (prairie smoke, purple avens)
Glandularia bipinnatifida var. bipinnatifida (prairie verbena, Dakota vervain)
Glycyrrhiza lepidota (wild licorice)
Helenium autumnale (common sneezeweed)
Helianthus maximiliani (Maximilian sunflower)
Helianthus pauciflorus ssp. pauciflorus (stiff sunflower)
Heliopsis helianthoides (ox-eye sunflower, false sunflower)
Heterotheca villosa var. villosa (golden aster)
Heuchera richardsonii (alum root)
Hydrophyllum virginianum (Virginia waterleaf)
Hypoxis hirsuta (yellow star grass)
Ipomoea leptophylla (bush morning glory)
Iris missouriensis (Rocky Mountain iris, western blue flag)
Lespedeza capitata (roundheaded bush clover)
Liatris aspera (rough blazing star, gayfeather)
Liatris punctata (dotted blazing star, gayfeather)
Liatris pycnostachya (prairie blazing star, gayfeather)
Liatris squarrosa (blazing star)
Lilium michiganense (Turk's cap lily, Michigan lily)
Lilium philadelphicum (wood lily)
Linum lewisii (wild blue flax)
Lithospermum canescens (hoary puccoon)
Lithospermum caroliniense (hairy puccoon, hispid gromwell)
Lithospermum incisum (fringed puccoon, narrow-leaved puccoon)
Lobelia spicata (pale lobelia)
Mimosa quadrivalvis var. angustata (catclaw sensitive briar)
Monarda fistulosa (wild bergamot, horsemint, beebalm)
Nothocalais cuspidata (prairie dandelion)
Nuphar lutea (yellow pond lily, cow lily, spatter dock)
Oenothera cespitosa (gumbo evening primrose, gumbo lily)
Oenothera flava (shortfin evening primrose)
Osmorhiza berteroi (mountain sweet cicely)
Osmorhiza claytoni (sweet cicely, sweet jarvil)
Penstemon albidus (white beardtongue)
Penstemon angustifolius (whorled penstemon)
Penstemon grandiflorus (large-flowered penstemon)
Phlox hoodii (phlox)
Phlox pilosa (prairie phlox, downy phlox)
Physostegia virginiana (obedient plant, false dragonhead)
Pulsatilla patens ssp. multifida (pasque flower, wild crocus)
Ratibida columnifera (prairie coneflower, long-headed coneflower, Mexican hat)
Ratibida pinnata (gray-headed coneflower, yellow coneflower)
Rudbeckia laciniata (cut-leaf coneflower)
Senecio plattensis (prairie ragwort, prairie goundsel)
Silphium integrifolium (rosinweed)
Silphium laciniatum (compass plant)
Silphium perfoliatum (cup plant)
Sisyrinchium angustifolium (narrow-leaved blue-eyed grass)
Sisyrinchium campestre (white-eyed grass, prairie blue-eyed grass)
Solidago canadensis (meadow goldenrod)
Solidago missouriensis (Missouri goldenrod, prairie goldenrod)

Solidago nemoralis (gray goldenrod, old-field goldenrod)
Solidago speciosa (showy goldenrod)
Tetraneuris acaulis var. acaulis (stemless goldflower, stemless rubber weed, butte marigold)
Thalictrum dasycarpum (tall or purple meadow rue)
Townsendia exscapa (Easter daisy)
Tradescantia bracteata (spiderwort)
Verbena hastata (blue verbena, blue vervain)
Vernonia fasciculata (ironweed)
Viola canadensis (Canadian white violet)
Viola pedatifida (prairie violet)
Viola pubescens (downy or smooth yellow violet)
Yucca glauca (yucca, soapweed)
Zizia aptera (heart-leaved golden alexanders)
Zizia aurea (golden alexanders)

Grasses/Grass-like plants

Agrostis exarata (spikebent, spike red top)
Andropogon gerardii (big bluestem)
Andropogon hallii (sand bluestem)
Bouteloua curtipendula (sideoats grama)
Bouteloua gracilis (blue grama)
Bouteloua hirsuta (hairy grama)
Bromus carinatus (California brome)
Bromus kalmii (prairie brome, wild chess)
Buchloe dactyloides (buffalograss)
Calamagrostis canadensis (bluejoint grass)
Calamagrostis stricta (bluejoint grass)
Calamovilfa longifolia (sandreed grass, prairie sandreed)
Carex aquatilis (water sedge)
Carex nebrascensis (Nebraska sedge)
Carex stipata (awl-fruited sedge)
Carex stricta (tussock sedge)
Carex utriculata (beaked sedge)
Danthonia spicata (poverty grass)
Deschampsia cespitosa (tufted hairgrass)
Eleocharis palustris (creeping spikesedge, spike rush)
Elymus canadensis (Canada wild rye)
Elymus glaucus (blue wild rye)
Elymus lanceolatus (thickspike wheatgrass)
Festuca ovina (sheep fescue)
Glyceria grandis (American mannagrass, tall mannagrass, reed meadowgrass)
Hierochloe odorata (sweet grass)
Juncus interior (inland rush)
Koeleria macrantha (June grass)
Leersia oryzoides (rice cut grass)
Oryzopsis hymenoides (Indian ricegrass)
Panicum virgatum (switchgrass)
Pascopyrum smithii (western wheatgrass)
Poa secunda (pine bluegrass)
Schizachyrium scoparium (little bluestem)
Scirpus acutus (hardstem bulrush)

Scirpus cyperinus (wool grass)
Scirpus maritimus (alkali bulrush, prairie bulrush, bayonet grass)
Scirpus tabernaemontani (great bulrush)
Sorghastrum nutans (Indian grass)
Spartina pectinata (prairie cordgrass, freshwater cordgrass
Sporobolus heterolepis (northern prairie dropseed)
Stipa comata (needle-and-thread grass)
Stipa nelsonii (Columbia needlegrass)
Stipa spartea (porcupine grass)
Typha angustifolia (narrow-leaved cattail)
Typha latifolia (cattail)

Shrubs (deciduous)

Amelanchier alnifolia (saskatoon, western serviceberry, Juneberry)
Amorpha canescens (leadplant)
Amorpha fruticosa (false indigo, Indigo bush)
Amorpha nana (dwarf wild indigo)
Artemisia frigida (prairie sagewort, fringed sage)
Chrysothamnus nauseosus (rabbit brush, chamisa)
Cornus racemosa (gray dogwood)
Cornus sericea (red-twig dogwood, red-osier dogwood)
Corylus americana (American hazelnut or filbert)
Corylus cornuta (beaked hazelnut or filbert)
Euonymus atropurpurea (wahoo, burning bush)
Lonicera dioica (limber or wild honeysuckle)
Prunus pumila var. besseyi (sand cherry)
Prunus virginiana (chokecherry)
Rhus glabra (smooth sumac)
Ribes cynosbati (prickly gooseberry, dogberry)
Ribes odoratum (buffalo currant, golden currant)
Rosa arkansana (prairie rose)
Rosa blanda (early wild rose, smooth rose)
Rosa woodsii (western wild rose, woods rose)
Rubus idaeus ssp. strigosus (red raspberry)
Rubus occidentalis (black raspberry, thimbleberry)
Salix bebbiana (Bebb willow, long-beaked willow)
Salix eriocephala (Missouri willow, diamond willow)
Salix exigua (sandbar willow)
Salix discolor (pussy willow)
Salix scouleriana (western pussy willow, Scouler's willow)
Sambucus canadensis (elderberry, common elder)
Sarcobatus vermiculatus (greasewood)
Shepherdia argentea (silverbuffaloberry)
Shepherdia canadensis (buffaloberry)
Sorbus scopulina (western mountain ash)
Spiraea alba (meadow sweet)
Symphoricarpos albus (snowberry)
Symphoricarpos occidentalis (wolfberry, buckbush)
Viburnum lentago (black haw, nannyberry)
Viburnum opulus var. americanum (high-bush cranberry, American cranberrybush viburnum)

Shrubs (evergreen)

Arctostaphylos uva-ursi (bearberry, kinnikinnik)
Artemisia tridentata (big sagebrush, Great Basin sagebrush)
Ceanothus velutinus (mountain balm, buckbush)
Cercocarpus montanus (mountain mahogany, silverleaf mountain mahogany)
Juniperus communis (common juniper)
Juniperus horizontalis (creeping juniper, creeping savin)

Trees (deciduous)

Acer negundo (box elder)
Acer saccharinum (silver maple)
Betula occidentalis (mountain birch, water birch)
Betula papyrifera (paper birch)
Celtis occidentalis (hackberry, sugarberry)
Fraxinus pennsylvanica (green ash)
Gleditsia triacanthos (honey locust)
Gymnocladus dioica (Kentucky coffee tree)
Juglans nigra (black walnut)
Ostrya virginiana (ironwood, hophornbeam)
Pinus contorta var. murrayana (lodgepole pine)
Populus deltoides (eastern cottonwood)
Populus tremuloides (quaking aspen)
Prunus americana (wild plum)
Prunus mexicana (Mexican plum)
Quercus macrocarpa (bur oak)
Salix amygdaloides (peachleaf willow)
Tilia americana (American linden, basswood)
Ulmus americana (American elm)
Ulmus rubra (red elm, slippery elm)

Trees (evergreen)

Juniperus scopulorum (Rocky Mountain juniper)
Juniperus virginiana (eastern red cedar)
Picea glauca (white spruce)
Pinus ponderosa (ponderosa pine)

Vines (deciduous)

Celastrus scandens (American bittersweet)
Clematis ligusticifolia (clematis)
Clematis virginiana (virgin's bower)
Parthenocissus quinquefolia var. quinquefolia (woodbine)
Vitis riparia (riverbank grape)

FEDERALLY LISTED ENDANGERED SPECIES

Natural Heritage Data Base
SD Department of Game, Fish & Parks
523 E. Capitol Avenue
Pierre, SD 57501
(605) 773-4227
(605) 773-6245 (fax)

The Nature Conservancy Field Office
1000 West Avenue North, Ste. 100
Sioux Falls, SD 57104
(605) 331-0619

South Dakota Resources Coalition
P.O. Box 7020
Brookings, SD 57007

SOUTH DAKOTA NOXIOUS SPECIES

Because the noxious weed lists have continually changed since we gathered them in 1994, we are not including them at this time. Not all States have noxious weed lists. Those that do, do not use the same standards of importance and are not comparable. States typically have included plants that interfere with agriculture (Canada thistle), or cause human health problems (poison ivy). Some States are now including a category of plants that invade and degrade the environment (purple loosestrife). Check with your State's Agriculture Department or Weed Scientist listed below. The noxious weed list can be used two ways on roadsides: l) check to not inadvertantly plant these invasive plants, and 2) note the plants you are legally responsible to control. Many States now check adjacent State lists to avoid planting their neighbors' problem plants. Because weeds do not respect political boundaries, and because by their very nature weeds continue to adapt and expand, monitoring and controlling invasives at State borders is a wise part of vegetation management.

(Weed and Seed Laws)

Department of Agriculture
Division of Regulatory Services
445 East Capitol, Anderson
Pierre, SD 57501

Leon J. Wrage, Agriculture
South Dakota State University
229 Ag. Hall, Box 2207A
Brookings, SD 57007
(605) 688-4591

SOUTH DAKOTA RESOURCES

Natural Heritage Data Base
SD Department of Game, Fish & Parks
523 E. Capitol Avenue
Pierre, SD 57501
(605) 773-4227

The Nature Conservancy Field Office
1000 West Avenue North, Ste. 100
Sioux Falls, SD 57104
(605) 331-0619

South Dakota Resources Coalition
P.O. Box 7020
Brookings, SD 57007

U.S. Fish and Wildlife Service
420 S. Garfield, Suite 400
Pierre, SD 57501
(605) 224-8693

Great Plains Native Plant Society
P.O. Box 461
Hot Springs, SD 57747

POTENTIAL NATURAL VEGETATION ZONES IN
TENNESSEE

Source: A.W. Kuchler's Potential Natural Vegetation Map, 1964, Revised 1985.
Presented in U.S.G.S. National Atlas of the U.S. Series,
U.S. Geological Survey, Reston, VA.

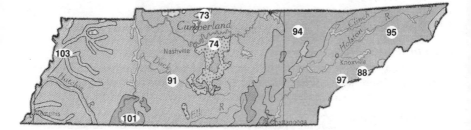

 Mosaic of numbers 66 and 91

74 Cedar glades
(Quercus-Juniperus-Sporobolus)

88 Southeastern spruce-fir forest
(Picea-Abies)

91 Oak-hickory forest
(Quercus-Carya)

94 Mixed mesophytic forest
(Acer-Aesculus-Fagus-Liriodendron-Quercus-Tilia)

95 Appalachian oak forest
(Quercus)

97 Northern hardwoods
(Acer-Betula-Fagus-Tsuga)

101 Oak-hickory-pine forest
(Quercus-Carya-Pinus)

103 Southern floodplain forest
(Quercus-Nyassa-Taxodium)

(Dominant plant species present in each vegetation type are listed in Appendix 8)

73 Mosaic of 66 (Bluestem Prairie) and 91 (Oak-Hickory Forest)
74 Cedar Glades (Quercus-Juniperus-Sporobolus)
88 Southeastern Spruce-Fir Forest (Picea Abies)
91 Oak-Hickory Forest (Quercus-Carya)
94 Mixed Mesophytic Forest (Acer-Aesculus-Fagus-Liriodendron-Quercus-Tilia)
95 Appalachian Oak Forest (Quercus)
97 Northern Hardwoods (Acer-Betula-Fagus-Tsuga)
101 Oak-Hickory-Pine Forest (Quercus-Carya-Pinus)
103 Southern Floodplain Forest (Quercus-Nyssa-Taxodium)

Botanical Expert

Carl Nordman, Botanist
Tennessee Department of Environment and Conservation
Division of Natural Heritage
401 Church St., 8th Floor L&C Tower
Nashville, TN 37243-0447
(615) 532-0440
(615) 532-0046 (fax)

Recommended Flora

Gleason, H.A. and A. Cronquist. 1991. Manual of Vascular Plants of Northeastern United States and Adjacent Canada, 2nd Edition. New York Botanical Garden, New York. 910 pgs. + map. ISBN 0893273651.

NATIVE PLANTS FOR LANDSCAPE USE IN TENNESSEE

Ferns

Adiantum capillus-veneris (southern maidenhair fern)
Adiantum pedatum (northern maidenhair fern)
Asplenium platyneuron (ebony spleenwort)
Asplenium trichomanes (maidenhair spleenwort)
Athyrium filix-femina (lady fern)
Botrychium virginianum (rattlesnake fern)
Cystopteris bulbifera (bladder fern)
Dennstaedtia punctilobula (hay-scented fern)
Dryopteris marginalis (marginal wood fern)
Onoclea sensibilis (sensitive fern, bead fern)
Osmunda cinnamomea (cinnamon fern)
Osmunda claytoniana (interrupted fern)
Osmunda regalis (royal fern)
Phegopteris hexagonoptera (broad beech fern)
Polystichum acrostichoides (Christmas fern)
Thelypteris novaboracensis (New York fern, tapering fern)
Woodwardia areolata (netted chain fern)

Forbs (annuals/biennials)

Campanulastrum americanum (American bellflower, tall bellflower)
Corydalis sempervirens (pale corydalis)
Lobelia spicata (pale lobelia)

Oenothera biennis (common evening primrose)
Rudbeckia hirta (black-eyed Susan)
Senecio glabellus (butterweed)
Senecio plattensis (prairie ragwort, prairie groundsel)

Forbs (perennials)

Acorus calamus (sweet flag, calamus)
Actaea pachypoda (white baneberry)
Allium canadense (wild garlic)
Allium cernuum (nodding onion)
Amsonia tabernaemontana (blue star)
Anemone virginiana (thimbleweed, tall anemone)
Antennaria spp. (pussytoes, everlasting)
Apocynum androsaemifolium (spreading dogbane)
Aquilegia canadensis (columbine)
Arisaema triphyllum (Jack-in-the-pulpit, Indian turnip)
Aruncus dioicus (goat's beard)
Asarum canadense (wild ginger)
Asclepias incarnata (swamp milkweed)
Asclepias tuberosa (butterfly weed)
Asclepias verticillata (whorled milkweed)
Aster divaricatus (white wood aster)
Aster dumosus (bushy aster)
Aster novae-angliae (New England aster)
Aster oblongifolius (aromatic aster)
Aster oolentangiensis (sky blue aster)
Aster pilosus (frost aster)
Aster puniceus (red-stem aster, swamp aster)
Astilbe biternata (false goatsbeard)
Astragalus canadensis (milk vetch, Canada milk vetch)
Baptisia alba (white false indigo)
Baptisia alba (cream false indigo, plains wild indigo)
Baptisia australis (blue wild indigo)
Camassia scilloides (wild hyacinth)
Cardamine diphylla (two-leaved toothwort)
Caulophyllum thalictroides (blue cohosh)
Chelone lyonii (turtlehead)
Chrysopsis mariana (Maryland golden aster)
Claytonia caroliniana (broad-leaved spring beauty)
Claytonia virginica (narrow-leaved spring beauty)
Collinsonia canadensis (stoneroot, citronella horsebalm)
Coreopsis auriculata (early coreopsis)
Coreopsis lanceolata (lance-leaved coreopsis)
Coreopsis tripteris (tall coreopsis)
Delphinium tricorne (dwarf larkspur)
Dicentra cucullaria (Dutchman's breeches)
Dicentra eximia (wild bleeding heart)
Dodecatheon meadia (shooting star)
Eryngium yuccifolium (rattlesnake master, button snake-root)
Erythronium americanum (eastern trout lily, yellow trout lily)
Eupatorium coelestinum (mist flower)
Eupatorium fistulosum (Joe-pye weed)

Eupatorium perfoliatum (boneset)
Eupatorium purpureum (Joe-pye weed)
Euphorbia corollata (flowering spurge)
Fragaria virginiana (wild strawberry)
Galium triflorum (sweet-scented bedstraw)
Gentiana andrewsii (bottle gentian)
Gentiana saponaria (closed gentian, soapwort gentian)
Geranium maculatum (wild geranium, cranesbill)
Hedyotis nigricans (bluets)
Helenium autumnale (common sneezeweed)
Helianthus strumosus (woodland sunflower)
Heliopsis helianthoides (ox-eye sunflower, false sunflower)
Hepatica nobilis var. acuta (sharp-lobed hepatica)
Heterotheca villosa var. villosa (golden aster)
Hibiscus moscheutos (swamp rose mallow, marshmallow hibiscus)
Houstonia caerulea (bluets)
Houstonia longifolia var. longifolia (long-leaved bluets, pale bluets)
Hymenocallis caroliniana (spider lily, rain lily)
Hypoxis hirsuta (yellow star grass)
Iris cristata (dwarf crested iris)
Lespedeza capitata (roundheaded bush clover)
Liatris aspera (rough blazing star, gayfeather)
Liatris spicata (marsh blazing star, gayfeather)
Liatris squarrosa (blazing star)
Lilium philadelphicum (wood lily)
Lithospermum canescens (hoary puccoon)
Lithospermum caroliniense (hairy puccoon, hispid gromwell)
Lobelia cardinalis (cardinal flower)
Lobelia siphilitica (great blue lobelia)
Lysimachia ciliata (fringed loosestrife)
Maianthemum canadense (wild lily-of-the-valley, Canada mayflower)
Maianthemum racemosum ssp. racemosum (false Solomon's seal,
    false spikenard)
Maianthemum stellatum (starry Solomon's seal)
Manfreda virginica (rattlesnake master, false aloe)
Mertensia virginica (bluebells)
Mitchella repens (partridge berry)
Monarda didyma (beebalm, oswego tea)
Nuphar lutea (yellow pond lily, cow lily, spatter dock)
Oenothera fruticosa (sundrops)
Oenothera macrocarpa (Missouri evening primrose)
Orontium aquaticum (golden club)
Osmorhiza claytoni (sweet cicely, sweet jarvil)
Pachysandra procumbens (Alleghany spurge)
Peltandra virginica (arrow arum)
Penstemon digitalis (beardtongue)
Penstemon smallii (small's beardtongue)
Phlox carolina (Carolina phlox)
Phlox divaricata (blue woodland phlox, sweet William)
Phlox divaricata ssp. laphamii (blue phlox, sweet William)
Phlox paniculata (summer phlox, perennial phlox)
Phlox pilosa (prairie phlox, downy phlox)

Phlox stolonifera (creeping phlox)
Podophyllum peltatum (May apple)
Polemonium reptans (Jacob's ladder, Greek valerian)
Polygonatum biflorum (Solomon's seal)
Potentilla simplex (common cinquefoil)
Pycnanthemum tenuifolium (slender mountain mint)
Pycnanthemum virginianum (mountain mint)
Ranunculus hispidus (early buttercup, tufted buttercup)
Rudbeckia laciniata (cut-leaf coneflower)
Ruellia humilis (wild petunia)
Salvia lyrata (cancer weed, lyre-leaf sage)
Sanguinaria candensis (bloodroot)
Sedum ternatum (wild stonecrop)
Senecio aureus (golden ragwort)
Sibbaldiopsis tridentata (three-toothed cinquefoil)
Silphium integrifolium (rosinweed)
Sisyrinchium angustifolium (narrow-leaved blue-eyed grass)
Sisyrinchium atlanticum (eastern blue-eyed grass)
Sisyrinchium mucronatum (eastern blue-eyed grass)
Solidago caesia (blue-stemmed goldenrod, wreath goldenrod)
Solidago canadensis (meadow goldenrod)
Solidago juncea (early goldenrod, plume goldenrod)
Solidago nemoralis (gray goldenrod, old-field goldenrod)
Solidago odora (sweet goldenrod)
Solidago rigida (stiff goldenrod)
Solidago rugosa (rough-leaved goldenrod)
Solidago speciosa (showy goldenrod)
Solidago ulmifolia (elm-leaved goldenrod)
Spigelia marilandica (Indian pink)
Stylophorum diphyllum (celandine poppy)
Tephrosia virginiana (goat's rue)
Thalictrum dioicum (early meadow rue)
Thalictrum pubescens (tall meadow rue)
Thalictrum thalictroides (rue anemone)
Thermopsis villosa (bush pea)
Tiarella cordifolia (foam flower)
Tradescantia ohiensis (Ohio spiderwort)
Tradescantia virginiana (Virginia spiderwort, spider lily)
Trientalis borealis ssp. borealis (starflower)
Trillium erectum (wakerobin, purple trillium)
Trillium undulatum (painted trillium)
Uvularia grandiflora (bellwort, merrybells)
Uvularia sessilifolia (wildoats, merrybells)
Verbena hastata (blue verbena, blue vervain)
Verbena stricta (hoary vervain)
Vernonia noveboracensis (New York ironweed)
Veronicastrum virginicum (Culver's root)
Viola affinis (Florida violet)
Viola canadensis (Canada violet)
Viola conspersa (American dog violet)
Viola pedata (bird-foot violet)
Viola pubescens (downy or smooth yellow violet)

Viola soraria (common blue violet, meadow violet)
Zizia aptera (heart-leaved golden alexanders)
Zizia aurea (golden alexanders)

Grasses/Grass-like plants

Agrostis scabra (ticklegrass, fly-away grass)
Andropogon gerardii (big bluestem)
Andropogon glomeratus (bushy bluestem)
Andropogon ternarius (splitbeard bluestem)
Andropogon virginicus (broom sedge)
Arundinaria gigantea (giant cane)
Bouteloua curtipendula (sideoats grama)
Calamagrostis canadensis (bluejoint grass)
Carex pensylvanica (Pennsylvania sedge)
Carex plantaginea (plantain-leaved sedge)
Carex stipata (awl-fruited sedge)
Carex stricta (tussock sedge)
Chasmanthium latifolium (inland sea oats, wild oats, river oats, broad-leaf uniola)
Danthonia spicata (poverty grass)
Elymus canadensis (Canada wild rye)
Elymus hystrix var. hystrix (bottlebrush grass)
Eragrostis spectabilis (purple lovegrass, tumblegrass)
Juncus effusus (soft rush)
Leersia oryzoides (rice cut grass)
Melica nitens (three-flower melic grass)
Muhlenbergia capillaris (gulf muhly, hair grass)
Panicum virgatum (switchgrass)
Saccharum giganteum (sugarcane plume grass)
Schizachyrium scoparium (little bluestem)
Scirpus atrovirens (dark green bulrush)
Scirpus cyperinus (wool grass)
Scirpus tabernaemontani (great bulrush)
Sorghastrum nutans (Indian grass)
Spartina pectinata (prairie cordgrass, freshwater cordgrass)
Tripsacum dactyloides (eastern gama grass)
Typha latifolia (cattail)

Shrubs (deciduous)

Alnus serrulata (smooth alder)
Amelanchier arborea (downy serviceberry, shadbush, Juneberry)
Amorpha fruticosa (false indigo, Indigo bush)
Aronia melanocarpa (black chokeberry)
Callicarpa americana (American beautyberry, French mulberry)
Calycanthus floridus (Carolina allspice, sweet shrub)
Castanea pumila (chinquapin)
Ceanothus americanus (New Jersey tea, red root)
Cephalanthus occidentalis (buttonbush)
Cornus alternifolia (pogoda dogwood, alternate-leaved dogwood)
Cornus amomum (swamp dogwood, silky dogwood)
Cornus drummondii (rough-leaf dogwood)
Corylus americana (American hazelnut or filbert)
Corylus cornuta (beaked hazelnut or filbert)

Diervilla sessilifolia (southern bush honeysuckle)
Dirca palustris (leatherwood, ropebark)
Euonymus americana (strawberry bush, brook euonymus, hearts-a-bustin')
Euonymus atropurpurea (wahoo, burning bush)
Forestiera acuminata (swamp privet)
Frangula caroliniana (Carolina buckthorn)
Hydrangea arborescens (wild hydrangea)
Hypericum hypericoides ssp. hypericoides (St. Andrew's cross)
Ilex verticillata (winterberry, black alder)
Itea virginica (Virginia willow, sweetspire, tassel-white)
Lindera benzoin (spicebush)
Lyonia ligustrina (male-berry, male-blueberry)
Physocarpus opulifolius (ninebark)
Rhododendron arborescens (smooth azalea)
Rhododendron calendulaceum (flame azalea)
Rhododendron canescens (wild, piedmont, or sweet azalea)
Rhododendron periclymenoides (pinxterbloom azalea)
Rhododendron viscosum (swamp azalea)
Rhus copallinum (dwarf or winged sumac)
Rhus glabra (smooth sumac)
Rhus hirta (staghorn sumac)
Ribes cynosbati (prickly gooseberry, dogberry)
Rosa carolina (Carolina rose)
Rosa setigera (Illinois or prairie rose)
Rubus occidentalis (black raspberry, thimbleberry)
Rubus odoratus (thimbleberry)
Sambucus canadensis (elderberry, common elder)
Sambucus racemosa var. pubens (scarlet elderberry, red-berried elder)
Spiraea tomentosa (steeplebush, hardhack)
Staphylea trifolia (bladdernut)
Styrax americana (American silverbells)
Symphoricarpos orbiculatus (coralberry, Indian currant)
Vaccinium arboreum (sparkleberry, farkleberry)
Vaccinium corymbosum (highbush blueberry)
Viburnum acerifolium (maple leaf viburnum)
Viburnum dentatum (southern arrowwood)
Viburnum nudum (possumhaw viburnum)
Viburnum nudum var. cassinoides (wild raisin)
Viburnum prunifolium (black haw, nanny berry)
Viburnum rufidulum (southern or rusty black haw)

Shrubs (evergreen)

Epigaea repens (trailing arbutus)
Gaylussacia brachycera (box huckleberry)
Kalmia latifolia (mountain laurel)
Rhododendron carolinianum (Carolina rhododendron)
Rhododendron catawbiense (purple rhododendron, red laurel)
Rhododendron maximum (rosebay, great laurel)

Trees (deciduous)

Acer negundo (box elder)
Acer pensylvanicum (striped maple)

Acer rubrum (red maple)
Acer saccharinum (silver maple)
Acer saccharum (sugar maple)
Acer spicatum (mountain maple)
Aesculus flava (sweet buckeye, yellow buckeye)
Aesculus glabra (Ohio buckeye, horse chestnut)
Aesculus pavia var. pavia (red buckeye)
Betula lenta (cherry birch)
Betula nigra (river birch)
Carpinus caroliniana (blue beech, hornbeam, musclewood)
Carya alba (mockernut hickory)
Carya cordiformis (bitternut, swamp hickory)
Carya illinoinensis (pecan)
Carya ovata (shagbark hickory)
Catalpa speciosa (northern catalpa)
Celtis laevigata (sugarberry, hackberry)
Celtis occidentalis (hackberry, sugarberry)
Cercis canadensis (redbud)
Chionanthus virginicus (fringe tree, old man's beard)
Cladrastis kentukea (yellowwood)
Cornus florida (flowering dogwood)
Crataegus crus-galli (cockspur hawthorn)
Crataegus marshallii (parsley hawthorn)
Crataegus mollis (downy hawthorn)
Crataegus phaenopyrum (Washington hawthorn)
Crataegus punctata (dotted hawthorn, white thorn)
Diospyros virginiana (persimmon)
Fagus grandifolia var. caroliniana (beech)
Fraxinus americana (white ash)
Fraxinus pensylvanica (green ash)
Gleditsia triacanthos (honey locust)
Gymnocladus dioica (Kentucky coffee tree)
Halesia tetraptera (Carolina silverbell)
Hamamelis virginiana (witch hazel)
Ilex decidua (possum-haw, deciduous holly)
Juglans nigra (black walnut)
Liquidambar styraciflua (sweet gum)
Liriodendron tulipifera (tulip tree)
Magnolia acuminata (cucumber tree)
Malus angustifolia (southern crabapple, wild crabapple)
Nyssa sylvatica (black gum, tupelo)
Ostrya virginiana (ironwood, hophornbeam)
Oxydendrum arboreum (sourwood)
Platanus occidentalis (sycamore, plane-tree)
Populus deltoides (eastern cottonwood)
Prunus americana (wild plum)
Prunus angustifolia (chickasaw plum)
Prunus mexicana (Mexican plum)
Prunus pensylvanica (fire or pin cherry)
Prunus serotina (black cherry)
Ptelea trifoliata (wafer ash, common hoptree)
Quercus alba (white oak)

Quercus bicolor (swamp white oak)
Quercus coccinea (scarlet oak)
Quercus falcata (southern red oak, Spanish oak)
Quercus lyrata (overcup oak)
Quercus macrocarpa (bur oak)
Quercus marilandica (blackjack oak)
Quercus muhlenbergii (chinkapin oak, chestnut oak)
Quercus palustris (pin oak)
Quercus phellos (willow oak)
Quercus rubra (red oak)
Quercus shumardii (shumard oak)
Quercus stellata (post oak)
Quercus velutina (black oak)
Salix nigra (black willow)
Sassafras albidum (sassafras)
Sorbus americana (mountain ash)
Taxodium distichum (bald cypress)
Tilia americana (American linden, basswood)
Ulmus americana (American elm)
Ulmus rubra (red elm, slippery elm)

Trees (evergreen)

Ilex opaca (American holly, Christmas holly)
Juniperus virginiana (eastern red cedar)
Pinus echinata (shortleaf pine)
Pinus rigida (pitch pine)
Pinus strobus (eastern white pine)
Pinus taeda (loblolly pine)
Pinus virginiana (Virginia pine)
Tsuga canadensis (eastern hemlock)

Vines (deciduous)

Bignonia capreolata (cross vine)
Campsis radicans (trumpet creeper, trumpet vine)
Celastrus scandens (American bittersweet)
Clematis crispa (leatherflower)
Clematis pitcheri (leather flower, purple clematis)
Clematis virginiana (virgin's bower)
Lonicera sempervirens (coral honeysuckle)
Parthenocissus quinquefolia (Virginia creeper)
Passiflora incarnata (passion flower, maypop)
Vitis riparia (riverbank grape)
Vitis rotundifolia (muscadine grape)
Wisteria frutescens (wisteria)

FEDERALLY LISTED ENDANGERED SPECIES

Blue Ridge goldenrod (Solidago spithamaea)
Cumberland rose (conradina verticillata)
Cumberland sandwort (Arenaria cumberlandensis)
Green pitcher-plant (Saracenia oreophila)
Large-flowered skullcap (Scutellaria montana)

Leafy prairie-clover (Dalea (Petalostemum) foliosa)
Price's potato-bean (Apios priceana)
Pyne's (Guthrie's) ground-plum (Astragalus bibullatus)
Roan Mountain bluet (Hedyotis purpurea var. Montana)
Rock cress (Arabis perstellata)
Rock hnome lichen (Gymnoderma lineare)
Ruth's golden aster (Pityopsis (Heterotheca Chrysopsis) ruthii)
Small shorled pogonia (Isotria medeoloides)
Spreading avens (Geum radiatum)
Tennessee purple coneflower (Echinacea tennesseensis)
Tennessee yellow-eyed grass (Xyris tennesseenisis)
Virginia spiraea (Spiraea virginiana)

TENNESSEE NOXIOUS SPECIES

Because the noxious weed lists have continually changed since we gathered them in 1994, we are not including them at this time. Not all States have noxious weed lists. Those that do, do not use the same standards of importance and are not comparable. States typically have included plants that interfere with agriculture (Canada thistle), or cause human health problems (poison ivy). Some States are now including a category of plants that invade and degrade the environment (purple loosestrife). Check with your State's Agriculture Department or Weed Scientist listed below. The noxious weed list can be used two ways on roadsides: l) check to not inadvertantly plant these invasive plants, and 2) note the plants you are legally responsible to control. Many States now check adjacent State lists to avoid planting their neighbors' problem plants. Because weeds do not respect political boundaries, and because by their very nature weeds continue to adapt and expand, monitoring and controlling invasives at State borders is a wise part of vegetation management.

(Weed and Seed Laws)

Department of Agriculture
Division of Plant Industry
Box 40627, Melrose Sta.
Nashville, TN 37204

Gilbert Rhodes, U of T
Agricultural Extension Service
363 Ellington Plant Science
Knoxville, TN 37901
(423) 974-7208

TENNESSEE RESOURCES

Divsion of Natural Heritage
401 Church Street
Life and Casualty Tower, 14th Floor
Nashville, TN 37243
(615) 532-0431

The Nature Conservancy Field Office
50 Vantage Way, Ste. 250
Nashville, TN 37228
(615) 255-0303

Tennessee Native Plant Society
Department of Botany
University of Tennessee
Knoxville, TN 37916

Warner Park Nature Center
7311 Highway 100
Nashville, TN 37221
(615) 352-6299

POTENTIAL NATURAL VEGETATION ZONES IN

TEXAS

Source: A.W. Kuchler's Potential Natural Vegetation Map, 1964, Revised 1985.
Presented in U.S.G.S. National Atlas of the U.S. Series,
U.S. Geological Survey, Reston, VA.

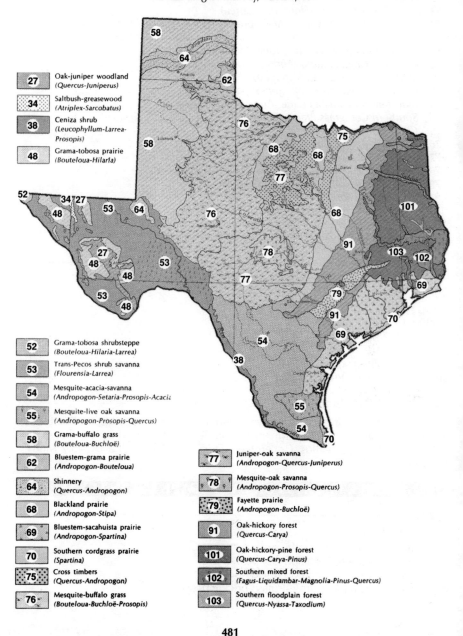

27 Oak-juniper woodland
(*Quercus-Juniperus*)

34 Saltbush-greasewood
(*Atriplex-Sarcobatus*)

38 Ceniza shrub
(*Leucophyllum-Larrea-Prosopis*)

48 Grama-tobosa prairie
(*Bouteloua-Hilaria*)

52 Grama-tobosa shrubsteppe
(*Bouteloua-Hilaria-Larrea*)

53 Trans-Pecos shrub savanna
(*Flourensia-Larrea*)

54 Mesquite-acacia-savanna
(*Andropogon-Setaria-Prosopis-Acacia*)

55 Mesquite-live oak savanna
(*Andropogon-Prosopis-Quercus*)

58 Grama-buffalo grass
(*Bouteloua-Buchloë*)

62 Bluestem-grama prairie
(*Andropogon-Bouteloua*)

64 Shinnery
(*Quercus-Andropogon*)

68 Blackland prairie
(*Andropogon-Stipa*)

69 Bluestem-sacahuista prairie
(*Andropogon-Spartina*)

70 Southern cordgrass prairie
(*Spartina*)

75 Cross timbers
(*Quercus-Andropogon*)

76 Mesquite-buffalo grass
(*Bouteloua-Buchloë-Prosopis*)

77 Juniper-oak savanna
(*Andropogon-Quercus-Juniperus*)

78 Mesquite-oak savanna
(*Andropogon-Prosopis-Quercus*)

79 Fayette prairie
(*Andropogon-Buchloë*)

91 Oak-hickory forest
(*Quercus-Carya*)

101 Oak-hickory-pine forest
(*Quercus-Carya-Pinus*)

102 Southern mixed forest
(*Fagus-Liquidambar-Magnolia-Pinus-Quercus*)

103 Southern floodplain forest
(*Quercus-Nyassa-Taxodium*)

(Dominant plant species present in each vegetation type are listed in Appendix 8)

27   Oak-Juniper Woodland (Quercus-Juniperus)
34   Saltbrush-Geasewood (Artiplex-Sarcobatus)
38   Ceniza Shrub (Leucophyllum-Larrea-Prosopis)
48   Grama-Tobosa-Prairie (Bouteloua-Hilaria)
52   Grama-Tobosa Shrubsteppe (Bouteloua-Hilaria-Larrea)
53   Trans-Pecos Savanna (Flourensia-Larrea)
54   Mesquite-Acacia-Savanna (Andropogon-Setaria-Prosopis-Acacia)
55   Mesquite-Live Oak Savanna (Andropogon- Prosopis-Quercus)
58   Grama-Buffalo Grass (Bouteloua-Buchloë)
62   Bluestem-Grama Prairie (Andropogon-Bouteloua)
64   Shinnery (Quercus-Andropogon)
68   Blackland Prairie (Andropogon-Stipa)
69   Bluestem-Sacahuista Prairie (Andropogon-Spartina)
70   Southern Cordgrass Prairie (Spartina)
75   Cross Timbers (Quercus-Andropogon)
76   Mesquite-Buffalo Grass (Bouteloua-Buchloë- Prosopis)
77   Juniper-Oak Savanna (Andropogon-Quercus-Juniperus)
78   Mesquite-Oak Savanna (Andropogon-Prosopis-Quercus)
79   Fayette Prairie (Andropogon-Buchloë)
91   Oak-Hickory Forest (Quercus-Carya)
101 Oak-Hickory-Pine Forest (Quercus-Carya-Pinus)
102 Southern Mixed Forest (Fagus-Liquidambar-Magnolia-Pinus-Quercus)
103 Southern Floodplain Forest (Quercus-Nyssa-Taxodium)

Botanical Expert

Jackie M. Poole, Botanist, Wildlife Diversity Program
Wildlife Division
Texas Parks and Wildlife Department
3000 I-35 South, Suite 100
Austin, TX 78744
(512) 912-7019
(512) 912-7058 (fax)
internet: jackie.poole@tpwd.state.tx.us

Recommended Flora

Hatch, S.L.; K.N. Gandhi; L.E. Brown. 1990. Checklist of the Vascular Plants of Texas. Texas Agricultural Experiment Station, Texas A&M University, College Station, TX. 158 pgs. + illus. Government Document Number: Z TA245.7 M681 no.1655

NATIVE PLANTS FOR LANDSCAPE USE IN TEXAS

Cacti

Opuntia atrispina
Opuntia imbricata (tree cholla, walkingstick cholla)
Opuntia lindheimeri (Texas prickly pear)
Opuntia macrorhiza (common prickly pear)
Opuntia phaeacantha (purple-fruited prickly pear)

Ferns

Adiantum capillus-veneris (southern maidenhair fern)
Anemia mexicana (Mexican fern)
Asplenium platyneuron (ebony spleenwort)
Asplenium trichomanes (maidenhair spleenwort)
Astrolepis sinuata ssp. sinuata (bulb lip fern)
Athyrium filix-femina (lady fern)
Botrychium virginianum (rattlesnake fern)
Cheilanthes lindheimeri (fairy swords)
Cystopteris bulbifera (bladder fern)
Cystopteris fragilis (fragile fern)
Marsilea macropoda (water clover)
Onoclea sensibilis (sensitive fern, bead fern)
Osmunda cinnamomea (cinnamon fern)
Osmunda regalis (royal fern)
Pellaea atropurpurea (purple cliff brake)
Pellaea ovata (cliff brake)
Phegopteris hexagonoptera (broad beech fern)
Polystichum acrostichoides (Christmas fern)
Thelypteris kunthii (southern shield fern, wood fern, river fern)
Woodwardia areolata (netted chain fern)

Forbs (annuals/biennials)

Amblyolepis setigera (huisache daisy, honey daisy)
Aphanostephus skirrhobasis (lazy daisy)
Argemone albiflora ssp. texana (white prickly poppy)
Argemone mexicana (yellow prickly poppy)
Argemone sangiunea (red prickly poppy)
Baileya multiradiata (desert marigold)
Castilleja indivisa (Indian paintbrush)
Centaurea americana (basket flower)
Cleome serrulata (Rocky Mountain beeplant)
Coreopsis tinctoria (tickseed, goldenwave, plains coreopsis, calliopsis)
Dimorphocarpa wislizeni (spectacle pod)
Dracopsis amplexicaulis (clasping leaf coneflower)
Dysodiopsis tagetoides (dyssodia, dogweed, fetid marigold)
Dyssodia papposa (dyssodia, dogweed, fetid marigold)
Erodium texanum (fillaree, stork's bill)
Eryngium leavenworthii (Leavenworth eryngo)
Erysimum capitatum (western wallflower, prairie rocket)
Eschscholzia californica ssp. mexicana (Mexican gold poppy)
Euphorbia marginata (snow-on-the-mountain)
Eustoma russellianum (prairie or catchfly gentian, Texas bluebell)
Gaillardia pulchella (Indian blanket, firewheel)
Glandularia canadensis (rose vervain, sweet William)
Helianthus argophyllus (silverleaf sunflower)
Helianthus petiolaris (plains sunflower)
Hymenopappus artemisiifolius (old plainsman, woolly white)
Ipomopsis longiflora (white-flowered gilia)
Ipomopsis rubra (standing cypress)
Kallstroemia grandiflora (desert poppy, Mexican poppy)
Lepidium montanum (mountain peppergrass)

Lesquerella gordonii (Gordon's bladderpod)
Lesquerella gracilis (bladderpod)
Lindheimera texana (Texas star, Lindheimer daisy)
Linum rigidum (yellow flax)
Linum rupestre (rock flax)
Lobelia spicata (pale lobelia)
Lupinus concinnus (annual lupine, bajada lupine)
Lupinus havardii (Havard bluebonnet, Big Bend bluebonnet, chisos bluebonnet)
Lupinus subcarnosus (Texas bluebonnet)
Machaeranthera tanacetifolia (tahoka daisy, tansy aster)
Marshallia caespitosa var. caespitosa (Barbara's buttons)
Monarda citriodora (horsemint, lemon beebalm, lemon mint)
Nemophila phacelioides (baby blue eyes)
Oenothera albicaulis (pale evening primrose)
Oenothera biennis (common evening primrose)
Oenothera elata ssp. hookeri (giant evening primrose)
Oenothera primiveris (bottle evening primrose, Yellow desert primrose)
Palafoxia callosa (small palafoxia)
Pectis angustifolia (limoncillo, fetid marigold)
Phacelia congesta (blue curls)
Phlox drummondii (Drummond's phlox)
Prionopsis ciliata
Proboscidea louisianica (unicorn plant, proboscis flower, ram's horn)
Rudbeckia hirta (black-eyed Susan)
Sabatia campestris (prairie rose gentian, prairie sabatia, meadow pink)
Sedum nuttallianum (yellow stonecrop)
Senecio ampullaceus (Texas groundsel)
Senecio glabellus (butterweed)
Senecio plattensis (prairie ragwort, prairie groundsel)
Simsia calva (awnless bush sunflower)
Streptanthus platycarpus (broadpod twist flower)
Teucrium laciniatum (dwarf germander, cutleaf germander)
Thelesperma filifolium var. filifolium (thelesperma, greenthread)
Thymophylla tenuiloba var. tenuiloba (dyssodia, dogweed, fetid marigold)
Townsendia exscapa (Easter daisy)
Verbesina encelioides (cowpen daisy)
Xanthisma texanum (sleepy daisy)

Forbs (perennials)

Abronia fragrans (sweet sand verbena)
Abutilon wrightii
Acacia angustissima (fern acacia, whiteball acacia)
Ageratina altissima var. altissima (white snakeroot)
Allium canadense (wild garlic)
Allium cernuum (nodding onion)
Allium drummondii (Drummond or wild onion)
Allium macropetalum (desert onion)
Allium stellatum (wild pink onion)
Alophia drummondii (purple pleatleaf)
Amoreuxia wrightii (yellow show)
Amsonia ciliata (blue funnel lily, blue star)
Amsonia tabernaemontana (blue star)

Anemone berlandieri (ten-petal anemone)
Anemone caroliniana (Carolina anemone, southern thimbleweed)
Antennaria marginata (pussytoes, everlasting)
Antennaria parlinii ssp. fallax (pussytoes, everlasting)
Apocynum androsaemifolium (spreading dogbane)
Aquilegia canadensis (columbine)
Aquilegia chrysantha (yellow columbine)
Arisaema triphyllum (Jack-in-the-pulpit, Indian turnip)
Artemisia ludoviciana (white sage, prairie sage, artemisia)
Asclepias asperula (antelope horns)
Asclepias incarnata (swamp milkweed)
Asclepias oenotheriodes (hierba de zizotes)
Asclepias speciosa (showy milkweed)
Asclepias tuberosa (butterfly weed)
Asclepias verticillata (whorled milkweed)
Aster ericoides (heath aster, white wreath aster)
Aster oblongifolius (aromatic aster)
Aster oolentangiensis (sky blue aster)
Astragalus canadensis (milk vetch, Canada milk vetch)
Bahia absinthifolia (bahia, yerba raton)
Baptisia alba (white false indigo)
Baptisia alba var. macrophyllla (cream false indigo, plains wild indigo)
Baptisia australis (blue wild indigo)
Berlandiera lyrata (green eyes, chocolate flower)
Callirhoe digitata (finger poppy mallow)
Callirhoe involucrata (purple poppy mallow, winecup)
Callirhoe papaver (poppy mallow)
Calylophus berlandieri (square-bud primrose, sundrops)
Calylophus hartwegii
Calylophus serrulatus (yellow evening primrose)
Camassia scilloides (wild hyacinth)
Campanula rotundifolia (harebell)
Castilleja integra (Indian paintbrush)
Castilleja sessiliflora (downy painted cup)
Claytonia virginica (narrow-leaved spring beauty)
Clitoria mariana (Atlantic pigeon wings)
Cooperia drummondii (rain lily, prairie lily)
Cooperia pedunculata (rain lily)
Coreopsis grandiflora (coreopsis)
Coreopsis lanceolata (lance-leaved coreopsis)
Coreopsis tripteris (tall coreopsis)
Dalea aurea (golden dalea)
Dalea candida (white prairie clover)
Dalea purpurea (purple prairie clover)
Delphinium carolinianum (blue larkspur)
Desmodium illinoense (Illinois tick-trefoil, Illinois tickclover)
Dichondra argentea (silver ponyfoot)
Dichondra carolinensis (ponyfoot)
Dodecatheon meadia (shooting star)
Echinacea angustifolia (narrow-leaved purple coneflower)
Echinacea purpurea (purple coneflower)
Engelmannia pinnatifida (Engelmann daisy)

Erigeron modestus (prairie fleabane)
Eriogonum annuum (buckwheat)
Eriogonum tenellum (buckwheat)
Eriogonum wrightii (Wright buckwheat)
Eryngium yuccifolium (rattlesnake master, button snake-root)
Erythrina herbacea (coral bean)
Eupatorium coelestinum (mist flower)
Eupatorium fistulosum (Joe-pye weed)
Eupatorium greggii (palmleaf thoroughwort)
Eupatorium perfoliatum (boneset)
Euphorbia corollata (flowering spurge)
Fragaria virginiana (wild strawberry)
Gaillardia pinnatifida (yellow gaillardia, blanket flower)
Gaillardia suavis (gaillardia, blanket flower)
Galium triflorum (sweet-scented bedstraw)
Gaura coccinea (scarlet gaura)
Gaura suffulta (wild honeysuckle, bee blossom)
Glandularia bipinnatifida var. bipinnatifida (prairie verbena, Dakota vervain)
Glycyrrhiza lepidota (wild licorice)
Habranthus tubispathus (copper lily)
Hedyotis nigricans (bluets)
Hedysarum boreale (sweet vetch, sweet broom)
Helenium autumnale (common sneezeweed)
Helianthus maximiliani (Maximilian sunflower)
Helianthus simulans (narrow-leaved sunflower, swamp sunflower)
Heliopsis helianthoides (ox-eye sunflower, false sunflower)
Heterotheca canescens (golden aster, camphor-weed)
Heterotheca villosa var. villosa (golden aster)
Heuchera rubescens var. versicolor (coral bells, alumroot)
Hibiscus laevis (halberd-leaved marsh mallow)
Hibiscus lasiocarpus (woolly rose mallow)
Hibiscus moscheutos (swamp rose mallow, marshmallow hibiscus)
Hieracium longipilum (hairy hawkweed)
Hymenocallis caroliniana (spider lily, rain lily)
Hypoxis hirsuta (yellow star grass)
Indigofera miniata (scarlet indigo)
Ipomoea leptophylla (bush morning glory)
Iris virginica (southern blue flag)
Kosteletzkya virginica (seashore mallow)
Lespedeza capitata (roundheaded bush clover)
Lesquerella fendleri (bladderpod)
Liatris aspera (rough blazing star, gayfeather)
Liatris elegans (gayfeather)
Liatris mucronata (narrow-leaf gayfeather)
Liatris punctata (dotted blazing star, gayfeather)
Liatris pycnostachya (prairie blazing star, gayfeather)
Liatris squarrosa (blazing star)
Linum lewisii (wild blue flax)
Lithospermum caroliniense (hairy puccoon, hispid gromwell)
Lithospermum incisum (fringed puccoon, narrow-leaved puccoon)
Lobelia cardinalis (cardinal flower)
Lobelia siphilitica (great blue lobelia)

Maianthemum racemosum ssp. racemosum (false Solomon's seal, false spikenard)
Manfreda virginica (rattlesnake master, false aloe)
Melampodium cinereum (black-foot)
Melampodium leucanthum (Blackfoot daisy, rock daisy)
Mimosa quadrivalvis var. angustata (catclaw sensitive briar)
Mimosa quadrivalvis var. nuttalii (catclaw sensitive briar)
Mitchella repens (partridge berry)
Monarda fistulosa (wild bergamot, horsemint, beebalm)
Monarda punctata (beebalm)
Nothocalais cuspidata (prairie dandelion)
Nuphar lutea (yellow pond lily, cow lily, spatter dock)
Nymphaea odorata (white water lily)
Oenothera brachycarpa (evening primrose)
Oenothera grandis
Oenothera lacinata (cut-leaved evening primrose)
Oenothera macrocarpa (Missouri evening primrose)
Oenothera speciosa (showy white evening primrose)
Penstemon albidus (white beardtongue)
Penstemon ambiguus (sand penstemon)
Penstemon baccharifolius (rock penstemon)
Penstemon barbatus (red penstemon, scarlet bugler)
Penstemon cobaea (cobaea penstemon, wild foxglove)
Penstemon digitalis (beardtongue)
Penstemon fendleri (fendler penstemon, purple foxglove)
Penstemon grandiflorus (large-flowered penstemon)
Penstemon jamesii (James' penstemon)
Penstemon murrayanus (red penstemon, cupleaf beardtongue)
Petrophytun caespitosum (dwarf spiraea, petrophytum, tufted rockmat)
Phlox carolina (Carolina phlox)
Phlox divaricata ssp. laphamii (blue phlox, sweet William)
Phlox nana (Santa Fe phlox, white-eyed phlox, canyon phlox)
Phlox pilosa (prairie phlox, downy phlox)
Physostegia digitalis (obedient plant)
Physostegia intermedia (obedient plant)
Physostegia virginiana (obedient plant, false dragonhead)
Pinaropappus roseus (white rock lettuce)
Pluchea camphorata (camphor-weed)
Podophyllum peltatum (May apple)
Polygonatum biflorum (Solomon's seal)
Porophyllum scoparium (poreleaf)
Potentilla simplex (common cinquefoil)
Psilostrophe tagetina (woolly paper-flower)
Pycnanthemum tenuifolium (slender mountain mint)
Ranunculus hispidus (early buttercup, tufted buttercup)
Ranunculus macranthus (large buttercup)
Ratibida columnifera (prairie coneflower, long-headed coneflower, Mexican hat)
Rhexia virginica (meadow beauty)
Rudbeckia fulgida (black-eyed Susan, orange coneflower)
Rudbeckia grandiflora (large coneflower)
Rudbeckia subtomentosa (sweet black-eyed Susan)
Ruellia humilis (wild petunia)

Ruellia nudiflora (wild petunia, violet ruellia)
Salvia arizonica (Arizona sage)
Salvia azurea (blue sage)
Salvia azurea var. grandiflora (blue sage)
Salvia coccinea (tropical sage)
Salvia engelmannii (Engelmann sage)
Salvia farinacea (mealy sage)
Salvia lyrata (cancer weed, lyre-leaf sage)
Sanguinaria candensis (bloodroot)
Scutellaria drummondii (Drummond skullcap)
Senna lindheimeriana (Lindheimer senna, velvetleaf senna)
Senna roemeriana (two-leaved senna)
Silene laciniata (southern Indian pink, catchfly, Mexican campion)
Silene stellata (starry campion)
Silphium albiflorum (compass plant)
Silphium laciniatum (compass plant)
Sisyrinchium angustifolium (narrow-leaved blue-eyed grass)
Sisyrinchium campestre (white-eyed grass, prairie blue-eyed grass)
Sisyrinchium chilense (prairie blue-eyed grass)
Solidago caesia (blue-stemmed goldenrod, wreath goldenrod)
Solidago canadensis (meadow goldenrod)
Solidago missouriensis (Missouri goldenrod, prairie goldenrod)
Solidago nemoralis (gray goldenrod, old-field goldenrod)
Solidago odora (sweet goldenrod)
Solidago rigida (stiff goldenrod)
Solidago rugosa (rough-leaved goldenrod)
Solidago sempervirens (seaside goldenrod)
Solidago speciosa (showy goldenrod)
Solidago ulmifolia (elm-leaved goldenrod)
Sphaeralcea angustfolia (globe mallow)
Sphaeralcea coccinea (scarlet globe mallow)
Spigelia marilandica (Indian pink)
Stachys coccinea (Texas betony)
Stanleya pinnata (desert or prince's plume)
Talinum aurantiacum (flame flower)
Tephrosia lindheimeri (Lindheimer tephorsia)
Tephrosia virginiana (goat's rue)
Tetraneuris acaulis var. acaulis (stemless goldflower, stemless rubber weed, Butte marigold)
Tetraneuris scaposa var. scaposa (four-nerve daisy, yellow daisy, bitterweed)
Thalictrum dasycarpum (tall or purple meadow rue)
Thymophylla micropoides (dyssodia)
Thymophylla pentachaeta var. pentachaeta (parralena)
Tinantia anomala (false dayflower)
Tradescantia gigantea (giant spiderwort)
Tradescantia hirsuticaulis (hairy spiderwort)
Tradescantia ohiensis (Ohio spiderwort)
Varilla texana (saladillo)
Verbena halei (slender or mint vergain)
Verbena stricta (hoary vervain)
Vernonia baldwinii (ironweed, western ironweed)
Vernonia lindheimeri (woolly ironweed)
Viguiera dentata (goldeneye)

Viola missouriensis (Missouri violet)
Viola pedata (bird-foot violet)
Wedelia acapulcensis var. hispida (wedelia)
Zinnia grandiflora (Rocky Mountain zinnia, yellow zinnia, plains zinnia)
Zizia aurea (golden alexanders)

Grasses/Grass-like plants

Agrostis exarata (spikebent, spike red top)
Agrostis scabra (ticklegrass, fly-away grass)
Andropogon gerardii (big bluestem)
Andropogon glomeratus (bushy bluestem)
Andropogon hallii (sand bluestem)
Andropogon ternarius (splitbeard bluestem)
Andropogon virginicus (broom sedge)
Aristida purpurea (purple three awn)
Aristida purpurea var. longiseta (red three awn)
Arundinaria gigantea (giant cane)
Bouteloua curtipendula (sideoats grama)
Bouteloua eriopoda (black grama)
Bouteloua gracilis (blue grama)
Bouteloua hirsuta (hairy grama)
Bouteloua rigidiseta (Texas grama)
Buchloe dactyloides (buffalograss)
Carex cherokeensis (sedge)
Chasmanthium latifolium (inland sea oats, wild oats, river oats, broad-leaf uniola)
Chloris crinita (two-flowered trichloris)
Cladium jamaicense (sawgrass)
Danthonia spicata (poverty grass)
Digitaria californica (cottontop)
Digitaria cognata (fall witchgrass)
Distichlis spicata (seashore saltgrass)
Eleocharis palustris (creeping spikesedge, spike rush)
Elymus canadensis (Canada wild rye)
Eragrostis intermedia (plains lovegrass)
Eragrostis spectabilis (purple lovegrass, tumblegrass)
Hilaria belangeri (curly mesquite)
Hilaria mutica (tobosa grass)
Juncus effusus var. solutus (soft rush)
Juncus interior (inland rush)
Koeleria macrantha (June grass)
Leersia oryzoides (rice cut grass)
Leptochloa dubia (green sprangletop)
Melica nitens (three-flower melic grass)
Muhlenbergia capillaris (gulf muhly, hair grass)
Muhlenbergia lindheimeri (Lindheimer muhly)
Muhlenbergia montana (mountain muhly)
Muhlenbergia porteri (bush muhly)
Muhlenbergia reverchonii (seep muhly)
Muhlenbergia rigida (purple muhly)
Oryzopsis hymenoides (Indian ricegrass)
Panicum obtusum (vine mesquite)
Panicum virgatum (switchgrass)
Pappophorum bicolor (pink pampus grass)

Pascopyrum smithii (western wheatgrass)
Piptochaetium fimbriatum (pinyon rice grass, burrograss)
Poa arachnifera (Texas bluegrass)
Rhynchospora colorata (star-rush whitetop)
Saccharum giganteum (sugarcane plume grass)
Schizachyrium scoparium (little bluestem)
Scirpus acutus (hardstem bulrush)
Scirpus cyperinus (wool grass)
Scirpus maritimus (alkali bulrush, prairie bulrush, bayonet grass)
Scirpus tabernaemontani (great bulrush)
Scleropogon brevifolius (burro grass, plains bristlegrass)
Sorghastrum nutans (Indian grass)
Spartina patens (marsh hay cordgrass, salt meadow cordgrass)
Spartina pectinata (prairie cordgrass, freshwater cordgrass)
Spartina spartinae (Gulf cordgrass)
Sporobolus airoides (alkali sacaton)
Sporobolus compositus var. compositus (tall dropseed)
Sporobolus cryptandrus (sand dropseed)
Sporobolus flexuosus (mesa dropseed)
Sporobolus giganteus (giant dropseed)
Sporobolus heterolepis (northern prairie dropseed)
Sporobolus pyramidatus (whorled dropseed)
Stipa comata (needle-and-thread grass)
Stipa nelsonii (Columbia needlegrass)
Tripsacum dactyloides (eastern gama grass)
Typha latifolia (cattail)
Zizaniopsis milacea (Texas wild rice, marsh millet)

Shrubs (deciduous)

Abutilon hypoleucum (Rio Grande abutilon)
Acacia berlandieri (guajillo)
Acacia greggii var. wrightii (catclaw, Wright acacia)
Acacia rigidula (black brush, chapano prieto, catclaw, gavia)
Acacia roemeriana (Roemer acacia, catclaw)
Agave harvardiana (Harvard agave)
Agave neomexicana (century plant, New Mexico agave)
Ageratina havanensis (mistflower)
Alnus serrulata (smooth alder)
Aloysia gratissima (beebrush, whitebrush, privet lippia)
Aloysia macrostachya (Rio Grande or woolly beebush)
Amelanchier arborea (downy serviceberry, shadbush, Juneberry)
Amelanchier utahensis (Utah serviceberry)
Amorpha canescens (leadplant)
Amorpha fruticosa (false indigo, Indigo bush)
Aniscanthus quadrifidus var. wrightii (flame acanthus, hummingbird bush)
Artemisia filifolia (sand sage)
Atriplex canescens (four-wing saltbush, wingscale)
Atriplex confertifolia (spiny saltbush, shadscale saltbush, hop sage)
Baccharis halimifolia (sea myrtle, groundsel bush)
Bauhinia congesta (orchid tree, anacacho orchid tree)
Bouvardia ternifolia (smooth bouvardia)
Calliandra eriophylla (fairy duster, mesquitilla)

Callicarpa americana (American beautyberry, French mulberry)
Castanea pumila (chinquapin)
Ceanothus americanus (New Jersey tea, red root)
Ceanothus greggii var. vestitus (desert ceanothus)
Celtis pallida (desert hackberry, granjeno)
Cephalanthus occidentalis (buttonbush)
Choisya dumosa (Mexican orange, zorrillo)
Chrysothamnus nauseosus (rabbit brush, chamisa)
Clethra alnifolia (summer sweet)
Colubrina texensis (Texas snakewood, hog plum)
Condalia ericoides (javelina bush, tecomblate)
Condalia hookeri (condalia, brasil)
Cornus drummondii (rough-leaf dogwood)
Dalea formosa (feather plume, feather dalea)
Dalea frutescens (black dalea)
Dalea greggii (indigo bush, Gregg dalea)
Dalea scoparia (broom dalea, broom pea)
Dasylirion wheeleri (Sotol, desert pampas grass, Desert spoon)
Diospyros texana (Texas or Mexican persimmon, chapote)
Ephedra trifurca (ephedra, joint fir)
Eupatorium odoratum (blue mistflower, crucita)
Euonymus americana (strawberry bush, brook euonymus, hearts-a-bustin')
Euonymus atropurpurea (wahoo, burning bush)
Eysenhardtia texana (kidneywood, vara dulce)
Fallugia paradoxa (Apache plume)
Fendlera rupicola (false mock orange, cliff fendler bush)
Forestiera acuminata (swamp privet)
Forestiera pubescens (desert olive, elbow-bush, forestiera)
Forestiera reticulata (nutleaf forestiera)
Fouquieria splendens (ocotillo, candlewood)
Frangula caroliniana (Carolina buckthorn)
Fraxinus greggii (littleleaf ash, Gregg ash, escobilla)
Hamamelis vernalis (vernal witch hazel)
Hesperaloe parviflora (red-flowered yucca)
Hibiscus coulteri (desert rose mallow, Coulter hibiscus)
Hibiscus denudatus (rock hibiscus)
Hibiscus martianus (heart-leaf hibiscus)
Holodiscus dumosus (bush rock-spires, cream bush, ocean spray)
Hypericum hypericoides ssp. hypericoides (St. Andrew's cross)
Ilex verticillata (winterberry, black alder)
Itea virginica (Virginia willow, sweetspire, tassel-white)
Krascheninnikovia lanata (winterfat)
Lantana urticoides (trailing lantana, calico bush)
Lindera benzoin (spicebush)
Lonicera albiflora (white honeysuckle)
Lycium carolinianum (Christmas berry, matrimony vine)
Lyonia ligustrina (male-berry, male-blueberry)
Malvaviscus drummondii (Turk's-cap mallow, Texas wax mallow,
   Mexican apple, Manzanilla)
Mimosa borealis (pink mimosa, fragrant mimosa)
Nolina texana (sacahuista, basket grass, Texas beargrass)
Parkinsonia texana var. texana (palo verde)

Parthenium argentatum (guayuule)
Parthenium incanum (mariola)
Poliomintha incana (mintbush)
Prunus gracilis (Oklahoma plum)
Prunus virginiana (chokecherry)
Ptelea trifoliata (wafer ash, common hoptree)
Quercus sinuata var. breviloba (shin oak)
Rhododendron canescens (wild, piedmont, or sweet azalea)
Rhododendron oblongifolium (Texas azalea)
Rhododendron prinophyllum (roseshell azalea, early azalea)
Rhus aromatica (fragrant sumac)
Rhus copallinum (dwarf or winged sumac)
Rhus glabra (smooth sumac)
Rhus lanceolata (prairie flameleaf sumac, lanceleaf sumac)
Rhus microphylla (desert sumac, littleleaf sumac, correosa)
Ribes odoratum (buffalo currant, golden currant)
Robinia neomexicana (New Mexico locust, mescal bean)
Rosa arkansana (prairie rose)
Rosa carolina (Carolina rose)
Rosa setigera (Illinois or prairie rose)
Rosa stellata (desert rose)
Rosa woodsii (western wild rose, woods rose)
Salvia ballotaeflora (shrubby blue sage)
Salvia regla (royal sage, mountain sage)
Sambucus canadensis (elderberry, common elder)
Sambucus mexicana (Mexican elderberry)
Sarcobatus vermiculatus (greasewood)
Senna wislizenii (shrubby senna, canyon senna)
Sideroxylon lanuginosum ssp. lanuginosum (chittamwood, gum elastic tree)
Stewartia malacodendron (silky camellia)
Styrax americanus (American silverbells)
Symphoricarpos orbiculatus (coralberry, Indian currant)
Symphoricarpos oreophilus (mountain snowberry)
Tecoma stans (yellow bells, trumpet flower)
Vaccinium arboreum (sparkleberry, farkleberry)
Viburnum acerifolium (maple leaf viburnum)
Viburnum dentatum (southern arrowwood)
Viburnum nudum (possumhaw viburnum)
Viburnum prunifolium (black haw, nanny berry)
Viburnum rufidulum (southern or rusty black haw)
Yucca arkansana (Arkansas yucca, softleaf yucca)
Yucca baccata (blue yucca, banana yucca, fleshy-fruited yucca)
Yucca constricta (Buckley yucca)
Yucca elata (soaptree yucca, palmella)
Yucca glauca (yucca, soapweed)
Yucca rupicola (twistleaf yucca)
Yucca treculeana (trecul yucca)

Shrubs (evergreen)

Avicennia germinans (black mangrove)
Ceanothus fendleri (Fendler ceanothus, buckbrush)
Cercocarpus montanus (mountain mahogany, silverleaf mountain mahogany)

Chrysactinia mexicana (damianita)
Cordia podocephala (cluster cordia)
Ericameria laricifolia (larchleaf goldenweed, turpentine bush)
Garrya ovata ssp. lindheimerii (Lindheimer silk tassel)
Garrya wrightii (Wright's catclaw, Wright's silk tassel)
Ilex vomitoria (yaupon)
Juniperus monosperma (one-seed juniper)
Larrea tridentata (creosote bush)
Leucophyllum frutescens (cenizo, Texas sage, purple sage)
Mahonia repens (creeping barberry)
Mahonia swaseyi (Texas barberry)
Mahonia trifoliolata (agarito, trifoliate barberry)
Myrica cerifera (wax myrtle, southern bayberry, candleberry)
Pithecellobium ebano (Texas ebony, ebano)
Purshia ericaefolia (heath cliffrose)
Rhus choriophylla (evergreen sumac)
Rhus virens (evergreen sumac, tobacco sumac)
Sabal minor (dwarf palmetto)
Salvia greggii (autumn sage)
Vauquelinia angustifolia (guauyul, palo prieto)
Viguiera stenoloba (resin bush)

Trees (deciduous)

Acacia farnesiana (huisache, sweet acacia)
Acer barbatum (Florida maple, southern sugar maple)
Acer grandidentatum (bigtooth maple)
Acer leucoderme (chalk maple)
Acer negundo (box elder)
Acer rubrum (red maple)
Aesculus glabra (Ohio buckeye, horse chestnut)
Aesculus glabra var. arguta (white buckeye, Texas buckeye)
Aesculus pavia var. pavia (red buckeye)
Betula nigra (river birch)
Carpinus caroliniana (blue beech, hornbeam, musclewood)
Carya alba (mockernut hickory)
Carya cordiformis (bitternut, swamp hickory)
Carya illinoinensis (pecan)
Carya ovata (shagbark hickory)
Carya texana (black hickory)
Celtis laevigata (sugarberry, hackberry)
Celtis laevigata var. reticulata (netleaf hackberry)
Celtis occidentalis (hackberry, sugarberry)
Cercis canadensis (redbud)
Chilopsis linearis (desert willow, trumpet flower)
Chionanthus virginicus (fringe tree, old man's beard)
Cornus florida (flowering dogwood)
Cotinus obovatus (smoke tree)
Crataegus crus-galli (cockspur hawthorn)
Crataegus marshallii (parsley hawthorn)
Cyrilla racemiflora (leatherwood, yiti)
Diospyros virginiana (persimmon)
Fagus grandifolia var. caroliniana (beech)

Fraxinus americana (white ash)
Fraxinus berlandieriana (Mexican ash, Fresno)
Fraxinus cuspidata (flowering ash)
Fraxinus pensylvanica (green ash)
Fraxinus texensis (Texas ash)
Fraxinus velutina (Arizona ash, Velvet ash, desert ash)
Gleditsia triacanthos (honey locust)
Halesia diptera (American snowdrop tree, two-winged silverbell)
Hamamelis virginiana (witch hazel)
Ilex decidua (possum-haw, deciduous holly)
Juglans major (Arizona walnut)
Juglans microcarpa (Texas walnut, river walnut, little walnut)
Juglans nigra (black walnut)
Leucaena retusa (goldenball lead-tree)
Liquidambar styraciflua (sweet gum)
Magnolia pyramidata (pyramid magnolia)
Magnolia virginiana (sweetbay, swampbay)
Malus angustifolia (southern crabapple, wild crabapple)
Nyssa sylvatica (black gum, tupelo)
Ostrya virginiana (ironwood, hophornbeam)
Platanus occidentalis (sycamore, plane-tree)
Populus deltoides (eastern cottonwood)
Populus fremontii (western cottonwood)
Populus tremuloides (quaking aspen)
Prosopis pubescens (tornillo, screwbean mesquite)
Prunus angustifolia (chickasaw plum)
Prunus mexicana (Mexican plum)
Prunus serotina (black cherry)
Quercus alba (white oak)
Quercus falcata (southern red oak, Spanish oak)
Quercus gambelii (Gambel's oak, Rocky Mountain white oak)
Quercus gravesii (Grave's oak, chisos red oak)
Quercus grisea (gray oak, Mexican blue oak)
Quercus incana (blue jack oak)
Quercus laceyi (lacey oak)
Quercus laurifolia (laurel oak)
Quercus lyrata (overcup oak)
Quercus macrocarpa (bur oak)
Quercus marilandica (blackjack oak)
Quercus muhlenbergii (chinkapin oak, chestnut oak)
Quercus phellos (willow oak)
Quercus shumardii (shumard oak)
Quercus stellata (post oak)
Quercus texana (Texas red oak, Spanish oak)
Quercus velutina (black oak)
Salix nigra (black willow)
Sapindus saponaria var. drummondii (soapberry)
Sassafras albidum (sassafras)
Taxodium distichum (bald cypress)
Tilia americana (American linden, basswood)
Ulmus americana (American elm)
Ulmus crassifolia (cedar elm)
Ulmus rubra (red elm, slippery elm)

Trees (evergreen)

Acacia constricta (whitethorn, mescat acacia)
Arbutus xalapensis (Texas madrone)
Cupressus arizonica (Arizona cypress)
Ehretia anacua (anacua, sandpaper tree, knock-away)
Ilex opaca (American holly, Christmas holly)
Juniperus ashei (rock or post cedar, Ashe or Mexican juniper)
Juniperus deppeana (alligator or western juniper)
Juniperus pinchotii (red-berry juniper)
Juniperus scopulorum (Rocky Mountain juniper)
Juniperus virginiana (eastern red cedar)
Magnolia grandiflora (southern magnolia)
Persea borbonia (red bay)
Pinus cembroides (Mexican pinyon)
Pinus echinata (shortleaf pine)
Pinus edulis (pinyon pine, Colorado pinyon)
Pinus palustris (longleaf pine)
Pinus ponderosa (ponderosa pine)
Pinus strobiformis (southwestern white pine)
Pinus taeda (loblolly pine)
Prunus caroliniana (cherry laurel)
Pseudotsuga menziesii (Douglas fir)
Quercus arizonica (Arizona white oak)
Quercus emoryi
Quercus fusiformis (escarpment live oak)
Quercus virginiana (live oak, coastal live oak, southern live oak)

Vines (deciduous)

Bignonia capreolata (cross vine)
Campsis radicans (trumpet creeper, trumpet vine)
Celastrus scandens (American bittersweet)
Clematis drummondi (Texas virgin's bower, old man's beard)
Clematis pitcheri (leather flower, purple clematis)
Clematis texensis (scarlet clematis)
Lonicera sempervirens (coral honeysuckle)
Maurandya antirrhiniflora (snapdragon vine)
Parthenocissus quinquefolia (Virginia creeper)
Parthenocissus quinquefolia var. quinquefolia (woodbine)
Passiflora incarnata (passion flower, maypop)
Passiflora lutea (yellow passion flower, may pop)
Vitis arizonica (Arizona grape, canyon grape)
Vitis riparia (riverbank grape)
Vitis rotundifolia (muscadine grape)
Wisteria frutescens (wisteria)

Vine (evergreen)

Gelsemium sempervirens (yellow jessamine, Carolina jessamine)

FEDERALLY LISTED ENDANGERED SPECIES

Ashy dogweed (Thymophylla tephroleuca)
Black lace cactus (Echinocereus reichenbachii (melanocentrus) var. albertii)
Bunched cory cactus (Coryphantha ramillosa)
Chisos Mountain hedgehog cactus (Echinocereus chisoensis var. chisoensis)
Davis' green pitaya (Echinocereus virdiflowus var. davisii)
Hinckley's oak (Quercus hinckleyi)
Johnston's frankenia (Frankenia johnstonii)
Large-fruited sand-verbena (Abronia macrocarpa)
Little Aguja pondweed (Potamogeton clystocarpus)
Lloyd's Mariposa cactus (Echinomastus (Sclerocactus) mariposensis)
Lloyd's hedgehog cactus (Echinocereus lloydii)
Navasota ladies'-tresses (Spiranthes parksii)
Nellie cory cactus (Coryphantha (Escobaria) minima)
Slender rush-pea (Hoffmannseggia tenella)
Sneed pincushion cactus (Coryphantha sneedii var. sneedii)
South Texas ambrosia (Ambrosia cheiranthifolia)
Star cactus (Astrophytum asterias)
Terlingua Creek cats-eye (Cryptantha crassipes)
Texas ayenia (Ayenia limitaris)
Texas poppy-mallow (Callirhoe scabriuscula)
Texas prairie dawn-flower (Texas biterweed) Hymenoxys texana)
Texas snowbells (Styrax texana)
Texas trailing phlox (Phlox nivalis ssp. texensis)
Texas wild-rice (zizania texana)
Tobusch fishhook cactus (Ancistrocactus tobuschii)
Waler's manioc (Manihot walkerae)
White bladderpod (Lesquerella pallida)

TEXAS NOXIOUS SPECIES

Because the noxious weed lists have continually changed since we gathered them in 1994, we are not including them at this time. Not all States have noxious weed lists. Those that do, do not use the same standards of importance and are not comparable. States typically have included plants that interfere with agriculture (Canada thistle), or cause human health problems (poison ivy). Some States are now including a category of plants that invade and degrade the environment (purple loosestrife). Check with your State's Agriculture Department or Weed Scientist listed below. The noxious weed list can be used two ways on roadsides: l) check to not inadvertantly plant these invasive plants, and 2) note the plants you are legally responsible to control. Many States now check adjacent State lists to avoid planting their neighbors' problem plants. Because weeds do not respect political boundaries, and because by their very nature weeds continue to adapt and expand, monitoring and controlling invasives at State borders is a wise part of vegetation management.

(Seed Law)

Department of Agriculture
Plant Quality Program
P.O. Box 12847
Austin, TX 78711

Paul Baumann
Soil and Crop Sciences
Texas A&M University
College Station, TX 77843
(409) 845-0877

Wildlife Diversity Program
Texas Parks and Wildlife Dept.
3000 IH-35 South, Ste. 100
Austin, TX 78705
(512) 912-7011

The Nature Conservancy Field Office
P.O. Box 1440
San Antonio, TX 78295
(210) 224-8774

Native Plant Society of Texas
P.O. Box 891
Georgetown, TX 78627

Native Prairies Association of Texas
3503 Lafayette Avenue
Austin, TX 78722

Lady Bird Johnson Wildflower Center
4801 La Crosse Avenue
Austin, TX 78739
(512) 292-4200

Mercer Arboretum and Botanic
Gardens
2306 Aldine-Westfield
Humble, TX 77338

Chihuahuan Desert Research Institute
P.O. Box 1334
Alpine, TX 79831

Wayne McCully, Harlow Landphair
Texas Transportation Institute
College Station, TX 77843
(409) 845-8539

POTENTIAL NATURAL VEGETATION ZONES IN
— UTAH —

Source: A.W. Kuchler's Potential Natural Vegetation Map, 1964, Revised 1985.
Presented in U.S.G.S. National Atlas of the U.S. Series,
U.S. Geological Survey, Reston, VA.

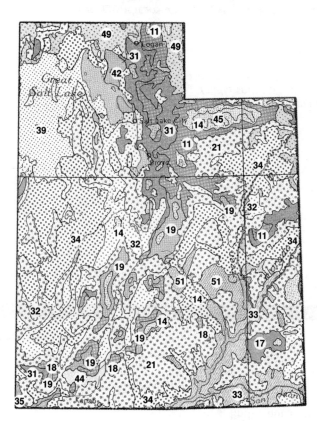

11 Douglas fir forest *(Pseudotsuga)*	**31** Mountain mahogany-oak scrub *(Cercocarpus-Quercus)*	**42** Tule marshes *(Scirpus-Typha)*
14 Western spruce-fir forest *(Picea-Abies)*	**32** Great Basin sagebrush *(Artemisia)*	**44** Wheatgrass-bluegrass *(Agropyron-Poa)*
17 Pine-Douglas fir forest *(Pinus-Pseudotsuga)*	**33** Blackbrush *(Coleogyne)*	**45** Alpine meadows and barren *(Agrostis, Carex, Festuca, Poa)*
18 Arizona pine forest *(Pinus)*	**34** Saltbush-greasewood *(Atriplex-Sarcobatus)*	**49** Sagebrush steppe *(Artemisia-Agropyron)*
19 Spruce-fir-Douglas fir forest *(Picea-Abies-Pseudotsuga)*	**35** Creosote bush *(Larrea)*	**51** Galleta-three awn shrubsteppe *(Hilaria-Aristida)*
21 Juniper-pinyon woodland *(Juniperus-Pinus)*	**39** Desert: vegetation largely absent	

(Dominant plant species present in each vegetation type are listed in Appendix 8)

11	Douglas Fir Forest (Pseudotsuga)
14	Western Spruce-Fir Forest (Picea-Abies)
17	Pine-Douglas Fir Forest (Pinus Pseudotsuga)
18	Arizona Pine Forest (Pinus)
19	Spruce Fir-Douglas Fir Forest (Picea-Abies-Pseudotsuga)
21	Juniper-Pinyon Woodland (Juniperus-Pinus)
31	Mountain Mahogany-Oak Scrub (Cercocarpus-Quercus)
32	Great Basin Sagebrush (Artemisia)
33	Blackbrush (Coleogyne)
34	Saltbrush-Geasewood (Artiplex-Sarcobatus)
35	Creosote Bush (Larrea)
39	Desert: Vegetation Largely Absent
42	Tule Marshes (Scirpus-Typha)
44	Wheatgrass-Bluegrass (Agropyron-Poa)
45	Alpine Meadows and Barren (Agrostis, Carex, Festuca, Poa)
49	Sagebrush Steppe (Artemisia-Agropyron)
51	Galleta-Three Awn Shrubsteppe (Hilaira-Aristida)

Botanical Expert

Duane Atwood, Assistant Curator
Herbarium
Brigham Young University
Provo, UT 84602

Recommended Flora

Welsh, S.L. 1993. A Utah Flora. 2nd Edition, Revision. Brigham Young University. Provo, UT. 986 pgs. maps. ISBN 0842523138.

NATIVE PLANTS FOR LANDSCAPE USE IN UTAH

Cacti

Echinocereus engelmannii (hedgehog cactus, strawberry cactus)
Opuntia basilaris (beavertail cactus)
Opuntia erinacea (grizzly, hedgehog, or Mohave prickly pear)
Opuntia macrorhiza (common prickly pear)
Opuntia phaeacantha (purple-fruited prickly pear)

Ferns

Adiantum capillus-veneris (southern maidenhair fern)
Adiantum pedatum (northern maidenhair fern)
Aspidotis densa (rock brake, cliff brake, Indian's dream)
Asplenium trichomanes (maidenhair spleenwort)
Athyrium filix-femina (lady fern)
Cheilanthes gracillima (lace fern)
Cystopteris bulbifera (bladder fern)
Cystopteris fragilis (fragile fern)

Forbs (annuals/biennials)

Baileya multiradiata (desert marigold)
Collomia linearis (collomia)
Eriogonum inflatum (desert trumpet)
Erysimum capitatum (western wallflower, prairie rocket)
Eschscholzia californica ssp. mexicana (Mexican gold poppy)
Gaillardia arizonica (Arizona blanket flower)
Hymenoxys cooperi (Cooper's goldflower)
Ipomopsis aggregata (sky rocket, scarlet gilia)
Layia glandulosa (tidy tips)
Lupinus concinnus (annual lupine, bajada lupine)
Machaeranthera tanacetifolia (tahoka daisy, tansy aster)
Mimulus guttatus (golden monkey flower)
Nemophila breviflora (Great Basin nemophila)
Oenothera albicaulis (pale evening primrose)
Oenothera deltoides (fragrant primrose, desert evening primrose)
Oenothera primiveris (bottle evening primrose, yellow desert primrose)
Salvia columbariae (chia)
Townsendia exscapa (Easter daisy)

Forbs (perennials)

Abronia fragrans (sweet sand verbena)
Allium cernuum (nodding onion)
Allium macropetalum (desert onion)
Anaphalis margaritacea (pearly everlasting)
Anemone multifida (early thimbleweed, cut-leaf anemone, Pacific anemone)
Aquilegia chrysantha (yellow columbine)
Aquilegia coerulea (Rocky Mountain or blue columbine)
Aquilegia flavescens (yellow columbine)
Aquilegia formosa (scarlet columbine)
Arnica cordifolia (heartleaf arnica)
Artemisia ludoviciana (white sage, prairie sage, artemisia)
Asclepias asperula (antelope horns)
Asclepias incarnata (swamp milkweed)
Aster ascendens (purple aster, Pacific aster)
Aster foliaceus (leafy aster)
Aster laevis (smooth aster)
Aster sibiricus (Sibirian or arctic aster)
Balsamorrhiza sagittata (balsamroot)
Calochortus nuttallii (sego lily, mariposa lily)
Caltha leptosepala (white marsh marigold, elkslip)
Campanula rotundifolia (harebell)
Castilleja angustifolia var. dubia (desert paintbrush)
Castilleja linariifolia (Indian paintbrush)
Dichelostemma congestum (wild hyacinth)
Dryas octopetala (mountain dryas, white mountain avens)
Epilobium angustifolium (fireweed, willow herb)
Epilobium canum var. latifolia (hummingbird trumpet)
Epilobium latifolium (dwarf fireweed)
Erigeron compositus (alpine daisy)
Erigeron speciosus (showy fleabane)
Eriogonum racemosum (red root buckwheat)

Eriogonum umbellatum (sulfur buckwheat)
Erythronium grandiflorum (glacier lily, yellow fawn lily, dogtooth violet)
Eupatorium maculatum (spotted Joe-pye weed)
Gaillardia aristata (blanket flower, gaillardia, brown-eyed Susan)
Gaillardia pinnatifida (yellow gaillardia, blanket flower)
Galium triflorum (sweet-scented bedstraw)
Gaura coccinea (scarlet gaura)
Gentiana parryi (Parry gentian)
Geranium viscossisimum (sticky wild geranium)
Geum triflorum (prairie smoke, purple avens)
Hedysarum boreale (sweet vetch, sweet broom)
Heliomeris multiflora (showy goldeneye)
Heterotheca villosa var. villosa (golden aster)
Heuchera parvifolia (saxifrage, alum root)
Heuchera rubescens (mountain alumroot, red alumroot, wild coralbells)
Houstonia caerulea (bluets)
Lesquerella fendleri (bladderpod)
Lewisia rediviva (bitter root)
Linnaea borealis (twinflower)
Linum lewisii (wild blue flax)
Lithospermum incisum (fringed puccoon, narrow-leaved puccoon)
Lobelia cardinalis (cardinal flower)
Lupinus argenteus (silvery lupine)
Maianthemum racemosum ssp. racemosum (false Solomon's seal,
    false spikenard)
Maianthemum stellatum (starry Solomon's seal)
Mertensia ciliata (mountain bluebells)
Mimulus cardinalis (crimson monkey flower)
Mimulus lewisii (Lewis monkey flower, great purple monkey flower)
Minuartia obtusiloba (cushion sandwort)
Mirabilis multiflora (wild four o'clock)
Monardella odoratissima (coyote mint, mountain pennyroyal)
Oenothera cespitosa (gumbo evening primrose, gumbo lily)
Oenothera flava (shortfin evening primrose)
Osmorhiza berteroi (mountain sweet cicely)
Pedicularis groenlandica (elephant heads)
Penstemon ambiguus (sand penstemon)
Penstemon barbatus (red penstemon, scarlet bugler)
Penstemon cyananthus (Platte River penstemon, Wasatch penstemon)
Penstemon eatonii (firecracker penstemon)
Penstemon rostriflorus (Bridge's penstemon, mountain scarlet penstemon)
Penstemon speciosus (sagebrush penstemon)
Penstemon strictus (Rocky Mountain penstemon)
Pentaphylloides floribunda (potentilla, shrubby cinquefoil)
Petrophyton caespitosum (dwarf spiraea, petrophytum, tufted rockmat)
Phacelia sericea (silky phacelia)
Polemonium foliosissimum (Jacob's ladder)
Polemonium pulcherrimum (alpine Jacob's ladder, skunk leaf)
Polemonium viscosum (sky pilot)
Potentilla arguta (white cinquefoil, prairie cinquefoil, tall cinquefoil)
Psilostrophe tagetina (woolly paper-flower)
Pulsatilla patens ssp. multifida (pasque flower, wild crocus)

Ranunculus alismifolius (meadow buttercup)
Ranunculus cardiophyllus (buttercup)
Saxifraga bronchialis (spotted saxifrage, matted saxifrage)
Saxifraga cespitosa (tufted saxifrage)
Sidalcea neomexicana (checker mallow, prairie mallow)
Silene acaulis (moss campion)
Solidago canadensis (meadow goldenrod)
Solidago missouriensis (Missouri goldenrod, prairie goldenrod)
Solidago multiradiata (northern goldenrod, mountain goldenrod)
Sphaeralcea ambigua (desert mallow)
Sphaeralcea coccinea (scarlet globe mallow)
Sphaeralcea grossulariifolia (gooseberry leaf globemallow)
Sphaeralcea munroana (Munro's globe mallow, white-leaved globe mallow)
Sphaeralcea parvifolia (globe mallow)
Stanleya pinnata (desert or prince's plume)
Tetraneuris acaulis var. acaulis (stemless goldflower, stemless rubber weed, butte marigold)
Thermopsis rhombifolia var. montana (golden pea, buckbean)
Verbena hastata (blue verbena, blue vervain)
Viola canadensis (Canada violet)
Viola nuttallii (yellow violet)
Viola vallicola (yellow violet)
Xylorhiza tortifolia var. tortifolia (Mojave aster)
Yucca baccata (blue yucca, banana yucca, fleshy-fruited yucca)
Yucca brevifolia (Joshua tree)
Zizia aptera (heart-leaved golden alexanders)

Grasses/Grass-like plants

Agrostis exarata (spikebent, spike red top)
Agrostis scabra (ticklegrass, fly-away grass)
Aristida purpurea (purple three awn)
Aristida purpurea var. longiseta (red three awn)
Bouteloua curtipendula (sideoats grama)
Bouteloua eriopoda (black grama)
Bouteloua gracilis (blue grama)
Calamagrostis canadensis (bluejoint grass)
Calamovilfa longifolia (sandreed grass, prairie sandreed)
Carex aquatilis (water sedge)
Carex nebrascensis (Nebraska sedge)
Carex utriculata (beaked sedge)
Danthonia californica (California oatgrass)
Danthonia intermedia (timber oatgrass)
Deschampsia cespitosa (tufted hairgrass)
Distichlis spicata (seashore saltgrass)
Eleocharis palustris (creeping spikesedge, spike rush)
Elymus canadensis (Canada wild rye)
Elymus glaucus (blue wild rye)
Elymus lanceolatus (thickspike wheatgrass)
Festuca idahoensis (Idaho fescue, blue bunchgrass)
Festuca ovina (sheep fescue)
Glyceria grandis (American mannagrass, tall mannagrass, reed meadowgrass)
Hierochloe odorata (sweet grass)

Koeleria macrantha (June grass)
Leymus cinereus (Great Basin wild rye)
Muhlenbergia montana (mountain muhly)
Muhlenbergia porteri (bush muhly)
Muhlenbergia wrightii (spike muhly)
Pascopyrum smithii (western wheatgrass)
Phleum alpinum (alpine timothy)
Poa alpina (alpine bluegrass)
Poa secunda (pine bluegrass)
Pseudoroegneria spicata (bluebunch wheatgrass)
Schizachyrium scoparium (little bluestem)
Scirpus acutus (hardstem bulrush)
Scirpus maritimus (alkali bulrush, prairie bulrush, bayonet grass)
Sporobolus airoides (alkali sacaton)
Sporobolus compositus var. compositus (tall dropseed)
Sporobolus cryptandrus (sand dropseed)
Sporobolus flexuosus (mesa dropseed)
Stipa comata (needle-and-thread grass)
Stipa nelsonii (Columbia needlegrass)
Trisetum spicatum (spike trisetum)

Shrubs (deciduous)

Alnus incana (speckled alder, mountain alder)
Amelanchier alnifolia (saskatoon, western serviceberry, Juneberry)
Amelanchier utahensis (Utah serviceberry)
Artemisia frigida (prairie sagewort, fringed sage)
Atriplex canescens (four-wing saltbush, wingscale)
Atriplex confertifolia (spiny saltbush, shadscale saltbush, hop sage)
Ceanothus greggii var. vestitus (desert ceanothus)
Chamaebatiaria millefolium (fernbush, desert sweet, tansy bush)
Chrysothamnus nauseosus (rabbit brush, chamisa)
Cornus sericea (red-twig dogwood, red-osier dogwood)
Crataegus douglasii (black hawthorn)
Ephedra nevadensis (Mormon tea)
Ephedra viridis (Mormon tea)
Eriogonum fasciculatum (California buckwheat)
Fallugia paradoxa (Apache plume)
Forestiera pubescens (desert olive, elbow-bush, forestiera)
Holodiscus dumosus (bush rock-spires, cream bush, ocean spray)
Krascheninnikovia lanata (winterfat)
Lonicera involucrata (black twinberry, bear berry honeysuckle)
Lycium andersonii (Anderson wolfberry)
Parthenium incanum (mariola)
Physocarpus malvaceus (mallow ninebark)
Poliomintha incana (mintbush)
Prosopis glandulosa (honey mesquite)
Prunus virginiana (chokecherry)
Psilostrophe cooperi (paperflower, yellow paper daisy)
Purshia tridentata (antelope brush)
Rhus glabra (smooth sumac)
Rhus trilobata (squawbush, basketbush, skunkbush)
Ribes aureum (golden currant)

Ribes cereum (wax currant, western red currant, squaw currant)
Ribes laxiflorum (trailing black currant)
Robinia neomexicana (New Mexico locust, mescal bean)
Rosa nutkana (nootka rose)
Rosa woodsii (western wild rose, woods rose)
Rubus parviflorus (western thimbleberry)
Salix bebbiana (Bebb willow, long-beaked willow)
Salix scouleriana (western pussy willow, Scouler's willow)
Salvia dorrii (grayball sage)
Sambucus cerulea (blue elderberry)
Sarcobatus vermiculatus (greasewood)
Shepherdia argentea (silver buffaloberry)
Shepherdia canadensis (buffaloberry)
Sorbus scopulina (western mountain ash)
Symphoricarpos oreophilus (mountain snowberry)

Shrubs (evergreen)

Arctostaphylos patula (greenleaf manzanita)
Arctostaphylos uva-ursi (bearberry, kinnikinnik)
Artemisia nova (black sagebrush)
Artemisia tridentata (big sagebrush, Great Basin sagebrush)
Ceanothus fendleri (Fendler ceanothus, buckbrush)
Ceanothus velutinus (mountain balm, buckbush)
Cercocarpus ledifolius (curl-leaf mountain mahogany)
Cercocarpus montanus (mountain mahogany, silverleaf mountain mahogany)
Encelia farinosa (brittle bush)
Grayia spinosa (spiny hopsage)
Juniperus communis (common juniper)
Kalmia polifolia (swamp laurel, bog laurel)
Larrea tridentata (creosote bush)
Mahonia fremontii (Fremont barberry, holly grape)
Paxistima myrsinites (Oregon box, myrtle boxwood, mountain lover)
Purshia stansburiana (cliff rose)
Quercus turbinella (shrub live oak)

Trees (deciduous)

Acer glabrum (Rocky Mountain maple)
Acer grandidentatum (bigtooth maple)
Acer negundo (box elder)
Betula occidentalis (mountain birch, water birch)
Celtis laevigata var. reticulata (netleaf hackberry)
Chilopsis linearis (desert willow, trumpet flower)
Fraxinus velutina (Arizona ash, Velvet ash, desert ash)
Populus fremontii (western cottonwood)
Populus tremuloides (quaking aspen)
Prosopsis pubescens (tornillo, screwbean mesquite)
Quercus gambelii (Gambel's oak, Rocky Mountain white oak)
Salix amygdaloides (peachleaf willow)
Salix laevigata (red willow)

Trees (evergreen)

Abies concolor (western white fir)

Abies lasiocarpa (subalpine fir)
Juniperus osteosperma (Utah juniper)
Juniperus scopulorum (Rocky Mountain juniper)
Picea engelmannii (Engelmann spruce)
Picea pungens (blue spruce, Colorado spruce)
Pinus flexilis (limber pine)
Pinus ponderosa (ponderosa pine)
Pseudotsuga menziesii (Douglas fir)

Vines (deciduous)

Clematis columbiana (purple virgin's bower)
Clematis ligusticifolia (clematis)
Vitis arizonica (Arizona grape, canyon grape)

FEDERALLY LISTED ENDANGERED SPECIES

Autumn buttercup (Ranunculus acriformis var. Aestivalis)
Barneby reed-mustard (Schoenocrambe barnebyiJ)
Barneby ridge-cress (peppercress) (Lepidium barnebyanum)
Clay phacelia (Phacelia argillacea)
Clay reed-mustard (Schoenocrambe argillacea)
Dwarf bear-poppy (Arctomecon humilis)
Heliotrope milk-vetch (Astrgalus montii)
Jones cycladenia (Cycladenia humilis var. jonesii)
Kodachrome bladderpod (Lesquerella tumulosa)
Last Chance townsendia (Townsendia aprica)
Maguire daisy (Erigeron maguirei var. maguirei)
Maguire primrose (Primula maguirei)
Navajo sedge (Carex specuicola)
San Rafael cactus (Pediocactus despainii)
Shrubby reed-mustard (toad-flax cress) (Schoenocrambe suffrutescens)
Siler pincushion cactus (Pediocactus sileri)
Uinta Basin hookless cactus (Sclerocactus glaucus)
Ute ladies'-tresses (Spiranthes diluvialis)
Welsh's milkweed (Asclepias selshii)
Wright fishhook cactus (Sclerocactus wrightiae)

UTAH NOXIOUS SPECIES

Because the noxious weed lists have continually changed since we gathered them in 1994, we are not including them at this time. Not all States have noxious weed lists. Those that do, do not use the same standards of importance and are not comparable. States typically have included plants that interfere with agriculture (Canada thistle), or cause human health problems (poison ivy). Some States are now including a category of plants that invade and degrade the environment (purple loosestrife). Check with your State's Agriculture Department or Weed Scientist listed below. The noxious weed list can be used two ways on roadsides: I) check to not inadvertantly plant these invasive plants, and 2) note the plants you are legally responsible to control. Many States now check adjacent State lists to avoid planting their neighbors' problem plants. Because weeds do not respect political boundaries, and because by their very nature weeds continue to adapt and expand, monitoring and controlling invasives at State borders is a wise part of vegetation management.

(Weed and Seed Laws)

Department of Agriculture
Division of Plant Industry
350 North Redwood Road
Salt Lake City, UT 84116

Steven A. Dewey
Plants/Soils/Biometeorology
Utah State University
Logan, UT 84322
(801) 797-2256

UTAH RESOURCES

Natural Heritage Program
Division of Wildlife Resources
1596 West North Temple
Salt Lake City, UT 84116
(801) 538-5511

The Nature Conservancy Field Office
559 East South Temple
Salt Lake City, UT 84102
(801) 531-0999

Utah Native Plant Society
3631 South Carolyn St.
Salt Lake City, UT 84106

POTENTIAL NATURAL VEGETATION ZONES IN
VERMONT

Source: A.W. Kuchler's Potential Natural Vegetation Map, 1964, Revised 1985.
Presented in U.S.G.S. National Atlas of the U.S. Series,
U.S. Geological Survey, Reston, VA.

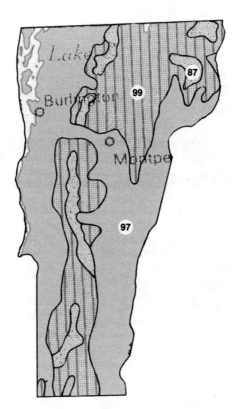

87	Northeastern spruce-fir forest *(Picea-Abies)*
97	Northern hardwoods *(Acer-Betula-Fagus-Tsuga)*
99	Northern hardwoods-spruce fores *(Acer-Betula-Fagus-Picea-Tsuga)*

(Dominant plant species present in each vegetation type are listed in Appendix 8)

87 *Northeastern Spruce-Fir Forest (Picea-Abies)*
97 *Northern Hardwoods (Acer-Betula-Fagus-Tsuga)*
99 *Northern Hardwoods-Spruce Forests (Acer-Betula-Fagus-Picea-Tsuga)*

Botanical Expert

Everett Marshall, Data Manager
Vermont Nongame and Natural Heritage
Vermont Fish and Wildlife Department
103 S. Main St.
Waterbury, VT 05671-0501
(802) 241-8715

Recommended Flora

Gleason, H.A.; A. Cronquist. 1991. Manual of Vascular Plants of Northeastern United States and Adjacent Canada, 2nd Edition. New York Botanical Garden, New York. 910 pgs. + map. ISBN 0893273651.

Missouri Botanical Garden. Flora of North America (when available). Missouri Botanical Garden. Flora of North America Project. St. Louis, MO.

NATIVE PLANTS FOR LANDSCAPE USE IN VERMONT

Ferns

Adiantum pedatum (northern maidenhair fern)
Asplenium platyneuron (ebony spleenwort)
Asplenium trichomanes (maidenhair spleenwort)
Athyrium filix-femina (lady fern)
Botrychium virginianum (rattlesnake fern)
Cystopteris bulbifera (bladder fern)
Cystopteris fragilis (fragile fern)
Dennstaedtia punctilobula (hay-scented fern)
Dryopteris carthusiana (shield fern, toothed wood fern, spinulose shield fern)
Dryopteris cristata (crested wood fern, buckler fern)
Dryopteris marginalis (marginal wood fern)
Gymnocarpium dryopteris (oak fern)
Matteuccia struthiopteris (ostrich fern)
Onoclea sensibilis (sensitive fern, bead fern)
Osmunda cinnamomea (cinnamon fern)
Osmunda claytoniana (interrupted fern)
Osmunda regalis (royal fern)
Polystichum acrostichoides (Christmas fern)
Thelypteris novaboracensis (New York fern, tapering fern)
Woodsia ilvensis (rusty woodsia)

Forbs (annuals/biennials)

Corydalis sempervirens (pale corydalis)
Oenothera biennis (common evening primrose)
Rudbeckia hirta (black-eyed Susan)

Forbs (perennials)

Acorus calamus (sweet flag, calamus)
Actaea pachypoda (white baneberry)
Ageratina altissima var. altissima (white snakeroot)
Allium tricoccum (wild leek)
Anaphalis margaritacea (pearly everlasting)
Anemone canadensis (Canada anemone, windflower)
Anemone virginiana (thimbleweed, tall anemone)
Antennaria neglecta (pussytoes)
Anennaria plantaginifolia (plantain-leaved everlasting)
Apocynum androsaemifolium (spreading dogbane)
Aquilegia canadensis (columbine)
Arisaema triphyllum (Jack-in-the-pulpit, Indian turnip)
Asarum canadense (wild ginger)
Asclepias incarnata (swamp milkweed)
Aster divaricatus (white wood aster)
Aster novae-angliae (New England aster)
Aster pilosus (frost aster)
Aster puniceus (red-stem aster, swamp aster)
Caltha palustris (marsh marigold, cowslip)
Campanula rotundifolia (harebell)
Cardamine diphylla (two-leaved toothwort)
Caulophyllum thalictroides (blue cohosh)
Chelone glabra (turtlehead)
Claytonia caroliniana (broad-leaved spring beauty)
Clintonia borealis (clintonia, blue-bead lily)
Coptis trifolia ssp. groenlandica (goldthread)
Cornus canadensis (bunchberry)
Desmodium canadense (Canada tick-trefoil, Canada tickclover)
Dicentra cucullaria (Dutchman's breeches)
Epilobium angustifolium (fireweed, willow herb)
Erythronium americanum (eastern trout lily, yellow trout lily)
Eupatorium maculatum (spotted Joe-pye weed)
Eupatorium perfoliatum (boneset)
Euthamia graminifolia var. graminifolia (grass-leaved goldenrod)
Fragaria virginiana (wild strawberry)
Galium triflorum (sweet-scented bedstraw)
Gentiana clausa (bottle gentian)
Geranium maculatum (wild geranium, cranesbill)
Geum rivale (purple avens, water avens)
Hepatica nobilis var. acuta (sharp-lobed hepatica)
Hydrophyllum virginianum (Virginia waterleaf)
Iris versicolor (blue flag)
Lilium canadense (wild yellow lily, Canada lily)
Linnaea borealis (twinflower)
Lysimachia ciliata (fringed loosestrife)
Maianthemum canadense (wild lily-of-the-valley, Canada mayflower)
Smilacina racemosum ssp. racemosum (false Solomon's seal, false spikenard)
Mitchella repens (partridge berry)
Monarda fistulosa (wild bergamot, horsemint, beebalm)
Nuphar lutea (yellow pond lily, cow lily, spatter dock)
Osmorhiza claytoni (sweet cicely, sweet jarvil)

Penstemon digitalis (beardtongue)
Pentaphylloides floribunda (potentilla, shrubby cinquefoil)
Potentilla simplex (common cinquefoil)
Pyrola elliptica (shinleaf)
Sanguinaria candensis (bloodroot)
Senecio aureus (golden ragwort)
Solidago caesia (blue-stemmed goldenrod, wreath goldenrod)
Solidago canadensis (meadow goldenrod)
Solidago juncea (early goldenrod, plume goldenrod)
Solidago nemoralis (gray goldenrod, old-field goldenrod)
Solidago rugosa (rough-leaved goldenrod)
Streptopus roseus (rosy twisted stalk)
Thalictrum dioicum (early meadow rue)
Thalictrum pubescens (tall meadow rue)
Tiarella cordifolia (foam flower)
Trientalis borealis ssp. borealis (starflower)
Trillium undulatum (painted trillium)
Uvularia grandiflora (bellwort, merrybells)
Uvularia sessilifolia (wildoats, merrybells)
Verbena hastata (blue verbena, blue vervain)
Viola canadensis (Canada violet)
Viola conspersa (American dog violet)
Viola pubescens (downy or smooth yellow violet)
Zizia aurea (golden alexanders)

Grasses/Grass-like plants

Agrostis scabra (ticklegrass, fly-away grass)
Andropogon gerardii (big bluestem)
Calamagrostis canadensis (bluejoint grass)
Carex pensylvanica (Pennsylvania sedge)
Carex plantaginea (plantain-leaved sedge)
Carex stipata (awl-fruited sedge)
Carex stricta (tussock sedge)
Carex rostrata var. utriculata (beaked sedge)
Danthonia spicata (poverty grass)
Deschampsia cespitosa (tufted hairgrass)
Eleocharis palustris (creeping spikesedge, spike rush)
Elymus canadensis (Canada wild rye)
Elymus hystrix var. hystrix (bottlebrush grass)
Eragrostis spectabilis (purple lovegrass, tumblegrass)
Glyceria grandis (American mannagrass, tall mannagrass, reed meadowgrass)
Hierochloe odorata (sweet grass)
Juncus effusus var. solutus (soft rush)
Leersia oryzoides (rice cut grass)
Schizachyrium scoparium (little bluestem)
Scirpus acutus (hardstem bulrush)
Scirpus atrovirens (dark green bulrush)
Scirpus cyperinus (wool grass)
Scirpus validus (great bulrush)
Trisetum spicatum (spike trisetum)
Typha latifolia (cattail)

Shrubs (deciduous)

Alnus incana (speckled alder, mountain alder)
Amelanchier arborea (downy serviceberry, shadbush, Juneberry)
Aronia melanocarpa (black chokeberry)
Cephalanthus occidentalis (buttonbush)
Cornus amomum var. Schaetzeana (swamp dogwood, silky dogwood)
Cornus racemosa (gray dogwood)
Corylus cornuta (beaked hazelnut or filbert)
Diervilla lonicera (bush honeysuckle)
Ilex verticillata (winterberry, black alder)
Prunus virginiana (chokecherry)
Rhus typhina (staghorn sumac)
Ribes cynosbati (prickly gooseberry, dogberry)
Rosa blanda (early wild rose, smooth rose)
Rosa carolina (Carolina rose)
Rubus idaeus ssp. strigosus (red raspberry)
Rubus occidentalis (black raspberry, thimbleberry)
Rubus odoratus (thimbleberry)
Salix discolor (pussy willow)
Sambucus canadensis (elderberry, common elder)
Sambucus racemosa var. pubens (scarlet elderberry, red-berried elder)
Spiraea alba (meadow sweet)
Spiraea tomentosa (steeplebush, hardhack)
Vaccinium angustifolium (low-bush blueberry)
Viburnum acerifolium (maple leaf viburnum)
Viburnum lentago (black haw, nannyberry)
Viburnum nudum var. cassinoides (wild raisin)
Viburnum opulus var. americanum (high-bush cranberry, American
  cranberrybush viburnum)

Shrubs (evergreen)

Epigaea repens (trailing arbutus)
Gaultheria hispidula (creeping snowberry)
Gaultheria procumbens (wintergreen, checkerberry)
Juniperus communis (common juniper)
Kalmia angustifolia (sheep laurel, lambkill kalmia)
Kalmia polifolia (swamp laurel, bog laurel)
Ledum groenlandicum (Labrador tea, muskeg tea)
Taxus canadensis (Canada yew)

Trees (deciduous)

Acer negundo (box elder)
Acer pensylvanicum (striped maple)
Acer rubrum (red maple)
Acer saccharinum (silver maple)
Acer saccharum (sugar maple)
Acer spicatum (mountain maple)
Betula papyrifera (paper birch)
Carpinus caroliniana (blue beech, hornbeam, musclewood)
Carya cordiformis (bitternut, swamp hickory)
Carya ovata (shagbark hickory)

Crataegus punctata (dotted hawthorn, white thorn)
Fagus grandifolia var. grandifolia (beech)
Fraxinus americana (white ash)
Hamamelis virginiana (witch hazel)
Juglans cinerea (butternut, white walnut)
Larix laricina (tamarack, American larch)
Ostrya virginiana (ironwood, hophornbeam)
Populus deltoides (eastern cottonwood)
Populus grandidentata (large-toothed aspen)
Populus tremuloides (quaking aspen)
Prunus nigra (Canada plum)
Prunus pensylvanica (fire or pin cherry)
Prunus serotina (black cherry)
Quercus alba (white oak)
Quercus rubra (red oak)
Sorbus americana (mountain ash)
Tilia americana (American linden, basswood)
Ulmus americana (American elm)

Trees (evergreen)

Abies balsamea (balsam fir)
Juniperus virginiana (eastern red cedar)
Picea glauca (white spruce)
Pinus resinosa (red pine, Norway pine)pine)
Thuja occidentalis (arbor vitae, northern white cedar)
Tsuga canadensis (eastern hemlock)

Vines (deciduous)

Celastrus scandens (American bittersweet)
Clematis virginiana (virgin's bower)
Parthenocissus quinquefolia (Virginia creeper)
Parthenocissus quinquefolia var. quinquefolia (woodbine)
Vitis riparia (riverbank grape)

Jesup's milk-vetch (Astrgalus robbinsii var. jesupi)
Northeastern (Barbed bristle) bulrush (Scirpus ancistrochaetus)

VERMONT NOXIOUS SPECIES

Because the noxious weed lists have continually changed since we gathered them in 1994, we are not including them at this time. Not all States have noxious weed lists. Those that do, do not use the same standards of importance and are not comparable. States typically have included plants that interfere with agriculture (Canada thistle), or cause human health problems (poison ivy). Some States are now including a category of plants that invade and degrade the environment (purple loosestrife). Check with your State's Agriculture Department or Weed Scientist listed below. The noxious weed list can be used two ways on roadsides: l) check to not inadvertantly plant these invasive plants, and 2) note the plants you are legally responsible to control. Many States now check adjacent State lists to avoid planting their neighbors' problem plants. Because weeds do not respect political boundaries, and because by their very nature weeds continue to adapt and expand, monitoring and controlling invasives at State borders is a wise part of vegetation management.

(Seed Law)

Department of Agriculture
Division of Plant Industry
116 State Street, Drawer 20
Montpelier, VT 05320

Sid Boseworth
University of Vermont
Plant & Soils
Burlington, VT 05405
(802) 650-0478

VERMONT RESOURCES

Nongame & Natural Heritage Program
103 South Main Street
Waterbury, VT 05671
(802) 241-3700

The Nature Conservancy Field Office
27 State Street
Montpelier, VT 05602
(802) 229-4425

POTENTIAL NATURAL VEGETATION ZONES IN

VIRGINIA

Source: A.W. Kuchler's Potential Natural Vegetation Map, 1964, Revised 1985.
Presented in U.S.G.S. National Atlas of the U.S. Series,
U.S. Geological Survey, Reston, VA.

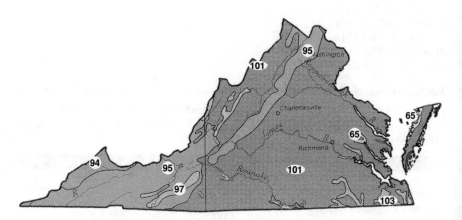

65	Northern cordgrass prairie *(Distichlis-Spartina)*		**97**	Northern hardwoods *(Acer-Betula-Fagus-Tsuga)*
94	Mixed mesophytic forest *(Acer-Aesculus-Fagus-Liriodendron-Quercus-Tilia)*		**101**	Oak-hickory-pine forest *(Quercus-Carya-Pinus)*
95	Appalachian oak forest *(Quercus)*		**103**	Southern floodplain forest *(Quercus-Nyassa-Taxodium)*

VEGETATION REFERENCES

Vegetation Types Present
(Dominant plant species present in each vegetation type are listed in Appendix 8)

65   *Northern Cordgrass Prairie (Distichlis-Spartina)*
94   *Mixed Mesophytic Forest (Acer-Aesculus-Fagus Liriodendron-Quercus-Tilia)*
95   *Appalachian Oak Forest (Quercus)*
97   *Northern Hardwoods (Acer-Betula-Fagus-Tsuga)*
101 *Oak-Hickory-Pine Forest (Quercus-Carya-Pinus)*
103 *Southern Floodplain Forest (Quercus-Nyssa-Taxodium)*

Botanical Expert

J. Christopher Ludwig, Staff Botanist
Virginia Department of Conservation and Recreation
Division of Natural Heritage
1500 E. Main St., Suite 312
Richmond, VA 23219
(804) 225-4855
(804) 371-2674 (fax)

Recommended Flora

Harvill, A.M.; T.R. Bradley; C.E. Stevens; T.F. Wieboldt; D.M.E. Ware; D.W. Ogle;
G.W. Ramsey; G.P. Fleming. 1992 Atlas of the Virginia Flora, 3rd Edition. Virginia
Botanical Associates, Rt. 1, Box 63, Burkeville, VA 23922.

NATIVE PLANTS FOR LANDSCAPE USE IN VIRGINIA

Cactus

Opuntia humifusa (prickly pear)

Ferns

Adiantum pedatum (northern maidenhair fern)
Asplenium platyneuron (ebony spleenwort)
Asplenium trichomanes (maidenhair spleenwort)
Athyrium filix-femina (lady fern)
Botrychium virginianum (rattlesnake fern)
Cystopteris bulbifera (bladder fern)
Dennstaedtia punctilobula (hay-scented fern)
Dryopteris carthusiana (shield fern, toothed wood fern, spinulose shield fern)
Dryopteris cristata (crested wood fern, buckler fern)
Dryopteris marginalis (marginal wood fern)
Onoclea sensibilis (sensitive fern, bead fern)
Osmunda cinnamomea (cinnamon fern)
Osmunda claytoniana (interrupted fern)
Osmunda regalis (royal fern)
Phegopteris hexagonoptera (broad beech fern)
Polystichum acrostichoides (Christmas fern)
Thelypteris novaboracensis (New York fern, tapering fern)
Woodsia ilvensis (rusty woodsia)
Woodwardia areolata (netted chain fern)
Woodwardia virginica (Virginia chain fern)

Forbs (annuals/biennials)

Campanulastrum americanum (American bellflower, tall bellflower)
Corydalis sempervirens (pale corydalis)
Lobelia spicata (pale lobelia)
Oenothera biennis (common evening primrose)
Rudbeckia hirta (black-eyed Susan)
Senecio plattensis (prairie ragwort, prairie groundsel)

Forbs (perennials)

Acorus calamus (sweet flag, calamus)
Actaea pachypoda (white baneberry)
Allium canadense (wild garlic)
Allium cernuum (nodding onion)
Allium tricoccum (wild leek)
Anemone virginiana (thimbleweed, tall anemone)
Antennaria spp. (pussytoes, everlasting)
Apocynum androsaemifolium (spreading dogbane)
Aquilegia canadensis (columbine)
Arisaema triphyllum (Jack-in-the-pulpit, Indian turnip)
Aruncus dioicus (goat's beard)
Asarum canadense (wild ginger)
Asclepias incarnata (swamp milkweed)
Asclepias tuberosa (butterfly weed)
Asclepias verticillata (whorled milkweed)
Aster divaricatus (white wood aster)
Aster dumosus (bushy aster)
Aster laevis (smooth aster)
Aster novae-angliae (New England aster)
Aster oblongifolius (aromatic aster)
Aster pilosus (frost aster)
Aster puniceus (red-stem aster, swamp aster)
Astilbe biternata (false goatsbeard)
Astragalus canadensis (milk vetch, Canada milk vetch)
Caltha palustris (marsh marigold, cowslip)
Cardamine concatenata (two-leaved toothwort)
Caulophyllum thalictroides (blue cohosh)
Chelone glabra (turtlehead)
Chrysogonum virginianum (green-and-gold)
Chrysopsis mariana (Maryland golden aster)
Cimicifuga racemosa (bugbane, black cohosh)
Claytonia caroliniana (broad-leaved spring beauty)
Claytonia virginica (narrow-leaved spring beauty)
Clintonia borealis (clintonia, blue-bead lily)
Collinsonia canadensis (stoneroot, citronella horsebalm)
Coreopsis auriculata (early coreopsis)
Coreopsis lanceolata (lance-leaved coreopsis)
Coreopsis tripteris (tall coreopsis)
Coreopsis verticillata (whorled coreopsis)
Delphinium tricorne (dwarf larkspur)
Dicentra cucullaria (dutchman's breeches)
Dicentra eximia (wild bleeding heart)
Dodecatheon meadia (shooting star)

Epilobium angustifolium (fireweed, willow herb)
Erythronium americanum (eastern trout lily, yellow trout lily)
Eupatorium coelestinum (mist flower)
Eupatorium fistulosum (Joe-pye weed)
Eupatorium perfoliatum (boneset)
Eupatorium purpureum (Joe-pye weed)
Euphorbia corollata (flowering spurge)
Euthamia graminifolia var. nuttallii (grass-leaved goldenrod)
Fragaria virginiana (wild strawberry)
Galium triflorum (sweet-scented bedstraw)
Gentiana clausa (bottle gentian)
Gentiana saponaria (closed gentian, soapwort gentian)
Geranium maculatum (wild geranium, cranesbill)
Helenium autumnale (common sneezeweed)
Helianthus strumosus (woodland sunflower)
Heliopsis helianthoides (ox-eye sunflower, false sunflower)
Hepatica nobilis var. acuta (sharp-lobed hepatica)
Heuchera americana (alumroot)
Hibiscus moscheutos (swamp rose mallow, marshmallow hibiscus)
Hydrastis canadensis (golden seal)
Hydrophyllum virginianum (Virginia waterleaf)
Hypoxis hirsuta (yellow star grass)
Iris cristata (dwarf crested iris)
Iris virginica (southern blue flag)
Kosteletzkya virginica (seashore mallow)
Lespedeza capitata (roundheaded bush clover)
Liatris spicata (marsh blazing star, gayfeather)
Liatris squarrosa (blazing star)
Lilium canadense (wild yellow lily, Canada lily)
Lilium michauxii (Carolina lily)
Linum virginianum (woodland flax)
Lithospermum canescens (hoary puccoon)
Lobelia cardinalis (cardinal flower)
Lobelia siphilitica (great blue lobelia)
Lupinus perennis (wild lupine)
Lysimachia ciliata (fringed loosestrife)
Maianthemum canadense (wild lily-of-the-valley, Canada mayflower)
Maianthemum racemosum ssp. racemosum (false Solomon's seal,
   false spikenard)
Mertensia virginica (bluebells)
Mitchella repens (partridge berry)
Monarda didyma (beebalm, oswego tea)
Monarda fistulosa (wild bergamot, horsemint, beebalm)
Nuphar lutea (yellow pond lily, cow lily, spatter dock)
Oenothera fruticosa (sundrops)
Orontium aquaticum (golden club)
Osmorhiza claytoni (sweet cicely, sweet jarvil)
Peltandra virginica (arrow arum)
Penstemon digitalis (beardtongue)
Phlox carolina (Carolina phlox)
Phlox divaricata (blue woodland phlox, sweet William)
Phlox paniculata (summer phlox, perennial phlox)

Phlox stolonifera (creeping phlox)
Physostegia virginiana (obedient plant, false dragonhead)
Podophyllum peltatum (May apple)
Polemonium reptans (Jacob's ladder, Greek valerian)
Polygonatum biflorum (Solomon's seal)
Potentilla simplex (common cinquefoil)
Pycnanthemum tenuifolium (slender mountain mint)
Pycnanthemum virginianum (mountain mint)
Pyrola americana
Ranunculus hispidus (early buttercup, tufted buttercup)
Rhexia virginica (meadow beauty)
Rudbeckia fulgida (black-eyed Susan, orange coneflower)
Rudbeckia laciniata (cut-leaf coneflower)
Ruellia caroliniensis (wild petunia)
Salvia lyrata (cancer weed, lyre-leaf sage)
Sanguinaria candensis (bloodroot)
Sedum ternatum (wild stonecrop)
Senecio aureus (golden ragwort)
Silene stellata (starry campion)
Silene virginica (fire pink)
Silphium perfoliatum (cup plant)
Sisyrinchium angustifolium (narrow-leaved blue-eyed grass)
Sisyrinchium atlanticum (eastern blue-eyed grass)
Sisyrinchium mucronatum (eastern blue-eyed grass)
Solidago caesia (blue-stemmed goldenrod, wreath goldenrod)
Solidago canadensis (meadow goldenrod)
Solidago juncea (early goldenrod, plume goldenrod)
Solidago nemoralis (gray goldenrod, old-field goldenrod)
Solidago odora (sweet goldenrod)
Solidago rugosa (rough-leaved goldenrod)
Solidago sempervirens (seaside goldenrod)
Solidago speciosa (showy goldenrod)
Solidago ulmifolia (elm-leaved goldenrod)
Streptopus roseus (rosy twisted stalk)
Tephrosia virginiana (goat's rue)
Thalictrum dioicum (early meadow rue)
Thalictrum pubescens (tall meadow rue)
Thalictrum thalictroides (rue anemone)
Tiarella cordifolia (foam flower)
Tradescantia ohiensis (Ohio spiderwort)
Tradescantia virginiana (Virginia spiderwort, spider lily)
Trientalis borealis ssp. borealis (starflower)
Trillium erectum (wakerobin, purple trillium)
Trillium undulatum (painted trillium)
Uvularia grandiflora (bellwort, merrybells)
Uvularia sessilifolia (wildoats, merrybells)
Verbena hastata (blue verbena, blue vervain)
Vernonia noveboracensis (New York ironweed)
Veronicastrum virginicum (Culver's root)
Viola canadensis (Canada violet)
Viola conspersa (American dog violet)
Viola pedata (bird-foot violet)

Viola pubescens (downy or smooth yellow violet)
Viola soraria (common blue violet, meadow violet)
Zephyranthes atamasca (atamasco lily, Easter lily)
Zizia aptera (heart-leaved golden alexanders)
Zizia aurea (golden alexanders)

Grasses/Grass-like plants

Agrostis perennans (ticklegrass, fly-away grass)
Andropogon gerardii (big bluestem)
Andropogon glomeratus (bushy bluestem)
Andropogon ternarius (splitbeard bluestem)
Andropogon virginicus (broom sedge)
Arundinaria gigantea (giant cane)
Bouteloua curtipendula (sideoats grama)
Calamagrostis canadensis (bluejoint grass)
Carex pensylvanica (Pennsylvania sedge)
Carex plantaginea (plantain-leaved sedge)
Carex stipata (awl-fruited sedge)
Carex stricta (tussock sedge)
Chasmanthium latifolium (inland sea oats, wild oats, river oats, broad-leaf uniola)
Danthonia spicata (poverty grass)
Deschampsia flexuosa (tufted hairgrass)
Distichlis spicata (seashore saltgrass)
Elymus hystrix var. hystrix (bottlebrush grass)
Eragrostis spectabilis (purple lovegrass, tumblegrass)
Juncus effusus var. solutus (soft rush)
Leersia oryzoides (rice cut grass)
Muhlenbergia capillaris (gulf muhly, hair grass)
Panicum virgatum (switchgrass)
Saccharum giganteum (sugarcane plume grass)
Schizachyrium scoparium (little bluestem)
Scirpus atrovirens (dark green bulrush)
Scirpus cyperinus (wool grass)
Scirpus tabernaemontani (great bulrush)
Sorghastrum nutans (Indian grass)
Spartina patens (marsh hay cordgrass, salt meadow cordgrass)
Tripsacum dactyloides (eastern gama grass)
Typha latifolia (cattail)

Shrubs (deciduous)

Alnus serrulata (smooth alder)
Amelanchier arborea (downy serviceberry, shadbush, Juneberry)
Baccharis halimifolia (sea myrtle, groundsel bush)
Castanea pumila (chinquapin)
Ceanothus americanus (New Jersey tea, red root)
Cephalanthus occidentalis (buttonbush)
Clethra alnifolia (summer sweet)
Comptonia peregrina (sweet fern)
Cornus alternifolia (pogoda dogwood, alternate-leaved dogwood)
Cornus amomum ssp. amonum (swamp dogwood, silky dogwood)
Cornus racemosa (gray dogwood)
Cornus sericea (red-twig dogwood, red-osier dogwood)

Corylus americana (American hazelnut or filbert)
Corylus cornuta (beaked hazelnut or filbert)
Diervilla lonicera (bush honeysuckle)
Dirca palustris (leatherwood, ropebark)
Euonymus americana (strawberry bush, brook euonymus, hearts-a-bustin')
Euonymus atropurpurea (wahoo, burning bush)
Frangula caroliniana (Carolina buckthorn)
Hydrangea arborescens (wild hydrangea)
Hypericum hypericoides ssp. hypericoides (St. Andrew's cross)
Hypericum prolificum (shrubby St. John's wort)
Ilex verticillata (winterberry, black alder)
Itea virginica (Virginia willow, sweetspire, tassel-white)
Lindera benzoin (spicebush)
Lonicera dioica (limber or wild honeysuckle)
Lyonia ligustrina (male-berry, male-blueberry)
Physocarpus opulifolius (ninebark)
Prunus virginiana (chokecherry)
Rhododendron atlanticum (dwarf, or coastal azalea)
Rhododendron calendulaceum (flame azalea)
Rhododendron periclymenoides (pinxterbloom azalea)
Rhododendron prinophyllum (roseshell azalea, early azalea)
Rhododendron viscosum (swamp azalea)
Rhus aromatica (fragrant sumac)
Rhus copallinum (dwarf or winged sumac)
Rhus glabra (smooth sumac)
Rhus hirta (staghorn sumac)
Ribes cynosbati (prickly gooseberry, dogberry)
Rosa carolina (Carolina rose)
Rubus idaeus ssp. strigosus (red raspberry)
Rubus occidentalis (black raspberry, thimbleberry)
Rubus odoratus (thimbleberry)
Sambucus canadensis (elderberry, common elder)
Sambucus racemosa var. pubens (scarlet elderberry, red-berried elder)
Spiraea alba (meadow sweet)
Spiraea tomentosa (steeplebush, hardhack)
Staphylea trifolia (bladdernut)
Vaccinium angustifolium (low-bush blueberry)
Vaccinium arboreum (sparkleberry, farkleberry)
Vaccinium corymbosom (highbush blueberry)
Viburnum acerifolium (maple leaf viburnum)
Viburnum dentatum (southern arrowwood)
Viburnum nudum (possumhaw viburnum)
Viburnum nudum var. cassinoides (wild raisin)
Viburnum prunifolium (black haw, nanny berry)

Shrubs (evergreen)

Epigaea repens (trailing arbutus)
Gaultheria procumbens (wintergreen, checkerberry)
Ilex glabra (inkberry, bitter gallberry)
Kalmia latifolia (mountain laurel)
Leucothoe axillaris (coast leucothoe)
Pieris floribunda (fetter-bush, mountain andromeda)

Rhododendron catawbiense (purple rhododendron, red laurel)
Rhododendron maximum (rosebay, great laurel)
Taxus canadensis (Canada yew)

Trees (deciduous)

Acer barbatum (Florida maple, southern sugar maple)
Acer negundo (box elder)
Acer pensylvanicum (striped maple)
Acer rubrum (red maple)
Acer saccharinum (silver maple)
Acer saccharum (sugar maple)
Acer spicatum (mountain maple)
Aesculus flava (sweet buckeye, yellow buckeye)
Amelanchier canadensis (shadblow serviceberry, Juneberry)
Betula lenta (cherry birch)
Betula nigra (river birch)
Carpinus caroliniana (blue beech, hornbeam, musclewood)
Carya alba (mockernut hickory)
Carya cordiformis (bitternut, swamp hickory)
Carya ovata (shagbark hickory)
Celtis laevigata (sugarberry, hackberry)
Celtis occidentalis (hackberry, sugarberry)
Cercis canadensis (redbud)
Chionanthus virginicus (fringe tree, old man's beard)
Cornus florida (flowering dogwood)
Crataegus crus-galli (cockspur hawthorn)
Crataegus punctata (dotted hawthorn, white thorn)
Cyrilla racemiflora (leatherwood, yiti)
Diospyros virginiana (persimmon)
Fagus grandifolia var. caroliniana (beech)
Fagus grandifolia var. grandifolia (beech)
Fraxinus americana (white ash)
Fraxinus pensylvanica (green ash)
Gleditsia triacanthos (honey locust)
Halesia tetraptera (Carolina silverbell)
Hamamelis virginiana (witch hazel)
Ilex decidua (possum-haw, deciduous holly)
Ilex opaca (American holly, Christmas holly)
Juglans cinerea (butternut, white walnut)
Juglans nigra (black walnut)
Liquidambar styraciflua (sweet gum)
Liriodendron tulipifera (tulip tree)
Magnolia acuminata (cucumber tree)
Magnolia virginiana (sweetbay, swampbay)
Malus angustifolia (southern crabapple, wild crabapple)
Nyssa sylvatica (black gum, tupelo)
Ostrya virginiana (ironwood, hophornbeam)
Oxydendrum arboreum (sourwood)
Platanus occidentalis (sycamore, plane-tree)
Populus deltoides (eastern cottonwood)
Populus grandidentata (large-toothed aspen)
Prunus americana (wild plum)

Prunus angustifolia (chickasaw plum)
Prunus pensylvanica (fire or pin cherry)
Prunus serotina (black cherry)
Ptelea trifoliata (wafer ash, common hoptree)
Quercus alba (white oak)
Quercus bicolor (swamp white oak)
Quercus coccinea (scarlet oak)
Quercus falcata (southern red oak, Spanish oak)
Quercus laurifolia (laurel oak)
Quercus lyrata (overcup oak)
Quercus marilandica (blackjack oak)
Quercus muhlenbergii (chinkapin oak, chestnut oak)
Quercus palustris (pin oak)
Quercus phellos (willow oak)
Quercus rubra (red oak)
Quercus shumardii (shumard oak)
Quercus stellata (post oak)
Quercus velutina (black oak)
Salix nigra (black willow)
Sassafras albidum (sassafras)
Sorbus americana (mountain ash)
Taxodium distichum (bald cypress)
Thuja occidentalis (arbor vitae, northern white cedar)
Tilia americana (American linden, basswood)
Tsuga canadensis (eastern hemlock)
Tsuga caroliniana (Carolina hemlock)
Ulmus americana (American elm)
Ulmus rubra (red elm, slippery elm)

Trees (evergreen)

Juniperus virginiana (eastern red cedar)
Persea borbonia (red bay)
Pinus echinata (shortleaf pine)
Pinus rigida (pitch pine)
Pinus strobus (eastern white pine)
Pinus taeda (loblolly pine)
Pinus virginiana (Virginia pine)
Quercus virginiana (live oak, coastal live oak, southern live oak)

Vines (deciduous)

Bignonia capreolata (cross vine)
Campsis radicans (trumpet creeper, trumpet vine)
Celastrus scandens (American bittersweet)
Clematis virginiana (virgin's bower)
Lonicera sempervirens (coral honeysuckle)
Parthenocissus quinquefolia (Virginia creeper)
Passiflora incarnata (passion flower, maypop)
Vitis riparia (riverbank grape)
Vitis rotundifolia (muscadine grape)

Vine (evergreen)

Gelsemium sempervirens (yellow jessamine, Carolina jessamine)

Eastern prairie fringed orchid (Platanthera leucophaea)
Northeastern (Barbed bristle) bulrush (Scirpus ancistrochaetus)
Peter's Mountain mallow (Iliamna corei)
Sensitive joint-vetch (Aeschynomene virginica)
Shale barren rock-cress (Arabis serotina)
Small whorled pogonia (Isotria medoloides)
Smooth coneflower (Echinacea laevigata)
Swamp pink (Helonias bullata)
Virginia round-leaf birch (Betula uber)
Virginia spiraea (Spiraea virginiana)

VIRGINIA NOXIOUS SPECIES

Because the noxious weed lists have continually changed since we gathered
them in 1994, we are not including them at this time. Not all States have
noxious weed lists. Those that do, do not use the same standards of importance
and are not comparable. States typically have included plants that interfere with
agriculture (Canada thistle), or cause human health problems (poison ivy). Some
States are now including a category of plants that invade and degrade the
environment (purple loosestrife). Check with your State's Agriculture Department
or Weed Scientist listed below. The noxious weed list can be used two ways on
roadsides: l) check to not inadvertantly plant these invasive plants, and 2) note
the plants you are legally responsible to control. Many States now check
adjacent State lists to avoid planting their neighbors' problem plants. Because
weeds do not respect political boundaries, and because by their very nature
weeds continue to adapt and expand, monitoring and controlling invasives at
State borders is a wise part of vegetation management.

(Weed Law)

Department of Agriculture
Plant Protection Office
P.O. Box 1163
Richmond, VA 23209

Scott Hagood
Virginia Tech, Weed Science
410 Price Hall
Blacksburg, VA 24061
(540) 231-6762

VIRGINIA RESOURCES

Division of Natural Heritage
Department of Conservation
1500 East Main Street, Ste. 312
Richmond, VA 23219
(804) 786-7951

The Nature Conservancy Field Office
1233-A Cedars Court
Charlottesville, VA 22903
(804) 295-6106

Virginia Native Plant Society
P.O. Box 844
Annandale, VA 22003

Chesapeake Bay Foundation
1001 E. Main St.
Richmond, VA 23219

Eastern Native Plant Alliance
P.O. Box 6101
McLean, VA 22106

Orland E. White Arboretum at Blandy
Experimental Farm
U.S. Route 50 East
Route 2, P.O. Box 210
Boyce, VA 22620

POTENTIAL NATURAL VEGETATION ZONES IN
WASHINGTON

Source: A.W. Kuchler's Potential Natural Vegetation Map, 1964, Revised 1985.
Presented in U.S.G.S. National Atlas of the U.S. Series,
U.S. Geological Survey, Reston, VA.

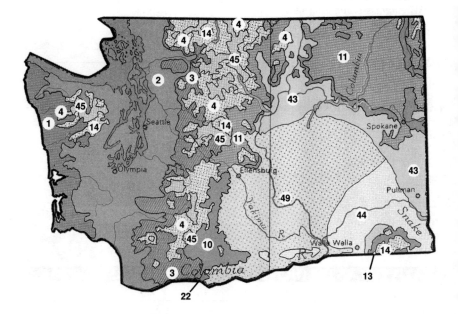

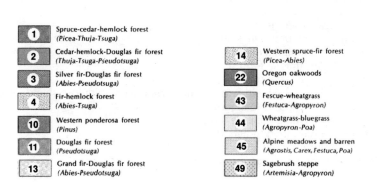

1	Spruce-cedar-hemlock forest *(Picea-Thuja-Tsuga)*	
2	Cedar-hemlock-Douglas fir forest *(Thuja-Tsuga-Pseudotsuga)*	
3	Silver fir-Douglas fir forest *(Abies-Pseudotsuga)*	
4	Fir-hemlock forest *(Abies-Tsuga)*	
10	Western ponderosa forest *(Pinus)*	
11	Douglas fir forest *(Pseudotsuga)*	
13	Grand fir-Douglas fir forest *(Abies-Pseudotsuga)*	

14	Western spruce-fir forest *(Picea-Abies)*
22	Oregon oakwoods *(Quercus)*
43	Fescue-wheatgrass *(Festuca-Agropyron)*
44	Wheatgrass-bluegrass *(Agropyron-Poa)*
45	Alpine meadows and barren *(Agrostis, Carex, Festuca, Poa)*
49	Sagebrush steppe *(Artemisia-Agropyron)*

(Dominant plant species present in each vegetation type are listed in Appendix 8)

1 Spruce-Cedar-Hemlock Forest (Picea-Thuja-Tsuga)
2 Cedar-Hemlock-Douglas Fir Forest (Thuja-Tsuga-Pseudotsuga)
3 Silver Fir-Douglas Fir Forest (Abies-Pseudotsuga)
4 Fir-Hemlock Forest (Abies-Tsuga)
10 Western Ponderosa Forest (Pinus)
11 Douglas Fir Forest (Pseudotsuga)
13 Grand Fir-Douglas Fir Forest (Abies-Pseudotsuga)
14 Western Spruce-Fir Forest (Picea-Abies)
22 Oregon Oakwoods (Quercus)
43 Fescue-Wheatgrass (Festuca-Agropyron)
44 Wheatgrass-Bluegrass (Agropyron-Poa)
45 Alpine Meadows and Barren (Agrostis, Carex, Festuca, Poa)
49 Sagebrush Steppe (Artemisia-Agropyron)

Botanical Expert

John Gamon, Botanist
Natural Heritage
Department of Natural Resources
P.O. Box 47016
Olympia, WA 98504-7016
(360) 902-1661
(360) 902-1783 (fax)
internet: john.gamon@wadnr.gov

Recommended Flora

Hitchcock, C.L. and A. Cronquist. 1973. Flora of the
Pacific Northwest. University of Washington Press, Seattle, WA.
730 pgs. + illus.

NATIVE PLANTS FOR LANDSCAPE USE IN WASHINGTON

Ferns

Adiantum pedatum (northern maidenhair fern)
Aspidotis densa (rock brake, cliff brake, Indian's dream)
Asplenium trichomanes (maidenhair spleenwort)
Athyrium filix-femina (lady fern)
Blechnum spicant (deer fern)
Botrychium virginianum (rattlesnake fern)
Cheilanthes gracillima (lace fern)
Cystopteris fragilis (fragile fern)
Dryopteris arguta (coast wood fern)
Dryopteris carthusiana (shield fern, toothed wood fern, spinulose shield fern)
Gymnocarpium dryopteris (oak fern)
Polypodium glycyrrhiza (licorice fern)
Polypodium scouleri (rock polypody)
Polystichum imbricans (dwarf western sword fern)
Polystichum munitum (western sword fern)

Forbs (annuals/biennials)

Clarkia amoena (farewell-to-spring, herald-of-summer)
Cleome serrulata (Rocky Mountain beeplant)
Collinsia parviflora var. grandiflora (blue lips)
Collomia grandiflora (collomia)
Erysimum capitatum (western wallflower, prairie rocket)
Gilia capitata (globe gilia, blue gilia)
Helianthus annuus (common sunflower)
Ipomopsis aggregata (sky rocket, scarlet gilia)
Layia glandulosa (tidy tips)
Lupinus bicolor (pigmy-leaved lupine, miniature lupine)
Mentzelia laevicaulis (blazing star, evening star, stick leaf)
Nemophila breviflora (Great Basin nemophila)

Forbs (perennials)

Achlys triphylla (vanilla leaf)
Aconitum columbianum (western monkshood)
Allium cernuum (nodding onion)
Allium validum (swamp onion)
Anaphalis margaritacea (pearly everlasting)
Anemone multifida (early thimbleweed, cut-leaf anemone, Pacific anemone)
Apocynum androsaemifolium (spreading dogbane)
Aquilegia flavescens (yellow columbine)
Aquilegia formosa (scarlet columbine)
Armeria maritima (sea pink, thrift)
Arnica cordifolia (heartleaf arnica)
Artemisia douglasiana (Douglas mugwort)
Artemisia ludoviciana (white sage, prairie sage, artemisia)
Aruncus dioicus var. vulgaris (sylvan goat's beard)
Asarum caudatum (wild ginger)
Aster ascendens (purple aster, Pacific aster)
Aster foliaceus (leafy aster)
Aster laevis (smooth aster)
Astragalus canadensis (milk vetch, Canada milk vetch)
Balsamorrhiza sagittata (balsamroot)
Calochortus macrocarpus (bigpod mariposa)
Campanula rotundifolia (harebell)
Claytonia lanceolata (spring beauty)
Clematis hirsutissima (clematis, vase flower, leather flower, lion's beard)
Clintonia uniflora (bride's bonnet, queen cup, bead lily)
Delphinium glareosum (delphinium)
Delphinium glaucum (tower larkspur)
Dicentra cucullaria (Dutchman's breeches)
Dicentra formosa (western bleeding heart)
Disporum smithii (fairy bells)
Dodecatheon hendersonii (Henderson's shooting stars)
Dodecatheon jeffreyi (Jeffrey's shooting stars)
Dryas drummondii (yellow dryas)
Dryas octopetala (mountain dryas, white mountain avens)
Epilobium angustifolium (fireweed, willow herb)
Epilobium latifolium (dwarf fireweed)
Erigeron compositus (alpine daisy)

Erigeron speciosus (showy fleabane)
Eriogonum umbellatum (sulfur buckwheat)
Eriophyllum lanatum (woolly sunflower, Oregon sunshine)
Erythronium grandiflorum (glacier lily, yellow fawn lily, dogtooth violet)
Erythronium oregonum (Oregon fawn lily)
Fragaria chiloensis (coast strawberry)
Fritillaria lanceolata (checker lily, mission bells, chocolate lily)
Gaillardia aristata (blanket flower, gaillardia, brown-eyed Susan)
Galium triflorum (sweet-scented bedstraw)
Geranium viscossisimum (sticky wild geranium)
Geum triflorum (prairie smoke, purple avens)
Glycyrrhiza lepidota (wild licorice)
Gutierrezia sarothrae (broom snakeweed, matchbrush)
Hedysarum boreale (sweet vetch, sweet broom)
Heterotheca villosa var. villosa (golden aster)
Heuchera micrantha (common alumroot)
Iris missouriensis (Rocky Mountain iris, western blue flag)
Iris tenax (Oregon iris)
Lewisia rediviva (bitter root)
Lilium columbianum (Columbia lily, Oregon lily, wild tiger lily)
Linnaea borealis (twinflower)
Linum lewisii (wild blue flax)
Luetkea pectinata (Alaska spiraea, partridge foot)
Lupinus arcticus (arctic lupine)
Maianthemum dilatatum (false lily-of-the-valley)
Maianthemum racemosum ssp. racemosum (false Solomon's seal,
    false spikenard)
Maianthemum stellatum (starry Solomon's seal)
Mertensia ciliata (mountain bluebells)
Mimulus primuloides (primrose monkey flower)
Minuartia obtusiloba (cushion sandwort)
Monardella odoratissima (coyote mint, mountain pennyroyal)
Myosotis asiatica (forget-me-not)
Nothochelone nemorosa (woodland penstemon)
Osmorhiza berteroi (mountain sweet cicely)
Oxalis oregana (redwood sorrel)
Penstemon davidsonii (blue color mat, alpine penstemon)
Penstemon deustus (hot rock penstemon)
Penstemon fruticosus (shrubby penstemon)
Penstemon rupicola (penstemon)
Penstemon serrulatus (Cascade penstemon, coast penstemon)
Penstemon speciosus (sagebrush penstemon)
Pentaphylloides floribunda (potentilla, shrubby cinquefoil)
Phacelia sericea (silky phacelia)
Phlox diffusa (mat phlox)
Phlox speciosa (showy phlox)
Polemonium occidentale (Jacob's ladder)
Polemonium pulcherrimum (alpine Jacob's ladder, skunk leaf)
Potentilla arguta (white cinquefoil, prairie cinquefoil, tall cinquefoil)
Pulsatilla patens ssp. multifida (pasque flower, wild crocus)
Ranunculus alismifolius (meadow buttercup)
Ranunculus cardiophyllus (buttercup)
Satureja douglasii (yerba buena)

Saxifraga bronchialis (spotted saxifrage, matted saxifrage)
Saxifraga cespitosa (tufted saxifrage)
Saxifraga oppositifolia (purple saxifrage)
Sedum spathulifolium (common stonecrop, broad-leaved sedum)
Silene acaulis (moss campion)
Sisyrinchium bellum (blue-eyed grass)
Sisyrinchium californicum (golden-eyed grass)
Solidago canadensis (meadow goldenrod)
Solidago missouriensis (Missouri goldenrod, prairie goldenrod)
Solidago multiradiata (northern goldenrod, mountain goldenrod)
Sphaeralcea grossulariifolia (gooseberry leaf globemallow)
Sphaeralcea munroana (Munro's globe mallow, white-leaved globe mallow)
Streptopus roseus (rosy twisted stalk)
Tellima grandiflora (fringe cup)
Thermopsis rhombifolia var. montana (golden pea, buckbean)
Tiarella trifoliata var. unifoliata (sugar scoop, western foam flower)
Tolmiea menziesii (piggyback plant, youth-on-age, thousand mothers)
Trientalis borealis ssp. latifolia (western starflower)
Trillium ovatum (coast trillium, western wakerobin)
Vancouveria hexandra (inside-out flower)
Verbena stricta (hoary vervain)
Viola canadensis (Canada violet)
Viola glabella (smooth yellow or stream violet)
Viola langsdorfii (Alaska violet)
Viola nuttallii (yellow violet)
Viola vallicola (yellow violet)
Wyethia angustifolia (narrowleaf mule ears)
Zizia aptera (heart-leaved golden alexanders)

Grasses/Grass-like plants

Agrostis exarata (spikebent, spike red top)
Agrostis scabra (ticklegrass, fly-away grass)
Aristida purpurea var. longiseta (red three awn)
Bromus carinatus (California brome)
Calamagrostis canadensis (bluejoint grass)
Carex aquatilis (water sedge)
Carex macrocephala (bighead sedge)
Carex nebrascensis (Nebraska sedge)
Carex stipata (awl-fruited sedge)
Carex utriculata (beaked sedge)
Carex vernacula (sedge)
Danthonia californica (California oatgrass)
Danthonia intermedia (timber oatgrass)
Danthonia spicata (poverty grass)
Deschampsia cespitosa (tufted hairgrass)
Dichanthelium acuminatum var. acuminatum (panic grass)
Distichlis spicata (seashore saltgrass)
Eleocharis palustris (creeping spikesedge, spike rush)
Elymus canadensis (Canada wild rye)
Elymus glaucus (blue wild rye)
Elymus lanceolatus (thickspike wheatgrass)
Festuca idahoensis (Idaho fescue, blue bunchgrass)

Festuca ovina (sheep fescue)
Glyceria grandis (American mannagrass, tall mannagrass, reed meadowgrass)
Hierochloe occidentalis (vanilla grass, California sweet grass)
Hierochloe odorata (sweet grass)
Koeleria macrantha (June grass)
Leersia oryzoides (rice cut grass)
Leymus cinereus (Great Basin wild rye)
Leymus mollis (American dune grass, beach wild rye)
Oryzopsis hymenoides (Indian ricegrass)
Pascopyrum smithii (western wheatgrass)
Phleum alpinum (alpine timothy)
Poa alpina (alpine bluegrass)
Poa secunda (pine bluegrass)
Pseudoroegneria spicata (bluebunch wheatgrass)
Scirpus acutus (hardstem bulrush)
Scirpus maritimus (alkali bulrush, prairie bulrush, bayonet grass)
Scirpus tabernaemontani (great bulrush)
Sporobolus airoides (alkali sacaton)
Sporobolus cryptandrus (sand dropseed)
Stipa comata (needle-and-thread grass)
Stipa nelsonii (Columbia needlegrass)
Trisetum spicatum (spike trisetum)
Typha latifolia (cattail)

Shrubs (deciduous)

Alnus viridis ssp. sinuata (Sitka alder, mountain alder)
Amelanchier alnifolia (saskatoon, western serviceberry, Juneberry)
Artemisia frigida (prairie sagewort, fringed sage)
Atriplex canescens (four-wing saltbush, wingscale)
Atriplex confertifolia (spiny saltbush, shadscale saltbush, hop sage)
Betula nana (bog birch, dwarf birch)
Ceanothus integerrimus (deer brush)
Ceanothus sanguineus (redstem ceanothus, wild lilac)
Chrysothamnus nauseosus (rabbit brush, chamisa)
Cornus sericea (red-twig dogwood, red-osier dogwood)
Corylus cornuta (beaked hazelnut or filbert)
Crataegus douglasii (black hawthorn)
Empetrum nigrum (crowberry)
Holodiscus discolor (cream bush, ocean spray, mountain spray)
Krascheninnikovia lanata (winterfat)
Lonicera involucrata (black twinberry, bear berry honeysuckle)
Oemleria cerasiformis (Indian plum, oso berry)
Philadelphus lewisii (wild mock orange, syringa)
Physocarpus capitatus (western ninebark)
Physocarpus malvaceus (mallow ninebark)
Prunus virginiana (chokecherry)
Purshia tridentata (antelope brush)
Rhus glabra (smooth sumac)
Ribes aureum (golden currant)
Ribes cereum (wax currant, western red currant, squaw currant)
Ribes laxiflorum (trailing black currant)
Ribes sanguineum (pink-flowered currant, red flowering currant)

Rosa nutkana (nootka rose)
Rosa woodsii (western wild rose, woods rose)
Rubus idaeus ssp. strigosus (red raspberry)
Rubus parviflorus (western thimbleberry)
Rubus spectabilis (salmon berry)
Rubus ursinus (western blackberry)
Salix arctica (arctic willow)
Salix bebbiana (Bebb willow, long-beaked willow)
Salix scouleriana (western pussy willow, Scouler's willow)
Salvia dorrii (grayball sage)
Sambucus cerulea (blue elderberry)
Sambucus racemosa var. melanocarpa (black elderberry)
Sarcobatus vermiculatus (greasewood)
Shepherdia canadensis (buffaloberry)
Sorbus scopulina (western mountain ash)
Spiraea douglasii (western spiraea, hardhack spiraea)
Spiraea splendens var. splendens (subalpine spiraea)
Symphoricarpos albus (snowberry)
Vaccinium parvifolium (red huckleberry)
Vaccinium uliginosum (alpine blueberry, bog blueberry)
Viburnum edule (moosewood viburnum)
Viburnum opulus var. americanum (high-bush cranberry, American
  cranberrybush viburnum)

Shrubs (evergreen)

Arctostaphylos columbiana (hairy manzanita)
Arctostaphylos nevadensis (pinemat manzanita)
Arctostaphylos uva-ursi (bearberry, kinnikinnik)
Artemisia tridentata (big sagebrush, Great Basin sagebrush)
Ceanothus velutinus (mountain balm, buckbrush)
Cercocarpus ledifolius (curl-leaf mountain mahogany)
Gaultheria shallon (salal)
Grayia spinosa (spiny hopsage)
Juniperus communis (common juniper)
Kalmia polifolia (swamp laurel, bog laurel)
Ledum groenlandicum (Labrador tea, muskeg tea)
Mahonia aquifolium (Oregon grape)
Mahonia nervosa var. nervosa (Cascade Oregon grape)
Myrica californica (California wax myrtle)
Paxistima myrsinites (Oregon box, myrtle boxwood, mountain lover)
Phyllodoce empetriformis (pink mountain heather)
Rhododendron macrophyllum (Pacific rhododendron, California rose-bay)
Vaccinium ovatum (evergreen huckleberry)

Trees (deciduous)

Acer circinatum (Oregon vine maple)
Acer glabrum (Rocky Mountain maple)
Acer macrophyllum (bigleaf maple, canyon maple)
Alnus rhombifolia (white alder)
Betula occidentalis (mountain birch, water birch)
Betula papyrifera (paper birch)
Celtis laevigata var. reticulata (netleaf hackberry)

Cornus nuttallii (Pacific dogwood, mountain dogwood)
Fraxinus latifolia (Oregon ash)
Larix occidentalis (western larch, western tamarack)
Populus balsamifera (black cottonwood)
Populus tremuloides (quaking aspen)
Quercus garryana (Oregon post oak)
Salix amygdaloides (peachleaf willow)

Trees (evergreen)

Abies grandis (grand fir, giant fir)
Abies lasiocarpa (subalpine fir)
Abies procera (noble fir)
Arbutus menziesii (Pacific madrone, Oregon laurel, laurelwood)
Chamaecyparis nootkatensis (Alaska cedar, yellow cedar, Nootka cedar)
Juniperus scopulorum (Rocky Mountain juniper)
Picea engelmannii (Engelmann spruce)
Picea sitchensis (Sitka spruce)
Pinus contorta (beach pine)
Pinus contorta var. murrayana (lodgepole pine)
Pinus monticola (western white pine)
Pinus ponderosa (ponderosa pine)
Pseudotsuga menziesii (Douglas fir)
Taxus brevifolia (western yew, Pacific yew)
Thuja plicata (western red cedar)
Tsuga heterophylla (western hemlock)
Tsuga mertensiana (mountain hemlock)

Vines (deciduous)

Clematis columbiana (purple virgin's bower)
Lonicera ciliosa (orange honeysuckle)

FEDERALLY LISTED ENDANGERED SPECIES

Bradshaw's desert-parsley (lomatium) (Lomatium bradshawii)
Marsh sandwort (Arenaria paludicola)
Nelson's checker-mallow (Sidalcea nelsoniana)
Water howellia (Howellia aquatilis)

WASHINGTON NOXIOUS SPECIES

Because the noxious weed lists have continually changed since we gathered them in 1994, we are not including them at this time. Not all States have noxious weed lists. Those that do, do not use the same standards of importance and are not comparable. States typically have included plants that interfere with agriculture (Canada thistle), or cause human health problems (poison ivy). Some States are now including a category of plants that invade and degrade the environment (purple loosestrife). Check with your State's Agriculture Department or Weed Scientist listed below. The noxious weed list can be used two ways on roadsides: l) check to not inadvertantly plant these invasive plants, and 2) note the plants you are legally responsible to control. Many States now check adjacent State lists to avoid planting their neighbors' problem plants. Because weeds do not respect political boundaries, and because by their very nature weeds continue to adapt and expand, monitoring and controlling invasives at State borders is a wise part of vegetation management.

(Weed Law)

Department of Agruiculture
Weed Control Board
1851 S. Central Place, #211
Kent, WA 98031

Joseph Yenish
Crop and Soil Sciences
Johnson 201A, Box 646240
Pullman, WA 99164
(509) 335-2961

WASHINGTON RESOURCES

Natural Heritage Program
Department of Natural Resources
P.O. Box 47016
Olympia, WA 98504
(360) 902-1340

The Nature Conservancy Field Office
217 Pine Street, Ste. 1100
Seattle, WA 98101
(206) 343-4344

Washington Native Plant Society
P.O. Box 28690
Seattle, WA 98118

Nature Scaping Wildlife Botanical
Gardens
11000 NE 149th Street
Vancouver, WA 98682

Sarah Reichard
Center for Urban Horticulture
University of Washington
P.O. Box 354115
Seattle, WA 98195
(206) 616-5020

POTENTIAL NATURAL VEGETATION ZONES IN
——— WEST VIRGINIA ———

Source: A.W. Kuchler's Potential Natural Vegetation Map, 1964, Revised 1985.
Presented in U.S.G.S. National Atlas of the U.S. Series,
U.S. Geological Survey, Reston, VA.

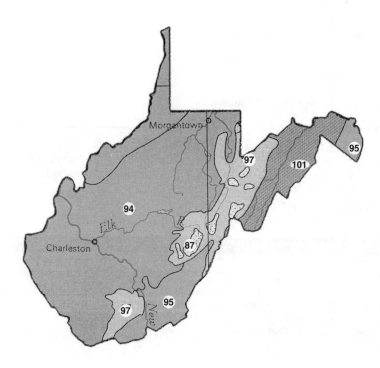

87	Northeastern spruce-fir forest *(Picea-Abies,*
94	Mixed mesophytic forest *(Acer-Aesculus-Fagus-Liriodendron-Quercus-Tilia)*
95	Appalachian oak forest *(Quercus)*
97	Northern hardwoods *(Acer-Betula-Fagus-Tsuga)*
101	Oak-hickory-pine forest *(Quercus-Carya-Pinus)*

(Dominant plant species present in each vegetation type are listed in Appendix 8)

87   *Northeastern Spruce-Fir Forest (Picea-Abies)*
94   *Mixed Mesophytic Forest (Acer-Aesculus-Fagus*
     Liriodendron-Quercus-Tilia)
95   *Appalachian Oak Forest (Quercus)*
97   *Northern Hardwoods (Acer-Betula-Fagus-Tsuga)*
101 *Oak-Hickory-Pine Forest (Quercus-Carya-Pinus)*

Botanical Experts

Paul J. "P.J." Harmon
West Virginia Division of Natural Resources
P.O. Box 67
Elkins, WV 26241
(304) 637-0245
(304) 637-0250 (fax)
internet: pharmon@mail.dnr.state.wv.us

Recommended Flora

Harmon, P.J.; J.T. Kartesz; C.M. Jessee; B.R. McDonald; B.D. Sargent. 1966. Checklist of the Vascular Flora of West Virginia. West Vrginia Natural Heritage Program, Wildlife Resources Bulletin 95-1. WV Division of Natural Resources, Wildlife Resources Section. Elkins, WV ($5/copy).

Strausbaugh, P.D. and E.L. Core. 1977. Flora of West Virginia, 2nd Edition. Seneca Books, Grantsville, WV. ISBN 0890920109.

NATIVE PLANTS FOR LANDSCAPE USE IN WEST VIRGINIA

Ferns

Adiantum pedatum (northern maidenhair fern)
Asplenium platyneuron (ebony spleenwort)
Asplenium trichomanes (maidenhair spleenwort)
Athyrium filix-femina (lady fern)
Botrychium virginianum (rattlesnake fern)
Cystopteris bulbifera (bladder fern)
Cystopteris fragilis (fragile fern)
Dennstaedtia punctilobula (hay-scented fern)
Dryopteris carthusiana (shield fern, toothed wood fern, spinulose shield fern)
Dryopteris cristata (crested wood fern, buckler fern)
Dryopteris marginalis (marginal wood fern)
Gymnocarpium dryopteris (oak fern)
Onoclea sensibilis (sensitive fern, bead fern)
Osmunda cinnamomea (cinnamon fern)
Osmunda claytoniana (interrupted fern)
Osmunda regalis (royal fern)
Phegopteris hexagonoptera (broad beech fern)
Polystichum acrostichoides (Christmas fern)
Thelypteris novaboracensis (New York fern, tapering fern)
Thelypteris simulata (Massachusetts fern)
Woodwardia areolata (netted chain fern)

Forbs (annuals/biennials)

Campanulastrum americanum (American bellflower, tall bellflower)
Corydalis sempervirens (pale corydalis)
Gentianopsis crinita (fringed gentian)
Lobelia spicata (pale lobelia)
Oenothera biennis (common evening primrose)
Rudbeckia hirta (black-eyed Susan)
Senecio plattensis (prairie ragwort, prairie groundsel)

Forbs (perennials)

Acorus calamus (sweet flag, calamus)
Actaea pachypoda (white baneberry)
Ageratina altissima var. altissima (white snakeroot)
Allium canadense (wild garlic)
Allium cernuum (nodding onion)
Allium tricoccum (wild leek)
Anaphalis margaritacea (pearly everlasting)
Anemone canadensis (Canada anemone, windflower)
Anemone virginiana (thimbleweed, tall anemone)
Antennaria spp. (pussytoes, everlasting)
Apocynum androsaemifolium (spreading dogbane)
Aquilegia canadensis (columbine)
Arisaema triphyllum (Jack-in-the-pulpit, Indian turnip)
Asarum canadense (wild ginger)
Asclepias incarnata (swamp milkweed)
Asclepias tuberosa (butterfly weed)
Asclepias verticillata (whorled milkweed)
Aster divaricatus (white wood aster)
Aster dumosus (bushy aster)
Aster laevis (smooth aster)
Aster novae-angliae (New England aster)
Aster oblongifolius (aromatic aster)
Aster pilosus (frost aster)
Aster puniceus (red-stem aster, swamp aster)
Astilbe biternata (false goatsbeard)
Astragalus canadensis (milk vetch, Canada milk vetch)
Baptisia australis (blue wild indigo)
Caltha palustris (marsh marigold, cowslip)
Camassia scilloides (wild hyacinth)
Cardamine diphylla (two-leaved toothwort)
Caulophyllum thalictroides (blue cohosh)
Chelone glabra (turtlehead)
Chrysogonum virginianum (green-and-gold)
Chrysopsis mariana (Maryland golden aster)
Cimicifuga racemosa (bugbane, black cohosh)
Claytonia caroliniana (broad-leaved spring beauty)
Claytonia virginica (narrow-leaved spring beauty)
Clintonia borealis (clintonia, blue-bead lily)
Collinsonia canadensis (stoneroot, citronella horsebalm)
Coreopsis auriculata (early coreopsis)
Coreopsis lanceolata (lance-leaved coreopsis)
Coreopsis tripteris (tall coreopsis)

Delphinium tricorne (dwarf larkspur)
Desmodium canadense (Canada tick-trefoil, Canada tickclover)
Dicentra cucullaria (dutchman's breeches)
Dicentra eximia (wild bleeding heart)
Dodecatheon meadia (shooting star)
Epilobium angustifolium (fireweed, willow herb)
Erythronium americanum (eastern trout lily, yellow trout lily)
Eupatorium coelestinum (mist flower)
Eupatorium fistulosum (Joe-pye weed)
Eupatorium maculatum (spotted Joe-pye weed)
Eupatorium perfoliatum (boneset)
Eupatorium purpureum (Joe-pye weed)
Euphorbia corollata (flowering spurge)
Euthamia graminifolia (grass-leaved goldenrod)
Euthamia graminifolia var. graminifolia (grass-leaved goldenrod)
Fragaria virginiana (wild strawberry)
Galium triflorum (sweet-scented bedstraw)
Gentiana andrewsii (bottle gentian)
Gentiana clausa (bottle gentian)
Gentiana saponaria (closed gentian, soapwort gentian)
Geranium maculatum (wild geranium, cranesbill)
Helenium autumnale (common sneezeweed)
Helianthus strumosus (woodland sunflower)
Heliopsis helianthoides (ox-eye sunflower, false sunflower)
Hepatica nobilis var. acuta (sharp-lobed hepatica)
Heuchera americana var. hirsuticaulis (alumroot)
Hibiscus moscheutos (swamp rose mallow, marshmallow hibiscus)
Houstonia caerulea (bluets)
Houstonia longifolia var. longifolia (long-leaved bluets, pale bluets)
Hydrastis canadensis (golden seal)
Hydrophyllum virginianum (Virginia waterleaf)
Hypoxis hirsuta (yellow star grass)
Iris cristata (dwarf crested iris)
Iris versicolor (blue flag)
Iris virginica var. shrevei (blue flag)
Lespedeza capitata (roundheaded bush clover)
Liatris aspera (rough blazing star, gayfeather)
Liatris spicata (marsh blazing star, gayfeather)
Lilium canadense (wild yellow lily, Canada lily)
Lilium michiganense (Turk's cap lily, Michigan lily)
Lilium philadelphicum (wood lily)
Linum virginianum (woodland flax)
Lithospermum canescens (hoary puccoon)
Lobelia cardinalis (cardinal flower)
Lobelia siphilitica (great blue lobelia)
Lupinus perennis (wild lupine)
Lysimachia ciliata (fringed loosestrife)
Maianthemum canadense (wild lily-of-the-valley, Canada mayflower)
Maianthemum racemosum ssp. racemosum (false Solomon's seal,
    false spikenard)
Maianthemum stellatum (starry Solomon's seal)
Manfreda virginica (rattlesnake master, false aloe)

Mertensia virginica (bluebells)
Mitchella repens (partridge berry)
Monarda didyma (beebalm, oswego tea)
Monarda fistulosa (wild bergamot, horsemint, beebalm)
Nuphar lutea (yellow pond lily, cow lily, spatter dock)
Oenothera fruticosa (sundrops)
Osmorhiza claytoni (sweet cicely, sweet jarvil)
Penstemon digitalis (beardtongue)
Penstemon hirsutus (hairy beardtongue)
Phlox divaricata (blue woodland phlox, sweet William)
Phlox paniculata (summer phlox, perennial phlox)
Phlox stolonifera (creeping phlox)
Physostegia virginiana (obedient plant, false dragonhead)
Podophyllum peltatum (May apple)
Polemonium reptans (Jacob's ladder, Greek valerian)
Polygonatum biflorum (Solomon's seal)
Potentilla simplex (common cinquefoil)
Pycnanthemum tenuifolium (slender mountain mint)
Pycnanthemum virginianum (mountain mint)
Pyrola elliptica (shinleaf)
Rhexia virginica (meadow beauty)
Rudbeckia fulgida (black-eyed Susan, orange coneflower)
Rudbeckia laciniata (cut-leaf coneflower)
Ruellia humilis (wild petunia)
Salvia lyrata (cancer weed, lyre-leaf sage)
Sanguinaria candensis (bloodroot)
Senecio aureus (golden ragwort)
Silene stellata (starry campion)
Silene virginica (fire pink)
Silphium perfoliatum (cup plant)
Sisyrinchium angustifolium (narrow-leaved blue-eyed grass)
Solidago caesia (blue-stemmed goldenrod, wreath goldenrod)
Solidago canadensis (meadow goldenrod)
Solidago juncea (early goldenrod, plume goldenrod)
Solidago nemoralis (gray goldenrod, old-field goldenrod)
Solidago odora (sweet goldenrod)
Solidago rigida (stiff goldenrod)
Solidago rugosa (rough-leaved goldenrod)
Solidago speciosa (showy goldenrod)
Solidago ulmifolia (elm-leaved goldenrod)
Streptopus roseus (rosy twisted stalk)
Stylophorum diphyllum (celandine poppy)
Tephrosia virginiana (goat's rue)
Thalictrum dioicum (early meadow rue)
Thalictrum pubescens (tall meadow rue)
Thalictrum thalictroides (rue anemone)
Thermopsis villosa (bush pea)
Tiarella cordifolia (foam flower)
Tradescantia ohiensis (Ohio spiderwort)
Tradescantia virginiana (Virginia spiderwort, spider lily)
Trientalis borealis ssp. borealis (starflower)
Trillium cernuum (nodding trillium)

Trillium erectum (wakerobin, purple trillium)
Trillium undulatum (painted trillium)
Uvularia grandiflora (bellwort, merrybells)
Uvularia sessilifolia (wildoats, merrybells)
Verbena hastata (blue verbena, blue vervain)
Vernonia noveboracensis (New York ironweed)
Veronicastrum virginicum (Culver's root)
Viola canadensis (Canada violet)
Viola conspersa (American dog violet)
Viola pedata (bird-foot violet)
Viola pubescens (downy or smooth yellow violet)
Viola soraria (common blue violet, meadow violet)
Zizia aptera (heart-leaved golden alexanders)
Zizia aurea (golden alexanders)

Grasses/Grass-like plants

Andropogon gerardii (big bluestem)
Andropogon glomeratus (bushy bluestem)
Andropogon virginicus (broom sedge)
Arundinaria gigantea (giant cane)
Calamagrostis canadensis (bluejoint grass)
Carex pensylvanica (Pennsylvania sedge)
Carex plantaginea (plantain-leaved sedge)
Carex stipata (awl-fruited sedge)
Carex stricta (tussock sedge)
Carex utriculata (beaked sedge)
Danthonia spicata (poverty grass)
Deschampsia cespitosa (tufted hairgrass)
Eleocharis palustris (creeping spikesedge, spike rush)
Elymus canadensis (Canada wild rye)
Elymus hystrix var. hystrix (bottlebrush grass)
Eragrostis spectabilis (purple lovegrass, tumblegrass)
Juncus effusus var. solutus (soft rush)
Leersia oryzoides (rice cut grass)
Panicum virgatum (switchgrass)
Schizachyrium scoparium (little bluestem)
Scirpus atrovirens (dark green bulrush)
Scirpus cyperinus (wool grass)
Scirpus tabernaemontani (great bulrush)
Sorghastrum nutans (Indian grass)
Spartina pectinata (prairie cordgrass, freshwater cordgrass)
Sporobolus compositus var. compositus (tall dropseed)
Tripsacum dactyloides (eastern gama grass)
Typha latifolia (cattail)

Shrubs (deciduous)

Alnus incana (speckled alder, mountain alder)
Alnus serrulata (smooth alder)
Amelanchier arborea (downy serviceberry, shadbush, Juneberry)
Amorpha fruticosa (false indigo, indigo bush)
Calycanthus floridus (Carolina allspice, sweet shrub)
Castanea pumila (chinquapin)

Ceanothus americanus (New Jersey tea, red root)
Cephalanthus occidentalis (buttonbush)
Comptonia peregrina (sweet fern)
Cornus alternifolia (pogoda dogwood, alternate-leaved dogwood)
Cornus amomum ssp. obliqua (swamp dogwood, silky dogwood)
Cornus racemosa (gray dogwood)
Corylus americana (American hazelnut or filbert)
Corylus cornuta (beaked hazelnut or filbert)
Dirca palustris (leatherwood, ropebark)
Euonymus americana (strawberry bush, brook euonymus, hearts-a-bustin')
Euonymus atropurpurea (wahoo, burning bush)
Hydrangea arborescens (wild hydrangea)
Hypericum hypericoides ssp. hypericoides (St. Andrew's cross)
Hypericum prolificum (shrubby St. John's wort)
Ilex verticillata (winterberry, black alder)
Lindera benzoin (spicebush)
Lonicera dioica (limber or wild honeysuckle)
Lyonia ligustrina (male-berry, male-blueberry)
Physocarpus opulifolius (ninebark)
Prunus virginiana (chokecherry)
Rhododendron arborescens (smooth azalea)
Rhododendron calendulaceum (flame azalea)
Rhododendron periclymenoides (pinxterbloom azalea)
Rhododendron prinophyllum (roseshell azalea, early azalea)
Rhododendron viscosum (swamp azalea)
Rhus aromatica (fragrant sumac)
Rhus copallinum (dwarf or winged sumac)
Rhus glabra (smooth sumac)
Rhus hirta (staghorn sumac)
Ribes cynosbati (prickly gooseberry, dogberry)
Rosa carolina (Carolina rose)
Rosa setigera (Illinois or prairie rose)
Rubus idaeus ssp. strigosus (red raspberry)
Rubus occidentalis (black raspberry, thimbleberry)
Rubus odoratus (thimbleberry)
Sambucus canadensis (elderberry, common elder)
Sambucus racemosa var. pubens (scarlet elderberry, red-berried elder)
Spiraea alba (meadow sweet)
Spiraea tomentosa (steeplebush, hardhack)
Staphylea trifolia (bladdernut)
Symphoricarpos orbiculatus (coralberry, Indian currant)
Vaccinium angustifolium (low-bush blueberry)
Vaccinium corymbosom (highbush blueberry)
Viburnum acerifolium (maple leaf viburnum)
Viburnum dentatum (southern arrowwood)
Viburnum lentago (black haw, nannyberry)
Viburnum nudum var. cassinoides (wild raisin)
Viburnum opulus var. americanum (high-bush cranberry, American
    cranberrybush viburnum)
Viburnum prunifolium (black haw, nanny berry)

Shrubs (evergreen)

Epigaea repens (trailing arbutus)
Gaultheria hispidula (creeping snowberry)
Gaultheria procumbens (wintergreen, checkerberry)
Juniperus communis (common juniper)
Kalmia latifolia (mountain laurel)
Rhododendron catawbiense (purple rhododendron, red laurel)
Rhododendron maximum (rosebay, great laurel)
Taxus canadensis (Canada yew)

Trees (deciduous)

Acer negundo (box elder)
Acer pensylvanicum (striped maple)
Acer rubrum (red maple)
Acer saccharinum (silver maple)
Acer saccharum (sugar maple)
Acer spicatum (mountain maple)
Aesculus flava (sweet buckeye, yellow buckeye)
Aesculus glabra (Ohio buckeye, horse chestnut)
Betula lenta (cherry birch)
Betula nigra (river birch)
Betula papyrifera (paper birch)
Carpinus caroliniana (blue beech, hornbeam, musclewood)
Carya alba (mockernut hickory)
Carya cordiformis (bitternut, swamp hickory)
Carya ovata (shagbark hickory)
Celtis laevigata (sugarberry, hackberry)
Celtis occidentalis (hackberry, sugarberry)
Cercis canadensis (redbud)
Chionanthus virginicus (fringe tree, old man's beard)
Cornus florida (flowering dogwood)
Crataegus crus-galli (cockspur hawthorn)
Crataegus mollis (downy hawthorn)
Crataegus phaenopyrum (Washington hawthorn)
Crataegus punctata (dotted hawthorn, white thorn)
Diospyros virginiana (persimmon)
Fagus grandifolia (beech)
Fraxinus pensylvanica (green ash)
Gleditsia triacanthos (honey locust)
Gymnocladus dioica (Kentucky coffee tree)
Hamamelis virginiana (witch hazel)
Juglans cinerea (butternut, white walnut)
Juglans nigra (black walnut)
Liquidambar styraciflua (sweet gum)
Liriodendron tulipifera (tulip tree)
Magnolia acuminata (cucumber tree)
Malus angustifolia (southern crabapple, wild crabapple)
Nyssa sylvatica (black gum, tupelo)
Ostrya virginiana (ironwood, hophornbeam)
Oxydendrum arboreum (sourwood)
Platanus occidentalis (sycamore, plane-tree)
Populus deltoides (eastern cottonwood)

Populus grandidentata (large-toothed aspen)
Populus tremuloides (quaking aspen)
Prunus americana (wild plum)
Prunus angustifolia (chickasaw plum)
Prunus pensylvanica (fire or pin cherry)
Prunus serotina (black cherry)
Ptelea trifoliata (wafer ash, common hoptree)
Quercus alba (white oak)
Quercus bicolor (swamp white oak)
Quercus coccinea (scarlet oak)
Quercus falcata (southern red oak, Spanish oak)
Quercus macrocarpa (bur oak)
Quercus marilandica (blackjack oak)
Quercus muhlenbergii (chinkapin oak, chestnut oak)
Quercus palustris (pin oak)
Quercus rubra (red oak)
Quercus stellata (post oak)
Quercus velutina (black oak)
Salix nigra (black willow)
Sassafras albidum (sassafras)
Sorbus americana (mountain ash)
Tilia americana (American linden, basswood)
Ulmus americana (American elm)
Ulmus rubra (red elm, slippery elm)

Trees (evergreen)

Ilex opaca (American holly, Christmas holly)
Juniperus virginiana (eastern red cedar)
Pinus echinata (shortleaf pine)
Pinus rigida (pitch pine)
Pinus strobus (eastern white pine)
Pinus virginiana (Virginia pine)
Tsuga canadensis (eastern hemlock)

Vines (deciduous)

Campsis radicans (trumpet creeper, trumpet vine)
Celastrus scandens (American bittersweet)
Clematis virginiana (virgin's bower)
Parthenocissus quinquefolia (Virginia creeper)
Passiflora incarnata (passion flower, maypop)
Vitis riparia (riverbank grape)

FEDERALLY LISTED ENDANGERED SPECIES

Harperella (Ptillimnium nodosum (fluviatila)
Northeastern (Barbed bristle) bulrush (Scirpus ancistrochaetus)
Running buffaco clover (Trifolium stonloniferum)
Shale barren roack-cress (Arabis serotina)
Virginia spiraea (Spiraea virginiana)

WEST VIRGINIA NOXIOUS SPECIES

Because the noxious weed lists have continually changed since we gathered them in 1994, we are not including them at this time. Not all States have noxious weed lists. Those that do, do not use the same standards of importance and are not comparable. States typically have included plants that interfere with agriculture (Canada thistle), or cause human health problems (poison ivy). Some States are now including a category of plants that invade and degrade the environment (purple loosestrife). Check with your State's Agriculture Department or Weed Scientist listed below. The noxious weed list can be used two ways on roadsides: l) check to not inadvertantly plant these invasive plants, and 2) note the plants you are legally responsible to control. Many States now check adjacent State lists to avoid planting their neighbors' problem plants. Because weeds do not respect political boundaries, and because by their very nature weeds continue to adapt and expand, monitoring and controlling invasives at State borders is a wise part of vegetation management.

(Weed Law)

Department of Agriculture
Division of Plant Industry
1900 Kanawha Boulevard East
Charleston, WV 25305

John Hinz
West Virginia University
P.O. Box 6100
Morgantown, WV 26506
(304) 293-2219

WEST VIRGINIA RESOURCES

The Nature Conservancy
723 Kanawha Boulevard East
Charleston, WV 25301
(304) 345-4350

West Virginia Native Plant Society
P.O. Box 2755
Elkins, WV 26241

Barbara Sargent, Environmental
Resources Specialist
West Virginia Natural Heritage
Program
(304) 637-0245
(304) 637-0250 (fax)
internet: bsargent@mail.dnr.state.wv.us

POTENTIAL NATURAL VEGETATION ZONES IN
WISCONSIN

Source: A.W. Kuchler's Potential Natural Vegetation Map, 1964, Revised 1985.
Presented in U.S.G.S. National Atlas of the U.S. Series,
U.S. Geological Survey, Reston, VA.

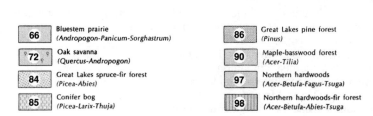

66	Bluestem prairie	(Andropogon-Panicum-Sorghastrum)
72	Oak savanna	(Quercus-Andropogon)
84	Great Lakes spruce-fir forest	(Picea-Abies)
85	Conifer bog	(Picea-Larix-Thuja)
86	Great Lakes pine forest	(Pinus)
90	Maple-basswood forest	(Acer-Tilia)
97	Northern hardwoods	(Acer-Betula-Fagus-Tsuga)
98	Northern hardwoods-fir forest	(Acer-Betula-Abies-Tsuga

(Dominant plant species present in each vegetation type are listed in Appendix 8)

66   Bluestem Prairie (Andropogon-Panicum-Sorghastrum)
72   Oak Savanna (Quercus-Andropogon)
84   Great Lakes Spruce-Fir Forest (Picea-Abies)
85   Conifer Bog (Picea-Larix-Thuja)
86   Great Lakes Pine Forest (Pinus)
90   Maple-Basswood Forest (Acer-Tilia)
97   Northern Hardwoods (Acer-Betula-Fagus-Tsuga)
98   Northern Hardwoods-Fir Forests (Acer-Betula-Abies-Tsuga)

Botanical Expert

Kelly Kearns, Native Plant Specialist
Ecosystem and Diversity Conservation Section
Bureau of Endangered Resources
Wisconsin Department of Natural Resources, Box 7921
Madison, WI 53707
(608) 267-5066
(608) 266-2925 (fax)
internet: kearns@dnr.state.wi.us

Recommended Flora

Curtis, J. 1987. The Vegetation of Wisconsin: An Ordination of Plant Communities. University of Wisconsin Press, Madison, WI. 657 pgs. + illus. maps. ISBN 0299019403.

Checklist of Vascular Plants of Wisconsin, University of Wisconsin-Madison Herbarium. Mark A. Wetks, Theodore S. Cochrane, Merel R. Block, Hugh H. I. H. S. Final version anticipated early 1999.

NATIVE PLANTS FOR LANDSCAPE USE IN WISCONSIN

Cactus

Opuntia humifusa (prickly pear)

Ferns

Adiantum pedatum (northern maidenhair fern)
Asplenium platyneuron (ebony spleenwort)
Athyrium filix-femina (lady fern)
Botrychium virginianum (rattlesnake fern)
Cystopteris bulbifera (bladder fern)
Cystopteris fragilis (fragile fern)
Dryopteris carthusiana (shield fern, toothed wood fern, spinulose shield fern)
Dryopteris cristata (crested wood fern, buckler fern)
Gymnocarpium dryopteris (oak fern)
Onoclea sensibilis (sensitive fern, bead fern)
Osmunda cinnamomea (cinnamon fern)
Osmunda claytoniana (interrupted fern)
Osmunda regalis (royal fern)
Polystichum acrostichoides (Christmas fern)
Woodsia ilvensis (rusty woodsia)

Forbs (annuals/biennials)

Campanula americanum (American bellflower, tall bellflower)
Corydalis sempervirens (pale corydalis)
Gentianopsis crinita (fringed gentian)
Lobelia spicata (pale lobelia)
Oenothera biennis (common evening primrose)
Rudbeckia hirta (black-eyed Susan)

Forbs (perennials)

(sweet flag, calamus)
Actaea pachypoda (white baneberry)
Allium canadense (wild garlic)
Allium cernuum (nodding onion)
Allium tricoccum (wild leek)
Anaphalis margaritacea (pearly everlasting)
Anemone canadensis (Canada anemone, windflower)
Anemone cylindrica (thimbleweed, candle anemone)
Anemone patens (windflower)
Anemone virginiana (thimbleweed, tall anemone)
Angelica atropurpurea (angelica)
Antennaria neglecta (pussytoes, everlasting)
Apocynum androsaemifolium (spreading dogbane)
Aquilegia canadensis (columbine)
Arisaema triphyllum (Jack-in-the-pulpit, Indian turnip)
Artemisia campestri ssp. caudata (field wormwood)
Artemisia ludoviciana (white sage, prairie sage, artemisia)
Asarum canadense (wild ginger)
Asclepias amplexicaulis (milkweed)
Asclepias incarnata (swamp milkweed)
Asclepias syriaca (common milkweed)
Asclepias tuberosa (butterfly weed)
Asclepias verticillata (whorled milkweed)
Asclepias viridiflora
Aster azureus (sky blue aster)
Aster cordifolius var. sagittifolius (blue heart-leaved aster)
Aster ericoides (heath aster, white wreath aster)
Aster laevis (smooth aster)
Aster linariifolius
Aster lucidulus (swamp aster)
Aster macrophyllus (large-leaved aster)
Aster novae-angliae (New England aster)
Aster oblongifolius (aromatic aster)
Aster oolentangiensis (sky blue aster)
Aster pilosus (frost aster)
Aster puniceus (red-stem aster, swamp aster)
Aster sericeus (silky aster)
Aster simplex (marsh aster)
Aster umbellatus (flat-top aster)
Astragalus canadensis (milk vetch, Canada milk vetch)
Baptisia alba (white false indigo)
Baptisia alba var. macrophyllla (cream false indigo, plains wild indigo)
Caltha palustris (marsh marigold, cowslip)

Campanula rotundifolia (harebell)
Cardamine diphylla (two-leaved toothwort)
Castilleja sessiliflora (downy painted cup)
Caulophyllum thalictroides (blue cohosh)
Chelone glabra (turtlehead)
Cimicifuga racemosa (bugbane, black cohosh)
Claytonia virginica (narrow-leaved spring beauty)
Clintonia borealis (clintonia, blue-bead lily)
Coptis trifolia ssp. groenlandica (goldthread)
Coreopsis lanceolata (lance-leaved coreopsis)
Coreopsis palmata (stiff coreopsis)
Cornus canadensis (bunchberry)
Dalea candida (white prairie clover)
Dalea purpurea (purple prairie clover)
Desmodium canadense (Canada tick-trefoil, Canada tickclover)
Desmodium illinoense (Illinois tick-trefoil, Illinois tickclover)
Dicentra cucullaria (Dutchman's breeches)
Dodecatheon meadia (shooting star)
Echinacea purpurea (purple coneflower)
Epilobium angustifolium (fireweed, willow herb)
Eryngium yuccifolium (rattlesnake master, button snake-root)
Erythronium americanum (eastern trout lily, yellow trout lily)
Eupatorium maculatum (spotted Joe-pye weed)
Eupatorium perfoliatum (boneset)
Eupatorium purpureum (Joe-pye weed)
Euphorbia corollata (flowering spurge)
Euthamia graminifolia var. graminifolia (grass-leaved goldenrod)
Fragaria virginiana (wild strawberry)
Galium triflorum (sweet-scented bedstraw)
Gentiana andrewsii (bottle gentian)
Gentiana saponaria (closed gentian, soapwort gentian)
Geranium maculatum (wild geranium, cranesbill)
Geum rivale (purple avens, water avens)
Geum triflorum (prairie smoke, purple avens)
Helenium autumnale (common sneezeweed)
Helianthus gigenteus (giant sunflower)
Helianthus laetiflorus (showy sunflower)
Helianthus pauciflorus ssp. pauciflorus (stiff sunflower)
Helianthus strumosus (woodland sunflower)
Heliopsis helianthoides (oxeye sunflower)
Hepatica nobilis var. acuta (sharp-lobed hepatica)
Heterotheca villosa var. villosa (golden aster)
Heuchera richardsonii (alum root)
Houstonia longifolia var. longifolia (long-leaved bluets, pale bluets)
Hydrophyllum virginianum (Virginia waterleaf)
Hypericum pyramidatum (great St. John's wort)
Hypoxis hirsuta (yellow star grass)
Iris versicolor (blue flag)
Iris virginica var. shrevei (blue flag)
Lespedeza capitata (roundheaded bush clover)
Liatris aspera (rough blazing star, gayfeather)
Liatris cylindracea (dwarf blazing star, gayfeather)

Liatris pycnostachya (prairie blazing star, gayfeather)
Lilium michiganense (Michigan lily)
Lilium philadelphicum (wood lily)
Lilium superbum (Turk's cap lily)
Linnaea borealis (twinflower)
Lithospermum canescens (hoary puccoon)
Lithospermum caroliniense (hairy puccoon, hispid gromwell)
Lithospermum incisum (fringed puccoon, narrow-leaved puccoon)
Lobelia cardinalis (cardinal flower)
Lobelia siphilitica (great blue lobelia)
Lupinus perennis (wild lupine)
Lycopus americanas (bugleweed)
Lysimachia ciliata (fringed loosestrife)
Maianthemum canadense (wild lily-of-the-valley, Canada mayflower)
Mentha arvensis (mint)
Mertensia virginica (bluebells)
Mitchella repens (partridge berry)
Monarda didyma (Oswego tea)
Monarda fistulosa (wild bergamot, horsemint, beebalm)
Nuphar lutea (yellow pond lily, cow lily, spatter dock)
Oenothera serrulata (evening primrose)
Osmorhiza claytoni (sweet cicely, sweet jarvil)
Penstemon digitalis (beardtongue)
Penstemon gracilis (large penstemon)
Penstemon grandiflorus (large-flowered penstemon)
Pentaphylloides floribunda (potentilla, shrubby cinquefoil)
Phlox divaricata ssp. laphamii (blue phlox, sweet William)
Phlox pilosa (prairie phlox, downy phlox)
Physostegia virginiana (obedient plant, false dragonhead)
Podophyllum peltatum (May apple)
Polemonium reptans (Jacob's ladder, Greek valerian)
Polygonatum biflorum (Solomon's seal)
Pontederia cordata (pickerelweed)
Potentilla arguta (white cinquefoil, prairie cinquefoil, tall cinquefoil)
Potentilla simplex (common cinquefoil)
Pulsatilla patens ssp. multifida (pasque flower, wild crocus)
Pycnanthemum virginianum (mountain mint)
Pyrola elliptica (shinleaf)
Ranunculus hispidus (early buttercup, tufted buttercup)
Ratibida columnifera (prairie coneflower, long-headed coneflower, Mexican hat)
Ratibida pinnata (gray-headed coneflower, yellow coneflower)
Rudbeckia hirta (black-eyed Susan)
Rudbeckia laciniata (cut-leaf coneflower)
Rudbeckia subtomentosa (sweet black-eyed Susan)
Sagitaria latifolia (arrowhead)
Sanguinaria candensis (bloodroot)
Scutellaria galesiculata (marsh skullcap)
Senecio aureus (golden ragwort)
Sibbaldiopsis tridentata (three-toothed cinquefoil)
Silene stellata (starry campion)
Silphium integrifolium (rosinweed)
Silphium laciniatum (compass plant)

Silphium perfoliatum (cup plant)
Silphium terebinthinaceum (prairie dock)
Sisyrinchium campestre (white-eyed grass, prairie blue-eyed grass)
Smilacena racemosam (false Solomon's seal, false spikenard)
Smilacena stellatum (starry Solomon's seal)
Solidago gigantea (giant goldenrod)
Solidago juncea (early goldenrod, plume goldenrod)
Solidago missouriensis (Missouri goldenrod, prairie goldenrod)
Solidago nemoralis (gray goldenrod, old-field goldenrod)
Solidago rigida (stiff goldenrod)
Solidago speciosa (showy goldenrod)
Solidago ulmifolia (elm-leaved goldenrod)
Streptopus roseus (rosy twisted stalk)
Stylophorum diphyllum (celandine poppy)
Tephrosia virginiana (goat's rue)
Thalictrum dasycarpum (tall or purple meadow rue)
Thalictrum dioicum (early meadow rue)
Thalictrum thalictroides (rue anemone)
Tradescantia ohiensis (Ohio spiderwort)
Trientalis borealis ssp. borealis (starflower)
Trillium cernuum (nodding trillium)
Trillium erectum (wakerobin, purple trillium)
Uvularia grandiflora (bellwort, merrybells)
Uvularia sessilifolia (wildoats, merrybells)
Verbena hastata (blue verbena, blue vervain)
Verbena stricta (hoary vervain)
Vernonia fasciculata (ironweed)
Veronicastrum virginicum (Culver's root)
Viola canadensis (Canada violet)
Viola conspersa (American dog violet)
Viola pedata (bird-foot violet)
Viola pedatifida (prairie violet)
Viola pubescens (downy or smooth yellow violet)
Viola soraria (common blue violet, meadow violet)
Zizia aptera (heart-leaved golden alexanders)
Zizia aurea (golden alexanders)

Grasses/Grass-like plants

Agrostis scabra (ticklegrass, fly-away grass)
Andropogon gerardii (big bluestem)
Bouteloua curtipendula (sideoats grama)
Bouteloua hirsuta (hairy grama)
Bromus kalmii (prairie brome, wild chess)
Calamagrostis canadensis (bluejoint grass)
Calamovilfa longifolia (sandreed grass, prairie sandreed)
Carex aquatilis (water sedge)
Carex lacustris (lake sedge)
Carex pensylvanica (Pennsylvania sedge)
Carex plantaginea (plantain-leaved sedge)
Carex stipata (awl-fruited sedge)
Carex stricta (tussock sedge)
Carex utriculata (beaked sedge)

Danthonia spicata (poverty grass)
Eleocharis palustris (creeping spikesedge, spike rush)
Elymus canadensis (Canada wild rye)
Elymus hystrix var. hystrix (bottlebrush grass)
Elymus lanceolatus (thickspike wheatgrass)
Eragrostis spectabilis (purple lovegrass, tumblegrass)
Glyceria grandis (American mannagrass, tall mannagrass, reed meadowgrass)
Hierochloe odorata (sweet grass)
Juncus effusus var. solutus (soft rush)
Juncus interior (inland rush)
Koeleria macrantha (June grass)
Leersia oryzoides (rice cut grass)
Panicum virgatum (switchgrass)
Schizachyrium scoparium (little bluestem)
Scirpus acutus (hardstem bulrush)
Scirpus americana (3-square bulrush)
Scirpus atrovirens (dark green bulrush)
Scirpus cyperinus (wool grass)
Scirpus fluviatilis (river bulrush)
Scirpus maritimus (alkali bulrush, prairie bulrush, bayonet grass)
Scirpus tabernaemontani (great bulrush)
Scirpus validus (soft stem bulrush)
Sorghastrum nutans (Indian grass)
Sparganium eurycarpum (giant burreed)
Spartina pectinata (prairie cordgrass, freshwater cordgrass)
Sporobolus compositus var. compositus (tall dropseed)
Sporobolus cryptandrus (sand dropseed)
Sporobolus heterolepis (northern prairie dropseed)
Stipa spartea (porcupine grass)
Typha latifolia (cattail)

Shrubs (deciduous)

Alnus incana (speckled alder, mountain alder)
Amelanchier arborea (downy serviceberry, shadbush, Juneberry)
Amorpha canescens (leadplant)
Amorpha fruticosa (false indigo, Indigo bush)
Aronia melanocarpa (black chokeberry)
Artemisia frigida (prairie sagewort, fringed sage)
Ceanothus americanus (New Jersey tea, red root)
Cephalanthus occidentalis (buttonbush)
Comptonia peregrina (sweet fern)
Cornus alternifolia (pogoda dogwood, alternate-leaved dogwood)
Cornus racemosa (gray dogwood)
Cornus sericea (red-twig dogwood, red-osier dogwood)
Corylus americana (American hazelnut or filbert)
Corylus cornuta (beaked hazelnut or filbert)
Diervilla lonicera (bush honeysuckle)
Dirca palustris (leatherwood, ropebark)
Euonymus atropurpurea (wahoo, burning bush)
Ilex verticillata (winterberry, black alder)
Physocarpus opulifolius (ninebark)
Prunus virginiana (chokecherry)

Ptelea trifolista (hoptree)
Ribes cynosbati (prickly gooseberry, dogberry)
Rosa arkansana (prairie rose)
Rosa blanda (early wild rose, smooth rose)
Rosa carolina (Carolina rose)
Rosa setigera (Illinois or prairie rose)
Salix bebbiana (Bebb willow, long-beaked willow)
Salix discolor (pussy willow)
Sambucus canadensis (elderberry, common elder)
Sambucus racemosa var. pubens (scarlet elderberry, red-berried elder)
Shepherdia canadensis (buffaloberry)
Spiraea alba (meadow sweet)
Spiraea tomentosa (steeplebush, hardhack)
Staphylea trifolia (bladdernut)
Symphoricarpos albus (snowberry)
Symphoricarpos orbiculatus (coralberry, Indian currant)
Vaccinium angustifolium (low-bush blueberry)
Viburnum acerifolium (maple leaf viburnum)
Viburnum lentago (black haw, nannyberry)
Viburnum opulus var. americanum (high-bush cranberry, American
 cranberrybush viburnum)

Shrubs (evergreen)

Andromeda polifolia var. glaucophylla (bog rosemary)
Arctostaphylos uva-ursi (bearberry, kinnikinnik)
Gaultheria hispidula (creeping snowberry)
Gaultheria procumbens (wintergreen, checkerberry)
Juniperus communis (common juniper)
Juniperus horizontalis (creeping juniper, creeping savin)
Kalmia polifolia (swamp laurel, bog laurel)
Ledum groenlandicum (Labrador tea, muskeg tea)

Trees (deciduous)

Acer rubrum (red maple)
Acer saccharinum (silver maple)
Acer saccharum (sugar maple)
Acer spicatum (mountain maple)
Betula nigra (river birch)
Betula papyrifera (paper birch)
Carpinus caroliniana (blue beech, hornbeam, musclewood)
Carya cordiformis (bitternut, swamp hickory)
Carya ovata (shagbark hickory)
Celtis occidentalis (hackberry, sugarberry)
Crataegus crus-galli (cockspur hawthorn)
Crataegus mollis (downy hawthorn)
Crataegus punctata (dotted hawthorn, white thorn)
Fagus grandifolia var. grandifolia (beech)
Fraxinus americana (white ash)
Fraxinus pensylvanica (green ash)
Hamamelis virginiana (witch hazel)
Juglans nigra (black walnut)
Larix laricina (tamarack, American larch)

Malus ioensis var. ioensis (prairie crabapple)
Ostrya virginiana (ironwood, hophornbeam)
Populus deltoides (eastern cottonwood)
Prunus americana (wild plum)
Prunus nigra (Canada plum)
Prunus pensylvanica (fire or pin cherry)
Prunus serotina (black cherry)
Quercus alba (white oak)
Quercus bicolor (swamp white oak)
Quercus macrocarpa (bur oak)
Quercus muhlenbergii (chinkapin oak, chestnut oak)
Quercus rubra (red oak)
Quercus velutina (black oak)
Salix amygdaloides (peachleaf willow)
Salix nigra (black willow)
Sorbus americana (mountain ash)
Tilia americana (American linden, basswood)
Ulmus americana (American elm)
Ulmus rubra (red elm, slippery elm)

Trees (evergreen)

Abies balsamea (balsam fir)
Juniperus virginiana (eastern red cedar)
Picea glauca (white spruce)
Pinus banksiana (Jack pine)
Pinus resinosa (red pine, Norway pine)
Pinus strobus (eastern white pine)
Thuja occidentalis (arbor vitae, northern white cedar)
Tsuga canadensis (eastern hemlock)

Vines (deciduous)

Celastrus scandens (American bittersweet)
Clematis occidentalis var. occidentalis (purple clematis)
Clematis virginiana (virgin's bower)
Lonicera dioica (limber or wild honeysuckle)
Parthenocissus quinquefolia var. quinquefolia (woodbine)

FEDERALLY LISTED ENDANGERED SPECIES

Dwarf lake iris (Iris lacustris)
Eastern paririe fringed orchid (Platanthera leucophaea)
Fassett's locoweed (Oxytropis campesstris var. chartacea)
Northern wild monkshood (Aconitum noveboracense)
Pitcher's thistle (Cirsium pitcheri)
Prairie bush-clover (lespedeza leptostachya)

WISCONSIN NOXIOUS SPECIES

Because the noxious weed lists have continually changed since we gathered
them in 1994, we are not including them at this time. Not all States have
noxious weed lists. Those that do, do not use the same standards of importance
and are not comparable. States typically have included plants that interfere with
agriculture (Canada thistle), or cause human health problems (poison ivy). Some
States are now including a category of plants that invade and degrade the
environment (purple loosestrife). Check with your State's Agriculture Department
or Weed Scientist listed below. The noxious weed list can be used two ways on
roadsides: l) check to not inadvertantly plant these invasive plants, and 2) note
the plants you are legally responsible to control. Many States now check
adjacent State lists to avoid planting their neighbors' problem plants. Because
weeds do not respect political boundaries, and because by their very nature
weeds continue to adapt and expand, monitoring and controlling invasives at
State borders is a wise part of vegetation management.

(Weed and Seed Laws)

Department of Agriculture
Bureau of Plant Industry
P.O. Box 8911
Madison, WI 53708

Chris Boerboom, Agronomy
University of Wisconsin
1575 Linden Drive
Madison, WI 53706
(608) 262-1392

WISCONSIN RESOURCES

Natural Heritage Program
WDNR, P.O. Box 7921
Madison, WI 53707-7921
(608) 264-6057

The Nature Conservancy
633 W. Main St.
Madison, WI 53703
(608) 251-8140

Wild Ones
P.O. Box 23576
Milwaukee, WI 53223-0576

University of Wisconsin Arboretum
1207 Seminole Highway
Madison, WI 53711
(608) 262-2746

Evelyn Howell
John Harrington
Restoration and Management
University of Wisconsin
25 Agriculture Hall
Madison, WI 53706
(608) 263-6964

POTENTIAL NATURAL VEGETATION ZONES IN
WYOMING

Source: A.W. Kuchler's Potential Natural Vegetation Map, 1964, Revised 1985.
Presented in U.S.G.S. National Atlas of the U.S. Series,
U.S. Geological Survey, Reston, VA.

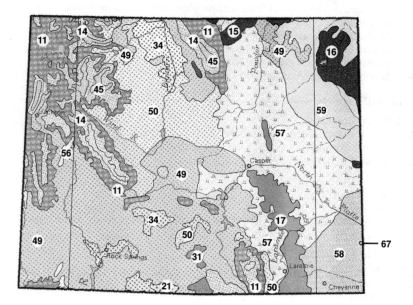

11	Douglas fir forest (Pseudotsuga)		**45**	Alpine meadows and barren (Agrostis, Carex, Festuca, Poa)
14	Western spruce-fir forest (Picea-Abies)		**49**	Sagebrush steppe (Artemisia-Agropyron)
15	Eastern ponderosa forest (Pinus)		**50**	Wheatgrass-needlegrass shrubsteppe (Agropyron-Stipa-Artemisia)
16	Black Hills pine forest (Pinus)		**56**	Foothills prairie (Agropyron-Festuca-Stipa)
17	Pine-Douglas fir forest (Pinus-Pseudotsuga)		**57**	Grama-needlegrass-wheatgrass (Bouteloua-Stipa-Agropyron)
21	Juniper-pinyon woodland (Juniperus-Pinus)		**58**	Grama-buffalo grass (Bouteloua-Buchloë)
31	Mountain mahogany-oak scrub (Cercocarpus-Quercus)		**59**	Wheatgrass-needlegrass (Agropyron-Stipa)
34	Saltbush-greasewood (Atriplex-Sarcobatus)		**67**	Sandhills prairie (Andropogon-Calamovilfa)

(Dominant plant species present in each vegetation type are listed in Appendix 8)

11 Douglas Fir Forest (Pseudotsuga)
14 Western Spruce-Fir Forest (Picea-Abies)
15 Eastern Ponderosa Forest (Pinus)
16 Black Hills Pine Forest (Pinus)
17 Pine-Douglas Fir Forest (Pinus-Pseudotsuga)
21 Juniper-Pinyon Woodland (Juniperus-Pinus)
31 Mountain Mahogany-Oak Scrub (Cercocarpus-Quercus)
34 Saltbrush-Geasewood (Artiplex-Sarcobatus)
45 Alpine Meadows and Barren (Agrostis, Carex, Festuca, Poa)
49 Sagebrush Steppe (Artemisia-Agropyron)
50 Wheatgrass-Needlegrass Shrubsteppe (Agropyron-Stipa-Artemisia)
56 Foothills Prairie (Agropyron-Festuca-Stipa)
57 Grama-Needlegrass-Wheatgrass (Bouteloua-Stipa-Agropyron)
58 Grama-Buffalo Grass (Bouteloua-Buchloë)
59 Wheatgrass-Needlegrass (Agropyron Stipa)
67 Sandhills Prairie (Andropogon-Calamovilfa)

Botanical Experts

Walt Fertig, Botanist
Wyoming Natural Diversity Database
1604 Grand Avenue
Laramie, WY 82070
(307) 745-5026

Dr. Robert Dorn
P.O. Box 147
Cheyenne, WY 82003
(307) 634-6328

Dr. Ronald L. Hartman, Curator
Rocky Mountain Herbarium
University of Wyoming
(307) 766-2236

Recommended Flora

Dorn, R.D. 1992. Vascular Plants of Wyoming, 2nd Edition. Mountain West Publishing, Box 1471, Cheyenne, WY 82003. 340 pgs. + illus.

NATIVE PLANTS FOR LANDSCAPE USE IN WYOMING

Ferns

Athyrium filix-femina (lady fern)
Cystopteris fragilis (fragile fern)

Forbs (annuals/biennials)

Cleome serrulata (Rocky Mountain beeplant)
Dyssodia papposa (dyssodia, dogweed, fetid marigold)
Erysimum capitatum (western wallflower, prairie rocket)
Helianthus annuus (common sunflower)
Helianthus petiolaris (plains sunflower)

Ipomopsis aggregata (sky rocket, scarlet gilia)
Lepidium montanum (mountain peppergrass)
Linum rigidum (yellow flax)
Machaeranthera tanacetifolia (tahoka daisy, tansy aster)
Mentzelia decapetala (blazing star, evening star, stick leaf)
Mentzelia laevicaulis (blazing star, evening star, stick leaf)
Mimulus guttatus (golden monkey flower)
Nemophila breviflora (Great Basin nemophila)
Oenothera albicaulis (pale evening primrose)
Rudbeckia hirta (black-eyed Susan)
Senecio plattensis (prairie ragwort, prairie groundsel)
Senecio serra
Senecio triangularis
Townsendia exscapa (Easter daisy)

Forbs (perennials)

Abronia fragrans (sweet sand verbena)
Aconitum columbianum (western monkshood)
Allium cernuum (nodding onion)
Anaphalis margaritacea (pearly everlasting)
Anemone canadensis (Canada anemone, windflower)
Anemone cylindrica (thimbleweed, candle anemone)
Anemone multifida (early thimbleweed, cut-leaf anemone, Pacific anemone)
Antennaria microphylla (pussytoes, everlasting)
Antennaria parvifolia (pussytoes, everlasting)
Antennaria rosea (pussytoes, everlasting)
Apocynum androsaemifolium (spreading dogbane)
Aquilegia coerulea (Rocky Mountain or blue columbine)
Aquilegia flavescens (yellow columbine)
Arnica cordifolia (heartleaf arnica)
Artemisia ludoviciana (white sage, prairie sage, artemisia)
Asclepias speciosa (showy milkweed)
Aster ascendens (purple aster, Pacific aster)
Aster ericoides (heath aster, white wreath aster)
Aster foliaceus (leafy aster)
Aster laevis (smooth aster)
Aster oblongifolius (aromatic aster)
Aster sibiricus (Sibirian or arctic aster)
Astragalus americanus (American milk vetch, rattlepod)
Astragalus canadensis (milk vetch, Canada milk vetch)
Balsamorrhiza sagittata (balsamroot)
Calochortus gunnisonii (lily)
Calochortus nuttallii (sego lily, mariposa lily)
Caltha leptosepala (white marsh marigold, elkslip)
Campanula rotundifolia (harebell)
Castilleja angustifolia var. dubia (desert paintbrush)
Castilleja linariifolia (Indian paintbrush)
Castilleja miniata (Indian paintbrush)
Castilleja sessiliflora (downy painted cup)
Castilleja sulphurea (splitleaf Indian paintbrush)
Claytonia lanceolata (spring beauty)
Clematis hirsutissima (clematis, vase flower, leather flower, lion's beard)

Cornus canadensis (bunchberry)
Delphinium glaucum (tower larkspur)
Dryas octopetala (mountain dryas, white mountain avens)
Dugaldia hoopesii (orange sneezeweed, owls' claws)
Echinacea angustifolia (narrow-leaved purple coneflower)
Epilobium angustifolium (fireweed, willow herb)
Epilobium latifolium (dwarf fireweed)
Erigeron compositus (alpine daisy)
Erigeron peregrinus (fleabane)
Erigeron speciosus (showy fleabane)
Eriogonum ovalifolium (buckwheat)
Eriogonum umbellatum (sulfur buckwheat)
Eriophyllum lanatum (woolly sunflower, Oregon sunshine)
Erythronium grandiflorum (glacier lily, yellow fawn lily, dogtooth violet)
Eupatorium maculatum (spotted Joe-pye weed)
Gaillardia aristata (blanket flower, gaillardia, brown-eyed Susan)
Galium triflorum (sweet-scented bedstraw)
Gaura coccinea (scarlet gaura)
Gentiana parryi (Parry gentian)
Geranium viscossisimum (sticky wild geranium)
Geum rivale (purple avens, water avens)
Geum triflorum (prairie smoke, purple avens)
Glycyrrhiza lepidota (wild licorice)
Gutierrezia sarothrae (broom snakeweed, matchbrush)
Hedysarum boreale (sweet vetch, sweet broom)
Helenium autumnale (common sneezeweed)
Helianthus maximiliani (Maximilian sunflower)
Helianthus pauciflorus ssp. pauciflorus (stiff sunflower)
Heliomeris multiflora (showy goldeneye)
Heterotheca villosa var. villosa (golden aster)
Heuchera parvifolia (saxifrage, alum root)
Ipomoea leptophylla (bush morning glory)
Iris missouriensis (Rocky Mountain iris, western blue flag)
Lewisia rediviva (bitter root)
Liatris punctata (dotted blazing star, gayfeather)
Linnaea borealis (twinflower)
Linum lewisii (wild blue flax)
Lithospermum incisum (fringed puccoon, narrow-leaved puccoon)
Lupinus argenteus (silvery lupine)
Lupinus polyphyllus (meadow lupine, bog lupine)
Maianthemum canadense (wild lily-of-the-valley, Canada mayflower)
Maianthemum racemosum ssp. racemosum (false Solomon's seal,
    false spikenard)
Maianthemum stellatum (starry Solomon's seal)
Mertensia ciliata (mountain bluebells)
Mimulus lewisii (Lewis monkey flower, great purple monkey flower)
Minuartia obtusiloba (cushion sandwort)
Monarda fistulosa (wild bergamot, horsemint, beebalm)
Oenothera cespitosa (gumbo evening primrose, gumbo lily)
Oenothera flava (Shortfin evening primrose)
Opuntia polyacantha (prickly pear)
Osmorhiza berteroi (mountain sweet cicely)

Osmorhiza occidentalis
Pedicularis bracteosa (elephant heads)
Pedicularis groenlandica (elephant heads)
Pedicularis parryi (elephant heads)
Penstemon albidus (white beardtongue)
Penstemon angustifolius (whorled penstemon)
Penstemon cyananthus (Platte River penstemon, Wasatch penstemon)
Penstemon deustus (hot rock penstemon)
Penstemon glaber var. alpinus (blue penstemon, alpine penstemon)
Penstemon grandiflorus (large-flowered penstemon)
Penstemon strictus (Rocky Mountain penstemon)
Petrophyton caespitosum (dwarf spiraea, petrophytum, tufted rockmat)
Phacelia sericea (silky phacelia)
Polemonium occidentale (Jacob's ladder)
Polemonium pulcherrimum (alpine Jacob's ladder, skunk leaf)
Polemonium viscosum (sky pilot)
Potentilla arguta (white cinquefoil, prairie cinquefoil, tall cinquefoil)
Pulsatilla patens ssp. multifida (pasque flower, wild crocus)
Ranunculus alismifolius (meadow buttercup)
Ranunculus cardiophyllus (buttercup)
Ratibida columnifera (prairie coneflower, long-headed coneflower, Mexican hat)
Rudbeckia laciniata (cut-leaf coneflower)
Saxifraga bronchialis (spotted saxifrage, matted saxifrage)
Saxifraga cespitosa (tufted saxifrage)
Saxifraga odontoloma
Sidalcea neomexicana (checker mallow, prairie mallow)
Solidago canadensis (meadow goldenrod)
Solidago missouriensis (Missouri goldenrod, prairie goldenrod)
Solidago multiradiata (northern goldenrod, mountain goldenrod)
Solidago rigida (stiff goldenrod)
Sphaeralcea coccinea (scarlet globe mallow)
Stanleya pinnata (desert or prince's plume)
Tetraneuris acaulis var. acaulis (stemless goldflower, stemless rubber weed, butte marigold)
Thalictrum dasycarpum (tall or purple meadow rue)
Thermopsis rhombifolia var. montana (golden pea, buckbean)
Verbena hastata (blue verbena, blue vervain)
Verbena stricta (hoary vervain)
Viola canadensis (Canada violet)
Viola nuttallii (yellow violet)
Yucca glauca (yucca, soapweed)
Zizia aptera (heart-leaved golden alexanders)

Grasses/Grass-like plants

Agrostis exarata (spikebent, spike red top)
Agrostis scabra (ticklegrass, fly-away grass)
Andropogon gerardii (big bluestem)
Andropogon hallii (sand bluestem)
Aristida purpurea var. longiseta (red three awn)
Bouteloua curtipendula (sideoats grama)
Bouteloua gracilis (blue grama)
Bromus anomalus (nodding brome)

Bromus carinatus (California brome)
Bromus ciliatus (fringed brome)
Buchloe dactyloides (buffalograss)
Calamagrostis canadensis (bluejoint grass)
Calamovilfa longifolia (sandreed grass, prairie sandreed)
Carex aquatilis (water sedge)
Carex nebrascensis (Nebraska sedge)
Carex stipata (awl-fruited sedge)
Carex utriculata (beaked sedge)
Carex vernacula (sedge)
Danthonia californica (California oatgrass)
Danthonia intermedia (timber oatgrass)
Danthonia spicata (poverty grass)
Deschampsia cespitosa (tufted hairgrass)
Distichlis spicata (seashore saltgrass)
Eleocharis palustris (creeping spikesedge, spike rush)
Elymus canadensis (Canada wild rye)
Elymus glaucus (blue wild rye)
Elymus lanceolatus (thickspike wheatgrass)
Festuca idahoensis (Idaho fescue, blue bunchgrass)
Festuca saximontana (fescue)
Glyceria grandis (American mannagrass, tall mannagrass, reed meadowgrass)
Hierochloe odorata (sweet grass)
Juncus interior (inland rush)
Koeleria macrantha (June grass)
Leymus cinereus (Great Basin wild rye)
Oryzopsis hymenoides (Indian ricegrass)
Panicum virgatum (switchgrass)
Pascopyrum smithii (western wheatgrass)
Phleum alpinum (alpine timothy)
Poa alpina (alpine bluegrass)
Poa secunda (pine bluegrass)
Pseudoroegneria spicata (bluebunch wheatgrass)
Schizachyrium scoparium (little bluestem)
Scirpus acutus (hardstem bulrush)
Scirpus maritimus (alkali bulrush, prairie bulrush, bayonet grass)
Sorghastrum nutans (Indian grass)
Spartina pectinata (prairie cordgrass, freshwater cordgrass)
Sporobolus airoides (alkali sacaton)
Sporobolus cryptandrus (sand dropseed)
Stipa comata (needle-and-thread grass)
Stipa nelsonii (Columbia needlegrass)
Stipa spartea (porcupine grass)
Trisetum spicatum (spike trisetum)
Typha latifolia (cattail)

Shrubs (deciduous)

Alnus incana (speckled alder, mountain alder)
Amelanchier alnifolia (saskatoon, western serviceberry, Juneberry)
Amelanchier utahensis (Utah serviceberry)
Amorpha canescens (leadplant)
Amorpha fruticosa (false indigo, Indigo bush)

Artemisia frigida (prairie sagewort, fringed sage)
Atriplex canescens (four-wing saltbush, wingscale)
Atriplex confertifolia (spiny saltbush, shadscale saltbush, hop sage)
Betula nana (bog birch, dwarf birch)
Chrysothamnus nauseosus (rabbit brush, chamisa)
Cornus sericea (red-twig dogwood, red-osier dogwood)
Crataegus douglasii (black hawthorn)
Elaeagnus commutata (silverberry, wild olive, wolf willow)
Holodiscus dumosus (bush rock-spires, cream bush, ocean spray)
Lonicera involucrata (black twinberry, bear berry honeysuckle)
Physocarpus malvaceus (mallow ninebark)
Prunus virginiana (chokecherry)
Purshia tridentata (antelope brush)
Rhus glabra (smooth sumac)
Rhus trilobata (squawbush, basketbush, skunkbush)
Ribes aureum (golden currant)
Ribes cereum (wax currant, western red currant, squaw currant)
Ribes odoratum (buffalo currant, golden currant)
Rosa arkansana (prairie rose)
Rosa nutkana (nootka rose)
Rosa woodsii (western wild rose, woods rose)
Rubus parviflorus (western thimbleberry)
Salix arctica (arctic willow)
Salix bebbiana (Bebb willow, long-beaked willow)
Salix discolor (pussy willow)
Salix scouleriana (western pussy willow, Scouler's willow)
Sambucus racemosa var. melanocarpa (black elderberry)
Sarcobatus vermiculatus (greasewood)
Shepherdia argentea (silver buffaloberry)
Shepherdia canadensis (buffaloberry)
Sorbus scopulina (western mountain ash)
Spiraea splendens var. splendens (subalpine spiraea)
Symphoricarpos albus (snowberry)
Symphoricarpos oreophilus (mountain snowberry)

Shrubs (evergreen)

Arctostaphylos uva-ursi (bearberry, kinnikinnik)
Artemisia nova (black sagebrush)
Artemisia tridentata (big sagebrush, Great Basin sagebrush)
Ceanothus velutinus (mountain balm, buckbush)
Cercocarpus ledifolius (curl-leaf mountain mahogany)
Cercocarpus montanus (mountain mahogany, silverleaf mountain mahogany)
Grayia spinosa (spiny hopsage)
Juniperus communis (common juniper)
Juniperus horizontalis (creeping juniper, creeping savin)
Kalmia polifolia (swamp laurel, bog laurel)
Paxistima myrsinites (Oregon box, myrtle boxwood, mountain lover)
Phyllodoce empetriformis (pink mountain heather)

Trees (deciduous)

Acer glabrum (Rocky Mountain maple)
Acer grandidentatum (bigtooth maple)

Acer negundo (box elder)
Betula occidentalis (mountain birch, water birch)
Fraxinus pensylvanica (green ash)
Populus deltoides (eastern cottonwood)
Populus tremuloides (quaking aspen)
Prunus americana (wild plum)
Prunus pensylvanica (fire or pin cherry)
Salix amygdaloides (peachleaf willow)

Trees (evergreen)

Abies lasiocarpa (subalpine fir)
Juniperus osteosperma (Utah juniper)
Juniperus scopulorum (Rocky Mountain juniper)
Picea engelmannii (Engelmann spruce)
Picea pungens (blue spruce, Colorado spruce)
Pinus flexilis (limber pine)
Pinus ponderosa (ponderosa pine)
Pseudotsuga menziesii (Douglas fir)

Vines (deciduous)

Clematis columbiana (purple virgin's bower)
Clematis ligusticifolia (clematis)
Parthenocissus quinquefolia var. quinquefolia (woodbine)
Vitis riparia (riverbank grape)

Ute ladies' tresses (Spiranthes diluvialis)

WYOMING NOXIOUS SPECIES

Because the noxious weed lists have continually changed since we gathered them in 1994, we are not including them at this time. Not all States have noxious weed lists. Those that do, do not use the same standards of importance and are not comparable. States typically have included plants that interfere with agriculture (Canada thistle), or cause human health problems (poison ivy). Some States are now including a category of plants that invade and degrade the environment (purple loosestrife). Check with your State's Agriculture Department or Weed Scientist listed below. The noxious weed list can be used two ways on roadsides: l) check to not inadvertantly plant these invasive plants, and 2) note the plants you are legally responsible to control. Many States now check adjacent State lists to avoid planting their neighbors' problem plants. Because weeds do not respect political boundaries, and because by their very nature weeds continue to adapt and expand, monitoring and controlling invasives at State borders is a wise part of vegetation management.

(Weed and Seed Laws)

Department of Agriculture
Division of Technical Services
2219 Carey Avenue
Cheyenne, WY 82002

Tom Whitson, U of W
Plant/Soil/Insect Sciences
University Station, Box 3354
Laramie, WY 82070
(307) 766-3113

WYOMING RESOURCES

The Nature Conservancy
258 Main St. #200
Lander, WY 82820
(307) 332-2971

Wyoming Native Plant Society
1604 Grand Avenue,
Laramie, WY 82070

Natural Heritage
Wyoming Natural Diversity Database
1604 Grand Avenue
Laramie, WY 82070
(307) 745-5026

Part Three

a p p e n d i c e s

(Replaces the 1988 guidance by the Office of Environmental Policy
in response to the 1987 STURAA)

Statutory Requirement

Section 130 of the Surface Transportation and Uniform Relocation Assistance Act of 1987 (STURAA) amended 23 U.S.C. 319 by adding a requirement that native wildflower seeds or seedlings or both be planted as part of any landscaping project undertaken on the Federal-aid highway system. At least one-quarter of one percent of funds expended for a landscaping project must be used to plant native wildflowers on that project. This provision requires every landscaping project to include the planting of native wildflowers unless a waiver has been granted. Federal-Aid Highway Program Manual 6-2-5-1 has been changed to reflect the STURAA amendment.

Operation Wildflower

The Federal Highway Administration (FHWA) has administered a voluntary, cooperative program titled, "Operation Wildflower" with the National Council of State Garden Clubs and State highway agencies since 1973. Unlike Operation Wildflower, however, the program requirements of STURAA are mandatory. However, it does not prohibit the acceptance of native wildflower seeds or seedlings donated by civic organizations or other organizations or individuals to be used in landscaping projects. State Garden Clubs may continue to pay for or supply native wildflower seeds or seedlings. However, neither the donated funds nor the value of donated plant materials can be counted toward the minimum expenditure required by STURAA.

The new program requirement does not discontinue the program policies of Operation Wildflower. Federal funds are still available for participation in the cost of planting wildflowers supplied by garden clubs and other organizations or individuals even though the planting may not be part of a landscaping project.

Landscaping Project

The native wildflower planting requirement is applicable only to landscaping projects and not every Federal-aid highway construction project. A landscaping project is defined as, "an action taken as part of a highway construction project or as a separate action to enhance the esthetics of a highway through the placement of plant materials consistent with a landscape design plan."

States are encouraged to plant native wildflowers on highway projects as part of their erosion control measures. Additionally, a State could establish a landscaping project that involves only native wildflowers. The project would follow normal procedures for programming landscaping projects. Planting native wildflowers and associated grasses, trees, shrubs and vines as part of an erosion control, wetland mitigation or other restoration solution, or as part of a total vegetation management program is certainly encouraged.

Expenditure Formula

The one-quarter of one percent expenditure requirement is intended to establish a minimum amount of project landscaping expense devoted to planting native wildflowers. A State can expend more than this amount. The forumla is applied only to the cost associated with the landscaping project. It does not include the total highway construction cost. However, all work performed in association with the landscaping is to be included in the total landscaping expenses. This would include, but not be limited to, costs associated with development of the design plan, site preparation, irrigation systems, plant materials, installation, and establishment period costs.

Waivers

Although the wildflower requirement allows the FHWA Division Administrator to grant a waiver if the State certifies that:

1. Native wildflowers or seedlings cannot be grown satisfactorily; or
2. There is a scarcity of available planting areas; or
3. The available planting areas will be used for agricultural purposes, project waivers are discouraged.

FHWA encourages more than the minimum use of native wildflowers and welcomes creative arrangements to plant more rather than less than the requirement. Note waiver example on page 578.

Specification Considerations

Specifications should be based on realistic procedures and expectations. Specifications not only serve as guidelines to successful projects, but as education to those who use the specifications. Following are considerations we recommend when establishing specifications for native wildflower and native grass plantings. Remember the practice continues to be more of an art than a science. That means there is no one correct solution that will succeed on all roadsides; but rather that each State, and possibly natural region within a State, will need to decide what works best. Then by writing specifications, the State can require what works best in its particular situation.

1. DESIGN

a. Site Selection:

* Analysis of site conditions is everything. Without this information, you cannot match species to the harsh environmental conditions of a right-of-way.
* Chose high visibility sites like slopes, interchanges, rest areas, State or city entrances, *if* you are confident you can succeed.
* Chose sites outside City limits, *if* you are still at a novice level of experience.
* It is cheaper to protect existing native wildflowers and native grass remnants than to restore them.

b. Concept:

* Find a local remnant of native wildflowers and grasses to use as a model.
* Contact your State's Natural Heritage Program and/or The Nature Conservancy to find local preserves with similar environmental conditions.
* Visit the model to observe distribution of the flowers among the grasses, the species diversity, the seasonal changes, overall structure, micro-climate relationships, and how the community changes over time.
* Use the inventory list of this model to shop for species appropriate to your site.

c. Plan:

* Limit and site beds or planting areas with maintenance in mind, i.e., sweeping lines are easier to mow around.
* Include maintenance notes in your plan.
* Keep the design simple; for visibility at high MPH as well as the installing contractor.

2. MATERIALS

a. Native Wildflower Seed Mix:

* List all native wildflowers available through commercial or harvest sources in your area. Keep this as a check-off list or permanent part of the specification.
* Note species that are available in seedling form only or species that can be used for visibility, diversity, or special considerations.
* Aim for as long a list as possible to encourage diversity on all projects. Also a long list will be needed to meet the constraints of a site: dry, mesic, wet; soil types; sun or shade; time of bloom; heights; colors, and so on.
* Attempt to use a long list of at least 20 or more species to assure diversity and interest over time.
* Planting rate of pounds per acre varies with equipment and experience. Cost is the strongest determining factor. Five pounds per acre along with five to ten pounds of native grasses can get spectacular results linked to good site preparation and cooperative weather patterns.
* Seedlings to enhance the project can be added.
* Every native wildflower/grass seed mix should be site specific, since all are different.

b. Native Grass Seed Mix:

* Always use native grasses with native forbs or wildflowers.
* Always plant grasses and forbs at the same time.
* Use a minimum of three grass species in each mix.
* The seeding rate per acre is specialized and low, unlike agricultural seeding rates.
* Consider a cover/nurse crop of an annual or short-lived native species. Most States have a short-lived wild rye species that could serve this purpose.
* Base choice on grass characteristics of height, bunch or sod formers, cool or warm season, annual, perennial, plus moisture and soil tolerances.

c. All Seed and Seedlings:

* Seed should be from current production and no more than one year old, free of mold or insect disease.
* Seed origin should be furnished. You decide the region of adaptation boundaries.
* Chose seed collected and/or grown in your region.
* All seedlings should be grown from known seed origin.

d. Contractor:

* 30 days within award of contract, Contractor should provide written certification from supplier of seed/seedlings. As long as native seed is in short supply, this safeguard is necessary to avoid unwanted substitutions. One strategy is to call for a longer list than needed, so that the Contractor can chose what is available that season; i.e., list 35 species, when you are

willing to accept 25. This allows shopping room. The early certification guarantees an order is secure in a short supply market.

* Limit these contracts to contractors with experience, whenever possible.
* Educate experienced and potential contractors in an annual winter workshop. Include consultants, seed growers, designers and maintenance to learn with them.
* Certification of seed includes:
  Name and location of seed supplier (warning: labels can be switched)
  Origin and date of harvest
  Seed germination statement (standards are not consistent at this time)
  On delivery, certify weights of each species.
  Each lot of seed should be individually packed and stored in paper bag.
  Assign an inspector who understands this kind of planting and what to check.

3. SITE PREPARATION

a. Vegetation Removal Prior to Seeding:

* Kill existing vegetation with nonselective, non-residual herbicide, a glyphosate without surfactant if possible. After evidence of kill (7-14 days) mow to 2".
* Mow or rake off. Burning off dead vegetation is done in some areas.
* Avoid techniques using high pressure or hot water sterilization. They need further environmental study.
* Avoid the use of methyl bromide which will no longer be available after the year 2000. This application kills all biota (useful and non useful) and has adverse environmental impacts.

b. Avoid Soil Disturbance:

* Avoid deep tillage which pulls up new weed seed to compromise plantings.
* Scarify soil no deeper than 1/2 inch, to reduce weed and erosion problems.
* No till planters are now available to plant into existed dead stubble.
* Avoid adding imported topsoils unless certified weed-free.

c. Soil Amendments:

* Amendments should be limited due to cost concerns.
* Fertilizers assist weed growth. Native forbs and grasses, if matched to the site, should establish without fertilizers, if moisture is available.
* Amendments, if used, should be monitored for potential runoff impacts.
* Addition of peat moss has not proven beneficial to these plantings over time.

* Addition of native mychorizae has proven beneficial.
* Often, the addition of weed-free sand can benefit a soil for plant establishment.

4. INSTALLATION

a. Timing:

* Should be decided specifically for your region. The planting window for native plants does not necessarily coincide with agricultural or residential planting times. Some regions prefer spring or early summer, others prefer fall or dormant plantings.
* Difficulty arises in new construction projects and the contractor's schedule. When possible, let the planting contract separately to avoid problems for both contractors.

b. Equipment:

* Specialized drills, broadcasters, and hydroseeders are available with mixed preferences.
* Chose carefully and experiment on small projects to determine the best for your region.
* Bottom line, the seed only germinates if it makes contact with the soil and moisture.
* Whichever you chose, deliver the weed-free mulch separately.

c. Follow-up:

* Cover seed by harrowing, dragging, raking or cultipacking.
* Mulch with weed-free straw/hay or native grass straw. Consider disc-anchoring.
* Avoid irrigation. During periods of drought, supplementary watering might be in order.
* A high (6-8") mowing once or twice during the first season reduces weed competition.
* Record keeping - develop a 3-5 year record of specifics to analyze project later.

Q. *What is our operational definition of "native wildflowers"?*

A. Because no definition was given with the 1987 STURAA, we asked that question in a 1993 survey of all State Departments of Transportation. Of the 45 replies, some 25 use a definition similar to "those herbaceaous flowering plants that were known to exist in a region or a State at the time of European settlement". Since the survey, the Federal Native Plant Conservation Initiative, an interagency group formed by a Memorandum of Understanding (MOU) in 1994, has defined "native plant species" as "one that occurs naturally in a particular region, state, ecosystem, and habitat without direct or indirect human actions." As a result of this MOU, Federal Highways expects this definition to be used by State agencies. Having a common definition will aid in decision-making and guide seed growers concerning our needs. Whatever the definition, most State Highway Agencies will need a plant expert on staff to help match native plant species to the site conditions of any landscape project.

Q. *Under what conditions will waivers/exceptions be granted?*

A. On October 5, 1993, the Office of Environment and Planning stated "Because of the importance of thse benefits, no waivers are being granted for the STURAA requirement. After seven years experience with native wildflowers, it was thought that the original reasons for waivers had been overcome in the planning process of any project." That opinion remains valid.

Q. *Should volunteer participation be encouraged?*

A. In 1973 the Operation Wildflower initiative was announced. Some States continue the program of working with volunteer groups to plant wildflowers to this day. Because of FHWA's interest in public-private partnerships, we continue to encourage partnering with volunteer groups in the spirit of Operation Wildflower. These partnerships can promote support and ownership, as well as get more done. Through careful planning and selection of safe planting sites by State Highway Agencies, we expect to see more volunteer participation.

Q. *How can maintenance conflicts with wildflower plantings be resolved?*

A. When maintenance forces are included in the design process and educated about the goals beyond beautification in planting native wildflowers, maintenance forces will be supportive and help manage the plantings. Be considerate of mowing regimes when siting and designing a wildflower planting.

Some states have actually legislated "reduced" mowing policies. In these States, frequent mowing is only allowed on safety strips and sight lines. Major mowing is limited to accomodate wildlife rearing seasons, often to the month of September alone. Other States have voluntarily, in conjunction with economic limitations, reduced mowing to safety mowing, noxious weed control, and brush suppression.

This strategy has allowed natural re-vegetation on many roadsides, encouraging the return of native wildflowers and grasses already in the seed bank or neighborhood.

Q.   *How does the 1/4 of 1 percent requirement really work?*

A.   a. Although native wildflowers and grasses are encouraged as erosion control, restoration, and vegetation mangement seeding, the STURAA requirement only applies to landscaping. The State, in accordance with paragraph 12 b of FHPM 6-2-5-1, must assure that the costs associated with the native wildflower seeding amounts to *at least 1/4 of 1 percent of the total cost*. The Project Status Record is to be documented to reflect these costs.

b. The amount spent on native wildflower plantings are to be recorded using *Work Type Code YOO5*.

c. Compliance should be determined during review of the project's plans, specifications, and estimate (PS&E). The seed specification, planting rate, overall seed quantity, and installation method will form the basis for the wildflower cost estimate.

d. There need not be an associated highway construction project to plant wildflowers. The State can program a landscaping project, specifically for wildflowers, using a typical landscaping action. The expenditure requirement of the STURAA is automatically met since wildflowers account for 100 percent of the landscaping cost.

e. Federal participation is available at the level associated with a regular landscaping project.

f. If an organization or individual volunteers to plant or donate funds for planting native wildflowers on a landscaping project, the State still must meet its expenditure requirement. This could be done by providing services associated with planting, i.e., design plans, site preparation, installation, or maintenance during the establishment period.

g. There is no time limit as to when wildflowers are planted on a landscaping project. If the project is programmed for and includes specifications for planting native wildflowers, a later planting season is permitted to allow for weather, availability, and other variables that could compromise native wildflower establishment.

Q.   *Why is design of native wildflower plantings important?*

A.   Good design will aid in the success of the planting and its acceptance by the traveling public. On rural sites, design that considers the adjacent and historic landsape will include diversity and naturalness that will lessen the impact the road corridor makes through the countryside, as well as enhance the local character of the rural environment. In urban sites, design must also honor the adjacent and historic landscape and consider more formal, garden-like designs that enhance the man-made beauty of the City. Although a "new aesthetic" is emerging in America, sensible design is needed to move us from the more traditional aesthetic that the public accepts at this time. The public tends to accept design that appears controlled and taken care of.

Q.   *Why is the use of local or regional native species important?*

A.   Experience shows that native wildflower and grass species which are native to an area are well adapted to the climate and other variables of that area. The species still must be matched to microclimates of the project to assure successful establishment. From the design staff to the construction inspector, all should have access to an expert who understands each plant species life history, environmental tolerances, establishment requirements, and long-term management needs. Consequently, these native species decisions should be made on a site by site basis.

NATIVE WILDFLOWER REQUIREMENT AGREEMENT

In 1995 an exemption was granted the California Department of Transportation (Caltrans) by the Federal Highway Administration. Because the planting of native wildflowers might not be appropriate on all projects, especially urban sites, a type of banking alternative was developed by Caltrans. In 1998 the Wisconsin Department of Transportation (WisDOT) used the Caltrans exemption as a model for their own native wildflower banking system, viewed by the FHWA as a commitment to establish and/or protect more native wildflowers than the U.S.C. 319(b) landscaping requirement. Their example demonstrates the flexibility of FHWA. Furthermore, as Wisconsin's FHWA Division Administrator wrote upon signing the agreement, "the new program should lend great support to WisDOT's strategic landscaping objectives including: safety enhancement, effective erosion control, reduction in the use of herbicides, pesticides, and fertilizers, and reduction of overall roadside vegetation maintenance costs." The WisDOT programmatic waiver is possible when certain stipulated conditions are met (shown below). **This agreement may be handled through each State's FHWA Division Office.**

1. Native wildlfowers shall be used on Federal-aid highway planting projects as required by existing Federal law wherever it is practical, appropriate, and cost-effective.

2. WisDOT shall establish a fund to which Federal-aid highway planting project moneys may be deposited or combined for use with other native wildflower plantings to achieve larger scale plantings.

3. WisDOT shall use an established method to identify a number of high-quality sites on Federal-aid highway rights-of-way in the State to preserve or establish native vegetation that will serve as native wildflower banking areas. The banking sites shall be developed in sufficient area to compensate for the locations where wildflower plantings are found to be inappropriate.

4. WisDOT shall develop a policy and guidance regarding the use and preservation of native wildflowers for use by landscape (and maintenance) staff that reflects the terms and conditions of this agreement.

5. WisDOT may determine that it is inappropriate to use native wildflowers where any of the following conditions exist:

   a. Where the adjacent urban landscape demands a compatible formal planting design inconsistent with the use of native wildflowers,

   b. Where the required native wildflowers would result in poor planting design, regardless of adjacent landscape, or

   c. Where cultural practices necessary to sustain the rest of the planting would lead to the decline of the native wildflowers.

6. WisDOT shall determine that it is inappropriate to use non-native wildflowers whenever such species are perceived as a threat to the genetic integrity of similar native species in the region or whenever such species are considered invasive to natural areas, or competitive with native plantings.

America's Treeways Initiative

(Signed by T.D. Larson, Federal Highway Administrator, September 24, 1992)

This is to ask for your support and assistance in launching a new program called America's Treeways. The objective is to encourage volunteer groups to plant donated trees along our highways in a way that is safe both to volunteer groups and to the traveling public. In many ways, America's Treeways is similar to the Adopt-a-Highway concept and Operation Wildflower, and can be equally successful in tapping America's volunteer spirit to beautify roadsides throughout the country.

Our partners in this program bring a wide range of interests and expertise to the America Treeways program: AASHTO, the U. S. Forest Service, the National Association of State Foresters, the National Tree Trust, and Take Pride in America (part of the Department of Interior). We are pleased that AASHTO has been a part of this initiative from the start because we hope the State departments of transportation will actively support this program.

I am attaching a new brochure entitled "Plant a Legacy...Support America's Treeways". The title comes from a comment by the President during a tree planting ceremony in Sioux Falls, South Dakota, on September 18, 1989. "Every tree," he said, "is a compact between generations." We prepared the brochure to encourage the public to enlist in planting trees along our Nation's highways. To provide all FHWA offices with copies of the brochure promptly, we are distributing copies directly to the Division Offices as well as to the Region Offices. I ask that you and the Division Administrators provide copies to key State DOT officials and to encourage them to support this program, as several States already have through pilot programs this year in Michigan, Ohio, and Virginia.

Additional Copies of the brochure may be obtained from Ms. Noreen Bowles of Environmental Analysis Division (HEP-42), Office of Environment and Planning. Ms. Bowles may be reached at 202-366-9173. (No longer available.)

We were pleased that First Lady Barbara Bush helped us launch America's Treeways at a site along I-70 outside Dayton, Ohio, on May 12. Also in May, I had an opportunity to see, first hand, what America's Treeways is all about. I joined fourth graders from Page Elementary School in Arlington, Virginia, to help plant 100 seedlings at Chain Bridge Road and Georgetown Pike. Here, as I worked alongside these bright, industrious 10-year olds, was the "compact between generations" in action.

We in FHWA are fortunate that our work typically involves creating a legacy – a legacy of roads and bridges – that will serve many generations to come. In America's Treeways, we have another opportunity to reach out to future generations, this time by planting a legacy along America's Treeways.

Treeways Guidelines

ACTION: On September 24, 1992 the Federal Highway Administrator sent a memorandum to regional and federal lands highway program administrators. It asked for support and assistance in launching a new program called America's Treeways. The objective was to encourage volunteer groups to plant donated trees along our highways. The idea, similar to the Adopt-a-Highway concept and Operation Wildflower taps a volunteer spirit to beautify roadsides throughout the country. You received explanatory brochures. Now we give you the guidelines based on a five year highway planting experience.

We understand the budget constraints on landscape and maintenance programs across the nation. Many of you are theoretically supportive of the initiative but do not have the resources to follow through. For those States who still need some common sense guidelines, we suggest the following:

Tree Source

The first source in place to provide free trees is the National Tree Trust. The Tree Trust is a non-profit corporation designated by President Bush to receive the support of the U.S. Congress to support tree planting and preservation. The Tree Trust further serves as a clearinghouse of trees for highway plantings. It notifies DOTs of availability of species in time to plan for the following planting season. It coordinates delivery of seedlings in advance of planting dates so that adequate storage can be provided before an event. Other sources may be used, as long as the following criteria are met.

Species Selection

In light of the April 4, 1994 Executive Memorandum encouraging the use of native plants, we suggest you use native tree species wherever practicable.

1. When ordering trees, select tree species that grow in your region and use local ecotypes whenever available.

2. Select only species that are indigenous to your area for use outside the city limits of urban areas. Within urban areas, select only noninvasive introduced species when natives are unavailable.

3. Avoid species that are known to be invasive in your region: i.e., black locust, Russian olive, Norway maple, Siberian elm, tamarisk, etc.

4. Select tree planting locations in areas of the State where trees have historically grown.

5. Match tree species' tolerances to the site conditions as in soils, moisture, light, etc.

Design Considerations

Please select safe, yet visible, planting sites like rest areas, State entrances, City entrances, interchanges, junkyard screens, windbreaks, living snowfences, or public or corporate interfaces. The final design should:

6. Respect clear zone and visibility requirements for highway safety.
7. Consider District or local maintenance constraints.
8. Avoid straight lines, unless in a formal setting.
9. Incorporate a diversity of tree species, whenever possible.
10. Include clusters of trees and/or shrubs to ease mowing.
11. Allow for volunteer ideas, with final review by State landscape architects.

Volunteer Responsibilities

We suggest that a public announcement be made in each State that invites volunteer application for Treeways projects. Applicants will need to be advised of the following responsibilities involved in a project:

12. Must submit an application to obtain permit to plant.
13. Identify one or two key volunteer contacts.
14. Organize and guarantee a number of people in advance of selected planting date.
15. Be responsible for the initial design concept.
16. Arrange media coverage.
17. Participate in safety training before planting date.
18. Understand nursery planting standards or include supervisor who does.
19. Sign an arrangement to maintain (water and weed) the tree seedlings for 1-3 years.

State Highway Agencies

At a time when States are asked to do more with less, we suggest the following to strengthen your volunteer partnerships, assure safety, and minimize your investment of staff needed to coordinate Treeway Plantings.

20. Insist on a permit before proceeding.
21. Select the site with volunteer input.
22. Require safety training before the event.
23. Provide safety vests, hard hats, etc.
24. Prepare the site, according to the staked plan, in advance of the event.
25. Provide a safe, accessible, clearly marked staging area.
26. Supervise the event and provide safety signage.
27. Sign the site as a thank you whenever possible.
28. Submit a one page report with media coverage whenever possible.
29. Follow up on volunteer maintenance contract.

Q. *What does the Treeways Initiative mean to our agency?*

A. This initiative remains an opportunity to:

1. Use regionally native plants where practicable.
2. Welcome volunteers to safely plant donated trees.
3. Beautify roadsides as a legacy where appropriate.
4. Increase public support through partnerships.

Q. *How does the Initiative relate to existing mandates?*

A. It is supportive of the 1965 Beautification Act.

Q. *Will the FHWA assist States in implementing the Initiative?*

A. In 1999 the FHWA will offer a handbook, "Roadside Use of Native Plants." This handbook lists trees that are native in your State. The handbook also notes relevant resources. The FHWA is interested in research proposals releant to this Initiative, i.e. native tree establishment issues, etc.

Q. *In 1994 the FHWA surveyed State Highway Agencies to determine the level of participation in this Initiative. What was learned?*

A. A brief analysis revealed reasons for not participating and needs to strengthen the Treeways Initiative. The key reason for not participating was lack of funding and consequently lack of administrative and maintenance staff. The most important need noted was that of increased funding for maintenance.

ENVIRONMENTALLY AND ECONOMICALLY BENEFICIAL LANDSCAPING GUIDANCE

The Office of the Federal Environmental Executive issued final guidance to implement the April 1994 Presidential Executive Memorandum (E.M.) on landscaping practices found on page 596. The guidance, as published in the Federal Register on August 10, 1995, pages 40837-41, applies to all Federal Agencies and all federally-funded or assisted projects. It provides information and direction regarding the implementation of environmentally and economically beneficial practices.

Definitions

Native Plant: A native plant species is one that occurs naturally in a particular region, ecosystem and/or habitat without direct or indirect human actions.

Pesticide: A pesticide is "any substance or mixture of substances: (a) for preventing, destroying, repelling, or mitigating any pest, or (b) for use as a plant regulator, defoliant, or desiccant." [FIFRA Section 2 (u)].

Pest: A pest is "(1) any insect, rodent, nematode, fungus, weed, or (2) any other form of terrestrial or aquatic plant or animal life or virus, bacteria, or other micro-organism (except viruses, bacteria, or other micro-organisms on or in living man or other living animals) which the Administrator declares to be a pest." [FIFRA Section 2 (t)].

Compliance With The National Environmental Policy Act (NEPA)

As published in the August 10, 1995 Federal Register (pages 40837-41

The National Environmental Policy Act (NEPA) provides a mandate and a framework for federal agencies to consider all reasonably foreseeable environmental effects of their actions. Where Federal projects or federally-funded activities or projects considered in the NEPA process include landscape considerations, draft and final NEPA documentation and Record of Decision for the proposed action and alternatives, as applicable, shall reflect the recommendations established in this Guidance.

I. Use of Regionally Native Plants for Landscaping

Federal agencies, Federal projects or federally-funded projects shall incorporate regionally native plants in site design and implementation where cost-effective and to the maximum extent practicable. Federal agencies shall strive to avoid or minimize adverse impacts of proposed actions or projects on existing communities of native plants.

Federal agencies shall ensure that the appropriate site and soil analyses are performed during pre-design stages of the project. To aid in proper plant selection and to ensure success of the plantings, analyses should match plant characteristics with site and soil conditions. Site design and implementation as well as plant selection shall incorporate such considerations as their biological needs, minimal plant care, low water use, and minimal need for fertilizers and pesticides.

Plants selected shall be in character with the project site plant communities. Those plants selected for Federal landscape projects or federally-funded landscape projects shall be nursery propagated from sources as close as practicable to the project area. Native plants collected from existing indigenous populations shall not be used unless they are salvaged from an area where they would otherwise be destroyed in the near-term. Where native plant seeds are to be used for federal projects, they should be unadulterated by other plant species. Federal agencies should ensure that appropriate actions are taken to support the success of native plant species used for Federal or federally-funded landscaping projects.

2. Design, Use, or Promote Construction Practices That Minimize Adverse Impacts on the Natural Habitat

Federal agencies, Federal projects or federally-funded projects shall avoid or minimize adverse impacts to natural habitat. During preliminary selection of sites for Federal or federally-funded projects, Federal agencies shall avoid sites which are relatively undisturbed. If such areas cannot be avoided, Federal agencies should employ construction practices and procedures which minimize adverse impacts to natural habitat and incorporate existing vegetation and associated natural habitat into the project. Where new projects require use of a relatively undisturbed site, site clearing and preparation should be limited in order to prevent unnecessary adverse impacts. Where adverse impacts to natural habitat occur as a result of Federal or federally-funded projects, Federal agencies shall mitigate impacts to natural habitat on-site where feasible. On-site and off-site compensatory mitigation shall fully reflect lost natural values.

Federal site design and development should consider environmental elements, human factors, context, sustainability, and pertinent special issues. Development of the site should include assessments of the soil and subsurface material.

Project decision-makers, including designers, contract supervisors, contractors, field inspectors, site or facility master planners, and maintenance personnel shall either be knowledgeable of or informed of likely project related impacts to natural habitat. Where existing plantings are incorporated into the site design, they shall be adequately protected from construction activities. Project plans and specifications shall include explicit direction regarding construction practices to meet the goals of this guidance. On-site project managers and contractors shall ensure that practices which minimize impacts to natural habitat are followed during project construction. Such practices may include site management to control soil erosion and non-point source run-off and proper disposal of construction material and debris. Where practicable, personnel responsible for on-site construction practices, including contractors and construction inspectors, shall be knowledgeable about natural habitat resources.

3. Seek to Prevent Pollution

Federal agencies, Federal projects or federally-funded projects shall use chemical management practices which reduce or eliminate pollution associated with the use of chemical fertilizers and pesticides. Wherever practicable, Federal agencies shall employ practices which avoid or minimize the need for using fertilizers and pesticides. These practices include, but are not limited to selection of plant materials that limit growth of "weed" species; use of integrated pest management techniques and practices, use of chemical pesticides which biodegrade, and use of slow release fertilizers.

Federal agencies shall recycle and/or compost leaves, grass clippings, and landscape trimmings for further use as both soil amendments and mulches. Woody debris such as tree trunks, stumps, limbs, etc., resulting from federally-funded activities shall also be recycled as appropriate.

Federal agencies shall use landscape management practices, including plant selection and placement, which control and minimize soil erosion, runoff of chemicals, and pollution of groundwater. Federal agencies shall also consider energy and water conservation benefits in the siting and selection of plants.

Federal agencies and facilities subject to the requirements of Executive Order 12856 shall identify those chemicals used at their facilities for landscape-management and develop alternative landscape management practices to reduce or eliminate the use of those chemicals.

4. Implement Water and Energy Efficient Landscape Practices

Federal agencies, Federal Projects or federally-funded projects shall use water-efficient landscape design and management practices. These practices (such as Xeriscape) shall include planning and designing landscaping projects with consideration to: watering requirements, existing vegetation, topography, climate, intended use of the property and water-use zones. In addition, facility managers shall conduct soil analyses and, as appropriate, amend the soil at the project site to improve its ability to support plants and retain water. Initial site design as well as the addition of plants in established areas shall seek to establish water-use zones and promote efficient irrigation practices.

Where irrigation systems have been installed, irrigation scheduling should be adjusted seasonally to the evapotranspiration rate (ET) for the plants in that particular climate.

Irrigation with recycled or reclaimed water, where practicable, shall serve as a preferred alternative to the use of potable water. Finally Federal agencies and facilities, Federal projects and federally-funded projects, are encouraged to use water audits to identify additional opportunities for water-efficient landscape practices.

5. Create Outdoor Demonstration Projects

Federal agencies, Federal projects or federally-funded projects shall create and maintain outdoor demonstration projects exhibiting and promoting the benefits of economically and environmentally sound landscaping practices. These exhibits may include the selection and use of native plant species and the use of water-efficient and energy-conserving practices.

Exhibits may include small scale projects, such as interpretive or wildlife gardens, that focus on environmentally sound landscape management practices, site design, and development appropriate for residential, commercial, and institutional application. Additionally, demonstration projects may highlight larger projects, such as wetland or grassland restoration or woodland rehabilitation, that are more likely implemented by groups or state and local governments. Federal agencies are encouraged to from public/private partnerships with groups such as educational institutions, arboreta, commercial nurseries, botanic gardens and garden clubs, to advance the goals of the Executive Memorandum. Federal agencies are encouraged to work with and share information with other interested nonfederal parties to promote the use of environmentally and economically sound landscaping practices.

(As issued to the field along with final guidance on November 2, 1995 by Kevin E. Heanue)

Q. *What does this Executive Memorandum mean to our agency?*

A. In a nutshell, the E.M. suggests principles for environmentally and economically beneficial landscape practices. The intent is for Federal Agencies, facilities, and funded projects to implement these principles. The E.M. further intends to assist in planning and policy development for landscape management practices. Since federally funded projects are included, these principles should be applied to highway construction projects. They include:

l. Use regionally native plants for landscaping.
2. Design, use, or promote construction practices that minimize adverse effects on natural habitat.
3. Seek to prevent pollution.
4. Implement water and energy efficient practices.
5. Create outdoor demonstration projects implementing these principles.

Q. *A key definition established by the E.M. for Agency use is that of "native plant". What is considered a native plant species?*

A. **"A native plant species is one that occurs naturally in a particular region, ecosystem and/or habitat without direct or indirect human actions."** This definition is not new, but rather, borrowed from the 1994 Memorandum of Understanding that established the Federal Native Plant Conservation Committee.

(The following questions have been raised about the E.M.'s application to the FHWA and State Highway agencies, when Federal-aid funds are involved on construction projects.)

Q. *Does the E.M. apply to all Federal-aid highway projects involving landscaping?*

A. At every opportunity where they are determined to be appropriate and cost-effective, the guiding principles of the E.M. should be considered to the maximum extent practicable.

Q. *Does the E.M. include habitat mitigation projects?*

A. Although the guidelines do not address this question directly, the guidelines do assume that restorations (one type is mitigation) will be encouraged as large-scale demonstrations of the landscape principles. Successful mitigation projects have already used the principles of these guidelines. Successful projects take the best scientific information available and apply those solutions to mitigation problems.

Q. *Do the E.M. and the implementing guidance create an unfunded mandate?*

A. The E.M. and the guidelines do not require new programs to be established. They only suggest that existing project funds be used thoughtfully, with environmental protection and cost savings in mind.

Q. *Does the E. M. infringe on State flexibility?*

A. The intent of the guidelines is to give support to the many State highway agencies who have already taken this approach to landscape projects and encourage other States to duplicate their wisdom. States continue to have flexibility to chose solutions appropriate to their landscape problems.

Q. *How does the E.M. relate to existing mandates?*

A. Existing regulations, i.e., the 1965 Beautification, 1966 Historic Preservation, 1969 NEPA, 1973 Endangered Species, and the 1987 STURRA Acts are not affected by this guidance.

Q. *Are naturalized species or named varieties considered "native plants"?*

A. The definition of a native plant in the guidance states..."a native plant is one that occurs naturally in an area without direct or indirect human actions." Therefore, introduced exotic species or named varieties and hybrids should not be considered native plants. Such plants would not occur naturally in an area if it were not for human activities, such as species introduction, plant breeding, and other similar cultural activities.

Although the guidance encourages the collection and nursery propagation of native species, this does not mean such species become non-native once these human activities occur. Simple propagation does not alter a native species, as would intentional genetic selection for desired characteristics or other activities such as hybridizing. The guidance states that "plants selected for Federal landscape projects or federally-funded landscape projects shall be nursery-propagated, using plant materials from sources as close as practicable to the project area". In some cases this may require collection and propagation of regionally native plant material or seeds for a project until commercial seed/seedling sources become available.

Q. *May native species be dug from the wild to meet these recommendations?*

A. Commercial sources should always be your first source of plant materials. Securing natives species from the wild, except in salvage, is not acceptable. However, if the opportunity to salvage naturally growing native species in the path of construction occurs, an effort should be made to incorporate them into your design and implementation. Since wild-dug plants often diminish and have no guarantee of survival, commercial sources should be sought. Seed collection from the wild could be one solution to limited seed sources.

Q. *Will the use of fertilizers and herbicides be eliminated?*

A. Fertilizers and herbicides are important tools in landscape work, including erosion control and vegetation management. The guidelines seek to reduce the use of chemicals in the environment and increase the use of alternatives, i.e., compost, mulches, and integrated pest management. Elimination of chemical tools is not possible at this time.

Q. *Will irrigation solutions be allowed?*

A. Although reducing the use of limited natural resources is a large part of this E.M., eliminating the use of irrigation is unlikely. However, reducing the use of irrigation and encorgaging the use of alternative methods like xeriscape, drought tolerant plants, recycled water, and advanced irrigation technology will be the solutions desired.

Q. *Will new funding be available?*

A. At this time, additional funding for demonstration projects is not budgeted. However, we encourage innovative funding to demonstrate the principles of the E.M.

For example, Caltrans is partnering with a commercial seed source to find better establishment techniques of native plants. The Florida DOT, with the help of the Florida Federated Garden Clubs, is using a research grant for a native plant interpretative garden at each of the State's Welcome Centers to increase public awareness. Further partnerships with educational institutions, arboreta, commercial nurseries, botanic gardens and garden clubs are encouraged. These partnerships themselves will improve public awareness.

Q. *Will "cultural landscapes" have to be replaced with environmentally and economically beneficial landscapes?*

A. No. Cultural, historical, or existing landscapes are not expected to be replaced. The E.M. applies only to landscape projects implemented after th release of the Guidance on August 10, 1995, or realistically, projects funded beginning October 1, 1995.

Q. *Will FHWA assist States in implementing the E.M.?*

A. The FHWA will facilitate the implementation in every way possible. Further guidelines for the use of native plants in wildflower and treeway programs are in progress. State-by-State lists of what plants are native are also in progress. The FHWA is developing a training course/workshop mechanism to further share information about the E.M.'s approach. The FHWA will continue to share experiences and information for all States through the quarterly Greener Roadsides.

Memorandum

U.S. Department
of Transportation

**Federal Highway
Administration**

Subject::
INFORMATION: Guidance Implementing
Executive Order on Invasive Species

Date: August 1999

From:
James M. Shrouds
Director of Natural Environment

Reply to
Attn. of: HEPN-30

To:
Division Administrators
Federal Lands Highway Division Engineers

Each year approximately $23 billion nationwide is lost to invasive plant impacts to agriculture, industry, recreation, and the environment. An estimated 4600 acres of land are invaded daily by invasive plants. In response to these impacts and to those of invasive animal species, President Clinton signed Executive Order 13112 (E.O.) on February 2, 1999 (attached). The Invasive Species E.O., directs Federal agencies to expand and coordinate their efforts to combat the introduction and spread of plants and animals not native to the United States.

The Federal Highway Administration has developed guidance to implement the E.O. It provides a framework for preventing the introduction of and controlling the spread of invasive plant species on highway rights-of-way. Controlling invasive plants on rights-of-way can often be a complex effort involving various governmental jurisdictions, adjacent landowners and the general public. Our guidelines were developed with a goal of promoting improved cooperation, communication, and joint eradication efforts with agencies at all levels and the private sector. In order to reduce economic and ecological costs and improve eradication effectiveness, States may wish to incorporate elements of this guidance into their planning and implementation of construction, erosion control, landscaping, and maintenance measures.

A copy of the guidance is attached for your information and use. It is effective 90 days from the date of this memorandum. In addition, attached for your information is: (1) a paper providing answers to questions related to the E.O. and the implementing guidance; (2) a copy of Secretary Slater's Policy Statement on Invasive Species; and (3) the Executive Memorandum on Landscaping referenced in the E.O. If you have further questions, please contact Ms. Bonnie Harper-Lore of my staff at (651) 291-6104. Please share copies with those in the State DOTs that have responsibility for construction, erosion control, landscaping, and maintenance.

cc: Resource Center Directors

EXECUTIVE ORDER 13112
Invasive Species

6183 Federal Register / Vol. 64, No. 25 / Monday, February 8, 1999 /
Presidential Documents

Invasive Species

By the authority vested in me as President by the Constitution and the laws of the United States of America, including the National Environmental

Policy Act of 1969, as amended (42 U.S.C. 4321 et seq.), Nonindigenous Aquatic Nuisance Prevention and Control Act of 1990, as amended (16 U.S.C. 4701 et seq.), Lacey Act, as amended (18 U.S.C. 42), Federal Plant Pest Act (7 U.S.C. 150aa et seq.), Federal Noxious Weed Act of 1974, as amended (7 U.S.C. 2801 et seq.), Endangered Species Act of 1973, as amended (16 U.S.C. 1531 et seq.), and other pertinent statutes, to prevent the introduc-tion of invasive species and provide for their control and to minimize the economic, ecological, and human health impacts that invasive species cause, it is ordered as follows:

Section 1. Definitions

(a) "Alien species" means, with respect to a particular ecosystem, any species, including its seeds, eggs, spores, or other biological material capable of propagating that species, that is not native to that ecosystem.

(b) "Control" means, as appropriate, eradicating, suppressing, reducing, or managing invasive species populations, preventing spread of invasive species from areas where they are present, and taking steps such as restoration of native species and habitats to reduce the effects of invasive species and to prevent further invasions.

(c) "Ecosystem" means the complex of a community of organisms and its environment.

(d) "Federal agency" means an executive department or agency, but does not include independent establishments as defined by 5 U.S.C. 104.

(e) "Introduction" means the intentional or unintentional escape, release, dissemination, or placement of a species into an ecosystem as a result of human activity.

(f) "Invasive species" means an alien species whose introduction does or is likely to cause economic or environmental harm or harm to human health.

(g) "Native species" means, with respect to a particular ecosystem, a species that, other than as a result of an introduction, historically occurred or currently occurs in that ecosystem.

(h) "Species" means a group of organisms all of which have a high degree of physical and genetic similarity, generally interbreed only among themselves, and show persistent differences from members of allied groups of organisms.

(i) "Stakeholders" means, but is not limited to, State, tribal, and local government agencies, academic institutions, the scientific community, non-governmental entities including environmental, agricultural, and conservation organizations, trade groups, commercial interests, and private landowners.

(j) "United States" means the 50 States, the District of Columbia, Puerto Rico, Guam, and all possessions, territories, and the territorial sea of the United States.

Sec. 2. Federal Agency Duties.

(a) Each Federal agency whose actions may affect the status of invasive species shall, to the extent practicable and permitted by law,

(1) identify such actions;

(2) subject to the availability of appropriations, and within Administration budgetary limits, use relevant programs and authorities to: (i) prevent the introduction of invasive species; (ii) detect and respond rapidly to and control populations of such species in a cost-effective and environmentally sound manner; (iii) monitor invasive species populations accurately and reliably; (iv) provide for restoration of native species and habitat conditions in ecosystems that have been invaded; (v) conduct research on invasive species and develop technologies to prevent introduction and provide for environmentally sound control of invasive species; and (vi) promote public education on invasive species and the means to address them; and

(3) not authorize, fund, or carry out actions that it believes are likely to cause or promote the introduction or spread of invasive species in the United States or elsewhere unless, pursuant to guidelines that it has pre-scribed, the agency has determined and made public its determination that the benefits of such actions clearly outweigh the potential harm caused by invasive species; and that all feasible and prudent measures to minimize risk of harm will be taken in conjunction with the actions.

(b) Federal agencies shall pursue the duties set forth in this section in consultation with the Invasive Species Council, consistent with the Invasive Species Management Plan and in cooperation with stakeholders, as appro-priate, and, as approved by the Department of State, when Federal agencies are working with international organizations and foreign nations.

Sec. 3. Invasive Species Council.

(a) An Invasive Species Council (Council) is hereby established whose members shall include the Secretary of State, the Secretary of the Treasury, the Secretary of Defense, the Secretary of the Interior, the Secretary of Agriculture, the Secretary of Commerce, the Secretary of Transportation, and the Administrator of the Environmental Protection Agency. The Council shall be Co-Chaired by the Secretary of the Interior, the Secretary of Agriculture, and the Secretary of Commerce. The Council may invite additional Federal agency representatives to be members, including representatives from subcabinet bureaus or offices with significant responsibilities concerning invasive species, and may prescribe special procedures for their participation. The Secretary of the Interior shall, with concurrence of the Co-Chairs, appoint an Executive Director of the Council and shall provide the staff and administrative support for the Council.

(b) The Secretary of the Interior shall establish an advisory committee under the Federal Advisory Committee Act, 5 U.S.C. App., to provide infor-mation and advice for consideration by the Council, and shall, after consultation with other members of the Council, appoint members of the advisory committee representing stakeholders. Among other things, the advisory committee shall recommend plans and actions at local, tribal, State, regional, and ecosystem-based levels to achieve the goals and objectives of the Manage-ment Plan in section 5 of this order. The advisory committee shall act in cooperation with stakeholders and existing organizations addressing invasive species. The Department of the Interior shall provide the administra-tive and financial support for the advisory committee.

Sec. 4. Duties of the Invasive Species Council

The Invasive Species Council shall provide national leadership regarding invasive species, and shall:

(a) oversee the implementation of this order and see that the Federal agency activities concerning invasive species are coordinated, complemen-tary, cost-efficient, and effective, relying to the extent feasible and appropriate on existing organizations addressing invasive species, such as the Aquatic Nuisance Species Task Force, the Federal Interagency Committee for the Management of Noxious and Exotic Weeds, and the Committee on Environ-ment and Natural Resources

(b) encourage planning and action at local, tribal, State, regional, and ecosystem-based levels to achieve the goals and objectives of the

Management Plan in section 5 of this order, in cooperation with stakeholders and existing organizations addressing invasive species;

(c) develop recommendations for international cooperation in addressing invasive species;

(d) develop, in consultation with the Council on Environmental Quality, guidance to Federal agencies pursuant to the National Environmental Policy Act on prevention and control of invasive species, including the procurement, use, and maintenance of native species as they affect invasive species;

(e) facilitate development of a coordinated network among Federal agencies to document, evaluate, and monitor impacts from invasive species on the economy, the environment, and human health;

(f) facilitate establishment of a coordinated, up-to-date information-sharing system that utilizes, to the greatest extent practicable, the Internet; this system shall facilitate access to and exchange of information concerning invasive species, including, but not limited to, information on distribution and abundance of invasive species; life histories of such species and invasive characteristics; economic, environmental, and human health impacts; man-agement techniques, and laws and programs for management, research, and public education; and

(g) prepare and issue a national Invasive Species Management Plan as set forth in section 5 of this order.

Sec. 5. Invasive Species Management Plan

(a) Within 18 months after issuance of this order, the Council shall prepare and issue the first edition of a National Invasive Species Management Plan (Management Plan), which shall detail and recommend performance-oriented goals and objectives and specific measures of success for Federal agency efforts concerning invasive species. The Management Plan shall recommend specific objectives and measures for carrying out each of the Federal agency duties established in section 2(a) of this order and shall set forth steps to be taken by the Council to carry out the duties assigned to it under section 4 of this order. The Management Plan shall be developed through a public process and in consultation with Federal agencies and stakeholders.

(b) The first edition of the Management Plan shall include a review of existing and prospective approaches and authorities for preventing the intro-duction and spread of invasive species, including those for identifying path-ways by which invasive species are introduced and for minimizing the risk of introductions via those pathways, and shall identify research needs and recommend measures to minimize the risk that introductions will occur. Such recommended measures shall provide for a science-based process to evaluate risks associated with introduction and spread of invasive species and a coordinated and systematic risk-based process to identify, monitor, and interdict pathways that may be involved in the introduction of invasive species. If recommended measures are not authorized by current law, the Council shall develop and recommend to the President through its Co-Chairs legislative proposals for necessary changes in authority.

(c) The Council shall update the Management Plan biennially and shall concurrently evaluate and report on success in achieving the goals and objectives set forth in the Management Plan. The Management Plan shall identify the personnel, other resources, and additional levels of coordination needed to achieve the Management Plan's identified goals and objectives, and the Council shall provide each edition of the Management Plan and each report on it to the Office of Management and Budget. Within 18 months after measures have been recommended by the Council in any edition of the Management Plan, each Federal agency whose action is re-quired to implement such measures shall either take the action recommended or shall provide the Council with an explanation of why the action is not feasible. The Council shall assess the effectiveness of this order no less than once each 5 years after the order is issued and shall report to the Office of Management and Budget on whether the order should be revised.

Sec. 6. *Judicial Review and Administration*

(a) This order is intended only to improve the internal management of the executive branch and is not intended to create any right, benefit, or trust responsibility, substantive or procedural, enforceable at law or equity by a party against the United States, its agencies, its officers, or any other person.

(b) Executive Order 11987 of May 24, 1977, is hereby revoked.

(c) The requirements of this order do not affect the obligations of Federal agencies under 16 U.S.C. 4713 with respect to ballast water programs.

(d) The requirements of section 2(a)(3) of this order shall not apply to any action of the Department of State or Department of Defense if the Secretary of State or the Secretary of Defense finds that exemption from such requirements is necessary for foreign policy or national security reasons.

THE WHITE HOUSE,
February 3, 1999.
[FR Doc. 99–3184
Filed 2–5–99; 8:45 am]
Billing code 3195–01–P

Environmentally and Economically Beneficial Practices on Federal Landscaped Grounds

The Report of the National Performance Review contains recommendations for a series of environmental actions, including one to increase environmentally and economically beneficial landscaping practices at Federal facilities and federally funded projects.Environmentally beneficial landscaping entails utilizing techniques that complement and enhance the local environment and seek to minimize the adverse effects that the landscaping will have on it. In particular, this means using regionally native plants and employing landscaping practices and technologies that conserve water and prevent pollution.

These landscaping practices should benefit the environment, as well as generate long-term costs savings for the Federal Government. For example, the use of native plants not only protects our natural heritage and provides wildlife habitat, but also can reduce fertilizer, pesticide, and irrigation demands and their associated costs because native plants are suited to the local environment and climate.

Because the Federal Government owns and landscapes large areas of land, our stewardship presents a unique opportunity to provide leadership in this area and to develop practical and cost-effective methods to preserve and protect that which has been entrusted to us. Therefore, for Federal grounds, Federal projects, and federally funded projects, I direct that agencies shall, where cost-effective and to the extent practicable:

(a) Use regionally native plants for landscaping;
(b) Design, use, or promote construction practices that minimize adverse effects on the natural habitat;
(c) Seek to prevent pollution by, among other things, reducing fertilizer and pesticide use, using integrated pest management techniques, recycling green waste, and minimizing runoff. Landscaping practices that reduce the use of toxic chemicals provide one approach for agencies to reach reduction goals established in Executive Order No. 12856 ``Federal Compliance with Right-To-Know Laws and Pollution Prevention Requirements;''
(d) Implement water-efficient practices, such as the use of mulches, efficient irrigation systems, audits to determine exact landscaping water-use needs, and recycled or reclaimed water and the selecting and siting of plants in a manner that conserves water and controls soil erosion.Landscaping practices, such as planting regionally native shade trees around buildings to reduce air conditioning demands, can also provide innovative measures to meet the energy

consumption reduction goal established in Executive Order No. 12902, ``Energy Efficiency and Water Conservation at Federal Facilities;'' and

(e) Create outdoor demonstrations incorporating native plants, as well as pollution prevention and water conservation techniques, to promote awareness of the environmental and economic benefits of implementing this directive. Agencies are encouraged to develop other methods for sharing information on landscaping advances with interested non-Federal parties.

In order to assist agencies in implementing this directive the Federal Environmental Executive shall:

(a) Establish an interagency working group to develop recommendations for guidance, including compliance with the requirements of the National Environmental Policy Act, 42 U.S.C.4321, 4331-4335, and 4341-4347, and training needs to implement this directive. The recommendations are to be developed by November 1994; and

(b) Issue the guidance by April 1995. To the extent practicable, agencies shall incorporate this guidance into their landscaping programs and practices by February 1996. In addition, the Federal Environmental Executive shall establish annual awards to recognize outstanding landscaping efforts of agencies and individual employees. Agencies are encouraged to recognize exceptional performance in the implementation of this directive through their awards programs. Agencies shall advise the Federal Environmental Executive by April 1996 on their progress in implementing this directive. To enhance landscaping options and awareness, the Department of Agriculture shall conduct research on the suitability, propagation, and use of native plants for landscaping. The Department shall make available to agencies and the public the results of this research.

William J. Clinton
THE WHITE HOUSE,
April 26, 1994

POLICY STATEMENT
ON INVASIVE ALIEN SPECIES

From: Rodney E. Slater   Date: April 22, 1999
The Secretary of the
Department of Transportation

To: Secretarial Officers
Heads of Operating Administrations

On February 3, 1999, President Clinton signed Executive Order 13112, which calls on Executive Branch agencies to work to prevent and control the introduction and spread of invasive species.

Nonnative flora and fauna can cause significant changes to ecosystems, upset the ecological balance, and cause serious economic harm to our nation's agricultural and recreational sectors. For example, in Guam, the brown tree snake, which was introduced from New Guinea by military aircraft during World War II, eliminated 9 of 11 species of native birds, has inflicted harmful bites, and, by climbing on power lines and into electronic equipment, has caused major power outages. Zebra mussels introduced into the Great Lakes in the ballast water of cargo ships have colonized water pipes, boat hulls, and other surfaces, wreaking havoc on water systems, transportation, and native shellfish. Introduced plants, such as kudzu in the southeastern states and purple loosestrife in the north, have choked out native plant species and, through them, wildlife and fish.

The Department of Transportation has been in the forefront of our national efforts to prevent and control the introduction of invasive species. The Coast Guard, the Maritime Administration and the St. Lawrence Seaway Development Corporation cooperate with the international community to prevent and control the introduction and spread of invasive aquatic species to the nation's waterways. The Federal Highway Administration works with other federal agencies and state governments to combat the introduction and spread of invasive species. The Federal Aviation Administration cooperates with other federal and state agencies in developing a comprehensive strategy to reduce the risk of introducing invasive species at airports in Hawaii; cooperates in federal research for screening baggage, cargo, and passengers; and protects native species in the management of its facilities and FAA-funded and licensed facilities throughout the country. The Federal Railroad Administration works with other federal agencies to reduce the risk from invasive species, including cooperating with the Department of Agriculture to lessen the opportunity for spreading karnal bunt, a serious crop disease, across international borders.

At its recently held triennial meeting, the Assembly of the International Civil Aviation Organization (ICAO) adopted a resolution, which was drafted by the Department, that will enable ICAO to assist other United

Nations agencies in preventing the introduction of invasive species. The Assembly also called on its 185-member nations to support efforts to reduce the risk of introducing, through civil air transportation, potentially invasive species to areas outside the species' natural range.

I commend these efforts; however, the problem is formidable. Therefore, I direct the Secretarial offices and operating administrations to implement Executive Order 13112 by adhering to the attached policy statement.

DEPARTMENT OF TRANSPORTATION POLICY ON INVASIVE SPECIES

Background

Transportation systems facilitate the spread of species outside their natural range, both domestically and internationally. Of particular concern are those species that are likely to harm the environment, human health or economy.

In response to this concern, the Clinton Administration has mounted a national effort. On February 3, 1999, President Clinton issued Executive Order 13112, which calls for Executive Branch agencies to work to prevent the introduction and control the spread of invasive species and eliminate or minimize their associated economic, ecological and human health impacts.

The Department of Transportation's (DOT) efforts to prevent the introduction and spread of invasive species (a) are in keeping with the Department's strategic goals, which include both ensuring transportation safety and the protection and enhancement of the natural environment affected by transportation, (b) are in accord with its statutory mandate to protect against aquatic invasive species, (c) reflect Departmental participation on interagency committees, such as the Aquatic Nuisance Species Task Force, the Federal Interagency Committee for Management of Noxious and Exotic Weeds, the Native Plants Conservation Initiative, the Interagency Ecosystem Management Task Force, and the Interagency Working Group on Endangered Species, and (d) reflect compliance with the Presidential Memorandum on Environmentally and Economically Beneficial Practices on Federal Landscaped Grounds.

Policy

The Department's policy is to fully participate in Administration efforts to prevent the introduction and spread of invasive species by:

a. pursuing appropriate authorities and funding for implementation;
b. participating on interagency committees;
c. analyzing invasive species' effects in accordance with Section 2 of Executive Order 13112;
d. increasing coordinated research;
e. implementing, at DOT facilities and DOT-funded facilities, the Presidential memorandum on beneficial landscaping;
f. coordinating with international organizations, such as the International Maritime Organization, the International Civil Aviation Organization, and the International Organization for Standardization on cooperative efforts;
g. training agency personnel and informing the public;
h. coordinating with other federal agencies and with state, local and tribal governments; and
i. encouraging innovative designs for transportation equipment and systems.

FEDERAL HIGHWAY ADMINISTRATION GUIDANCE ON INVASIVE SPECIES

August 10, 1999

Background

On February 3, 1999, President Clinton signed Executive Order 13112 (E.O.) which calls on Executive Branch agencies to work to prevent and control the introduction and spread of invasive species. Nonnative flora and fauna can cause significant changes to ecosystems, upset the ecological balance, and cause economic harm to our Nation's agricultural and recreational sectors. For example, introduced plants, such as Kudzu in the southeastern States and purple loosestrife throughout the country, have choked out native plant species and consequently have altered wildlife and fish habitat. Transportation systems can facilitate the spread of plant and animal species outside their natural range, both domestically and internationally. Those species that are likely to harm the environment, human health, or economy are of particular concern.

The Department of Transportation's efforts to prevent the introduction and spread of invasive species are consistent with: (1) the Department's strategic goal of protecting the natural environment, service, and teamwork; (2) statutory mandates to protect against aquatic invasive species; (3) the Department's active participation on interagency committees such as the Federal Interagency Committee for Management of Noxious and Exotic Weeds (FICMNEW), the Native Plant Conservation Initiative (NPCI), the Interagency Ecosystem Management Task force, and the Interagency Working Group on Endangered Species; and (4) the 1994 Presidential Memorandum on Environmentally and Economically Beneficial Landscaping Practices. The U.S. Department of Transportation has traditionally been in the forefront of national efforts to prevent and control the introduction of invasive species. On April 22, 1999, Secretary Slater issued a policy statement directing DOT's operating administrations to implement E.O. 13112.

Highway corridors provide opportunities for the movement of invasive species through the landscape. Invasive plant or animal species can move on vehicles and in the loads they carry. Invasive plants can be moved from site to site during spraying and mowing operations. Weed seed can be inadvertently introduced into the corridor during construction on equipment and through the use of mulch, imported soil or gravel, and sod. Some invasive plant species might be deliberately planted in erosion control, landscape, or wildflower projects. Millions of miles of highway rights-of-ways traverse public and private lands. Many of these adjacent lands have weed problems and the highway rights-of-way provide corridors for further spread.

Under the E.O., State Departments of Transportation (DOTs) have new opportunities to address roadside vegetation management issues on both their construction activities and maintenance programs. Through new levels of cooperation and communication with other agencies and conservation organizations at all levels, the highway program offer a coordinated response against the introduction and spread of invasive species.

The E.O. builds on the National Environmental Policy Act (NEPA) of 1969, the Federal Noxious Weed Act of 1974, and the Endangered Species Act of 1973 to prevent the introduction of invasive species, provide for their control, and take measures to minimize economic, ecological, and human health impacts. In response to the proactive policy of the Office of the Secretary of Transportation and the E.O., the FHWA offers the following guidance:

Use of Federal Funds:

Under the E.O., Federal agencies cannot authorize, fund, or carry out actions that it believes are likely to cause or promote the introduction or spread of invasive species in the United States or elsewhere unless all reasonable measures to minimize risk of harm have been analyzed and considered. Complying with the E.O. means that Federal-aid and Federal Lands Highway Program funds cannot be used for construction, revegetation, or landscaping activities that purposely include the use of known invasive plant species. Until an approved national list of invasive plants is defined by the National Invasive Species Council, "known invasive plants" are defined as those listed on the official noxious weed list of the State in which the activity occurs. The FHWA recommends use of Federal-aid funds for new and expanded invasive species control efforts under each State DOTs' roadside vegetation management program.

FHWA NEPA Analysis:

Determinations of the likelihood of introducing or spreading invasive species and a description of measures being taken to minimize their potential harm should be made part of any process conducted to fulfill agency responsibilities under NEPA. Consideration of invasive species should occur during all phases of the environmental process to fulfill the requirements of NEPA. For example, during scoping, discussions with stakeholders should identify the potential for impacts from invasive species and include possible prevention and control measures. The actual NEPA analysis should include identification of any invasive terrestrial or aquatic animal or plant species that could do harm to native habitats within the project study area. This could involve the mapping all existing invasive populations on and adjacent to the project and a survey of existing soils for invasive potential. Also, the analysis should include the potential impact of the disturbances caused by construction on the spread of invasives. Finally, the analysis should include a discussion of any preventative measures or eradication measures that will be taken on the project. Measures may include the inspection and cleaning of construction equipment, commitments to ensure the use of invasive-free mulches, topsoils and seed mixes, and eradication strategies to be deployed should an invasion occur. Until the National Vegetation Management Plan specified in the E.O. is completed, NEPA analyses should rely on each State's noxious weed list to define the invasive plants that must be addressed and the measures to be implemented to minimize their harm. The FHWA strongly encourages statewide, right-of-way inventories of vegetation that map existing invasive plant infestations to provide information for NEPA analysis. In addition, the FHWA encourages the DOTs to develop their own vegetation management plans based on the E.O., their own statewide invasive plant inventories, and the National plan when available. In absence of a specific State or State DOT plans, the National plan will serve as policy and guidance to the States.

State DOT Activities and Funded Facilities:

The FHWA encourages the State DOTs to implement the Executive Memorandum on Beneficial Landscaping at every opportunity. This includes applying it to highway landscaping projects, rest area construction, scenic overlooks, State entrances, and Transportation Enhancement activities. In addition, FHWA recommends that roadside maintenance programs be given the necessary support to control and prevent invasive species.

Innovative Design:

The FHWA encourages the selection of construction and landscaping techniques and equipment that will contribute to accomplishing the intent of the E.O. These include bio-control delivery systems, more efficient equipment cleaners, improved seeding equipment for steep slopes, safer burn management equipment, easier-to-use Geographic Positioning Systems for invasive population inventories, and methods to minimize soil disturbance during vegetation management activities so as to reduce the opportunities for the introduction of invasive species.

Coordinated Research:

The FHWA environmental research program will promote studies on invasive plant control methods, and restoration of native species after control. We will make a concerted effort to support applied research relevant to State DOT vegetation management programs. Results will proactively be shared among States and other State and Federal resource agencies.

Training:

The FHWA suggests increased training of vegetation managers in maintenance districts, landscape units, and erosion control sections within each State DOT. Integrated vegetation management principles should be included in this training. The FHWA will provide training materials for identification of invasive plants, and restoration of native plants, plus encourage regional workshops in its four national Resource Centers. The FHWA supports increased public education, especially resulting from interagency partnerships. State agencies are also encouraged to take steps to increase public awareness about invasive plant species and the integrated management methods used to control and prevent invasives.

Interagency Cooperation:

The FHWA recommends that State DOTs participate in State invasive species councils as they are established. These interagency councils will likely include Federal agencies, State, local and tribal governments. Many States have already begun to organize these councils to promote cooperative work on invasive species issues within their State. These groups can share public awareness, training, data bases, policy, and research information and be a resource the National Invasive Species Council. The FHWA suggests that each State DOT cooperate with adjacent State DOTs to establish coordinated prevention and control measures for invasive species.

Interagency Committees:

The FHWA will continue to participate in the coordinated activities of FICMNEW, NPCI, and the Aquatic Nuisance Species Task Force (ANS). The FICMNEW initiates cooperative projects aimed at public awareness, policy, training, and research on invasive plant issues. The NPCI addresses non-native invasive species issues across agencies in an effort to protect and to restore native plant communities nationwide. The ANS focuses interagency efforts on those aquatic plant and animal species that impact our Nation's waterways. The FHWA encourages participation by State DOTs in the State Interagency Invasive Species Councils.

Where can we get more information about weed control?

Most State DOTs have an annual herbicide applicators' training session. Always check first with your State's Department of Agriculture and Department of Natural Resources or similar agencies for applicable regulations and technical information. Include the herbicide industry and their research results for control information on your State's target species. Your University and Extension Service should be included also. Check websites, such as that of the Federal Interagency Committee for Management of Noxious and Exotic Weeds (FICMNEW) at **http://bluegoose.arw.r9.fws.gov/FICMNEWFiles/FICMNEWHomePage**. Through this homepage, you can link to related sites for additional information and contacts. Finally, consult the 1999 FHWA handbook, *Roadside Use of Native Plants*, for more information.

What can the National Invasive Species Council do for us?

The Council is intended to avoid overlap and redundancy of work being done on invasive species control. By combining research projects, training efforts, public awareness tactics, cooperative agreements, and other resources, we all can avoid wasting precious time and funds in the battle against invasive plants. Its national view and participation should encourage beneficial connections and new partnerships. In the long run, this unprecedented cooperation should save money and diminish the impacts caused by invasive species.

What kinds of research will be supported?

The FHWA will support applied research projects that would apply to many States, develop innovative methods for control of key invasive plants, characterize roadside environments, benefit wildlife habitat, improve water quality, integrate vegetation management tools, improve native plant restoration techniques for rights-of-way, and increase public awareness about non-native invasive and native vegetation.

What technical support can we expect?

The FHWA will continue as a technical resource to each State Highway Agency. The FHWA will share recent research products and fund new research. The FHWA will cooperate with other Federal and State agencies in meaningful partnerships. The FHWA will publish invasive species information in its quarterly newsletter, *Greener Roadsides*. The FHWA will offer training workshops at our four Resource Centers. The FHWA will act as part of your network and connection to other related networks. An FHWA Vegetation Management website at **http://www.fhwa.dot.gov/environment** will be on line in the near future to make these connections. The FHWA will encourage roadside vegetation reviews by State and FHWA in 3 years to determine the results of the Executive Order's intent in each State.

How will environmental documents be affected?

Since the spread of invasive plant species is somewhat predictable and avoidable on construction and related projects, an analysis of site conditions and a plan for minimizing weed introduction and spread could be accomplished during the environmental process. On projects where the potential exists for the introduction or spread of invasive species, the environmental document should include a discussion of the potential impact of these species and any anticipated prevention or control measures to be taken.

Will State Vegetation Management Plans be required?

No. There is no requirement in Executive Order 13112 for State DOT vegetation management plans. Under the Order, the National Invasive Species Council has 18 months to provide a national plan. A State may wish to develop their own plan to specifically deal with species of concern. State DOTs should be involved in the development of any State plans and should be prepared to offer their own vegetation management objectives and solutions.

How can States use native plants as much as practicable as called for by the Presidential Memorandum on beneficial landscaping?

The use of native plants is practicable only when native plants and/or seed are reasonably available in the State. Some creativity will be necessary i.e., salvaging native plants in the way of construction, harvesting native plant seed from the project locality, notifying existing growers of your upcoming needs as far in advance as possible, and contract-growing native plants and native seed whenever you can prove cost-effectiveness as alternative to low bid.

Ira BICKFORD is the roadside vegetation manager for the Utah Department of Transportation. He has spent most of his professional career in the fields of biology and botany. His research interests include inter-relationships of plants, wildlife, and transportation. He has authored and co-authored several papers and articles on botany and transportation issues.

J. Baird CALLICOTT is professor of philosophy and religion studies at the University of North Texas and president of the International Society for Environmental Ethics. He is author of In Defense of the Land Ethic; Essays in Environmental Philosophy; Beyond the Land Ethic; More Essays in Environmental Philosophy, Earth's Insights; A Multicultural Survey of Ecological Ethics from the Mediterranean Basin to the Australian Outback, and more than a hundred book chapters, journal and encyclopedia articles and book reviews. He is editor or co-editor of Companion to A Sand County Almanac; Nature in Asian Traditions of Thought; Environmental Philosophy; and Earth Summit Ethics.

Bonnie L. HARPER-LORE is the vegetation specialist for the Federal Highway Administration. In that role she acts as a resource to all State departments of transportation. Her training focused on the design, restoration and management of native plant communities. She serves on the Federal Interagency Committee on Management of Exotic and Noxious Weeds (FICMNEW) and the Native Plant Conservation Initiative.

Kirk HENDERSON is county coordinator for Iowa's Integrated Roadside Vegetation Management (IRVM) program plus manager of the Roadside Program at the University of Northern Iowa. His primary focus is encouraging counties to use native plant species in roadside plantings. His office has produced and distributed a number of IRVM educational publications.

Evelyn A. HOWELL is professor of botany in the Department of Landscape Architecture and Institute for Environmental Studies at the University of Wisconsin-Madison. She has published many articles on prairie, woodland and wetland restoration and management. Howell has written restoration and management plans for various national and regional agencies.

Don JACOBOVITZ is assistant manager of the Orange County Roads and Drainage Department in Orlando, Florida. He is a graduate of the United States Military Academy at West Point. Jacobovitz also acquired a masters in enginering administration from Geroge Washington University and transportation engineering from the University of Central Florida. He aided in the research of this book as an Eisenhower Fellow from 1994-1995. Currently he is involved with the issue of right-of-way mowing in Florida.

Bill JOHNSON is State roadside environmental engineer with the North Carolina Department of Transportation. He is a graduate of North Carolina State University with a B.S. in agricultural engineering and additional course work in landscape architecture. He is head of the roadside environmental unit which has done extensive landscaping along North Carolina highways. Bill is responsible for the Department's nationally recognized wildflower program.

John T. KARTESZ is the Director of the Biota of North America Program (BONAP) of the North Carolina Botanical Garden, and the author of numerous publications, including the 1994 book - A Checklist of the Vascular Flora of the United States, Canada, and Greenland. Over the last three decades, he has developed one of the largest international vascular plant databases currently available, which includes nomenclatural, taxonomic, phytogeographic, and other biological attribute data. He is planning to publish much of his database via a forthcoming digital program, Synthesis of the North American Flora in early spring 1999.

Gary K. LORE is an environmental writer. For more than two decades he was a rights-of-way vegetation mananger in both the public and private sectors. His interests include environmental philosophy and ethics, nature writing, and natural history.

Wayne G. MCCULLY is research scientist and program manager for vegetation management in the Texas Transportation Institute, a unit of the Texas A&M University system. His academic training is in range science and plant physiology. His interests include selection and improvement of range plant materials, roadside vegetation establishment/management, plant ecology, reclamation and erosion control, and range improvement/management.

Darrel G. MORRISON is professor in the School of Environmental Design, University of Georgia and periodically consults on ecologically-based landscape design, management and restoration. His many design projects include the Museum of History at the Atlanta History Center and the Lady Bird Johnson Wildflower Center near Austin.

Larry E. MORSE is chief botanist for The Nature Conservancy, and is based at their international headquarters in Arlington, Virginia. His research emphsizes native plant conservation priorities and strategies, particularly in the United States and Canada.

William A. NIERING is professor of botany at Connecticut College, New London. His research interests include dynamics of plant communities and wetland ecology. Niering is author of several books including Wetlands and Wetlands of North America.

Reed F. NOSS is co-executive director of the Conservation Biology Institute, a non-profit research and educational organization based in Corvallis, Oregon. He is a former editor of Conservation Biology and is currently president-elect of the Society for Conservation Biology.

Peggy OLWELL is endangered species coordinator for the National Park Service. She received her bachelor's degree in botany from the University of North Carolina at Chapel Hill and her masters in biology from Southern Methodist University. She is currently chair of the Native Plant Conservation Initiative. Olwell is a member of The World Conservation Union's (IUCN) Plant Reintroduction Species Survival Commission.

Wayne R. PAULY is a restoration ecologist for the Dane Country Parks Department in Madison, Wisconsin. Pauley works with hundreds of volunteers to manage several thousand acres of Conservancy land. He may be reached by phone, (608) 246-3896.

John M. RANDALL is invasive weed specialist for The Nature Conservancy. He provides leadership, technical support and advice on weed control to TNC preserves nationwide. He is a founding member of the California Exotic Pest Plant Council. Randall holds a PhD in ecology from the University of California, Davis.

Sarah REICHARD is research assistant professor at the Center for Urban Horticulture at the University of Washington. Sarah's primary research interests are in the prevention of introduction and spread of introduced invasives, including prediction of invasive ability and early monitoring of new invasions. Reichard directs a new program on the conservation, propagation and growth of rare Washington plant species. She serves as vice-chair of the Conservation Committee for AABGA, a member of the ANLA working group on invasive plants, and a member of the IUCN Invasive Species Specialist Group.

Jil SWEARINGEN is IPM Coordinator for the National Parks Service, National Capital Region. Jil provides support to the region's parks for pest problems of all types, including invasive plants. Swearingen chairs the Native Plant Conservation Initiative's Alien Plant Working Group. Spurred by a strong interest in educating the public on this issue, she initiated a web-based project called "Weeds Gone Wild: Alien Plant Invaders of Natural Areas."

Randy WESTBROOKS is the national weed coordinator for the USDA Animal and Plant Health Inspection Service. His current focus is to facilitate the establishment of Regional and State Invasive Species Councils and to work with the National Invasive Species Council. Westbrooks holds a PhD in botany/weed science from North Carolina State University.

Maggie WILSON, with the U.S. EPA's Office of Pollution Prevention and Toxics, Risk Assessment Division, worked as a field botanist and as a researcher at the Smithsonian Institution while completing her Master's Degree at George Mason University. She completed research for this Handbook while in the doctoral program at GMU. Her interests include habitat restoration and technology transfer. She can be reached by email at: wilson.maggie@epa.gov.

Environmental Thought

Callicott, Baird J. 1989. *In Defense of the Land Ethic.* State University of New York Press, Albany, New York.

Callicott, Baird J. 1991. *The River of the Mother of God and other Essays by Aldo Leopold.* University of Wisconsin Press, Madison, Wisconsin.

Carson, Rachel. 1962. *Silent Spring.* Houghton Mifflin, Boston, Massachusetts.

Cronon, William, Ed. 1992. *Uncommon Ground: Toward Reinventing Nature.* W. W. Norton and Co., Inc., New York, New York.

Gore, Albert G. 1992. *Earth in the Balance.* Houghton Mifflin Company, New York, New York.

Hargrove, Eugene C. 1989. *Foundations of Environmental Ethics.* Environmental Ethics Books, Denton, Texas.

Jensen, Jens. 1939. *Siftings.* Ralph Fletcher Seymour, Chicago, Illinois.

Leopold, Aldo. 1949. *A Sand County Almanac.* Oxford University Press, Inc., Oxford, England.

Nash, Roderick. 1976. *The American Environment.* Addison-Wesley Publishing Company, Inc. Philippines.

Nash, Roderick Frazier. 1989. *The Rights of Nature; A History of Environmental Ethics.* University of Wisconsin Press, Madison, Wisconsin.

Noss, R.F. and A.Y. Cooperrider. 1994. *Saving Nature's Legacy: Protecting and Restoring Biodiveristy.* Island Press, Washington, DC.

Noss, R.F., M.A. O'Connell, and D. D. Murphy. 1997. *The Science of Conservation Planning: Habitat Conservation under the Endangered Species Act.* Island Press, Washington, DC.

Udall, Stewart L. 1963. *The Quiet Crisis.* Holt, Rinehart & Winston, Inc. New York, New York.

Identification

(General references only - check with your State for local field guides)

Britton, Nathaniel and Addison Brown. 1970. *An Illustrated Flora of the Northern United States and Canada.* Volumes 1-3. Dover Publications, Inc., New York.

Brockman, C. Frank. 1986. *Trees of North America.* Western Publishing, Racine, Wisconsin.

Fernald, Merritt L. 1950. *Gray's Manual of Botany.* Van Nostrand, New York.

Gleason, Henry A. And Arthur Cronquist. 1991. *Manual of Vascular Plants of Northeastern United States and Adjacent Canada*. D. Van Nostrand Company, New York.

Hitchcock, A.S. 1935. *Manual of the Grasses of the United States*. U.S. Government Printing Office, Washington, DC.

Hitchcock, C.L. and Ar. Cronquist. 1973. *Flora of the Pacific Northwest*. University of Washington Press, Seattle, Washington.

Kartesz, John. 1994. *A Synonymized Checklist of the Vascular Flora of the United States, Canada and Greenland*. Timber Press, Portland, Oregon.

Mohlenbrock, Robert H. 1987. Wildflowers, *A Quick Identification Guide to the Wildflowers of North America*. Macmillan Publishing Company, New York.

Newcomb, Lawrene. 1977. *Newcomb's Wildflower Guide*. Little, Brown, Boston, Massachusetts.

Peterson, Roger Tory and Margaret McKenny. 1968. *A Field Guide to Wildflowers*. Houghton Mifflin Company, Boston, Massachusetts.

Petrides, George A. 1972. *A Field Guide to Trees and Shrubs*. Houghton Mifflin, Boston, Massachusetts.

Plant Communities/Ecology

Barry, John M. 1980. *Natural Vegetation of South Carolina*. University Press, Columbia, South Carolina.

Bennett, Dean. 1988. *Maine's Natural Heritage, Rare Species and Unique Natural Features*. Down East Books, Camden, Maine.

Boon, William and Harlen Groe. 1990. *Nature's Heartland, Native Plant Communities of the Great Plains*, Iowa State University Press, Ames, Iowa.

Brown, David E. 1982. *Biotic Communities of the American Southwest*. Boyce Thompson Arboretum, Superior, Arizona.

Cain, Stanley A. 1944. *Foundations of Plant Geography*. Harper & Brothers, New York.

Curtis, John T. 1959. *The Vegetation of Wisconsin*. University of Wisconsin Press, Madison, Wisconsin.

Collins, Beryl Robichaud, and Karl H. Anderson. 1973. *Plant Communities of New Jersey*. Rutgers University Press, New Brunswick, New Jersey.

Daubenmire, R.F. 1959. *Plants and Environment*. John Wiley and Sons, New York.

Daubenmire, Rexford. 1968. *Plant Communities: A Textbook of Plant Synecology*. Harper & Row, New York.

Franklin, Jerry F. and C.T. Dyrness. 1988. *Natural Vegetation of Oregon and Washington*. Oregon State University Press, Eugene, Oregon.

Gleason, Henry A. and Arthur Cronquist. 1964. *The Natural Geography of Plants*. Columbia University Press, New York.

Hanson, Herbert and Ethan Churchill. 1961. *The Plant Community*. Reinhold, New York.

Jackson, Marion T. Editor. 1997. *The Natural Heritage of Indiana*. Indiana University Press, Bloomington and Indianapolis, Indiana.

Lorgensen, Neil. 1977. *A Guide to New England's Landscape*. Globe Pequot Press, Chester, Connecticut.

McClaran, Mitchel P. and Thomas R. Van Devender, Editors. 1995. *The Desert Grassland*. The University of Arizona Press, Tucson.

Minnesota Natural Heritage Program. 1993. *Minnesota's Native Vegetation: A Key to Natural Communities*. Version I.5, Biologial Report 20. Dept.of Natural Resources, St. Paul, Minnesota.

Olmsted, C.E. 1944. Photoperiodic responses of 12 geographic strains of sideoats grama. Bot. Gaz. 106:46-74.

Oosting, Henry J. 1956. *The Study of Plant Communities*. W.H. Freeman and Co., San Francisco, California.

Ornduff, Robert. 1974. *Introduction to California Plant Life*. University of California Press, Berkeley, California.

Reschke, Carol. 1990. *Ecological Communities of New York State*. New York Natural Heritage Program, Latham, New York.

Robichaux, Robert H. 1998. *Ecology of Sonoran Desert Plants and Plant Communities*. The University of Arizona Press, Tucson, Arizona.

Swink, Floyd and Gerould Wilhelm. 1979. *Plants of the Chicago Region*. The Morton Arboretum, Lisle, Illinois.

Tester, John R. 1995. *Minnesota's Natural Heritage, An Ecological Perspective*. University of Minnesota Press, Minneapolis, Minnesota.

Turesson, G. 1922. The species and variety as ecological units. *Hereditas* 3: 100-113.

Weaver, J.E. and T.J. Fitzpatrick. 1934. "The Prairie". *Ecological Monographs*, Vol. 4. Duke University Press, Durham, North Carolina.

Stubbendieck, J., Hatch, S.L. and C.H. Butterfield. 1992. *North American Range Plants*. University of Nebraska Press, Lincoln, Nebraska.

Weaver, J.E., F.E. Clements. 1938. *Plant Ecology*. McGraw-Hill, New York.

Wilsie, Carroll P. 1961. *Crop Adaptation and Distribution*. Chap. 4, The Ecotype Concept.

Landscaping

(Including selected regional references)

Brooklyn Botanic Garden Record. 1989. *Gardening with Wildflowers & Native Plants*. Brooklyn Botanic Garden, Brooklyn, New York.

DuPont, Elizabeth N. 1978. *Landscaping with Native Plants in the Middle Atlantic Region*. Brandywine Conservancy, Chadds Ford, Pennsylvania.

Hightshoe, Gary L. 1988. *Native Trees, Shrubs, and Vines for Urban and Rural America*. Van Nostrand Reinhold Company, New York.

Diekelmann, J. And R. Schuster. 1982. *Natural Landscaping*. McGraw-Hill Book Co., New York.

Holmes, Roger, Editor. 1993. *Taylor's Guide to Natural Gardening*. Houghton Mifflin Co. New York.

Jones Jr., Samuel B. and Leonard E. Foote. 1990. *Gardening with Native Wild Flowers*. Timber Press, Portland, Oregon.

Kruckeberg, Arthur R. 1982. *Gardening with Native Plants of the Pacific Northwest*. University of Washington Press, Seattle, Washington.

McHarg, Ian L.1969. *Design with Nature*, Natural History Press, Garden City, New York.

Phillips, Judith. 1987. *Southwestern Landscaping with Native Plants*. Museum of New Mexico Press, Santa Fe, New Mexico.

Roberts, Edith A. and Elsa Rehmann. 1996. *American Plants for American Gardens*. University of Georgia Press, Athens, Georgia.

Sternberg, Guy and Jim Wilson. 1995. *Landscaping with Native Trees*. Chapters Publishing Ltd., Shelburne, Vermont.

Taylor, Patricia A. 1996. *Easy Care Native Plants*. Henry Holt and Company, New York.

Wasowski, Sally and Andy Wasowski,1994. *Gardening with Native Plants of the South*. Taylor Publishing Company, Dallas, Texas.

Wilson, Jim. 1992. *Landscaping with Wildflowers, An Environmental Approach to Gardening*. Houghton Mifflin Company, New York.

Wilson, William H. W. 1984. *Landscaping with Wildflowers & Native Plants*. Chevron Chemical Company, San Francisco, California.

Native Plant Regional Source Directories

Northeast Region*: Sources of Propagated Native Plants and Wildflowers*. New England Wild Flower Society, Garden in the Woods, Hemenway Road, Framingham, Maine 01701.

Southeast*: Sources of Native Plants of the Southeastern United States*, 1993. Jan Midgley, 234 Oak Tree Trail, Wilsonville, Alabama 35186.

Midwest: *Midwest Native Plant and Seed Sources*, 1991. Maria Urice - National Wildflower Research Center, 4801 La Crosse Avenue, Austin, Texas 78739.

Northwest*: Hortus West, A Native Plant Directory and Journal*. P.O. Box 2870, Wilsonville, Oregon 97070.

Southwest: Nursery sources are listed in *Wildflower Handbook, a resource for Native Plant Landscapes*, 1992. NWRC, Austin, Texas.

MidAtlantic: Mark Gormell, Brandywine, Pennsylvania. (215) 388-7601.

California: *Nursery Sources for California Nature Plants*, 1995. California Department of Conservation, Office of Mine Reclamation, Sacramento, California.

Alaska: *Directory of Alaska Native Plant Sources.* Department of Natural Resources, Division of Agriculture, Plant Materials Center, HC02 Box 7440, Palmer, Alaska 99645.

Hawaii: *Directory of Sources for Native Hawaiian Plants.* Hawaiian Plant Conservation Center, NTBG, P.O. Box 3340, Lawai, Kauai, Hawaii 96765.

Weeds or Invasive Species

Agricultural Research Service of the United States Department of Agriculture. 1971. *Common Weeds of the United States.* Dover Publications, New York.

Doren, Robert F., Ed. 1991. *Proceedings of the Symposium on Exotic Pest Plants.* National Park Service, Denver, Colorado.

FICMNEW. 1996. *Pulling Together, National Strategy for Invasive Plant Management.* Federal Interagency Committee on the Management of Noxious and Exotic Weeds, Washington, DC.

McKnight, Bill N., ed. *1992. Biological Pollution: The Control and Impact of Invasive Exotic Species.* Indiana Academy of Science. Indianapolis, Indiana.

Paddock, David N., ed. *1992. Compendium on Exotic Species.* Natural Areas Association. Mukwonago, Wisconsin.

Phillips Petroleum Company. 1986. *Pasture and Range Plants.* Fort Hays State University, Kansas.

Randall, John M. and Janet Marinelli, eds. 1996. *Invasive Plants, Weeds of the Global Garden.* Brooklyn Botanic Gardens Inc. New York.

Simberloff, Daniel, Don C. Schmitz, and Tom C. Brown, Editors. 1997. *Strangers in Paradise, Impact and Management of Nonindigenous species in Florida.* Island Press, Washington, DC.

Stubbendieck, James, G. Friisoe, M. Bolick. 1994. *Weeds of Nebraska and the Great Plains.* Nebraska Department of Agriculture, Lincoln, Nebraska.

The Nature Conservancy. 1992. *Element Stewardship Abstracts.* The Nature Conservancy, Arlington, Virginia.

Westbrooks, Randy G. and R.E. Eplee. 1989. Federal Noxious Weeds in Florida. *Proceedings of the Southern Weed Science Society* 42:316-321.

Whitson, Tom D., et al. 1992. *Weeds of the West.* University of Wyoming, Laramie, Wyoming.

U.S. Congress. 1993. *Harmful Nonindgenous Species in the United States.* Office of Technology Assessment, Washington, DC.

Vegetation Restoration and Management

Falk, Donald A., Constance I. Millar, and Margaret Olwell, Editors. 1996. *Restoring Diversity, Strategies for Reintroduction of Endangered Plants.* Island Press, Washington, DC.

Falk, D.A. 1990. Discovering the Past, Restoring the Future. *Restoration and Management Notes* 8 92):71.

Gerling, Heather-Sinton, etal. 1996. *A Guide to Using Native Plants on Disturbed Lands,* Alberta Agriculture, Food and Rural Development, Edmonton, Canada.

Harper, Bonnie L. 1987. Return of the Natives. Transportation Research Board. Academy of Science. Washington, DC.

Harper-Lore, Bonnie. 1996. Using Native Plants as Problem-Solvers. *Environmental Management,* Vol. 20, No. 6. Springer-Verlag New York Inc. p. 827-830. New York, New York.

Harper-Lore Bonnie. 1998. Do Native Grasslands have a place on Roadsides? *Land and Water,* July/August, p.29-31. Fort Dodge, Iowa.

Howell, Evelyn A. and William R. Jordan III. 1991. Tallgrass Prairie Restoration in the Upper Midwest in *Scientific Management of Temperate Communities for Conservation.* Blackwell Scientific Publications. United Kingdom.

Jordan III, William R. Ongoing. *Restoration and Management Notes.* University of Wisconsin Arboretum, 1207 Seminole Highway, Madison, Wisconsin 53711.

Morgan, John P., D.R. Collicutt and J.D. Thompson. 1995. *Restoring Canada's Native Prairies - A Practical Manual.* Argyle, Manitoba, Canada.

Nilsen, Richard, Editor, 1991. *Helping Nature Heal, An Introduction to Environmental Restoration.* Ten Speed Press Publication, Berkeley, California.

NRVMA 1997. *How to Develop and Implement an Integrated Roadside Vegetation Management.* National Roadside Vegetation Management Association, 218 Rhett Drive Adams Run, Newark, Delaware.

Packard, Stephen and Cornelia F. Mutel, Editors. 1997. *The Tallgrass Restoration Handbook for Prairies, Savannas, and Woodlands.* Island Press, Washington, DC.

Pauly, Wayne. 1998. *How to Manage Small Prairie Fires.* Dane County Parks, Madison, Wisconsin.

Wisconsin Department of Natural Resources. 1991. Draft Rare Plant Propagation and Distribution Policy. Madison, Wisconsin.

Bedford, Barbara L. and E.M. Preston. 1988. Developing the scientific basis for assessing cumulative effects of wetland loss and degradation on landscape functions: Status, perspectives, and prospects. *Environmental Management* 12(5): 751-772.

Cowardin, L.M., V. Carter, F.C. Golet, and E.T. LaRoe. 1979. *Classification of Wetlands and Deepwater Habitats of the United States*. FWS/OBS-79/31. U.S. Fish and Wildlife Service, Washington, DC.

Eggers, Steve D. and Donald M. Reed. 1997. *Wetland Plants and Plant Communities of Minnesota and Wisconsin*. U.S. Army Corps of Engineers, St. Paul District, Minnesota.

Fassett, Norman. 1957. *A Manual of Aquatic Plants*. University of Wisconsin Press, Madison, Wisconsin.

Garbish, E.W. Jr. 1986. *Highways and Wetlands: Compensating Wetland Losses*. Contract Report DOT-FH-11-9442. FHWA, Office of Implementation, McLean, Virginia.

Hunt, Randall J. 1998. Do Created Wetlands Replace the Wetlands that are Destroyed? *U.S. Department of Interior - USGS fact sheet* FS-246-96.

Kadlec, J.A. 1962. Effects of a drawdown on waterfowl impoundment. *Ecology* 43:267-281.

Kantrud, H.A., G.L. Krapu, and G.A. Swanson. 1989. Prairie Basin Wetlands of the Dakotas: A Community Profile. U.S. Fish and Wildlife Service. Biological Report 85 (7.28). Washington, DC.

Kentula, M.E., R.P. Brooks, S.E. Gwin, C.C. Holland, A.D. Sherman, and J.C. Sifneos. 1992. *An Approach to Improving Decision Making in Wetland Restoration and Creation*. Edited by A.J. Hairston. U.S. Environmental Protection Agency, Environmental Research Laboratory, Corvallis, Oregon.

Kusler, Jon A. and Mary E. Kentula, Eds. 1990. *Wetland Creation and Restoration, the Status of the Science*. Island Press, Washington, DC.

Mitsch, William and James Gosselink. 1986. *Wetlands*. Van Nostrand Reinhold Company, New York.

National Research Council. 1992. *Restoration of Aquatic Ecosystems, Science Technology, and Public Policy*. National Academy Press, Washington, DC.

Niering, W.A. 1991. *Wetlands of North America*. Thomasson-Grant, Charlottesville, Virginia.

Niering, W.A. 1994. Wetland Vegetation Change: A Dynamic Process. *Wetland Journal* 6:4 (6-10)

Novitzki, R.P. 1989. Wetland Hydrology, p. 46-64. In S.K. Majumbar, R.P.Brooks, F.J. Brenner, and R.W. Tinner, Jr. (Eds.), *Wetlands Ecology and Conservation*. The Pennsylvania Academy of Science, Philadelphia, Pennsylvania.

Quammen, M.L. 1986. Measuring the success of wetlands mitigation. *National Wetlands Newsletter* 8(5):6-8.

Tiner, R.W., Jr. 1984. *Wetlands of the United States: Current Status and Recent Trends*. U.S. Fish and Wildlife Service, National Wetland Inventory, Washington, DC.

Van der Valk, A.G. 1981. Succession in wetlands: a Gleasonian approach. *Ecology* 62:688-696.

Van der Valk, A.G. Ed. 1989. *Northern Prairie Wetlands*. Iowa State University Press, Ames.

Van der Valk, A.G. and C.B. Davis. 1978. The role of seed banks in vegetation dynamics of prairie glacial marshes. *Ecology* 59:322-335.

Weller, M.W. 1975. Studies of cattail in relation to management of marsh wildlife. *Iowa State Journal of Research* 49:383-412.

Zedler, J.B. and R. Langis. 1991. Comparisons of constructed and natural salt marshes of San Diego Bay. *Restoration and Management Notes* 9(1):21-25.

American Association of Retired Persons
1909 K Street, NW
Washington, DC 20029

American Horticultural Society
7931 East Boulevard Drive
Alexandria, VA 22308
(703) 768-5700

American Nursery and Landscape Association
1250 I Street, NW
Washington, DC 20005
(202) 789-2900

American Planning Association
1313 East 60th Street
Chicago, IL 60637

American Rivers
801 Pennsylvania Avenue SE, Ste. 303
Washington, DC 20003
(202) 547-6900

American Society of Landscape Architects
4401 Connecticut Avenue, NW
Washington, DC 20008

American Trails
1400 16th Street NW
Washington, DC 20036

Association for the Study of Literature and Environment
University of Oregon, Louise Westling
Eugene, OR 97403

Boy Scouts of America
P.O. Box 152079
Irving, TX 75015
(214) 580-2434

Center for Environmental Ethics
University of North Texas
P.O. Box 310980
Denton, TX 76203
(940) 565-2727

Center for Watershed Protection
8737 Colesville Road, Ste. 300
Silver Spring, MD 20910

Columbia Basin Fish and Wildlife Authority
2501 SW First Avenue, Ste. 200
Portland, OR 97201

Defenders of Wildlife
1101 14th Street NW, Ste. 1400
Washington, DC 20005

Ducks Unlimited
1155 Connecticut Avenue, Ste. 800
Washington, DC 20036

Ecological Society of America
2010 Massachusetts Avenue NW,
Ste. 420
Washington DC, 20036

Environmental Defense Fund
257 Park Avenue South
New York, NY 10010
(212) 505-2100

Environmental Law Institute
1616 P St. NW, Ste. 200
Washington, DC 20036
(202) 939-3800

Federal Interagency Committee for Management of Noxious & Exotic Weeds (FICMNEW)
USDA Forest Service
P.O. Box 96090
Washington, DC 20090
(202) 205-0847

The Garden Clubs of America
598 Madison Avenue
New York, NY 10022
(212) 753-8287

Girl Scouts of the USA
830 Third Avenue
New York, NY 10022

Grasslands Heritage Foundation
P.O. Box 394
Shawnee Mission, KS 66201
(913) 262-3506

Greater Yellowstone Coalition
P.O. Box 187413
South Wilson
Bozeman, MT 59711
(406) 586-1593

International Erosion Control Association
P.O. Box 4904
Steamboat Springs, CO 80477
(303) 879-3010

Intl. Union for Conservation of Nature and Natural Resources (IUCN)
1400 16th Street NW
Washington DC, 20036
(202) 797-5454

Izaak Walton League of America, Inc.
707 Conservation Lane
Gaithersburg, MD 20878
(301) 548-0150

Keep America Beautiful, Inc.
9 West Broad Street
Stamford, CT 06902
(203) 323-8987

National Arboretum
3501 New York Avenue NE
Washington, DC 20002
(202) 475-4815

National Arborist Association
Route 101, Box 1094
Amherst, NH 03031
(603) 673-3311

National Association of Service and Conservation Corps
666 11th Street NW, Ste. 1000
Washington DC 20001
(202) 737-6272

National Association of State Foresters Hall of the States, Ste. 52
6444 N. Capitol Street, NW
Washington, DC 20001

National Audubon Society
950 Third Avenue
New York, NY 10022
(212) 546-9100

National Fish and Wildlife Foundation
1120 Connecticut Avenue NW, Ste. 900
Washington DC 20036
(202) 857-0166

National 4-H Council
7100 Connecticut Avenue
Chevy Chase, MD 20815
(301) 961-2800

National Forest Foundation
1099 14th Street NW, Ste. 5600
Washington, DC 20005
(202) 501-2473

National Museum of Natural History
Smithsonian Institution
Constitution Avenue 10th Street NW
Washington, DC 20560
(202) 357-1300

National Park Foundation
1101 17th Street NW, Ste. 1102
Washington, DC 20036
(202) 785-4500

National Roadside Vegetation Management Assoc.
218 Rhett Drive Adams Run
Newark, DE 19702

National Council of State Garden Clubs, Inc.
4401 Magnolia Avenue
St. Louis, MO 63110
(800) 550-6007

National Tree Trust
1120 G Street NW, Ste. 770
Washington DC 20005
(202) 628-8733

National Trust for Historic Preservation
1785 Massachusetts Avenue, NW
Washington, DC 20036
(202) 673-4000

National Wildflower Research Center (Ladybird Johnson Wildflower Center)
4801 LaCrosse Avenue
Austin, TX 78739
(512) 292-4200

National Wildlife Federation
8925 Leesburg Pike
Vienna, VA 22184
(800) 477-5560

Native Plant Conservation Initiative (NPCI)
Bureau of Land Management
Fish, Wildlife and Forests Group
1849 C Street NW LSB-204
Washington, DC 20240
(202) 452-0392

Natural Areas Association
P.O. Box 900
Chesterfield, MO 63006
(314) 878-7850

Natural Resources Defense Council
40 W. 20th Street,
New York, NY 10011
(212) 727-2700

New England Wildflower Society, Inc.
180 Hemenway Road
Framingham, MA 01701
(617) 237-4924

North American Weed Managers Association
2305 Nottingham Court
Fort Collins, CO 80526

Northwest Ecosystem Alliance
1421 Cornwall Avenue
Bellingham, WA 98227
(360) 671-9950

Outdoor Writers Association of America, Inc.
2017 Cato Avenue, Ste. 101
State College, PA 16801
(814) 234-1011

Pheasants Forever, Inc.
P.O. Box 75473
St. Paul, MN 55175
(651) 773-2000

Rails to Trails Conservancy
1400 16th Street, NW, Ste. 300
Washington, DC 20036
(202) 797-5400

Renew America
1400 16th Street NW, Ste. 710
Washington, DC 20036
(202) 232-2252

River Network
P.O. Box 878
7520 SW 6th Avenue, Ste. 1130
Portland, OR 97204
(503) 241-3506

Scenic America
21 Dupont Circle NW
Washington, DC 20036
(202) 833-4300

Sierra Club
408 C Street, NE
Washington, DC 20002
(202) 547-1141

Smithsonian Institution
1000 Jefferson Drive SW
Washington, DC 20560
(202) 357-2700

Society for Conservation Biology
Stanford University Center for Conservation Biology
Stanford, CA 94305
(415) 725-1852

Society for Ecological Restoration
1207 Seminole Highway, Ste. B
Madison, WI 53711
(608) 262-9547

Society of Environmental Journalists
P.O. Box 27280
Philadelphia, PA 19118
(215) 836-9970

Society for Range Management
1839 York Street
Denver, CO 80206
(303) 355-7070

Society of Wetland Scientists
P.O. Box 1897
Lawrence, KS 66044
(913) 843-1221

Soil and Water Conservation Society
7515 NE Ankeny Road
Ankeny, IA 50021
(515) 289-2331

The Nature Conservancy
4245 North Fairfax Drive, #100
Arlington, VA 22203-1606
(703) 841-5361

Transportation Research Board
2101 Constitution Avenue, NW
Washington, DC 20418
(202) 334-3214

Trout Unlimited
1500 Wilson Bloulevard, Ste. 310
Arlington, VA 22209
(703) 522-0200

Western Society of Weed Science
P.O. Box 963
Newark, CA 94560

Wilderness Society
900 17th Street, NW
Washington, DC 20006
(202) 833-2300

World Wildlife Fund
1250 24th Street, NW
Washington DC 20037
(202) 293-4800

Xerces Society
4828 SE Hawthorne Boulevard
Portland, OR 97215
(503) 232-6639

Resource Addresses drawn from:
Gordon, Rue E., 1997.
Conservation Directory, 42nd Edition.
National Wildlife Federation, Vienna,
VA; Wilson , Jim, 1992. *Landscaping
with Wildflowers*. Houghton-Mifflin
Company, Boston; and Wolfe, Joanne,
1998. *Wild Garden, Magazine*.
Eugene, OR

VEGETATION MANAGEMENT-RELATED WEB SITES

WWW.

APHIS, US Department of Agriculture, weed information
aphis.usda.gov/oa/weeds/weedhome.html

Association for the Study of Literature and the Environment
asle.umn.edu

California WILD, the Caltrans wildflower program
dot.ca.gov/hq/landarch/CaliforniaWILD/abtwild

Conservation Biology, Society for
conbio.rice.edu/scb/

Federal Highway Administration (FHWA), Wildflower Program
fhwa.dot.gov

Federal Interagency Committee on Management of Exotic and Noxious Weeds (FICMNEW)
refuges.fws.gov/FICMNEWFiles

Hawkeye Community College (Vegetation Management course focus)
hawkeye.cc.ia.us

International Erosion Control Association (IECA)
ieca.org

Iowa Integrated Roads, IRVM program (University of Northern Iowa)
uni.edu/~irvm/

Landscape Architecture/restoration ecology program (University of Wisconsin)
wisc.edu/la

National Roadside Vegetation Mangement Association (NRVMA)
nrvma.org

Native Plant Conservation Initiative (NPCI)
nps.gov/plants/index.htm

Natural Areas Association (NAA)
natareas.org/frame.htm

North American Weed Management Association (NAWMA)
fortnet.org/NAWMA

Restoration and Management Notes, a journal
wiscinfo.doit.wisc.edu/arboretum/rmn

Society of Ecological Restoration (SER)
ser.org

Society for Range Management (SRM)
srmden@ix.netcom.com

The Nature Conservancy (TNC), invasive management
tnc.org/science/src/weeds/links

Utah Department of Transportation (UDOT)
dot.state.ut.us/mnt/roadside/veggie

Weed Society of America (WSA)
piked2.agn.uiuc.edu/wssa/

Washington Department of Transportation (WDOT), roadside program
Western Society of Weed Science
wsweedscience.org

Wildflower Magazine, Canadian Wildflower Society
acorn-online.com/hedge/scws.html

The history of roadside development and management has occurred on different timelines in different States. However, most State Departments of Transportation share this common history. The Surface Transportation and Uniform Relocation Assistance Act formalized a native wildflower requirement. On that law and others, the case for use of native plants was built.

1932 - A midwest group known as Friends of the Native Landscape (Jens Jensen) reported an approach to the Illinois Department of Transportation for Roadside Planting and Development. Many States were pursuing this approach due to the economic pressures of the times.

1936 - Jesse M. Bennett wrote Roadsides, the Front Yard of the Nation. Although the book's title stuck, Bennett's words did not: "What is really desired, however, is attractive and useful roadsides which can be obtained by preserving or creating a natural or an approach to a natural condition in keeping with the adjacent or surrounding country. And the significant thing about this is outright economy in road maintenance." States like Texas thought this to be true.

1965 - The Highway Beautification Act, under Ladybird Johnson's influence, encouraged the removal of billboards, screening of junkyards, and landscaping of roadsides.

1969 - The NEPA (National Environmental Policy Act) established the notion of avoidance and minimization of disturbance. This law encouraged environmentally sensitive solutions.

1987 - STURAA (Surface Transportation and Uniform Relocation Assistance Act) is the act that includes the requirement to plant native wildflowers with of 1% of a highway project's landscape budget when federal funds are used. By 1987 some States were already planting more than that minimum. By 1994 only 38 States had program level support for native wildflowers.

1991 - ISTEA (Intermodal Surface Transportation Efficiency Act) provided funding for enhancements. One of the ten categories of enhancements was landscaping. All ISTEA projects were subject to the STURAA requirement of native wildflower use.

1994 - The Executive Memorandum (E.M.) On environmentally and economially beneficial landscaping was signed by President Clinton. The E.M. recommended the use of regional native plants, less fertilizers, less pesticides, less irrigation on federal grounds, lands, and federally funded landscape projects....as in highway construction projects.

1999 - An Executive Order (E.O) on invasive plants was signed by President Clinton. The E.O. ordered increased communication and cooperation of all agencies through a National Invasive Species Council. All agencies focused on prevention and control of invasive plant species, as well as followed-up with restoration of native plants as directed.

ALASKA

AK1 Hemlock-spruce forest
(Tsuga-Picea)

AK2 Spruce-birch forest
(Picea-Betula)

AK3 Black spruce forest
(Picea)

AK4 Muskeg
(Eriophorum-Sphagnum-Betula)

AK5 Alder thickets
(Alnus)

AK6 Cottonsedge tundra
(Eriophorum)

AK7 Watersedge tundra
(Carex)

AK8 Dryas meadows and barren
(Dryas-Carex-Betula)

AK9 Aleutian meadows
(Calamagrostis-Anemone)

AK10 Aleutian heath and barren
(Empetrum-Vaccinium)

HAWAII

HI1 Sclerophyllous forest, shrubland, and grassland
(Heteropogon-Opuntia-Prosopis)

HI2 Guava mixed forest
(Aleurites-Hibiscus-Mangilera-Psidium Schinus)

HI3 Ohia lehua fores
(Metrosideros-Cibotium)

HI4 Lama-manele forest
(Diospyros-Sapindus)

HI5 Koa forest
(Acacia)

HI6 Koa-mamani parkland
(Acacia Deschampsia-Myoporum-Sophora)

HI7 Grassland, microphyllous shrubland, and barren
(Deschampsia-Styphelia-Vaccinium)

PUERTO RICO

PR1 Subtropical dry forest
(Bosque seco subtropical)

PR2 Subtropical moist forest
(Bosque humedo subtropical)

PR3 Subtropical wet forest
(Bosque muy humedo subtropical)

PR4 Subtropical rain forest
(Bosque pluvial subtropical)

PR5 Lower montane wet forest
(Bosque muy humedo montano bajo)

PR6 Lower montane rain forest
(Bosque pluvial montano bajo)

48 CONTIGUOUS STATES

1 Spruce-Cedar-Hemlock-Forest
Dense forests of tall needleleaf evergreen trees, rarely with an admixture of broadleaf deciduous trees
Dominants:
Picea stichensis Sitka spruce
Thuja plicata western red cedar
Tsuga heterophylla western hemlock
Other components:
Abies grandis
Alnus rubra
Chamaecyparis lawsoniana
(southern part)
Pseudotsuga menziesii

2 Cedar-Hemlock-Douglas Fir Forest
Dense forests of very tall needleleaf evergreen trees
Dominants:
Pseudotsuga menziesii Douglas fir
Thuja plicata western red cedar
Tsuga heterophylla western hemlock
Other components:
Abies grandis
Acer circinatum
Acer macrophyllum
Berberis nervosa
Gaultheria shallon
Rubus spectabilis
In southernmost part only:
Pinus lambertiana
Pinus ponderosa

3 Silver Fir-Douglas Fir Forest Dense forests of tall needleleaf evergreen trees with patches of shrubby undergrowth
Dominants:
Abies amabilis Pacific silver fir
Pseudotsuga menziesii Douglas fir
Other components:
Abies grandis
Abies procera
Acer circinatum
Arctostaphylos nevadensis
Pachystima myrsinityes
Rhododendron macrophyllum
Thuja plicata
Tsuga heterophylla
Vaccinium membranaceum

4 Fir-Hemlock Forest Dense or medium dense forests of low to medium tall needleleaf evergreen trees
Dominants:
Abies lasiocarpa subalpine fir
Tsuga mertensiana mountain hemlock
Other components:
Abies amabilis
Picea engelmannii
Pinus albicaulis
Pinus contorta
Pinus monticola
Pseudotsuga menziesii
Vaccinum spp.
Xerophyllum tenax

5 Mixed Conifer Forest Tall, needleleaf, evergreen trees, occasionally with broadleaf trees and shrubs
Dominants:
Abies concolor white fir
Librocedrus decurrens incense cedar
Pinus lambertiana sugar pine
Pinus ponderosa ponderosa pine
Pseudotsuga menziesii Douglas fir
Other components:
Arctostaphylos mariposa

Arctostaphylos patula
Ceanothus integerrimus
Chamaebatia foliolosa
Pseudotsuga macrocarpa (southern part only, where it may dominate)
Quercus chrysolepis
Quercus kelloggii
Ribes nevadense
Ribes roezlii
Rubus parviflorus

6 Redwood Forest Dense forests of very tall needleleaf, evergreen trees, sometimes with much undergrowth
Dominants:
Pseudotsuga menziesii Douglas fir
Sequoia sempervirens redwood
Other components:
Abies grandis
Gaultheria shallon
Lithocarpus densiflorus
Myrica californica
Oxalis oregona
Polystichum munitum
Rhodendron macrophyllum
Tsuga heterophylla
Vaccinium ovatum
Vancouveria parviflora
Whipplea modesta

7 Red Fir Forest Tall dense forests of needleleaf evergreen trees with patches of shrubby undergrowth
Dominants:
Abies magnifica red fir
Other components:
Castanopsis sempervirens
Ceanothus cordulatus
Ipomopsis aggregata
Pinus contorta
Pinus jeffreyi
Pinus monticola
Populus tremuloides

8 Lodgepole Pine-Subalpine Forest Fairly dense to quite open needleleaf evergreen forest; medium tall in lower elevations to krummholz in high altitudes with numerous shrubs and

herbaceous plants
Dominants:
Pinus albicaulis whitebark pine
Pinus balfouriana foxtail pine
Pinus contorta lodgepone pine
Other components:
Aquilegia pubescens
Castilleja culbertsonii
Eriogonum incanum
Pedicularis attolens
Pentstemon heterodoxus
Pinus flexilis
Potentilla breweri
Ribes cereum
Salix petrophila

9 Pine-Cypress Forest Rather dense forest of low to medium tall needleleaf evergreen trees
Dominants:
Cupressus goveniana Gowen cypress
Cupressus macrocarpa Monterey cypress
Pinus contorta lodgepone (beach) pin
Pinus muricata bishop pine
Pinus radiata Monterey pine
Other components:
Arctostaphylos nummularia
Ledum glandulosum
Xerophyllum tenax

10 Western Ponderosa Forest
Medium dense to open forest of tall needleleaf evergreen trees with a fairly open ground cover of grasses and occasional shrubs
Dominants:
Pinus ponderosa ponderosa pine
Other components:
Achillea millefolium var. lanulosa
Agropyron spicatum
Arctostaphylos nevadensis (southern part)
Arctostaphylos uva ursi
Carex geyeri
Festuca idahoensis
Hieracium spp.
Lupinus spp.

Poa secunda
Purshia tridentata
Symphoricarpos albus (northern part)

11 Douglas Fir Forest Medium dense forest of medium tall needleleaf evergreen trees
Dominants:
Pseutotsuga menziesii Douglas fir
Other components:
Abies concolor
Larix occidentalis
Physocarpus malvaceus
Picea pungens
Picea glauca (northern part)
Pinus contorta
Pinus ponderosa (lower elevations)
Populus tremuloides

12 Cedar-Hemlock-Pine Forest Tall evergreen needleleaf forest, often very dense
Dominants:
Pinus monticola western white pine
Thuja plicata western red cedar
Tsuga heterophylla western hemlock
Other components:
Abies grandis
Larix occidentalis
Pinus ponderosa (lower elevations)
Pseutotsuga menziesii

13 Grand Fir-Douglas Fir Tall, needleleaf evergreen forest
Dominants:
Abies grandis grand fir
Pseutotsuga menziesii Douglas fir
Other components:
Larix occidentalis
Pinus monticola
Populus tremuloides

14 Western Spruce-Fir Forest Dense to open forests of low to medium tall needleleaf evergreen trees; open forests with a synusia of shrubs and herbaceous plants
Dominants:
Abies lasiocarpa subalpine fir

Picea engelmannii Engelmann spruce
Other components:
Arctostaphylos uva ursi
Arnica cordifolia
Calamagrostis canadensis
Carex spp.
Larix lyallii
Menziesia ferruginea
Pinus albicaulis (northern part)
Pinus contorta
Populus tremuloides
Pseutotsuga menziesii (lower
    elevations)
Shepherdia canadensis
Symphoricarpos albus
Tsuga mertensiana (western part)
Vaccinium spp.
Xerophyllum tenax

15 Eastern Ponderosa Forest Medium
dense to open forest of low to
medium tall needleleaf evergreen
trees with a fairly open ground cover
of grasses
Dominants:
Pinus ponderosa ponderosa pine
Other components:
Agropyron smithii
Bouteloua gracilis
Stipa comata

16 Black Hills Pine Forest Open to
dense forests of tall needleleaf
evergreen trees, often with much
undergrowth
Dominants:
Pinus ponderosa ponderosa pine
Pseutotsuga menziesii Douglas fir
Other components:
Acer glabrum
Alnus tenuifolia
Aristida spp.
Blepharoneuron tricholepis
Ceanothus fendleri
Chamaebatiaria millefolium
Festuca arizonica
Holodiscus dumosus
Jamesia americana

Juniperus communis var. montana
Picea pungens
Pinus flexilis
Prunus emarginata
Ribes spp.
Salix spp.

17 Pine-Douglas Fir Forest Open to
dense forests of tall needleleaf
evergreen trees, often with much
undergrowth
Dominants:
Pinus ponderosa ponderosa pine
Pseutotsuga menziesii Douglas fir
Other components:
Acer glabrum
Alnus tenuifolia
Aristida spp.
Blepharoneuron tricholepis
Ceanothus fendleri
Chamaebatiaria millefolium
Festuca arizonica
Holodiscus dumosus
Jamesia americana
Juniperus communis var. montana
Picea pungens
Pinus flexilis
Prunus emarginata
Ribes spp.
Salix spp.

18 Arizona Pine Forest Open to
dense forest of needleleaf evergreen
trees, medium tall or tall, frequently
with a herbaceous ground cover
Dominants:
Pinus ponderosa ponderosa pine
Other components:
Aristida spp.
Blepharoneuron tricholepis
Ceanothus fendleri
Festuca arizonica
Holodiscus dumosus
Muhlenbergia montana
Physocarpus monogynus
Pinus cembroides (southern part)
Pinus flexilis (upper elevations)
Pinus leiophylla var. chihuahuana

(southern part)
Poa fendleriana
Pseutotsuga menziesii (upper
    elevations)
Quercus gambelii
Stipa spp.

19 Spruce-Fir-Douglas Fir Forest
Open to dense forest of low to
medium tall needleleaf evergreen
trees with an admixture of broadleaf
deciduous low trees and shrubs
Dominants:
Abies concolor white fir
Picea pungens blue spruce
Pseutotsuga menziesii Douglas fir
Other components:
Acer glabrum
Amelanchier alnifolia
Chamaebatiaria millefolium
Pachystima myrsinites
Physocarpus malvacea
Populus tremuloides
Prunus virginiana
Sambucus glauca
Symphoricarpos vaccinoides

20 Southwestern Spruce-Fir Forest
Dense to open stands of low to
medium tall needleleaf evergreen
trees
Dominants:
Abies lasiocarpa var. arizonica
    corkbark fir
Picea engelmannii Engelmann spruce
Other components:
Abies lasiocarpa
Acer glabrum
Juniperus communis
Pachystima myrsinites
Pinus aristata
Pinus flexilis
Populus tremuloides
Ribes spp.
Salix bebbiana
Sambucus racemosa
Symphoricarpos vaccinoides

21 Juniper-Pinyon Woodland
Open
groves of low needleleaf evergreen
trees with varying admixtures of
shrubs and herbaceous plants
Dominants:
Juniperus monosperma oneseed
    juniper
Juniperus osteosperma Utah juniper
Pinus edulis pinyon pine (more in
    eastern part)
Pinus monophylla oneleaf pine (more
    in western part)
Other components:
Agropyron smithii
Artemisia tridentata (not in southern
    part)
Juniperus occidentalis
Artemisia arbuscula
Balsamorrhiza sagittata
Festuca idahoensis
Lithospermum ruderale
Lupinus sericeus
Poa secunda
Purshia tridentata
Sitanion spp.

22 Oregon Oakwoods
Broadleaf
deciduous forests of medium tall
trees, often with an undergrowth of
grass and some shrubs
Dominants:
Quercus garryana Oregon white oak
Other components:
Agrostis tenuis
Amelanchier spp.
Arbutus menziesii (southern part)
Bromus laevipes
Danthonia californica
Elymus glaucus
Festuca californica
Festuca rubra
Melica bulbosa
Rhus diversiloba

23 Mesquite Bosques Open to dense forests of low, broadleaf deciduous trees
Dominants:
Prosopis juliflora var. velutina mesquite
Other components:
Acacia greggii
Baccharis emoryi
Baccharis glutinosa
Cercidium floridum
Clematis neomesicana
Cucurbita digitata
Cucurbita foetidissima
Dalea spinosa
Hymenoclea monogyra
Lycium spp.
Olneya tesota
Populus fremontii
Prosopis pubescens
Salix gooddingii

24 Mosaic of Cedar-Hemlock-Douglas Fir Forest (2) and Oregon Oakwoods (26)

25 California Mixed Evergreen Forest
Medium tall to tall broadleaf and needleleaf evergreen forest with an admixture of broadleaf deciduous trees
Dominants:
Arbutus menziesii madrone
Castanopsis chrysophylla golden chinquapin
Lithocarpus densiflorus tanbark oak
Pseutotsuga menziesii Douglas fir
Quercus chrysolepis canyon live oak
Quercus wislizenii interior live oak
Umbellularia californica California laurel
Other components:
Acer macrophyllum
Aesculus californica
Arctostaphylos manzanita
Ceanothus aprryi
Ceanothus thyrsiflorus
Cornus nutallii

Quercus douglasii
Quercus garryana
Quercus kelloggii

26 California Oakwoods Medium tall or low broadleaf evergreen or semideciduous forests with an admixture of low to medium tall needleleaf evergreen trees
Dominants:
Pinus coulteri Coulter pine (higher elevations)
Pinus sabiniana digger pine
Quercus agrifolia coast live oak
Quercus chrysolepis canyon live oak
Quercus douglasii blue oak
Quercus lobata valley oak
Quercus wislizenii interior live oak
Other components:
Aesculus californica
Ceanothus cuneatus
Cercis occidentalis
Eriodyction californicum
Juglans californica (southern part)
Quercus englemannii (southern part)
Rhamnus californica
Rhus integrifolia (southern part)
Rhus ovata (southern part)
Ribes quercetorum
Umbellularia californica

27 Oak-Juniper Woodland Low open to dense forest of broadleaf and needleleaf evergreen trees and varying undergrowth
Dominants:
Juniperus deppeana alligator juniper
Juniperus monosperma oneseed juniper
Quercus emoryi Emory oak
Quercus oblongifolia Mexican blue oak (western part)
Other components:
Arctostaphylos pungens
Bouteloua curtipendula
Bouteloua gracilia
Bouteloua hirsuta
Ceanothus spp.

Cowania mexicana
Dasylirion wheeleri
Garrya spp.
Nolina microcarpa
Nolina texana
Pinus cembroides (higher elevations)
Pinus leiophylla var. chihuahuana
  (higher elevations)
Quercus grisea
Quercus hypoleucoides
Quercus turbinella
Quercus undulata
Rhus choriophylla
Rhus microphylla
Yucca schottii

28 Transition between Oak-Juniper
Woodland (27) and Mountain
Mahogany-Oak Scrub (31)

29 Chaparral Very dense vegetation
of broadleaf evergreen sclerophyll
shrubs
Dominants:
Adenostoma fasciculatum chamise
Arctostaphylos spp. manzanita
Ceanothus spp. California lilac
Other components:
Arctostaphylos glandulosa
Arctostaphylos glauca (southern part)
Arctostaphylos manzanita (northern
  part)
Arctostaphylos parryana
Arctostaphylos pungens (southern
  part)
Arctostaphylos viscida (northern part)
Ceanothus cuneatus
Ceanothus foliosus
Ceanothus impressus
Ceanothus integerrimus
Ceanothus leucodermis
Ceanothus sorediatus
Ceanothus spinosus
Ceanothus thyrsiflorus
Ceanothus velutinus
Cercocarpus betuloides
Fremontia californica
Heteromeles arbutifolia
Pickeringia montant

Prunus ilicifolia
Quercus dumosa
Rhamnus californica
Rhamnus corcea
Trichostema lanatum
Yucca whipplei (southern part)
Pinus lambertiana
Pinus ponderosa
Quercus kellogii
Quercus vaccinifolia

30 Coastal Sagebrush Moderately
dense vegetation of broadleaf
evergreen shrubs, rarely more than
1.5 meters tall
Dominants:
Eriogonum fasciculatum California
  buckwheat
Salvia apiana white sage
Salvia mellifera black sage
Other components:
Artemisia californica
Encelia californica
Eriophyllum confertiflorum
Haplopappus squarrosus
Haplopappus venetus
Horkelia cuneata
Rhus integrifolia
Salvia leucophylla

31 Mountain Mahogany-Oak Scrub
Dense to open vegetation of
deciduous or semideciduous shrubs
Dominants:
Cercocarpus ledifolius mountain
  mahogany
Quercus gambelii Gamble oak
Other components:
Acer grandidentatum
Amelanchier utahensis
Arctostaphylos spp.
Ceanothus velutinus
Cowania mexicana
Fallugia paradoxa
Pachystima myrsinites
Physocarupu malvaceus
Purshia trindentata
Quercus harvardii

Quercus turbinella
Quercus undulata
Rhus trilobata
Symphoricarpos spp.

32 Great Basin Sagebrush Fairly dense to open vegetation of low to medium tall shrubs
Dominants:
Artemisia tridentata big sagebrush
Other components:
Agropyron smithii (northern part)
Artemisia nova
Atriplex confertifolia (southern part)
Astragalus spp. (southern part)
Chrysothamnus spp. (southern part)
Coleogyne spp. (southern part)
Ephedra spp.
Eriogonum spp.
Lupinus spp.
Phacelia spp.
Tetradynia spp.

33 Blackbrush Dense to open stands of broadleaf evergreen shurbs, frequently with an open understory of grass
Dominants:
Coleogyne ramosissima blackbrush
Other components:
Artemisia tridentata
Ephedra spp.
Gutierrezia sarothrae
Haplopappus linearifolius
Hilaria jamesii

34 Saltbrush-Greasewood Open stands of low shrubs and dwarf shrubs
Dominants:
Atriplex confertifolia shadscale
Sarcobatus vermiculatus greasewood
Other components:
Allenrolifea occidentalis
Artemisia spinescens
Atriplex spp.
Distichlis spicatum
Eurotia lanata
Grayia spinosa

Kochia anericana
Lycium cooperi
Menodora spinescens (western part)
Suaeda torreyana

35 Creosote Open stands of low to medium tall shrubs and dwarf shrubs
Dominants:
Larrea divaricata creosote bush
Other components:
Baccharis sergiloides
Encelia farinosa
Franseria dumosa
Lycium andersonii
Sphaeralcea ambigua

36 Creosote Bush-Bur Sage Open stands of shrubs and dwarf shrubs
Dominants:
Franseria dumosa white bur sage
Larrea divaricata creosote bush
Other components:
Acacia greggii
Cercidium floridum
Cercidium microphyllum
Dalea californica
Dalea spinosa
Encelia farinosa
Ferrocactus acanthodes
Fouquiera splendens
Franseria deltoidea
Hilaria rigida
Lycium brevipes
Olneya tesota
Opuntia echinocarpa
Opuntia ramosissima
Opuntia wrightiana
Prosopis juliflora var. velutina

37 Palo Verde-Cactus Shrub Open to dense vegetation of shrubs and low trees, often with many succulants
Dominants:
Cercidium microphyllum Palo verde
Opuntia spp. prickly pear
Other components:
Acacia constricta
Acacia greggii

Calliandra eriophyllua
Celtis pallida
Cercidium floridum
Cereus giganteus
Condalia lycioides
Condalia spathulata
Echinocereus engelmannii
Encelia farinosa
Ephedra trifurca
Ferocactus wislizenii
Fouquiera splendens
Franseria deltoidea
Franseria fomosa
Janusia gracilis
Jatrophya cardiophylla
Larrea divaricata
Lycium spp.
Olneya tesota
Opuntia engelmannii
Opuntia fulgida
Opuntia spinosior
Opuntia versicolor
Prosopis juliflora var. velutina
Simmondsia chinensis

38 Ceniza Shrub Open to dense stands of broadleaf deciduous and evergreen shrubs with a patchy synusia of grass
Dominants:
Larrea divaricata creosote bush
Leucophyllum frutescens ceniza
Prosopis juliflora var. glandulosa mesquite
Other components:
Acacia spp.
Bouteloua spp.
Cercidium macrum
Condalia spp.
Dasylirion leiophyllum
Hilaria mutica
Opuntia spp.
Scleropogon brevifloius

39 Desert Vegetation largely absent

40 Fescue-Oatgrass Dense, medium tall meadow-like grassland
Dominants:
Carex tumulicola sedge
Danthonia californica oatgrass
Deschampsia holciformis hairgrass
Festuca idahoensis Idaho fescue
Other components:
Agrostis hallii
Brodiaea pulchella
Calamagrostis nutakensis
Calochortus luteus
Chrysopsis bolanderi
Grindelia hirsutula
Iris douglasiana
Lupinus formosus
Lupinus variicolor
Pteridium aquilinum var. pubescens
Ranunculus californicus
Sanicola acrtopoides
Sisyrinchium ellum
Stipa lepida

41 California Steppe Dense to medium dense, low to medium tall grassland
Dominants:
Stipa cernus needlegrass
Stipa pulchra speargrass
Other components:
Aristida divaricata
Avena spp. (annual species only)
Bromus (annual species only)
Elymus glaucus
Elymus triticoides
Eschscholtzia californica
Festuca (annual species only)
Gilia spp.
Lupinus bicolor
Lupinus luteolus
Melica spp.
Orthocarpus spp.
Plagiogothrys nothofulvus
Poa scabrella
Sisyrinchium bellum
Stipa coronata (southern part)
Stipa lepida

42 Tule Marshes Tall graminoid vegetation
Dominants:
Scirpus acutus common tule
Scirpus californicus California bulrush
Scirpus olneyi Olneyi bulrush
Scirpus validus tule
Typha domingensis cattail
Typha latifolia soft flag, cattail
Other components:
Carex senta
Heleocharis palustris
Typha angustifolia

43 Fescue-Wheatgrass Dense, low to medium tall grassland

Dominants:
Agropyron spicatum bluebunch
  wheatgrass
Festuca idahoensis Idaho fescue
Other components:
Achille millefolium var. lanulosa
Artemisia tripartita
Cllinsia parviflora
Hieracium albertinum
Lupinus sericeus
Potentilla balschkeana
Rosa nutkana
Rosa woodsii
Symphoricarpos albus

44 Wheatgrass-Bluegrass Dense, low to medium tall grassland
Dominants:
Agropyron spicatum bluebunch
  wheatgrass
Festuca idahoensis Idaho fescue
Poa secunda sandberg bluegrass
Other components:
Achille millefolium var. lanulosa
Astragalus spp.
Chrysothamnus nauseosus
Draba verna
Festuca pacifica
Lithophragma bulbifera
Lupinus sericeus
Plantago purshii

Stellaria nitens

45 Alpine Meadows and Barren Low to medium tall grassland with few woody plants
Dominants:
Argostis spp. bentgrass
Carex spp. sedges
Deschampsia caespitosa hairgrass
Festuca viridula fescue
Luzula spicata woodrush
Phleum alpinum mountain timothy
Poa spp. bluegrass
Trisetum spicatum spike trisetum
Other components:
Achillea spp.
Atennaria spp.
Aquilegia spp.
Arenaria spp.
Castilleja spp.
Draba spp.
Erigeron compositus
Oxyria digyna
Pentstemon fruticosus
Phacelia spp.
Phlox caespitosa
Polemonium spp.
Polygonum spp.
Potentilla diversifolia
Salix nivalis
Salix spp.
Saxifraga spp.
Selaginella spp.
Sibbaldia procumbens
Sieversia turbinata
Solidago spp.

46 Fescue-Mountain Muhly Prairie Dense, low to medium tall grassland
Dominants:
Festuca spp.
Muhlenbergia spp.

47 Grama-Galleta Steppe Low to medium tall grassland with few woody plants
Dominants:
Bouteloua gracilis blue grama

Hilaria jamesii galleta
Other components:
Andropogon hallii
Andropogon scoparius
Artemisis tridentata
Astragalus spp.
Atriplex canescens
Bouteloua curtipendula
Bouteloua hirsuta
Ephedra viridis
Opuntia whipplei
Oryzopsis hymenoides
Tetradymia spp.
Yucca glauca

48 Grama-Tobosa Prairie Open grassland of rather low growth with scattered succlents, etc.
Dominants:
Bouteloua gracilis blue grama
Hilaria mutica tobosa
Other components:
Bouteloua curtipendula
Bouteloua eriopoda
Bouteloua hirsuta
Gutierrezia spp.
Muhlenbergia spp.
Opuntia imbricata
Tridens pilosus
Yucca spp.

49 Sagebrush Steppe Dense to open grassland with dense to open shrub synusia
Dominants:
Agropyron spicatum bluebunch wheatgrass
Artemisia tridentata big sagebrush
Other components:
Artemisia arbuscula (western part)
Artemisia nova (eastern part)
Balsamorrhiza sagittata
Festuca idahoensis
Lithospermum ruderale
Lupinus sericeus
Oryzopsis hymenoides
Phlox spp.
Poa nevadensis

Poa secunda
Purshia tridentata
Sitanion spp.

50 Wheatgrass-Needlegrass Shrubsteppe Open grasslands, sometimes fairly dense, with scattered dwarf shrubs
Dominants:
Agropyron smithii western wheatgrass
Artemisia tridentata big sagebrush
Poa arida plains bluegrass
Stipa comata needle-and-thread grass
Other components:
Agropyron spicatum
Artemisia cana
Artemisia frigida
Atriplex canescens
Atriplex confertifolia
Carex filifolia
Curotia lanata
Koeleria cristata
Sarcobatus vermiculatus

51 Galleta-Three Awn Shrubsteppe Open grassland with low shrubs
Dominants:
Aristida longiseta three awn
Artemisia filifolia sandsage
Ephedra viridis Mormon tea
Hilaria jamesii galleta
Other components:
Aster cichoriaceus
Berberis fremontii
Bouteloua gracilis
Chrysopsis villosa
Chrysothamnus nauseosus
Chrysothamnus viscidiflorus
Ephedra torreyana
Euploca convolvulacea
Franseria acanthicarpa
Helianthys anomalus
Mentzelia pumila
Muhlenbergia pungens
Monroa squarrosa
Oenothera albicaulis
Oryzopsis hymenoides
Poliomintha incana

Quercus undulata
Sphaeralcea grossulariaefolia
Sporobolus cryptandrus
Stephanomeria pauciflora

52 Grama-Tobosa Shrubsteppe Short
grasses with a shrub synusia varying
from very open to dense
Dominants:
Bouteloua eriopoda black grama
Hilaria mutica tobosa
Larrea divaricata creosote bush
Other components:
Acacia constricta
Andropogon barbinodis
Aristida divaricata
Aristida glabrata
Aristida hamulosa
Aristida longiseta
Astragalus spp.
Baileya multiradiata
Bouteloua curtipendula
Bouteloua gracilis
Bouteloua spp.
Gutierrezia sarothrae
Hilaria belangeri
Hilaria jamesii
Mentzelia spp.
Muhlengergia porteri
Opuntia spp.
Prosopis juliflora var. torreyana
Sphaeralcea spp.
Sporobolus airoides
Sporobolus cryptandrus
Sporobolus flexuosus
Yucca baccata
Yucca elata
Zinnia grandiflora
Zinnia pumila

53 Trans-Pecos Shrub Savanna Shrubs
and dwarf shrubs, dense to scattered,
with short grass
Dominants:
Flourensis cernua tarbush
Larrea divaricata creosote bush
Other components:

Acacia constricta
Acacia greggii
Agave lechuguilla
Aristida spp.
Bouteloua breviseta
Bouteloua trifida
Dasylirion leiophyllum
Fouquiera splendens
Hilaria mutica
Muhlenbergia porteri
Muhlenbergia spp.
Opuntia spp.
Prosopis juliflora var. glandulosa
Scleropogon brevifolius
Yucca spp.

54 Mesquite-Acacia Oak Savanna
Dense to open grassland with
broadleaf deciduous low trees and
shrubs scattered singly or in groves
Dominants:
Acacia rigidula blackgrush acacia
Andropogon littoralis seacoast
   bluestem
Prosopsis juliflora var. glandulosa
   Mesquite
Setaria macrostachya plains bristle
   grass
Other components:
Acacia berlandieri
Acacia spp.
Andropogon saccharoides
Andropogon scoparius (eastern part)
Aristida spp.
Bouteloua filiformis (western part)
Bouteloua hirsuta
Buchloë dactyloides
Cenchrus myosuroides
Chloris spp.
Condalia spp.
Heteropogon contortus
Hilaria belangeri
Opuntia spp.
Pappophorum bicolor
Paspalum spp.
Sorghastrum nutans
Quercus virginiana
Trichloris spp.

55 Mesquite-Live Oak Savanna

Rather open medium tall grass with low to medium tall broadleaf evergreen trees and low broadleaf deciduous trees and shrubs, scattered singly or in groves

Dominants:

Andropogon littoralis seacoast bluestem

Prosopis juliflora var. glandulosa mesquite

Quercus virginiana var. maritima sand live oak

Other components:

Aristida roemeriana
Heteropogon contortus
Panicum virgatum
Paspalum spp.
Sorghastrum nutans
Trachypogon secundus

56 Foothills Prairie
Open to fairly dense grassland of usually rather short grasses

Dominants:

Agropyron spicatum bluebunch wheatgrass
Festuca idahoensis Idaho fescue
Festuca scabrella rough fescue
Stipa comata needle-and-thread grass

Other components:

Achillea millefolium
Agropyron smithii
Artemisia frigida
Bouteloua gracilis
Carex filifolia
Eriogonum spp.
Koeleria cristata
Pentstemon spp.
Poa secunda

57 Grama-Needlegrass-Wheatgrass

Rather short, open to fairly dense grassland

Dominants:

Agropyron smithii western wheatgrass
Bouteloua gracilis blue grama
Stipa comata needle-and-thread grass

Other components:

Agropyron spicatum
Andropogon scoparius
Artemisia frigida
Carex filifolia
Chrysopsis villosa
Gutierrezia sarothrae
Koeleria cristata
Liatris punctata
Muhlenbergia cuspidata
Poa secunda
Stipa viridula

58 Grama-Buffalo Grass
Fairly dense grassland of short grass with somewhat taller grasses in the eastern sections

Dominants:

Bouteloua gracilis blue grama
Buchloë dactyloides buffalo grass

Other components:

Agropyron smithii
Aristida purpurea
Bouteloua curtipendula
Bouteloua hirsuta
Gaura coccinea
Grindelia squarrosa
Haplopappus spinulosus
Lycurus phleoides
Muhlenbergia torreyi
Opuntia spp. (southern part)
Plantago purshii
Psoralea tenuiflora
Ratibida columinifera
Senecio spp.
Sitanion hystrix
Sphaeralcea coccinea
Sporobolus cryptandrus
Yucca glauca
Zinnia grandiflora

59 Wheatgrass-Needlegrass

Moderately dense, short or medium tall grassland

Dominants:

Agropyron smithii western wheatgrass
Bouteloua gracilis blue grama

Stipa comata needle-and-thread grass
Stipa viridula green needlegrass (not
  in CO)
Other components:
Agropyron trachycaulum
Antennaria spp.
Artemisia frigida
Carex spp.
Koeleria cristata
Mertensia spp.
Oryzopsis hymenoides
Pentstemon spp.
Plains only:
Andropogon scoparius
Artemisia dranuncula
Artemisia ludoviciana
Aster ericoides
Echinacea angustifolia
Liatris punctata
Psoralea argophylla
Solidage spp.
Stipa spartea
Colorado only:
Chrysothamnus viscidiflorus
Festuca arizonica
Muhlenbergia montana
Tetradymia canescens

60 Wheatgrass-Bluestem-Needlegrass
Dense, medium tall to tall grassland
Dominants:
Agropyron smithii western wheatgrass
Agropyron gerardi big bluestem
Stipa spartea needlegrass
Other components:
Agropyron trachycaulum
Andropogon scoparius
Artemisia frigida
A. ludoviciana
Aster ericoides
Bouteloua curtipendula
Bouteloua gracilis
Echinacea angustifolia
Koeleria cristata
Liatris punctata
Psoralea argophylla
Rosa arkansana

Solidago missouriensis
Solidago mollis
Stipa comata
Stipa viridula

61 Wheatgrass-Grama-Buffalo Grass
Short to medium tall grasses
Dominants:
Agropyron smithii western wheatgrass ·
Bouteloua gracilis blue grama
Buchloë dactyloides buffalo grass

62 Bluestem-Grama Prairie Dense,
medium tall grassland with many
forbs
Dominants:
Andropogon scoparius little bluestem
Bouteloua curtipendula side-oats
  grama
Bouteloua gracilis blue grama
Other components:
Agropyron smithii
Ambrosia stilostachya
Amorpha canescens
Andropogon gerardi
Buchloë dactyloides
Clematis fremontii
Dalea enneandra
Echinacea angustifolia
Erysimum asperum
Hedeoma hispida
Liatris punctata
Oenothera serrulata
Panicum virgatum
Paronychia jamesii
Psoralea tenuifolia
Scutellaria resinosa
Sorghastrum nutans
Sporobolus asper
Stenosiphon linifolius

63 Sandsage-Bluestem Prairie
Medium tall, medium dense grassland
with strong element of dwarf shrubs
Dominants:
Andropogon hallii sand bluestem
Andropogon scoparius little bluestem
Artemisia filifolia sandsage

Bouteloua hirsuta hairy grama
Other components:
Bouteloua gracilis
Buchloë dactyloides
Calamovilfa longifolia
Eragrostis trichodes
Helianthus petiolaris
Hordeum jubatum
Panicum virgatum
Redfieldia flexuosa
Sporobolus cryptandrus
Stipa comata
Yucca glauca

64 Shinnery Midgrass prairie with open to dense broadleaf deciduous shrubs and occasional needleleaf evergreen low trees or shrubs
Dominants:
Andropogon scoparius little bluestem
Quercus mohriana shin oak
Other components:
Acacia spp.
Andropogon hallii
Aristida spp.
Artemisia filifolia
Bouteloua gracilis
Bouteloua hirsuta
Buchloë dactyloides
Celtis reticulata
Cenchrus spp.
Eriogonum annum
Juniperus pinchotii
Prosopis juliflora var. glandulosa
Prunus angustifolia
Quercus havardii
Rhus aromatica var. pilosissima
Rhus trilobata
Sorghastrum nutans
Sporobolus cryptandrus
Yucca glauca

65 Northern Cordgrass Prairie
Usually dense, medium tall grassland
Dominants:
Distichlis spicata seashore saltgrass
Spartina alterniflora smooth cordgrass
Spartina patens saltmeadow cordgrass

Other components:
Gerardina maritima
Juncus gerardi
Limonium carolinianum
Plantago decipiens
Salcornia spp.
Triclochin maritima

66 Bluestem Prairie Dense vegetation of tall grasses and many forbs
Dominants:
Andropogon gerardi big bluestem
Andropogon scoparius little bluestem
Panicum virgatum switchgrass
Sorghastrum nutans Indian grass
Other components:
Amorpha canescens
Antennaria neglecta
Aster ericoides
Aster laevis
Baptisia leucantha
Baptisia leucophaea
Bouteloua curtipendula
Erigeron strigosus
Galium tinctorum
Helianthus grosseserratus
Koeleria cristata
Liatris aspera
Liatris punctata
Liatris scarriosa
Panicum leibergii
Panicum scribnerianum
Phlox pilosa
Psoralea argophylla
Psoralea floribunda
Ratibida columnifera
Ratibida pinnata
Rosa arkansana
Silphium laciniatum
Solidago altissima
Solidago missouriensis
Solidago rigida
Sporobolus heterolepis (northern part)
Stipa spartea (northern part)

67 Sandhills Prairie Medium dense to open grassland, tall to medium tall

Dominants:
Andropogon gerardi big bluestem
Andropogon hallii sand bluestem
Andropogon scoparius little bluestem
Calamovilfa longifolia sandreed
Stipa comata needle-and-thread grass
Other components:
Artemisia canadensis
Asclepias arenaria
Carex heliophila
Eragrostis trichodes
Erigeron spp.
Gilia longifolia
Oryzopsis hymenoides
Panicum virgatum
Petalostemum villosum
Sporobolus cryptandrus

68 Blackland Prairie Medium tall,
rather dense grassland
Dominants:
Andropogon scoparius little bluestem
Stipa leucotricha Texas needlegrass
Other components:
Andropogon gerardi
Andropogon saccharoides
Aristida purpurea
Bouteloua curtipendula
Bouteloua hirsuta
Bouteloua rigidiseta
Buchloë dactyloides
Panicum virgatum
Sorghastrum nutans
Sporobolus asper

69 Bluestem-Sacahuista Prairie
Medium tall, rather dense grassland

70 Southern Cordgrass Prairie
Medium tall to very tall grassland,
often very dense
Dominants:
Spartina alterniflora smooth cordgrass
Other components:
Carex spp.
Distichlis spicata
Juncus effusus
Juncus roemerianus
Mariscus jamaicensis

Panicum hemitomon
Panicum repens
Panicum virgatum
Phragmites communis
Sagittaria spp.
Scirpus americanus
Scirpus californicus
Scirpus olneyi
Scirpus validus
Spartina cynosuroides
Spartina patens
Spartina spartinae
Typha domingensis
Zizaniopsis miliacea

71 Palmetto Prairie Dense, medium
tall grasses with scattered palms and
shrubs
Dominants:
Aristida stricta wiregrass
Serenoa repens saw palmetto
Other components:
Andropogon spp.
Aristida spiciformis
Axonopus compressus
Axonopus furcatus
Lyonia fruticosa
Lyonia mitida
Paspalum distichum
Sabal palmetto
Vaccinium myrsinites

72 Oak Savanna Tall grass prairie
with broadleaf deciduous trees
scattered singly or in groves
Dominants:
Andropogon gerardi big bluestem
Andropogon scoparius little bluestem
Quercus macrocarpa bur oak
Other components:
Amphicarpa bracteata
Calamovilfa longifolia (in ND)
Carya ovata
Comandra richardsiana
Euphorbia corollata
Fraxinus pennsylvanica (in ND)
Monadra fistulosa
Panicum leibergii

Quercus alba
Quercus ellipsoidalis
Quercus velutina
Rosa spp.
Sorghastrum nutans
Sporobolus heterolepis
Stipa spartea

73 Mosaic of Oak-Hickory Forest (91) in Bluestem Prairie (66) A true mosaic (not a transition zone) of the two types, containing dominants and other components characteristic of those two types. See the composition descriptions of 66 and 91 for lists of species present in 73.

74 Cedar Glades Low to medium tall open grassland with scattered needleleaf evergreen shrubs and groves of low to medium tall broadleaf deciduous trees
Dominants:
Celtis laevigata hackberry (eastern part)
Juniperus virginiana red cedar
Quercus stellata post oak (western part)
Sporobolus neglectus poverty grass (western part)
Sporobolus vaginiflorus poverty grass (eastern part)
Ulmus alata winged elm (eastern part)
Other components:
Andropogon gerardi
Andropogon scoparius
Arenaria patula
Aristida longispica (eastern part)
Bouteloua curtipendula
Bumelia lanuginosa
Carya glabra
Celtis tenuifolia
Cercis canadensis
Cheilanthes lanosa
Croton monanthogynus
Forestiera langustrina (eastern part)
Leavenworthia spp.
Palafoxia callosa
Petalostemum purpureum

Pleurochaete squarrosa (eastern part)
Psoralea spp.
Quercus marilandica
Quercus muhlenbergii
Quercus velutina
Rhus aromatica
Sedum pulchellum
Symphoricarpos orbiculatus

75 Cross Timbers Medium tall grass with broadleaf deciduous trees scattered singly or in extensive groves
Dominants:
Andropogon scoparius little bluestem
Quercus marilandica blackjack oak
Other components:
Andropogon gerardi
Bouteloua curtipendula
Bouteloua hirsuta
Carya texana
Celtis spp.
Elymus canadensis
Eragostis spectabilis
Eragostis trichodes
Panicum scribnerianum
Panicum virgatum
Sorghastrum nutans
Sporobolus asper
Stipa leucotricha
Ulmus crassifolia (southern part)

76 Mesquite-Buffalo Grass Short grass with scattered low broadleaf deciduous trees and shrubs and low needleleaf evergreen shrubs
Dominants:
Buchloë dactyloides buffalo grass
Prosopsis juliflora var. glandulosa
Mesquite (southern part)
Other components:
Acacia greggii
Aristida purpurea
A. roemeriana
Bouteloua gracilis
Bouteloua hirsuta
Bouteloua trifida
Condalia obovata
Juniperus pinchotii

Juniperus virginiana (northeastern part)
Quercus virginiana var. fusiformis
Schedonnardus paniculatus
Yucca glauca

77 Juniper-Oak Savanna Savanna with a dense to very open synusia of broadleaf deciduous and evergreen low trees and shrubs and needleleaf evergreen low trees and shrubs
Dominants:
Andropogon scoparius little bluestem
Juniperus ashei ash juniper
Quercus virginiana live oak
Other components:
Andropogon gerardi (eastern part)
Aristida glauca
Aristida intermedia
Aristida purpurea
Bouteloua curtipendula (western part)
Bouteloua hirsuta
Buchloë dactyloides
Cercis canadensis var. texensis (eastern part)
Fraxinus texensis
Hilaria belangeri (western part)
Leptochloa dubia (western part)
Panicum obtusum (western part)
Quercus durandii var. breviloba
Quercus shumardii var. texana
Sorghastrum nutans (eastern part)
Sporobolus spp.
Tridens pilosus

78 Mesquite-Oak Savanna Low to medium tall grass with broadleaf deciduous shrubs and low trees scattered openly to densely
Dominants:
Andropogon scoparius little bluestem
Prosopis juliflora var. glandulosa Mesquite
Quercus spp. oak
Other components:
Aloysia ligustrina
Andropogon barbinodis
Aristida purpurea
Bouteloua curtipendula

Bouteloua hirsuta
Bouteloua rigidiseta
Brayodendron texanum
Buchloë dactyloides
Juniperus ashei
Quercus marilandica
Quercus stellata
Ulmus crassifolia

79 Fayette Prairie Medium tall, rather densegrassland with scattered open groves of broadleaf deciduous trees
Dominants:
Andropogon scoparius little bluestem
Buchloë dactyloides buffalo grass
Other components:
Andropogon saccgaroides
Andropogon ternarius
Aristida purpurea
Andropogon roemeriana
Paspalum dilatatum
Paspalum plicatulum
Stipa leucotricha
Groves of trees are oak-hickory (91)

80 Blackbelt Tall or medium tall broadleaf deciduous forest with concentrations of low needleleaf evergreen trees and patches of bluestem prairie (66)
Dominants:
Juniperus virginiana red cedar
Liquidambar styraciflua sweetgum
Quercus stellata post oak
Other components:
Carya spp.
Fraxinum americana
Liriodendron tuliperfera
Nyssa sylvatica
Quercus alba
Quercus falcata
Quercus muhlenbergii
Ulmus alata

81 Live Oak-Sea Oats Irregular, varying from open grasslands to dense shrub and groves of low broadleaf evergreen trees

Dominants:

Quercus virginiana var. maritima
sand live oak

Uniola paniculata sea oats

Other components:

Baccharis halimifolia
Cenchrus tribuloides
Croton punctatus
Ilex vomitoria
Iva frutescens
Juncus roemerianus
Myrica cerifera
Myrica pensylvanica
Opuntia spp.
Panicum amarum
Sabal palmetto
Salsola kali
Serenoa repens
Spartina alterniflora
Spartina patens
Yucca aloifolia

82 Cypress Savanna Open forest to
savanna with needleleaf deciduous
trees and some broadleaf evergreen
or deciduous trees and shrubs; trees
and shrubs also occur in groves
surrounded by open grassland

Dominants:

Aristida affinia three awn
Aristida patula three awn
Taxodium distichum bald cypress

Other components:

Acer rubrum var. drummondii
Annona glabra
Blechnum serrulatum
Cyperus haspan
Hypericum fasciculatum
Ilex cassine
Leersia hexandra
Magnolia virginiana
Mariscus jamaicensis
Myrica cerifera
Persea borbonia
Rhynchospora filifolia
Salix caroliniana
Saururus cernuus

Spartina bakeri
Stillingia aquatica
Taxodium distichum var. nutans
Tillandsia utriculata
Utricularia juncea

83 Everglades Medium tall to tall
grassland with scattered groves
(bayheads) of low to medium tall
broadleaf evergreen trees and shrubs

Grassland

Dominants:

Mariscus jamaicensis sawgrass

Other components:

Aristida affinia
Aristida patula
Boehmeria cylindrica
Cephalanthus occidentalis
Eleocharis spp.
Eragrostis elliottii
Erigeron quercifolius
Myrica cerifera
Osmunda regalis
Panicum hemitomon
Peltandra virginica
Polygonum acre
Pontederia spp.
Rhynchospora spp.
Sagittaria lancifolia
Salix caroliniana
Sambucus simpsonii
Scirpus spp.
Spartina bakeri
Typha angustifolia

Bayheads

Dominants:

Magnolia virginiana sweet bay
Persea borbonia red bay

Other components:

Annona glabra
Chrysobalanus icaco
Dryopteris spp.
Ilex cassine
Myrica cerifera
Osmunda cinnamomea
Osmunda regalis
Persea humilis

Rapanea guianensis
Sabal palmetto
Smilax laurifolia

84 Great Lakes Spruce-Fir Forest
Dense needleleaf evergreen forests, sometimes low but usually medium tall, with modest admixtures of broadleaf deciduous trees
Dominants:
Abies balsamea balsam fir
Picea glauca white spruce
Other components:
Acer rubrum
Acer spicatum
Betula papyrifera
Pinus resinosa
Pinus strobus
Populus tremuloides
Sorbus americana
Thuja occidentalis

85 Conifer Bog
Dense to open, low to medium tall forests of needleleaf evergreen or deciduous trees, often with dense undergrowth
Dominants:
Larix laricina larch
Picea mariana black spruce
Thuja occidentalis arbor vitae/white cedar
Other components:
Acer rubrum
Carex spp.
Chamaedaphne caliculata
Ilex verticillata
Kalmia polifolia
Ledum groenlandicum
Nemopanthus mucronatua
Sphagnum spp.

86 Great Lakes Pine Forest
Low to tall needleleaf evergreen forest, often with a synusia of broadleaf deciduous trees and shrubs
Dominants:
Pinus bankaiana Jack pine
Pinus resinosa red pine
Pinus strobus white pine

Other components:
Kalmis angustifolia
Populus grandidentata
Populus tremuloides
Quercus alba (southern part)
Quercus coccinea
Quercus ellipsoidalis
Quercus rubra
Quercus velutina

87 Northeastern Spruce-Fir Forest
Dense needleleaf evergreen forest, low to medium tall, with stunted growth in high altitudes, with a modest mixture of broadleaf deciduous trees
Dominants:
Abies balsamea balsam fir
Picea rubens red spruce
Other components:
Acer rubrum
Betula papyrifera
Betula populifolia
Populus grandidentata
Populus tremuloides
Sorbus americana

88 Southeastern Spruce-Fir Forest
Dense needleleaf evergreen low to medium tall forest, often with shrubby undergrowth
Dominants:
Abies fraseri Fraser fir
Picea rubens red spruce
Other components:
Acer spicatum
Rhododendron catawbiense
Rhubus canadensis
Sorbus americana

89 Northern Floodplain Forest
Low to tall broadleaf deciduous forest, open to dense, often with lianas
Dominants:
Populus deltoides cottonwood
Salix nigra black willow
Ulmus americana American elm
Other components:
Acer negundo

Acer rubrum
Acer saccharinum
Betula nigra (eastern part)
Celastrus scandens
Celtis occidentalis
Clematis virginiana
Fraxinus americana
Fraxinu pennsylvanica
Gleditsia triacanthos
Juglans nigra (southern part)
Parthenocissus quinquefolia
Platanus occidentalis (southern part)
Populus sargentii
Rhus radicans
Salix amygdaloides
Salix interior
Smila hispida
Symphoricarpos orbiculatus
Ulmus rubra

90 Maple-Basswood Forest Medium tall, broadleaf deciduous forest
Dominants:
Acer saccharum sugar maple
Tilia americana basswood
Other components:
Acer negundo
Carya cordiformis
Fraxinus pennsylvanica
Ostrya virginiana
Quercus macrocarpa
Quercus rubra
Ulmus americana
Ulmus rubra

91 Oak-Hickory Forest Medium to tall broadleaf deciduous forest
Dominants:
Carya cordiformis bitternut hickory
Carya ovata shagbark hickory
Quercus alba white oak
Quercus rubra northern red oak
Quercus velutina black oak
Other components:
Carya glabra
Carya texana (southern part)
Carya tomentosa (southern part)
Fraxinus americana

Juglans nigra
Prunus serotina
Quercus ellipsoidalis (northern part)
Quercus falcata (southern part)
Quercus imbricaria (northern part)
Quercus lyrata (southern part)
Quercus marilandica (southern part)
Quercus muhlenbergii
Quercus shumardii (southern part)
Quercus stellata (southern part)
Tilia americana
Ulmus americana

92 Ponderosa Shrub Forest
Moderately dense to open forests of tall needleleaf evergreen trees with shrubs and some grasses
Dominants:
Pinus ponderosa ponderosa pine
Other components:
Agropyron spicatum
Arctostaphylos patula
Arctostaphylos parryans var. pinetorum
Calamagrostis rubescens
Ceanothus velutinus
Cercocarpus ledifolius
Festuca idahoensis
Holodiscus discolor
Physocarpus capitatus
Pseudotusga menziesii
Purshia tridentata
Symphoricarpos spp.

93 Beech-Maple Forest Tall broadleaf deciduous forest
Dominants:
Acer saccharum sugar maple
Fagus grandifolia beech
Fraxinus pennsylvanica white ash
Ulmus americana American elm
Other components:
Aesculus glabra (southern part)
Carya ovata
Fraxinus americana
Juglans nigra
Liriodendron tulipifera
Prunus serotina

Quercus alba
Tilia americana
Ulmus americana
Ulmus rubra

94 Mixed Mesophytic Forest Tall
broadleaf deciduous forest
Dominants:
Acer saccharum sugar maple
Aesculus octandra buckeye
Fagus grandifolia beech
Liriodendron tulipifera tulip poplar
Quercus alba white oak
Quercus rubra northern red oak
Tilia heterophylla basswood
Other components:
Acer nigrum
Acer pensylvanicum
Acer rubrum
Amelanchier arborea
Betula alleghleniensis
Betula lenta
Carpinus caroliniana
Cornus florida
Fraxinus americana
Halesia carolina var. monticola
   (southern part)
Ilex opaca
Juglans nigra
Magnolia acuminata
Magnolia fraseri
Magnolia macrophylla (southern part)
Magnolia tripetala
Nyssa sylvatica
Ostrya virginiana
Oxydendrum arboreum
Prunus serotina
Tilia americana
Tsuga canadensis (northern part)

95 Appalachian Oak Forest Tall
broadleaf deciduous forest
Dominants:
Quercus alba white oak
Quercus rubra northern red oak
Other components:
Acer rubrum
Acer saccharum

Betula lenta
Carpinus caroliniana
Carya cordiformis
Carya glabra
Carya tomentosa
Castanea dentata
Fagus grandifolia
Liriodendron tulipifera
Pinus strobus (northern part)
Quercus coccinea
Quercus ilicifolia
Quercus muhlenbergii
Quercus prinus
Quercus velutina
Tsuga canadensis (northern part)

96 Mangrove Usually dense growth of
broadleaf evergreen shrubs and low
to medium tall trees with stilt roots,
with patches of tropical forest, esp. on
the Florida Keys
Dominants:
Avicennia nitida black mangrove
Rhizophora mangle red mangrove
Other components:
Batis maritima
Conocarpus erectus
Laguncularia racemosa
Salicornia perennis
Patches of tropical forest include:
Bursera simaruba
Coccoloba diversifolia
Dipholis salicifolia
Drypetes diversifolia
Exothea paniculata
Ficus aurea
Lysiloma bahamensis
Nectandra coriacea
Piscidia piscipula
Sapindus saponaria
Sideroxylon foetidissima
Simarouba glauca
Swietenia mahogoni

97 Northern Hardwoods Tall,
broadleaf deciduous forest with a
mixture of needleleaf evergreen trees

Dominants:
Acer saccharum sugar maple
Betula allegheniensis yellow birch
Fagus grandifolia beech
Tsuga canadensis hemlock
Other components:
Acer pensylvanicum
Acer rubrum
Acer spicatum
Fraxinus americana
Kalmia latifolia
Pinus strobus
Prunus serotina
Taxus canadensis
Tilia americana
Ulmus americana

98 Northern Hardwoods-Fir Forest
Dense medium tall forests of
broadleaf deciduous and needleleaf
evergreen trees
Dominants:
Abies balsamea balsam fir
Acer saccharum sugar maple
Betula papyrifera paper birch
Tsuga canadensis hemlock
Other components:
Acer rubrum
Acer spicatum
Betula allegheniensis
Fagus grandifolia
Picea glauca
Pinus resinosa
Pinus strobus
Tilia americana

99 Northern Hardwoods-Spruce Forest
Tall, dense forest of broadleaf
deciduous and needleleaf evergreen
trees
Dominants:
Acer saccharum sugar maple
Betula allegheniensis yellow birch
Fagus grandifolia beech
Picea rubens red spruce
Tsuga canadensis hemlock
Other components:
Abies balsamea

Acer rubrum
Acer spicatum
Betula papyrifera
Pinus strobus
Pinus resinosa
Tillia americana
Viburmum alnifolium

100 Northeastern Oak-Pine Forest
Medium tall forest of broadleaf
deciduous and needleleaf evergreen
trees; in places forest is low, even
shrubby
Dominants:
Pinus rigida pitch pine
Quercus coccinea scarlet oak
Quercus velutina black oak
Other components:
Gaylussacia baccata
Kalmia angustifolia
Kalmia latifolia
Pinus echinata
Quercus marilandica
Quercus prinus
Quercus stellata

101 Oak-Hickory-Pine Forest
Medium tall to tall forest of broadleaf
deciduous and needleleaf evergreen
trees
Dominants:
Carya spp. hickory
Pinus echinata shortleaf pine
Pinus taeda loblolly pine
Quercus alba white oak
Quercus stellata post oak
Other components:
Carya cordiformis
Carya glabra
Carya ovata
Carya tomentosa
Cornus florida
Diospyros virginiana
Liquidambar styraciflua
Liriodendron tuliperfera
Nyssa sylvatica
Oxydendrum arboreum
Persea borbonia (lower elevations)

Persea virginiana
Quercus coccinea
Quercus falcata
Quercus marilandica
Quercus prinus
Quercus rubra
Quercus shumardii
Quercus velutina

102 Southern Mixed Forest Tall forest of broadleaf deciduous and evergreen and needleleaf trees
Dominants:
Fagus grandifolia beech (not in central FL)
Liquidambar styraciflua sweetgum
Magnolia grandiflora southern magnolia
Pinus elliotti slash pine
Pinus taeda loblolly pine
Quercus alba white oak
Quercus laurifolia laurel oak
Other components:
Acer barbatum
Carpinus caroliniana (not in central FL)
Carya clabra (northern part)
Carya tomentosa (northern part)
Cornus florida
Ilex glabra
Ilex opaca
Liriodentron tuliperifera (not in central FL)
Myric cerifera
Ostrya virginiana (not in central FL)
Persea borbonia
Pinus echinata (northern part)
Pinus palustris
Quercus falcata
Quercus incana
Quercus laevis
Quercus marilandica
Quercus stellata
Quercus virginiana (FL and coastal regions)
Sabal palmetto (eastern part)
Serenoa repens

103 Southern floodplain forest
Dense, medium tall to tall forest of broadleaf deciduous and evergreen trees and shrubs and needleleaf deciduous trees
Dominants:
Nyssa aquatica tupelo
Quercus spp. oak
Taxodium distichum bald cypress
Other components:
Acer rubrum var. drummondii
Ampelopsis arborea
Berchemia scandens
Campsis radicans
Carya aquatica
Carya illinoensis
Celtis laevigata
Foresteria acuminata
Fraxinus caroliniana
Fraxinus profunda
Gleditsia aquatica
Ilex decidua
Liquidambar stryaciflua
Nyssa silvatica
Nyssa silvatica var. biflora
Persea borbonia
Planera aquarica
Platanus occidetalis
Populus deltoides
Populus heterophylla
Quercus falcata var. pagodaefolia
Quercus lyrata
Quercus michauxii
Quercus migra
Quercus shumardii
Salix nigra
Ulmus americana
Vitis spp.

104 Pocosin Low open forests of needleleaf evergreen trees and broadleaf evergreen low trees and shrubs and much moss
Dominants:
Ilex glabra gall berry
Pinus serotina pond pine
Other components:
Cyrilla racemiflora

Gordonia lasianthus
Magnolia virginiana
Myrica cerifera
Persea borbonia
Smilax laurifolia
Sphagnum spp.

105 Sand Pine Scrub Open woodland of low needleleaf evergreen trees and broadleaf deciduous or evergreen trees and shrubs

Dominants:

Pinus clausa sand pine
Quercus chapmanii Chapman oak
Quercus myrtifolia myrtle oak
Quercus virginiana var. maritima sand live oak

Other components:

Bumelia tenax
Carya floridana
Ceratiola ericoides
Chrysopsis graminifolia

Cladonia pycnocladia
Garberia fruticosa
Lyonia ferruginea
Osmanthus americanus
Rhynchospora dodocandra
Serenoa repens

106 Subtropical Pine Forest Medium tall forest of needleleaf and broadleaf evergreen trees and shrubs

Dominants:

Pinus elliottii var. densa South Florida slash pine

Other components:

Chiococca pinetorum
Coccothrinax argentata
Guettarda elliptica
Guettarda scabra
Metopium toxiferum
Myrica cericera
Tetrazygia bicolor

INDICATOR SPECIES COMPOSITION OF PLANT COMMUNITY TYPES

KUCHLER, 1985

Composition of Vegetation Types Including Dominant and Component Species

Our descriptive information regarding the vegetation of Alaska, Hawaii, and Puerto Rico, related to Kuchler's Potential Natural Vegetation map is limited. For further information on plant community types and their composition, please check with the Natural Heritage Program and/or The Nature Conservancy in each State.

ALASKA

In Alaska remoteness and a very sparse population have combined to preserve the vegetation. Even extensive fires cannot hide the potential natural vegetation, which is severely limited to relatively few types by extremely harsh environmental conditions. Introduced species are few, and disturbed vegetation types return to their original state when given an opportunity. One of the outstanding characteristics of the Alaskan vegetation is its uniformity over very large areas. Note the numerous plant communities which imply great diversity.

HAWAII

In Hawaii great complexity is the rule. More than two-thirds of all plant species on the Hawaiian Islands have been introduced. Some arrived long ago, others more recently; some spread fast, others more slowly. Some introduced species, such as the mesquite (Prosopis pallida) and the guava (Psidium guayava), have crowded out the native species and taken over their territory. Man has changed, removed, or replaced the vegetation. In addition, he introduced pigs and goats that soon spread without control into the hills and mountains where they became very destructive. Finally, the vegetation and its evolution are strongly affected by the age and the physical and chemical nature of individual lava flows that built up the islands. This volcanism occurred long ago in Kauai, in the west, but continues on the easternmost island of Hawaii.

PUERTO RICO

Our descriptive information and detailed lists are not complete for Puerto Rico. Please note written and resource references for more information on plant community types and their composition. Plant community types include: Subtropical dry forest, moist forest, wet forest, and rain forest; as well as Lower Montane wet forest, and rain forest. Puerto Rico's vegetation is under the same population pressures and environmental impacts as those of other States. Introduction of invasive species is a great threat to the diversity of this island's natural vegetation.

48 CONTIGUOUS STATES ———

WESTERN FORESTS
Needleleaf Forests

1 Spruce-Cedar-Hemlock Forest (Picea Thuja-Tsuga)

2 Cedar-Hemlock-Douglas Fir Forest (Thuja-Tsuga-Pseudotsuga)

3 Silver Fir-Douglas Fir Forest (Abies Pseudotsuga)

4 Fir-Hemlock Forest (Abies-Tsuga)

5 Mixed Conifer Forest (Abies-Pinus Pseudotsuga)

6 Redwood Forest (Sequoia-Pseudotsuga)

7 Red Fir Forest (Abies)

8 Lodgepole Pine-Subalpine Forest (Pinus-Tsuga)

9 Pine-Cypress Forest (Pinus-Cupressus)

10 Western Ponderosa Forest (Pinus)

11 Douglas Fir Forest (Pseudotsuga)

12 Cedar-Hemlock-Pine Forest (Thuja Tsuga-Pinus)

13 Grand Fir-Douglas Fir Forest (Abies Pseudotsuga)

14 Western Spruce-Fir Forest (Picea-Abies)

15 Eastern Ponderosa Forest (Pinus)

16 Black Hills Pine Forest (Pinus)

17 Pine-Douglas Fir Forest (Pinus Pseudotsuga)

18 Arizona Pine Forest (Pinus)

19 Spruce Fir-Douglas Fir Forest (Picea Abies-Pseudotsuga)

20 Southwestern Spruce Fir Forest (Picea Abies)

21 Juniper-Pinyon Woodland (Juniperus Pinus)

Broadleaf Forests

22 Oregon Oakwoods (Quercus)

23 Mesquite Bosques (Prosopis) Broadleaf and Needleleaf forests

24 Mosaic of 2 (Cedar-hemlock-Douglas fir forest) and 22 (Oregon oakwoods)

25 California Mixed Evergreen Forest (Quercus-Arbutus-Pseudotsuga)

26 California Oakwoods (Quercus)

27 Oak-Juniper Woodland (Quercus Juniperus)

28 Transition Between 27 Woodland) and 31 (Mountain Mahogany-Oak Scrub)

WESTERN SHRUB AND GRASSLAND
Shrub

29 Chaparral (Adenostoma-Arctostaphylos Ceanothus)

30 Coastal Sagebrush (Salvia-Eriogonum)

31 Mountain Mahogany-Oak Scrub (Cercocarpus-Quercus)

32 Great Basin Sagebrush (Artemisia)

33 Blackbrush (Coleogyne)

34 Saltbrush-Geasewood (Artiplex Sarcobatus)

35 Creosote Bush (Larrea)

36 Creosote Bush-Bur Sage (Larrea Franseria)

37 Palo Verde-Cactus Shrub (Cercidium Opuntia)

38 Ceniza Shrub (Leucophyllum-Larrea Prosopis)

39 Desert: Vegetation Largely Absent

Grasslands

40 Fescue-Oatgrass (Festuca-Danthonia)

41 California Steppe (Stipa)

42 Tule Marshes (Scirpus-Typha)

43 Fescue-Wheatgrass (Festuca Agropyron)

44 Wheatgrass-Bluegrass (Agropyron-Poa)

45 Alpine Meadows and Barren (Agrostis, Carex, Festuca, Poa)

46 Fescue-Mountain Muhly Prairie (Festuca-Muhlenbergia)

47 Grama-Galleta Steppe (Bouteloua Hilaria)

48 Grama-Tobosa-Prairie (Bouteloua Hilaria)

Shrub and Grasslands Combinations

49 Sagebrush Steppe (Artemisia Agropyron)

50 Wheatgrass-Needlegrass Shrubsteppe (Agropyron-Stipa-Artemisia)

51 Galleta-Three Awn Shrubsteppe (Hilaira Aristida)

52 Grama-Tobosa Shrubsteppe (Bouteloua-Hilaria-Larrea)

53 Trans-Pecos Savanna (Flourensia Larrea)

54 Mesquite-Acacia-Savanna (Andropogon Setaria-Prosopis-Acacia)

55 Mesquite-Live Oak Savanna (Andropogon- Prosopis-Quercus)

Grasslands

56 Foothills Prairie (Agropyron-Festuca Stipa)

57 Grama-Needlegrass-Wheatgrass (Bouteloua-Stipa-Agropyron)

58 Grama-Buffalo Grass (Bouteloua Buchloë)

59 Wheatgrass-Needlegrass (Agropyron Stipa)

60 Wheatgrass-Bluestem-Needlegrass (Agropyron-Andropogon-Stipa)

61 Wheatgras-Grama-Buffalo Grass (Andropogon-Bouteloua-Buchloë)

62 Bluestem-Grama Prairie (Andropogon Bouteloua)

63 Sandsage-Bluestem Prairie (Artemisia Andropogon)

64 Shinnery (Quercus-Andropogon)

65 Northern Cordgrass Prairie (Distichlis Spartina)

66 Bluestem Prairie (Andropogon-Panicum Sorghastrum)

67 Sandhills Prairie (Andropogon Calamovilfa)

68 Blackland Prairie (Andropogon-Stipa)

69 Bluestem-Sacahuista Prairie (Andropogon-Spartina)

70 Southern Cordgrass Prairie (Spartina)

71 Palmetto Prairie (Serenoa-Aristida)

Grassland and Forest Combinations

72 Oak Savanna (Quercus-Andropogon)

73 Mosaic of 66 (Bluestem Prairie) and 91 (Oak-Hickory Forest)

74 Cedar Glades (Quercus-Juniperus Sporobolus)

75 Cross Timbers (Quercus-Andropogon)

76 Mesquite-Buffalo Grass (Bouteloua Buchloë- Prosopis)

77 Juniper-Oak Savanna (Andropogon Quercus-Juniperus)

78 Mesquite-Oak Savanna (Andropogon Prosopis-Quercus)

79 Fayette Prairie (Andropogon-Buchloë)

80 Blackbelt (Liquidambar-Quercus Juniperus)

81 Live Oak-Sea Oats (Quercus-Uniola)

82 Cypress Savanna (Taxodium-Mariscus)

83 Everglades (Mariscus and Magnolia Persea)

EASTERN FORESTS
Needleleaf Forests

84 Great Lakes Spruce-Fir Forest (Picea Abies)

85 Conifer Bog (Picea-Larix-Thuja)

86 Great Lakes Pine Forest (Pinus)

87 Northeastern Spruce-Fir Forest (Picea Abies)

88 Southeastern Spruce-Fir Forest (Picea Abies)

Broadleaf Forests

89 Northern Floodplain Forest (Populus Salix-Ulmus)

90 Maple-Basswood Forest (Acer-Tilia)

91 Oak-Hickory Forest (Quercus-Carya)

92 Elm-Ash Forest (Ulmus-Fraxinus)

93 Beech-Maple Forest (Fagus-Acer)

94 Mixed Mesophytic Forest (Acer Aesculus-Fagus-Liriodendron-Quercus Tilia)

95 Appalachian Oak Forest (Quercus)

96 Mangrove (Avicennia-Rhizophora)

Broadleaf and Needleleaf Forests

97 Northern Hardwoods (Acer-Betula Fagus-Tsuga)

98 Northern Hardwoods-Fir Forests (Acer Betula-Abies-Tsuga)

99 Northern Hardwoods-Spruce Forests (Acer-Betula-Fagus-Picea-Tsuga)

100 Northeastern Oak-Pine Forest (Quercus Pinus)

101 Oak-Hickory-Pine Forest (Quercus-Carya Pinus)

102 Southern Mixed Forest (Fagus Liquidambar-Magnolia-Pinus-Quercus)

103 Southern Floodplain Forest (Quercus Nyssa-Taxodium)

104 Pocosin (Pinus-Ilex)

105 Sand Pine Scrub (Pinus-Quercus)

106 Subtropical Pine Forest (Pinus)

KUCHLER, 1985

Some species names listed in the 1964 edition and in the 1985 revision of Potential Natural Vegetation (Kuchler, 1964; 1985) have been changed based on current research into vegetation species relationships. The names of all species listed were compared with the currently accepted names listed in Kartesz (1994). If a species name has been changed, the old name is in italics followed by the currently accepted name in normal font. Some species names could not be located in Kartesz (1994) and, for this reason, the accepted name could not be verified. These species are designated by an asterisk (*).

Citation: J.T. Kartesz. 1994. A Synonymized Checklist of the Vascular Flora of the United States, Canada, and Greenland. Second Edition. Vol. 1: Checklist, Vol. 2: Thesaurus. Timber Press, Portland, Oregon.

Abies amabilis
Abies balsamea
Abies concolor
Abies fraseri
Abies grandis
Abies lasiocarpa
Abies lasiocarpa var. arizonica
Abies magnifica
Abies procera
Acacia berlandieri
Acacia constricta
Acacia greggii
Acacia rigidula
Acer barbatum
Acer circinatum
Acer glabrum
Acer grandidentatum
Acer macrophyllum
Acer negundo
Acer nigrum
Acer pensylvanicum
Acer rubrum
Acer rubrum var. drummondii
Acer saccharum
Acer spicatum
Achillea millefolium var. lanulosa
   Achillea millefolium var. occidentalis
Achillea millefolium
Adenostoma fasciculatum

Aesculus californica
Aesculus glabra
Aesculus octandra
   Aesculus flava
Agave lechuguilla
Agropyron smithii
   Pascopyrum smithii
Agropyron spicatum
   Pseudoroegneria spicata ssp. spicata
Agropyron trachycaulum
   Elymus trachycaulus ssp. trachycaulus
Agrostis hallii
Agrostis tenuis
   Agrostis capillaris
Allenrolfea occidentalis
Alnus rubra
Alnus tenuifolia
   Alnus incana ssp. tenuifolia
Aloysia ligustrina*
Ambrosia psilostachya
Amelanchier alnifolia
Amelanchier arborea
Amelanchier utahensis
Amorpha canescens
Ampelopsis arborea
Amphicarpa bracteata
Andropogon barbinodis
   Bothriochloa barbinodis var. barbinodis

Andropogon gerardi
Andropogon glomeratus
Andropogon hallii
Andropogon littoralis
   Schizachyrium scoparium ssp.
   littorale
Andropogon saccharoides
   Bothriochloa saccharoides
Andropogon scoparius
   Schizachyrium scoparium
   ssp.scoparium
Andropogon tener
   Schizachyrium tenerum
Andropogon ternarius
Andropogon virginicus
Annona glabra
Antennaria neglecta
Aquilegia pubescens
Arbutus menziesii
Arctostaphylos glandulosa
Arctostaphylos glauca
Arctostaphylos manzanita
Arctostaphylos mariposa
   Arctostaphylos viscida ssp.
   mariposa
Arctostaphylos nevadensis
Arctostaphylos nummularia
Arctostaphylos parryana
Arctostaphylos parryana var.
   pinetorum
Arctostaphylos patula
Arctostaphylos pungens
Arctostaphylos uva ursi
Arctostaphylos viscida
Arenaria patula
   Minuartia patula var. patula
Aristida affinis
   Aristida purpurascens var.
   purpurascens
Aristida divaricata
Aristida glabrata
   Aristida californica var. glabrata
Aristida glauca
   Aristida purpurea var. neafleyi
Aristida hamulosa
   Aristida ternipes var. hamulosa
Aristida intermedia

Aristida longespica var. geniculata
Aristida longiseta
   Aristida purpurea var. longiseta
Aristida longispica
Aristida patula
Aristida purpurea
Aristida roemeriana
   Aristida purpurea var. purpurea
Aristida spiciformis
Aristida stricta
Aristida tenuispica
   Aristida purpurascens var.
   tenuispica
Aristida wrightii
   Aristida purpurea var. wrightii
Arnica cordifolia
Artemisia arbuscula
Artemisia californica
Artemisia cana
Artemisia canadensis
   Artemisia campestris var. borealis
Artemisia dranunculus
Artemisia filifolia
Artemisia frigida
Artemisia ludoviciana
Artemisia nova
Artemisia spinescens
Artemisia tridentata
Artemisia tripartita
Asclepias arenaria
Aster cichoriaceus
   Machaeranthera canescens var.
   aristata
Aster ericoides
   Aster subulatus var. ligulatus
Aster exilis
Aster laevis
Astragalus platytropis
Atriplex canescens
Atriplex confertifolia
Avicennia nitida
   Avicennia germinans
Axonopus compressus
Axonopus furcatus
Baccharis emoryi
Baccharis halimifolia

Baccharis sergiloides
Baileya multiradiata
Balsamorrhiza sagittata
Baptisia leucantha
    Baptisia alba var. macrophylla
Batis maritima
Berberis fremontii
    Mahonia fremontii
Berberis nervosa
    Mahonia nervosa var. nervosa
Berchemia scandens
Betula alleghaniensis
Betula lenta
Betula nigra
Betula papyrifera
Betula populifolia
Blechnum serrulatum
Blepharoneuron tricholepis
Boehmeria cylindrica
Bouteloua breviseta
Bouteloua curtipendula
Bouteloua eriopoda
Bouteloua filiformis
    Bouteloua repens
Bouteloua gracilis
Bouteloua hirsuta
Bouteloua rigidiseta
Bouteloua trifida
Brayodendron texanum*
Brodiaea pulchella
    Dichelostemma congestum
Bromus laevipes
Buchloe dactyloides
Bumelia lanuginosa
    Sideroxylon lanuginosum ssp.
    lanuginosum
Bumelia tenax
    Sideroxylon tenax
Bursera simaruba
Calamagrostis canadensis
Calamagrostis nutkaensis
Calamagrostis rubescens
Calamovilfa longifolia
Calliandra eriophyllua
Calochortus luteus
Campsis radicans

Carex eleocharis
    Carex duriuscula
Carex filifolia
Carex geyeri
Carex heliophila
    Carex inops ssp. heliophila
Carex senta
Carex tumulicola
Carpinus caroliniana
Carya aquatica
Carya cordiformis
Carya floridana
Carya glabra
Carya illinoinensis
Carya ovata
Carya texana
Carya tomentosa
    Carya alba
Castanea dentata
Castanopsis chrysophylla
Castanopsis sempervirens
Castilleja culbertsonii
    Castilleja lemmonii
Ceanothus cordulatus
Ceanothus cuneatus
Ceanothus fendleri
Ceanothus foliosus
Ceanothus impressus
Ceanothus integerrimus
Ceanothus leucodermis
Ceanothus parryi
Ceanothus sorediatus
    Ceanothus oliganthus ssp.
    sorediatus
Ceanothus spinosus
Ceanothus thyrsiflorus
Ceanothus velutinus
Celastrus scandens
Celtis laevigata
Celtis occidentalis
Celtis pallida
Celtis reticulata
    Celtis laevigata var. reticulata
Celtis tenuifolia
Cenchrus myosuroides
Cenchrus tribuloides

Centella repanda
  Centella erecta
Cephalanthus occidentalis
Ceratiola ericoides
Cercidium floridum
  Parkinsonia florida
Cercidium macrum
  Parkinsonia texana var. macra
Cercidium microphyllum
  Parkinsonia microphylla
Cercis canadensis
Cercis canadensis var. texensis
Cercis occidentalis
  Cercis canadensis var. texensis
Cercocarpus betuloides
  Cercocarpus montanus var. glaber
Cercocarpus ledifolius
Cereus giganteus
  Carnegia gigantea
Chamaebatia foliolosa
Chamaebatiaria millefolium
Chamaecyparis lawsoniana
Chamaedaphne calyculata
Cheilanthes lanosa
Chiococca pinetorum
  Chiococca parvifolia
Chrysobalanus icaco
Chrysopsis bolanderi
  Heterotheca bolanderi
Chrysopsis graminifolia
  Pityopsis graminifolia var.
  graminifolia
Chrysopsis villosa
  Heterotheca villosa var. villosa
Chrysothamnus nauseosus
Chrysothamnus viscidiflorus
Cladonia pycnocladia
Clematis fremontii*
Clematis neomexicana
  Clematis ligusticifolia var.
  ligusticifolia
Clematis virginiana
Collinsia parviflora
Coccoloba diversifolia
Coccothrinax argentata
Coleogyne ramosissima

Comandra richardsiana
  Comandra umbellata ssp.
  umbellata
Condalia lycioides
  Ziziphus obtusifolia var. obtusifolia
Condalia obovata
  Condalia hookeri var. hookeri
Condalia spathulata
Conocarpus erectus
Cornus florida
Cornus nutallii
Cowania mexicana
  Purshia mexicana
Croton monanthogynus
Croton punctatus
Cryptantha hoffmannii
Cryptantha roosiorum
Cucurbita digitata
Cucurbita foetidissima
Cupressus goveniana
Cupressus macrocarpa
Cymopterus cinerarius
Cyperus haspan
Cyrilla racemiflora
Dalea enneandra
Dalea spinosa
  Psorothamnus spinosus
Danthonia californica
Dasylirion leiophyllum
Dasylirion wheeleri
Deschampsia cespitosa
Deschampsia holciformis
  Deschampsia cespitosa ssp.
  holciformis
Diospyros virginiana
Dipholis salicifolia
  Sideroxylon salicifolium
Distichlis spicata
Draba verna
Drypetes diversifolia
Echinacea angustifolia
Echinocereus engelmannii
Elymus canadensis
Elymus glaucus
Elymus triticoides
  Leymus triticoides

Elyonurus tripsacoides
Encelia californica
Encelia farinosa
Ephedra antisyphilitica
Ephedra torreyana
Ephedra trifurca
Ephedra viridis
Eragrostis elliottii
  Eragrostis campestris
Eragrostis spectabilis
Eragrostis trichodes
Erigeron compositus
Erigeron quercifolius
Erigeron strigosus
Eriodyction californicum
Eriogonum annuum
Eriogonum fasciculatum
Eriogonum incanum
Eriophyllum confertiflorum
Erysimum asperum
Eschscholzia californica
Eupatorium capillifolium
Euphorbia corollata
Euploca convolvulacea
  Heliotropium convolvulaceum
Eurotia lanata
  Krascheninnikovia lanata
Exothea paniculata
Fagus grandifolia
Fallugia paradoxa
Ferocactus wislizeni
Festuca arizonica
Festuca californica
Festuca idahoensis
Festuca pacifica
  Vulpia microstachys var. pauciflora
Festuca rubra
Festuca scabrella
  Festuca campestris
Festuca viridula
Ficus aurea
Flourensia cernua
Foresteria acuminata
Forestiera lingustrina
Fouquieria splendens
Franseria acanthicarpa

Ambrosia acanthicarpa
Franseria deltoidea
  Ambrosia deltoidea
Franseria dumosa
  Ambrosia dumosa
Fraxinus americana
Fraxinus caroliniana
Fraxinus latifolia
Fraxinus pennsylvanica
Fraxinus texensis
Fremontia californica
  Fremontodendron californicum
Galium tinctorium
Garberia fruticosa
  Garberia heterophylla
Gaultheria shallon
Gaura coccinea
Gaylussacia baccata
Gerardia maritima
  Agalinis maritima
Gilia longifolia
  Ipomopsis longifolia var. longifolia
Gleditsia aquatica
Gleditsia triacanthos
Gordonia lasianthus
Grayia spinosa
Grindelia hirsutula
Grindelia squarrosa
Guettarda elliptica
Guettarda scabra
Gutierrezia lucida
  Gutierrezia microcephala
Gutierrezia sarothrae
Halesia carolina var. monticola
  Halesia tetraptera var. monticola
Haplopappus gilmani
  Ericameria gilmanii
Haplopappus linearifolius
  Ericameria linearifolia
Haplopappus spinulosus
  Machaeranthera pinnatifida var. pinnatifida
Haplopappus squarrosus
  Hazardia squarrosa var. squarrosa
Hedeoma hispida
Eleocharis palustris

Helianthus grosseserratus
Helianthus anomalus
Helianthus petiolaris
Heteromeles arbutifolia
Heteropogon contortus
Hieracium albertinum
   Hieracium cynoglossoides
Hilaria belangeri
Hilaria jamesii
Hilaria mutica
Holodiscus discolor
Holodiscus dumosus
Hordeum jubatum
Horkelia cuneata
Hymenoclea monogyra
Hypericum fasciculatum
Ilex cassine
Ilex decidua
Ilex glabra
Ilex opaca
Ilex verticillata
Ilex vomitoria
Ipomea littoralis
Ipomea pes-caprae
Ipomopsis aggregata
Iris douglasiana
Iva frutescens
Jamesia americana
Janusia gracilis
Jatropha cardiophylla
Juglans californica
Juglans nigra
Juncus effusus
Juncus gerardi
Juncus roemerianus
Juniperus ashei
Juniperus communis
Juniperus communis var. montana
Juniperus deppeana
Juniperus monosperma
Juniperus occidentalis
Juniperus osteosperma
Juniperus pinchotii
Juniperus scopulorum
Juniperus virginiana
Kalmia angustifolia

Kalmia latifolia
Kalmia polifolia
Kochia americana
Koeberlinia spinosa
Koeleria cristata
   Koeleria macrantha
Laguncularia racemosa
Larix laricina
Larix lyallii
Larix occidentalis
Larrea divaricata
   Larrea tridentata var. tridentata
Ledum glandulosum
Ledum groenlandicum
Leersia hexandra
Leptochloa dubia
Leucophyllum frutescens
Liatris aspera
Liatris punctata
Liatris scarrosa
Librocedrus decurrens
   Calocedrus decurrens
Limonium carolinianum
Liquidambar styraciflua
Liriodendron tulipifera
Liriodendron tulipifera
Lithocarpus densiflorus
Lithophragma bulbifera
   Lithophragma glabrum
Lithospermum ruderale
Lupinus bicolor
Lupinus formosus
Lupinus luteolus
Lupinus sericeus
Lupinus variicolor
   Lupinus versicolor
Luzula spicata
Lycium andersonii
Lycium cooperi
Lycurus phleoides
Lyonia ferruginea
Lyonia fruticosa
Lyonia nitida*
Lysiloma bahamensis
   Lysiloma latisiliquum
Magnolia acuminata

Magnolia fraseri
Magnolia grandiflora
Magnolia macrophylla
Magnolia tripetala
Magnolia virginiana
Mariscus jamaicensis
    Cladium mariscus ssp. jamaicense
Melica bulbosa
Menodora spinescens
Mentzelia pumila
Menziesia ferruginea
Metopium toxiferum
Monadra fistulosa
Monroa squarrosa
Mortonia scabrella
    Mortonia sempervirens ssp.
    scabrella
Muhlenbergia cuspidata
Muhlenbergia montana
Muhlenbergia porteri
Muhlenbergia pungens
Muhlenbergia torreyi
Myrica californica
Myrica cerifera
Myrica pensylvanica
Nectandra coriacea
Nemopanthus mucronatus
Nolina microcarpa
Nolina texana
Nyssa aquatica
Nyssa silvatica
Nyssa silvatica var. biflora
    Nyssa biflora
Oenothera albicaulis
Oenothera serrulata
    Calylophus serrulatus
Olneya tesota
Opuntia engelmannii
Opuntia fulgida
Opuntia imbricata
Opuntia spinosior
Opuntia versicolor
Opuntia whipplei
Orthocarpus spp.
Oryzopsis hymenoides
Osmanthus americanus

Osmunda cinnamomea
Osmunda regalis
Ostrya virginiana
Oxalis oregana
Oxydendrum arboreum
Oxyria digyna
Pachystima myrsinites*
Palafoxia callosa
Panicum amarum
Panicum hemitomon
Panicum leibergii
    Dichanthelium leibergii
Panicum obtusum
Panicum repens
Panicum scribnerianum
    Dichanthelium oligosanthes var.
    scribnerianum
Panicum virgatum
Pappophorum bicolor
Paronychia jamesii
Parthenium incanum
Parthenocissus quinquefolia
Paspalum dilatatum
Paspalum monostachyum
Paspalum plicatulum
Pedicularis attollens
Peltandra virginica
Pentstemon fruticosus
Pentstemon heterodoxus
Pentstemon scapoides*
Persea borbonia
Persea humilis
Persea virginiana*
Petalostemon purpureum
    Dalea purpurea var. purpurea
Petalostemon villosum
    Dalea villosa var. villosa
Phleum alpinum
Phlox caespitosa
Phlox pilosa
Phragmites communis
    Phragmites australis
Physocarpus capitatus
Physocarpus malvaceus
Physocarpus monogynus
Picea engelmannii

Picea glauca
Picea mariana
Picea pungens
Picea rubens
Pickeringia montana
Pinus albicaulis
Pinus aristata
Pinus balfouriana
Pinus banksiana
Pinus cembroides
Pinus clausa
Pinus contorta
Pinus coulteri
Pinus echinata
Pinus edulis
Pinus elliottii
Pinus elliottii var. densa
Pinus flexilis
Pinus jeffreyi
Pinus lambertiana
Pinus leiophylla var. chihuahuana
Pinus monticola
Pinus muricata
Pinus ponderosa
Pinus radiata
Pinus resinosa
Pinus rigida
Pinus sabiniana
Pinus serotina
Pinus strobus
Pinus taeda
Piscidia piscipula
Planera aquatica
Plantago decipiens*
Platanus occidentalis
Pleurochaete squarrosa*
Poa arida
Poa fendleriana
Poa scabrella
Poliomintha incana
Polygonum acre
  Polygonum punctatum var.
  punctatum
Polystichum munitum
Populus deltoides
Populus fremontii

Populus grandidentata
Populus heterophylla
Populus sargentii
  Populus deltoides ssp. monilifera
Populus tremuloides
Populus trichocarpa
  Populus balsmamifera ssp.
  trichocarpa
Potentilla blaschkeana
  Populus gracilis var. nuttallii
Potentilla breweri
Potentilla diversifolia
Prosopis juliflora var. torreyana
  Prosopsis glandulosa var. torreyana
Prosopis juliflora var. velutina
  Prosopsis velutina
Prosopis juliflora var. glandulosa
  Prosopsis glandulosa var.
  glandulosa
Prosopis pubescens
Prunus angustifolia
Prunus emarginata
Prunus ilicifolia
Prunus serotina
Prunus virginiana
Pseudotsuga macrocarpa
Pseudotsuga menziesii
Psoralea argophylla
  Pediomelum argophyllum
Psoralea floribunda
  Psoralidium tenuiflorum
Psoralea tenuiflora
  Psoralidium tenuiflorum
Pteridium aquilinum var. pubescens
Purshia tridentata
Quercus agrifolia
Quercus alba
Quercus chapmanii
Quercus chrysolepis
Quercus coccinea
Quercus douglasii
Quercus dumosa
Quercus durandii var. breviloba
  Quercus sinuata var. breviloba
Quercus ellipsoidalis
Quercus emoryi

Quercus englemannii
Quercus falcata
Quercus falcata var. pagodaefolia
  Quercus pagoda
Quercus gambelii
Quercus garryana
Quercus grisea
Quercus havardii
Quercus hypoleucoides
Quercus ilicifolia
Quercus imbricaria
Quercus incana
Quercus kelloggii
Quercus laevis
Quercus lobata
Quercus lyrata
Quercus macrocarpa
Quercus marilandica
Quercus michauxii
Quercus nigra
Quercus mohriana
Quercus muehlenbergii
Quercus myrtifolia
Quercus oblongifolia
Quercus prinus
Quercus rubra
Quercus shumardii
Quercus stellata
Quercus turbinella
Quercus undulata
  Quercus x pauciloba
Quercus vacciniifolia
Quercus velutina
Quercus virginiana
Quercus virginiana var. fusiformis
  Quercus fusiformis
Quercus virginiana var. maritima
  Quercus maritima
Quercus wislizeni
Ranunculus californicus
Rapanea guianensis
  Myrsine floridana
Ratibida columnifera
Ratibida pinnata
Redfieldia flexuosa
Rhamnus californica

Frangula californica ssp. californica
Rhizophora mangle
Rhododendron catawbiense
Rhododendron macrophyllum
Rhus aromatica
Rhus aromatica var. pilosissima
  Rhus trilobata var. pilosissima
Rhus choriophylla
  Rhus virens var. choriophylla
Rhus diversiloba
  Toxicodendron diversilobum
Rhus integrifolia
Rhus radicans
  Toxicodendron radicans ssp.
  radicans
Rhus trilobata
Rhynchospora dodecandra
  Rhynchospora megalecarpa
Rhynchospora filifolia
Ribes cereum
Ribes nevadense
Ribes quercetorum
Ribes roezlii
Rosa arkansana
Rosa nutkana
Rubus canadensis
Rubus parviflorus
Rubus spectabilis
Rynchospora divergens*
Sabal palmetto
Sagittaria lancifolia
Salicornia perennis
  Sarcocornia perennis
Salix amygdaloides
Salix bebbiana
Salix caroliniana
Salix gooddingii
Salix nigra
Salix nivalis
  Salix reticulata ssp. nivalis
Salix petrophila
  Salix arctica
Salsola kali
Salvia apiana
Salvia leucophylla
Salvia mellifera

Sambucus glauca
   Sambucus cerulea var. cerulea
Sambucus racemosa
Sambucus simpsonii
   Sambucus canadensis
Sanicula arctopoides
Sapindus saponaria
Sarcobatus vermiculatus
Saururus cernuus
Schedonnardus paniculatus
Scirpus acutus
Scirpus americanus
Scirpus californicus
Scirpus olneyi
   Scirpus americanus
Scirpus validus
   Scirpus tabernaemontani
Scleropogon brevifolius
Scutellaria resinosa
Sedum pulchellum
Sequoia sempervirens
Serenoa repens
Sesuvium portulacastrum
Setaria macrostachya
Shepherdia canadensis
Sibbaldia procumbens
Sideroxylon foetidissimum
Sieversia turbinata
Silphium laciniatum
Simarouba glauca
Simmondsia chinensis
Sisyrinchium bellum
Sitanion hystrix
   Elymus elymoides
Smilax hispida
   Smilax tamnoides
Smilax laurifolia
Solidago altissima
   Solidago canadensis var. scarba
Solidago missouriensis
Solidago mollis
Solidago rigida
Sorbus americana
Sorghastrum nutans
Spartina alterniflora
Spartina bakeri

Spartina cynosuroides
Spartina patens
Spartina spartinae
Sphaeralcea ambigua
Sphaeralcea coccinea
Sphaeralcea grossulariifolia
Sporobolus airoides
Sporobolus asper
   Sporobolus compositus var. compositus
Sporobolus cryptandrus
Sporobolus flexuosus
Sporobolus heterolepis
Sporobolus neglectus
Sporobolus poiretti
   Sporobolus indicus
Sporobolus vaginiflorus
Stellaria nitens
Stenosiphon linifolius
Stephanomeria pauciflora
Stillingia aquatica
Stipa cernus
   Nassella cernua
Stipa comata
Stipa coronata
Stipa lepida
   Nassella lepida
Stipa leucotricha
   Nassella leucotricha
Stipa pinetorum
Stipa pulchra
   Nassella pulchra
Stipa spartea
Stipa viridula
   Nassella viridula
Suaeda torreyana
   Suaeda moquinii
Swietenia mahogoni
Symphoricarpos albus
Symphoricarpos orbiculatus
Symphoricarpos vaccinoides
   Symphoricarpos var. utahensis
Taxodium distichum
Taxodium distichum var. nutans
   Taxodium ascendens
Taxus canadensis

Tetradymia canescens
Tetrazygia bicolor
Thuja occidentalis
Thuja occidentalis
Thuja plicata
Tilia americana
Tilia heterophylla
   Tilia americana var. heterophylla
Tillandsia utriculata
Trichostema lanatum
Triclochin maritima*
Tridens pilosus
   Erioneuron pilosum
Trisetum spicatum
Tsuga canadensis
Tsuga heterophylla
Tsuga mertensiana
Typha angustifolia
Typha domingensis
Typha latifolia
Ulmus alata
Ulmus americana
Ulmus crassifolia
Ulmus rubra

Umbellularia californica
Uniola paniculata
Utricularia juncea
Vaccinium membranaceum
Vaccinium myrsinites
Vaccinium ovatum
Vancouveria parvifolium
Viburnum alnifolium
Vitis munsonia
   Vitis rotundifolia var. munsoniana
Whipplea modesta
Xanthoxylum insulare
Xerophyllum tenax*
Yucca aloifolia
Yucca baccata
Yucca elata
Yucca glauca
Yucca schottii
Yucca whipplei
Zinnia grandiflora
Zinnia pumila
   Zinnia acerosa
Zizaniopsis miliacea

INVASIVE PLANT LIST

From Invasive Plants, Weeds of the Global Garden,
John M. Randall & Janet Marinelli,
Editors,1996 Brooklyn Botanic Garden.

In this list you will find plant species you know to be pest plants in your region. However, others will surprise you. When making plant material selections in landscape, erosion control, and maintenance projects, simply think twice about planting a potentially invasive plant. This reference is available in bookstores for $9.95 or from the Brooklyn Botanic Garden via their web site, www.bbg.org.

Forbs and grasses

Highway Iceplant, *Carpobrotus edulis*
Cornflower, Bachelor's Button, *Centaurea cyanus*
Crownvetch, *Coronilla varia*
Wild Artichoke, Cardoon, *Cynara cardunculus*
Common foxglove, *Digitalis purpurea*
Water Hyacinth, *Eichhornia crassipes*
Japanese Knotweed, *Fallopia japonica*
Baby's-breath, *Gypsophila paniculata*
Dame's Rocket, *Hesperis matronalis*
Bird's-foot Trefoil, Deer Vetch, *Lotus corniculatus*
Purple Loosestrife, *Lythrum salicaria*
Sulfur Cinquefoil, *Potentilla recta*
Vinca, Periwinkle, Myrtle, *Vinca* minor, *V.*major
Giant Reed, *Arundo donax*
Pampas Grass, Jubata, *Cortaderia selloana*, *C. Jubata*
Tall Fescue, *Festuca arundinacea*
Cogongrass, *Imperata cylindrica*
Chinese Silver Grass, Eulalia, *Miscanthus sinensis*
Reed Canary Grass, *Phalaris arundinacea*

Vines

Porcelain Berry, *Ampelopsis brevipedunculata*
Oriental or Asiatic Bittersweet, *Celastrus orbiculatus*
English Ivy, *Hedera helix*
Jasmine, *Jasminum dichotomum*, *J. Fluminense*
Japanese or Hall's Honeysuckle, *Lonicera japonica*
Japanese Climbing Fern, *Lygodium japonicum*
Wood Rose, *Merremia tuberosa*

Shrubs

Shoebutton Ardisia, *Ardisia elliptica*
Japanese Barberry, *Berberis thunbergii*
butterfly Bush, *Buddleia davidii*

Cotoneaster, *Cotoneaster microphyllus, C. Pannosus, C. Microphyllus, C. Pannosus, C. Lacteus*
Singleseed Hawthorn, *Crataegus monogyna*
Scotch Broom, *Cytisus scoparius*
Russian Olive, *Elaeagnus angustifolia*
Autumn Olive, *Elaeagnus umbellata*
Winged Euonymus, Burning Bush, *Euonymus alatus*
Wintercreeper, *Euonymus fortunei*
English Holly, *Ilex aquifolium*
Privet, *Ligustrum vulgare, L. Sinense, L. Japonium*
Bush Honeysuckle, *Lonicera maackii, L. Morrowii, L. Tatarica*
Myoporum, *Myoporum laetum*
Heavenly Bamboo, *Nandina domestica*
Common or Euopean Buckthorn, *Rhamnus cathartica*
Smooth or Glossy Buckthorn, *Rhamnus frangula*
Multiflora Rose, *Rosa multiflora*
Beach Naupaka, *Scaevola sericea*
Brazilian Pepper, *Schinus terebinthifolius*
Japanese Spiraea, *Spiraea japonica*
Japanese yew, *Taxus cuspidata*
Guelder Rose, *Viburnum opulus var. opulus*

Trees

Earleaf Acacia, *Acacia auriculiformis*
Amur Maple, *Acer ginnala*
Norway maple, *Acer platanoides*
Alianthus, Tree-of-heaven, *Ailanthus altissima*
Bishopwood, *Bischofia javanica*
Paper Mulberry, *Broussonetia papyrifera*
Australian Pine, *Casuarina Euisetifolia*
Carrot Wood, *Cupaniopsis anacardioides*
Bluegum Eucalyptus, *Eucalyptus globulus*
Fig, *Ficus altissima, F. Benghalensis, F. Microcarpa*
Edible Fig, *Ficus carica*
Melaleuca, Cajeput Tree, *Melaleuca quinquenervia*
Chinaberry Tree, *Melia azedarach*
Princess Tree, *Paulownia tomentosa*
White Poplar, *Populus alba*
Black Locust, *Robinia pseudoacacia*
Chinese Tallow Tree, *Sapium sebiferum*
Queensland Umbrella Tree, *Schefflera actinophylla*
Tamarisk, *Tamarix ramoisissima, T. chinensis, T. parviflora*
Siberian Elm, *Ulmus pumila*